TSCA Handbook

Fourth Edition

McKenna Long & Aldridge LLP

Government Institutes
An imprint of
The Scarecrow Press, Inc.
Lanham, Maryland • Toronto • Oxford
2005

Government
Institutes

Published in the United States of America
by Government Institutes, an imprint of The Scarecrow Press, Inc.
A wholly owned subsidiary of
The Rowman & Littlefield Publishing Group, Inc.
4501 Forbes Boulevard, Suite 200
Lanham, Maryland 20706
http://govinst.scarecrowpress.com

PO Box 317
Oxford
OX2 9RU, UK

ISBN : 0-86587-733-5

™ The paper used in this publication meets the minimum requirements of American National Standard for Information Sciences—Permanence of Paper for Printed Library Materials, ANSI/NISO Z39.48-1992.
Manufactured in the United States of America.

SUMMARY OF CONTENTS

TABLE OF CONTENTS

PREFACE TO THE FOURTH EDITION

The first edition of the *TSCA HANDBOOK,* published in 1987, grew out of a TSCA compliance course that McKenna, Conner & Cuneo (predecessor to McKenna Long & Aldridge LLP), organized in that year and several trade journal articles on TSCA which our attorneys wrote in the 1970s and early 1980s. At that time, no one had published a comprehensive manual on the regulation of chemical substances and mixtures under TSCA. We designed the *TSCA HANDBOOK* to fill that need, and to serve as a ready reference for virtually anyone who manufactures, processes, distributes or uses chemicals. We have drawn upon our experience in chemical regulation to make the *TSCA HANDBOOK* as practical and informative as possible.

This Fourth Edition was prompted by important developments in the TSCA area that have taken place since the Third Edition was published in 1997. Since then, EPA has promulgated extensive changes to the Inventory Update Rule; created voluntary testing initiatives such as the High Production Volume testing program; issued a new enforcement policy regarding reporting environmental contamination under TSCA § 8(e); substantially revised the PCB regulations regarding contaminated sites; used rules to raise the maximum civil penalties that can be imposed under TSCA; and finalized a sweeping new rule on biotechnology.

The outward appearance of the *TSCA HANDBOOK* has changed dramatically over time, but the basic structure and organization remains largely unchanged from the Second Edition in 1989. We intentionally maintained the same basic structure so that those readers accustomed to the organization of the Second and Third Editions will find the Fourth Edition comfortingly familiar.

We intend periodically to revise the *TSCA HANDBOOK.* Please feel free to contact us with questions, comments or suggestions c/o Michael Boucher, McKenna Long & Aldridge LLP, 1900 K Street, N.W., Washington, D.C. 20006 (tel: 202-496-7500).

The Authors, August 2005

ACKNOWLEDGMENTS

The authors are indebted to **John DiFazio** of Consumer Specialty Products Association who donated his time and expertise to review and comment on various sections of this edition of the *TSCA HANDBOOK*. The authors also wish to thank **Skip Kazmarek** for his input regarding SEC reporting of environmental liabilities and **Nina MacLeay** for the many hours of TSCA research and preparing this edition for publication. Special thanks go to **David Mitchell** for assisting in the production of the final manuscript.

CHAPTER 1
TSCA OVERVIEW

1.1. INTRODUCTION

In 1971 the President's Council on Environmental Quality (CEQ) identified a "high-priority need for a program of testing and control of toxic substances" because the existing statutory mechanisms for protecting the environment against chemical hazards were neither cohesive nor adequate.[1] In addition, public concern was mounting over the risks from specific chemicals such as kepone, vinyl chloride, heavy metals, PCBs and chlorinated fluorocarbons. Responding to these concerns, Congress enacted the Toxic Substances Control Act (TSCA), which became law on October 11, 1976. 15 U.S.C. §§ 2601-2629 (2000 & Supp. I 2001).

There have been three major amendments to the Act, each adding an additional title, so that TSCA now contains four titles: Title I—Control of Toxic Substances; Title II—Asbestos Hazard Emergency Response; Title III—Indoor Radon Abatement; and Title IV—Lead Exposure Reduction. At the time of this edition, however, the U.S. Senate had proposed legislation (2003 S. 1486) to implement requirements under international treaties controlling hazardous substances, in part, by adding a new Title V to TSCA entitled, "Implementation of International Agreements." Although Titles II, III, and IV of TSCA are important, with the exception of brief descriptions in section 1.3 of this chapter, we confine the balance of this Handbook to a discussion of Title I—the Control of Toxic Substances, the regulations implementing Title I of TSCA, and relevant guidance from EPA. Title I has remained largely unchanged since its enactment in 1976.

1.1.1. Legislative Background

The 92nd through 94th Congresses debated proposed TSCA legislation, weighing the need to protect health and the environment from unreasonable risks due to untested chemicals against the counter-balancing goal of not overburdening the chemical industry with testing and other regulatory costs that might stifle innovation. Highlights of the testimony on the proposed legislation convey the substance and intensity of the congressional debate.

After introducing S. 3149 on March 16, 1976, Senator Tunney stressed the urgent need for toxic substances legislation:

---

[1] Council on Environmental Quality, *Toxic Substances* (Apr. 1971), *reprinted in* House Comm. on Interstate and Foreign Commerce, 94th Cong., *Legislative History of the Toxic Substances Control Act* 760 (1976) [*TSCA Legislative History*].

> I do not think there is a way to assure a risk free society. However, the Toxic Substances Control Act will end the situation where we play Russian roulette by introducing vast numbers of untested chemicals into the environment. This legislation will assure that we will no longer thave [sic] to wait for a body count or serious health damage to generate controls over hazardous chemicals.

122 Cong. Rec. S4397, S4398 (daily ed. Mar. 26, 1976), *reprinted in TSCA Legislative History* at 209.

Senator Pearson shared this view:

> Final congressional passage now of this legislation would first, come at a time when the need to prevent unreasonable risks of injury to health or the environment associated with the manufacture, processing, distribution, use or disposal of chemical substances has never been greater; second, close an untenable chasm in Federal legislation designed to protect human health and the environment, and third, culminate over 5 years of congressional consideration of and background work on legislation designed to control toxic substances.

Id. at S4399, *reprinted in TSCA Legislative History* at 214.

Russell Train, then Administrator of EPA, supported this major premise of the Act:

> It is time we started putting chemicals to the test, not people. It is time we gave the people of this country some reason to believe that every time they take a breath or eat or drink or touch, they are not taking their life into their hands.

Id. at S4401, *reprinted in TSCA Legislative History* at 217.

On July 14, 1976, the Committee on Interstate and Foreign Commerce of the House of Representatives submitted its report on H.R. 14,032. Adopting the same stance as the Senate, the House committee recognized the pervasiveness of chemicals in the air, water, and soil. It further noted that we have little or no knowledge of long-term health or environmental effects of dangerous chemicals that presently bombard the population and environment. H.R. Rep. No. 94-1341, at 3-6, *reprinted in TSCA Legislative History* at 411-14. The Committee resolved to change the present situation under which “the general population and the environment now serve as the laboratory for discovering adverse health and environmental effects.” *Id.* at 5, *reprinted in TSCA Legislative History* at 413.

Both the Senate and the House focused upon studies indicating the high incidence of cancer in the United States and its relationship to environmental factors. The Senate pointed to five chemicals which are known potent carcinogens—vinyl chloride, bischloromethyl ether (BCME), mercury, arsenic, and asbestos—for which effective regulation was lacking. According to Senator Tunney, cancer had become the number one killer of youngsters less than 15 years of age; he added that "[t]here does not seem to be any question that it is the environmental carcinogens that are producing this cancer in youngsters." 122 Cong. Rec. at S4398, *reprinted in TSCA Legislative History* at 211. Further discussion suggested that individuals often face a "silent death" when they are exposed to carcinogens daily yet are unaware of such exposure. *Id.*

The House committee echoed the Senate's recognition that many chemicals in the environment cause harm that is not immediately visible. The House included vinyl chloride, asbestos, and PCBs on the list of carcinogens. Disease prevention, as distinct from treatment, the House determined, should be the hallmark of toxic substances legislation. H.R. Rep. No. 94-1341, at 4, *reprinted in TSCA Legislative History* at 412. The Senate also stressed the need for prevention as the best cure:

> In order to protect against these dangers, the proposed Toxic Substances Control Act would close a number of major regulatory gaps, for while certain statutes, including the Clean Air Act, the Federal Water Pollution Control Act, the Occupational Safety and Health Act, and the Consumer Product Safety Act, may be used to protect health and the environment from chemical substances, none of these statutes provide the means for discovering adverse effects on health and environment before manufacture of new chemical substances. Under these other statutes, the Government regulator's only response to chemical dangers is to impose restrictions after manufacture begins.

S. Rep. No. 94-698, at 5, *reprinted in* 1976 U.S.C.C.A.N. 4491, 4494. In sum, Congress had two concerns: (1) neither industry nor the government was systematically assessing the adverse effects of exposure to chemicals already in commerce, and (2) the government lacked authority to assess the safety of new chemical substances prior to their introduction into commerce. With this as a backdrop, Congress went about the task of drafting TSCA.

1.1.2. Legislative Goals

Congress intended that TSCA impose on manufacturers the responsibility for providing data on the health and environmental effects of chemical substances and mixtures. Further, the EPA Administrator was given authority to regulate those chemical substances and mixtures which "present an unreasonable risk of injury to health or the environment" and to summarily redress those which are "imminent hazards." TSCA § 2(b)(2). Congress also provided EPA with comprehensive authority to regulate the manufacture, use, distribution in commerce, and disposal[2] of chemical substances.

The key elements of this authority are as follows:

- Required testing of chemicals which may present a significant risk or which are produced in substantial quantities and result in substantial human or environmental exposure.

- Premanufacture review of new chemical substances prior to their commercial production for introduction into the marketplace.

- Regulation of existing chemical substances that present an unreasonable risk of injury to human health or the environment.

- Specific prohibitions on the manufacture, use, distribution, and disposal of PCBs.

- Broad recordkeeping and reporting requirements to ensure that the EPA Administrator would continually have access to new information regarding adverse health or environmental effects associated with chemical substances.

TSCA is administered by EPA's Office of Pollution Prevention and Toxics (OPPT), which has developed a complex web of regulations designed to implement each of the above statutory grants of authority. To date, EPA's primary focus has been on premanufacture reviews, regulation of new chemicals and the myriad recordkeeping and reporting requirements of TSCA § 8. With the exception of testing, including a substantial and increasing reliance upon voluntary testing programs, EPA has done little else to regulate existing chemicals.

Unlike other federal statutes, which regulate a chemical risk after the chemical has been introduced into commerce, the major objective of TSCA is to characterize and understand the risks a chemical poses to humans and the environment *before* it is introduced into commerce. TSCA, however, requires that before undertaking regulatory action once introduced into commerce, the EPA Administrator balance the economic and social benefits derived from the use of a chemical against that chemical's identified risks. TSCA §§ 2, 6(c). Thus, the goal of TSCA is not to regulate all chemicals which

---

2 Under TSCA, EPA can regulate the disposal of "chemical substances" as defined by the Act. By contrast, the Resource Conservation and Recovery Act is limited to the regulation of the disposal of solid wastes and, within that category, hazardous wastes. 42 U.S.C. §§ 6901-6992k (2000 & Supp. I 2001).

present a risk but only those which present an "unreasonable" risk of harm to human health or the environment.

Congress limited the Administrator's authority to the regulation of "unreasonable" risks "because to do otherwise assumes that a risk-free society is attainable, an assumption that the Committee does not make." H.R. Rep. No. 94-1341, at 15, *reprinted in TSCA Legislative History* at 423. Nevertheless, Congress declined to expressly define the term "unreasonable risk." Rather, Congress recognized that implementation of the "unreasonable risk" standard for triggering regulatory authority under TSCA "will of necessity vary depending on the specific regulatory authority which the Administrator seeks to exercise." *Id.* at 14, *reprinted in TSCA Legislative History* at 422.

1.2. PRINCIPAL PROVISIONS OF TSCA

Subject to a few important exclusions (such as those for pesticides, foods, drugs, cosmetics and medical devices), TSCA § 3(2) defines the term "chemical substance" broadly to mean "any organic or inorganic substance of a particular molecular identity." EPA has even interpreted this definition to include genetically engineered microorganisms. TSCA § 8(b) requires EPA to compile and keep current a list or "inventory" of chemical substances manufactured, imported, or processed in the United States for commercial purposes. For regulatory purposes, TSCA divides the chemical universe between "existing" chemical substances, *i.e.*, those on the TSCA § 8(b) Inventory of Chemical Substances, and "new chemical substances," which are not on the Inventory.

1.2.1. TSCA § 4—Testing

EPA also may require testing of chemical substances and mixtures under TSCA § 4, if it finds that they "may present" an unreasonable risk of injury to health or the environment, or if they will be produced in substantial quantities resulting in significant human or environmental exposure. Manufacturers and/or processors of chemicals subject to a testing rule must bear the cost of testing, and TSCA § 4(c) provides for cost sharing among them.

1.2.2. TSCA § 5—Premanufacture Notification

Any company intending to manufacture or import a new chemical substance must give the Agency 90 days' prior notice under TSCA § 5. This "premanufacture notification" (PMN) requirement enables EPA to screen a new chemical before its commercial production or importation. If the new chemical "presents or will present" an unreasonable risk of injury to health or the environment, and if there is insufficient information "to permit a reasoned evaluation of the health and environmental effects of a chemical substance," the Agency can prohibit or limit its manufacture, processing, distribution in commerce, use, or disposal. TSCA § 5(e), (f).

1.2.3. TSCA § 6—Regulation of Existing Chemicals

If the manufacture, processing, distribution, use, or disposal of an existing chemical substance or mixture "presents . . . an unreasonable risk of injury to health or the environment," the Administrator has broad authority under TSCA § 6 to prohibit or limit production and to impose labeling or other requirements. The determination of unreasonable risk under TSCA § 6 requires a consideration of both risks and benefits. In addition, the Agency must conduct its TSCA § 6 rulemaking in accordance with the procedures of section 4 of the Administrative Procedure Act, 5 U.S.C. § 553 (1994), such as publishing a proposed rule, providing an opportunity for oral and written comment and publishing a final rule that sets forth the basis for EPA's finding of unreasonable risk. TSCA § 6. Thus, although the Agency has broad authority to regulate existing chemicals, this authority is limited by procedural safeguards that apparently have discouraged EPA from taking action under TSCA § 6 in all but a few cases over the last 29 years. In 2005 and beyond, however, there will be new pressure on EPA to act under section 6 (or on Congress to require or facilitate such action, if needed), as EPA acquires and publishes summaries of abundant new test data on so-called high production volume (HPV) chemicals (*see* section 1.4 below), as EPA continues to collect and publish information about industrial chemicals under the TSCA § 8(a) Inventory Update Rule (IUR), including manufacturing and import quantities and, beginning in 2006, use and exposure information, and as EPA also continues to collect and publish information about releases of "toxic" chemicals under the Emergency Planning and Community Right-to-Know Act (EPCRA) section 313 Toxic Release Inventory (TRI).

1.2.4. TSCA § 6(e)—PCB Regulation

TSCA § 6(e) prohibits the manufacture, processing, distribution in commerce or use of polychlorinated biphenyls (PCBs) except in a totally enclosed manner. Yet, section 6(e)(2)(B) authorizes the EPA Administrator to permit the manufacture, processing, distribution in commerce, or use of PCBs in other than a totally enclosed manner "if the Administrator finds that [a specific activity] will not present an unreasonable risk of injury to health or the environment." Additionally, any person may petition the Administrator for an exemption from the section 6(e) ban, which the Administrator may grant by rule upon finding that no unreasonable risk of injury to health or the environment would result and that good faith efforts had been made to develop a chemical substitute for PCBs. These exemptions, however, are limited to one year from the date they are granted. TSCA § 6(e)(3)(B).

1.2.5. TSCA § 8—Recordkeeping and Reporting

To complement its broad regulatory authority under sections 4, 5, 6 and 7, TSCA § 8 authorizes the Administrator to require manufacturers, processors and in some cases distributors to undertake recordkeeping and reporting. Under section 8(a), EPA can require companies to collect, maintain, and submit information on production and processing of chemicals (and mixtures, but only if "necessary for the effective enforcement of the [Act]"); under section 8(c), EPA can require manufacturers and processors of chemical substances and mixtures to maintain records of significant adverse reactions alleged to have been caused by their chemicals; under section 8(d), EPA can require companies to search their files and to provide lists and copies of health and safety studies they have on chemical substances and mixtures that they manufacture, process or distribute in commerce; and under section 8(e), companies must immediately report information concerning substantial risks associated with chemical substances and mixtures that they manufacture, process or distribute in commerce.

1.2.6. TSCA §§ 11, 15, 16 and 17—Enforcement

TSCA § 11 gives EPA broad authority to inspect establishments that hold chemicals and to subpoena information for enforcement of the Act. TSCA §§ 15, 16, and 17, respectively, list prohibited acts, their attendant civil and criminal penalties, and the jurisdiction of the district court for specific enforcement and seizure.

1.3. TSCA AMENDMENTS—TITLES II, III AND IV

In October 1986, Congress passed the Asbestos Hazard Emergency Response Act of 1986 (AHERA), Pub. L. No. 99-519, 100 Stat. 2970 (codified as amended at 15 U.S.C. §§ 2641-2655 (1994)), now Title II of TSCA. AHERA was designed to remedy major problems identified with EPA's present asbestos-in-schools program. It requires EPA to establish a comprehensive regulatory framework of inspection, management, planning, operations and maintenance activities, and appropriate abatement responses for controlling asbestos-containing materials in schools.

In October 1988, Congress added a third title to TSCA under which EPA must study indoor radon pollution, publish model construction standards for new buildings, give technical advice on abatement to states and federal agencies, and establish a grant program to assist states in developing their own radon control programs. Act of Oct. 28, 1988, Pub. L. No. 100-551, 102 Stat. 2755 (codified as amended at 15 U.S.C.A. §§ 2661-2671 (West 1982 & Supp. 1997)).

In October 1992, the fourth and currently final title was added to TSCA. Act of October 28, 1992, Pub. L. 102-55, 106 Stat. 3924 (codified at 15 U.S.C. §§ 2681-2691 (1994)). Title IV—Lead Exposure Reduction—requires EPA, the Occupational Safety and Health Administration and the Department of Housing and Urban Development to develop lead paint abatement training and certification programs for contractors who engage in lead-based paint activities, to identify lead-based paint hazards and communicate such hazards to the public through a lead hazard information pamphlet, and to define safe levels of lead in various media.

1.4. EPA'S IMPLEMENTATION OF TSCA

Although TSCA is now almost 30 years old, EPA's progress in gathering health and environmental effects data on new and existing chemical substances has been slow. For example, between 1979 (when EPA established the TSCA Inventory) and

September 30, 2002, the Agency reviewed 30,906 new chemical submissions (called "pre-manufacture notifications" or "PMNs") and an additional 9,052 exemption notices, but less than a third of the PMNs filed with EPA typically contain any data. About 15 percent of PMNs have some (primarily acute) mammalian toxicity data; about ten percent have measured data on physico-chemical properties and/or environmental fate attributes; and about five percent have some (mostly fish acute) ecotoxicity data.

The lack of data on new chemicals has forced EPA to base its premanufacture review of many new chemicals on so-called "structure activity relationships" (SAR) analysis, in which EPA predicts the characteristics and potential effects of the new chemical based upon the known characteristics and effects of structurally similar chemicals. Initially controversial, EPA's use of SAR analysis is now generally accepted. In 1988, in an attempt to increase the amount of data available on new chemicals, EPA implemented a policy to require testing of certain new chemicals. Making use of its TSCA § 5(e) authority, EPA began requiring testing of new chemicals that will be produced in high volumes or that fall within certain categories of concern, including since 1999 a category for persistent, bioaccumulative, and toxic (PBT) new chemicals.

As of September 30, 2004, EPA had issued 1,280 TSCA § 5(e) consent orders, 729 of which were with so-called Significant New Use Rules (SNURs) and 570 non-5(e) SNURs, covering 7.92 percent of the 32,559 TSCA § 5 notices, which include PMNs, Low Volume Exemptions (LVEs), Test Marketing Exemption Applications (TMEAs), Low Release/Low Exposure Exemptions (LoREX), and Polymer Exemptions.[3] In addition, as of September 30, 2004, PMN submitters voluntarily agreed to perform toxicity testing on over 300 chemicals before EPA completed its review of the PMN, and to withdraw 1,662 PMNs in the face of prospective EPA regulation under section5(e). Overall, EPA has taken or threatened to take some action on a new chemical in 3,812 cases, about 9 percent of all section 5 notices received by EPA as of September 30, 2004.

In response to the initial controversy over SAR analysis, EPA conducted a study in 1993 to evaluate its effectiveness as a tool to predict a chemical's toxicity. The study involved 144 chemicals that had been the subject of European Union (EU) pre-market notifications.[4] EPA conducted its typical SAR analysis on these 144 chemicals to predict their toxic properties and to carry out preliminary hazard assessments and then compared these predicted properties to the properties identified through tests conducted on these same compounds. From the study, EPA concluded that SAR analysis is useful and effective in identifying chemicals that may be toxic but has limitations in predicting the exact type and level of toxicity. Nevertheless, EPA believes

---

3 Before it became self-implementing in March 1995, the Polymer Exemption required an application to EPA.

4 The EU requires notifiers to perform certain up-front toxicity testing on new chemical substances and to include these data with the pre-market notification.

that selectively incorporating specific testing schemes into SAR analysis would improve its chemical review process. Since EPA's 1993 study, however, Congress has made no plans to amend TSCA Title I to require any up-front toxicity testing of new chemical substances. The EU's efforts to modernize its assessment and management of chemical substances under the proposed Registration, Evaluation and Authorization of Chemicals (REACH) legislation has prompted some reconsideration in the United States of the need for up-front toxicity testing of new chemicals (among other things), but it is unclear at present what action Congress will take in this area, if any.[5]

As EPA has gained experience in reviewing new chemical notifications, its PMN regulations also have evolved, most notably in several significant amendments in March 1995. Designed to streamline the PMN review process, these amendments allow EPA to review more notices in a shorter time with fewer resources. Briefly, they introduced sweeping changes in the polymer and low volume exemptions, a new exemption for low release/low exposure (LoREX) chemicals and a simplified process for issuing expedited significant new use rules for chemicals not the subject of TSCA § 5(e) orders.

In 1997, under the authority of TSCA § 5, EPA also promulgated new rules governing the way that EPA reviews and regulates the use of intergeneric microorganisms in commerce and commercial research (intergeneric microorganisms are created to contain genetic material from organisms in more than one taxonomic genera). Prior to 1997, EPA reviewed microbial products of biotechnology for ten years under the authority of a 1986 policy statement that declared intergeneric microorganisms "new chemicals" under TSCA § 5 and used pre-existing TSCA regulations intended for new chemicals to notify new biotechnology products. The 1997 rulemaking superseded EPA's biotechnology program under the 1986 policy.

By contrast, EPA's regulation of existing chemicals under TSCA § 6 remains almost nonexistent. Since the enactment of TSCA in 1976, EPA has used section 6 to control just six existing substances or chemical groups: (1) polychlorinated biphenyls (PCBs); (2) chlorofluorocarbons; (3) dioxin; (4) metalworking fluids; (5) asbestos; and (6) hexavalent chromium. Of these, Congress mandated the regulation of PCBs under section 6(e), and EPA ultimately abandoned regulation of dioxin and chlorofluorocarbons in favor of more comprehensive regulatory schemes under the Resource Conservation and Recovery Act and the Clean Air Act.

In general, EPA has found TSCA § 6 regulation of existing chemicals to be highly resource-intensive and procedurally difficult. The statute requires EPA to consider the effects of the chemical on health and the environment, the magnitude of the exposure to the chemical, the benefits of the chemical, the availability of substitutes, and the economic consequences of the rule, all before taking action under section 6. In

---

[5] *See* footnote 7 and the associated discussion of future developments with Title I of TSCA later in this chapter.

addition, EPA must conduct its section 6 rulemaking in accordance with the Administrative Procedure Act, so that no rule is promulgated under section 6 without input from the regulated community and the general public.

EPA's most celebrated and ultimately unsuccessful attempt to regulate an existing chemical under TSCA § 6 was its 1989 rule phasing out most uses of asbestos. The U.S. Court of Appeals for the Fifth Circuit overturned this rule, because the court felt that EPA lacked substantial evidence to justify a complete ban. *Corrosion Proof Fittings v. EPA*, 947 F.2d 1201 (5th Cir. 1991). EPA spent ten years preparing its rule, had a huge body of scientific evidence on the adverse health effects of asbestos and, still, its rule was overturned, because a ban was not justified. EPA has used the *Corrosion Proof Fittings* case to disparage the procedural safeguards of TSCA § 6 as unworkable, but the case really may illustrate the value of the legal standard of section 6, which requires EPA to use the least burdensome form of regulation and to base its decision upon substantial evidence.

On a positive note, EPA is making progress toward reviewing existing chemicals through a combination of TSCA § 4 test rules, enforceable consent agreements (ECAs), voluntary testing agreements, and voluntary testing programs. In 1998, EPA initiated two important new voluntary testing programs for industry, namely, the High Production Volume (HPV) Challenge Program and the Voluntary Children's Chemical Evaluation Program (VCCEP), which is in a pilot phase. Although only 23 chemicals currently are proposed for testing under the pilot VCCEP, as of May 28, 2004, industry has voluntarily undertaken to test 2,223 of the approximately 2,800 chemicals manufactured in, or imported into, the United States in amounts equal to or exceeding one million pounds per year. The HPV Challenge Program has become the centerpiece of EPA's existing chemicals program. For HPV chemicals that are not "sponsored" for voluntary testing, EPA is planning to develop a testing requirement under a TSCA § 4 test rule.

In addition, as of May 2004, the Agency had addressed approximately 154 chemicals in TSCA § 4 test rules (EPA did not issue its first test rule until 1984) and another 250 chemicals in so-called "Decisions not to Test." EPA has negotiated testing agreements or entered into ECAs to test approximately 60 additional chemicals, and industry is voluntarily testing a further 60 or so chemicals outside of the VCCEP and the HPV Challenge Program. The Agency blames the rulemaking process for its failure to require testing more often and has responded in recent years by significantly increasing its reliance upon voluntary testing initiatives. Hence, the HPV Challenge Program constitutes a new paradigm, with its enormous jump in the number of existing chemicals undergoing testing.

It is hard to predict what the future holds for Title I of TSCA. A 1994 GAO report recommended that Congress amend TSCA to reduce procedural requirements for EPA to regulate existing chemicals, to place a greater burden on industry to compile data on existing chemicals and to require a certain minimum amount of pre-market data in all

PMNs.[6] Congress has not acted upon the GAO report, however, leaving EPA to make do with its present statutory authority.

A 2005 GAO report also suggested options for improving the assessment and regulation of chemicals by EPA, which would shift the burden of proving the safety of chemicals from the government onto industry, like the proposed REACH legislation in the EU.[7] GAO recommended that Congress give EPA new authority to enter into testing agreements with companies, to require manufacturers to develop test data, and to share the information with States and foreign governments. GAO also recommended a systematic review of existing chemicals based on data submitted by industry and financial incentives to ensure the development of safer alternatives to toxic substances, as with the EU's REACH proposals. It is too soon, however, to predict how Congress will react to the most recent GAO report.

Under planned legislation to implement treaties concerning so-called persistent organic pollutants (POPs), EPA will acquire a TSCA mandate to reduce or eliminate specific chemical substances, but the basic regulatory structure of TSCA will not change for the many other chemicals not listed in the POPs treaties. The *status quo* is likely to change, however, with respect to the control of existing chemicals under TSCA § 6.

In 2004, EPA began to receive new test data on over 2,200 HPV chemicals under the HPV Challenge Program. EPA will soon publish additional data on industrial chemicals collected in 2002 under the TSCA § 8(a) IUR, which, beginning in 2006, will collect not only information about manufacturing and import quantities but also information about uses of, and exposures to, industrial chemicals. In addition, EPA also will soon publish the most recent annual data on releases of "toxic" chemicals under the EPCRA section 313 TRI. In other words, EPA is now receiving an enormous and increasing amount of new exposure and toxicity data on thousands of basic industrial chemicals, and these data will provide EPA with an abundant scientific record to consider action against certain existing chemicals under the authority of TSCA § 6. If EPA remains unwilling or unable to act under section 6, despite all of the new information, pressure will mount on Congress to require or facilitate EPA action under TSCA § 6.

Consequently, for the immediate future, EPA will surely continue to focus on new chemical regulation, voluntary testing of existing chemicals, and enforcement of the reporting and recordkeeping requirements of the Act. On the basis of plentiful new

---

[6] U.S. Gov't Accountability Office, *GAO/RCED-94-103*, *Toxic Substances Control Act: Legislative Changes Could Make the Act More Effective* 5 (Sept. 1994).

[7] U.S. Gov't Accountability Office, *GAO-05-458*, *CHEMICAL REGULATION: Options Exist to Improve EPA's Ability to Assess Health Risks and Manage its Chemical Review Program* # (June 2005).

information acquired from recent collection efforts, however, EPA also will need to revisit its authority under TSCA § 6 to act against existing chemicals posing documented risks.

CHAPTER 2
ADMINISTRATION OF EPA'S TOXIC SUBSTANCES PROGRAM

The EPA Administrator sets overall policy for implementation of several environmental statutes, including TSCA. Assistant Administrators oversee each of EPA's major environmental programs, and ten Regional Administrators impose the programs within their respective regions. *See* EPA Organization Chart, Figure II-1.

The Assistant Administrator for Prevention, Pesticides and Toxic Substances directs the Office of Prevention, Pesticides and Toxic Substances (OPPTS). OPPTS has two principal components: the Office of Pesticide Programs (OPP), and the Office of Pollution Prevention and Toxics (OPPT). *See* OPPTS Organization Chart, Figure II-2. The OPPT Director exercises day-to-day responsibility for TSCA administration. EPA Headquarters is 1200 Pennsylvania Avenue, N.W., Washington, D.C. 20460.

For important contact information for the OPPT New Chemical Program and sending documentation by mail or courier see Figure II-6.

2.1. OFFICE OF POLLUTION PREVENTION AND TOXICS

OPPT is organized into seven divisions and one committee: (1) Chemical Control; (2) Risk Assessment; (3) Economics, Exposure and Technology; (4) National Program Chemicals; (5) Information Management; (6) Pollution Prevention; (7) Environmental Assistance; and (8) TSCA Interagency Testing Committee. *See* OPPT Organization Chart, Figure II-3. A directory of OPPT organization, functions and key staff is available through the TSCA Assistance Office (tel: 202-554-1404).

2.1.1. Chemical Control Division

The Chemical Control Division (CCD) (tel: 202-564-0104) remains the most visible of OPPT's divisions. Headed by a director and associate director, CCD has four branches: (1) New Chemicals Notice Management; (2) New Chemicals Prenotice; (3) Chemical Information and Testing; and (4) Existing Chemicals. Each branch has a chief.

The New Chemicals Notice Management Branch (NCNMB) (tel: 202-564-9138) manages the review and disposition of TSCA § 5 premanufacture notices (PMNs) on new chemicals. The NCNMB branch chief assigns a program manager (PM) to each new chemical. The PM has overall responsibility for shepherding the PMN through the review process. Each PMN is reviewed by a team of EPA toxicologists, chemists, biochemists, engineers and experts in other disciplines who work together to predict the potential risks to humans and the environment from the PMN substance. Inquiries concerning a specific PMN already undergoing EPA review, including inquiries regarding development of section 5(e) consent order, should be directed to the PM responsible for that PMN.

The New Chemicals Prenotice Branch (NCPNB) currently has two "Prenotice Coordinators" (tel: 202-564-9262 & 564-9373), who are available to assist companies with substantive questions concerning technical and regulatory issues relating to the PMN requirements before a PMN is submitted. Requests for PMN consolidation are submitted to the coordinators. Routine inquiries on established PMN practices and procedures should be directed to the TSCA Assistance Office (tel: 202-554-1404).

The Chemical Information and Testing Branch (tel: 202-564-8469) develops TSCA § 4 test rules, negotiates testing consent agreements, and develops and implements information gathering rules under TSCA § 8 and import certifications under TSCA § 13.

The Existing Chemicals Branch (tel: 202-564-8164) develops significant new use rules, manages the evaluation of chemicals identified for "follow-up" after PMN review, and develops TSCA § 6 rules for existing chemicals. It also issues section 9(a) referral reports and section 21 petition responses.

2.1.2. Risk Assessment Division

The Risk Assessment Division (RAD) (tel: 202-564-7641) is responsible for identifying, evaluating and developing human and ecological risk assessment techniques, providing technical program management for the TSCA § 4 testing program and risk assessments and chemical profiles for the TSCA § 6 regulatory program, developing and implementing procedures for systematically screening information on new and existing chemicals, including section 8(e) information, managing the High Production Volume (HPV) Challenge Program, participating in development of the Master Testing List, and assisting in evaluations of requests for exemptions from testing. RAD is divided into four branches: (1) Existing Chemicals Assessment (tel: 202-564-7634); (2) High Volume Production Chemicals (tel: 202-564-7649); (3) New Chemicals Screening and Assessment (tel; 202-564-8907); and (4) Science Support (tel: 202-564-7633).

2.1.3. Economics, Exposure and Technology Division

The Economics, Exposure and Technology Division (EETD) (tel: 202-564-8770) provides economic, engineering and industrial chemical information to support OPPT programs and regulatory decisions. EETD consists of the: (1) Industrial Chemistry Branch; (2) Chemical Engineering Branch; (3) Design for Environment Branch; (4) Exposure Assessment Branch; and (5) Economics and Policy Analysis Branch.

The Industrial Chemistry Branch (ICB) (tel: 202-564-8569) maintains and updates the TSCA Chemical Substance Inventory, provides Inventory searching support, provides information on chemical identity and physical-chemical properties, and serves as the final expert on chemical nomenclature issues within OPPT and EPA. After the NCNMB and NCPNB, the ICB is a major contact point for industry. For example, all inquiries regarding whether a substance is on the Inventory or how a certain substance is defined for Inventory listing purposes should be addressed to the ICB. ICB houses the Chemical Inventory Section (CIS), which is the section responsible for maintaining, refining and updating the TSCA Chemical Substance Inventory.

The Chemical Engineering Branch (CEB) (tel: 202-564-8526) assesses potential occupational exposure to chemicals from manufacturing and processing operations, and evaluates releases of chemicals into the environment and the methods used to control such releases. The Design for Environment Branch (DEB) (tel: 202-564-3821) partners with individual industry sectors to compare and improve the performance, human and environmental risks and costs of existing and alternative products, processes and practices, and to promote the integration of cleaner, cheaper and smarter solutions into everyday business practices. Partnership projects include automotive refinishing, adhesives, computer displays, garment and textile care, flexographic, lithographic, screen and gravure printing, laundry and printed wiring board.

The Economics and Policy Analysis Branch (EPAB) (tel: 202-564-8786) conducts economic analyses of the costs and benefits of TSCA regulatory actions and their impact on small businesses and the chemical industry in general. The Exposure Assessment Branch (EAB) (tel: 202-564-8551) analyzes and assesses potential human and environmental exposures to chemical substances in support of OPPT risk assessment activities.

2.1.4. National Program Chemicals Division

The National Program Chemicals Division (NPCD) (tel: 202-566-0718) is responsible for the development and management of multi-media regulatory and non-regulatory control programs, and other private or public sector initiatives to reduce and manage risks from designated National Program Chemicals (NPCs) or other priority risk management chemicals, such as asbestos, lead and PCBs. NPCD also designs, develops and implements technical programs to support management of NPCs and other priority chemicals by providing expertise and technical leadership in the areas of statistical analysis, modeling, survey design, monitoring programs, chemical measurement and analytical methods. NPCD uses the authorities granted under TSCA §§ 5, 6, 7, 9 and 11, as appropriate and necessary, to carry out its responsibilities. NPCD has three branches: (1) Fibers and Organics (tel: 202-566-0514); (2) Lead, Heavy Metals and Inorganics (tel: 202-566-1980); and (3) Program Assessment and Outreach (tel: 202-566-0474).

2.1.5. Information Management Division

The Information Management Division (IMD) (tel: 202-564-0918) manages receipt and handling of all data and documents submitted under TSCA, the Emergency

Planning and Community Right to Know Act (EPCRA) and the Pollution Prevention Act (PPA). The IMD develops, implements, and evaluates policies and procedures for the control and security of TSCA confidential business information, and operates the Optus public docket and reading room. IMD consists of four branches: (1) Information Access (tel: 202-564-8617); (2) Information Technology and Support (tel: 202-564-8591); (3) Records and Dockets Management (tel: 202-564-8594); and (4) Science Information (tel: 202-564-8598). IMD also provides an information retrieval service that searches scientific literature, commercial databases, OPPT databases, and other EPA and federal databases to support OPPT activities. Consistent with its information management responsibilities, IMD houses the TSCA Document Control Office (DCO). Through the DCO, IMD receives, logs and then disseminates all confidential and non-confidential information submitted under TSCA.

2.1.6. Pollution Prevention Division

Within OPPT, the Pollution Prevention Division (PPD) (tel: 202-564-8636) has the responsibility for implementing the Pollution Prevention Act of 1990. This Act encourages the promotion of pollution prevention over EPA's traditional approaches of pollution control, treatment and cleanup.

PPD is divided into two branches: (1) Prevention Analysis and (2) Prevention Integration. The Prevention Analysis Branch (PAB) (tel: 202-564-8829) is primarily responsible for promoting pollution prevention measures within all EPA regulatory programs. The Prevention Integration Branch (PIB) (tel: 202-564-8834) manages and implements the Pollution Prevention State Grant Program under which more than $5 million in various program support and operating grants are available to states for implementing pollution prevention programs. PIB also oversees the Technical Assistance Program. Under this program, PIB manages the library and Outreach program, including publication of a monthly newsletter, and assists in the development of pollution prevention educational initiatives.

2.1.7. Environmental Assistance Division

The Environmental Assistance Division (EAD) (tel: 202-564-8198) provides comprehensive outreach, liaison and technical assistance activities to enhance development and implementation of OPPT pollution prevention and toxic chemical use control programs, develops assistance, outreach and information exchange strategies to increase awareness of and participation in these programs, responds to congressional correspondence and inquiries, prepares congressional testimony, provides regional offices with technical information in support of their risk assessment and risk management activities, and processes TSCA § 12(b) export notifications. EAD also operates the TSCA Assistance Office (staffed by an outside contractor), which is available from 8:30 a.m. to 5:00 p.m., eastern time (tel: 202-554-1404). Requests for documents can also be made by: (1) writing to the Environmental Assistance Division (7408), U.S. Environmental Protection Agency, TSCA Assistance Information Service, 1200 Pennsylvania Avenue, N.W., Washington, D.C. 20460; (2) faxing your request to

(202) 554-5603 (fax line open 24 hours per day); or (3) e-mailing your request to tsca-hotline@epamail.epa.gov.

2.1.8. TSCA Interagency Testing Committee

In 1976 under the Toxic Substances Control Act (TSCA), the U.S. Congress created the TSCA Interagency Testing Committee (ITC) as an independent advisory committee to the Administrator of the U.S. EPA. The ITC (tel: 202-564-7526) includes representatives from 16 U.S. government member organizations. The ITC was created to identify chemicals regulated by TSCA for which there are suspicions of toxicity or exposure and for which there are few, if any, ecological effects, environmental fate or health effects testing data. As mandated under section 4(e) of TSCA, the ITC must add these chemicals to the Priority Testing List and recommend them for testing or information reporting in May and November Reports to the Administrator. Chemicals are recommended for testing to meet the data needs of the ITC's 16 government member organizations. The ITC encourages manufacturers and importers of recommended chemicals to voluntarily submit studies to meet these U.S. government data needs. Since its first meeting in 1977, the ITC has reviewed more than 40,000 chemicals.

2.2. OFFICE OF GENERAL COUNSEL

The Office of General Counsel (OGC) provides legal services to the Agency's program offices, including OPPT. Headed by a general counsel and a principal deputy general counsel, OGC is organized into divisions that correspond to EPA's program offices. OGC's Pesticides and Toxic Substances Division serves as legal counsel to OPPTS. Its activities are coordinated by an associate general counsel. In addition, the assistant general counsel, Toxics Branch, advises the OPPT staff on various matters of statutory and regulatory interpretation.

2.3. OFFICE OF ENFORCEMENT AND COMPLIANCE ASSURANCE

The Office of Enforcement and Compliance Assurance (OECA) (202-564-2440) (http://www.epa.gov/oeca) serves as the principal adviser to the Administrator in matters of enforcement and compliance assurance, and provides the direction for and review of all administrative, civil, and criminal enforcement activities, including those under TSCA. OECA consists of eight components: (1) Office of Compliance; (2) The Federal Facilities Enforcement Office; (3) Office of Criminal Enforcement, Forensics and Training; (4) Office of Civil Enforcement; (5) Office of Site Remediation Enforcement; (6) Office of Federal Activities; (7) Office of Environmental Justice; and (8) Office of Planning, Policy Analysis and Communications. *See* OECA Organization Chart, Figure II-4.

Organized by industrial sector, the Office of Compliance (OC) (202-564-2280) assists industries and other regulated entities to improve their compliance with environmental laws. OC also works with EPA regions and Headquarters to establish national enforcement and compliance priorities, monitor compliance, develop and track performance and measure and evaluate results. OC has four Divisions: (1) Enforcement, Planning, Targeting and Data; (2) Compliance Assessment and Media Programs; (3) Compliance Assistance and Sector Programs; and (4) Agriculture.

The Federal Facilities Enforcement Office (FFEO) (tel: 202-564-2510) is responsible for ensuring that federal facilities take all necessary actions to prevent, control and abate environmental pollution. The FFEO is divided into two groups: (1) the Site Remediation Civil Enforcement Program (SRES); and (2) the Planning, Prevention and Compliance Program (PPCS).

The Office of Criminal Enforcement, Forensics and Training (OCEFT) (tel: 202-564-2480) directs EPA's criminal program, provides technical and forensic services for civil and criminal investigative support and provides training for federal, State and local environmental professionals. OCEFT also provides investigative and technical support to the federal government's homeland security program. OCEFT has four divisions: (1) Criminal Investigations; (2) Legal Counsel & resource Management; (3) National Enforcement Investigations Center; and (4) National Enforcement Training Institute.

The Office of Civil Enforcement (OCE) (tel: 202-564-2220) works with States, EPA Regional Offices, Tribes and other federal agencies to assure compliance with the nation's environmental laws by investigating violations, deterring violations of federal environmental laws through civil enforcement actions and providing incentives to those members of the regulated community to comply with the law. ORE is divided into five enforcement divisions: (1) Air; (2) RCRA (hazardous waste); (3) Water; (4) Toxics and Pesticides; and (5) Multimedia. The Toxics and Pesticides Enforcement Division (tel: 202-564-2325) has responsibility for case development, administrative enforcement proceedings, interface with the Justice Department, litigation policy, and regulatory development and review. The division is comprised of both attorneys and program staff and has two branches, eastern and western. Associate enforcement counsel in the Toxics and Pesticides Enforcement Division provide principal direction and review of pesticides and toxic substances civil enforcement activities. Associate enforcement counsel or a member of the staff for Toxics and Pesticides will act as counsel for OPPT and OPPTS in enforcement matters under TSCA.

The Office of Site Remediation Enforcement (OSRE) (tel: 202-564-5110) facilitates, coordinates and evaluates the enforcement of EPA's national hazardous waste cleanup programs. OSRE has two divisions: (1) Policy & Program Evaluation and (2) Regional Support.

The Office of Federal Activities (OFA) (tel: 202-564-5400) reviews all federal Environmental Impact Statements (EISs) prepared under the National Environmental Policy Act (NEPA), maintains a national EIS filing system, assures that EPA's own actions comply with NEPA and other environmental requirements, and provides technical assistance, compliance assistance, enforcement and capacity building. OFA has two divisions: (1) International Enforcement & Compliance and (2) NEPA Compliance.

The Office of Environmental Justice (OEJ) (tel: 202-564-2515) provides a central point for EPA to address environmental and human health concerns in all communities, including minority communities and/or low-income communities – a segment of the population that has been disproportionately exposed to environmental harm and risks.

The Office of Planning, Policy Analysis and Communications (OPPAC) (tel: 202-564-2530) recommends national policy on issues pertaining to environmental enforcement and compliance and addresses emerging and crosscutting issues, such as innovation in OECA's programs.

FIGURE II-1
U.S. ENVIRONMENTAL PROTECTION AGENCY

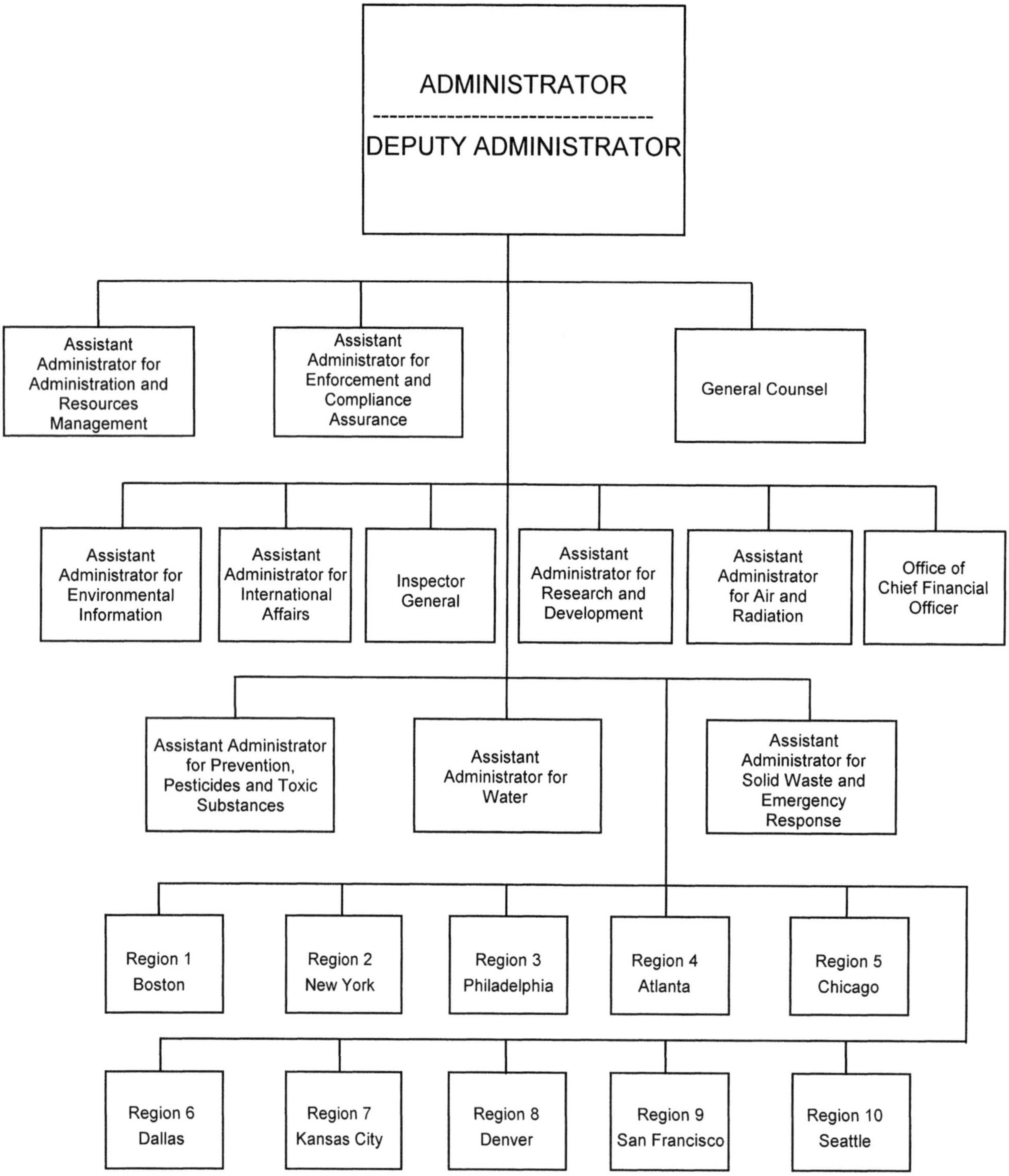

FIGURE II-2
OFFICE OF PREVENTION, PESTICIDES AND TOXIC SUBSTANCES

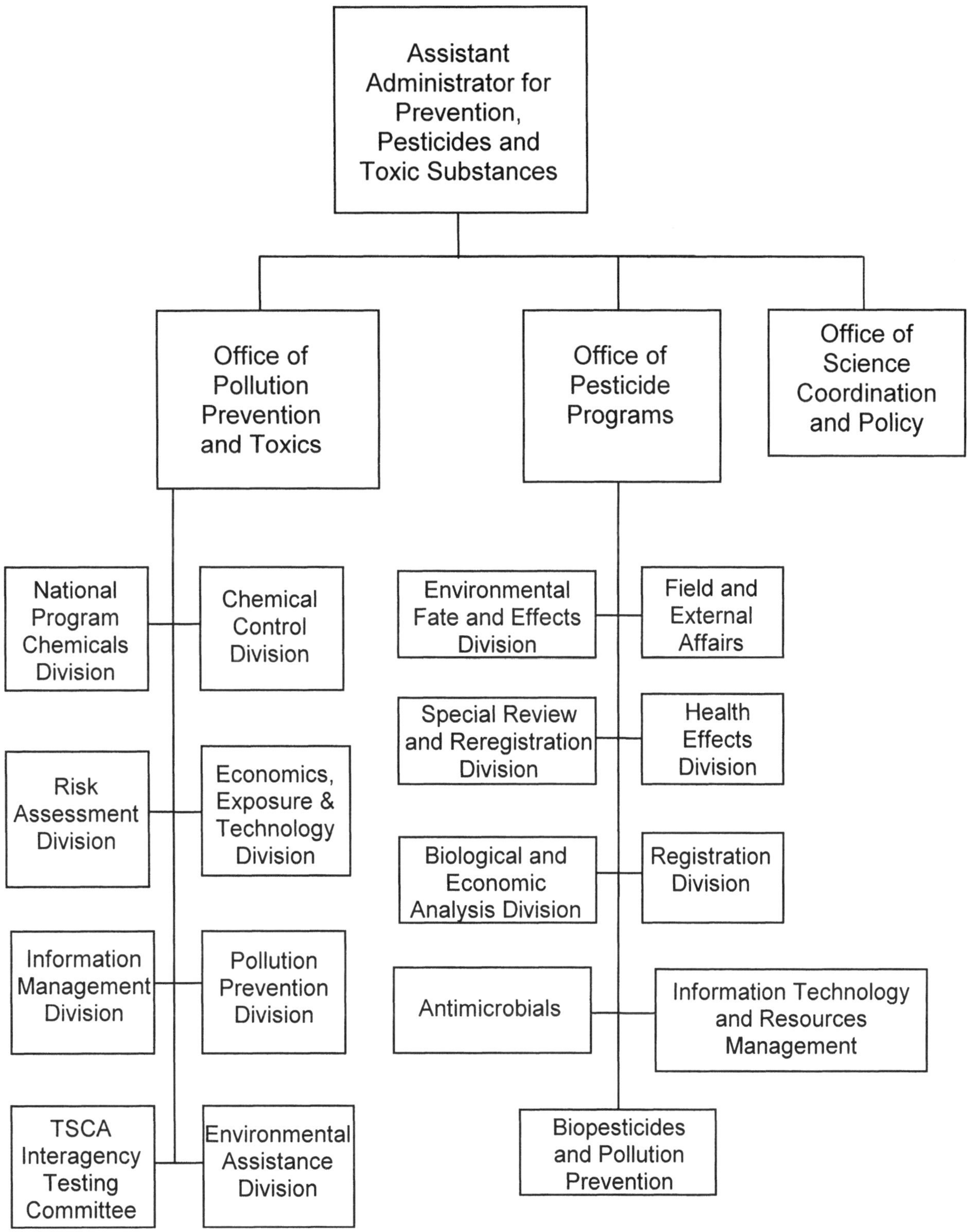

FIGURE II-3
OFFICE OF POLLUTION PREVENTION AND TOXICS

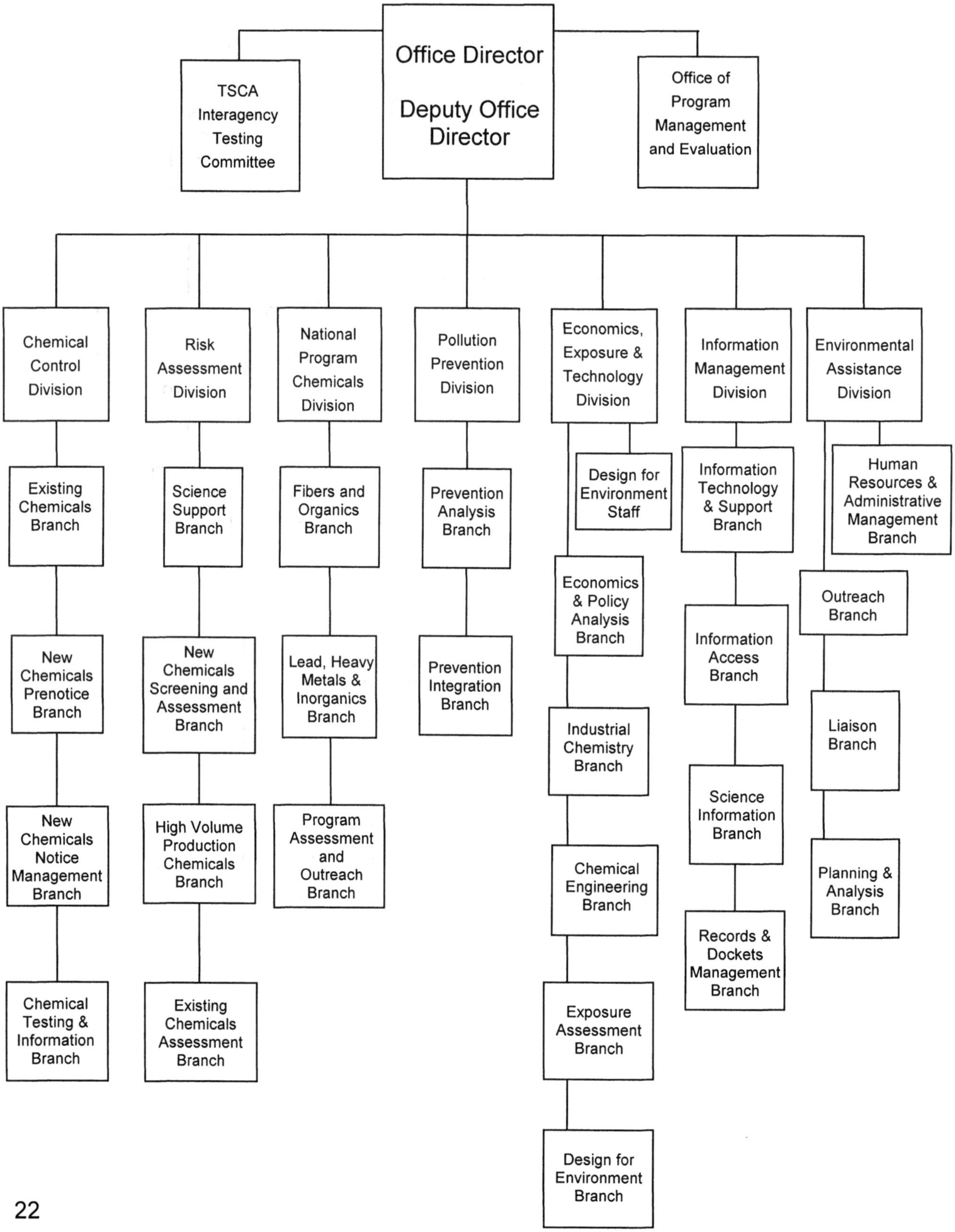

FIGURE II-4
OFFICE OF ENFORCEMENT AND COMPLIANCE ASSURANCE

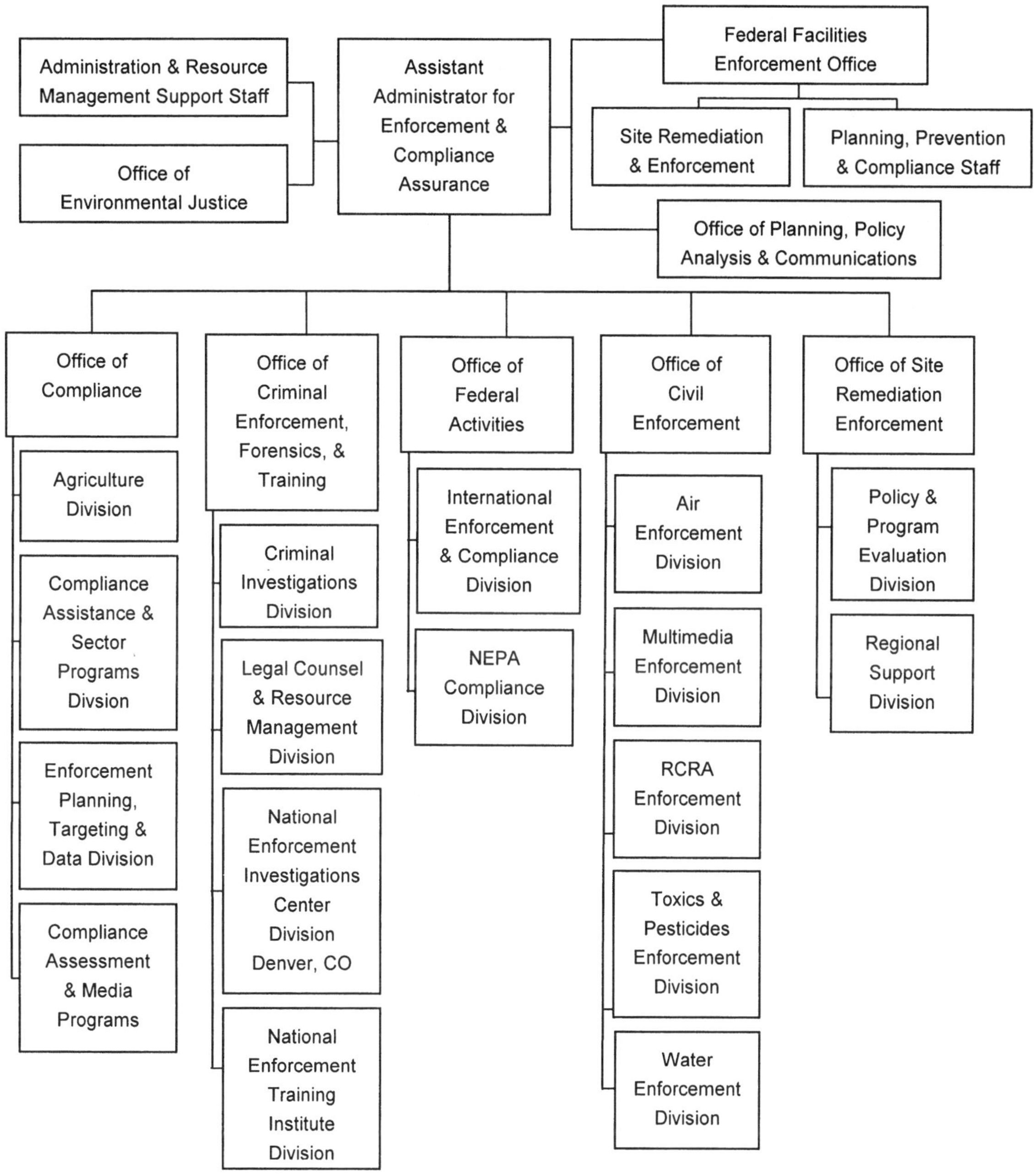

FIGURE II-5
TELEPHONE LIST FOR EPA OFFICES RELATED TO TSCA

Office	***Telephone Number***
Chemical Control Division (CCD)	(202) 564-0104
National Program Chemicals Division (NPCD)	(202) 566-0718
Risk Assessment Division (RAD)	(202) 564-7641
Economics, Exposure and Technology Division (EETD)	(202) 564-8770
Environmental Assistance Division (EAD) (TSCA Assistance Office)	(202) 564-8198 (202) 554-1404
Information Management Division (IMD)	(202) 564-0918
Office of Pollution Prevention and Toxics (OPPT)	(202) 564-3810
Pollution Prevention Division (PPD)	(202) 564-8636
Interagency Testing Committee	(202) 564-7526

EPA OPPT WEBSITE ADDRESS

EPA OPPT Programs	http://www.epa.gov/oppt/opptprg.htm

FIGURE II-6
CONTACT INFORMATION FOR THE OPPT NEW CHEMICALS PROGRAM

(http://www.epa.gov/opptintr/newchems/contact.htm)

I. General inquiries and prenotice communications:

US Mail

US EPA
Office of Pollution Prevention & Toxics
New Chemicals Program (7405M)
1200 Pennsylvania Avenue, NW
Washington, DC 20460

Courier

Use the following direct address to send material by courier. (The door guards will need a new chemicals program staff contact phone and room number):

US EPA
Office of Pollution Prevention & Toxics (New Chemicals Program)
EPA East Building, Room 4133
1201 Constitution Ave.
Washington, DC 20004-3302.

Main phone number: 202-564-8999
Fax: 202-564-9490

II. US Mail submissions of TSCA § 5 notices -- such as PMNs, PMN Exemption Notices (LVEs, TMEAs, LoRex applications), NOCs, any supporting information for previously submitted notices, etc.:

US Mail

US EPA
Office of Pollution Prevention and Toxics
Document Control Office (7407M)
1200 Pennsylvania Ave., NW
Washington, DC 20460

Courier

Courier submissions of TSCA § 5 notices are delivered to the Confidential Business Information Center (CBIC). The room at which submissions are accepted is only open until 4 pm. If a courier service comes after that time it will be turned away.

The address for sending by courier is:

US EPA
Office of Pollution Prevention and Toxics
US EPA
Confidential Business Information Center (CBIC)
EPA East Building, Room 6428
1201 Constitution Ave.
Washington, DC 20004-3302.

Contact Phone Numbers: 202-564-8930 and 202-564-8940.

Non-uniformed (bicycle, etc) couriers will be met at the 1201 Constitution Ave. entrance by CBIC personnel. Uniformed couriers are admitted to deliver directly to the CBIC.

CHAPTER 3
ACTIVITIES SUBJECT TO TSCA

TSCA applies to persons and companies that manufacture, process, distribute, use, or dispose of TSCA-regulated chemicals. As a result, questions often arise as to whether a particular activity constitutes "manufacture," "processing," "distribution," "use," or "disposal" for purposes of TSCA jurisdiction and enforcement. Unfortunately, these questions often cannot be answered clearly.

TSCA does not define "use" or "dispose," and the statutory definitions of "manufacture," "process," and "distribute" are worded so broadly that TSCA jurisdiction could extend to ridiculous lengths if the definitions were applied literally. EPA's implementing regulations generally define the terms more narrowly than the statute, and the preambles to those regulations sometimes provide further clarification, but in some cases the scope of TSCA jurisdiction remains unclear and varies among TSCA regulatory provisions.

For most major TSCA rules, EPA has issued at least one question and answer (Q&A) document, in part for the purpose of clarifying the Agency's positions with regard to the rule. As a practical matter, however, these Q&A documents sometimes seem to expand the scope of these terms beyond the definitions stated in the regulations, leaving the exact scope of the regulations unclear.

This chapter discusses in succession the terms "manufacture," "process," "distribute," "use," and "dispose," the TSCA obligations potentially applicable to each type of activity, and EPA's attempts to clarify these terms. The various chapters of this handbook discuss the full scope and regulatory implications of these activities.

3.1. "MANUFACTURE"

Under TSCA, manufacturers of chemical substances generally must: (1) sponsor tests and submit data to EPA if their chemical becomes subject to a test rule; (2) submit a premanufacture notice before manufacturing a chemical substance not on the TSCA Inventory or before manufacturing a chemical for a significant new use; (3) comply with EPA orders issued under section 5(e), 5(f) or 6(b) or rules promulgated under section 6(a); (4) avoid the manufacture of PCBs except for certain allowable inadvertent generation or permitted activities; (5) maintain records and submit reports as required by section 8; (6) submit to EPA inspections and subpoenas, as authorized by section 11; (7) submit notices of export as required by section 12(b); and (8) certify compliance with TSCA upon importation as required by section 13.

TSCA § 3(7) defines the term "manufacture" to mean

> import into the customs territory of the United States . . . produce, or manufacture.

Hence, the TSCA definition of "manufacture" encompasses not only the traditional notions of manufacturing and production, but also the importation of TSCA-regulated chemical substances or mixtures into the United States. Therefore, importers should be aware of their responsibilities as "manufacturers" under TSCA. *See ALM Corp. v. EPA*, 974 F.2d 380, 384 (3d Cir. 1992) (recognizing that TSCA reporting requirements imposed on domestic manufacturers also are imposed on importers).

3.1.1. Manufacture "for Commercial Purposes"

The TSCA definition of "manufacture" is potentially very broad, and does not clearly establish what types of operations EPA may regulate as "manufacturing." In fact, a federal appeals court has noted that the statutory definition of "manufacture" does "little more than include importing as a type of manufacture." *Dow Chemical Co. v. EPA*, 605 F.2d 673, 682 (3d Cir. 1979). The statute, however, does impose some limitations on the term. For example, TSCA § 5(i) states that for the purposes of section 5, TSCA jurisdiction over manufacturers is limited to persons who manufacture a chemical substance or mixture "for commercial purposes"; section 8(f) applies the same limitation to section 8.

EPA defines "manufacture for commercial purposes" under TSCA §§ 5, 8(a), 8(c), and 8(d) rules as follows:

> (e)(1) "Manufacture for commercial purposes" means to import, produce, or manufacture with the purpose of obtaining an immediate or eventual commercial advantage for the manufacturer, and includes, among other things, such "manufacture" of any amount of a chemical substance or mixture:
>
> (i) For distribution in commerce, including for test marketing.
>
> (ii) For use by the manufacturer, including use for product research and development, or as an intermediate.
>
> (2) "Manufacture for commercial purposes" also applies to substances that are produced coincidentally during the manufacture, processing, use, or disposal of another substance or mixture, including both byproducts that are separated from that other substances [sic] or mixture and impurities that remain in that substance or mixture.

> Such byproducts and impurities may, or may not, in themselves have commercial value. They are nonetheless produced for the purpose of obtaining a commercial advantage since they are part of the manufacture of a chemical product for a commercial purpose.

40 C.F.R. § 717.3(e); *see also id.* §§ 712.3(h), 704.3, 716.3, 720.3(r). For purposes of compiling the TSCA Inventory, the Agency defines "manufacture for commercial purposes" to mean "manufacture or import: (1) [f]or distribution in commerce, including for test marketing purposes, or (2) [f]or use by the manufacturer, including for use as an intermediate." *Id.* § 710.2(p).

Courts apparently will permit EPA to define "commercial purposes" broadly. The court in *Dow Chemical* ruled that EPA may define "manufacture for commercial purposes" to extend to manufacture of a small amount of a chemical solely for research and development (R&D). *See Dow Chemical Co.*, 605 F.2d at 686. In its rule to implement section 8(d), EPA had taken the position that anyone who manufactured solely for R&D a small quantity of one of the chemical substances covered by the section 8(d) implementing rule had manufactured the R&D substance "for a commercial purpose," and, therefore, was subject to section 8(d) requirements. Dow Chemical challenged the rule, contending that manufacture solely for R&D was not "for a commercial purpose," and as such, R&D was not subject to the requirements of section 8(d). The court concluded that the "commercial purposes" limitation of TSCA § 8(f) did not exclude R&D chemicals from coverage under section8(d) and that EPA was acting within its authority under TSCA § 8(d) when it sought to require submission of health and safety studies on R&D chemicals. *Id.* This precedent could extend to other section 8 provisions, and to section 5 as well, since the statutory language of section 5(i) is identical to that of section 8(f).

3.1.2. "Extraction" as "Manufacturing"

The rules implementing TSCA §§ 5, 8(a), and 8(d) expand the statutory definition of "manufacture" by defining "manufacturer" to include persons who extract a chemical from another chemical substance or mixture of substances:

> "Manufacturer" means a person who imports, produces, or manufactures a chemical substance. A person who extracts a component chemical substance from a previously existing chemical substance or a complex combination of substances is a manufacturer of that component chemical substance.

40 C.F.R. § 704.3; *see also* 40 C.F.R. §§ 716.3, 720.3(t).

The Agency apparently has interpreted "extraction" to include purification processes. In its Q&A document on the Comprehensive Assessment Information Rule (CAIR), for example, EPA sets forth the following question and answer:

> We buy Chemical X (a CAIR listed substance) as a raw material from a supplier at 80% purity. We purify this raw material to make 90% pure Chemical X, and then sell it to our customers. Since we do not actually "manufacture" any more Chemical X than we buy, must we report as a manufacturer of Chemical X?
>
> Yes. "Manufacture" of a substance includes, by definition, the purification of that substance (40 CFR sec. 704.3).

EPA, *Comprehensive Assessment Information Rule Question and Answer Document* 9-10 (Dec. 1988).

The cited definition of "manufacture" (40 C.F.R. § 704.3), however, does not directly address purification. Apparently EPA is referring to that portion of the definition which includes as a manufacturer a person who "extracts a component chemical substance from a previously existing chemical substance or a complex combination of substances." Whether purification of a market-grade chemical substance constitutes "extraction" under this definition is unclear.

The concept of purification as manufacture is inconsistent with the preamble to an earlier model reporting rule, the Preliminary Assessment Information Rule (PAIR). 47 Fed. Reg. 26,992 (June 22, 1982). The preamble to the final PAIR defines "purification" as "manufacturing" only in a single circumstance—where a company is purifying mined raw materials to make them marketable for the first time as a PAIR-listed substance:

> Questions were asked during the comment period about the application of this rule to mining of chemical substances. The concern was that listed chemical substances are present in mined substances in variable or undefined concentrations and that a single chemical substance may be reported as "manufactured" more than once in the stream of commerce. Commenters felt that it must be made clear precisely at what point they are "manufacturing" a specific chemical substance that is present in a mined substance. We have provided clarification both here and in the rule.
>
> Any method of extraction, refinement, or purification of the mined substance to make it marketable as a listed chemical substance is to be regarded as "manufacture of a listed chemical substance" for the purposes of this rule.

47 Fed. Reg. 26,992, 26,993 (June 22, 1982).

EPA apparently intends to reassure the commenters that "manufacture" of a chemical substance occurs only once. Moreover, this is the only place in the preamble that the Agency equates purification with manufacture—the PAIR regulations themselves are silent on this point. The preamble never states or implies that an entity that purchases a market-grade PAIR-listed substance and further purifies it is "manufacturing" that substance.

3.1.3. Toll Manufacturers

Companies often use independent firms, *i.e.*, toll manufacturers, to manufacture chemical substances to their specifications. This raises the question concerning which of these companies is a "manufacturer" for TSCA purposes.

The toll manufacturer is always a manufacturer of the substances. Under the premanufacture and significant new use notification regulations, however, the purchasing or contracting company also is a manufacturer if: (1) the toll manufacturer produces the substance exclusively for that purchasing company; and (2) the purchasing company specifies the identity of the substance and controls the amount produced and the basic technology for the plant process. 40 C.F.R. § 720.3(t). In such circumstances, EPA believes that the contracting company is the most knowledgeable party and therefore should submit the notice. *See id.* § 720.22(a)(2). The Agency considers both parties liable, however, if the toll manufacturer produces the substance before the PMN is submitted or before EPA completes its review of the PMN. 48 Fed. Reg. 21,727 (May 13, 1983).

In informal guidance, EPA also deems both parties responsible for maintaining records of any allegations that the substance caused significant adverse effects. Office of Toxic Substances, EPA, *TSCA Section 8(c) Final Rule — Questions and Answers Document I*, at 3 (Nov. 1983) (response to question 7). The section 8(c) implementing regulations at 40 C.F.R. part 717 and the preambles to the proposed and final rules, however, do not mention toll manufacturers.

3.2. "PROCESS"

Processors of chemical substances must: (1) provide EPA with data under test rules, in some circumstances; (2) notify EPA prior to processing a chemical for a significant new use; (3) comply with EPA orders issued under section 5(e), 5(f) or 6(b) or rules promulgated under section 6(a); (4) avoid processing PCBs, except as permitted by EPA; and (5) comply with the record-keeping and reporting requirements of sections 8(c), 8(d) and 8(e); (6) submit to EPA inspections and subpoenas, as authorized by section 11; and (7) submit notices of export as required by section 12(b).

TSCA § 3(10) defines "process" to mean

> the preparation of a chemical substance or mixture, after its manufacture, for distribution in commerce—
>
> (A) in the same form or physical state as, or in a different form or physical state from, that in

which it was received by the person so preparing such substance or mixture, or

(B) as part of an article containing the chemical substance or mixture.

TSCA § 3(11) further defines the term "processor" as "any person who processes a chemical substance or mixture."

3.2.1. "Processing" versus "Use"

If interpreted literally, the broad statutory definitions of "process" and "processor" would encompass an enormous range of activities. At times, the breadth of the term "process" has blurred the distinction between processing and mere use of a chemical.

OPPT has issued no guidance distinguishing between processing and use for the purposes of TSCA. OPPT did clarify these terms, however, in its Toxic Release Inventory (TRI) Reporting Rule under section 313 of title III of the Superfund Amendments and Reauthorization Act of 1986 (SARA), 42 U.S.C. § 11023 (2000). Because OPPT administers both statutes and because the SARA definition of "process" is identical to the TSCA definition, EPA's guidance is significant for TSCA purposes.

The preamble to the TRI Reporting Rule distinguishes between "processing" and "use" by defining processing as an "incorporative" activity. 53 Fed. Reg. 4506 (Feb. 16, 1988). Thus, processing is any activity in which a chemical or its degradate or reaction product is placed into or incorporated in a commercially distributed substance, mixture, or article. The preamble exemplifies processing as: (1) use of chemicals as raw materials or intermediates in the manufacture of other chemicals; (2) the formulation of mixtures or other products where the incorporated chemical imparts some desired property to the product, *e.g.*, a pigment, surfactant, or solvent; (3) repackaging; and (4) incorporating the chemical into an article for industrial, trade, or consumer use. *See id.* at 4506.

By contrast, the preamble to the TRI Reporting Rule defines "use" as "non-incorporative" activity, where the chemical does not intentionally become part of a product distributed in commerce. The preamble offers the following examples: (1) chemical processing aids, such as catalysts, solvents, or reaction terminators; (2) manufacturing aids such as lubricants, refrigerants, or metalworking fluids; and (3) chemicals used for other purposes at a facility, such as cleaners, degreasers, or fuels. *Id.* Because these chemicals are not incorporated into commercial products, they are not processed for purposes of TRI reporting or by analogy for TSCA purposes either.

3.2.2. "Processing" as Defined in TSCA Rules

Subsections 5(i) and 8(f) limit the application of sections 5 and 8 to those who process "for commercial purposes." In addition, OPPT has recognized that for the purposes of some section 8 rules, literal application of the statutory language would cover so many activities that the regulations would be inequitable and OPPT would be administratively overburdened. For example, EPA has identified shoemakers who apply dye to shoes or hardware stores that mix pigments into a can of paint technically as "processors" of the dye or pigments and all the chemicals in them.

To avoid such regulatory breadth, OPPT: (1) exempted processors from the PAIR (unless the manufacturer cannot supply the necessary information); (2) exempted processors from the initial section 8(b) Inventory reporting requirements (although processors were eligible to add substances to the Inventory if the manufacturers did not); and (3) limited application of the section 8(c) Rule to processors that formulate or repackage. *See* 45 Fed. Reg. 13,648 (Feb. 29, 1980); 42 Fed. Reg. 64,572 (Dec. 23, 1977); 50 Fed. Reg. 46,768 (Nov. 27, 1985). Although EPA exempted these activities under the foregoing rules, companies and persons who conduct such activities should not assume that they are exempt from the obligations of a "processor" for any other TSCA purposes. Indeed, EPA broadly defines "processor" under the section 8(d) health and safety study reporting rule, and intends to interpret processor broadly when enforcing section 8(e) substantial risk reporting obligations.

3.2.3. Toll Processors

The TSCA obligations of processors extend to those companies that mix, formulate or repackage chemical substances for another company, *i.e.*, toll processors. EPA has not yet stated whether the other contracting company is a processor as well. While the PMN regulations address the responsibilities of companies that contract with toll manufacturers, they do not discuss the responsibilities of companies that use toll processors, presumably because processors are not subject to PMN requirements. *See* 40 C.F.R. §§ 720.3, 720.22(a)(2). The significant new use regulations, which do apply to processors, incorporate the definitions section of the PMN regulations, and add some additional definitions, but never discuss toll processors or the responsibilities of companies that use them. In a guidance letter, however, EPA took the position that contracting companies must comply with TSCA § 8(c) with respect to the chemicals processed for them. Letter from Joseph J. Merenda, Director, Existing Chemical Assessment Division (Feb. 8, 1988).

3.3. "DISTRIBUTE"

Distributors of chemical substances (who are not also manufacturers or processors) must: (1) comply with rules issued under section 6(a); (2) refrain from distributing PCBs except as permitted by EPA; (3) report "substantial risk information" to EPA under section 8(e); (4) submit to EPA inspections and subpoenas, as authorized by section 11; and (5) submit export notices as required by section 12(b).

According to TSCA § 3(4):

> The terms "distribute in commerce" and "distribution in commerce" when used to describe an action taken with

> respect to a chemical substance or mixture or article containing a substance or mixture means to sell, or the sale of, the substance, mixture, or article in commerce; to introduce or deliver for introduction into commerce, or the introduction or delivery for introduction into commerce of, the substance, mixture, or article; or to hold, or the holding of, the substance, mixture, or article after its introduction into commerce.

The term "commerce" is defined under TSCA § 3(3) to mean "trade, traffic, transportation, or other commerce (A) between a place in a State and any place outside of such State, or (B) which affects trade, traffic, transportation, or commerce described in clause (A)."

The TSCA definition of distribution encompasses more than sales or transportation, but its full scope is not clear. For example, if applied literally, "holding" a chemical after its introduction in commerce constitutes "distribution," making even the purchaser a "distributor," since the purchaser necessarily holds the substance briefly before using it. EPA has not clarified the term "holding" or attempted to prosecute an individual for TSCA violations who is only holding a chemical for personal use rather than for further distribution in commerce. The TSCA legislative history is also silent on the meaning of the term. As interpreted in practice, however, the term applies to persons who purchase a chemical and then hold it for purposes of later distribution—not persons who hold a chemical for their own use. This interpretation prevents a distributor from escaping liability by temporarily ceasing active distribution, without extending coverage of TSCA to ridiculous lengths.

3.4. "USE"

Users of chemical substances (who are not also manufacturers, processors, or distributors) must: (1) comply with regulations issued under section 6(a); (2) refrain from using PCBs except as permitted by EPA; (3) refrain from using any chemical substance they know or have reason to know has been manufactured, processed, or distributed in violation of TSCA; (4) submit to EPA inspections and subpoenas, as authorized by section 11; and (5) submit export notices as required by section12(b).

TSCA § 15(2) states that it is unlawful for a person to

> use for commercial purposes a chemical substance or mixture which such person knew or had reason to know was manufactured, processed, or distributed in commerce in violation of section 5 or 6, a rule or order under section 5 or 6, or an order issued in an action brought under section 5 or 7.

Thus, any chemical user who is on notice that its supplier has violated section 5, 6, or 7 could also be liable for a TSCA violation as a consequence of merely using the substance.

The Agency's original Section 5 Enforcement Response Policy (Section 5 ERP) assessed penalties for unlawful use as well as for unlawful manufacture. Office of Compliance Monitoring, EPA, *TSCA Section 5 Enforcement Response Policy* 7, 10 (Oct. 30, 1987) (draft). EPA did this partly for administrative convenience because most of the unlawful use cases which EPA brought in the mid 1980s were TSCA § 5 enforcement actions against companies that had manufactured a new chemical without filing a PMN and then had used the chemical in-house. By charging the use as well as manufacturing violations, EPA effectively doubled the calculated civil penalty.

Under its revised Section 5 ERP issued August 5, 1988, however, the Agency restricted the situations in which it would charge commercial use violations to two instances:

1. Where a company processes or uses a chemical substance which it did not manufacture and it has reason to know is not on the Inventory.

2. Where a chemical substance was manufactured or imported illegally on just a few occasions and processed over a long period of time, the substance would have been subject to a TSCA § 5(e) or 5(f) order, and the activity could have caused substantial endangerment to health or the environment.

Office of Compliance Monitoring, EPA, *TSCA Section 5 Enforcement Response Policy* 10 (Aug. 5, 1988). In cases involving an imminent hazard, however, the Agency may still charge a manufacturer with both unlawful manufacturing and unlawful use. *Id.* at 11.

Note that the Section 5 ERP states that EPA will charge persons who *process* chemicals they know were manufactured unlawfully with unlawful use violations. It is not clear whether the Agency has statutory authority for this position since TSCA § 15 only prohibits the *use* of a chemical that the user knows (or has reason to know) was manufactured, processed or distributed in violation of TSCA; it does not prohibit the *processing* of such chemicals. EPA apparently takes the position that processing and even certain distribution can constitute use, at least for purposes of section 15(2).

3.4.1. SNURs

TSCA § 5(a)(1)(B) allows EPA to promulgate "significant new use rules" (SNURs), which apply to processors and manufacturers. In a SNUR, EPA determines that a particular use of a specific chemical substance already on the TSCA Inventory constitutes a "significant new use" which should undergo prior EPA review. A SNUR requires anyone who intends to manufacture or process the identified chemical for a "significant new use" to give ninety days prior notice to the Agency. (*See* chapter 7 for a more detailed discussion of SNURs.) In effect, the SNUR transforms the existing chemical into a new chemical, requiring notification to EPA before the chemical is manufactured or processed for the new use.

EPA's procedural regulations for developing SNURs, however, do not define "use" or "significant new use." Rather, each individual SNUR lists that particular activity which the Agency deems to constitute a significant new use of that chemical, after applying the factors set forth in TSCA § 5(a)(2).[8] Considering all of the SNURs developed under EPA's case-by-case approach, the Agency apparently believes that "use" means virtually any activity involving a chemical. For example, some SNURs designate manufacturing or importing as significant new uses, whereas others designate processing or distributing (without certain safeguards) as significant new uses. *See, e.g.,* 40 C.F.R. §§ 721.1500, 721.3000. The Agency has even designated mere release to water or disposal as a significant new use. *See, e.g., id.* §§ 721.85, 721.90.

In 2002, EPA notably attempted to expand its SNUR jurisdiction to include even the existing and well-established commercial uses of certain previously notified chemical substances known as perfluoroalkyl sulfonates (PFAS). 67 Fed. Reg. 11,008 (March 11, 2002) (codified at 40 C.F.R. § 721.9582). Concerned about the persistent and bioaccumulative properties of PFAS, EPA based its original proposed rule, published at 65 Fed. Reg. 62,328 (Oct. 18, 2000), on its understanding that the 3M Company was the only producer of this class of chemicals and on 3M's agreement to phase out its production of these chemicals entirely, thereby rendering any subsequent use a "new" use.[9] Following the publication of the original proposed SNUR, the photolithography, semiconductor and photographic industries presented substantial data to EPA demonstrating the existence of producers, other than 3M, of PFAS and the ongoing uses of PFAS in these particular industries. The substantial data provided to EPA included analyses of the protection of human health and the environment inherent in these particular uses as well as analyses of waste streams and disposal methods. The final SNUR ultimately reflected the existence of these ongoing uses. The PFAS SNUR is discussed further in Chapter 7 of this Handbook.

Release and disposal obviously are not "use" of a chemical in the usual sense of the word. In fact, TSCA §§ 4(a), 5(a), 6(a), 7(a), 9(a) and 15 all treat manufacturing, processing, distribution in commerce, use, and disposal as separate and distinct

---

[8] EPA's procedural regulations define "commercial use" and "immediate use," but the definitions focus entirely on defining "commercial" and "immediate." They contain no explanation of the word "use."

[9] EPA's originally proposed SNUR, published on October 18, 2000, specified the chemicals that were the subject of the proposed action and referred to those chemicals as perfluorooctyl sulfonates ("PFOS"). The final SNUR reflects the fact that the chemicals at issue are more accurately identified as PFAS.

activities. Thus, it is not clear that EPA even has the authority under TSCA to define "use" to include all these many other activities.

This is particularly true with respect to disposal, because the TSCA legislative history indicates that Congress considered use and disposal to be two distinct activities. Section 15(2) of one Senate version of TSCA, S. 3149, 94th Cong. (1976), specifically provided that either the use or the disposal of an illegally manufactured chemical constitutes a violation of TSCA. *Id.*, *reprinted in* S. Rep. No. 94-698, at 62 (1976). The provision for a separate violation for disposal was dropped, suggesting the TSCA § 15(2) use prohibition does not apply to disposal. Thus, EPA's assertion that disposal can constitute a prohibited "use" of a chemical finds rebuttal in the statutory language and congressional intent.

3.5. "DISPOSE"

"Dispose" or "disposal" is another activity not defined in TSCA. Disposers of chemical substances (who are not also manufacturers, processors, distributors, or users) must: (1) comply with regulations issued under section 6(a); (2) dispose of PCBs according to the requirements of the PCB disposal regulations; (3) submit to EPA inspections and subpoenas, as authorized by section 11; and (4) submit export notices as required by section 12(b).

3.5.1. TCDD Disposal Regulations

Under TSCA § 6(a)(6), EPA may establish a requirement "prohibiting or otherwise regulating any manner or method of disposal of such substance or mixture . . . by its manufacturer or processor or by any other person who uses, or disposes of, it for commercial purposes." On March 11, 1980, using its section 6(a)(6) and section 6(d) authority, EPA issued a proposed rule, effective immediately, to control the disposal of wastes contaminated with 2,3,7,8-tetrachlorodibenzo-p-dioxin (TCDD). 45 Fed. Reg. 15,592 (Mar. 11, 1980). EPA's purpose in regulating disposal was to prevent Vertac, Inc. from removing approximately 3,445 drums of TCDD-contaminated waste from the company's Jacksonville facility. By its terms, however, the rule also required any person "who dispose[d] of chemical substances or mixtures for commercial purposes who wishe[d] to dispose of waste containing TCDD [to] notify the [EPA] sixty (60) days prior to their intended disposal of such wastes." 40 C.F.R. § 775.190(b).

The TCDD disposal rule defined "[d]ispose of chemical substances or mixtures for commercial purposes" as "disposal by any person who disposes of chemical substances or mixtures for the purpose of obtaining commercial advantage, as well as disposal by any person incidental to his commercial activities." 40 C.F.R. § 775.183(c). Thus, the rule applied to all commercial disposers of waste who intended to dispose of TCDDs and to any commercial users of TCDDs who intended to dispose of TCDD-contaminated wastes. The rule, however, never defined "dispose" or "disposal." In 1985, EPA revoked the TCDD disposal rule when promulgating regulations to control the disposal of dioxin-contaminated waste under the Resource Conservation and

Recovery Act (RCRA), and removed the TCDD regulations under TSCA from the *Code of Federal Regulations*.

3.5.2. PCB Regulations

EPA's regulations controlling polychlorinated biphenyls (PCBs) define "disposal" as:

> [I]ntentionally or accidentally to discard, throw away, or otherwise complete or terminate the useful life of PCBs or PCB Items. Disposal includes spills, leaks, and other uncontrolled discharges of PCBs as well as actions related to containing, transporting, destroying, degrading, decontaminating, or confining PCBs and PCB Items.

40 C.F.R. § 761.3. This broad definition ensures that the PCB regulations cover virtually any release of PCBs into the environment. In that respect, it is similar to definitions of "disposal" contained in hazardous waste control statutes such as RCRA and the Comprehensive Environmental Response, Compensation, and Liability Act (CERCLA). (*See* chapter 11 for a more detailed discussion of the PCB disposal regulations.) The definition, however, applies only to disposal of PCBs; it does not cover other chemicals or apply to disposal activities under other TSCA regulations.

3.5.3. Section 5(e) Consent Orders

TSCA § 5(e) permits EPA to issue an administrative order regulating a new chemical substance if the Agency finds that it has insufficient information to permit a reasoned evaluation of the hazards posed by the substance, and, in the absence of such information, the manufacture, processing, distribution in commerce, use *or disposal* of the substance may present an unreasonable risk. As discussed in detail in chapter 7, EPA uses this authority to enter into consent orders with PMN submitters governing disposal. Some of these consent orders require the affected manufacturer to use specified methods to dispose of any wastes that contain or are associated with manufacture of the PMN substance; all other methods of disposal are prohibited. The orders, however, generally do not define disposal. Thus, the party to the consent order might have to enter separate discussions with EPA to determine whether certain activities such as recycling constitute "disposal" under the consent order.

CHAPTER 4
THE TSCA INVENTORY

TSCA § 8(b) requires EPA to compile a list of chemical substances manufactured or processed for commercial purposes in the United States. This list, which EPA refers to as the TSCA Inventory, is a massive, complex, multi-volume compilation of more than 82,000 chemicals (as of 2005). The Agency adds new chemicals to the Inventory each year, and periodically "delists" chemicals that were improperly included.

The Inventory provides EPA with an important tool for identifying, prioritizing, and evaluating chemicals, and for developing a profile of the chemical industry in the United States. While the Inventory's list of chemicals is current, much of the information originally provided about production volumes and plant sites is out of date. An EPA regulation known as the "Inventory Update Rule," first published in 1986 and extensively amended in 2003, provides a framework for updating the Inventory data base. 51 Fed. Reg. 21,447 (June 12, 1986) and 68 Fed. Reg. 848 (Jan. 7, 2003).

The extent to which EPA regulates a chemical substance under TSCA and the obligations that TSCA imposes on manufacturers and processors of a chemical depend largely on whether the substance is "existing" or "new." The TSCA Inventory comprises the universe of "existing" chemical substances, and all substances not on the Inventory are considered "new." The Industrial Chemistry Branch, Economics Exposure and Technology Division (EETD) of the Office of Pollution Prevention and Toxics (OPPT) manages the Inventory, and is responsible for additions, corrections, and deletions, as well as for development of Inventory reporting requirements and technical and policy documents.

4.1. INITIAL COMPILATION OF THE INVENTORY

To develop the Inventory as required by TSCA § 8(b), EPA promulgated Inventory Reporting Regulations in December 1977. 42 Fed. Reg. 64,572 (Dec. 23, 1977). These regulations enabled the Agency to compile the initial "list" of chemical substances mandated by TSCA and thereby facilitated regulation of the chemical industry by triggering the PMN requirements.

The 1977 Inventory Reporting Regulations and the extensive explanatory comments accompanying them were EPA's first attempt to refine the statutory definitions of "chemical substance" and the exclusions from that definition, which is set forth in TSCA § 3(2). While EPA has deleted the Initial Inventory reporting regulations that no longer have effect, the Agency still relies on portions of those rules and the comments submitted when those rules were promulgated in responding to questions about the scope of TSCA regulation.[10] Because chemicals not appearing on the Inventory are subject to TSCA § 5 premanufacture notification (PMN) requirements, most manufacturers and processors wanted their chemicals to be included on the initial TSCA Inventory so that they would not later become subject to PMN requirements. As a result, the Inventory Reporting Regulations and comments were, and remain, an important source of guidance in interpreting the PMN requirements.

The 1977 Inventory Reporting Regulations established an initial two-phased reporting period. During the first phase manufacturers and importers of bulk chemicals were required to submit activities reports, which EPA reviewed and processed to publish the Initial Inventory in June 1979. During the second phase, processors of chemicals could voluntarily report their chemicals if the manufacturers failed to do so during the first phase. Companies that imported chemicals as part of a mixture or article were permitted to submit voluntary reports during either phase, or to have a trade association or agent report for them during the first phase. The Agency published the results of the second phase reporting in two Cumulative Supplements to the Initial Inventory, in 1979 and 1980. The initial Inventory and Cumulative Supplements are collectively referred to as the Revised Inventory.

In order to be eligible for inclusion on the initial Inventory, a substance had to be: (1) a "chemical substance"; (2) manufactured, imported or processed for a commercial purpose in the United States between January 1, 1975 and the date of publication of the Initial Inventory (June 1, 1979); and (3) not specifically excluded from the Inventory. These criteria and the current regulatory provisions are discussed below.

4.1.1. "Chemical Substance"

TSCA § 3(2)(A) defines the term "chemical substance" as follows:

> [A]ny organic or inorganic substance of a particular molecular identity, including -- (i) any combination of such substances occurring in whole or in part as a result of a chemical reaction or occurring in nature and (ii) any element or uncombined radical.

This statutory definition was incorporated into the 1977 Inventory Reporting Regulations, and appears in the current regulations at 40 C.F.R. § 710.3(d) (TSCA Chemical Inventory Regulations).

---

10 In 1995, EPA revised subpart 710 to remove provisions associated with the Initial Inventory reporting period that are not referenced in other TSCA regulations. 60 Fed. Reg. 31,917 (June 19, 1995).

The Inventory Reporting Regulations also incorporate the statutory exclusions from the definition of "chemical substance" set forth in TSCA § 3(2)(B). These exclusions encompass: (1) any "mixture," as defined by TSCA; (2) any pesticide when manufactured, processed, or distributed in commerce for use as a pesticide; (3) tobacco or any tobacco product, but not including any derivative products; (4) any radioactive source material, special nuclear material, or radioactive by-product material; (5) any pistol, firearm, revolver, shells, and cartridges; and (6) any food, food additive, drug, cosmetic, or device, when manufactured, processed, or distributed in commerce for use as a food, food additive, drug, cosmetic, or device. *See* 40 C.F.R. § 710.3(d). (The pesticide and food and drug exclusions are discussed in detail in Chapter 13.)

EPA guidance on Inventory reporting issued in 1977 established two basic categories of chemical substances. Substances with compositions that can be represented by a definite chemical structural diagram and have a definite molecular formula are denoted "Class 1" substances. Office of Toxic Substances, EPA, *Reporting for the Chemical Substance Inventory* at 105 (Dec. 1977). In contrast, substances with compositions that cannot be fully represented by a definite structural diagram, or which are composed of different known or unknown species, are denoted "Class 2" substances. *Id.* Certain substances which do not have a definite structural diagram, *e.g.*, polymers, can nonetheless be categorized as Class 1 substances. For example, polymers prepared from Class 1 monomers or reactants are considered Class 1 substances, whereas polymers, such as alkyd resins, prepared in whole or in part from Class 2 monomers or reactants, are considered Class 2 substances. EPA has incorporated this classification scheme into the premanufacture notification regulations. 40 C.F.R. § 720.45. (*See* Chapter 6.)

Whether or not a particular substance was a reportable chemical substance for purposes of the Inventory Reporting Regulations also depended upon whether it was a "mixture." Mixtures were specifically excluded from Inventory reporting (although chemical components of a mixture remain individually subject to reporting). *See* 40 C.F.R. § 710.3(d), which parallels the statutory exclusion of mixtures from the definition of "chemical substance." *See also Reporting for the Chemical Substance Inventory* at 5. The term "mixture" is defined in TSCA § 3(8). EPA has stated that the distinction between a chemical substance and a mixture is a function of its "source, origin, or method of preparation." *Reporting for the Chemical Substance Inventory* at 5. Since the definition of chemical substance includes "any *combination of...substances. . .* occurring in nature" (emphasis added), any material extracted or removed from nature is a "chemical substance" and, therefore, not a mixture even though it may be comprised of different chemicals. *See* TSCA § 3(2)(A)(i). Interestingly, under the term "mixture," TSCA includes any combination of chemical substances that occurs, in whole or in part, as a result of a reaction of two or more substances and that does not contain a new chemical substance, if that combination could have been created without a chemical reaction by mixing chemical substances.

In short, a mixture is a "combination of two chemical substances" that "does not occur in nature" and is not "the result of a chemical reaction."

Although naturally occurring substances were reportable, EPA considered them to be automatically included on the Inventory. Therefore, manufacturers and importers did not have to report them. 40 C.F.R. § 710.4(b).

4.1.2. Manufactured or Imported for a "Commercial Purpose"

In addition to being a "chemical substance" by definition under TSCA § 3(2)(A), the substance also must have been manufactured or imported for a commercial purpose in the United States since January 1, 1975 to be eligible for inclusion in the Inventory. A "commercial purpose" includes manufacture or import for distribution in commerce (including test marketing), or for use by the manufacturer or importer (including use as an intermediate). 40 C.F.R. § 710.2(p).

4.1.3. Specifically Excluded Substances

Several categories of substances were specifically excluded from the Inventory. These categories include not only those chemicals explicitly excluded from the TSCA definition of "chemical substance" but also several others excluded pursuant to section 8(b) and TSCA's implementing regulations. *See* 40 C.F.R. § 710.4(c), (d). EPA has incorporated these same exclusions into the PMN regulations. (*See* Chapter 5, New Chemical Review.)

4.1.3.1. Small Quantities for Research and Development

TSCA § 8(b)(1) specifically excludes from the Inventory "any chemical substance which is manufactured or processed only in small quantities . . . solely for purposes of scientific experimentation or analysis or chemical research on, or analysis of, such substance or another substance, including such research or analysis for the development of a product." The Inventory Reporting Regulations established a quantitative limit for "small quantities" of such research and development chemicals. Under the Inventory Reporting Regulations, a chemical substance "manufactured, imported or processed in quantities less than 1,000 pounds annually" was presumed to be a research and development (R&D) substance, but nevertheless could be reported if the manufacturer certified that it was not for R&D. *See* 40 C.F.R. § 710.3(d) (see note under "small quantities"). EPA deleted this quantitative limit, however, in its final TSCA § 5 PMN rules. *Id.* § 720.3(cc). Indeed, the Agency has declined to establish a quantitative limit for "small quantities" of R&D substances. Instead, EPA evaluates the particular use of a substance in determining whether such activity constitutes R&D. (The R&D exemption is discussed in detail in Chapter 5, New Chemical Review.)

4.1.3.2. Impurities

An impurity is defined as "a chemical substance which is unintentionally present with another chemical substance." 40 C.F.R. § 710.2(m). Impurities are specifically excluded from Inventory reporting. *Id.* § 710.4(d)(1). Although EPA recognized the potential hazards of certain impurities, the Agency determined as a matter of policy that:

> [T]his first inventory should not distinguish among chemical substances which are identical except with respect to their impurities. The Agency recognized the potential hazards of some impurities and intends to use the alternative authorities of sections 4, 6, 7, and 8 to prevent and reduce any unreasonable risks posed by impurities.

42 Fed. Reg. 64,588 (Dec. 23, 1977) (EPA response to comment 61).

4.1.3.3. By-Products

As a matter of policy, EPA also determined that "byproducts which have no commercial purpose" should be excluded from the Inventory. *Id.* at 64,587 (EPA response to comment 52); *see* 40 C.F.R. § 710.4(d)(2). In addition, EPA excluded by-products which had some limited commercial purposes. *See id.* note. Thus, for example, by-products burned as fuel, or disposed of as waste, including disposal in a landfill or for enriching the soil, have commercial value and could be reported for the Inventory, but such reporting was not required. Furthermore, such substances were not subject to PMN requirements even if they were not listed in the original Inventory. Although disposal of a by-product for purposes of enriching the soil did not trigger Inventory reporting, fertilizers in general are not considered by-products. They are considered to be manufactured for a specific commercial purpose and therefore subject to TSCA reporting.

4.1.3.4. Chemicals Produced from Incidental Reactions

Chemical substances produced as the result of incidental reactions were excluded from the Inventory. *See* 40 C.F.R. § 710.4(d)(3), (4). EPA excluded incidentally produced chemicals from Inventory reporting because they are not intentionally produced for commercial purposes and are not necessary for the essential structure or function of the desired chemical substance. 42 Fed. Reg. at 64,587 (Dec. 23, 1977) (EPA response to comment 53).

4.1.3.5. Non-Isolated Intermediates

Intermediates, which are defined as chemicals that are both manufactured and partially or totally consumed in the chemical reaction process, or are intentionally present in order to affect the rate of chemical reactions by which other chemical substances or mixtures are being manufactured, were subject to Inventory reporting. *Id.* at 64,588 (EPA response to comment 68). Yet, the Agency excluded non-isolated intermediates from reporting. Non-isolated intermediates are defined as intermediates that are not intentionally removed from the equipment in which they are manufactured. 40 C.F.R. § 710.4(d)(8). (*See* Chapter 5 for a more detailed discussion of non-isolated intermediates.)

4.2. HOW SUBSTANCES WERE REPORTED

EPA developed five different initial Inventory reporting forms. Form A was for chemicals listed on the TSCA "Candidate List of Chemical Substances." Form B was for chemicals that did not appear on the Candidate List, but had known Chemical Abstracts Service (CAS) Registry numbers. Form C was for chemicals that did not appear on the Candidate List and had no known CAS numbers, or whose chemical identities were claimed to be confidential. Form D was for voluntary reporting of trademarked products comprised of chemicals, but was not a substitute for any of the reports required by the Inventory reporting regulations.[11] Form E was for use in reporting for the Revised Inventory in 1979 - chemicals processed for non-exempt uses which the manufacturer or importer had not reported.

4.2.1. Information Reported

For all chemicals manufactured or imported after January 1, 1975 but before June 1, 1979, manufacturers and importers had to report the chemical identity, production or import volume, and whether its use was site-limited. "Small manufacturers had reduced reporting requirements (by company headquarters, rather than individual plant sites) or were exempt. Processors were entirely exempt from initial Inventory reporting. During the second reporting phase (June 1 to December 31, 1979) processors were permitted (but not required) to report those substances that they processed but that the manufacturer or importer did not report for the Initial Inventory.

4.2.2. Special Reporting Problems

Several types of substances posed special reporting problems for both EPA and affected manufacturers and importers.

4.2.2.1. Mixtures

TSCA § 3(2)(B) excludes mixtures from the definition of "chemical substances." Mixtures were specifically exempt from the Inventory reporting requirements "because they are not manufactured for distribution in commerce as chemical substances *per se* and have no commercial purposes separate from the mixture or article of which they may be a part." 42 Fed. Reg. 64,585 (Dec. 23, 1977) (EPA response to comment 36).

A mixture is defined in relevant part as:

> [A]ny combination of two or more chemical substances if the combination does not occur in nature and is not, in whole or in part, the result of a chemical reaction . . . .

---

[11] EPA no longer identifies chemical substances by their trademark identities.

40 C.F.R. § 710.4(d). The definition goes on to include combinations which actually resulted from chemical reactions if the combination could have been manufactured without the chemical reactions. *Id.* The *components* of mixtures, however, were not excluded from reporting requirements.

The term "mixture" under TSCA caused confusion because it differed in several respects from the commonly understood meaning of that term. For example, many compositions generally considered to be "mixtures" fall within the definition of "chemical substances" under TSCA. EPA provided the following clarification of the definition of the term "mixture" for purposes of Inventory reporting:

> In general, a combination of two or more chemical substances is a "mixture" if they have been combined by actually mixing them together.
>
> If, however, the combination occurs in nature, it is a "chemical substance" and is not a "mixture." If, further, the combination is prepared by a chemical reaction, it is a "chemical substance" and not a "mixture," unless the combination could actually have been manufactured for commercial purposes at this time without a chemical reaction, *e.g.*, by mixing its separate components with each other.

42 Fed. Reg. at 64,585 (Dec. 23, 1977) (EPA response to comment 36).

EPA's policy on Inventory reporting of mixtures must be distinguished from the Agency's policy for naming substances on the Inventory. Because the Inventory functions as an index for determining whether a substance is "existing" or "new" for TSCA § 5 PMN purposes, the Inventory entries must be as specific as possible. With respect to the identification of discrete chemical substances, the Inventory could be quite precise, but the Agency recognized that describing mixtures with the same degree of precision is difficult. The Agency's initial position, therefore, was that it would allow considerably more latitude to submitters in naming mixtures. Thus, EPA required the listing of each identified constituent of a reaction "mixture" (exclusive of by-products). If, however, not all of the constituents were identified or known to be present each time a reaction is carried out, a Class 2 substance name was used. Furthermore, the Agency permitted an even less specific name such as "reaction product of A and B" (where A and B are the starting reactants) as a name of last resort, although such a name is often a very non-specific chemical description of the reaction mixture and hence a poor Inventory entry. An Inventory with a large number of such non-descriptive entries would not function accurately in defining existing and new substances; hence, the Agency determined that mixtures could not be included in the Inventory. Product mixtures resulting from chemical reactions are included on the Inventory. Only formulated mixtures are excluded. The reason for the exclusion is not that formulated mixtures cannot be defined. In fact, many reaction product mixtures cannot be exactly defined but they are included. Formulated mixtures are not included, because they are arbitrary, *i.e.*, by simply varying the ratio of chemical components, one can come up with a large number of such formulations. Therefore, to minimize reporting burden for industry, EPA requires the reporting of only the chemical components comprising the mixtures.

4.2.2.2. Polymers

To report polymers for the Inventory, submitters had to describe the polymer composition by listing all monomers and other reactants used at greater than two percent (by weight) in the manufacture. EPA, Office of Toxic Substances, Reporting for the Chemical Substance Inventory at 7 (Dec. 1977). The manufacturer or importer, however, could elect whether to list monomers used at two percent or less. *Id.*

Although the Agency wanted the Inventory accurately to reflect the identities of polymers, EPA recognized that it was not essential for the Inventory listing to identify all of a polymer's constituent monomers in order to achieve this goal. 42 Fed. Reg. at 64,589 (EPA response to comment 78). In recognition of the practical constraints of polymer chemistry, the Agency derived the "two percent reporting rule."[12] The difficulty of distinguishing monomers present at two percent or less from impurities, the fact that minor process changes can produce minute amounts of new monomers, and the low toxicity of monomers present in this range prompted EPA to adopt its two percent reporting rule. *Id.* (For further discussion of the two percent rule on polymers, see Chapter 6.)

4.2.2.3. Pesticides

TSCA specifically excludes pesticides, as defined in the Federal Insecticide, Fungicide, and Rodenticide Act (FIFRA), 7 U.S.C.A. §§ 136-136y, from the definition of chemical substances "when manufactured, processed, or distributed in commerce for use as a pesticide." TSCA § 3(2)(B)(ii). Substances intended solely for use as a pesticide are subject to FIFRA. If a substance has multiple uses, however, those uses not subject to FIFRA are subject to TSCA. OPPT considers a substance to be a pesticide at the time an application is filed either for an experimental use permit or registration under FIFRA. 51 Fed. Reg. 15,098 (Apr. 22, 1986). Prior to the filing of either type of application, the substance is presumed by OPPT to be a chemical substance under TSCA. *Id.* In addition, intermediates and inerts used in the production of pesticides are subject to TSCA. (*See* Chapter 13, Relationship between TSCA and Other Laws.)

---

12 The "two percent rule" is not really a "rule" in the sense of being part of the Inventory Reporting Regulations. Rather, it is an EPA interpretation of the Inventory Reporting Regulations, which, if they were read literally without application of the two percent rule, would require (a) a PMN on every polymer which was "new" simply because the manufacturer had added a small amount of a new monomer and (b) a listing of each new monomer in the Inventory description of the polymer, even though the monomer constituted less than two percent of the polymer.

4.2.2.4. Articles

"Articles" were excluded from Inventory reporting. EPA defines an article for TSCA purposes as a manufactured item "formed to a specific shape or design during manufacture," whose "end use function(s)" are dependent upon its shape or design during end use, and which has generally "no change of chemical composition during its end use." 40 C.F.R. § 710.2(d). Fluids or particles, regardless of their shape or design, are not considered articles. *Id.* EPA guidance indicates that paint in a can or ink in a pen, for example, are not considered part of the articles that contains them.

4.2.2.5. Quality Control Chemicals

The TSCA § 8(b) R&D exemption includes small quantities of chemical substances used solely for quality control testing and for the development of a chemical substance or product. In response to a comment on the use of quality control chemicals, EPA stated that:

> Chemicals used for quality control testing and for the development of a product are considered "small quantities for research and development" if they fall within the definition provided in § 710.3(d).

42 Fed. Reg. at 64,586 (Dec. 23, 1977) (EPA response to comment 43); *see* Office of Toxic Substances, EPA, *New Chemical Information Bulletin: Exemptions for Research and Development and Test Marketing* 2 (Nov. 1986).

4.3. CORRECTING AN INVENTORY SUBMISSION

Companies sometimes made errors in reporting substances for inclusion on the Inventory. Often these errors are not discovered until years later. Under limited circumstances, EPA will accept corrections to a company's Inventory submissions. 45 Fed. Reg. 50,544 (July 29, 1980). The corrections must be submitted by the company which currently owns the rights to the chemical, must be accompanied by adequate documentation, and must fall into one of the following three categories:

(1) Corrections of the chemical identity of previously reported materials, as a result of:

- typographical errors in recording the chemical identity on the Inventory reporting forms;
- refinement of the identity of the reported substance;
- identification of new components in the material; and
- discovery that the chemical substance is different from that reported previously.

(2) Corrections to identify previously unrecognized isolated intermediates.

(3) Corrections made in response to communications from EPA which identify reporting errors.

See 45 Fed. Reg. at 50,544-45.

Mechanisms for correcting the Inventory provide an important (although limited) means for companies to rectify an error in reporting without becoming subject to the PMN requirements. EPA has published useful guidance for making Inventory corrections. EPA, *The TSCA Inventory: Submitting Successful Corrections* (Mar. 4, 1987).

To document the first two categories of corrections, the submitter must provide a copy of the Inventory reporting form previously submitted for the final product and any other related intermediates, a new Inventory reporting form and, if the correction is for an isolated intermediate, a detailed description of the chemical relationship between the intermediate and the final product, along with documentation showing that the intermediate was isolated between January 1, 1975 and July 1, 1979. 45 Fed. Reg. at 50,544-45. Documentation of the third category of correction also requires a copy of the EPA communication identifying the error, as well as a new Inventory reporting form. *Id.* at 50,545.

In addition to the above, companies must document that the chemical presently being manufactured is the same one that was manufactured when it was reported for the initial Inventory. EPA has accepted such items as shipping vouchers, plant notebooks indicating batch records, and dated documentation of production from the period of original submission.

EPA has indicated informally that in very limited circumstances it will allow third-party corrections, *i.e.*, corrections submitted by a company other than the original reporting company. If a company that did not originally report a substance cannot obtain an Inventory correction through a normal correction filing by the original reporting company, the Agency may allow a correction based upon information received from such a non-reporting company. For example, EPA will entertain an Inventory correction request from a non-reporting company where it can be demonstrated that the original reporting company no longer has any commercial interest in the substance to be corrected, and the non-reporting company faces the difficult if not impossible task of persuading the original reporting company to submit a correction package. To date, EPA has received a very limited number of correction requests from non-reporting companies.

EPA uses Form C for reporting most Inventory corrections, but Forms A, B, and E may be submitted, if applicable. These reporting forms can be requested from the Industrial Chemistry Branch of OPPT. Correction forms submitted to EPA should reference the form number on which the incorrectly reported chemical was submitted.

Inventory correction packages should be submitted to the OPPT Document Control Officer at the same address where PMNs and IUR reports are submitted.

The submitter will be notified by EPA in writing as to whether the Agency has accepted or rejected the Inventory correction. If the correction is accepted, the substance becomes included in the TSCA Inventory retroactively to the time of the initial Inventory reporting period. It is important to note that even when the Agency accepts an Inventory correction, the erroneously listed chemical remains on the Inventory until EPA makes a formal *Federal Register* announcement of the removal of the incorrectly listed substance from the Inventory. This is because EPA does not want to disrupt commercial activity by the unpublished deletion of a chemical which manufacturers may be producing in reliance upon the Inventory listing.

OPPT will accept corrections to Inventory listings even if the substance was placed on the Inventory through the PMN submission process, but OPPT has never published separate guidance on the procedures that a PMN submitter should follow to make such a correction. In practice, the procedures for correcting initial Inventory listings are easily adapted to the PMN scenario. Corrections to PMN substances can be coordinated through the Industrial Chemistry Branch. By contrast with corrections to reports for the initial Inventory, however, corrections to PMNs trigger a further review of the modified PMN so that the Agency can determine if the chemical, as corrected, poses some new risk warranting further regulation.

4.4. MAINTAINING AND UPDATING THE INVENTORY DATA BASE

EPA continuously adds to the Inventory new chemicals which have cleared TSCA § 5 PMN review and for which a notice of commencement of manufacture has been filed. Periodically, EPA also removes from the Inventory chemical substances that were incorrectly identified or reported. The Agency will publish periodically a notice of its intent to delist a chemical in the *Federal Register* and solicit comments on the proposed delisting. *See, e.g.*, 60 Fed. Reg. 33,201 (June 27, 1995) (TSCA Chemical Substance Inventory; Removal of 136 Incorrectly Reported Chemical Substances from the TSCA Inventory). Companies desiring to manufacture or import a delisted chemical for a commercial purpose subsequent to the date on which it was formally removed from the TSCA Inventory first must comply with the TSCA § 5 PMN requirements. As a result of this ongoing process, EPA maintains the Inventory as a list of chemicals currently in commerce, not just chemicals manufactured for commercial use during the 1975-1979 reporting period for the Initial Inventory.

4.4.1. Inventory Update Rule

In June 1986, EPA issued an Inventory Update Rule (IUR) requiring manufacturers and importers of certain chemicals listed on the Inventory to report current data on their production volumes, plant sites, and site-limited activities. 51 Fed. Reg. 21,438 (June 12, 1986). The Agency also published detailed reporting instructions for manufacturers and importers subject to the IUR. Info. Mgmt. Div., U.S.

Envtl. Prot. Agency, *Instructions for Reporting for the Partial Updating of the TSCA Chemical Inventory Data Base* (Apr. 1986). The initial 120-day reporting period commenced on August 25, 1986 and ended on December 23, 1986. Currently, IUR reporting is required every four years.

In January 2003, EPA amended the IUR and refers to the amended rule as the Inventory Update Rule Amendments (IURA). 68 Fed. Reg. 848 (January 7, 2003). The IURA is intended to accomplish three goals: to better match chemical substances reporting requirements with the EPA's information needs, to update information regarding potential exposures to a subset of chemical substances, and to increase the utility of reported information. 68 Fed. Reg. at 852-53. The amendments retained the unrevised IUR for the 2002 reporting period, but promulgated significant changes for the 2006 reporting period and beyond (40 C.F.R. pt. 710, subpts. B and C, respectively).

Beginning in 2006, the following categories of substances listed on the Inventory are exempt from IUR requirements: (1) polymers; (2) microorganisms; (3) naturally occurring chemical substances; and (4) certain forms of natural gas. 40 C.F.R. § 710.46(a). Polymers, microorganisms, and certain forms of natural gas are not entitled to this exemption, however, if they are subject to any of the following: (1) a proposed or final rule under TSCA § 4, 5(a)(2), 5(b)(4), or 6; (2) an order under TSCA § 5(e) or 5(f); or (3) relief granted pursuant to a civil action under section 5 or 7 of TSCA. *Id.* § 710.46. Partial IUR exemptions apply to (1) certain substances termed "petroleum process streams," identified at 40 C.F.R. section 710.46(b)(1); (2) inorganic chemical substances; and (3) certain substances for which EPA has a low interest in having the processing and use information collected under the IUR. *Id.* § 710.46(b). Although partial reporting is required for inorganic chemical substances during the 2006 reporting period, in subsequent reporting periods, manufacturers of such substances will be subject to full IUR reporting. *Id.* § 710.46(b)(3). In other words, in post-2006 IUR reporting periods, manufacturers of inorganic substances will be subject to the processing and use information reporting requirements.

For the 2006 reporting period and beyond, any company that manufactures or imports for commercial purposes 25,000 pounds or more of a "reportable substance" at any single site during the calendar year prior to the reporting period is obligated to submit updated information. 40 C.F.R. § 710.48. "Small" manufacturers are exempt from reporting, unless the reportable substance is subject to any of the following: (1) a proposed or final rule under TSCA § 4, 5(b)(4), or 6; (2) an order under TSCA § 5(e); or

(3) relief granted pursuant to a civil action under section 5 or 7 of TSCA.[13] *Id.* § 710.49. In addition, companies that manufacture or import a reportable substance in small quantities solely for R&D or as part of an article or who manufacture a reportable substance as an impurity, by–product, or in a manner incidental to its end use are exempt from IUR reporting. *Id.* § 710.50.

A company subject to the IUR must report the specific chemical identity, plant site and production volume in pounds, whether the substance is manufactured or imported, and whether a manufactured substance is site-limited. 40 C.F.R. § 710.52(c)(3)(i)-(iv). The IURA, however, requires additional exposure-related information: (1) the number of workers reasonably likely to be exposed to the substance, (2) the physical form in which the substance is sent off-site, (3) the percentage of total reported production volume for each physical form, and (4) the maximum concentration of the substance at the time it either leaves the site or used to produce a difference substance. *Id.* § 710.52(c)(3)(vi)-(ix).

IURA requires more specific information regarding plant sites. 40 C.F.R. § 710.52(c)(2). For each site at which at least 25,000 lbs. (11, 340 kg) of a reportable chemical substance is manufactured, the manufacturer must report the following: (1) the name of a person who will serve as technical contact for the submitter company, and who will be able to answer questions about the information submitted by the company to EPA, the parent company name and Dun and Bradstreet Number, the contact person's full mailing address, the contact person's telephone number and the contact person's e-mail address; and (2) the name, full street address of each site, Dun and Bradstreet Number for each plant site reported, and the county or parish (or other jurisdictional indicator) in which the plant site is located. *Id.*

A claim of confidentiality for a site can be asserted by submitters only if the linkage of the site with a reportable chemical is confidential and not publicly available. 40 C.F.R. § 710.58(c). To assert such a claim, the submitter must do the following: (1) submit with the IURA report written answers as to (a) whether the site information has been linked with a chemical identity in any other reporting scheme and (b) whether identifying the site and chemical substance being disclosed would harm the submitter's competitive position. *Id.* § 710.58(c)(1).

---

[13] A manufacturer/importer is "small," if it meets one of the following standards: (1) when the manufacturer's or importer's total annual sales, when combined with those of its parent company, are less than $40 million; however, if annual production or importation volume of a particular substance at any individual site is greater than 45,400 kilograms (100,000 pounds), the manufacturer or importer will not qualify as "small" for purposes of reporting on the production or importation of that substance at that site; and (2) when a manufacturer's or importer's total annual sales, when combined with those of its parent company, are less than $4 million, regardless of the quantity of substances produced or imported by that manufacturer or importer. § 704.3.

For manufacturers with production volumes of 300,000 lbs. or greater, the IURA requires additional exposure-related information on the processing and use of each reportable substance, to the extent the information is "readily obtainable." 40 C.F.R. § 710.52(c)(4). In its March 2004 draft "Instructions for Reporting for the 2006 Partial Updating of the TSCA Chemical Inventory Database," EPA explains it means by "readily obtainable" as follows:

> **Readily obtainable information** is information known to or readily obtainable by management and supervisory employees of the submitter company who are responsible for manufacturing, processing, technical services, or marketing of the reportable chemical substance. Where reporting in ranges is prescribed, **readily obtainable information** may employ estimates utilizing best professional judgment based on past experience for similar chemical substances in the same or similar markets and/or any reasonable projections of likely processing and use scenarios for the chemical substance. If information (including estimates) necessary to complete any portion of Part III is not readily obtainable, the submitter is not required to respond.
>
> The **readily obtainable standard** applies to processing and use information reported in Part III of Form U and described in sections 4.8 and 4.9 of these Instructions. The **readily obtainable standard** for processing and use information is intended to require less effort on the part of the submitter than the "known to or reasonably ascertainable by" standard that applies to all other IUR reporting. The **readily obtainable standard** limits the burden associated with processing and use reporting by making extensive file searches and customer surveys unnecessary. The **readily obtainable standard** is identical to the standard currently in effect under EPA's TSCA § 8(a) Preliminary Assessment Information Rule (PAIR) (*See* 40 CFR 712.7).

Econ., Exposure & Tech. Div., U.S. Envtl. Prot. Agency, *Instructions for Reporting for the 2006 Partial Updating of the TSCA Chemical Inventory Database* at 4-2 (draft, March 2004). (*Note:* Companies reporting for the 2006 IUR should consult EPA's final reporting instructions, which were unavailable at the time of this publication.)

Submitters manufacturing over 300,000 lbs. will be required to report the following: (1) type of industrial processing or use operations at each site; (2) five-digit North American Industry Classification System (NAICS) codes best describing activities; (3) industrial function of each chemical substance during processing or use operation for each NAICS code reported; (4) percentage of submitter's production volume used in each industrial function category; (5) number of sites where the various processing or use operations occur; (6) number of workers reasonably likely to be exposed to the chemical substance in each processing or use operation; (7) categories of commercial and consumer uses of the reportable chemical substance; (8) indication of the presence of the reportable chemical substance in or on consumer products intended for use by children; (9) percentages of the submitter's production volume associated with each commercial and consumer product category; and (10) maximum concentration of the reportable chemical substance in each commercial and consumer product category. Companies can report this information either in writing by completing an original numbered reporting form available from EPA or on diskette. 40 C.F.R. § 710.52(c)(4).

The IURA also requires each manufacturer or importer subject to the rule to maintain specific records documenting the information submitted to EPA. The amendments extend the records retention period from 4 years to 5 years. 40 C.F.R. § 710.57. Additionally, the IURA changes the reporting period from a corporate fiscal year to a calendar year. 40 C.F.R. §§ 710.48, 710.52, and 710.53. Importantly, for those substances manufactured at less than 25,000 pounds, companies must maintain production volume records to justify the decision not to report.

The IURA now allows companies to claim as CBI their production volume range, as well as their specific production volume number. 40 C.F.R. § 710.52(c)(3)(iv) and (v). The amendments allow submitters to assert a confidentiality claim for specific production volume information while releasing the more general production volume range as public information. Guidance for asserting confidentiality claims is provided in EPA's instructions for the IUR reporting period in question, as stated in sections 710.59 and 710.58(a).

4.4.2. Special Reporting Problems

As originally promulgated, the IUR created a number of special reporting problems that still persist. One such problem arises when a company divests a division or subsidiary that had manufactured or imported reportable chemical substances during the reporting period. The question of which corporate entity bears the responsibility for reporting depends upon the terms of the transaction. If the sales contract specifies who is responsible for reporting, EPA looks to that specified party. If not, EPA considers the person who bought the plant site to have also purchased the responsibility to report. Office of Pollution Prevention & Toxics, U.S. Envtl. Protection Agency, *TSCA IUR Questions and Answers* 2 (August 1994). EPA also has stated that when one company toll manufactures a chemical substance for another, the company doing the toll manufacturing has the IUR reporting obligation. *Id.*

Other questions pertain to the parent company-subsidiary relationship and the small manufacturer exemption. EPA has indicated that the reporting obligation rests with the company subject to the rules, even if it is a subsidiary of a larger company. 51 Fed. Reg. 21,445 (June 12, 1986). EPA also has stated that the definition of "small manufacturer" includes the total annual sales of parent firms and subsidiaries, because

"EPA believes that a broadly defined sales criterion is the best available measure of a diversified firm's full financial resources available for regulatory compliance." *Id.*

4.4.3. IURA Litigation

In March 2003, several trade associations, including The Fertilizer Institute, the Consumer Specialty Products Association, and the American Chemistry Council, petitioned the U.S. Court of Appeals for the District of Columbia Circuit to review the final IURA rules, 68 Fed. Reg. 848 (January 7, 2003). *The Fertilizer Institute v. EPA*, No. 03-1077 and consolidated cases (D.C. Cir. 2002). Because ongoing discussions between the associations and EPA appeared to allow for resolution of the issues outside the courtroom, the court ordered that the cases be held in abeyance. A tentative settlement agreement was recorded in 2004, and the parties agreed to continue the stay until EPA published a final rule and both a question-and-answer document and reporting instructions for the 2006 IUR. In light of public comment and potential litigation, EPA proposed revisions to the IURA, which were not final at the time of this publication. 70 Fed. Reg. 3,658 (January 26, 2005).

4.4.4. Proposed IURA Revision

Pursuant to the above-mentioned settlement agreement, EPA proposes to amend the list of commercial and consumer product use categories in the IURA. Specifically, EPA proposes the following changes to the list of consumer categories: (1) to combine "Soaps and Detergents" and "Polishes and Sanitation Goods" to form a new "Cleaning Products (non-pesticidal)" category; (2) to remove category "Photographic chemicals"; and (3) to add an "Agricultural products (non-pesticidal)" category. 70 Fed. Reg. at 3,662-63.

EPA also proposes to move the submission period from August 25-December 23 of the reporting year to the January 1-April 30 immediately following the reporting year. 70 Fed. Reg. at 3,660. EPA will require separate reporting of manufacture and import volumes, a return to pre-IURA requirements. 70 Fed. Reg. at 3,663. EPA also will restrict the reporting of processing and use information to domestic processing and use activities only: The industrial processing or use operations (§ 710.52(c)(4)(i)(A)) and commercial and consumer uses (§ 710.52(c)(4)(ii)(A)) reported by submitters would be limited to domestic operations and uses. *Id.* To compensate industry for the burden of increased information requirements, EPA is proposing to reduce the frequency of IUR reporting from every four years to every five years. 70 Fed. Reg. at 3,660.

EPA further explained the partial exemption for chemicals for which the IURA processing and use information is of "low current interest." 70 Fed. Reg. at 3,661. A request for listing/delisting must provide written rationale or justification for partial exemption request, including relevant documents and specific cites to information in those documents. The burden is on the petitioner to establish "low current interest" qualification and EPA advises petitioners to include any additional information that would inform the Agency's decision. In determining whether a partial exemption applies, EPA will consider the totality of available information.

The IURA partially exempts certain petroleum refinery process streams from downstream processing and use reporting requirements described in section 710.52(c)(4). 70 Fed. Reg. at 3,661-62. The IURA revisions modify the IURA partial exemption name by adding the word "refinery." Additionally, the IURA revisions update the list of partial exemptions by adding certain streams which have been added to the TSCA Inventory since the 1983 publication was compiled.

Under the IURA, substances qualifying as polymers are fully exempt from reporting. 40 C.F.R. § 710.46(a)(1). Substances included in this IURA exemption are listed in either the 1985 Edition of the Inventory and the Master Inventory File. The proposed IURA revisions define polymers based only upon the "Master Inventory File" and not the 1985 edition of the Inventory. 70 Fed. Reg. at 3,663. Lastly, the IURA requires manufacturers of chemicals in amounts greater than 25,000 pounds to report the total volume of each reportable chemical substance manufactured at each site. 40 C.F.R. § 710.52(c)(3)(iv). Any manufacturer claiming confidentiality for the total volume requirement must indicate whether the total volume range which corresponds with the specific volume figure required by section 710.52(c)(3)(iv) is also confidential. *Id.* § 710.52(c)(3)(v). The IURA revisions remove this requirement. 70 Fed. Reg. at 3,663.

4.5. HOW TO USE THE INVENTORY

The "TSCA Chemical Substance Inventory: 1985 Edition" consists of non-confidential substance identities and generic names for confidential substances and is comprised of one volume and six indices (contained in five volumes) as aids to the user. EPA maintains the Master File which contains both the confidential and non-confidential identities.

In 1990, the Agency issued a supplement to the 1985 edition of the Inventory for the purpose of assisting companies preparing to respond to the 1990 IUR. Since 1990, EPA has not issued any more hard copy updates to the Inventory, but the Agency updates the Inventory every six months and makes current information available on CD-ROM. The CD-ROMs include some chemical synonyms, generic names, PMN case numbers and EPA accession numbers for substances with confidential chemical identities.

4.5.1. Volume I: TSCA Inventory

The first volume of the 1985 edition lists, in ascending order by CAS Registry Number, the CAS Index or Preferred Names of non-confidential chemical substances included on the Inventory. This list is titled "Chemical Substance Identities." Accompanying each entry is the molecular formula of the substance (if known). Some CAS Registry Numbers have an asterisk (*) designating a substance of unknown or variable composition, complex reaction products, or biological materials (UVCB substances). A CAS Registry Number with an asterisk also may have a dagger (†), which indicates a UVCB substance that is more precisely defined in Appendix A:

"Chemical Substance Definitions." Some CAS Registry Numbers also may be accompanied by one or more EPA "flags" to indicate that EPA has taken certain regulatory action on the listed substance.[14]

Following the Chemical Substance Identities section are two appendices: Appendix A (mentioned above), and Appendix B: "Generic Names for Confidential Identities." Appendix B lists generic names for those substances submitted under the reporting regulations whose identities were claimed as confidential by their submitters. These generic names are ordered by a unique five or six digit accession number. Any applicable EPA flags for the substance(s) covered by the generic name accompany the accession number. The remaining four volumes of the 1985 TSCA Inventory consist of various indices.

4.5.2. Volumes II and III: Substance Name Index

This is a listing of all CAS Index or Preferred Names, EPA submitter names, and CAS synonyms in alphabetical order for the substances in the Chemical Substance Identities section. Accompanying each name is the CAS Registry Number and, if appropriate, the molecular formula, asterisk, dagger, and EPA flags.

4.5.3. Volume IV: Molecular Formula Index

This index lists all substances appearing in the Chemical Substance Identities section which have molecular formulas. It is ordered alphabetically with each chemical element and its particular numerical suffix considered a separate unit. Beneath each molecular formula are listed, in alphabetical order, the CAS Index Names for substances having the same molecular formula. Accompanying each name is the CAS Registry Number and any applicable EPA flags.

4.5.4. Volume V: UVCB Index, Section 4 Rule Index, Section 5(e) Order/Sections 5(f)/6(a) Rule Index and Significant New Use Rules (SNUR) Index

The UVCB Index lists substances of unknown or variable composition, complex reaction products, and biological materials (UVCB Substances).

---

14 For example:

P: indicates a commenced PMN substance, *i.e.*, a substance that has been added to the Inventory as a result of a PMN submission and a notice of commencement of manufacture.

S: indicates a substance identified in a proposed or final significant new use rule.

XU: indicates a substance exempt from reporting under the Inventory Update Rule.

4.5.4.1. UVCB Index

This index lists the CAS Preferred Names for all substances that do not have definite chemical structures or molecular formulas like those contained in the Chemical Substance Identities section. Accompanying each name is the CAS Registry Number and any applicable EPA flags. The names are grouped into subsets with each subset consisting of closely related substances. The subsets highlight a structural feature of the substance, a significant precursor or a general description. The subsets are ordered alphabetically by subset heading name. The subset headings developed for the index are listed preceding the index itself in a general hierarchy of subsets within each subset heading. The subsets are arranged in order of increasing specificity. This hierarchy list serves as a guide to the most appropriate subsets for the substances of interest. Most of the substances in this index have been assigned to more than one subset heading. Subset headings are meant to classify like substances and are not substances themselves.

4.5.4.2. Section 4 Index, Sections 5(e), 5(f) Index, Significant New Use Rules Index

This section 4 index contains a reference list of substances subject to either an Advanced Notice of Proposed Rulemaking, a Notice of Proposed Rulemaking or a Final Rule for testing under TSCA § 4. The Significant New Use Rule (SNUR) Index contains a reference list of substances identified in proposed and final SNURs. The sections 5(e) and 5(f) index lists those chemicals subject to a section 5(e) order or a 5(f) rule or order.

4.6. SEARCHING THE INVENTORY

Volume I of the 1985 edition contains instructions on how to use the Inventory. The appropriate procedure for searching the Inventory depends on the amount of information known about the substance in question. The easiest way to determine if a substance is listed in the printed Inventory is to search for its CAS Registry Number in Vol. I. If the CAS Registry Number for the substance is already known, then it is only necessary to determine if it is included in the Chemical Substance Identities section. If the CAS Registry Number is not known, indices such as the Molecular Formula Index can assist in determining whether the chemical appears on the Inventory.

A useful approach is to determine if the substance is well defined; *i.e.*, whether it has a chemical structure or formula. If so, the searcher can consult the Molecular Formula Index for the specific molecular formula. If present, the substance name(s) listed for that formula can be reviewed to determine if any correspond to the substance of interest. If the substance has a chemical name, look for the name in the Substance Name Index to determine its CAS Registry Number. If both of these indices can be searched, it is wise to cross-check and to make sure both techniques result in the same CAS number.

If the substance is not well defined (*i.e.*, it has no chemical structure or formula), the searcher should consult the hierarchy of subset headings preceding the UVCB Index to identify possible subset classifications for the substance. If the UVCB Index listing has a dagger following the CAS Registry Number, the searcher should confirm that the definition given in Appendix A matches the chemical of interest. As a final step, the CAS Number located in the UVCB Index should be checked against the Volume I Inventory listings to ensure that all three descriptions match.

4.6.1. Inventory Search Assistance

The 1985 edition and 1990 supplement are available in printed form from the Superintendent of Documents, Government Printing Office, Washington, D.C. 20402, (tel: 202-783-3238) under document control codes S/N 055-000-00254-1 (1985 edition) and S/N 055-000-00361-1 (1990 supplement). The Inventory also is available on CD-ROM from the National Technical Information Service (NTIS), 5285 Port Royal Road, Springfield, Virginia 22161 (tel: 703-605-6060 or 800-363-2068) under order number SUB5423.

The Inventory also is available to the public on several commercial on-line databases. These services include the following:

Chemlist
maintained by Scientific and Technical Network International (STNI)
(800) 753-4227

Dialog Information Services
maintained by Thompson Publishing
(800) 3DIALOG

Solutions Software Corp.
877-373-4726

Because new substances are continually being added to the Inventory, the CD-ROM version of the Inventory is never completely current. Further, EPA does not publish the identities of over 15,000 unique substances that have been claimed confidential by their submitters. In recognition of this problem, EPA provides a service whereby EPA will search the Master Inventory File (which contains both confidential and non-confidential chemical identities). Finally, a basic understanding of TSCA Inventory nomenclature policies is mandatory before undertaking any search of the Inventory.

4.6.2. Searches for Confidential Identities: *Bona fide* Requests

Because confidential chemicals are not listed by specific chemical identity, and new non-confidential chemicals are continually being added, the only way to determine if a substance is or is not on the Inventory is to search the Master File version of the Inventory. This version includes both the confidential and non-confidential chemical identities and is kept current by EPA. Unless a PMN is filed, which necessitates an Inventory search, EPA will search the confidential Inventory only if the person requesting the search can demonstrate a *bona fide* intent to manufacture or import the substance for a commercial purpose. 40 C.F.R. § 720.25(b)(1). This service is available only to those who intend to manufacture or import for a commercial purpose. Thus, processors and users cannot file such a statement of *bona fide* intent.

In order to establish this *bona fide* intent to manufacture or import the substance, the request must be in writing and include the following information: the specific chemical identity, a signed statement of intent to manufacture or import for a commercial purpose, a description of the research and development activities conducted to date on the substance, a description of the major intended use of the substance, an infrared spectrum or alternative spectra, anticipated date that a PMN would be submitted, the address of the site where manufacturing or processing most likely would occur, and a description of the most probable manufacturing process. 40 C.F.R. § 720.25(b)(2).

After gathering the information necessary to file a *bona fide* request, the requester has much of what is needed to complete a PMN. For this reason, many choose to file a PMN rather than a *bona fide* request on a chemical of uncertain Inventory status which they wish to manufacture. If the chemical in fact is on the confidential Inventory, EPA will notify the PMN submitter (just as it will notify the *bona fide* requester). But if it is not on the Inventory, the PMN submitter has gained valuable time (over the *bona fide* requester) in getting its chemical to market since it is well into the PMN review process.

The information provided to EPA in a *bona fide* request can be claimed confidential. This claim must be made at the time the request is submitted. Unless the information in the *bona fide* request has been claimed confidential, EPA will release the *bona fide* request in response to a Freedom of Information Act request. Although EPA does not require substantiation at the time the claim of confidentiality is made, the Agency advises *bona fide* submitters to anticipate at least the following substantiation questions when making claims of confidentiality:

1. What period of time is desired by the business for confidential treatment (*e.g.*, until a certain date, until the occurrence of a specified event, or permanently)?

2. What measures were taken by the business to guard against undesired disclosure of the information to others?

3. To what extent has the information been disclosed to others, and what precautions have been taken to avoid further disclosure?

4. What pertinent confidentiality determinations, if any, have been made by EPA or other federal agencies?

5. Do you assert that disclosure of the information would be likely to result in substantial harmful effects on the business's competitive position, and if so, what would those harmful effects be, why should they be viewed as substantial, and how would you describe the causal relationship between disclosure and such harmful effects?

See 40 C.F.R. § 720.85(b)(3)(iv).

If some of the information is claimed confidential by a foreign supplier or manufacturer, the information can be supplied directly to EPA by the foreign company. The *bona fide* request must be submitted to:

OPPT Document Control Officer
Office of Pollution Prevention and Toxics
U.S. Environmental Protection Agency
1200 Pennsylvania Avenue, NW
Washington, D.C. 20460

Each *bona fide* request is assigned an EPA Document Control Number. The Document Control Officer then forwards the request to the Industrial Chemistry Branch, where the submission is reviewed to ensure that the submitter has provided all the required information. Only then is the Inventory search performed. A member of the Industrial Chemistry Branch will contact the submitter by telephone if EPA has identified any problems with the submission. In theory, EPA will answer a *bona fide* request within 30 days of receipt. 40 C.F.R. § 720.25(b)(8). In some cases, EPA's response may take longer.

EPA will not honor a request to search the confidential Inventory if the Agency determines that the submitter has failed to establish a *bona fide* intent. If the submitter does establish such intent, the Agency will notify the submitter by letter of the results of its search. It is important to note that, under EPA's regulations, the disclosure of a confidential chemical identity to a *bona fide* requester is not considered public disclosure of confidential business information (CBI) under TSCA § 14. 40 C.F.R. § 720.25(b)(7).

4.6.3. *Bona fide* Requests and IUR Reports

EPA also will honor a request to search the Master Inventory File in conjunction with the IUR. If after searching the TSCA Inventory a manufacturer is still uncertain about the Inventory status of a chemical it is manufacturing or importing, it can request that EPA search the Master Inventory File. In order to request this search, the manufacturer must substantiate the fact that it is actually manufacturing or importing the substance in question, and must include all of the information required with a *bona fide* request, except for the description of R&D activities. *See* EPA, Office of Prevention, Pesticides and Toxic Substances, *Instructions for Reporting for the 1994 Partial Updating of the TSCA Chemical Inventory Data Base* at 3-4 (June 1994). Manufacturers or importers should be cautious about using this procedure, however, unless they have a high degree of confidence that the chemical is listed on the confidential Inventory. Otherwise, a *bona fide* request in the IUR context constitutes disclosure of a TSCA § 5 violation.

CHAPTER 5
NEW CHEMICAL REVIEW: OVERVIEW AND EXEMPTIONS

Any person intending to manufacture or import a chemical substance first must determine whether the substance is listed on the TSCA Inventory. If it is listed, manufacture or importation may begin immediately. If it is not listed, the manufacturer or importer must determine whether the chemical substance is excluded altogether from regulation under TSCA or exempt from premanufacture notification (PMN) requirements under TSCA § 5(h). If the substance is neither excluded nor exempt, the prospective manufacturer or importer must satisfy PMN requirements before commencing activity with the substance.

This chapter discusses the PMN requirements and exemptions. Chapter 6 provides detailed guidance on complying with PMN requirements, and Chapter 7 discusses how EPA exercises its authority to control the manufacture of new chemical substances and suggests responses to relevant Agency actions.

5.1. OVERVIEW OF TSCA § 5

TSCA § 5 authorizes EPA to evaluate and, in certain instances, to regulate new chemical substances. Specifically, section 5(a)(1) requires a manufacturer (which, by definition, includes an importer) of a new chemical substance to file a PMN at least 90 days prior to the commencement of commercial production or importation. This 90-day review period provides EPA its first, but not its only, opportunity to evaluate risks posed by new chemical substances and reflects the House and Senate conferees' view that

> the most desirable time to determine the health and environmental effects of a substance, and to take action to protect against any potential adverse effects, occurs before commercial production begins. Not only is human and environmental harm avoided or alleviated, but the cost of any regulatory action in terms of loss of jobs and capital investment is minimized.

H.R. Conf. Rep. No. 94-1679, at 65, *reprinted in* 1976 U.S.C.C.A.N. 4539, 4550.

5.2. PMN REQUIREMENTS

The information that is required in a PMN is set forth in TSCA § 5(d): (1) the identity of the chemical, categories of use, amounts manufactured, by-products, employees exposed, and the manner or method of disposal, to the extent known or "reasonably ascertainable;" (2) any test data related to the effects of the chemical on health or the environment that are in the submitter's possession or control; and (3) a description of any other data concerning the health and environmental effects of the chemical, to the extent such data are known to, or "reasonably ascertainable" by, the submitter. By using the phrase "reasonably ascertainable," Congress intended to create an objective standard encompassing information of which a reasonable person similarly situated might be expected to have knowledge.

Under TSCA, manufacturers, importers, and processors of chemical substances bear the responsibility for developing adequate data regarding the effects of commercial chemicals on human health and the environment. Section 5(b)(2)(B) obligates a PMN submitter to produce data showing that the manufacture, processing, distribution in commerce, use, and disposal of a new chemical, or any combination of these activities, "will not present an unreasonable risk of injury to health or the environment." Yet, TSCA does not expressly authorize EPA to require, or obligate the PMN submitter to produce, *specific* tests in conjunction with a PMN, except where a chemical substance is otherwise subject to a TSCA § 4 test rule. Thus, unlike some chemical control laws outside the United States (*e.g.*, the European Union), TSCA does not require a "base set" of specified (premarket) data on new chemical substances.

EPA promulgated the basic regulations implementing TSCA § 5 over a seven-year period ending in 1986.[15] Under these regulations, EPA requires that the PMN be submitted on a standard form (EPA Form No. 7710-25) or electronically (pursuant to EPA media specifications), in which case the Certification and Submitter Identification sections of the standard form still must be submitted on paper. 40 C.F.R. § 720.40(a). All information submitted must be true and accurate.

The PMN must contain the following specific information concerning the manufacture, processing, distribution in commerce, use and disposal of the new chemical substance: (1) chemical identity, including the currently correct or preferred Chemical Abstracts Service (CAS) name and the CAS Registry Number, if available; (2) impurities anticipated to be present; (3) known synonyms or trade names; (4) a description of by-products, if any; (5) estimated production or import volumes; (6)

---

[15] Notification regulations were first proposed on January 10, 1979 (44 Fed. Reg. 2242), re-proposed on October 16, 1979 (44 Fed. Reg. 59,764), and adopted on May 13, 1983 (48 Fed. Reg. 21,722). In response to comments from industry, EPA clarified portions of the rule on September 13, 1983 (48 Fed. Reg. 41,132) and stayed the effective date of provisions regarding the exemption for R&D substances, the definition of "possession and control," and data requirements for related chemicals pending continuing EPA review; the final rule became effective on October 26, 1983. Revisions were proposed on December 27, 1984 (49 Fed. Reg. 50,201) and finalized on April 22, 1986 (51 Fed. Reg. 15,096). Additional amendments were proposed on February 8, 1993 (58 Fed. Reg. 7661) and promulgated on March 29, 1995 (60 Fed. Reg. 16,298). A further amendment on April 11, 1997 clarified that the notification regulations apply to microorganisms only to the extent provided by 40 C.F.R. § 725. 62 Fed. Reg. 17,909.

intended uses, including percentages of the substance in end-use formulations; and (7) site and process information, including expected worker, user, and consumer exposures and releases to the environment. 40 C.F.R. § 720.45 (*see* chapter 6). Pursuant to TSCA § 5(b), the PMN submission must include any test data in the submitter's possession or control concerning health and environmental effects of the new substance and by such other data on these effects as are known to, or reasonably ascertainable by, the submitter. *Id.* § 720.50 (*see* chapter 6).

After a PMN is submitted, the submitter may withdraw it voluntarily from review at any time. 40 C.F.R. § 720.75(e). Although the Agency must be forewarned in writing of the submitter's intent to withdraw the PMN, the submitter need not offer or furnish EPA an explanation for the withdrawal.

5.2.1. PMN Review Period

Under section 5(a), EPA must review the PMN within 90 days. Under section 5(c), EPA may extend the review period for an additional 90 days for "good cause." Also, the submitter and the Agency may suspend the review period for a specific period of time or indefinitely by mutual consent. During its PMN review, EPA must assess the potential risks associated with the manufacture, processing, distribution, use, and disposal of the new chemical substance based upon information supplied by the submitter and available from various Agency databases, the existing scientific literature and the Agency's own expertise and professional judgment.

If EPA takes no regulatory action by the end of the PMN review period (90 days or up to 180 days, with an extension), the submitter may begin commercial manufacture or importation of the new chemical substance immediately, without prior explicit Agency approval. Within 30 days of beginning commercial manufacture or importation, however, the manufacturer or importer must file a Notice of Commencement of Manufacture or Import (NOC) with EPA. 40 C.F.R. § 720.102. (For a complete discussion of NOC requirements, see chapter 6.) The NOC certifies that commercial manufacture or importation has occurred in fact. After receiving the NOC, EPA adds the new chemical substance to the TSCA Inventory, at which time the substance becomes an "existing" chemical for regulatory purposes under TSCA.

5.2.2. EPA Regulation of PMN Substances

TSCA § 5 was intended to provide EPA

> an opportunity to review and evaluate information with respect to the substance to determine if manufacture, processing, distribution in commerce, use or disposal should be limited, delayed or prohibited because data is insufficient to evaluate the health and environmental effects or because the substance or the new use presents or will present an unreasonable risk of injury to health or the environment.

H.R. Conf. Rep. No. 94-1679, at 65, *reprinted in* 1976 U.S.C.C.A.N. 4539, 4550.

TSCA provides EPA with three means to prevent, delay, or limit manufacture (including by importation) after the initial 90-day PMN review period expires. First, under section 5(c) the Agency may delay manufacture for an additional 90 days for "good cause." Second, under section 5(e)(1)(A)(i) EPA may propose an order to limit or prohibit manufacture if the Agency determines that the available information is "insufficient to permit a reasoned evaluation" of the health and environmental effects of the new chemical substance. Third, under section 5(f)(2) EPA may propose a section 6(a) rule limiting or conditioning manufacture, and under section 5(f)(3)(B) may propose an order totally banning manufacture if "there is a reasonable basis to conclude that the manufacture [import] . . . presents or will present an unreasonable risk of injury to health or the environment." Each of these regulatory options is discussed in detail in chapter 7.

5.3. EXCLUSIONS FROM PMN REQUIREMENTS

The notification requirements of TSCA § 5(a) apply only to "chemical substances." Although TSCA's definition of "chemical substance" is quite broad, it specifically excludes mixtures, pesticides (as defined by the Federal Insecticide, Fungicide, and Rodenticide Act), tobacco and tobacco products, radioactive materials regulated under the Atomic Energy Act, firearms and shells, articles, and any food, food additive, drug, cosmetic, or device (as defined by the Federal Food, Drug, and Cosmetic Act). TSCA § 3(2)(B). These substances are excluded from TSCA jurisdiction by definition and, as such, are not subject to TSCA PMN requirements unless they are also intended for a "TSCA use" (*see* chapter 13 for a detailed discussion of TSCA exclusions).

5.4. PMN EXEMPTIONS THAT REQUIRE EPA APPROVAL

TSCA § 5(h) authorizes EPA to exempt from PMN requirements chemical substances intended for test marketing, research and development (R&D), and other uses. Some exemptions, like the test marketing exemption, require prior application and EPA approval. Others, like R&D, are "self-executing;" *i.e.*, they do not require an application or an approval, and serve to exempt a manufacturer or importer of the PMN requirement for the exempt substance as long as the manufacturer/importer complies with requirements pertaining to these exemptions.

5.4.1. Test Market Exemption

TSCA § 5(h)(1) authorizes EPA to exempt a new chemical substance from the PMN requirements when the substance is manufactured for test marketing purposes if the Agency determines that the proposed test marketing activity will not present an unreasonable risk to human health or the environment. The test market exemption (TME) permits a company to assess the commercial viability of a new chemical and to receive customer feedback on product performance before filing a PMN. The test marketer, however, must apply for this exemption and must demonstrate that the proposed activity is legitimate test marketing which will not present an unreasonable risk. EPA must publish in the *Federal Register* both its receipt of the TME application and its decision to grant or deny the application.

EPA reviews a TME application in essentially the same manner as a PMN (*see* chapter 6). Yet, under TSCA § 5(h)(6) EPA must review a TME application within 45 days of its receipt. According to EPA, however, the Agency's failure to complete its review of a TME application within 45 days does not constitute an automatic approval. Rather, unlike a PMN submitter, a TME applicant must await EPA approval prior to initiating activity.

EPA regulations implementing the TME are published at 40 C.F.R. section 720.38. They provide that a TME application need not be submitted on a PMN form. Rather, it may be submitted in letter form. The application, however, must contain the following information:

- all existing data regarding health and environmental effects, including physical/chemical properties or, in the absence of toxicity data, a discussion of structural analogues;
- the maximum amount to be imported/manufactured;
- the maximum number of persons who may be exposed;
- the estimated routes and durations of exposures;
- the maximum number of persons who may be provided the chemical substance during test marketing;
- a description of the test marketing activity, with particular attention to how the proposed activity differs from R&D and full scale commercial production.

5.4.2. Low Volume Exemption

Under TSCA § 5(h)(4) and upon expiration of a mandatory 30-day review period, EPA exempts from full PMN requirements certain new chemicals manufactured in "low" volumes. 40 C.F.R. § 723.50. A manufacturer or importer who intends to produce or import a chemical substance in quantities of 10,000 kilograms or less per year may apply for the low volume exemption (LVE). The LVE is available to multiple manufacturers and importers, except that EPA will not approve subsequent LVE applications "unless it can determine that the potential human exposure to, and environmental release of, the new chemical substance at the higher, aggregate production volume will not present an unreasonable risk of injury to human health or the environment" (the exemption standard in TSCA § 5(h)(4)). *Id.* § 723.50(f)(1).

EPA substantially amended the LVE on March 29, 1995 (60 Fed. Reg. 16,336). Prior to this amendment, only one company could hold an LVE for any given chemical, and that company was limited to manufacturing or importing no more than 1,000 kilograms per year. Although the superseded LVE became unavailable to new applicants on or after May 30, 1995 (the effective date of the 1995 LVE amendment), all exemptions granted previously under the 1,000 kilogram exemption remain binding and effective, even though the relevant provisions no longer exist in the *Code of Federal Regulations*. 40 C.F.R. § 723.50(m).

An LVE applicant must submit to EPA an exemption application on the standard PMN form (EPA Form No. 7710-25) at least 30 days before the manufacture or import of the new chemical substance begins. 40 C.F.R. § 723.50(e). The LVE application must include the following information: (1) the identity of the manufacturer or importer; (2) the identity of the chemical substances; (3) the identity of any known impurities; (4) any known synonyms and trade names; (5) any by-products; (6) the intended production volume; (7) a description of intended categories of use; (8) for manufacturer-controlled sites only, the identity of manufacturing sites, process descriptions, and worker exposure and environmental release information; (9) for sites not controlled by the manufacturer, processing and use operation descriptions, estimated number of processing and use sites, and worker exposure/environmental release information; (10) an indication on the first page of the application that the submission is a "TSCA § 5(h)(4) exemption notice" and whether the application is submitted under 40 C.F.R. section 723.50(c)(1) or (c)(2); (11) any test data in the possession or control of the applicant regarding the new chemical's effects on human health and the environment; and (12) required certifications. *Id.* § 723.50(e)(2). In addition, if the applicant claims any part of the application as confidential business information (CBI) in accordance with section 723.50(*l*), the applicant must submit an additional copy of the exemption application with the CBI deleted. To encourage use of the LVE, EPA has eliminated filing fees for their submission. *See id.* § 700.45(c).

A manufacturer or importer need not provide information on worker exposures or environmental releases if such information is not known or readily available to it. *Id.* § 723.50(c)(2)(viii). In the absence of such information, however, EPA will generate exposure and release estimates using the basic process descriptions for the proposed manufacturing, processing, and use operations of the new chemical. 60 Fed. Reg. 16,336, 16,339 (Mar. 29, 1995). Understandably, EPA estimates generally will be very conservative, due to uncertainties over actual operating conditions at manufacturing, processing, and use sites. Thus, applicants should supply their own exposure and release data wherever possible. EPA will perform risk assessments upon the new chemical substance, and will assume manufacture or importation at an annual volume of 10,000 kilograms. 40 C.F.R. § 723.50(e)(2)(vi). A manufacturer or importer who intends to produce or import a new chemical at an annual volume of less than 10,000 kilograms may request that EPA perform risk assessments at this lower level by indicating the actual production or importation volume in the appropriate box on the application form and by marking the adjacent binding option box. Of course, manufacturers and importers who elect to specify annual production or importation levels below 10,000 kilograms may not subsequently manufacture or import more than the amount of the new substance specified and exempted, unless a new LVE application is submitted and approved for the higher volume.

Where a manufacturer or importer voluntarily provides EPA information on human exposure controls and/or environmental release controls to support an LVE application, the manufacturer or importer must maintain those controls throughout the duration of the exemption. 40 C.F.R. § 723.50(j)(1). If EPA identifies potential human risks that it believes may be sufficiently mitigated by pollution prevention techniques and/or exposure or release controls, the Agency may conditionally approve an LVE, pending submission of an amended LVE application setting forth these techniques or controls. 60 Fed. Reg. at 16,337. If insufficient time remains in the 30-day review period to submit such information, the manufacturer or importer may request a temporary suspension of the review period to prepare and submit the amended LVE application. 40 C.F.R. § 723.50(g)(1).

EPA does *not* require the filing of an NOC for an LVE chemical and does not place it on the TSCA Inventory. Consequently, LVE chemicals remain "new" chemical substances for purposes of TSCA § 5 and are subject to PMN requirements at any point in time that they no longer qualify for an LVE or PMN exemption.

5.4.2.1. LVE Review

In order to grant an LVE, EPA must determine that the chemical substance will not present an "unreasonable risk of injury to health or the environment." TSCA § 5(h)(4). EPA makes this determination based upon the information contained in the LVE application. If EPA concludes that the substance itself or any reasonably anticipated metabolites, environmental transformation products, by-products, or impurities of the substance may cause serious acute or chronic health effects or significant environmental effects, the Agency will deny the LVE application. 40 C.F.R. § 723.50(d).

If EPA has taken no action upon expiration of the 30-day review period, the manufacturer or importer may consider its LVE exemption approved and may begin to produce or manufacture the new chemical in accordance with the terms of its exemption application and of section 723.50 generally. *Id.* § 723.50(g)(2). If, during the application review period, the applicant obtains possession, control, or knowledge of new information that materially adds to, changes, or otherwise makes significantly more complete the information contained in the LVE application, the applicant must send this information to EPA within ten days of receipt and no later than five days before the end of the application review period. *Id.* § 723.50(i).

The LVE submitter's obligation to observe precisely all statements made in the exemption application about exposure and release controls, chemical uses, and manufacturing (importation) sites is the main drawback to using the LVE. Once the LVE is approved, any change in manufacturing sites, chemical uses, human exposure and environmental release controls, or manufacturing and import volumes will require the submission of a new LVE application under the new conditions, except that an applicant may manufacture or import the new chemical at a site not listed in the original LVE application, without submitting a new LVE application, if: (1) the magnitude, frequency, and duration of exposure of individual workers at the new site is equal to or less than worker exposure at the site for which EPA performed its original risk assessment; and (2) the manufacturer or importer either (a) does not release the new chemical to surface waters at the new site, or (b) maintains surface water concentrations of the new chemical at or below 1 part per billion or at an alternative concentration level approved by the Agency. 40 C.F.R. § 723.50(j)(4) - 723.50(j)(6)(i). Changes to the physical form of a new chemical approved under an LVE also will require a new LVE application whenever such a change may increase the human exposure to, or environmental release of, the new chemical substance over those exposures or releases resulting from the physical form approved in the original application. *Id.* § 723.50(j)(4).

5.4.2.2. LVE Revocation

If new information causes a chemical substance to become ineligible for the LVE, EPA will revoke the exemption. For example, EPA may learn that a company has manufactured more than the permitted 10,000 kilograms, or the Agency may receive information in a TSCA § 8(e) substantial risk notice indicating that the compound may present a substantial risk to health or the environment (*see* chapter 10). Under such circumstances, EPA would no longer be able to make the required finding that the LVE chemical will be produced in annual quantities less than 10,000 kilograms and "will not present an unreasonable risk" as required by TSCA § 5(h)(4).

Before revoking the LVE, however, EPA must notify the manufacturer or importer in writing of the Agency's intent to revoke. 40 C.F.R. § 723.50(h)(2)(i)(A). After receiving such notice, the manufacturer or importer within 15 days may file objections or an explanation of its "diligence and good faith efforts" in attempting to comply with the terms of the exemption. *Id.* § 723.50(h)(2)(ii). If the LVE holder was manufacturing, processing, distributing, or using the LVE chemical at the time of the notice and files objections or an explanation, the LVE holder may continue to manufacture the LVE chemical until EPA makes a final eligibility determination. *Id.* § 723.50(h)(2)(i)(B).

EPA will notify the manufacturer or importer of its final LVE eligibility determination by telephone within 15 days of receiving objections or a "due diligence" explanation and will follow up such expedited notification with a certified letter. 40 C.F.R. § 723.50(h)(2)(iii). If the determination is favorable, EPA will leave the LVE in effect. *Id.* § 723.50(h)(2)(iv). If EPA determines that the manufacturer or importer does not satisfy the LVE criteria and did not act with due diligence and in good faith to meet such criteria, the manufacturer or importer must discontinue its activities with the new chemical within seven days of receiving the written eligibility determination from the Agency. *Id.* § 723.50(h)(2)(v). If the Agency finds that the manufacturer or importer has not satisfied LVE requirements but has adequately demonstrated due diligence and good faith in its attempts to comply with LVE standards, the manufacturer or importer may continue its activities with the new chemical provided that it submits a PMN to EPA within 15 days of receiving the Agency's written eligibility determination. *Id.* § 723.50(h)(2)(vi).

EPA created the due diligence/good faith provisions to address industry concerns that the immediate cessation of manufacturing or importation could unfairly disrupt marketing plans and customer relations where EPA had not actually discovered any unreasonable risks but simply could not make the required affirmative finding that the LVE chemical presents no unreasonable risks to health or the environment. Therefore, in those instances where a company no longer qualifies for an LVE but has operated with due diligence and in good faith, the Agency permits continued manufacture or import until a PMN is filed and clears review. Of course, the Agency may determine that an LVE chemical should be regulated under TSCA § 5(e) or (f). If it does so, the LVE holder must cease manufacturing, importing, processing, or using the LVE chemical, notwithstanding its due diligence and good faith. *See* 40 C.F.R. § 723.50(h)(2)(vi)(B).

5.4.2.3. Customer Notification

Manufacturers and importers of LVE substances must notify processors and industrial users: (1) that the substance may be used only in accordance with the use restrictions specified in the exemption application; and (2) of any and all applicable exposure and release controls. 40 C.F.R. § 723.50(k)(1). Notification by labeling, written notice, or any other adequately informative method is allowed. *Id.*

If a manufacturer or importer learns that a customer is using or processing the LVE substance in violation of use restrictions or without exercising required exposure or release controls, it must stop distribution of the substance to the customer, or to the customer's distributor, unless it is able to provide certain prescribed, written assurances from the customer. 40 C.F.R. § 723.50(k)(3). If the customer subsequently fails to comply with use restrictions or release or exposure controls, the manufacturer or importer must again halt distribution, notify EPA within 15 days, and await the Agency's notification of whether, and under what conditions, distribution of the LVE substance to the customer may resume. *Id.* § 723.50(k)(4).

5.4.3. LoREX Exemption

EPA also exempts from the PMN requirements new chemicals that are released at low levels and result in minimal human exposure during production, regardless of production or import volumes. To satisfy the TSCA § 5(h)(4) exemption standard of no substantial risk and to qualify for the so-called "LoREX" (low release/exposure) exemption, however, a manufacturer or importer must meet a variety of stringent exposure and release-related criteria.

First, regarding exposure of consumers and the general public to the new chemical substance, there must be no dermal exposure, no inhalation exposure (except in the case of authorized incineration), and no exposure in drinking water greater than one milligram per year. 40 C.F.R. § 723.50(c)(2)(i). Second, with respect to the exposure of workers, there must be no dermal exposure and no inhalation exposure, but dermal and inhalation exposure controls used in accordance with applicable EPA guidance will satisfy these occupational criteria. *Id.* § 723.50(c)(2)(ii). Third, there must be no ambient surface water releases resulting in surface water concentrations greater than 1 part per billion, unless EPA approves a higher surface water concentration supported by evidence provided in the LoREX exemption application. *Id.* § 723.50(c)(2)(iii). Lastly, ambient air releases are allowed only for the purposes of incineration and only at a maximum annual average concentration of 1 microgram per cubic meter, calculated using the following formula:

> (kg per day of release after treatment) x (number of release days per year) x (9.68 x 10^{-6} micrograms per m^3).

Application for, and administration of, the LoREX exemption are almost identical to the requirements for an LVE, described in section 5.4.2 above (30-day review period, application on standard PMN form, no filing fee, record-keeping, etc.). In addition to observing the customer notification requirements for an LVE chemical, however, a manufacturer or importer of a LoREX substance may only distribute it to customers who agree in writing not to distribute the substance further until it has been reacted, incorporated into an article, or otherwise rendered into a state or physical form in which human exposures and environmental releases above the exemption's eligibility criteria are "not likely" to occur. 40 C.F.R. § 723.50(k)(2).

Because of the stringent exposure and release criteria, industry has not made widespread use of the LoREX exemption. Some companies, however, have pursued compliance with the LoREX exemption criteria as an alternative to negotiating a consent order with EPA under section 5(e) of TSCA, where such an order was expected. For such companies, the opportunity voluntarily to propose and support exposure and release controls of their own in an exemption application was preferable to the imposition of such controls in an Agency order.

5.5. PMN EXEMPTIONS THAT DO NOT REQUIRE EPA APPROVAL

In addition to the test-marketing exemption under TSCA § 5(h)(1) and the LVE and LoREX exemptions that EPA has authorized under its TSCA § 5(h)(4) authority, TSCA § 5(h) also exempts certain other categories of new chemical substances from PMN requirements without requiring prior application and Agency approval. The following exemptions under Section 5(h) are sometimes referred to as "self-executing."

5.5.1. Research and Development Exemption

TSCA § 5(h)(3) exempts from PMN and SNUR requirements small quantities of new chemicals used solely for R&D under the supervision of a technically qualified individual, if the manufacturer or importer notifies persons engaged in R&D of any health risks associated with the substance. Unlike the foregoing exemptions under

TSCA §§ 5(h)(1) and (4), the manufacturer or importer need not apply for the R&D exemption.

EPA regulations establishing requirements for the R&D exemption appear at 40 C.F.R. section 720.36. EPA requires that manufacturers or importers supervise the R&D with a technically qualified individual, evaluate any potential risks associated with the R&D substance, notify persons involved in the R&D of those risks, and maintain certain records of their R&D activity. In evaluating risks, the manufacturer and importer must consider all health and environmental effects data in their "possession or control." This includes information in the files of agents and employees engaged in the R&D and marketing of the new chemical. When R&D activity is conducted in laboratories using prudent laboratory practices, this risk assessment need not be performed.

Manufacturers and importers must maintain records pertaining to their risk evaluations of each new R&D chemical, the nature and method of their notification of any potential risk and, if they distribute the R&D chemical, the identity and amount of the distributed chemical and the identity of the recipient. In addition, those who manufacture or import an R&D substance in quantities greater than 100 kilograms per year must maintain records of the chemical identity, production volume, and disposition of the substance.

5.5.1.1. Meaning of R&D

R&D consists of several levels of activities, including "tests of the physical, chemical, production, and performance characteristics of a chemical substance." 51 Fed. Reg. 15,096, 15,097 (Apr. 22, 1986). Tests of the physical and chemical properties typically occur at the laboratory stage, while tests of production characteristics involve manufacturing equipment and production processes. Analysis of performance characteristics can include "carefully monitored tests using limited quantities of the chemical substance by the manufacturer or potential customer." 49 Fed. Reg. 50,201, 50,202 (Dec. 27, 1984). In addition, EPA considers the use of quality control chemicals to test the performance characteristics of a chemical substance or mixture to fall within the R&D exemption.

According to EPA, the following activities may be considered R&D:

- Chemical synthesis and physical/chemical properties testing in the laboratory.
- Health and environmental effects testing.
- Tests or demonstrations of equipment or production processes, [which may involve] full-scale commercial runs . . . .
- Efficacy and performance tests . . . .

- Consumer panel testing of the performance characteristics of a new chemical substance.

Exemptions Bulletin at 3.

The definition of an R&D substance applies not only to the substance that is itself the subject of R&D, but also to a substance used to produce or analyze an R&D substance. Also, chemicals used for quality testing (quality control indicators) fall within the definition of R&D.

EPA has distinguished R&D from test marketing as follows:

> R&D focuses on the analysis of the chemical or physical characteristics, the performance, or the production characteristics of a chemical substance, a mixture containing the substance, or an article. Test marketing focuses on customers' acceptance of a chemical substance, and the probable demand for a product in a market where it will be competing with other goods.

Office of Toxic Substances, EPA, *New Chemical Information Bulletin* 2 (Nov. 1986) [*Exemptions Bulletin*].

5.5.1.2. Sale of R&D Chemicals

An R&D substance may be sold or distributed for further R&D without losing its R&D exemption. To preserve the exemption, however, it is critical that the recipient use the substance *solely* for R&D purposes. In addition, EPA permits the sale of existing chemical substances which contain the R&D substance as an impurity.

> For example, an R&D substance tested for its effectiveness as a process aid (*e.g.*, a catalyst or a reagent) or an intermediate may exist as an impurity in the final product resulting from the R&D. If the final product is an existing chemical, it may be used for non-exempt commercial purposes without a PMN being submitted on the R&D substance, as long as the product was produced in the course of legitimate R&D, and the manufacturer or importer meets all the requirements of the exemption for R&D and the PMN rule.

51 Fed. Reg. at 15,097.

EPA also permits the sale of an R&D substance as part of an article without requiring a PMN, if that article was produced in the course of legitimate R&D. EPA has adopted this position because the

> risks from R&D substances contained in finished articles will generally be very low, while the costs, both to industry and the public, that could be associated with storing or disposing of finished articles, once R&D is completed, could be relatively high.

49 Fed. Reg. at 50,203.

In the PMN regulations, EPA defines an article as a manufactured item with a specific shape or design whose end-use function is dependent upon that shape or design. 40 C.F.R. § 720.3(c). Thus, a rug containing an R&D substance within a pigment used to dye the rug during legitimate R&D could be distributed commercially before the R&D substance completes the PMN review process. The same R&D substance, however, could not be lawfully distributed through the bulk sale of pigment, even if the pigment is sold in a can. In this instance, the substance in the can has no definite shape or design whose function or end-use is dependent on that form, and the substance is intended to be removed from the can. Therefore, the substance is not part of an article. Similarly, items manufactured in a particular shape or design solely for purposes of shipping are not considered articles. *Id.* For example, EPA does not consider chemical substances formed into crystals or ingots to be articles, because these shapes generally are intended for convenience of handling or shipping and not for their end-use.

5.5.1.3. Use and Disposal of Residual R&D Substances

Often manufacturers have a surplus of an R&D chemical after the R&D activities are completed. After the PMN has cleared EPA review, of course, the R&D substance can be used. Such use, however, does not entitle the PMN submitter to file an NOC if the batch was manufactured for R&D purposes.

EPA permits the disposal of wastes from R&D activities and certain commercial uses of surplus R&D material. 40 C.F.R. § 720.36(d)-(e). Wastes from R&D substances can be disposed of in virtually any manner, provided that the disposal otherwise complies with any other applicable federal, state, and local regulations. Acceptable commercial uses include burning the wastes as fuel, or reacting or processing the wastes to form other existing chemical substances for commercial purposes. These uses of R&D chemicals manufactured solely for legitimate R&D do not trigger PMN or NOC obligations.

5.5.1.4. Small Quantities

The R&D exemption contemplates the use of only "small quantities" of a new chemical substance. "Small quantities" are those "not greater than reasonably necessary for such purposes." 40 C.F.R. § 720.3(cc). EPA declined to establish quantitative limits on production because they might hamper innovation, and because the volume necessary for R&D can vary substantially, depending on the type of chemical and R&D. 49 Fed. Reg. at 50,202.

Despite the absence of quantitative limits, EPA frequently questions whether the amount of a chemical substance produced under the R&D exemption is greater than reasonably necessary for the intended R&D. The burden remains on the manufacturer to establish that the production volume is appropriate to the R&D chemical.

5.5.1.5. Technically Qualified Individual

EPA requires that a technically qualified individual (TQI) supervise all stages of the R&D activities. This individual must be a person who by "education, training, or experience, or a combination of these factors" can appreciate the risks from exposure to a chemical substance and minimize such risks. 40 C.F.R. § 720.3(ee). EPA does not require that the TQI be professionally certified or even be present during the R&D testing. Rather, it is sufficient that he or she supervises the persons actually responsible for the testing.

5.5.1.6. Evaluation, Notification, and Record-Keeping of Risks

Manufacturers and processors must evaluate information in their possession and control to determine whether R&D substances pose a potential risk to human health or the environment, and must notify those engaged in R&D of any such risks. TSCA § 5(h)(3); 40 C.F.R. § 720.36(b)(1)(i), (c)(1). Laboratories using "prudent laboratory practices," however, are exempt from the risk evaluation and notification requirements. Similarly, EPA does not require risk evaluation and notification for the distribution of R&D substances between two laboratories using prudent laboratory practices.

The Agency has not published regulations or guidelines specifying what constitutes "prudent laboratory practices." EPA recommends, however, that manufacturers and processors follow standard procedures to control exposure and consult the following handbooks for guidance: National Research Council, *Prudent Practices for Handling Hazardous Chemicals in Laboratories* (1981); U.S. Department of Health and Human Services, *NIH Guidelines for the Laboratory Use of Chemical Carcinogens* (May 1981). *Exemptions Bulletin* at 8.

EPA summarized the risk evaluation and notification requirements in the following table:

REQUIREMENTS FOR NOTIFICATION OF RISKS			
Who must be notified	**Method of Notification**	**Content of Notification**	**Authority**
Persons employed by a Firm for R&D work	Any appropriate means	Risks associated with R&D substance*	720.36(a)(2)
Persons not in a firm's employ to whom it distributes R&D substances	In writing	Risks associated with R&D substance* Requirement that substance be used only for R&D	720.36(c)(2)

* In the case of workers in laboratories using prudent laboratory practices, or distribution from one such laboratory to another, EPA does not require evaluation of risks.

Exemptions Bulletin at 8.

The R&D rule requires that records be kept documenting compliance with either the risk evaluation and notification provisions or prudent laboratory practices. EPA summarized these requirements in the following table:

RECORD-KEEPING REQUIREMENTS		
Who Must Keep Records	**Requirement**	**Authority**
All manufacturers using the R&D exemption (except labs using prudent lab practices)	Copies of or citations to information reviewed to determine risks; Documentation of the nature & method of risk notification	720.78(b) (1)(i) & (ii)
Labs using prudent lab practices	Documentation of prudent lab practices	720.78 (b)(iii)
Manufacturers distributing R&D substances to persons outside their employ	Names and addresses of those who received substance; Identity of substance; Amount distributed; Copies of written notification	720.78 (b)(iv)
Producers of more than 100 kg/yr	Record of identity of substance; Production volume; Disposition	720.78 (b)(2)

Exemptions Bulletin at 9.

5.5.1.7. *R&D Pesticides*

As a matter of policy, EPA has expressly exempted new chemicals undergoing R&D for possible use as pesticides from the risk assessment, notification, and record-keeping requirements of the new R&D rule. 40 C.F.R. § 720.36(g). In order to qualify for this exemption, "the exclusive intention of the subsequent R&D activities of the person manufacturing the new substance and conducting the R&D activities [must be] to develop the substance as a pesticide." 51 Fed. Reg. 15,096, 15,097 (Apr. 22, 1986). A new pesticide chemical may qualify for this exemption, however, "even if the potential properties of the substances as a pesticide are unknown at the time it is first manufactured." *Id.*

A manufacturer can show an exclusive pesticidal intent by having a patent for use of the chemical as a pesticide, or simply by operating as a company or laboratory devoted entirely to pesticide R&D. By contrast, a company with a broad range of marketing activities would need other positive evidence to establish the prerequisite exclusive pesticide intent. Where the R&D activity is not solely for pesticidal purposes, the manufacturer or importer must fulfill the risk assessment, notification, and record-keeping requirements of the R&D rule—until the submission of an experimental use permit, a registration application, "or other activities . . . which provide evidence of exclusive pesticide intent." *Id.*

Although exempted from the requirements of the R&D rule, EPA considers that pesticide R&D remains subject to other applicable TSCA provisions, especially TSCA § 8(e). The section 8(e) provision requires notification to EPA of information concerning substantial risks associated with the candidate pesticide (*see* chapter 10). Furthermore, although the preamble to the R&D rule implies that R&D pesticide intermediates and R&D pesticide inert ingredients may qualify for the R&D exemption for pesticides, the Agency apparently did not intend this result. Rather, EPA permits only the pesticide active ingredient to qualify for this exemption from the requirements of the R&D rule; the R&D inerts and R&D intermediates remain subject to the risk assessment, notification, and record-keeping requirements.

5.5.2. Polymer Exemption

Under the authority of TSCA § 5(h)(4), EPA exempts from PMN requirements new chemical substances which: (1) meet the definition of a "polymer;" (2) are not specifically excluded by rule; and (3) meet the prescribed general exemption criteria, provided that the manufacturer or importer submits a required annual report to EPA and maintains certain records. 40 C.F.R. § 723.250(a). EPA has determined that the exemption of new chemical substances covered by the so-called "polymer" exemption "will not present an unreasonable risk of injury to human health or the environment." 60 Fed. Reg. 16,316 (Mar. 29, 1995).

Prior to EPA's overhaul of the polymer exemption in 1995 (60 Fed. Reg. 16,316 (effective May 30, 1995)), manufacturers and importers were required to submit an exemption application, as in the case of the LVE and the LoREX exemption today. The application requirement no longer exists for eligible and qualified polymers and has been replaced by a one-time, post-manufacture reporting requirement. The 1995 overhaul of the polymer exemption greatly reduced the reporting burden to industry and facilitated rapid, market-driven process changes, previously hindered by the 21-day EPA review period for polymer exemption applications.

Manufacturers and importers of new polymers may elect to proceed under the new polymer exemption or may file PMNs. 60 Fed. Reg. at 16,335 (codified at 40 C.F.R. § 723.250(i)). Manufacturers of polymers granted exemptions under the superseded regulations can continue to manufacture or import in compliance with their earlier exemption requirements or can elect to follow the procedural and record-keeping requirements of the 1995 polymer exemption. EPA will not place new polymers on the TSCA Inventory unless manufacturers or importers elect to proceed under the normal PMN/NOC process, but EPA intends that polymers already listed on the Inventory will remain on it with the old low molecular weight species content and maximum residual reactant restrictions still in force. 60 Fed. Reg. at 16,326.

5.5.2.1. Polymer Definition

In 1995, EPA adopted for exemption purposes the definition of "polymer" developed by the Organization for Economic Cooperation and Development (OECD) and agreed upon by OECD Member Countries in May 1993:

> Polymer means a chemical substance consisting of molecules characterized by the sequence of one or more types of monomer units and comprising a simple weight majority of molecules containing at least 3 monomer units which are covalently bound to at least one other monomer unit or other reactant and which consists of less than a simple weight majority of molecules of the same molecular weight. Such molecules must be distributed over a range of molecular weights wherein differences in the molecular weight are primarily attributable to differences in the number of monomer units. In the context of this definition, sequence means that the monomer units under consideration are covalently bound to one another and form a continuous string within the molecule, uninterrupted by units other than monomer units.

60 Fed. Reg. 16,332 (codified at 40 C.F.R. § 723.250(b)).

This definition ensures that exempt substances have the structural characteristics common to the category of substances on which EPA has based its finding of no unreasonable risk. 60 Fed. Reg. at 16,317. All polymers must meet this definition to be eligible for the exemption.

5.5.2.2. *Ineligible Polymers*

Five classes of polymers are not eligible for the polymer exemption:

- *Cationic polymers.* A polymer which is a "cationic polymer," as defined in 40 C.F.R. section 723.250(b), or is reasonably anticipated to become a cationic polymer in a natural aquatic environment is ineligible, unless (1) the polymer is a solid material that is not soluble or dispersible in water and will be used only in the solid phase, or (2) the combined (total) functional group equivalent weight of cationic groups in the polymer is equal to or greater than 5,000 daltons. 40 C.F.R. § 723.250(d)(1). EPA has ongoing ecotoxicity concerns for polymers in this category. 60 Fed. Reg. at 16,318.

- *Elemental limitations.* A polymer is ineligible if it does not contain as an integral part of its composition at least two of the atomic elements carbon, hydrogen, nitrogen, oxygen, silicon, and sulfur. In addition, a polymer is ineligible if it contains as an integral part of its composition, other than as impurities, any elements other than (1) carbon, hydrogen, nitrogen, oxygen, silicon, and sulfur, (2) sodium, magnesium, aluminum, potassium, calcium, chlorine, bromine, and iodine as the monatomic counter-ions Na^{+}, Mg^{+2}, Al^{+3}, K^{+}, Ca^{+2}, Cl^{-}, Br^{-}, or I^{-}, (3) fluorine, chlorine, bromine, and iodine covalently bound to carbon, and (4) less than 0.20 weight percent of any combination of the atomic elements lithium, boron, phosphorous, titanium, manganese, iron, nickel, copper, zinc, tin, and zirconium. 40 C.F.R. § 723.250(d)(2).

- *Polymers which degrade, decompose, or depolymerize.* Polymers which are designed or reasonably anticipated to degrade, decompose, or depolymerize are ineligible. This includes polymers which could substantially decompose after manufacture and use, even if they are not intended to do so. Degradation, decomposition, or depolymerization mean those types of chemical change that convert a polymeric substance into simpler, smaller substances through processes including, but not limited to, oxidation, hydrolysis, attack by solvents, heat, light, or microbial action. 40 C.F.R. § 723.250(d)(3).

- *Polymers prepared from monomers and reactants not on the TSCA Inventory.* A polymer prepared from monomers and/or reactants not already on the TSCA Inventory or not exempt from PMN requirements (TSCA § 5) is ineligible. This exclusion does not apply to monomers and reactants which are either (1) not charged to the reaction vessel or (2) not incorporated in the polymer at levels greater than two percent, as these would not ordinarily be considered part of the polymer's identity for PMN purposes (see the full description of the so-called "Two Percent Rule" in chapter 6). 40 C.F.R. § 723.250(d)(4). As a practical matter, only importers of polymers will be able to take advantage of the Two Percent Rule for monomers or other reactants that are not listed on the Inventory. Domestic manufacturers are precluded by TSCA § 15(2) from using non-listed chemicals in their manufacturing process in any amount regardless of the Two Percent Rule.

- *Water-absorbing polymers with number average molecular weights 10,000 daltons and greater.* For purposes of the polymer exemption, a "water-absorbing polymer" is a polymeric substance that is capable of absorbing its weight of water. EPA believes this category of polymers should remain subject to the full PMN review process. 60 Fed. Reg. at 16,317.

A polymer which falls into one of the five categories above is expressly disqualified from the polymer exemption, and any further inquiry into the remaining requirements of the exemption (*e.g.*, the general exemption criteria) is moot.

5.5.2.3. General Exemption Criteria

To be eligible for the polymer exemption, a polymer must meet one of three sets of criteria:

- *Polymers with number average molecular weight greater than or equal to 1,000 and less than 10,000 daltons.* In addition to possessing the required number average molecular weight ($\geq$ 1,000 and < 10,000 daltons), the polymer must contain less than 10 percent oligomeric material below molecular weight 500 daltons and less than 25 percent oligomeric material below molecular weight 1,000 daltons. Furthermore, the polymer may contain reactive functional groups in three situations only. The first is where the reactive functional groups are all included in a list of "approved" groups, regardless of the polymer's combined (total) reactive group equivalent weight. Second, the polymer contains certain other listed and approved reactive functional groups only and has a total reactive group equivalent weight greater than or equal to 1,000 daltons. Third, if any reactive functional groups not listed in the first two situations are present, the polymer has a total reactive group equivalent weight greater than or equal to 5,000 daltons. 40 C.F.R. § 723.250(e)(1).

- *Polymers with number average molecular weight greater than or equal to 10,000 daltons.* In addition to possessing the required number average molecular weight ($\geq$ 10,000 daltons), the polymer must contain less than two percent oligomeric material below molecular weight 500 and less than five percent oligomeric material below molecular weight 1,000. 40 C.F.R. § 723.250(e)(2).

- *Polyesters.* The polymer is a polyester and is manufactured solely from a list of approved reactants which the Agency believes present a low hazard potential. 40 C.F.R. § 723.250(e)(3). "Polyester" is defined as a chemical substance that meets the definition of a polymer and whose polymer molecules contain at least two carboxylic acid ester linkages, at least one of which links internal monomer units together. *Id.* § 723.250(b). EPA plans to expand the list of eligible polyester precursors from time to time as additional candidates are identified. 60 Fed. Reg. at 16,324. To this end, EPA encourages industry petitions for additional reactants, provided such requests are supported by relevant health and environmental effects information and candidate precursors are already listed on the TSCA Inventory. *Id.*

5.5.2.4. *Exemption Report*

Manufacturers and importers must submit an annual report identifying themselves, a technical contact, and the number of new polymers (*i.e.*, polymers not on the TSCA Inventory) manufactured or imported for the first time under the exemption in the preceding year. 40 C.F.R. § 723.250(f). This report is due (*i.e.*, must be postmarked) by January 31 of the year following the initial manufacture or import. A company may report on a site-by-site basis rather than submit a consolidated report, so long as such reporting is not duplicative. 60 Fed. Reg. at 16,325. The Agency believes that this annual reporting requirement will alleviate the reporting burden to industry while providing EPA a direct mechanism for monitoring compliance with, and use of, the polymer exemption. *Id.*

5.5.2.5. *Record-Keeping*

To justify their reliance on the polymer exemption, manufacturers and importers must maintain certain records at the site of manufacture or import for a period of at least five years from the date of initial manufacture or import. 40 C.F.R. § 723.250(j). Failure or refusal to establish and maintain records is a violation of TSCA § 15. *Id.* § 723.250(l)(3). Specifically, the records must contain the following information to demonstrate compliance with the requirements of the exemption:

- *Chemical identity information.* 40 C.F.R. § 723.250(j)(2)(i). To the extent known or reasonably ascertainable, 40 C.F.R. section 723.250(g) requires manufacturers and importers to maintain records of a specific chemical name and a CAS Registry Number (or EPA Accession Number) for each "reactant" that is either (1) used at greater than two percent by weight to manufacture the polymer or (2) chemically combined (incorporated) at greater than two percent by weight in the polymer. *Id.* § 723.250(g)(1).

Manufacturers and importers who decide not to maintain this information for a reactant based upon the weight of the reactant "incorporated" in the polymer, as opposed to the weight charged to the reaction vessel, must maintain either analytical data or theoretical calculations (where an analytical determination is impossible or unnecessary) to support this decision. *Id.* § 723.250(j)(2)(vii). Although the Agency encourages the use of CAS nomenclature, manufacturers and importers do not have an affirmative duty to obtain or use such nomenclature, since EPA does not add polymers manufactured or imported under the exemption to the TSCA Inventory. 60 Fed. Reg. at 16,325. Manufacturers and importers also are required to maintain a representative structural diagram of the polymer, "if possible." 40 C.F.R. § 723.250(g)(2).

- *Proof that the polymer is eligible and not specifically excluded.* 40 C.F.R. § 723.250(j)(2)(ii)-(iv). Manufacturers and importers relying on the polymer exemption must maintain information sufficient to demonstrate that the new polymer is not of a kind specifically excluded under 40 C.F.R. section 723.250(d) (*see* section 5.5.2.2 above). They also must maintain information showing that the polymer meets one of the three sets of general eligibility criteria specified in 40 C.F.R. section 723.250(e) (*see* section 5.5.2.3 above). Where it can be documented that an analytical determination is impossible or unnecessary, EPA will accept theoretical calculations to demonstrate that the new polymer meets the number-average molecular weight and the low molecular weight exemption criteria. Otherwise, the Agency requires analytical data. Acceptable analytical tests for number-average molecular weight include gel permeation chromatography (GPC), vapor pressure osmometry (VPO), and similar tests.

- *Production records.* 40 C.F.R. § 723.250(j)(2)(iii). Manufacturers and importers must keep records of production or import volumes for the first three years of manufacture or import. They must also document the date that manufacture or import commenced.

- *Certification.* 40 C.F.R. § 723.250(j)(2)(viii). Pursuant to 40 C.F.R. section 723.250(h), manufacturers and importers must maintain written certification that (1) the new polymer is manufactured or imported for a purpose other than for research and development, (2) the new polymer meets the definition of a "polymer," is not specifically excluded, and meets all other applicable exemption eligibility criteria, and (3) all statements in the written certification are truthful.

5.5.3. "Polaroid" Exemption

In response to a petition from the Polaroid Corporation, EPA exempted new chemical substances used in or for instant photographic and "peel-apart" film articles. 40 C.F.R. § 723.175. Under the terms of the so-called "Polaroid" exemption, manufacturers of instant photographic materials may commence manufacture of new chemical substances for these products immediately upon submitting an exemption application pursuant to 40 C.F.R. section 723.175. These new chemical substances, however, cannot be distributed in commerce until a PMN is filed and the review period has ended.

Under the "Polaroid" exemption, these new chemical substances must be manufactured or processed in a "special production area" (defined as a "demarcated area within which all manufacturing, processing and use" takes place) until they are incorporated into the photographic article. *Id.* § 723.175(b)(13). The rule also requires the use of engineering controls and worker protective equipment to control exposure.

The exemption application must identify the manufacturer, the new chemical substance and its impurities, describe the physical/chemical properties, by-products and production volume, provide any test data, identify the photographic article that will contain the new chemical substance, describe the methods used to control and treat waste water, and certify that the manufacturing, processing and use of the exempted chemical substance will comply with the terms of the exemption. *Id.* § 723.175(i).

5.5.4. New Chemicals Imported As Part of An Article

Under 40 C.F.R. section 720.22(b)(1), a new chemical substance is exempt from the PMN requirements if it is imported into the United States for commercial purposes "as part of an article." EPA defines "article" to mean the following:

> [A] manufactured item (1) which is formed to a specific shape or design during manufacture, (2) which has end use function(s) dependent in whole or in part upon its shape or design during end use, and (3) which has either no change of chemical composition during its end use or only those changes of composition which have no commercial purpose separate from that of the article and that may occur as described in § 720.36(g)(5), except that fluids and particles are not considered articles regardless of shape or design.

40 C.F.R. § 720.3(c).

EPA's definition of article specifically excludes "fluids and particles . . . regardless of shape or design." *Id.* Yet, some imported articles, such as transformers, contain fluids that are entirely contained and have no commercial purpose apart from the article. EPA exempted such fluids from the Inventory reporting requirements.

> Chemical substances or mixtures will be considered to be imported as a part of an article, if the substance or mixture is not intended to be removed from that article and has no end use or commercial purposes separate from the article of which it is a part. Importers may report these chemical substances but are not required to do so. For example, *transformer fluids in transformers, lighter fluids in cigarette lighters, and crankcase oil in automobiles are not intended to be removed from the articles of which they are a part and have no commercial purpose separate from these articles. Accordingly, these chemical substances need not be reported.* These same chemical substances, however, if imported in drums, cans, or other containers, must be reported as required by these regulations.

42 Fed. Reg. 64,572, 64,583 (Dec. 23, 1977) (EPA response to comment 21) (emphasis added).

The foregoing also represents EPA's current position interpreting the PMN exclusion under 40 C.F.R. section 720.22(b)(1) for imported articles. Thus, importers of articles that contain fluids or particles which are not intended to be removed and which have no separate commercial purpose are excluded from the PMN requirements. Conversely, EPA considers that a substance cannot be "a part" of an article if it is released and, upon release, has a commercial purpose. Thus, according to EPA, articles which contain fluids designed to be used or released in order for the article to function, like ink in pens or windshield wiper fluid in cars, are not encompassed by this exemption.

5.5.5. Impurities, By-Products, and Non-Isolated Intermediates

EPA has excluded from the PMN requirements impurities, by-products, non-isolated intermediates, and chemicals formed incidentally when exposed to the environment or to other chemicals. 40 C.F.R. § 720.30(h). These exemptions are essentially identical to those from the initial Inventory at 40 C.F.R. section 710.4. In fact, EPA often uses its discussion of these exemptions in the preamble and response to comments in its initial Inventory reporting rule to clarify the scope and applicability of these same exemptions from the PMN requirements.

Impurities. Impurities are exempt from the PMN requirements under 40 C.F.R. section 720.30(h)(1). EPA defines an impurity as a "chemical substance which is unintentionally present with another chemical substance." 40 C.F.R. § 720.3(m). Although impurities are exempt from separate PMN reporting under section 5, they must be identified as impurities in the PMN on a new chemical substance (*see* chapter 6).

By-products. EPA exempts by-products from PMN requirements and permits their commercial use in limited situations. EPA defines a by-product as follows:

> [A] chemical substance produced without a separate commercial intent during the manufacture, processing, use, or disposal of another chemical substance or mixture.

40 C.F.R. § 720.3(d). Under 40 C.F.R. section 720.30(h)(2), EPA exempts any by-product that is not used for commercial purposes.

EPA also exempts by-products intended for certain limited commercial uses, as it did in the Inventory reporting requirements. Thus a by-product is exempt if its commercial use is one of the following:

> (1) to be burned as a fuel, (2) to be disposed of as a waste, including in a landfill or for enriching soil, or (3) to have component chemical substances extracted from it for commercial purposes (this last exclusion applies only to the by-product; it does not apply to the component substances extracted from the by-product, which must be listed on the TSCA Inventory or be used for purposes that are otherwise exempt from the PMN requirements).

40 C.F.R. § 720.30(g). Now, as then, EPA encourages conservation and recycling of energy and resources contained in waste materials that otherwise might be discarded because of TSCA reporting burdens.

Non-Isolated Intermediates. Non-isolated intermediates are exempt from the Agency's PMN regulations under 40 C.F.R. section 720.30(h)(8). EPA defines a non-isolated intermediate as follows:

> [A]ny intermediate that is not intentionally removed from the equipment in which it is manufactured, including the reaction vessel in which it is manufactured, equipment which is ancillary to the reaction vessel, and any equipment through which the chemical substance passes during a continuous flow process, but not including tanks or other vessels in which the substance is stored after its manufacture.

40 C.F.R. § 720.3(w). Thus, EPA exempts from the PMN requirements chemical substances manufactured and consumed in the manufacture of another chemical substance and not intentionally removed from the reaction vessels.

The term "equipment" in the definition of non-isolated intermediate includes the following: the "reaction vessel" in which the intermediate is produced and consumed, the equipment "ancillary" to that reaction vessel, and any equipment through which the chemical substance passes during continuous flow. EPA considers that an intermediate is "isolated" once it is removed from the process equipment, stored, or transferred to shipping containers. Mechanical or gravity transfer through a closed system, however, is not considered "isolation." In addition, an intermediate is not considered isolated merely because a trace amount has not been reacted and eventually becomes incorporated into the final product which is removed from the vessel or because the intermediate appears as a waste product.

EPA used the following examples to illustrate its position on non-isolated intermediates:

> (1) *Reaction in the Same Vessel:* Reactants A and B are charged to a reaction vessel to form a chemical substance X. Then C is added to react with X to form another substance Y which is then drummed for shipment. In this example X is considered to be nonisolated since it is not intentionally removed from the process equipment of manufacture. Y will be considered to be isolated since it is intentionally removed by drumming for transport.
>
> (2) *Reaction in One Vessel with Purification in Another and Transfer to a Second Vessel:* The reaction is carried out in one reactor and the reaction mixture is then pumped through an enclosed drum filter to another vessel for the next reaction step. The reaction intermediate is considered to be nonisolated since there is no intentional removal and all transfer is mechanical and through closed equipment. However, if the filtration is not closed or if the transfer is manual (for example, involving the removal of the intermediate as a filter cake), then the intermediate would be considered to be isolated since the transfer would not be through closed equipment. A similar interpretation applies to other processing steps between manufacture and subsequent reaction (*e.g.*, distillation, drying, size reduction, etc.).

Letter from Edwin F. Tinsworth, Acting Director, Office of Toxic Substances, to Chemical Manufacturers Association (July 15, 1986).

5.5.6. Chemicals Formed Incidental to Exposure to Other Chemicals

During congressional debate on TSCA, the House Committee on Interstate and Foreign Commerce stated the following:

> [I]t has come to the attention of the Committee that there are activities incidental to the end use or storage of certain substances or mixtures which under a literal reading of the definition [of manufacture] would make a person engaging in them a manufacturer and thus subject to the provisions of the bill applying to manufacturers.

> For example, there are certain substances or mixtures, such as adhesives, paints, inks, and drying oils, which during storage or upon end use, when exposed to environmental factors such as air, moisture, or sunlight, undergo a chemical reaction which produces a different substance or mixture. Similarly, plastic resins subjected to heat for purposes of molding undergo a thermal setting which produces a different substance. In such cases, the chemical reaction is merely incidental to the end use or storage of the original substance or mixture. The substance or mixture produced is not used as a chemical substance or mixture, per se. It is not the Committee's intent that a person, such as a painter, who is engaged in the end use or storage activity in which such a chemical reaction occurs is to be considered a manufacturer because of the reaction.

H.R. Rep. No. 94-1341, at 13, *reprinted in* House Comm. on Interstate and Foreign Intelligence, *Legislative History of the Toxic Substances Control Act* 421 (1976).

In consideration of the expressed wishes of Congress, EPA exempts from the PMN requirements new chemical substances which result from chemical reactions incidental to storage or end-use. 40 C.F.R. § 720.30(h)(5). The exemption covers the following:

> Any chemical substance which results from a chemical reaction that occurs upon end use of another chemical substance, mixture, or article such as an adhesive, paint, miscellaneous cleanser or other housekeeping product, fuel additive, water softening and treatment agent, photographic film, battery, match, or safety flare, and which is not itself manufactured or imported for distribution in commerce or for use as an intermediate.

Id.

The use of epoxy illustrates this exemption. When mixed together, the two separate components of the epoxy will react spontaneously to form another chemical substance. Because this substance is formed upon the end use of another existing chemical and is not intended for distribution in commerce or use as an intermediate, it is exempt from the PMN requirements under 40 C.F.R. section 720.30(h)(5).

5.5.7. Chemicals Formed During the Manufacture of an Article

EPA also exempts from the PMN requirements the following:

> [A]ny other chemical substance formed during the manufacture of an article destined for the marketplace

> without further chemical change of the chemical substance except for those chemical changes that occur as described elsewhere in this paragraph.

40 C.F.R. § 720.30(h)(6).

Thus, for example, EPA exempts new chemicals formed upon use of rubber molding or curable plastic compounds, inks, drying oils, adhesives or paints, and metal finishing compounds. *Id.*

5.5.8. Chemicals Formed Incidental to the Use of Certain Additives

Under 40 C.F.R. section 720.30(h)(7), EPA exempts from the PMN requirements new chemicals formed incidental to the use of certain enumerated additives when these additives function as intended or chemicals formed incidental to the use of any chemical intended *solely* to impart a specific physiochemical characteristic functions as intended. For example, EPA exempts a new chemical substance formed incidental to the addition of bleach to cotton if the manufacturer adds the bleach only to change a specific physiochemical characteristic of the cotton and not to make a major compositional change. 43 Fed. Reg. 9256 (Mar. 1, 1978). This exemption is known variously as the additives exemption, the salts exemption or the (h)(7) exemption.

Even though EPA interprets this exemption narrowly, it has broad implications. As companies learn more about the chemical make-up of their products, they may discover constituents in their products that form incidentally upon use of an additive but have some useful function. According to the Agency, a crude test for determining whether a chemical substance is truly "incidental" is whether the final product could function equally well without the incidentally created chemical. If the product could perform equally well or in the same way without it, then the new substance is incidental and not functional. If, by contrast, the chemical is essential to the structure or functioning of the product, it would not be incidental, but functional. For example, if the resulting new chemical significantly improves a product's performance, it probably would not be considered incidental. The discovery of the heretofore unknown functionality of such "incidental" chemicals may require the manufacturer to correct its original Inventory submission or to file a PMN for the chemical.

5.5.8.1. Polymer Salts

The (h)(7) exemption is often difficult in application. To illustrate, in late 1988, the printing inks and coatings industry alerted EPA to a long-standing and common practice in these industries whereby polymer manufacturers or their customers added various hydroxides and/or organic amines to liquid polymer solutions to increase the solubility of the base polymers. In solution, however, the hydroxides or amines react with the polymer's acid functional groups to form transient salts. When the ink or coating is used, the hydroxide or amine evaporates, and the polymer reverts to its insoluble form and creates the desired film, which then dries as the water and any co-solvents evaporate.

At the time the original Inventory was created, neither EPA nor the polymer industry considered this issue. A few manufacturers listed the transient salts on the original Inventory, but others believed that such salts were ineligible for listing because the Inventory regulations exclude any chemical substance formed when a pH neutralizer, or a chemical substance that is intended to impart a specific physicochemical characteristic, functions as intended. 40 C.F.R. § 710.4(d)(7). EPA exempted the same substances from PMN requirements when the Agency promulgated the PMN regulations in 1983, and, accordingly, many companies did not file PMNs for these transient salts.

EPA subsequently rejected the ink and coating industry's arguments and contended that PMNs must be submitted when these transient salts are created. EPA's position created an uproar in many quarters because the practice of mixing an acid-functional polymer with a base in water was widespread, and many of the companies engaging in it considered themselves to be "formulators," not manufacturers subject to TSCA PMN requirements.

A series of public meetings, submissions, and discussions about the proper scope of the exemption culminated in a June 29, 1994 EPA letter to interested parties which states that the exemption excludes a new substance from both the TSCA Inventory and PMN requirements if three conditions are met:

> 1. The substance is formed from a chemical reaction that involves the use of a chemical substance of the type described under 40 C.F.R. 710.4(d)(7) or 720.30(h)(7);
>
> 2. The substance does not function to provide one or more primary properties that would determine the use of the product or product mixture distributed in commerce, even though it may impart certain physicochemical characteristics to the product or mixture of which it is a part; and
>
> 3. The substance is not itself the one intended for distribution in commerce as a chemical substance *per se*. Although it may be a component of the product, product mixture, or formulation actually distributed in commerce, it has no commercial purpose separate from the product, product mixture, or formulation of which it is a component.

Letter from Joseph S. Carra, Deputy Director, Office of Pollution Prevention and Toxics, EPA, at 2-3 (June 29, 1994).

Under the foregoing guidance in the June 29, 1994 letter, the polymer salts that initially stirred the controversy apparently would be exempt, as EPA illustrated by an example in the letter. The letter states that if an acid polymer is converted to its soluble amine salt during an ink formulation process in which other ingredients are added, the polymer salt formed as a result of a chemical reaction that brings the insoluble acid polymer into solution is exempt for the following reasons:

- The polymer salt does not itself contribute a primary property that is essential to the functioning of the ink as a viable commercial product;
- The polymer salt is not itself the product intended for distribution in commerce as a chemical substance per se; and
- The polymer salt has no commercial purpose separate from the ink formulation.

Id. at 3-4.

Even with this new guidance, determining whether a particular chemical substance is exempt can be challenging. For example, the guidance indicates that, to be exempt, a substance must not provide one of the "primary properties" that would determine the product's use. Yet, EPA has not defined this concept. Thus, the guidance remains open to subjective interpretation. EPA has indicated some willingness to allow companies that previously had relied on the (h)(7) exemption to report the situation to EPA and to file PMNs without ceasing manufacture during the PMN review period.

CHAPTER 6
PREPARING THE PMN AND SEEING IT THROUGH EPA

After determining that a chemical substance is not listed on the Inventory, and not excluded or exempted from the section 5 requirements, the company intending to manufacture or import the chemical for commercial purposes must file a premanufacture notification (PMN) under section 5(a). A company then must decide whether to file a full PMN or, if the chemical qualifies, a low volume exemption (LVE) or low release/low exposure (LoREX) exemption application.[16] Although the standard PMN form can be used for any of these applications, each has its own distinct requirements. This chapter discusses how to prepare a PMN and the exemption applications, and how to see them successfully through EPA.

6.1. DETERMINING THE TYPE OF PMN

If a chemical does not qualify for the LVE or LoREX exemption, the manufacturer must file a PMN. EPA has published an *Instruction Manual for Reporting Under the TSCA Section 5 New Chemicals Program Premanufacture Notification of New Chemical Substances Instruction Manual* (Feb. 2003) to assist submitters in preparing the PMN. Both the PMN form (EPA Form 7710-25 (Rev. 5-95)) and the *Instruction Manual* are available from the TSCA Assistance Office or can be downloaded from the following EPA website: http://www.epa.gov/opptintr/newchems/guideman.htm. In addition, a submitter can call the Prenotice Coordinator with questions on preparing the PMN (or exemption applications). There are essentially three types of PMNs: (1) full or standard PMN (*i.e.*, single submitter and single chemical); (2) consolidated PMN (*i.e.*, single submitter and multiple chemicals); and (3) joint PMN (*i.e.*, two submitters and single or multiple chemicals). All are submitted on the same PMN form.

6.1.1. Full PMN

A company prepares a full or standard PMN by filling out EPA's PMN form for each new chemical. In general, EPA intends that the submitter use one PMN form for each new chemical when submitting standard PMNs or exemption applications.

---

16 If a company intends to manufacture or import a new chemical substance solely for test marketing purposes, it can submit a test marketing exemption (TME) application. (*See* chapter 5.)

6.1.2. Consolidated PMNs

EPA developed the consolidated PMN in response to requests from submitters who had been filing groups of PMNs for structurally similar chemicals. According to EPA, "[t]hese notices contained a large amount of duplicative information, such as exposure, release, or use data." 48 Fed. Reg. 21,734 (May 13, 1983). Thus, EPA developed the consolidated PMN to cover two or more new chemicals similar in structure or use. EPA does not intend the consolidated PMN to be used for a series of intermediates and a final product, but rather intends it for chemicals with the same or similar structures and uses. A manufacturer should submit a written request for consolidation and identify the chemical substances to be consolidated. The Prenotice Coordinator will grant approval to file a consolidated PMN over the phone, but only a maximum of six chemicals can be approved. Where the Prenotice Coordinator and the OPPT chemists determine that the chemicals are not sufficiently similar, they will disapprove a consolidation request.

6.1.3. Joint Submissions

In some cases, another person may have some of the information required to complete a PMN, but may be unwilling to reveal that information to the PMN submitter. For example, a foreign supplier may possess the specific chemical identity but refuse to reveal it to the domestic importer who is filing the PMN. In order to accommodate these situations, EPA developed the "joint submission." 40 C.F.R. § 720.40(e).

To file a joint PMN, each joint submitter must complete a PMN form, sign the certification statement, and assert any confidential business information (CBI) claims. Each party should identify the other joint submitter and should indicate which information the other submitter will supply. Each submitter is required to complete all mandatory sections of the form to the extent the information "is known to or reasonably ascertainable by the person." The review period will not begin until EPA has received all of the required information from both parties.

6.1.4. Special Cases: LVE and LoREX Exemption

The information requirements for the LVE and LoREX exemption applications differ slightly from those of a full PMN. In completing an LVE or LoREX exemption application, submitters are required to provide exposure and environmental release information for manufacturer-controlled sites, and must certify to the following:

(A) The manufacturer intends to manufacture or import the new chemical substance for commercial purposes, other than in small quantities solely for research and development, under the terms of this section.

(B) The manufacturer is familiar with the terms of this section and will comply with those terms.

(C) The new chemical substance for which the notice is submitted meets all applicable exemption conditions.

(D) For substances manufactured under paragraph (c)(1) of this section [the LoREX exemption provision], the manufacturer intends to commence manufacture of the exempted substance for commercial purposes within one year of the date of the expiration of the 30-day review period.

40 C.F.R. § 723.50(e)(2)(xi).

6.2. COMPLETING THE PMN FORM

6.2.1. The Submitter's Basic Obligations

The PMN form requires information on the submitter's identity, specific chemical identity, production volume, use, exposures (worker, user and consumer), and environmental fate. The submitter must provide this information to "the extent it is known to or reasonably ascertainable by the submitter." 40 C.F.R. § 720.45. In essence, the PMN represents the submitter's best estimates of the future production, distribution, and use of the new substance at the time the notice is filed. Unless EPA issues an order or rule on the PMN under section 5(e) or 5(f), the submitter is free to deviate from these projections after the PMN clears review (*i.e.*, the submitter is not "locked in" to the estimates represented in the PMN). The submitter, however, may not change the chemical identity, since this is the only chemical which EPA will consider in reviewing the PMN. The submitter is required to maintain records of the information contained in the notice for five years from the date of commencement of manufacture. 40 C.F.R. § 720.78. An original and two copies of a standard PMN including all attachments and studies must be submitted. If information is claimed confidential, a sanitized copy also must be submitted. *Id.* § 720.40(d)(2).

6.2.2. PMN Processing Fees

EPA requires manufacturers, importers, and processors to pay fees for PMNs and significant new use notices. 40 C.F.R. § 700.45. Submitters, however, are not required to pay fees for LVE, LoREX or test marketing exemption applications. A fee of $2,500 is required for each PMN submitted to the Agency, with the following exceptions: 1) a fee of $1,000 is required for a PMN on an intermediate chemical substance, and 2) a fee of $100 is required for a PMN submitted by a qualifying "small business concern."

Submitters are required to assign a unique user fee identification number for each PMN submission. This number should be a six-character alphanumeric identifier assigned by the submitter preceded by the letters "TS." Each user fee payment check must bear the corresponding user fee identifying number. The submitter must certify that the user fee has been paid before EPA will begin processing the PMN. An effective way to accomplish this is to provide a photocopy of the check with the PMN.

Checks, themselves, should be mailed directly to: Environmental Protection Agency, HQ Accounting Operations Branch (PM-226), P.O. Box 360399M, Pittsburgh, PA 15251-6399, ATTN: TSCA User Fee. This is a different address than the one to which the PMN is submitted.

Submissions received without the appropriate user fee are deemed incomplete and EPA will not review them. Submitters of notices which are determined to be incomplete due to fee deficiencies (or other errors or omissions) will be contacted by the Agency within the first 30 days after their notice is received. 40 C.F.R. § 720.65(b). The review period for a PMN notice will *not* commence until EPA receives a complete notice and the appropriate fee. Indeed, EPA will require those who submit deficient notices to prepare and return a new PMN, complete in its entirety (with the corresponding fee), before the review period will begin to run. *See also* section 6.7.1 below.

6.2.3. Premarket Data Requirements

Submitters are not required to develop any minimum amount of data on the new chemical prior to submission of the PMN. Nevertheless, the submitter should file sufficient data to demonstrate that the manufacture, processing, distribution in commerce, use, and disposal of the substance will not present an unreasonable risk. 40 C.F.R. § 720.40(h). Importantly, however, the submitter must submit any test data in its possession or control related to environmental or health effects of manufacturing, processing, distributing, using, or disposing of the new chemical substance, or any mixture or article containing it. *Id.* § 720.50. EPA's definition of "possession or control" includes data in the files of employees engaged in R&D, test marketing or commercial production of the substance and agents if the files are kept in the agent's capacity as an agent of the submitter. *Id.* § 720.3(y).

The requirement to submit test data on the new chemical applies to data on the chemical in its pure, technical grade, or formulated form. The submitter must provide a full report or standard literature citation for health effects data, ecological effects data, environmental fate characteristics, physical and chemical properties, exposure, and monitoring data. This applies even to incomplete studies, reports, and tests. If the data do not appear in the open scientific literature, a full report must be provided. *Id.* § 720.50(a)(1) - (3).

6.2.3.1. Agricultural Screening Data

In 1986, the Agency also clarified that a PMN submitter must furnish agricultural screening data with PMNs. EPA, *New Chemical Information Bulletin, Submission of Agricultural Screening Data in PMNs* 2 (Dec. 1986) (available from the TSCA Assistance Office). According to EPA, many companies routinely screen all new chemical substances for potential biological activity. If the company thereafter intends the chemical for a TSCA use, *e.g.*, use as a pesticide intermediate, it must submit any agricultural screening data with the PMN. Companies may submit summaries of primary agricultural screening results, rather than detailed descriptions of the test protocol and results. *Id.* The Agency may request more detailed information on a voluntary basis.

6.2.3.2. All Other Data

In addition to test data, submitters also must submit any other information and data on the new chemical to the extent that it is "known to or reasonably ascertainable by the person." 40 C.F.R. § 720.40(d). EPA does not require submission of exposure data for non-U.S. populations or ecosystems, or submission of efficacy data. *Id.* § 720.50(d)(2), (3). But EPA does require submission of health and environmental effects data, even if they involve non-U.S. populations. *Id.*

6.2.3.3. New Data During Review Period

If during the review period the submitter comes into possession, control, or knowledge of any "new information that materially adds to, changes, or otherwise makes significantly more complete" the information contained in the PMN, the submitter must give the information to EPA within ten days of its receipt, but in no event less than five days before the end of the review period. 40 C.F.R. § 720.40(f). If the new information becomes available within the last five days of the review period, EPA must be notified immediately.

6.2.4. Practical Tips

Do not leave any sections of the notice form blank. If the information is unknown or inapplicable, then state as much in those sections. Any "blank" section or part may prompt EPA to consider the notice incomplete (*see* sections 6.2.2 and 6.7.1). The submitter should check the notice form to make sure that it clearly identifies all confidential information. In addition, if any information has been claimed confidential, the submitter must provide EPA a copy with the CBI deleted (the so-called "sanitized" copy) at the same time it files the PMN or exemption application.

6.3. PMN FORM PART I: GENERAL INFORMATION

6.3.1. Submitter Identification—Section A

The company that intends to manufacture or import a new chemical substance must submit the PMN. 40 C.F.R. § 720.22(a). Only manufacturers that are licensed, incorporated, or doing business in the United States may submit a PMN. The "manufacturer" includes a company that contracts with another company (toll or contract manufacturer) to make a chemical substance for it. In this case, the company that contracts with the toll manufacturer is considered a manufacturer if it specifies the chemical identity and the basic production technology, and the toll manufacturer produces the substance exclusively for it. A company that simply orders a non-specific chemical having certain properties, however, is not a manufacturer under this definition and, therefore, is not eligible to file a PMN.

Importers of new chemical substances also are subject to the PMN requirements (unless the substance is excluded or exempted). *Id.* § 720.22(b). An importer is the company primarily liable for the payment of duties; it can be either the consignor, the importer of record, the actual owner, or any transferee. *Id.* § 720.3(1). In the case where several parties are involved in the import transaction, the "principal" importer is responsible for submitting the notice. The principal importer is the importer who selects the substance to be imported, knows that the substance actually will be imported rather than manufactured domestically, and specifies the identity of the substance and the actual amount to be imported. As with a manufacturer, a principal importer must be licensed, incorporated, or doing business in the United States. *Id.* § 720.3(z).

6.3.1.1. Agents

Manufacturers or importers required to submit a PMN may designate an agent to submit the PMN for them. The agent is often a consultant or an attorney. Both the agent and the manufacturer or importer must sign the certification statement. *Id.* § 720.40(e).

6.3.1.2. Technical Contact

The submitter also must list its technical contact. The technical contact serves as the company's representative on the PMN and is generally the person who actually prepared the PMN or is familiar with the details of the chemical substance. The technical contact should be based in the United States, fluent in English, and technically qualified.

6.3.1.3. Previous Communications with EPA

The submitter must indicate any prenotice communication, test market exemption, LVE, PMN or *bona fide* request previously made of the Agency.

6.3.2. Chemical Identity—Section B

EPA considers the specific identity of the new chemical substance to be critical information in the PMN. Indeed, if the submitter fails to describe the chemical identity adequately, EPA will declare the PMN incomplete and will not start the review period. *See* sections 6.2.2 and 6.7.1. Even if a substance is classified as a trade secret under the Occupational Safety and Health Administration (OSHA) Hazard Communication Standard (29 C.F.R. § 1910.1200), the submitter still must report its specific chemical identity to EPA.

In 1995, EPA amended the PMN rule to require that submitters provide the correct Chemical Abstracts (CA) Index name or CA Preferred Name for each chemical substance included in the notice. The amended rule also requires that submitters provide a valid Chemical Abstracts Service (CAS) Registry Number (CASRN) consistent with the CA name if one has been assigned.

Submitters can use either of two methods for obtaining or developing CA nomenclature for the PMN substance(s), but must indicate on the PMN form which method was used. 40 C.F.R. § 720.45(a)(3). Under Method 1, the submitter obtains the correct chemical identification number from the CAS Inventory Expert Service. Submitters must include with the PMN a copy of the chemical identification report obtained from CAS. Alternatively, under Method 2, the submitter can obtain chemical information from any chemical information service or consultant, or can retrieve or develop the proper CA identification itself.

Regardless of the method used, EPA ultimately may disagree with the identification assigned. If Method 1 has been used, EPA will work with CAS to resolve the disagreement. Under these circumstances, there is no delay in the review of the PMN. When Method 2 has been used to develop the chemical identity information and EPA disagrees with the identity, the PMN will be declared incomplete, and EPA will not process or review it further until the submitter provides full and correct identity information. 40 C.F.R. § 720.45(a)(3)(ii).

EPA has prepared a series of Inventory nomenclature papers to describe how various classes of substances or types of complex reaction products should be identified for TSCA purposes. The Inventory papers (dated March 29, 1995) are available from the TSCA Assistance Office or from the EPA website: http://www.epa.gov/opptintr/newchems/invntory.htm.

EPA classifies chemicals into three categories: Class 1 substances, Class 2 substances, and polymers. 40 C.F.R. § 720.45(a). This classification scheme is the same one that was used in the initial Inventory reporting rules.

6.3.2.1. Class 1 Substances

Class 1 substances are those whose composition (except for impurities) can be represented by a structural diagram. For Class 1 substances, the submitter must include a specific chemical name using the standard rules of chemical nomenclature, the molecular formula, the CASRN (if known), and a structural diagram. *Id.* § 720.45(a)(1).

6.3.2.2. Class 2 Substances

Class 2 substances are those whose composition cannot be represented by a definite, complete structural diagram. Class 2 substances are often derived from natural sources or complex chemical reactions. For Class 2 substances, the submitter must include the specific chemical name, the molecular identity, the immediate precursor compounds, a description of the reaction process, the range of composition and the typical composition, and a representative or partial structural diagram. *Id.* EPA recommends that the submitter contact the prenotice coordinator by letter in order to obtain specific guidance before submitting a PMN on a complex reaction product.

6.3.2.3. *Polymers*

In 1995, EPA amended its definition of polymer to adopt the exact wording of the internationally recognized definition developed by the Organization of Economic Cooperation and Development (OECD). Polymer is defined as:

> a chemical substance consisting of molecules characterized by the sequence of one or more types of monomer units and comprising a simple weight majority of molecules containing at least 3 monomer units which are covalently bound to at least one other monomer unit or other reactant and which consists of less than a simple weight majority of molecules of the same molecular weight. Such molecules must be distributed over a range of molecular weights wherein differences in the molecular weight are primarily attributable to differences in the number of monomer units. In the context of this definition, sequence means that the monomer units under consideration are covalently bound to one another and form a continuous string within the molecule, uninterrupted by units other than monomer units.

40 C.F.R. § 723.250(b).

With the 1995 change in the polymer exemption, chemicals manufactured pursuant to the exemption no longer require an exemption application, and are not listed on the TSCA Inventory. Persons intending to manufacture a new polymeric chemical substance that is not eligible for the polymer exemption still must file a PMN. In the PMN, the submitter must indicate the lowest number-average molecular weight of any composition of the polymer and must identify the method used to make the determination. *Id.* § 720.45(a)(2). In addition, the submitter must provide the maximum weight percent of species below 500 and 1000 molecular weight. Supporting analytical data should be attached to the PMN form or, if the values are estimates, a description of the basis for the estimate.

Submitters are also required to provide the chemical name and CASRN of each reactant, including those used at two percent or less, and the maximum residual of each monomer in the polymer. Reactants include precursors, monomers, free radical initiators, crosslinking agents, chain-terminating chemicals, salt forming chemicals, or any other reactant intended to be incorporated into the structure of the polymer. Trade names are not acceptable substitutes for chemical names. *Id.* If the identity of a reactant is unknown, the submitter must arrange with the supplier to provide the chemical identity to EPA either in a joint submission or in a letter supporting the PMN.

The Two Percent Reporting Rule for Polymers. As discussed in chapter 4 on the TSCA Inventory, EPA only required the reporting of monomers and other reactants in a polymer present at two percent or greater for purposes of compiling the initial Inventory. Similarly, although the final PMN rule requires that *all* constituents of a polymer be listed on the PMN, EPA allows the submitter to elect which constituents, present at two percent or less, will be incorporated into the Inventory description of the polymer. 40 C.F.R. § 720.45(a)(2)(iii).

A monomer or other reactant is eligible for exclusion from the Inventory description if it is incorporated into the polymer at less that two percent or is charged to the reaction vessel at less than two percent. The PMN submitter may determine which monomers or other reactants constitute the polymer identity on the basis of either method. Submitters who adopt the "percent incorporated" method will want to monitor carefully any changes in manufacturing processes (such as a change in catalyst or solvent, or change in method and/or order of charging the reactants) that affect the incorporation of substances not included in the Inventory description. EPA has published a guidance document on the polymer exemption that discusses the Two Percent Rule. Office of Pollution Prevention and Toxics, EPA, *Polymer Exemption Guidance Manual* (June 26, 1997). The Guidance Manual is available from the TSCA Assistance Office or can be downloaded from the EPA website: http://epa.gov/opptintr/newchems/guideman.htm.

Free Radical Initiators. One particular area of confusion in the past has been whether to include free radical initiators in the description of a polymer. The Agency has defined the phrase "monomers and other reactants" such that it

> applies to those reactive agents that are used intentionally to become chemically part of the polymer composition. These reactive agents include all monomers, *e.g.*, vinyl chloride, acrylamide, terephthalic acid, and any other reactive agents that are intended to be incorporated into the polymer. Reactants other than monomers include crosslinking agents, chain-terminating agents, *free radical initiators*, and any other reactant which is intended to be incorporated into the structure of the polymer. This may include such substances as monohydric alcohols, *e.g.*, methanol, and monofunctional amines, *e.g.*, butyl amine, and acids or bases used to form a salt of the polymer.

Letter from Charles L. Elkins, Director, Office of Toxic Substances (Feb. 9, 1987) (emphasis in original).

Free radical initiators are used in the manufacture of certain classes of polymers. Fragments of these initiators may become chemically incorporated into the polymer as it is manufactured. At one time, EPA took the position that such chemical incorporations did not mean that the initiator necessarily became part of the Inventory description of the polymer. Instead, the Agency asserted that the intent of the manufacturer in using the initiator determined whether the initiator became part of the polymer description:

> The Agency recognizes that "intent" plays an important role in a company's determination of whether or not to include a free radical initiator in the polymer description. Likewise, you reference correspondence from John Ritch, former director of EPA's Industry Assistance Office, dated October 20, 1980, that "seemed to once again leave the question of whether or not to include initiators to 'intent.'" The Agency acknowledges that it is the manufacturer's responsibility to make a good faith effort in determining whether or not a free radical initiator added at a concentration of greater than two weight percent is intended to be chemically incorporated into the polymer. While recognizing the manufacturer's "intent" as the determining factor, the Agency reserves the right to raise questions relating to a reactant role for an initiator when it is used at greater than two weight percent if there is obvious indication of significant incorporation of initiator into a polymer composition.

Id.

EPA eventually recognized that members of the polymer manufacturing industry needed more clarification of the Agency's position, and that the "intent" standard was unnecessarily confusing. Accordingly, on June 28, 1989, EPA issued a *Federal Register* notice to clarify industry obligations. 54 Fed. Reg. 27,174.

The clarification states that a polymer that is manufactured with one or more free radical initiators, in which at least one initiator is used at greater than two percent by weight, is considered to be on the Inventory if it falls into one of the following categories: (1) the identical polymer description, without any initiator(s), was on the Inventory as of July 28, 1989; or (2) the identical polymer description, including the same initiator(s) in the name, is on the Inventory. To help future manufacturers of polymers with free radical initiators determine whether a polymer falls into one of these categories, EPA flags by the letter "N" after the CASRN in the TSCA Inventory listing those polymers that were on the Inventory as of July 28, 1989 which do not have the initiators in the polymer name.

As of July 28, 1989, any polymer manufactured using greater than two percent by weight of an initiator is subject to PMN requirements, unless the polymer is on the Inventory, is eligible for a categorical exception or is demonstrably present at less than two percent, *i.e.*, unless the polymer meets one of the two criteria given above, or EPA agrees with a claim by the manufacturer or importer that the initiator(s) used at greater than two percent by weight are not incorporated into the polymer structure.

EPA considers an initiator to be incorporated into the polymer structure if it is known to be incorporated or can be reasonably ascertained that its use primarily involves chemical incorporation of one or more initiator fragments (other than a hydrogen atom) into the polymer. Manufacturers who claim that a free radical initiator used at greater than two percent by weight is not being incorporated into the polymer must provide information to support that assertion. For example, the manufacturer might submit: (1) a description of the activity of the initiator and the extent to which this activity will operate; (2) an explanation of what is intended by this activity role; (3) the extent of incorporation of initiator-derived fragments; (4) any measures taken to prevent or limit incorporation; (5) any product properties or performance factors that would make incorporation undesirable; and (6) any other technical, economic, or utility considerations that would sustain the manufacturer's claims.

6.3.2.4. Impurities and By-Products

EPA also requires the submitter to list any impurities and by-products as part of the description of chemical identity on the PMN form. 40 C.F.R. § 720.45(b), (d). An impurity is a chemical substance unintentionally present with another chemical substance, while a by-product is a chemical substance produced without a separate commercial intent. *Id.* § 720.3(d), (m).

6.3.2.5. Generic Name

The submitter must provide a generic chemical name if the specific chemical identity has been declared confidential. EPA has provided guidelines in Appendix B of the TSCA Inventory for developing a generic name. In addition, the submitter can contact the Prenotice Coordinator for help in developing a generic chemical name, which can be downloaded from the EPA website: http://epa.gov/opptintr/newchems/guideman.htm. Failure to provide a generic chemical name when the specific chemical name has been declared CBI will render the notice incomplete (*see* sections 6.2.2 and 6.7.1).

6.3.2.6. Synonyms, Trade Identification

Finally, the submitter must provide any synonyms and trade names under which the substance has been or will be marketed. 40 C.F.R. § 720.45(c).

6.3.3. Production, Use, and Import Information—Section C

6.3.3.1. Production Volume

EPA requires the submitter to furnish "reasonable estimates" of the maximum production volume during the first twelve months of production and the maximum twelve-month production during the first three years of production. 40 C.F.R. § 720.45(e). EPA uses these production figures to estimate the potential exposure of workers, users, and consumers and to perform an economic analysis on the chemical. In fact, the production figure (along with the sales price) is a critical factor in determining when a chemical can support the cost of any required testing (either voluntary or pursuant to a section 5(e) order). Production volume is also a crucial factor in the Agency's determination of whether to grant an LVE. By limiting the production to

10,000 kilograms or less per year, the submitter limits potential exposure and hence potential risk to the chemical and establishes its eligibility to seek an LVE.

6.3.3.2. Use

EPA defines use of a chemical substance in terms of both function and application. EPA has clarified the terms as follows:

> "Function" is related to the inherent physical and chemical properties of the substance (*e.g.*, degreaser, catalyst, plasticizer, ultraviolet absorber). "Application" refers to the use of the substance in particular processes or products (*e.g.*, a degreaser may be used for cleaning of fabricated metal parts).

Instruction Manual (cited in section 6.1 above) at II, section C. With respect to use, the submitter must estimate the percent of total production volume for each category of use for the first three years (with the percent formulated), and whether the intended use is site-limited, industrial, commercial, or consumer. 40 C.F.R. § 720.45(f).

The submitter must provide a generic use description if a specific category of use has been declared confidential. The generic use description should provide a "sufficient indication of potential exposure." *Instruction Manual* at II, section C. If a generic use description does not indicate potential exposure, EPA will accept a description of the "degree of containment" (*e.g.*, contained use, destructive use). The *Instruction Manual* sets forth a list of acceptable containment descriptions. *Id.*

6.3.3.3. Hazard Information

As part of its risk assessment, EPA also will examine any hazard warning statement, label, material safety data sheet (MSDS), or other information which the submitter intends to provide to any person. Submitters are not required to develop any hazard warning statements, but any that have been developed must be submitted with the notice.

6.4. PMN FORM PART II: HUMAN EXPOSURE AND ENVIRONMENTAL RELEASE

EPA requires submitters to provide a description of the manufacturing and processing operations for the new chemical substances both at sites controlled by the submitter and sites controlled by others. EPA utilizes these descriptions in estimating the potential human and environmental exposure to the new chemical substance.

6.4.1. Industrial Sites Controlled by the Submitter—Section A

The submitter must provide a description of the operation, including where the operation will occur; must indicate whether it is a manufacturing, processing, or use operation and whether it is a continuous run or a batch operation; must indicate the amount and duration of the operation; and must supply a process description. 40 C.F.R. § 720.45(g).

The process description must include a diagram that identifies the major unit operation steps and chemical conversions, the entry point for feedstocks, and the points of release to the environment. The submitter also must provide information on occupational exposure and environmental release and disposal. Even if workers wear protective equipment, the submitter must describe each specific activity during which workers may be exposed along with the physical form of the chemical at the time of potential exposure, and the maximum number of workers potentially exposed.

The submitter also must identify the number of release points to the environment, the amount of the new chemical potentially released at each point, and the medium into which it will be released (air, surface water, ground, etc.).

6.4.2. Industrial Sites Controlled by Others—Section B

To the extent known or reasonably ascertainable, the submitter also must describe processing and use operations controlled by others involved with the new chemical substance. 40 C.F.R. § 720.45(h). The description must include an estimate of the number of sites involved, situations in which exposure to workers or the environment is likely to occur, the percent of the new chemical as formulated in products, and any methods used to control worker exposure and environmental release.

6.4.3. Pollution Prevention Information (Optional)

EPA encourages submitters to provide additional information not reported elsewhere in the PMN regarding efforts to minimize pollution associated with manufacturing, processing, use and disposal of the PMN substance. The information provided is taken into consideration during the review of the PMN.

6.5. PMN FORM PART III: LIST OF ATTACHMENTS

Finally, the submitter must list any attachments to the notice, such as an MSDS, and indicate whether any of them is confidential. The attachments will include the MSDS, any continuation sheets, the CAS Inventory Expert Service Report (if Method 1 was used to identify the chemical) and studies, reports or other relevant data that are submitted as part of the PMN.

6.6. PROTECTING CONFIDENTIAL BUSINESS INFORMATION

TSCA § 14 permits submitters to claim as confidential any information submitted to EPA and also prohibits EPA employees from "knowingly" disclosing this information. The claim of confidentiality must be asserted at the time the information is submitted. 40 C.F.R. § 720.80(b).

EPA can disclose CBI, however:

- To any officer or employee of the United States in connection with official duties pertaining to the protection of human health or the environment;
- To contractors when such disclosure is necessary for their job performance;
- To protect human health and the environment when the Administrator determines that disclosure is necessary; and
- To any proceeding under TSCA when relevant.

TSCA § 14(a). In addition, TSCA § 14(b) specifically authorizes disclosure of health and safety studies or data obtained from such studies on chemical substances currently in commercial distribution, or subject to the PMN requirements or subject to testing under TSCA § 4. EPA cannot disclose data that reveals manufacturing or production processes or the portion of a mixture composed of a particular chemical substance. TSCA § 14(b).

6.6.1. EPA's Handling of CBI

EPA has developed elaborate procedures for handling CBI under TSCA § 14. These procedures include security clearance and training for EPA employees and contractors permitted access to CBI, storage of CBI in secured areas, computer security for CBI, and special methods for creating, transferring, and destroying CBI.

EPA grants TSCA CBI access separately for each section of TSCA. Before handling TSCA CBI, an EPA employee or contractor must attend a special briefing and must pass a written examination. Those employees and contractors who are authorized access to TSCA CBI are added to an "authorized access list." EPA uses this authorized access list to check whether an individual has TSCA CBI access.

The Document Control Officer (DCO) maintains the Document Tracking System in order to track the location and disposition of TSCA CBI. The DCO assigns materials in the Document Tracking System a document control number and a machine-readable bar code, which are used to track a document from the time it is received at EPA until it is either transferred to another location or destroyed. All TSCA CBI have a green TSCA CBI cover sheet which clearly identifies the document as CBI. "CBI" is stamped on the first and last pages of each confidential document.

EPA stores TSCA CBI in "secured" areas which are accessible only with the use of a special key card. Persons who do not have authorized access to TSCA CBI can gain entry to a secured area only by signing the visitors log and by being escorted at all times by an authorized person.

EPA also has developed procedures for transferring custody of TSCA CBI. TSCA CBI can be transferred from one authorized person to another only by hand and only if the transferor receives a CBI loan receipt. TSCA CBI can only be transferred to individuals at other facilities by hand or through registered mail, a courier, or the United States Postal Service Express Mail. Regardless of the method, the CBI must be double-wrapped and the outside stamped "To Be Opened by Addressee Only."

6.6.2. Asserting CBI in a PMN

To assert a CBI claim, the submitter must check the appropriate box on the PMN form next to the item of information which is CBI. The claims of confidentiality do not have to be substantiated when the PMN form is submitted. A claim of confidential treatment of the specific chemical identity or use, however, must be substantiated when the Notice of Commencement of Manufacture (NOC) is submitted. 40 C.F.R. § 720.85(b).

Any submitter who claims the specific chemical identity and use confidential must provide a generic chemical identity and a generic use description. *Id.* § 720.87. If any information on the PMN or exemption is declared confidential, the submitter must furnish a copy with all the CBI deleted; this is referred to by EPA as a "sanitized" version of the PMN. *Id.* § 720.80. Any CBI contained in attachments to the PMN can be sanitized, when appropriate. TSCA § 5(d)(1) requires that a section 5 notice be made available to interested persons subject to the confidentiality provisions of TSCA § 14. In addition, EPA must publish a *Federal Register* notice announcing its receipt of the section 5 notice. Failure to provide a sanitized copy when claiming CBI will result in EPA's declaring the PMN or exemption application "incomplete" (*see* sections 6.2.2 and 6.7.1). EPA places this sanitized copy in the public file in the OPPT Public Reading Room at EPA Headquarters.

In order to substantiate a CBI claim, a manufacturer must provide a generic chemical name and answer a series of questions set forth at 40 C.F.R. section 720.85(b)(3)(iv). The questions concern the submitter's efforts to protect confidentiality, the harm to the manufacturer's competitive position in the event of disclosure, extent of disclosure to others, whether any other federal agency or court has made any pertinent findings with respect to confidentiality determinations, and the purpose of manufacture or import.

6.7. EPA'S REVIEW PROCEDURES FOR THE PMN

EPA has developed a detailed new chemical review process to review PMNs, SNURs, and the various exemptions. In March 1997, EPA issued a document entitled *Chemistry Assistance Manual for Premanufacture Notification Submitters* which explains its review process in detail. This document is available from the TSCA Assistance Office or can be downloaded from the EPA website: http://www.epa.gov/opptintr/newchems/chem-pmn/index.htm. EPA's review system consists of seven major stages designed to ensure that the Agency examines all aspects of a new chemical, including its physical and chemical properties, potential toxicity, exposure of workers, users and consumers, and economic benefits. (*See* Figure VI-1.) If at one of several stages of this review EPA determines that the new chemical does not present a cause for concern, it can "drop" the chemical from further review. Although "dropped" from review, the new chemical substance cannot be manufactured or imported until the 90-day review period is completed. The review status for PMNs and LVEs can be determined from reviewing the EPA website at: http://www.epa.gov/opptintr/newchems/status1.htm.

6.7.1. Filing and Receiving the PMN

The submitter can file a PMN or exemption application either by hand-delivering it to the OPPT DCO at EPA Headquarters or by mailing it. If sent by mail, an overnight mail service or registered mail should be used to insure prompt delivery to the Agency. Mailing instructions can be found at the EPA website: http://www.epa.gov/opptintr/newchems/contact.htm. Whether hand delivered or mailed, the package should contain two envelopes; the inner envelope should be stamped "confidential." EPA will send the submitter a letter acknowledging receipt of the submission and identifying the PMN or exemption number that has been assigned.

The Confidential Data Branch reviews a PMN or exemption application to determine if the submission is "complete" (*i.e.*, if the submitter has provided all the required information, has furnished a "sanitized" copy if necessary, and has sent the applicable fee to EPA's HQ Accounting Operations Branch in Pittsburgh). EPA will ask the submitter to correct any minor errors identified in the submission. The failure to date the form, typographical mistakes, and contradictory information are examples of common errors in the forms. EPA can request a correction up to day 30 of the review period. The submitter then has 15 days after being notified of an error within which to forward the corrected notice pages to EPA. Pursuant to section 5(c), EPA can extend the review period for failure to respond within this 15-day period.

By contrast, a PMN lacking any of the required information is deemed "incomplete." EPA does not consider it a valid PMN or exemption application and, therefore, does not start the 90-day or 30-day clock. EPA notifies the submitter of the problem by telephone and then by registered mail. The review period will not start to run until the submitter either submits the missing information or indicates that it is not known or reasonably ascertainable. 40 C.F.R. § 720.65(c)(2)(i).

If the submission is complete, the day of receipt is the first day of the 90-day or 30-day review period. EPA reviews a complete submission for CBI. EPA then prepares a section 5(d)(2) notice for publication in the *Federal Register*. The DCO assigns the submission a document control number, a case number, and logs it into several information systems, including OPPT's confidential data system that contains the scientific and regulatory information from all section 5 cases. This data system is used to identify structural, functional and/or use analogues for a new submission. The public and confidential versions of the Inventory also are searched by chemists from the Chemical Inventory Section; both groups may call the submitter with questions concerning identity. If the PMN or exemption chemical is located on the Inventory, EPA notifies the submitter of this fact and assigns the submission a disposition code. In general, EPA will not return a submission to the original submitter. If the substance is not on the Inventory, it proceeds to the next stage of review.

The submitter may withdraw the notice from review at any time by sending to the OPPT DCO a written notice to that effect. The withdrawal will be effective upon receipt of the statement by the DCO. 40 C.F.R. § 720.75(e).

6.7.2. Initial Review

6.7.2.1. Chemical Review (CR) Meeting

The Chemical Review (CR) meeting is held between days eight and twelve of the review process. Chemists from the Industrial Chemistry Branch/Economics Exposure and Technology Division (ICB/EETD) review the chemical nomenclature, including the generic name, the chemical structure, physical and chemical properties, use, and related data. In the case of polymers, EPA can terminate review of the PMN at this point if it determines that the chemical substance poses no risk to human health or the environment. A CR "drop" is prepared and EPA conducts no further review on the chemical substance. For those chemicals which are not dropped, EPA prepares a partially completed chemistry report summarizing the CR discussion and the need for further information.

6.7.2.2. Structure-Activity Team (SAT) Meeting

The SAT meeting occurs between days nine and thirteen of the review period. The SAT predicts the potential human health or environmental hazards of the new chemical substance by evaluating the physical/chemical properties, data on analogous substances, knowledge of chemical reactions, and any data on the new chemical itself. The SAT is an interdisciplinary group of chemists, biologists, toxicologists and information specialists.

At the SAT meeting, the team reviews the results of the CR meeting and a member presents the environmental fate profile. The SAT reviews information on related chemicals from the PMN files and the published literature in order to arrive at a hazard concern rating. The results of the SAT meeting are then summarized in a written SAT report which also includes a listing of the substance's physical/chemical properties, a discussion of chemical fate in wastewater treatment and in the environment, toxicity test data summaries, and the basis for Quantitative Structure-Activity Relationships (QSARs).

6.7.2.3. Profile of Exposure and Release

During review days 10-19, occupational exposure, environmental releases (including environmental persistence and bioaccumulation) and consumer exposure are assessed.

6.7.2.4. Focus Meeting

The Branch Chief, New Chemicals Notice Management Branch (NCNMB), which is the branch responsible for coordinating the new chemical review program, chairs the Focus meeting. At the Focus meeting, held between days 15 and 19 of the review period, representatives from the CR and SAT meetings review the results of those meetings in order to determine which issues, if any, need further investigation. If no further work is necessary, the chemical may be "dropped" from additional review. This is referred to as a "Focus drop"—which usually occurs by PMN review day 20.

If toxicity concerns are identified at the Focus meeting, however, the case enters "Standard Review." The case (even if dropped) may also be referred for "Follow-Up" investigation of potential increased production volumes or other uses that could lead to increased exposure, which in turn could increase risk. At the conclusion of the Focus meeting, a set of "Focus notes" summarizing the meeting and an assignment sheet for those chemicals going into Standard Review are produced. Members from the various support branches are assigned to each of the cases, including a Program Manager who coordinates the PMN review and works with the submitter in resolving any problems.

6.7.3. Standard Review

6.7.3.1. Workplan Meeting

Between days 23 and 27, a Workplan meeting is held to address the issues raised at the Focus meeting and to review scheduling. The NCNMB Program Manager leads the Workplan meeting, which is attended by a technical integrator and the case review team. The case review team consists of the economist, engineer, hazard reviewer, and exposure assessor. The technical integrator coordinates the technical review of the case and is responsible for developing a list of specific questions to be addressed by the technical case team members. The technical integrator also is responsible for working with these team members in order to resolve any outstanding technical issues.

6.7.3.2. Risk Assessment Disposition

Also, between days 57 and 61, a Risk Assessment meeting is held to determine whether the new chemical may present a potential health or environmental hazard and, if so, whether there is sufficient exposure to the chemicals to present a significant risk. Appropriate testing recommendations also are discussed. A Risk Assessment report is prepared summarizing the results of the meeting.

6.7.3.3. Decision Meeting

Between days 79 and 82, the division directors of CCD, EETD, and RA, and the deputy director of OPPT meet to review the PMN cases and to determine whether any regulatory action will be taken.

At this meeting the division directors decide on the appropriate course of action, which may include a decision to initiate a consent or unilateral section 5(e) order or section 5(f) order or rule; to enter into a voluntary agreement with the submitter for "up-front" testing; to refer the case to "Follow-Up"; to drop the case from further review; or to request additional case review and another division directors' briefing. The program manager prepares a Division Directors' Briefing Summary which summarizes the discussion and sets forth the regulatory decision.

6.7.4. Submitters' Post Review Duties

6.7.4.1. Notice of Commencement of Manufacture

If EPA fails to take any action on the new chemical substance, the submitter is free to manufacture or import the substance for commercial purposes on the 91st day after PMN submission. The PMN submitter is not obligated to commence manufacture, however. If the PMN submitter does commence commercial manufacture or importation, it must notify EPA within 30 days after commercial manufacture or import begins. 40 C.F.R. § 720.102. The PMN submitter must submit this "notice of commencement of manufacture" (NOC) in writing and must provide the specific chemical identity, a generic name if the chemical identity is claimed confidential, PMN number, and the date when commercial manufacture actually commenced, including whether the substance was manufactured in the United States or imported. The date of commencement for manufacture is the date of completion of the first amount (batch, drum, etc.). The date of commencement for import is the date when the new substance clears customs. The NOC also must include the name and address of the submitter, the name of the authorized official, the name and telephone number of the technical contact in the United States, and the address of the site where commencement of the manufacture occurred.

This NOC constitutes a certification that commercial manufacture or importation has actually occurred; thus, it cannot be submitted in advance. In addition, if the submitter originally claimed the chemical identity as confidential and wants this confidentiality retained, the submitter must substantiate this claim in accordance with the procedures set forth in 40 C.F.R. section 720.85(b), when filing the NOC. Unless the manufacturer provides this substantiation, EPA lists the specific chemical identity on the public TSCA Inventory.

6.7.4.2. Record-Keeping

The submitter must maintain records of the information contained in the PMN or exemption application for a period of five years from the date of commencement of manufacture. In particular, the submitter must maintain documentation pertaining to the production volume for the first three years of manufacture and "other data . . . in the submitter's possession or control." 40 C.F.R. § 720.78(a).

FIGURE VI-1
EPA PMN REVIEW PROCESS

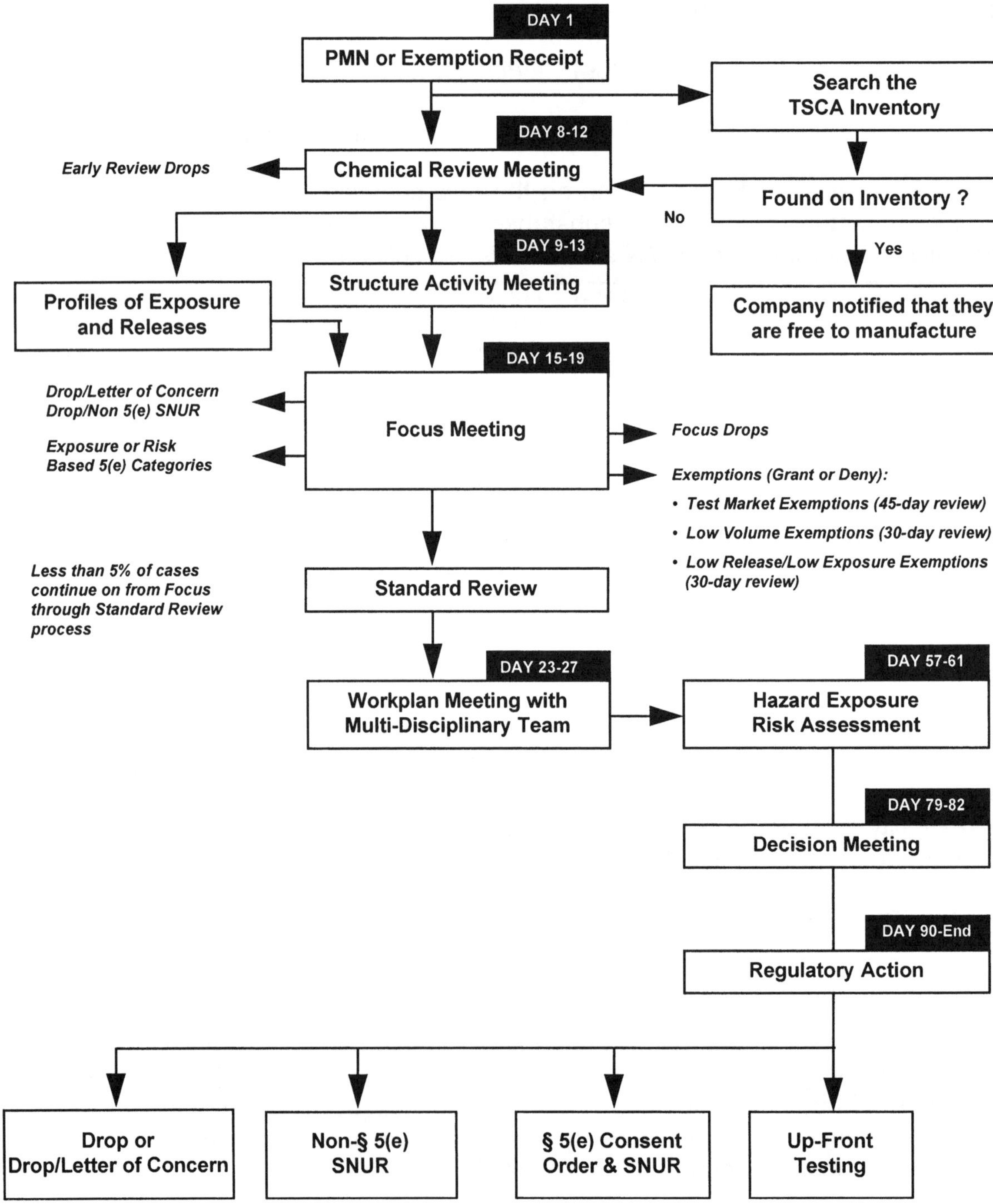

Source: EPA New Chemicals Program Bulletin (EPA-743-F-95-001) (May 1995)

CHAPTER 7
REGULATION OF NEW CHEMICALS AND USES

In the vast majority of cases, EPA reviews premanufacture notices (PMNs) within the initial 90-day review period. In such cases, EPA does not notify the PMN submitter that it may begin commercial manufacture or importation. Explicit Agency approval is not required, and the PMN submitter may commence commercial manufacture as soon as the review period expires. In some cases, EPA requires additional time in which to review the PMN. TSCA § 5(c) authorizes EPA to extend the PMN review period by one additional 90-day period for "good cause." Finally, in a small percentage of cases (fewer than 15 percent), EPA exercises its right to control the manufacture, processing, distribution, use or disposal of new chemical substances.

EPA has two regulatory tools to control the manufacture, processing, distribution, use or disposal of new chemical substances. First, under section 5(e) EPA may limit or prohibit manufacture of the new chemical if the Agency determines that available information is insufficient to permit a reasoned evaluation of the health and environmental effects of the PMN substance and, in the absence of such information, the chemical *may* present an unreasonable risk to health or the environment, or the chemical *may* enter the environment in substantial quantities, or there *may* be substantial human exposure. Second, under section 5(f) EPA may limit or ban manufacture if it has a reasonable basis to conclude that the manufacture *presents* or *will present* an unreasonable risk of injury to health or the environment before EPA can take action under TSCA § 6 to protect against that risk. EPA generally exercises its section 5(e) authority rather than its section 5(f) authority because it is easier for EPA to demonstrate that a new chemical *may* present a risk than that it *will* present a risk.

7.1. EPA REGULATION UNDER TSCA § 5(e)

Under TSCA § 5(e), EPA can issue an administrative order regulating a new chemical substance if the Agency finds that (1) there is insufficient information to reasonably evaluate the risk, *and* (2) *either* the chemical may present an unreasonable risk to health or the environment, *or* it will be produced in substantial quantities with the result that either substantial quantities will enter the environment or there will be substantial or significant human exposure to the substance. The section 5(e) order can ban or limit manufacture, distribution, use, or disposal of the chemical pending development of data sufficient for EPA to reasonably evaluate the chemical's risk. Unilateral section 5(e) orders must be proposed at least 45 days before the end of the PMN review period, *i.e.*, by day 135 of a 180-day review period where EPA has extended the standard review period an additional 90 days "for good cause." Unilateral orders become effective on the day the review period ends.

EPA often will negotiate a "consent order" with the PMN submitter to limit the commercial production, use, or disposal of the substance rather than to ban manufacture altogether.[17] Faced with the prospect of a unilateral order, a submitter must decide whether to fight the unilateral order, to negotiate a consent order or to withdraw the PMN. The cost of challenging a unilateral order or complying with a consent order may be too great, in which case the submitter will withdraw the PMN. Many if not most submitters try to negotiate a consent order with EPA. As of September 30, 2004, EPA had issued 1,280 section 5(e) consent orders. Overall, EPA has taken or threatened to take some action on a new chemical in 3,812 cases, about 9 percent of all section 5 notices received by EPA as of September 30, 2004. Copies of unilateral and consent orders (with confidential business information (CBI) deleted) are available for review in the Office of Pollution Prevention and Toxics (OPPT) Public Reading Room at EPA Headquarters in Washington, D.C.

In what has become a trend in the area of new chemical regulation, EPA announced in November 1996 that it would allow Union Carbide Corporation to manufacture a new chemical substance without imposing a section 5(e) consent order, even though the chemical was of a class that EPA almost always regulates under section 5(e). Instead, Union Carbide agreed to several *voluntary* control measures, which dramatically shortened the review period for its PMN. Two factors influenced EPA's decision to accept the voluntary measures in lieu of regulation under section 5(e): (1) the new chemical is safer than chemicals currently on the market; and (2) Union Carbide had obtained patents on the chemical, thereby precluding other companies from manufacturing the chemical once it is listed on the Inventory. Although this is an important regulatory development with potential to greatly reduce the time to market for chemicals traditionally regulated under section 5(e), companies may find it difficult to satisfy the second factor, *i.e.*, preventing a subsequent manufacturer from entering the market without observing the same controls.

7.1.1. EPA's Standard Section 5(e) Consent Order

TSCA § 5(e) does not provide explicit authority for EPA to enter "consent" orders. EPA developed the consent order concept to permit the introduction of new chemicals into the market while at the same time controlling any potential risk during the time needed to develop the required data. EPA has two standard consent orders - a risk-based consent order (triggered by a finding that the chemical may present an unreasonable risk to health or the environment) and an exposure-based consent order (triggered by a finding that the chemical will be produced in substantial quantities and either substantial quantities will enter the environment or there will be substantial human exposure). For exposure-based consent orders, EPA has quantified the criteria that trigger regulation under section 5(e). *See* Figure VII-2 at the end of this chapter.

---

[17] EPA has identified 55 categories of chemicals that are likely to be subject to a section 5(e) order. The categories are listed in Figure VII-1 at the end of this chapter.

In a risk-based consent order, EPA usually permits non-exempt commercial manufacture to proceed if the manufacturer agrees to certain restrictions on the production, distribution, use, or disposal of the new chemical, until the information EPA considers necessary to evaluate potential hazards is developed. In an exposure-based consent order, EPA usually permits non-exempt commercial manufacture to proceed without restriction until certain production volumes are reached which trigger the obligation to submit specified test data. *See* Figure VII-3 for a summary of the testing generally required by exposure-based consent orders. If a specific chemical presents both health and exposure concerns, EPA will combine the two types of consent orders.

In general, EPA takes a minimum of three months to negotiate and issue a section 5(e) consent order. Negotiations of complex orders can take even longer. Much of this time is spent in the myriad levels of Agency review. Industry has objected to the amount of time involved in issuing these orders, because even a three-month delay in commercial manufacture can have a severe impact on a company's marketing plans.

In response to these objections, EPA has created a two-track system of consent order preparations.[18] If the PMN submitter agrees to certain standard Agency terms at the beginning of negotiations, EPA will expedite the consent order. Under the expedited process, OPPT will prepare the order, send it through the Agency review process, and provide the PMN submitter the final order for signature after it has been signed by the Director of the Chemical Control Division within OPPT. The order becomes effective when the submitter signs it and returns it to EPA. EPA estimates that, under the expedited approach, it can prepare a standard consent order in 60 working days, compared to as much as 120 working days under the standard procedure. Figure VII-4 shows the schedule for non-expedited section 5(e) consent order development.

Consent orders consist of two sections: a preamble and a consent order. In the preamble, EPA sets forth the terms of the order, the contents of the PMN, the Agency's assessment of exposure to and risk from the PMN substance, its conclusions of law, and the data that EPA believes it needs to conduct a reasoned evaluation of risk. Here, EPA specifies the basis upon which it has determined that there is insufficient information on the chemical and that either it may present an unreasonable risk or it will be produced in substantial quantities with significant human or environmental exposure. Generally, EPA assesses the risk of the chemical by examining available data on the

---

[18] In addition, in 1995, EPA modified the Low Volume Exemption (LVE) and promulgated a new Low Release Low Exposure (LoREX) Exemption with the intent that the limitations inherent in these exemptions would replace the section 5(e) process. Thus, where a new chemical substance is eligible for an LVE or LoREX exemption, the manufacturer is assured speedy review of the exemption application and EPA is assured equivalent controls and/or production limits. These exemptions are discussed in more detail in chapter 5.

chemical and on structurally analogous substances. The submitter need not accept the Agency's risk assessment, but instead can agree to the terms of the order without admitting the facts or the conclusions underlying the Agency's risk determination.

In the "consent order" section, EPA sets forth the conditions and limitations on manufacturing, processing, disposal, and use pending the development of additional information on the PMN substance. A standard order consists of five distinct parts:

Part I	Terms of Manufacture, Import, Processing, Distribution in Commerce, Use and Disposal Pending Submission and Evaluation of Information
Part II	Record-Keeping
Part III	Successor Liability upon Transfer of Consent Order
Part IV	Modification and Revocation of Consent Order
Part V	Effect of Consent Order

Part I of the order prohibits the company from manufacturing, importing, processing, distributing in commerce, using or disposing of the PMN substance in the United States, for any non-exempt commercial purpose, except under the conditions of the consent order, pending the development of information necessary for a reasoned evaluation of the effects of the chemical and the completion of EPA's review of that information. Consent orders do not limit manufacture for exempt commercial purposes, such as research and development (R&D), export only, and excluded, non-TSCA (*e.g.*, pesticide, food, and drug) uses. (*See* chapter 5 for a discussion of the exemptions and chapter 13 for a discussion of the exclusions.) Thus, a signatory to a consent order can manufacture the new chemical substance without complying with the provisions of the consent order if the chemical is exempt from the PMN process or is excluded from TSCA all together.

Part I also contains the conditions of manufacture, import, processing, distribution, use and disposal. These conditions will vary depending upon whether the consent order is exposure- or risk-based, and, if risk-based, whether the risk is to human health or the environment. For example, a typical exposure-based consent order prohibits the company from manufacturing or importing the PMN substance beyond various production limits unless and until the company conducts specified studies on the PMN substance and submits the final study reports to EPA. EPA bases these "trigger quantities" on an estimate of the volume of PMN substance necessary to generate sufficient income to support the cost of the testing. In addition, the company must notify any person handling the PMN substance of any testing results indicating that the chemical presents a risk of injury to human health or the environment.

A typical risk-based consent order requires the company to institute specific worker protection and hazard communication practices (health risk only), or to limit disposal practices or releases of the PMN substance to water (environmental risk only). In some cases, EPA also restricts the manner in which the substance can be manufactured, imported, or processed and imposes stringent notification obligations on the company whenever it distributes the PMN substance to another company, even for disposal. Testing triggers also can be part of the risk-based consent order. More commonly, however, EPA specifies the information required to conduct its evaluation of the effects of the PMN substance, and states that submission of this information is not required but the order's restrictions on manufacture, import, processing, distribution in commerce, use and disposal will remain in effect until EPA modifies or revokes the order based on submission of this or other relevant data.

Part II specifies which records the company must keep regarding its compliance with the terms of the consent order. Companies must keep these records for five years after the date on which they were created and must make them available to EPA in the event of a TSCA inspection. Both exposure- and risk-based consent orders will have a record-keeping section.

Part III sets forth the procedures by which the PMN submitter may transfer its rights and obligations under the consent order (including the right to manufacture the PMN substance). It is important to note that if this transfer occurs before the notice of commencement of manufacture or import is filed, the successor company must file a new PMN for the chemical and negotiate its *own* TSCA § 5(e) consent order before beginning to manufacture or import the chemical.

Part IV provides that the consenting company may petition EPA at any time to modify or revoke a consent order. For example, a company may find that market conditions have changed and that it needs to manufacture more of the chemical than permitted by the consent order before return on the chemical can support the cost of the required tests. These petitions need not take any particular form, but the submitter must provide the Agency with sufficient justification for the requested relief. EPA has no deadline under the consent order within which it must respond to these petitions. For this reason, some petitioners also characterize their requests for modification as petitions under TSCA § 21 in order to take advantage of the 90-day provision within which EPA must act to grant or deny such petitions.

Under its standard consent order provisions, EPA will grant requests to modify or revoke a consent order if the results of the required tests or other new information indicate that there are no longer grounds for action under section 5(e). Additionally, the Agency will authorize other modifications if it determines that such modifications are useful, appropriate, and consistent with the structure and intent of the order as issued.

Part V sets forth the effect of the consent order. By signing the standard Agency consent order, a company agrees to waive three rights: (1) to file objections to the order (other than petitions to modify or revoke the order); (2) to receive service of the order no later than 45 days before the end of the review period; and (3) to challenge the validity of the order. This waiver does not affect any other rights that the company may have under TSCA or otherwise.

7.1.2. EPA Evaluation of Section 5(e) Data

EPA's standard section 5(e) consent order contemplates several possible regulatory scenarios after receiving the required data. EPA may determine that the test data are: (1) scientifically invalid; (2) scientifically equivocal; or (3) valid and unequivocal. EPA considers that its standard section 5(e) consent order enables the Agency to take continued regulatory action based on the submitted data without resorting to its TSCA § 4 or § 6 authority.

7.1.2.1. Invalid Data

If EPA determines that submitted test results are scientifically invalid, EPA will notify the company in writing of this finding. In the standard consent order EPA defines the term "scientifically invalid" to mean any significant departure from the EPA-approved protocol or the Good Laboratory Practice Standards at 40 C.F.R. part 792 (without prior or subsequent Agency approval) that prevents a reasoned evaluation of the health or environmental effects of the PMN substance. Upon notification that its test results are scientifically invalid, the company has two options (1) re-conduct the study or (2) challenge EPA's finding. If the company adopts one of these two options, generally it may continue to manufacture the PMN substance beyond the applicable production limit. If the company does nothing, it is prohibited from further manufacture or import of the PMN substance beyond the applicable production limit.

If a specific event beyond the control of the company has prevented the development of scientifically valid data, the company may submit a report documenting this extenuating fact within two weeks of its occurrence. If EPA agrees that the company was not at fault, the company can continue to manufacture beyond the applicable production limit provided that it re-initiates the study within a reasonable period of time (generally three months) and submits the data within a specified time thereafter.

7.1.2.2. Equivocal Data

EPA may determine that the data are scientifically equivocal. In the standard consent order EPA defines the term "scientifically equivocal data" to mean data which, although developed in apparent conformity with the Good Laboratory Practice Standards and EPA-approved protocols, are inconclusive, internally inconsistent, or otherwise insufficient to permit a reasoned evaluation of the potential risk of injury to human health or the environment from the PMN substance. In this instance, the Agency will allow the company to continue to manufacture or import the PMN substance but will maintain the other restrictions in the consent order. To be relieved of the remaining restrictions, the company must re-conduct the study and produce data sufficient to resolve EPA's concerns.

7.1.2.3. Valid, Unequivocal Data

Valid, unequivocal data can take one of two forms. The data indicate that the chemical either presents or does not present an unreasonable risk of injury to human health or the environment. If EPA determines that the data indicate an unreasonable risk, EPA will notify the company of its finding and instruct the company to undertake certain actions to mitigate exposures or to better characterize the risks presented by the

PMN substance. Within two weeks of receipt of such notice, the company must cease all production, importation, processing, distribution, use, and disposal unless the company complies with the additional requirements specified in EPA's notice or submits a written report refuting EPA's finding and/or the appropriateness of these additional requirements. The company may continue to manufacture, import, process, distribute in commerce, use and dispose of the PMN substance pending EPA's response to the company's written objections.

If the data indicate that the chemical will not present an unreasonable risk, the company must continue to obey all terms of the consent order until otherwise notified in writing by EPA. If EPA determines that continued regulation is unnecessary, the Agency will revoke the order. If the Agency takes no action, the company can petition EPA for modification or revocation of the consent order based upon the submitted test data.

7.1.3. Problems of Section 5(e) Consent Orders

The Agency's standard consent order under section 5(e) poses three significant problems for the signatory company: (1) a consent order can extend section 5(e) jurisdiction over a PMN substance almost indefinitely; (2) it relieves the Agency (and denies the company the protections) of the more exacting standards of TSCA §§ 4 and 6; and (3) it places the PMN submitter at a possible competitive disadvantage since EPA does not automatically revoke the consent order upon submission of required data, and since subsequent manufacturers or importers of the same substance are not bound to the terms of the order. To address the latter concern, the Agency generally issues a final significant new use rule (SNUR) to impose the same terms and conditions upon subsequent manufacturers, importers or processors. Since establishing its generic SNUR, the Agency has acted promptly to issue follow-on SNURs after entering into section 5(e) consent orders.

7.1.3.1. Potentially Infinite Duration

EPA generally loses its section 5 jurisdiction over a chemical once the PMN review period has expired. Upon receiving a notice of commencement of manufacture (NOC), EPA lists the chemical on the TSCA Inventory, and it becomes an "existing chemical." Thereafter, anyone, including the PMN submitter, may lawfully manufacture the chemical for commercial purposes. Should problems arise with the chemical after commercial manufacture, EPA must regulate the chemical under TSCA provisions other than section 5, such as section 4 (testing of chemical substances or mixtures), section 6 (regulation of hazardous substances and mixtures which present an unreasonable risk), or section 7 (imminent hazard).

The section 5(e) consent order, however, effectively extends section 5 jurisdiction over a chemical long after the PMN review period has expired, permitting EPA to take action on the basis of data submitted under the order (even though the chemical is listed on the Inventory) without having to satisfy the more rigorous criteria under section 4 or 6. To date, the Agency has refused to incorporate section 4 or 6 criteria into these consent orders.

7.1.3.2. No Automatic Revocation

Consent orders do not contain any provision automatically revoking the order upon submission of the required data. In fact, EPA expressly refuses to insert such language into consent orders on the grounds that even data "exonerating" the PMN substance do not necessarily mean that the chemical presents no unreasonable risk. Even when test data are negative, the Agency still may find a risk unreasonable unless the company maintains engineering controls, worker protections, or other limitations that the Agency may wish to impose. Thus, the Agency maintains a right to use the consent order to regulate a PMN substance long after it is listed on the Inventory and required data are submitted.

7.1.3.3. Anticompetitive Effects

As the only signatory to the consent order, the PMN submitter alone is bound by its terms and limitations. Once the company notifies EPA that non-exempt commercial manufacture or importation of the PMN substance has begun, EPA lists the substance on the TSCA Inventory, and any other person may manufacture or import it *without* facing any of the consent order restrictions imposed on the original PMN submitter. Initially, EPA did not automatically issue a SNUR for every chemical subject to a section 5(e) consent order. Instead, EPA issued a SNUR only if the potential market for the chemical indicated a likelihood of other follow-on manufacturers. Under the so-called Generic SNUR Rule, promulgated in 1989, however, EPA now must issue a SNUR for every PMN substance subject to a section 5(e) consent order or publish its reasons for not doing so. 40 C.F.R. § 721.1670(a). Thus, EPA has eliminated the previous competitive disadvantage to the consent order signatory by issuing a SNUR which applies the same restrictions to subsequent manufacturers and importers. The signatory always remains at a competitive disadvantage vis-à-vis importers, however, since EPA cannot impose SNUR requirements at foreign manufacturing sites for want of TSCA jurisdiction.

7.1.4. Exposure Controls versus Data Development

Submitters often object to EPA's use of production limits in risk-based consent orders, arguing that exposure controls reduce risk and thereby obviate the need for testing. EPA responds that it often accepts more risk under consent orders than ideally it wishes, in order to permit manufacture to commence, but that it will not do so indefinitely. Thus, EPA maintains that the additional data remains necessary so EPA can evaluate potential risk. Submitters also argue that EPA should revoke the consent order once the data are submitted, regulating the chemical thereafter under TSCA provisions applicable to existing chemicals. EPA categorically rejects this argument and refuses to release its jurisdiction under a consent order until it has evaluated the data.

7.2. NEGOTIATING SECTION 5(e) CONSENT ORDERS

EPA has a detailed three-stage process for developing non-routine section 5(e) consent orders. (*See* Figure VII-4, EPA's Schedule for Developing Non-Expedited Section 5(e) Consent Orders.)[19] At the outset, the program manager asks the submitter to voluntarily suspend the PMN review period. Some submitters agree to suspend for a period of several months, while others prefer to hold a closer rein on the process by suspending for successive but much shorter periods.

7.2.1. Intra-Agency Process

The Agency's program manager (PM), who coordinates development of the consent order, prepares an initial draft and distributes it to case team members for review. After incorporating any comments of the case team, the PM distributes the second draft to the PMN submitter. After receiving comments from the PMN submitter, the PM prepares a third internal draft for review and concurrence up the chain of command (section chief, staff attorney, branch chief). The Office of General Counsel only reviews "nonroutine" consent orders.

Upon receiving all the necessary concurrences, the PM sends two copies of the Agency's final consent order to the submitting company. Because the language of these consent orders has evolved over many years, EPA now considers much of it "standard" and modifies it only reluctantly. Indeed, the Agency encourages submitters to confine their comments to those consent order sections specific to their PMN chemical (*e.g.*, the administrative history of the case, and the specific limitations being placed on the chemical).

After signing the final order, the submitter returns it to EPA for final signature. Upon receipt of the signed order, the PM again sends it up the chain of command for final concurrence and signature. Once signed by the director of the Chemical Control Division, the consent order also binds EPA. EPA then provides the PMN submitter one signed consent order and the Agency retains the other, placing a "sanitized" copy—one without CBI—in the public file located in the OPPT Public Reading Room at EPA Headquarters. The consent order becomes effective the day following the lapse of the PMN review period. If the review period has been suspended voluntarily beyond the statutory period, EPA and the submitter may revoke jointly any remaining time.

Because of its internal review schedule, EPA generally takes about three months to prepare a section 5(e) consent order from the first internal draft to the final signature. This delay results primarily because each level within OPPT has an allotted time to review the draft and final order, and OPPT has an increased overall workload with

---

19 This is the development process for nonroutine consent orders, not the expedited approach discussed above.

declining staff. Development of a consent order can take much longer, however, if serious disagreement arises between the Agency and the submitter over its terms or if a PM faces several consent orders simultaneously. Predictably, industry has complained about the amount of time required to develop these consent orders and its adverse impact on market introduction and customer relations.

7.2.2. Expediting the Process

Despite these built-in delays, the submitter can do several things to expedite the consent order. First and foremost, the company should establish a good working relationship with the PM (and thereby with the Agency). The submitter's credibility with the Agency will go a long way in making the negotiations productive and efficient. Second, the submitter also should work with the PM to address problems as they arise during internal draft development. In this way the PMN submitter can clarify issues, suggest alternative approaches, and provide additional information in a timely manner.

EPA's draft order will contain brackets around all CBI. The submitter should check carefully to make sure that all information deemed confidential is properly bracketed and all factual information (*e.g.*, chemical name, production volume, and uses) is accurate and complete. Interlineate the draft itself with comments and return it to the Agency for review, along with a cover letter highlighting the comments and the underlying reasons. Merely objecting to provisions of the order is not productive; the submitter should explain the basis for its concerns and, where possible, offer an alternative approach.

Due to the demand on Agency resources, EPA prefers to negotiate by telephone rather than in person. Nevertheless, EPA will grant requests for a meeting if face-to-face discussions might break an impasse or provide helpful new information. Importantly, the PMN submitter must provide EPA with any new data on the PMN substance developed or obtained during consent order development. 40 C.F.R. § 720.40(f).

Many submitters retain outside consultants or counsel to assist in these negotiations. The Agency cannot discuss CBI related to the consent order, however, unless the submitter notifies EPA that certain outside parties represent the submitter in negotiations and may have access to the submitter's CBI. Such authorization can take the following form:

Re: PMN P97-XXXX: Designation of Counsel

Dear Program Manager:

XYZ Company has retained Mr./Ms. A of the law firm of ABC as counsel to represent XYZ Company in negotiations with the U.S. Environmental Protection Agency concerning the issuance of a TSCA § 5(e) Consent Order on premanufacture notice P97-XXXX. Therefore, Mr./Ms. A and members of his/her law firm are authorized to receive and discuss XYZ Company confidential business information in conjunction with P97-XXXX.

Sincerely,

[Signature of authorized company official who signed the PMN]

The submitter or its counsel should deal only with the PM or the New Chemicals Branch (NCB) staff attorney. The PM is the official contact between EPA and the submitter during the development of the order. The PM may misinterpret any contacts with other PMN team members without prior clearance as an attempt to circumvent established Agency procedure.

7.3. CHALLENGES UNDER SECTION 5(e) CONSENT ORDERS

Although the signatory company waives the three rights under a section 5(e) consent order (see discussion of standard consent order part V in section 7.1.1 above), this waiver does not prevent subsequent challenge to an Agency decision based upon the submitted data. Rather, companies who disagree with the Agency's determination of invalidity, equivocality, or unreasonable risk have essentially three methods of challenging an Agency decision: (1) a TSCA § 21 petition; (2) a petition under the consent order; or (3) an action under the Administrative Procedure Act.

7.3.1. Petitions under TSCA § 21

TSCA contains no provision for judicial review of Agency actions taken under section 5(e) consent orders. TSCA § 19 expressly provides for judicial review only of "a rule under section 4(a), 5(a)(2), 5(b)(4), 6(a), 6(e) or 8" and, therefore, does not apply to actions taken under a section 5(e) order. Although TSCA § 5(e) provides for judicial review of decisions made under section 5, a company has waived its rights to invoke this provision under the waiver language of the consent order. The consent order, however, does preserve a company's rights not explicitly waived. One such "right" is that provided under section 21 of "any person" to petition for the initiation of "a proceeding for the issuance, amendment, or repeal of . . . an order under section 5(e) or 6(b)(2)."

TSCA § 21 requires the Administrator to grant or deny such a petition within 90 days after it is filed. If the Administrator denies a petition for the issuance of an order (or fails to act on such a petition within 90 days), the petitioner may seek judicial review in federal district court in order to compel the Administrator to initiate the requested proceeding. In this proceeding, the petitioner is entitled to *de novo* review by the court (a review of the entire matter as if for the first time).

By contrast, if the Administrator denies a petition to amend or repeal an order (or fails to act on such a petition within 90 days), TSCA § 21 does not expressly provide for judicial review of such denial (or failure to act). Importantly, however, the legislative history indicates that Congress did not intend to commit such actions to unreviewable Agency discretion or to deny judicial review under the Administrative Procedure Act (APA), 5 U.S.C. sections 701-706 (1994):

> The conference substitute provides different treatment for review of petitions for amendment or repeal of rules or orders, because the Administrator already will have addressed the general subject matter in an existing rule or order and the Administrator's determination will have been subject to review under section 19 of this Act.
>
> . . . .
>
> . . . Therefore, if the Administrator denies a petition to *amend or repeal an action* under section 4, *5(e)*, 6, or 8, the conference substitute permits review of such denial only under the *Administrative Procedure Act*.

H.R. Rep. No. 1679, at 98-99, *reprinted in* 1976 U.S.C.C.A.N. 4539, 4583-84 (emphasis added). Accordingly, an Agency denial of a petition under TSCA § 21 to repeal or modify the consent order is subject to judicial review under the APA.

7.3.2. Petitions under the Consent Order

The standard consent order under TSCA § 5(e) permits a company to petition EPA for modification or revocation of provisions of the consent order. Once the Agency has reviewed a company's data and determined that, despite a company's comments and expert opinions to the contrary, the data are scientifically invalid, equivocal, or indicative of an unreasonable risk, the Agency may continue to prohibit manufacture or require further testing in accordance with the consent order. If, upon petition for Agency review, the Agency remains unchanged in its decision, the company may seek APA review in federal court.

A petition under either TSCA § 21 or the consent order is time-consuming. Since the Administrator has 90 days to act on a petition under TSCA § 21, any attempt to file suit before the 90 days has lapsed would be premature—meaning a court would likely consider the action not yet "ripe" for judicial review. The modification and revocation section of the consent order sets no timetable whatsoever for Agency action on petitions for relief. While a reasonable period is implied, EPA could prolong its consideration of the company's petition and thereby delay the company's effective access to the courts. In the interim, while awaiting Agency action on its petition for relief, the company would need to comply with the order.

7.3.3. Review under the Administrative Procedure Act (APA)

Section 10 of the APA, among other things, provides a right to judicial review of "final" Agency actions which are not committed to unreviewable Agency discretion and for which there is no other adequate remedy. Since TSCA does not expressly provide a judicial remedy for adverse decisions under a consent order, APA review is available unless the Agency action is not final or by law is committed to unreviewable Agency discretion.

7.4. UNILATERAL SECTION 5(e) ORDERS

If EPA determines that exposure or engineering controls cannot reduce the potential risk of a PMN substance to acceptable levels, or that it cannot negotiate a mutually agreeable consent order, the Agency will issue a proposed unilateral section 5(e) order. Although TSCA § 5(e)(1)(A) permits the Administrator to limit the manufacture, processing, distribution, use or disposal of the PMN substance, the Agency generally uses these orders to ban a PMN substance outright. In practice, therefore, a "unilateral" order bans the commercial manufacture, processing, distribution, use, and disposal of the PMN substance. Of course, the PMN submitter is free to develop additional data and re-submit the PMN.

Unlike a consent order, a unilateral order *does* receive top priority in OPPT. This is because under section 5(e)(1)(B), EPA must issue the proposed order no later than 45 days before the end of the review period (day 135 of the 180-day review period).

The proposed unilateral order is similar in structure to a consent order—it consists of a preamble and an order. The preamble sets forth EPA's findings of fact and conclusions of law with respect to the PMN substance and the Agency's evaluation of available toxicity, exposure, and economic information, and its opinion on the type of information necessary to conduct a reasoned evaluation of the chemical. The order bans the PMN substance from commercial production, processing, distribution, use, and disposal, pending the development of specified information.

Upon receipt of a proposed order, the PMN submitter has 30 days to file "objections specifying with particularity the provisions of the order deemed objectionable and stating the grounds therefor." TSCA § 5(e)(1)(C). The filing of these objections is critical because they prevent the proposed order from taking effect. *Id.* Upon receiving objections, the Administrator must apply to a federal district court for an injunction to prohibit or limit the commercial manufacture, processing, distribution, use, or disposal. TSCA § 5(e)(2)(A)(i). If, after evaluating the objections, the Administrator determines that there is no basis to ban or limit the PMN substance under section 5(e), the order will not be finalized.

To date, EPA has not applied to federal district court for such an injunction, although the Agency has proposed 13 unilateral section 5(e) orders. PMN submitters subject to such proposed unilateral orders either have withdrawn the PMN chemical from review or have successfully negotiated a consent order. On occasion, after issuing a proposed unilateral order EPA has agreed to negotiate because of significant additional analyses of potential toxicity and exposure supplied by the submitter. Submitters usually file this additional information with the Agency in the form of "draft objections."

7.4.1. Statutory Standard for Unilateral Section 5(e) Orders

In the conference report accompanying Senate Bill 3149, which became TSCA, Congress indicated that it included the objections procedure under TSCA § 5(e) (and § 5(f)) to prevent EPA from taking action without a reasonable and substantial basis:

> However, to protect against unilateral action by the Administrator without an adequate basis for action, the conference substitute borrows the procedure from section 701(e) of the Federal Food, Drug, and Cosmetic Act which permits the filing of objections by manufacturers and processors specifying with particularity the provisions of the order deemed objectionable and stating the grounds for the objections.
>
> If such objections are filed, then the Administrator is instructed to seek an injunction in a Federal district court to prohibit or limit the manufacture, processing, distribution in commerce, use or disposal of the substance. Of course, if the objections filed with the Administrator indicate to the Administrator that the injunction is not necessary, then the Administrator is not required to seek the injunction.

H.R. Rep. No. 1679, at 68-69, *reprinted in* 1976 U.S.C.C.A.N. at 4553-54. Clearly, Congress wanted EPA to have an adequate factual basis for its determinations under section 5(e) before issuing a unilateral order and/or applying for injunctive relief to prohibit manufacture or processing.

As the conference report notes, section 5(e) is modeled on section 701(e) of the Federal Food, Drug, and Cosmetic Act (FFDCA). The FFDCA section 701(e)(2) procedure is identical to the TSCA § 5(e) objections procedure, except that the FFDCA includes a right to a public hearing and an Agency decision based on substantial record evidence. Both the administrative hearing under the FFDCA and the federal court hearing required by TSCA follow the filing of objections and thereby enable the judicial trier of fact to evaluate whether the Agency has "an adequate basis for action." H.R. Rep. No. 1679, at 68, *reprinted in* 1976 U.S.C.C.A.N. at 4553. Accordingly, the Agency's determinations under section 5(e), like determinations under FFDCA section 701(e), must be supported by substantial evidence.

Similarly, section 706 of the APA requires that a reviewing court hold unlawful and set aside Agency action, findings, and conclusions found to be arbitrary, capricious, an abuse of discretion, or otherwise not in accordance with law. At least two courts have ruled that, in assessing the adequacy of factual support in the administrative record, the substantial evidence test and the arbitrary or capricious test are one and the same. *Olenhouse v. Commodity Credit Corp.*, 42 F.3d 1560 (10th Cir. 1994); *Association of Data Processing Service Organizations v. Board of Governors*, 745 F.2d 677 (D.C. Cir. 1984). Thus, in the context of TSCA § 5(e) the distinction between the substantial evidence test and the arbitrary or capricious test may be largely illusory.

7.4.2. Objecting to Unilateral Section 5(e) Orders

Objections to a proposed section 5(e) order must state with particularity those provisions of the order deemed objectionable. In order to satisfy this statutory standard, a company must address EPA's findings of fact about the PMN chemical and its conclusion about the need for a section 5(e) order. Thus, the objections should discuss EPA's findings on potential toxicity, human and environmental exposure, risk and information needed to assess risk, as well as pertinent economic considerations.

The objections themselves should address each assumption upon which EPA has based its proposed order. If the order is based on the "may present an unreasonable risk" trigger of section 5(e)(1)(A)(ii)(I), the submitter should address the following areas as applicable: (1) EPA's reliance on the toxicity of chemicals that are structurally analogous to the PMN substance, including any differences between the two substances in structure, physical and chemical properties, metabolism, and fate; (2) EPA's reliance on test data on the structural analogue used to support its risk determination; (3) the existence of a more appropriate structural analogue, if any; (4) EPA's interpretation of any test data submitted with the PMN; and (5) based on discussion of the previous factors, the reasons why the PMN substance does not present an unreasonable risk. Since risk is a function of both toxicity and exposure, the objections also should examine and discuss potential worker, user and consumer exposure.

In order to address these matters effectively, company and outside experts may be necessary in the areas of toxicology, structure activity relationships, engineering, chemistry, and risk assessment. Company personnel with knowledge of industrial hygiene and the chemistry and function of the PMN substance also may be critical.

If EPA based its order on the substantial production/substantial exposure trigger of TSCA § 5(e)(1)(A)(ii)(II), the submitter must address both the issues of substantial production and significant or substantial human exposure.[20] EPA will determine "substantial production" based on the company's production estimates in its PMN. A

20 EPA's criteria for substantial production/substantial exposure are summarized in Figure VII-2.

company may need to change its production estimates to reflect different market conditions since submitting the PMN. Therefore, the company should provide any such new production projections to EPA since reduced production volume can reduce potential exposure and risk.

The company should address the issue of significant or substantial human exposure for all possible exposure scenarios—manufacturing, processing and use. The company should discuss the number of workers exposed, the length of exposure (number of hours per day and number of days per year), the type of exposure (*e.g.*, inhalation, dermal), and the types of protective equipment routinely worn. The potential exposure of processors and users should be analyzed in a similar manner.

The submitter also should consider proposing to the Agency an alternative testing scheme. In the event that, notwithstanding the submitter's objections, the Agency determines that testing is still required, the Agency may permit the submitter to conduct a different test or to employ a tiered testing sequence. EPA must be convinced that an alternative test would provide information sufficient to conduct a reasoned evaluation of the PMN substance. For example, the submitter could conduct a genotoxicity battery in the first tier in order to determine whether the weight of such evidence warrants conducting upper-tier mutagenicity assays or a two-year bioassay.

7.5. EPA REGULATION UNDER TSCA § 5(f)

If EPA determines that a new chemical substance presents or will present an unreasonable risk before the Agency can issue a rule under section 6 to protect against such risk, the Administrator must act under section 5(f) to control the risk. Under section 5(f) the Administrator either (a) may issue a proposed *rule* (which becomes immediately effective upon publication in the *Federal Register*) to *limit or delay* the manufacture, production, use, or disposal, or (b) may issue a proposed *order* and, if the submitter's objections thereto are unpersuasive, must file for an injunction in federal district court to *prohibit* the chemical's manufacture, processing or distribution in commerce before expiration of the PMN review period. EPA will publish a proposed rule if it does not intend to ban the chemical outright. If the Agency determines that an outright ban is necessary to control the risk, it must issue a proposed order.

7.5.1. Proposed Section 5(f) Rules

TSCA § 5(f)(2) authorizes the Administrator to issue an immediately effective proposed rule under section 6(a) that limits or delays manufacture of a chemical substance undergoing PMN review. Under section 6(a) the Administrator may take the following actions:

- limit the amount of the substance that can be manufactured, processed, or distributed;
- prohibit a particular use or a particular use in a concentration in excess of a certain level;

- limit the amount that can be manufactured, processed or distributed for a particular use, or in a concentration in excess of a certain level;
- require labeling of the substance or articles containing the substance;
- require records of the manufacturing or processing operations used and testing that is reasonably necessary to assure compliance with the rule;
- prohibit or otherwise regulate the commercial use;
- prohibit or otherwise regulate the disposal; and/or
- require notification to distributors, other persons in possession of the substance, and the general public of the risk associated with the substance and require the manufacturer to offer to replace or repurchase the substance.

Pursuant to section 6(d)(2)(B), the proposed rule is immediately effective upon publication in the *Federal Register*.

Judicial relief from a section 5(f) rule is probably unavailable because TSCA § 6(d)(2)(A) provides that "[s]uch a proposed rule which is made so effective shall not, for purposes of judicial review, be considered final agency action." Presumably, an affected party could challenge EPA's failure to complete the rulemaking in an expeditious manner as directed by TSCA § 6(d)(2)(B). Any challenge to the merits of the rule, however, would have to wait until EPA issues the final section 6 rule.

As of fiscal year 2003, EPA has proposed only three section 5(f)(2) rules covering four chemicals. 40 C.F.R. pt. 747. Each of the rules prohibits the addition of nitrosating agents, such as nitrates, to the PMN chemical when used in metalworking fluids, in order to prevent formation of nitrosamines, which are known carcinogens. These proposed rules also require distributors of the substances to notify their customers of the restrictions prior to shipping the substance and to notify machine shop workers of the health hazards through labels on metalworking fluids containing the substance. Although *proposed* in 1984, the rules became effective immediately after publication.

7.5.2. Proposed Section 5(f) Orders

If the Administrator determines that it is necessary to ban the chemical from commercial manufacture, distribution, processing, use, and disposal, EPA must issue a proposed order under section 5(f)(3) and, if the submitter files objections, apply for an injunction. The proposed order takes effect upon the expiration of the review period unless the submitter files objections in accordance with TSCA § 5(e)(1)(C) (the objection procedures for section 5(e) orders also applies to section 5(f) orders). The Administrator must apply to federal court for an injunction before the expiration of the review period unless EPA determines on the basis of the objections filed that the substance does not or will not present an unreasonable risk. TSCA § 5(f)(3)(D). To date, EPA has not proposed any banning orders under TSCA § 5(f).

If the Administrator applies to a district court for an injunction banning the commercial introduction of a new chemical substance, the district court must issue such an injunction if it finds a reasonable basis for concluding that the substance presents or will present an unreasonable risk of harm before a rule under TSCA § 6 can be promulgated. TSCA § 5(f)(3)(B). Hence, the court may not use the normal equity standard for determining whether to issue an injunction. Rather, "the standard set out in section 5(f)(3)(B) of [TSCA] is intended to totally replace the normal injunction standard." H.R. Rep. No. 1679, at 70, *reprinted in* 1976 U.S.C.C.A.N. at 4555.

7.6. SIGNIFICANT NEW USE RULES (SNURs)

Like persons who filed for the initial Inventory, PMN submitters also must describe the intended uses of their chemicals. After EPA places a chemical on the TSCA Inventory, however, the original submitters or others may discover additional uses for the chemical not anticipated at the time of the initial Inventory or PMN submission. Such new uses could substantially increase human or environmental exposure to the chemical—exposure that EPA did not evaluate during the initial Inventory or PMN review.

If EPA determines by rule that a particular use of a chemical already on the Inventory constitutes or would constitute a "significant new use," the Agency can issue a significant new use rule (SNUR). A SNUR requires that anyone who wants to manufacture or process a chemical substance for a use that EPA has determined is a "significant new use" must give 90 calendar days' prior notice to EPA. TSCA §§ 5(a)(1)(B), 5(a)(2); 40 C.F.R. pt. 721. This notice is referred to as a "significant new use notice" or SNUN, but is functionally equivalent to a PMN. Thus, in effect, a SNUR turns an "existing" chemical into a "new" chemical for purposes of TSCA § 5 by requiring the manufacturer or processor to submit a SNUN on the existing substance before undertaking the significant new use.[21] A SNUR potentially has a broader application than the PMN regulations, however, because it *applies to processors* as well as manufacturers and importers and obligates every person subject to the SNUR (not just the first manufacturer/importer) to file the SNUN.

---

[21] The information that must be submitted in a SNUN is virtually identical to the information that must be submitted under the PMN regulations.

Persons required to submit a SNUN must do so at least 90 days prior to manufacturing, importing, or processing the SNUR substance for the significant new use. The notice must be submitted on the standard PMN form and contain the same information as a full PMN. 40 C.F.R. § 721.10(a). The submitter must send the appropriate $2500 fee to the same address at which EPA receives PMN fees. (*See* chapter 6.) If two or more persons are required to submit the notice, they may file a joint SNUN. 40 C.F.R. § 721.25(b). EPA processes a SNUN in the same manner as a full PMN (except to the extent that PMN review would be inconsistent with 40 C.F.R. part 721). Documentation of information contained in the SNUN must be maintained for five years after submission of the notice to EPA. 40 C.F.R. § 721.40. EPA calculates penalties for failure to submit a SNUN by using its section 5 Enforcement Response Policy. (*See* chapter 14 for a discussion of that policy.)

If, after reviewing a SNUN, EPA fails to initiate any action under section 5, 6, or 7, then TSCA § 5(g) requires the Administrator to publish a notice in the *Federal Register* giving EPA's reasons for not initiating any action. Absent any such action when the 90-day review period has elapsed, the submitter may manufacture, import or process the chemical for the significant new use without the need for explicit approval from EPA. Unlike a PMN submitter, the Agency does not require the SNUN submitter to file an NOC when the new use has commenced.

7.6.1. SNUR Standard

TSCA does not set criteria for determining when EPA may deem a new use "significant," but does charge EPA to consider "all relevant factors," including:

> (A) the projected volume of manufacturing and processing of a chemical substance,
>
> (B) the extent to which a use changes the type or form of exposure of human beings or the environment to a chemical substance,
>
> (C) the extent to which a use increases the magnitude and duration of exposure of human beings or the environment to a chemical substance, and
>
> (D) the reasonably anticipated manner and methods of manufacturing, processing, distribution in commerce, and disposal of a chemical substance.

TSCA § 5(a)(2). A new "use" need not be a use at all, but can be any method of manufacturing, processing or disposing of the product that EPA determines to be significant under the TSCA § 5(a)(2) criteria.

EPA generally considers a significant new use to be any increased production volume, different type or greater extent of exposure, different disposal method, or different manufacturing site.[22] Indeed, EPA has gone even further, by attempting to designate ***existing*** manufacture and importation for ***any*** use as "significant new uses" for purposes of promulgating a SNUR. In 2000, EPA proposed (and ultimately promulgated) a SNUR for a class of chemicals known as perfluoroalkyl sulfonates (PFAS), used primarily in the textile, carpet and apparel industries. 65 Fed. Reg. 62,319 (October 18, 2000).[23] The proposed SNUR reflected EPA's concerns regarding the purported persistent bioaccumulative nature of this class of chemicals, and represented the culmination of discussions between EPA and 3M Company, which agreed to discontinue the manufacture of the chemicals pursuant to a negotiated phase-out schedule. Several different industries, who had been manufacturing, importing and using PFAS chemicals and their analogues for years in a variety of other applications (including the manufacture of photoresists and aviation hydraulic fluids), worked with EPA to demonstrate that their "use" of PFAS was preexisting and that their small volume uses in controlled workplace settings were not the source of EPA's stated concerns regarding impacts to health or the environment. As a result, EPA narrowed the specific chemicals to which the SNUR applied, while retaining the definition of "significant new use" as the manufacture and importation of the subject chemicals for any use. 67 Fed. Reg. 11,008 (March 11, 2002); 40 C.F.R. § 721.9582. Although the proposed SNUR, as originally drafted, triggered significant issues regarding EPA's authority under TSCA § 5(a)(2) to impose a SNUR on an existing use, the issue has not been adjudicated since the parties interested in the PFAS SNUR resolved their differences with EPA.

7.6.2. Who Must Report

All persons who intend to manufacture, import, and/or process for commercial purposes a chemical substance identified in a SNUR (published at 40 C.F.R. pt. 721, subpt. E) must file a SNUN if they intend to engage in the identified significant new use. Even manufacturers, importers or processors who themselves do not engage in a significant new use but nevertheless intend to distribute the substance to others must submit a SNUN *unless* they can document that: (1) they have notified in writing each person who purchases or otherwise receives the chemical from them of the specific section in subpart E of part 721 that identifies the substance and its designated significant new uses; (2) each such recipient has knowledge of that specific section of subpart E; or (3) each such recipient cannot undertake any significant new use

---

22 In 1994, EPA proposed a SNUR for refractory ceramic fibers, 59 Fed. Reg. 13,294 (Mar. 21, 1994), and published an Advance Notice of Proposed Rulemaking for a SNUR on lead and lead compounds, 59 Fed. Reg. 49,484 (Sept. 28, 1994). If finalized, these SNURs would represent the first use of SNURs to regulate chemical substances with widespread existing uses and further blur the distinction between the Agency's authority under TSCA §§ 5 and 6 to regulate existing chemical substances.

23 The proposed SNUR, as originally published, inaccurately described the category of chemicals at issue as perfluorooctyl sulfonates ("PFOS"). The final SNUR accurately identifies the category of chemicals as PFAS.

described in the specific section of subpart E. 40 C.F.R. § 721.5. By contrast, a company that processes for a significant new use a chemical substance listed in subpart E must submit a SNUN only if it: (1) knows the specific chemical identity of the chemical substance being processed; and (2) processes the chemical substance with specific knowledge that the substance is listed in subpart E of part 721. *Id.* Clearly the Agency places primary responsibility on manufacturers and importers that distribute SNUR-regulated chemicals to spread the word about the SNUR restrictions and will prosecute the distributor rather than its customers for SNUR violations where the required notice was not given.

The following persons are exempt from complying with SNURs and need not file a SNUN:

- persons who have been granted a Test Marketing Exemption (TME) for the significant new use;
- persons who manufacture, import or process the chemical only in small quantities for research and development;
- persons who manufacture, import or process the substance only as an impurity;
- persons who manufacture, import or process the substance only as a by-product which is used subsequently only by organizations that burn it as fuel, dispose of it as a waste or extract from it component chemical substances;
- persons who import or process the substance as part of an article;
- persons who manufacture the substance solely for export and comply with the labeling requirement of TSCA § 12(a)(1)(B);
- persons who submit a SNUN prior to the promulgation date of the section of subpart E which identifies the substance and who have received written notification of compliance from EPA prior to the effective date of such section. EPA will issue such notice only if one of the following occurs: (1) EPA is unable to make the finding that the activities described in the SNUN will or may present an unreasonable risk under reasonably foreseeable circumstances; or (2) EPA and the person negotiate a consent order under section 5(e), with such order taking effect on the effective date of the section in subpart E which identifies the substance;

- persons who are operating under a consent order issued under section 5(e). If the terms of the consent order are inconsistent with the SNUR, complying with the consent orders exempts the person from the SNUN requirement.

40 C.F.R. § 721.45.

The regulations also exempt any person who "has applied for and been granted an exemption under section 5(h)(5) of [TSCA]." *Id.* This exemption, which is available for chemicals that exist temporarily and to which there is no human or environmental exposure, seems primarily to encompass non-isolated intermediates. Yet, EPA has never required manufacturers of non-isolated intermediates to apply for an exemption under this section. Rather, the Agency has granted a blanket exemption to all such manufacturers. In fact, EPA has never issued regulations to implement section 5(h)(5). Since there is no procedure for applying for such an exemption, presumably manufacturers of SNUR-listed chemicals who produce them only as non-isolated intermediates are exempt from SNUN requirements as well, even though they have not literally "applied for and been granted" an exemption, as the regulations state.

EPA also has established a procedure whereby a manufacturer or processor can petition the Agency to allow use of alternative measures to control exposure to, or environmental release of, a chemical substance without submitting a SNUN. If EPA determines that the alternative measures provide substantially the same degree of protection as the methods specified in the SNUR, no SNUN is necessary. 40 C.F.R. § 721.30. Persons who intend to employ such alternative control measures must submit a request to EPA for a determination of equivalency before commencing manufacture, importation or processing involving the alternate controls. Such requests must be submitted to:

Office of Pollution Prevention and Toxics
Document Control Office (7407M)
U.S. Environmental Protection Agency
1200 Pennsylvania Avenue, N.W.
Washington, D.C. 20460
ATT'N: SNUR Equivalency Determination

EPA will review requests for determinations of equivalency within 45 days of receipt and mail the results to the submitter. Upon receipt of notice from EPA, the submitter may commence operations using the alternative control methods.

A manufacturer, importer or processor of a chemical identified in subpart E who already has begun commercial distribution (the "supplier") and who subsequently acquires knowledge that the purchaser or "recipient" is engaging in a significant new use of that chemical without having submitted the required SNUN must stop supplying that recipient and submit a SNUN. The supplier need not take such action, however, if it can document each of the following: (1) it has notified the recipient and the EPA Office of Compliance Monitoring (OCM) about the unlawful activity in writing within fifteen working days of learning for the first time that the recipient is engaging in a significant new use without submitting a SNUN; (2) within fifteen working days after notifying the recipient, the recipient has responded to the supplier in writing that it is aware of the terms of subpart E and will not engage in the significant new use; and (3) the supplier has promptly provided OCM with a copy of the recipient's written assurances. 40 C.F.R. § 721.5. Any supplier notified by EPA or with independent knowledge that a recipient is engaging in a significant new use, even after the recipient has provided written assurances to the contrary, must immediately cease distribution to that recipient until either the supplier or the recipient has submitted a SNUN and the review period has expired or EPA otherwise informs the supplier that shipments may resume.

7.6.3. Determining Inventory Status

Chemicals listed in 40 C.F.R. part 721, subpart E often are listed by generic names because manufacturers have claimed the specific chemical identities as confidential. In order to determine whether a specific chemical is subject to a SNUR, a *bona fide* request will have to be filed with the Agency. The requirements to establish a *bona fide* intent under the SNUR provisions are identical to those under the PMN and Inventory Update rules. (*See* chapters 4 and 5.) If EPA is satisfied that the manufacturer or processor has shown a *bona fide* intent to manufacture, import or process the chemical substance, EPA will notify the manufacturer or processor of its findings within 30 days of receipt of the notice of *bona fide* intent. 40 C.F.R. § 721.11.

7.6.4. Use of SNURs to Support Section 5(e) Consent Orders

As discussed earlier in this chapter, when EPA has concerns about a new chemical substance but does not want to prohibit its manufacture, the Agency will enter into a consent order with the PMN submitter, allowing limited production under carefully controlled conditions. Once the chemical is placed on the Inventory, however, other manufacturers could begin producing the substance without complying with the restrictions in the consent order, giving them a competitive advantage over the original manufacture. As a result, manufacturers subject to section 5(e) consent orders urged EPA to designate as a "significant new use" any manufacture of such substances not in compliance with the same restrictions placed upon the original manufacturers in the consent orders. *See* 40 C.F.R. § 721.160. Once EPA issues such a SNUR, any manufacturer who intends to depart from the conditions imposed under the SNUR must file a SNUN 90 days before doing so.

As of September 30, 2004, EPA has entered into approximately 1280 section 5(e) consent orders and has issued more than 729 SNURs. *See* 40 C.F.R. §§ 721.225 - 721.9975. EPA initially experienced a large backlog of SNURs because any rulemaking, even a relatively simple SNUR, requires commitment of substantial Agency resources. In 1994-95, EPA was very active in this area and issued forty-seven final SNURs affecting nearly one hundred chemical substances. The Agency's difficulties in developing SNURs to support the section 5(e) consent order program provided much of the incentive for the "generic SNUR" rulemaking process, which is discussed below.

The use of SNURs to support the section 5(e) consent order program unfortunately has blurred the distinction between "use" and other activities such as manufacturing, processing, distribution and disposal. TSCA consistently refers to "use" as something distinct from these other activities. To apply a section 5(e) consent order to third parties, the SNUR must designate as a significant new "use" any *manufacturing* that does not comply with the consent order's restrictions. Similarly, when a section 5(e) consent order contains restrictions on processing, distribution or disposal, the corresponding SNUR must designate as a significant new "use" any such activities not in compliance with the consent order's restrictions. EPA's designation of manufacturing and processing as "uses" may present difficulties for courts attempting to interpret the regulations because elsewhere TSCA draws a fairly clear distinction between use and these other activities. TSCA § 5(a)(1)(B) states that notice to EPA (a SNUN) is required before a person can "manufacture or process any chemical substance *for* a [significant new] use." *Id.* (emphasis added). In rules where EPA has designated manufacturing as a significant new use, however, the Agency has not explained how a person can manufacture a substance "*for* manufacture." For that matter, in the SNURs that designate certain types of disposal as significant new "uses," EPA has not explained how a person can "manufacture a chemical" *for* disposal.

Chemical manufacturers have not challenged EPA on these grounds, perhaps in large part because they protect PMN submitters subject to section 5(e) orders. Still, it remains to be seen whether EPA can enforce these rules, if challenged.

7.6.5. Generic SNUR Rule

On July 27, 1989, EPA promulgated sweeping changes to its procedures for issuing SNURs. 54 Fed. Reg. 31,298 (codified as amended at 40 C.F.R. pt. 721). The rule, known as the "Generic SNUR Rule," establishes standardized significant new uses and record-keeping requirements and creates two new procedures for promulgating SNURs on an expedited basis without undergoing notice and comment.

7.6.5.1. Summary of the Generic SNUR Rule

Found in part 721 of the TSCA regulations, the Generic SNUR Rule is divided into five subparts: (1) subpart A contains general provisions for SNUR compliance, such as definitions for terms found in other subparts, an indication of who must submit SNUNs and who is exempt, and specific requirements for the notice itself and procedures for submitting the notice; (2) subpart B lists standardized significant new uses that by rule EPA can apply to any existing chemical; (3) subpart C establishes record-keeping requirements which by rule EPA can impose upon manufacturers, importers, or processors of any chemical that becomes subject to a SNUR; (4) subpart D establishes two expedited rulemaking procedures that EPA can use to establish SNURs for chemical substances that are undergoing or have completed PMN review and creates a procedure by which persons affected by an expedited SNUR may petition the Agency to modify or revoke it; and (5) subpart E lists the chemicals that are subject to part 721 and the new uses of each chemical that EPA has designated as "significant." EPA can establish significant new uses other than those in subpart B, and can impose record-keeping requirements other than those in subpart C, but only by notice-and-comment rule-making.

The key to the Generic SNUR Rule lies in its standardized significant new uses (subpart B) and its expedited rulemaking procedures (subpart D). The standardized significant new uses are simply a list of all the various restrictions EPA has placed on new chemicals through the section 5(e) consent order process. Since creating the generic SNUR, the Agency has used the expedited procedures in subpart D to promulgate a SNUR corresponding to a section 5(e) consent order by publishing a single *Federal Register* notice that cites standard provisions comparable to the restrictions in the consent order. Once this expedited SNUR is in place, any subsequent manufacturers (or processors) must either comply with the consent order's restrictions embodied in the SNUR, or submit a SNUN. During its review of the SNUN, EPA can address the notifier's proposed activities involving the chemical that do not comply with the consent order/SNUR. This SNUN could result in another section 5(e) consent order applicable to these new uses.

7.6.5.2. Standardized Significant New Uses

The Generic SNUR Rule establishes five categories of standardized significant new uses. From this "menu" EPA picks the controls that will apply to a particular chemical based upon the known effects of the chemical and the conditions of manufacture and processing.

Protection in the Workplace. 40 C.F.R. section 721.63 designates as a standardized "significant new use" any manner of manufacturing, importing or processing associated with any use of the chemical substance if the manufacturer, importer or processor has not established a program whereby each person who is reasonably likely to be exposed to the chemical is provided with and required to wear appropriate protective equipment.

If the exposure will be dermal, EPA can declare any manufacturing or processing to constitute a significant new use if the employer's equipment does not include: (1) equipment selected and used in accordance with the Occupational Safety and Health Administration (OSHA) regulations at 29 C.F.R. sections 1910.132 and 1910.133; (2) gloves; (3) full body chemical protection clothing; (4) chemical goggles or equivalent eye protection; and/or (5) clothing which covers any other exposed areas of the arms, legs and torso. Even if the persons subject to the rule provide and require the use of all the equipment EPA deems appropriate, EPA can still declare the manufacture or processing to be a significant new use if the employer is unable to demonstrate that each item of clothing will provide an impervious barrier to prevent dermal exposure during normal and expected duration and conditions of exposure within the work area. The employer can demonstrate the effectiveness of the clothing by testing it or by citing the specifications from the clothing manufacturer.

If workers are reasonably likely to be exposed by inhalation, EPA can declare as a significant new use any manufacturing or processing associated without having established a program whereby each person who is likely to be exposed is provided with and required to wear a respirator approved by the National Institutes of Occupational Safety and Health (NIOSH), and the respirators are used in accordance with 29 C.F.R. section 1910.134 and 42 C.F.R. part 84. 40 C.F.R. section 721.63(a)(5) lists fifteen types of respirators that meet minimum requirements for use of a respirator.

If the SNUR substance is present in the work area only as a mixture, EPA can set a concentration limit for the substance. An employer is exempt from the worker protection provisions of section 721.63 if the concentration of the SNUR substance in the mixture does not exceed the concentration set by EPA in the SNUR.

Hazard Communication Program. 40 C.F.R. section 721.72 designates as a standardized significant new use any manner or method of manufacture, importation or processing associated without having established a hazard communication program. When EPA promulgates an expedited SNUR, the Agency can designate as a significant new use any manufacture, import or processing associated if the program does not contain the following elements: (1) a written hazard communication program available, upon request, to all employees, contractor employees, and their designated representatives, which, at a minimum, will describe how the requirements of the Generic SNUR Rule for labels, material safety data sheets (MSDSs), and other forms of warning material will be satisfied; (2) a labeling program under which containers of the SNUR substance in the workplace are labeled in accordance with criteria listed in the Generic SNUR Rule; (3) each employer maintains or develops an MSDS for the substance; and (4) each employer ensures that employees are provided with information and training on the substance.

If the substance is present in the work area only as a mixture, EPA can set a concentration limit for the substance. An employer is exempt from the hazard communication program provisions of section 721.72 if the concentration of the substance in the mixture does not exceed the set concentration.

An employer need not take additional actions to comply with a SNUR if existing programs or procedures satisfy the hazard communication program requirements. Most of the provisions parallel those of OSHA's Hazard Communication Standard (HCS), but the EPA rule differs in four respects: (1) EPA makes the hazard determination, rather than the employer; (2) EPA provides language for labels and MSDSs, whereas OSHA allows employers to develop appropriate language; (3) EPA does not provide trade secret protection whereas OSHA's HCS does; and (4) EPA requires listing of environmental (as distinct from health and safety) hazards on labels and MSDSs, whereas OSHA does not have such jurisdiction. Furthermore, under the hazard communication program of the SNUR EPA can require labeling, etc., based on a finding that a substance *may* present a risk. OSHA's hazard communication restrictions generally apply to chemicals which do present known hazards.

Industrial, Commercial, and Consumer Activities. 40 C.F.R. section 721.80 designates as a significant new use any of the following: (1) use in non-enclosed processes; (2) any manner or method of manufacture or processing in non-enclosed processes associated with any use; (3) use beyond the site of manufacture or import; (4) processing beyond the site of manufacture or import; (5) any manner or method of manufacture (excluding import) of the substance associated with any use; (6) use other than as an intermediate; (7) use other than as a site-limited intermediate; (8) use as an intermediate where the concentration of the intermediate substance in the product intended for distribution in commerce exceeds a concentration specified by EPA; (9) any use other than as described in the PMN for the substance; (10) use other than as allowed by the section 5(e) consent order for the substance; (11) non-industrial use; (12) commercial use; (13) non-commercial use; (14) use in a consumer product; (15) aggregate manufacture and importation volume for any use greater than as specified by EPA; (16) aggregate manufacture and importation volume for any use greater than that allowed by the section 5(e) consent order for the substance; (17) aggregate manufacture and importation volume for any use greater than that specified by EPA unless the manufacturer or importer has submitted results of the health or environmental effects studies EPA identified for the substance; (18) annual manufacture and importation volume for any use greater than that specified by EPA; (19) annual manufacture and importation for any use greater than that allowed by the section 5(e) consent order for that substance; (20) annual manufacture and importation volume for any use greater than that specified by EPA unless the manufacturer or importer has submitted the results of the health or environmental effects studies identified by EPA; (21) use in the form of: (a) a powder; (b) a solid; (c) a liquid; or (d) a gas; (22) any manner or method of manufacture of the substance in any of those forms that is associated with any use; (23) any manner or method of processing of the substance in any of those forms that is associated with any use; and (24) use involving an application method that generates: (a) a vapor, mist, or aerosol; or (b) a dust.

Disposal. The new subpart A defines "process stream" to mean:

> all reasonably anticipated transfer, flow, or disposal of a chemical substance, regardless of physical state or concentration, through all intended operations of processing, including the cleaning of equipment.

40 C.F.R. § 721.3.

Section 721.85 designates as a standardized significant new use any method of disposal of the process stream associated with any use of the SNUR substance, or with any manner or method of manufacturing or processing associated with any use of the substance, other than by methods designated in the SNUR by EPA. These may include: (1) incineration; (2) landfill; and/or (3) deep well injection. This section, however, does not supersede any applicable federal, state, or local laws and regulations.

Release to Water. Section 721.90 designates as a significant new use any predictable or purposeful release of a manufacturing stream, process stream, or use stream associated with any use of the SNUR substance, from any site: (1) into the waters of the United States; (2) into the waters of the United States without application of certain treatment technologies that will be specified in the SNUR by EPA; (3) into the waters of the United States without primary wastewater treatment and secondary wastewater treatment as defined in 40 C.F.R. part 133; or (4) into the waters of the United States if, by using a formula specified in the regulations, the concentration in the receiving waters would exceed a limit set by EPA in the SNUR.

7.6.6. Expedited SNURs for New Chemical Substances Subject to Section 5(e) Orders

Section 721.160 establishes the procedures which EPA can use to promulgate SNURs for chemicals that have been the subject of a final order issued under section 5(e) of TSCA. The presumption under the regulations is that EPA *will* issue a SNUR for every new chemical substance that was the subject of a section 5(e) order. If the Agency does not issue a SNUR, it must issue a notice in the *Federal Register* explaining why a SNUR is not required. 40 C.F.R. § 721.160(a)(2). The specific requirements of the SNUR must be based on and consistent with the provisions of the section 5(e) order. If EPA designates additional activities as significant new uses, that designation must be done in accordance with the provisions of 40 C.F.R. section 721.170 (procedures for issuing non-5(e) SNURs). EPA's procedural options for issuing section 5(e) SNURs include: (1) direct final rule-making; (2) interim final rule-making; and (3) notice-and-comment rule-making.

Direct Final Rule-Making. EPA will issue SNURs using the direct final rule-making option unless it determines that another process is more appropriate. When EPA uses the direct final rule-making procedure, it will issue a final rule in the *Federal Register.* The *Federal Register* notice will state that, unless EPA receives written notice within 30 days of publication that someone wishes to submit adverse or critical comments, the rule will be effective 60 days from the date of publication. If EPA receives notice within 30 days that someone wishes to submit adverse or critical comments, the Agency will issue a notice in the final rule section of the *Federal Register* withdrawing the portions of the direct final rule for which a notice of intent to comment was received, and the Agency will publish a proposal in the proposed rule section of the *Federal Register.* The proposal will establish a 30-day comment period. EPA then will consider any timely comments submitted in response to the proposal, and issue a final rule only if the Agency decides to establish notification requirements under part 721.

Interim Final Rule-Making. EPA will use interim final rule-making procedures when the Agency believes that a significant new use is likely to take place before a direct final rule would become effective. When EPA uses the interim final rule-making procedure to issue a SNUR, the Agency issues it in the "final rule" section of the *Federal Register*, and the SNUR takes effect upon publication. Persons still have 30 days after publication to submit comments which the Agency will consider when it develops the final rule. Rules issued under this procedure, although immediately effective, automatically expire 180 days after publication unless, within that period, EPA issues a final rule in the *Federal Register*.

Notice-and-Comment Rule-Making. EPA uses traditional notice-and-comment procedures where the Agency anticipates adverse comments to the SNUR. Under this procedure, EPA issues a proposal in the *Federal Register* and allows a 30-day comment period before issuing a final rule. Unlike the interim rule, however, this proposed rule is not immediately effective.

Timetable for Issuing Expedited Section 5(e) SNURs. EPA must issue a proposed rule, a direct final rule, or an interim final rule within 180 days of receipt of a valid NOC for any substance that was the subject of a section 5(e) consent order. 40 C.F.R. § 721.160.

7.6.7. Expedited SNURs for New Chemical Substances Not Subject to Section 5(e) Orders

Section 721.170 establishes the procedures and criteria under which EPA can issue expedited SNURs for chemicals that have passed through the PMN process without becoming subject to a section 5(e) consent order. EPA initially determined that some of the standardized significant new uses that are listed in subpart B should not be applied to non-5(e) chemicals. In 1995, however, EPA amended the rule to allow the Agency to designate as a significant new use any one or more of the activities set forth in subpart B. 40 C.F.R. § 721.170(c)(1). EPA can promulgate a non-5(e) SNUR on an existing chemical if it determines that activities different from those described in the PMN may result in significant changes in exposure or release levels or concern exists about the substance's health or environmental effects.

7.6.7.1. Concern Criteria

EPA may promulgate a non-5(e) SNUR if the substance meets one or more of the concern criteria listed in 40 C.F.R. section 721.170(b). The concern criteria are basically the same criteria that EPA uses when determining whether a new chemical substance should be subject to a section 5(e) consent order. Thus, the criteria call for a SNUR if exposures likely to result from new uses not specified in the PMN would have called for a section 5(e) order if the PMN had identified them.

EPA may determine that concern exists if it makes any one of the following findings:

- the substance may cause carcinogenic effects, because it: (a) has been shown by valid test data to cause carcinogenic effects in humans or in at least one species of test animal; (b) has been shown to be a possible carcinogen based on the weight of the evidence with short-term tests indicative of the potential to cause carcinogenic effects; (c) is closely analogous to another substance that has been shown by test data to cause carcinogenic effects in humans or in at least one species of laboratory animal, provided that if there is more than one such analogue, the greatest weight will be given to the relevant data for the most appropriate analogues; or (d) is known or can reasonably be anticipated to be metabolized in humans or transformed in the environment to a substance which may have the potential to cause carcinogenic effects.

- the substance has been shown by valid test data to cause acutely toxic effects in at least one species of laboratory animal, or is closely analogous to another such substance.
- the substance may cause serious chronic, acute, or developmentally toxic effects under reasonably anticipated conditions of exposure, based on evidence similar to that listed for carcinogenic effects.
- the substance may cause significant adverse environmental effects under reasonably anticipated conditions of release.
- concern exists about the health or environmental effects of one or more of the impurities or by-products of the substance because the impurity or by-product meets one of the criteria listed above.
- no substance may be regulated on this basis unless EPA also determines that the significant new use may be accompanied by changes in exposure or release levels that may be significant in relation to these health or environmental concerns.

40 C.F.R. § 721.170.

7.6.7.2. Procedures for Issuing Non-5(e) SNURs

EPA may issue non-5(e) SNURs by the same three processes available to it for section 5(e) SNURs: direct final rule-making; interim final rule-making; and notice-and-comment rule-making. 40 C.F.R. § 721.170(d)(4). EPA will use the direct final rule-making process to issue non-5(e) SNURs unless it determines that one of the other processes is more appropriate. One difference between section 5(e) and non-5(e) SNURs is that EPA has 270 days from the date it receives the NOC to issue a proposed, interim final or direct final non-5(e) SNUR.

7.6.8. Record-Keeping Requirements

Subpart C establishes record-keeping requirements that apply to manufacturers, importers and processors. The provisions of subpart C apply only when referenced in a

SNUR for specific uses of a specific substance. When promulgating a SNUR, the Agency will specify the appropriate record-keeping requirements from among those listed in section 721.125 of subpart C.

Under section 721.125, manufacturers, importers and processors may be required to keep for five years from the date of their creation any of the following records:

- records documenting dates and volume of manufacture and import of the substance;
- records documenting volumes of the substance purchased in the United States by processors, dates of purchase, and names and addresses of suppliers;
- records documenting the names and addresses of all persons outside the site of manufacture, importation or processing to whom the manufacturer, importer or processor directly sells or transfers the substance, transfer dates, and quantities transferred on each date;
- records documenting establishment and implementation of a program for the use of any applicable personal protective equipment required under section 721.63, or the hazard communication program required under section 721.72;
- records documenting the determination required by section 721.63(a)(3) that the chemical protective clothing is impervious to the substance;
- copies of labels and MSDSs required by section 721.72;
- records documenting compliance with any applicable industrial, commercial, and consumer use limitations;
- records documenting compliance with any applicable disposal requirements; and
- records documenting establishment and implementation of procedures that ensure compliance with any applicable water discharge limitation.

7.6.9. Procedures for Limitation or Revocation of Expedited SNURs

Using the expedited procedures in subpart D, any affected person may request modification or revocation of any SNUR requirements that were added to subpart E by writing to the Director of OPPT and stating the basis for the request. All such letters should be sent to:

> Office of Pollution Prevention and Toxics
> Document Control Office (7407M)
> U.S. Environmental Protection Agency
> 1200 Pennsylvania Avenue N.W.
> Washington, D.C. 20460
>
> ATT'N: Request to amend significant new use rule.

The request must be accompanied by information sufficient to support the request. EPA may modify or revoke an expedited SNUR on the Agency's own initiative or in response to a written request if the Agency finds:

- test data or other information provide a reasonable basis for concluding that activities designated as significant new uses will not present an unreasonable risk;
- EPA has promulgated a rule under TSCA § 4 or 6, or EPA or another agency has taken action under another law that eliminates the need for the SNUR;
- EPA has received SNUNs for some or all of the activities designated as significant new uses, reviewed those SNUNs, and concluded that there is no need for additional SNUNs;
- EPA has examined new information or re-examined test data or other information and concluded that the substance does not meet the concern criteria in section 721.170(b), or that a rational basis no longer exists for a finding that the substances may present an unreasonable risk;
- for a substance added to subpart E by the procedures in section 721.160, certain activities involving the substance were designated significant new uses pending the completion of testing, and adequate test data have been submitted to EPA.

40 C.F.R. § 721.185.

FIGURE VII-1
CATEGORIES OF CHEMICALS LIKELY TO BE SUBJECT TO A SECTION 5(E) ORDER

(The effects of concern to EPA are in parentheses.)

1. Acid Chlorides
(environmental toxicity/fate)
2. Acid and Amphoteric Dyes
(environmental toxicity/fate)
3. Acrylamides
(oncogenicity, neurotoxicity, heritable mutations, reproductive/ developmental/environmental toxicity/fate)
4. Acrylates/Methacrylates
(oncogenicity)
5. Aldehydes
6. Aliphatic Amines
(environmental toxicity)
7. Alkoxysilanes
(chronic lung toxicity, environmental toxicity/fate)
8. Aluminum Compounds
9. Aminobenzothiazole Azo Dyes
(oncogenicity/mutagenicity, liver, thyroid, environmental toxicity/fate)
10. Anhydrides, Carboxylic Acid
(lung toxicity, developmental toxicity)
11. Anilines
(environmental toxicity/fate)
12. Anionic Surfactants
(environmental toxicity)
13. Azides
14. Benzotriazoles
(environmental toxicity/fate)
15. Benzotriazole-hindered phenols
(systemic, reproductive, environmental toxicity)
16. Boron Compounds
17. Cationic Dyes
(environmental toxicity)
18. Cationic (Quaternary Ammonium) Surfactants
(environmental toxicity/fate)
19. Cobalt
20. Dianilines
(oncogenicity/mutagenicity, retinopathy, systemic, reproductive toxicity)
21. Diazoniums
(environmental toxicity)
22. Dichlorobenzidine-based Pigments
(oncogenicity mutagenicity, environmental toxicity)
23. Diisocyanates
24. Dithiocarbamates
(environmental toxicity)
25. Epoxides
(oncogenicity, reproductive, toxicity (male), environmental toxicity)
26. Esters
(environmental toxicity)

27. Ethylene Glycol Ethers
(chronic toxicity, developmental toxicity)
28. Hindered Amines
(systemic toxicity, reproductive toxicity (male))
29. Hydrazines and Related Compounds
(oncogenicity, chronic toxicity, environmental toxicity/fate)
30. Imides
(environmental toxicity)
31. Lanthanides or Rare Earth Metals
32. β-Naphthylamines, sulfonated
(oncogenicity)
33. Neutral Organics
(environmental toxicity/fate)
34. Nickel Compounds
(environmental toxicity)
35. Nonionic Surfactants
(environmental toxicity)
36. Organotins
37. PBT Chemicals
38. Peroxides
(oncogenicity, environmental toxicity)
39. Phenolphthaleins
40. Phenols
(environmental toxicity)
41. Phosphates, Inorganic
42. Phosphinate Esters
43. Polyanionic Polymers (& Monomers)
(environmental toxicity)
44. Polycationic Polymers
(environmental toxicity/fate)
45. Polynitroaromatics
(environmental toxicity/fate)
46. Respirable, Poorly Soluable Particulates
47. Rosin
(environmental toxicity)
48. Stilbene, derivatives of 4,4-bis (triazin-2-ylamino)-(Tinopal®)
(reproductive/developmental toxicity)
49. Substituted Triazines
(environmental toxicity)
50. Thiols
51. Triarylmethane pigments/dyes with non-solubilizing groups
(oncogenicity/mutagenicity, reproductive developmental toxicity, environmental toxicity)
52. Vinyl Esters
(oncogenicity, neurogenicity, reproductive toxicity, environmental toxicity)
53. Vinyl Sulfones
(mutagenicity/oncogenicity, environmental toxicity)
54. Soluble complexes of Zinc (excluding Zn^{++})
(environmental toxicity)
55. Zirconium Compounds
(environmental toxicity)

FIGURE VII-2
CRITERIA TRIGGERING TSCA § 5(E) EXPOSURE-BASED CONSENT ORDERS

1. Substantial Production Volumes

All non-polymer PMN chemicals (as specified at 40 C.F.R. section 723.250) with estimated production volumes greater than or equal to 100,000 kilograms per year.

2. Significant or Substantial Human Exposure

Workers	
• high number of workers exposed	≥ 1,000 workers
• acute worker inhalation	≥ 100 workers exposed by inhalation to ≥ 10 mg/day
• chronic worker exposure	
inhalation	≥ 100 workers exposed to 1-10 mg/day for ≥ 100 days/year
dermal	≥ 250 workers exposed by routine dermal contact for ≥ 100 days/year
Consumers	Presence of the chemical in any consumer product where (1) the physical state of the chemical in the product and (2) the manner of use would make exposures likely.
Ambient/General Population	
• ambient drinking water exposure	≥ 70 mg/year exposure via drinking water
• ambient air exposure	≥ 70 mg/year exposure via air
• ambient groundwater exposure	≥ 70 mg/year exposure via groundwater
• aggregate ambient exposure over all media	≥ 10,000 kg/year release to environmental media

3. Substantial Environmental Release

Surface Water	≥ 1,000 kg/year total release to surface water calculated after wastewater treatment

FIGURE VII-3
RECOMMENDED TSCA § 5(E)
EXPOSURE-BASED POLICY: TESTING*

Health Testing

For those PMN substances that meet human exposure criteria and warrant testing as determined by EPA, chemical manufacturers may be asked to perform some or all of the following health "core" tests on the PMN substance:

1) Bacterial reverse mutation (formerly "Ames") test (OPPTS 870.5100/OECD 471)

2) Mammalian erythrocyte micronucleus (intraperitoneal route) (OPPTS 870.5395/OECD 474)

3) Repeated dose 28-day oral toxicity in rodents (OPPTS 870.3050 or OECD 407)

4) Acute oral toxicity (OPPTS 870.1100/OECD 401, or OECD 425 ["Acute Oral Toxicity: Up-and-Down Procedure"])

Environmental Toxicity Testing

For those PMN substances that meet the substantial environmental release criterion and warrant testing as determined by EPA, chemical manufacturers may be asked to perform some or all of the following environmental "core" tests on the PMN substance if the chemical is expected to be acutely toxic:

1) Algal toxicity (OPPTS 850.5400/OECD 201 ("Alga, Growth Inhibition Test"))

2) Aquatic invertebrate acute toxicity, freshwater daphnids (OPPTS 850.1010/OECD 202 ("Daphnia sp. Acute Immobilisation Test and Reproduction Test"))

3) Fish acute toxicity (OPPTS 850.1075/OECD 203)

If the chemical is expected to be chronically toxic, then chronic toxicity tests of aquatic organisms will be recommended.

FIGURE VII-3 (continued)

Environmental Fate Testing

For those PMN substances that meet the drinking water, ground water, total release to environment media, or total release to surface water exposure-based policy criteria and warrant testing as determined by EPA, chemical manufacturers may be asked to perform some or all of the following environmental fate testing, depending upon predicted solubility and which of the above criteria are met.

1) Water solubility - OPPTS 830.7840 or 835.7860; OECD 105

2) Fate in wastewater treatment - Porous Pot test (OPPTS 835.3220); or Semi-Continuous Activated Sludge test (OPPTS 835.3210; OECD 302A); or Modified Zahn-Wellens/EMPA test (OPPTS 835.3200; OECD 302B); or Activated Sludge Sorption Isotherm test (OPPTS 835.1110)

3) Aerobic biodegradation - Ready Biodegradability test (OPPTS 835.3110; OECD 301A-F); or Sealed Vessel CO2 Production test (OPPTS 835.3120)

4) Anaerobic biodegradation - Anaerobic Biodegradability of Organic Chemicals (OPPTS 835.3400)

5) Soil biodegradation - OPPTS 835.3300; OECD 304A

6) Photolysis (photodegradation) - OPPTS 835.2210

7) Hydrolysis as a function of pH (stability in water) - OPPTS 835.2110 or 835.2130, or OECD 111

*This information is available at the EPA TSCA 5(e) Exposure-Based Policy: Testing website at: http://www.epa.gov/opptintr/newchems/expbasedtesting.htm.

FIGURE VII-4

EPA'S SCHEDULE TO DEVELOP NON-EXPEDITED SECTION 5(E) CONSENT ORDERS

This schedule assumes no new issues for development of the consent order.

ACTION	TIME PERIOD ALLOWED (in work days)
• EPA § 5(e) regulatory decision and telephone notification	
• EPA sends Action Letter to submitter	7 days
• Submitter decision to negotiate order	Approx. 20 days (depending on time needed by submitter
• EPA internal § 5(e) draft to work group	15 days
• Work group comments	10 days
• First draft to submitter	7 days
• Comments from submitter	Approx. 20 days (depending on time needed by submitter)
• Second draft and accompanying paperwork finalized by EPA	5 days
• Chemical Control Division Director concurrence	5 days
• Transmittal/Office of General Counsel (only in "non-routine" cases)	7 days
• Letter and final order to submitter for signature	5 days
• Final signed copies received from submitter	15 days (depending on time needed by submitter)
• Chemical Control Division Director signature	4 days
TOTAL	120 work days (approx.)

CHAPTER 8
BIOTECHNOLOGY

EPA maintains that TSCA's broad definition of "chemical substance" gives it authority to regulate microorganisms. *See* 62 Fed. Reg. 17,909, 17,913.[24] EPA first asserted this authority in its 1984 statement, "Proposed Policy Regarding Certain Microbial Products," part of the "Proposal for a Coordinated Framework for Regulation of Biotechnology" published by the Executive Office of the President, Office of Science and Technology Policy (OSTP). 49 Fed. Reg. 50,886 (Dec. 31, 1984). In 1986, OSTP published the final federal "Coordinated Framework for Regulation of Biotechnology," 51 Fed. Reg. 23,302 (June 26, 1986). At the same time, EPA published its final policy statement, which established the TSCA reporting requirements for genetically engineered microorganisms. 51 Fed. Reg. 23,313 (June 26, 1986). Under the 1986 Policy Statement, EPA required section 5 PMN filing for "new" microorganisms and section 8(e) substantial risk reporting for all microorganisms, and requested voluntary compliance with other section 8 reporting requirements.

In 1988, EPA drafted a proposed biotechnology rule to implement the 1986 Policy Statement, but the White House Office of Management and Budget (OMB) returned it to EPA for reconsideration. EPA did not publish this proposed rule in the *Federal Register*, but over the next six years EPA solicited comments on the proposal from OMB, other government agencies, industry, academia, and public interest groups. Then on September 1, 1994, 59 Fed. Reg. 45,526, EPA published a proposed biotechnology rule and on April 11, 1997 promulgated its final rule, 62 Fed. Reg. 17,909, codified primarily at 40 C.F.R. part 725. EPA established a new part 725, because it believed the specific characteristics of new microorganisms justified consolidating all requirements and procedures applicable to them. The 1997 Biotechnology Rule supercedes the 1986 Policy Statement.

The 1997 Biotechnology Rule requires a Microbial Commercial Activity Notice (MCAN) for new microorganisms, and a TSCA experimental release application (TERA) for research and development (R&D) activities releasing a new microorganism into the environment. The rule also established a two-tiered exemption from the MCAN requirement for microorganisms meeting specified criteria.

Several agencies other than EPA regulate biotechnology products, and some products subject to potential TSCA regulation may also be subject to regulation under other statutes. EPA regulates biotechnology products under both the Federal

---

24 Section 3(2) defines "chemical substance" as "any organic or inorganic substance of a particular molecular identity, including (i) any combination of such substances resulting in whole or in part from a chemical reaction or occurring in nature. . . ."

Insecticide, Fungicide, and Rodenticide Act (FIFRA) and TSCA, the Food and Drug Administration (FDA) under the Federal Food, Drug, and Cosmetic Act (FFDCA), the United States Department of Agriculture (USDA) under the Federal Plant Pest Act and the Plant Quarantine Act, and the Department of Labor under the Occupational Safety and Health Act (OSHA).

8.1. 1986 FRAMEWORK FOR REGULATION OF BIOTECHNOLOGY

On June 26, 1986, OSTP published the Coordinated Framework for Regulation of Biotechnology. 51 Fed. Reg. 23,302. EPA, FDA, USDA, OSHA and the National Institutes of Health (NIH) also published agency-specific policy statements. EPA's 1986 Policy Statement served as the Agency's policy until when it was superceded by the Biotechnology Rule. Because the 1986 Policy Statement laid the predicate for the 1997 Biotechnology Rule, it is discussed briefly below.

8.1.1. Microorganisms as Chemical Substances

In its 1986 Policy Statement, EPA stated:

> Microorganisms and their DNA molecules are "chemical substances" under section 3 of TSCA, and thus are subject to all the provisions of TSCA, except to the extent they are manufactured, processed, or distributed in commerce for use as pesticides, foods, food additives, drugs, cosmetics, and medical devices.

51 Fed. Reg. at 23,324. Under its TSCA policy, EPA considered a living organism to be a "combination of such [chemical] substances occurring in whole or in part as a result of a chemical reaction or occurring in nature." As such, the microorganism falls within the definition of "chemical substance" at TSCA § 3(2)(A) as "an organic substance of a particular molecular identity." 49 Fed. Reg. at 50,886. The 1997 Biotechnology Policy continued this treatment.

Substantial controversy surrounded EPA's assertion of TSCA jurisdiction over microorganisms. Even through TSCA was originally intended to fill existing gaps in environmental laws for industrial chemicals and did not directly address biotechnology products, EPA justified its position by noting that Congress intended TSCA to "provide authority over substances not covered by other health and environmental laws." *Id.* at 50,887. Despite the initial controversy, EPA asserts unchallenged TSCA authority over genetically altered microorganisms.

8.1.2. PMN Reporting

Under the 1986 Policy Statement, EPA required PMNs for all "new" microorganisms. EPA defined new microorganisms as intergeneric combinations of genetic material, *i.e.*, new organisms created by combining genetic material from at least two different genera of microorganisms. EPA excluded inter-generic combinations in which the genetic material added to the recipient microorganism consisted only of well-characterized, non-coding regulatory regions, explaining that the resulting organisms do not possess new combinations of traits but, rather, exhibit only quantitative changes in preexisting traits. 51 Fed. Reg. 23,313, 23,317 (June 26, 1986). EPA defined a coding regulatory region as a segment of genetic material that controls the activities of other regions that produce protein peptide molecules or acts as a site for the initiation of nucleic acid or protein synthesis, and included operators, promoters, origins of replication, terminators and ribosome-binding regions. 51 Fed. Reg. at 23,332.

EPA did not consider an organism as "new" even if it had been altered so long as it was not the product of intergeneric transfers, and therefor did not subject it to PMN requirements. Examples of these "altered" microorganisms include intraspecific microorganisms formed by deliberate combinations of genetic material from the same species, deletion products and mutations. Intrageneric organisms and organisms resulting from transfers of well-characterized, non-coding regulatory regions were exempted from PMN requirements because EPA concluded that they posed a lower level of uncertainty and risk than intergeneric microorganisms. *Id.* at 23,325-26. The 1997 Biotechnology Rule continued this treatment.

Naturally occurring microorganisms are not subject to reporting for the TSCA Inventory. EPA concluded that "[n]aturally occurring substances and substances derived from nature with limited human intervention" are implicitly included in the TSCA Inventory. *Id.* at 23,325. Therefore, EPA did not consider them new chemical substances. The 1997 Biotechnology Rule also continued this treatment.

8.1.3. Substantial Risk Information/TSCA § 8(e) Reporting

The 1986 Policy Statement made clear that biotechnology products, including those undergoing R&D or involving contained uses, were subject to TSCA § 8(e). EPA required manufacturers, processors and distributors of these substances to notify EPA immediately of any information which reasonably supported the conclusion that the microorganism presented a substantial risk to human health or the environment. EPA considered the following information to be reportable under section 8(e): "(1) pathogenicity to humans, plants, animals, or microbes; (2) significant ability to displace other organisms in the intended use area; (3) significant potential to transfer genetic material to other organisms; and (4) any other significant potential to cause harm to human health or the environment." 51 Fed. Reg. at 23,331. EPA's response to the public comments to the 1997 Biotechnology Rule make clear that this requirement remains in effect.

8.2. THE 1997 BIOTECHNOLOGY RULE

After EPA published the 1986 Policy Statement, EPA sought to issue regulations for commercialized, genetically engineered microorganisms. On September 1, 1994, EPA published a proposed rule, 59 Fed. Reg. 45,526, and then promulgated a final biotechnology rule on April 11, 1997. 62 Fed. Reg. 17,909. The 1997 Biotechnology Rule became effective on June 10, 1997, is codified primarily at 40 C.F.R. part 725, and supercedes the 1986 Policy Statement. Part 725 establishes all reporting requirements under TSCA § 5 for manufacturers, importers, and processors of new microorganisms for commercial purposes, including R&D. When EPA released the 1997 Biotechnology Rule, Administrator Browner stated, "Today's action achieves the Clinton Administration's objective to protect public health and the environment, while protecting flexibility for the development of our nation's emerging biotechnology industry." EPA Press Release, "EPA Issues New Notification and Screening Requirements for Biotech Products" (March 27, 1997).

8.2.1. Regulated Microorganisms

The 1997 Biotechnology Rule defines "microorganism" to mean an organism in the kingdoms Monera (Procaryotae), Protista, Fungi, and the Chlorophyta and the Rhodophyta of the Plantae, as well as viruses and virus-like particles. 40 C.F.R. § 725.3. Therefore, this definition includes, but is not limited to, bacteria, protozoa, fungi, mycoplasmas, mycoplasma-like organisms, spiroplasmas, microphytoplanktons, green and red algea, viruses, and virus-like particles (*e.g.*, viroids, satellites, and virusoids).

A "new" microorganism means a microorganism not included on the TSCA Inventory. *Id.* Naturally occurring microorganisms are implicitly (even though not explicitly) listed on the TSCA Inventory (as are all naturally occurring substances). Rather, "new microorganisms" are those resulting from deliberate combinations of genetic material from organisms in different genera ("intergeneric microorganisms"). As with the 1986 Policy Statement, genetically modified microorganisms are not "new" unless they are intergeneric microorganisms. Further, microorganisms resulting from the addition of well-characterized, intergeneric material containing only non-coding regulatory regions such as operators, promoters, origins of replication, terminators, and ribosome-binding regions are not new. *Id.*, *see also* 40 C.F.R. § 725.8.

Some microorganisms are not subject to the 1997 Biotechnology Rule either because they are not subject to TSCA jurisdiction or are not subject to TSCA § 5 reporting. 40 C.F.R. § 725.8. These include: (1) any microorganism excluded from the definition of "chemical substance" in TSCA § 3 and 40 C.F.R. section 720.3(e);[25] (2) any "microbial mixture," defined in section 725.3 as "any combination of microorganisms or microorganisms and other chemical substances, if the combination does not occur in nature and is not an article (note that this exclusion does not extend

---

[25] When publishing its 1997 Biotechnology Rule, EPA reiterated that TSCA's definition of "chemical substance" excludes pesticides, tobacco and tobacco products, food, food additives, drugs (including human drugs, animal drugs, and animal biologics), cosmetics, and substances that are used as medical devices. 62 Fed. Reg. 17,921-17,922.

to the microorganisms and other chemical substances which are part of the microbial mixture); and (3) any microorganism manufactured and processed solely for export if labeled in accordance with TSCA § 12(a)(1)(B) when distributed in commerce, and the manufacturer and processor can document that the person to whom the microorganism will be distributed intends to export it or process it solely for export.

EPA uses the following terms to describe microorganisms and their roles in developing a reportable microorganism:

1. A "subject microorganism" is the subject of the microbial submission.

2. The "recipient microorganism" is the strain into which the intergeneric DNA is introduced and which generally determines the taxonomic designation of the subject microorganism.

3. "Donor microorganisms" are those which contribute DNA to the subject microorganism, or those which contribute DNA to intermediate microorganisms used to construct the subject microorganism.

4. "Intermediate microorganisms" do not contribute DNA, but may be used to temporarily contain a vector used to construct the subject microorganism, to aid in a triparental mating, etc.

5. "Final construct" describes the DNA sequences contributed by the donor microorganisms, and where applicable, the recipient's DNA sequences immediately flanking the inserted donor microorganisms' DNA. The construct includes structural genes (usually genes which encode an enzyme that is of commercial importance), vector DNA, and marker genes (such as antibiotic resistance). Information on the final construct should focus on the intergeneric DNA, and intrageneric DNA that affects the expression, stability, and mobility of the intergeneric DNA.

U.S. Environmental Protection Agency, Office of Pollution Prevention and Toxics, *Points to Consider in the Preparation of TSCA Biotechnology Submissions for Microorganisms* at 17-18 (June 2, 1997).

8.2.2. Prenotice Consultations and *Bona Fide* Submissions

EPA encourages persons, who are considering reporting microorganism activity or who are unsure whether TSCA applies to their microorganisms, to consult with EPA before preparing any submission. Early discussion with EPA may help to identify data requests and preliminary concerns associated with the specific microorganism, and may result in guidance tailored to the submitter's microorganism. Meetings and written communications during this stage may be claimed confidential. *See* U.S.

Environmental Protection Agency, Office of Pollution Prevention and Toxics, *Points to Consider in the Preparation of TSCA Biotechnology Submissions for Microorganisms* at 7 (June 2, 1997).

Companies planning to manufacture, import, or process intergeneric microorganisms for commercial purposes may also submit to EPA a *bona fide* notice to determine their reporting obligations. This process is available because confidential identities and uses are not listed on the public version of the TSCA Inventory. If a company's microorganism is listed on the confidential version of the Inventory and is not subject to a Significant New Use Rule (SNUR), then no section 5 submission would be required. The review process for a *bona fide* notice generally takes 30 days after EPA receives the notice. 40 C.F.R. § 725.15.

8.2.3. Premanufacture Review of Microorganisms Intended for General Commercial Use

8.2.3.1. MCAN Submission

TSCA § 5 applies only to microorganisms manufactured, imported, or processed for commercial purposes. EPA defined manufacture, import, or process for commercial purposes as "manufacture or process for purposes of obtaining an immediate or eventual commercial advantage." 40 C.F.R. §725.3. Whether an activity has an immediate or eventual commercial advantage is determined by indicia of commercial intent.

For new commercial microorganisms, any manufacturer, importer, or processor must file a MCAN with EPA, unless the activity is eligible for a specific exemption. 40 C.F.R. § 725.105. Further, a MCAN is required under section 725.105(c) for any person who intends to manufacture, import, or process for commercial purposes, a microorganism identified at 40 C.F.R. section 725, subpart M as having one or more significant new uses; and who intends to engage in a designated significant new use of the microorganism or intends to distribute it in commerce.

The purpose of a MCAN is to provide EPA the information necessary to identify and list a microorganism on the TSCA Inventory and to determine whether the microrganism may present an unreasonable risk of injury to human health or the environment. The MCAN must be submitted at least 90 days before commercial manufacture import or processing of a new microorganism, or before the manufacture, import, or processing of an existing microorganism for a significant new use. *Id.* at 45,571 (codified at 40 C.F.R. § 725.150). EPA does not require use of a specific MCAN form, but requires the following information to enable accurate and unambiguous identification:

1. submitter identification;
2. microorganism identity;
    a) description of recipient and new microorganism;

b) genetic construction of new microorganism (including the pertinent and distinguishing genotypic characteristics of a microorganism, such as the identity of the introduced genetic material and the methods used to construct the microorganism. This also may include information on the vector construct, the cellular location, and the number of copies of the introduced genetic material);

c) phenotypic and ecological characteristics (traits resulting from the interaction of a microorganism's genotype and the environment, and which may include intentionally added biochemical and physiological traits);

3. byproducts;
4. total production volume;
5. use; and
6. worker exposure and environmental release.

See 40 C.F.R. § 725.155. Information to the extent known to or reasonably ascertainable by the submitter must be provided. Information on human or ecological exposure solely outside the United States, however, is not required. *Id.*

Each MCAN also must contain all test data in the submitter's possession or control related to the new microorganism or any microbial mixture or article containing the new microorganism and its effects on health or the environment. This includes test data concerning the new microorganism in a pure culture or formulated form as used or as intended. A full report or standard literature citation must be submitted for the following test data:

(i) health effects data;

(ii) ecological effects data;

(iii) physical and chemical properties data;

(iv) environmental fate characteristics; and

(v) monitoring data and other test data related to human exposure or environmental release.

If the data do not appear in the open scientific literature the submitter must provide a full report, including experimental methods and materials, results, discussion and data analysis, conclusions, references, and the name and address of the laboratory that developed the data.

Each person should also submit, in writing, all other information known to or reasonably ascertainable by that person that would permit EPA to make a reasoned evaluation of health and environmental effects.

8.2.3.2. General Commercial Exemptions

EPA has created exceptions to the MCAN requirement where it can otherwise find that the microorganism does not present an unreasonable risk to human health or the environment. These exemptions for microorganisms differ from those available for traditional chemicals. For example, microorganisms are not eligible for the low volume exemption (LVE), but are entitled to the test marketing exemption (TME). 40 C.F.R. pt. 725, subpt. F.

8.2.3.2.1. Test Marketing Exemption

Test marketing activities usually involve limited sale or distribution of a substance within a limited period of time to determine its competitive value when its market is uncertain.

EPA strongly suggests that an applicant contact EPA for a prenotice consultation regarding TME eligibility. A TME application is due at least 45 calendar days before the applicant intends to start test marketing. The TME application must contain submitter identification and microorganism identity; phenotypic and ecological characteristics; quantity and exposure data; a description of the test marketing activity, including its duration and how it can be distinguished from full-scale commercial production and research and development; and health and environmental effects data. The application must provide EPA sufficient information to permit a reasoned evaluation of the health and environmental effects of the planned test marketing activity. No later than 45 days after EPA receives a TME application, the Agency will either approve or deny it. Test marketing activities may begin only after receipt of EPA approval. In approving a TME application, EPA may impose any restrictions necessary to ensure that the activity will not present an unreasonable risk of injury to health and the environment. 40 C.F.R. pt. 725, subpt. F.

In general, EPA suggests that manufacturers who intend to test market a new microorganism file a MCAN rather than request a TME. There may be situations, however, in which a TME is appropriate, such as for microorganisms that EPA reviewed at the R&D stage. *See* 40 C.F.R. § 725.94; *see also Points to Consider in the Preparation of TSCA Biotechnology Submissions for Microorganisms*, Office of Pollution Prevention and Toxics, U.S. Environmental Protection Agency, June 2, 1997, at page 11.

8.2.3.2.2. Tier I and Tier II Exemptions

EPA also established two tiered exemptions for specific recipient microorganisms. The following recipient microorganisms are eligible for either exemption:

(i) Acetobacter aceti;

(ii) Aspergillus niger;

(iii) Aspergillus oryzae;

(iv) Bacillus licheniformis;

(v) Bacillus subtilis;

(vi) Clostridium acetobutylicum;

(vii) Escherichia coli K-12;

(viii) Penicillium roqueforti;

(ix) Saccharomyces cerevisiae; and

(x) Saccharomyces uvarum.

The Tier I exemption is a complete exemption from the MCAN requirement. To qualify for the Tier I exemption, the recipient microorganism must be one of the ten species listed above and the introduced genetic material must be limited in size, of known function and associated nucleotide sequences, poorly mobilizable, and free of certain nucleotide sequences that encode toxins. 40 C.F.R. §§ 725.420, 725.421. In addition, the use site must meet certain containment and control standards. 40 C.F.R. § 725.422.

To obtain a Tier I exemption, a manufacturer must submit a certification to EPA at least ten days before commercial manufacture stating that the microorganism meets the Tier I exemption criteria and maintain documentation that the manufacturer meets the exemption conditions. EPA need not receive notice of subsequent use of the recipient microorganism as long as the manufacturer continues to comply with all of the Tier I exemption conditions. 40 C.F.R. § 725.424.

The Tier II exemption provides for expedited EPA review and approval or denial of microorganisms meeting the Tier I requirements except for containment and control. 40 C.F.R. § 725.428. The Tier II exemption application must be submitted 45 days before commencing manufacture or import. 40 C.F.R. § 725.450. EPA strongly suggests that for a Tier II exemption the submitter contact the Agency for a prenotice consultation regarding eligibility for the exemption. *Id.*

When seeking an exemption from a MCAN requirement, a Letter of Application should provide EPA sufficient information showing the exempted activities will not present an unreasonable risk of injury to health or the environment. This information should include:

(i) effects on health and the environment;

(ii) magnitude of human and environmental exposure;

(iii) benefits of the new microorganism and the availability of substitutes; and

(iv) the reasonably ascertainable economic consequences of granting or denying the exemption, including effects on the national economy, small business, and technological innovation.

After considering the application and any other available relevant information, EPA makes a preliminary determination that the new microorganism will not present an unreasonable risk of injury to health or the environment. EPA will then propose a rule to grant the exemption. If EPA decides that it cannot make this preliminary determination then EPA will deny the application and provide the applicant EPA's reasons in writing.

8.2.3.2.3. MCAN Submission Statement

Each person subject to the notification requirements must complete, sign, and submit a MCAN or exemption request. MCANs must contain the following statement, signed and dated by an authorized official:

> I certify that to the best of my knowledge and belief: The company named in this submission intends to manufacture, import, or process for a commercial purpose, other than in small quantities solely for research and development, the microorganism identified in this submission. All information provided in this submission is complete and truthful as of the date of submission. I am including with this submission all test data in my possession or control and a description of all other data known to or reasonably ascertainable by me as required by 40 CFR 725.160 or 725.260.

40 C.F.R. § 725.25. For Tier I exemption certifications and Tier II exemption applications, the last sentence of this certification statement is not required. 40 C.F.R. §§ 725.424 and 725.455.

8.2.3.2.4. EPA Review of MCAN Submissions

Upon receipt, EPA reviews the MCAN to determine whether the intended activity may present an unreasonable risk to health or the environment. EPA may reach one of three decisions, based on a balancing of the risks and benefits presented by the microorganism: (1) the available information does not indicate that the risks are unreasonable; (2) information is insufficient to determine that the risks are unreasonable; or (3) information is insufficient to make a reasoned evaluation of risk, and the substance may present an unreasonable risk or the microorganism will be produced in substantial quantities, and the microorganism may reasonably be anticipated to enter the environment, or there may be significant or substantial human or environmental exposure to the microorganism. EPA encourages prenotice consultation and keeps a public docket for each section 5 notice, in part to eliminate any surprise by its decisions.

The MCAN review period is 90 days, which EPA may extend for an additional 90 days for "good cause." 40 C.F.R. § 725.56. "Good cause" includes:

(i) EPA has reviewed the submission and seeks more information;

(ii) EPA has received significant additional information during the review period;

(iii) The submitter has failed to correct a submission; and

(iv) EPA has determined that there is a significant possibility that the microorganism will be regulated under TSCA § 5(e) or § 5(f), but cannot initiate regulatory action within the initial 90 days.

On review, EPA may issue a section 5(e) consent order if the product presents an unreasonable risk of injury to health or the environment or that the microorganism may enter the environment in substantial quantities and cause significant human or environmental exposure to the microorganism, and the submitted information is insufficient to reasonably evaluate the risk. EPA may restrict manufacture, processing or use; require recordkeeping and reporting; and, if necessary, ban commercialization of the microorganism. To reduce uncertainty about microorganism behavior, such as survival and dissemination, EPA may use its 5(e) authority to negotiate consent orders to allow limited field tests. This can enable the submitter to proceed with product development while providing EPA with data that reduces uncertainty.

Manufacture or import of the microorganism may not commence until the review period, including all extensions and suspensions, has expired. If the review period expires without notice from EPA, the MCAN submitter may commence commercial manufacture or import. 40 C.F.R. § 725.170.

Following review, companies must submit to EPA a notice of commencement of manufacture or import (NOC) form. The NOC must contain the specific microorganism identity, MCAN number, and the date when manufacture or import commences. The timing of the NOC for microorganisms is the same as for traditional chemicals; that is, the manufacture must submit the NOC within 30 days of commencing manufacture or import of the new microorganism. 40 C.F.R. § 725.190.

Upon receiving the NOC, EPA will add a new microorganism to the TSCA Inventory. EPA identifies and lists microorganisms on the TSCA Inventory by a taxonomic designation and a consistent set of supplemental information on phenotypic and genotypic traits necessary to identify the microorganism as precisely as possible. 40 C.F.R. § 725.12. If the submitter claimed the microorganism identity as confidential in the MCAN, the submitter must reassert and substantiate the claim in the NOC. Otherwise, EPA will list the specific microorganism identity on the public Inventory.

8.2.4. Research and Development

EPA has established exemptions from full MCAN reporting for R&D activity. EPA's requirements for R&D reporting depends upon several factors, such as whether the R&D will take place in a contained structure, whether it will be supervised by another federal agency, and whether EPA already has determined that the microorganism in question poses no unreasonable risk of injury to human health or the environment. 40 C.F.R. pt. 725, subpt. E. These requirements are discussed below.

Some biotechnology R&D activity may not be subject to TSCA. Researchers considering their obligations under TSCA § 5 must first determine whether the microorganism's use or potential use is specifically excluded. TSCA specifically excludes from its jurisdiction substances used to produce foods, drugs, cosmetics and medical devices. *See* §§ 8.1.1 and 8.2.1, supra. Researchers, however, who intend to develop a product with multiple uses, who are unsure of their product's final use or potential use, or who intend to develop a product which could be subject to either FIFRA or TSCA, must consider whether TSCA applies. *See* 62 Fed. Reg. 17,909, 17921-22. Unlike R&D on typical pesticide chemicals, EPA asserts FIFRA jurisdiction over biotechnology pesticides at the R&D stage. *See* 40 C.F.R. § 172.3(a).

Next, because TSCA § 5(i) states that only manufacturing, importing, and processing for "commercial purposes" are subject to TSCA § 5, researchers must determine whether their research is for commercial purposes. If not, section 5 does not apply. *See* 40 C.F.R. § 725.205(b). All research by a commercial entity, however, is considered to be for commercial purposes. *See The Dow Chemical Company v. EPA*, 605 F.2d 673 (3d Cir. 1979). Consequently, if a business directly funds research for potential product development then the research is considered to be for commercial purposes, even if an academic institution conducts it.

Researchers not at a commercial entity should consider whether any funding comes directly from a commercial source. 40 C.F.R. § 725.205(b)(1). Any direct industry involvement in or direct funding of an activity at a noncommercial institution is for commercial purposes. This includes using company funds wholly or partially to develop the microorganisms or using a company-provided microorganism in the research. Moreover, if any research is funded by contract, joint venture, or another financial arrangement to eventually produce a commercial product, the research is for commercial purposes. For example, EPA considers as commercial any R&D laboratory work or field tests conducted under a research contract between a company and a university or a researcher if the company holds patent rights or trade secrets in the work.

If researchers do not fall under section 725.205(b)(1) they should next consider the potential indirect indicators of commercial intent under section 725.205(b)(2). They should consider, for example, whether the research is to develop a commercially viable improvement of a product already on the market, or whether they are seeking commercial funding or a patent.

If the R&D activity does not fall under section 725.205(b)(1) or (b)(2) the activity may be considered noncommercial. For example, an outright gift of funds from a company to a university or a researcher without the company directing or controlling the research or use of its results is not direct funding under section 725.205(b)(1). Research conducted using such a gift would be considered noncommercial R&D, assuming the researcher also does not believe the microorganism has the potential to be developed as a commercial product in the future and does not intend to obtain an immediate or eventual commercial advantage as described under section 725.205(b)(2). Therefore, laboratory work or field tests or other environmental testing using funds from an outright gift from a company to the university with no strings attached would be considered noncommercial R&D.

If funding does not come from a commercial source then the researcher must consider whether he or she intends to pursue developing the new microorganism as a commercial product in the future, should testing show potential commercial viability. For example, under section 725.205(b)(2)(iv), if the researcher has engaged in serious discussions with a company concerning marketing or commercializing the microorganism if initial research is successful, that research would be commercial R&D. *See* 62 Fed. Reg. 17,909, 17,922-23. The researcher is responsible for judging when commercial intent exists. In the initial research stage, a researcher may not see a commercial purpose. But if a researcher later determines that the microorganism has a potential commercial use which he or she intends to pursue then from that point on the researcher must comply with the 1997 Biotechnology Rule.

8.2.4.1. Research Conducted in a Contained Structure

EPA exempts R&D taking place in a "contained structure" from all reporting requirements except record-keeping, containment, and employee notice. 40 C.F.R. §§ 725.234, 725.235. The exemption focuses on containment because living microorganisms released into the environment have the potential to increase beyond the released amount. Under this contained structure exemption, R&D must be supervised by a technically qualified individual (TQI), defined at section 725.3 as a person who is:

(1) capable of understanding health and environmental risks, because of education, training, or experience;

(2) responsible for enforcing appropriate conduct of scientific experimentation, analysis, or research to minimize such risks; and

(3) responsible for the safety assessments and clearances for procuring, storing, using, and disposing of the microorganism.

The TQI must select and use appropriate containment and control measures for the microorganism. Containment and control measures must take into account the organism's ability to survive in the environment; potential routes of release in air, solids, liquids, waste materials, and in or on people or other organisms such as insects and rodents; and procedures for transfer between facilities. Another authorized individual of the R&D facility must approve the TQI's selection. 40 C.F.R. § 725.234. If the researcher decides to conduct research outside the contained setting, such as by field testing, the researcher will need to use a different exemption, such as the TERA. *See* 62 Fed. Reg. 17,909, 17,921.

8.2.4.2. Research Under Other Federal Agency Jurisdiction

EPA exempts from all reporting requirements any R&D subject to the jurisdiction of another federal agency or program requiring compliance with NIH Guidelines for Research Involving Recombinant DNA Molecules. 40 C.F.R. § 725.232. This includes all research at a university or institution adhering to the NIH Guidelines to receive federal funds, whether a federal agency funds it or not. EPA developed this exemption to avoid duplicating oversight with other federal authority. Researchers complying with the NIH Guidelines voluntarily or through vehicles such as contracts or local regulations are not eligible for this exemption, because their research lacks federal agency oversight. *See* 62 Fed. Reg. 17,909, 17,924.

8.2.4.3. Specific Microorganisms

From prior review based on PMNs that were voluntarily submitted under the 1986 Policy Statement and resultant field test data, EPA exempts R&D activities for two specifically listed microorganisms, *Bradyrhizobium japonicum* and *Rhizobium meliloti*. 40 C.F.R. § 725.239. Under this exemption, EPA restricts recipient microorganisms, introduced genetic material, and conditions of use. Field testing for these microorganisms must occur on ten or fewer terrestrial acres. Persons who intend use this exemption must submit a certification of compliance before initiating the activity. 40 C.F.R. § 725.238.

8.2.4.4. TSCA Experimental Release Application

The TSCA experimental release application (TERA) applies to R&D activities that do not qualify for the contained structure exemption and are not otherwise specifically exempted from the TERA requirement. The TERA must include submitter and microorganism identifications identical to those required in a MCAN, as well as a detailed description of the proposed R&D activity and information on monitoring, confinement, mitigation and emergency termination procedures. 40 C.F.R. § 725.255. The TERA must also contain all available data concerning actual or potential effects of the microorganism on human health or the environment in the submitter's possession and control and a describe other data known to or reasonably ascertainable by the submitter that will permit EPA to make a reasoned evaluation of the planned test. 40 C.F.R. § 725.260.

EPA must review the TERA within 60 days of receipt, but may extend this for an additional 60 days for "good cause." 40 C.F.R. § 725.270. If EPA determines that the activity does not pose an unreasonable risk of injury to human health or the environment, EPA will notify the submitter that it may proceed. *Id.* EPA may include requirements and conditions in its approval. If EPA concludes that it cannot make this determination, EPA will deny the TERA and provide its reasons for doing so in writing. *Id.*

EPA's TERA approval legally binds the submitter. The submitter must conduct the research and development activity only as the TERA describes and in accordance with any requirements and conditions that EPA prescribes. If, after approval, it is necessary to alter the activity in a manner that would result in its being different from that subject to the TERA and EPA's approval, the submitter must inform EPA and may not modify the activity without EPA's prior approval.

EPA encourages submitters to advise state and local authorities of their field test plans, although this is not a requirement. Under the 1994 proposed rule, EPA considered requiring persons who prepare TERA submissions to notify appropriate state authorities. EPA, however, did not impose this requirement in the 1997 Biotechnology Rule because under the 1986 Policy Statement, it had developed procedures to coordinate review with state and local authorities. An EPA review coordinator contacts by telephone the appropriate state agencies where the test will be conducted to inform them of the submission. If the state requests, EPA will provide a nonconfidential copy of the submission to the state contact. EPA also will provide to the state nonconfidential reports, assessments and public comments added to the Public Docket upon request. EPA considers state comments during the review process. Finally, EPA provides the state a copy of any document which addresses the field test performance conditions. Consequently, EPA felt these procedures would make researcher notification redundant. If submitters have informed State and local authorities, EPA requires submitters to so inform EPA in their submissions. *See* 62 Fed. Reg. 17,909, 17,928.

Although a manufacturer may submit a MCAN for any R&D activity, EPA expects most researchers will choose to submit a TERA. In addition to the shorter TERA review period, EPA would likely issue a TSCA § 5(e) consent order to address any uncertainties in the MCAN. This order would need to be modified each time the manufacturer wanted to vary its terms.

8.2.5. Confidential Business Information

All information, including any health and safety study and supporting documentation, enters the public file, unless the submitter claims materials to be confidential. 40 C.F.R. § 725.95. Although EPA treats confidential business information (CBI) for microorganisms similar to that for traditional chemicals, EPA developed questions unique to biotechnology products that a submitter must answer to substantiate CBI claims. *See* 40 C.F.R. § 725.94; *see also Points to Consider in the Preparation of TSCA Biotechnology Submissions for Microorganisms*, Office of Pollution Prevention and Toxics, U.S. Environmental Protection Agency, June 2, 1997, at Attachment 3, page 51. EPA requires submitters to substantiate their CBI claims for MCANs, TMEs, Tier I exemption certification statements, and Tier II exemption applications at the time of submission. Because of the uncertainty involved in R&D,

however, EPA does not require submitters to substantiate CBI claims with TERA applications. 40 C.F.R. § 725.94.

8.2.6. *Federal Register* Publication

After receiving the MCAN or exemption request, EPA publishes a notice in the *Federal Register* describing the submission. TSCA § 5(d)(2); 40 C.F.R. § 725.40 The Notice includes the identity of the new microorganism, use, the information submitted including occupational exposure, production volume, and test data, and the submitter's identity. For CBI, EPA will use a generic description. The public is generally given 30 days from the Notice to comment. When the appropriate review period for the exemption request expires, EPA publishes a notice in the *Federal Register* indicating whether EPA has approved or denied the request, and the reasons for the decision.

8.2.7. Microorganisms Subject to Significant New Use Rules

40 C.F.R. part 725, subpart L requires manufacturers, importers and processors to report significant new uses of microorganisms that EPA has described in subpart M. To date, EPA has determined only one significant new use under subpart M. That significant new use is any use other than R&D in the degradation of chemicals via injection into subsurface groundwater involving the microorganisms identified as the *Burkholderia cepacia* complex. 40 C.F.R. pt. 725, subpt. M; 68 *Federal Register* 35,320, June 13, 2003.

8.2.8. Compliance and Enforcement

EPA may conduct inspections under TSCA § 11 to assure compliance with the 1997 Biotechnology Rule, to verify that information required by EPA under the rule is true and correct, and to audit data submitted to EPA. 40 C.F.R. § 725.75.

The following actions are violations of TSCA § 15:

(i) Failure to comply with the 1997 Biotechnology Rule;

(ii) Manufacture or import before a MCAN is submitted and the MCAN review period expires;

(iii) Submitting an NOC before commencing manufacture or import;

(iv) Using a microorganism which a person knew or had reason to know was manufactured, processed, or distributed in commerce in violation of TSCA § 5 or 40 C.F.R. part 725;

(v) Failure to conduct a research and development activity as described in an approved TERA and in accordance with any requirements and conditions EPA prescribed;

(vi) Failure or refusal to establish and maintain records or to permit access to or copying of records; and

(vii) Failure or refusal to permit EPA entry or inspection as required by TSCA § 11.

40 C.F.R. § 725.70. Violators may be subject to the civil and criminal penalties in TSCA § 16 for each violation. EPA may seek to enjoin the manufacture or processing of a microorganism that violates part 725 and to seize any microorganism manufactured or processed in violation of part 725, under TSCA § 7 and section 17.

8.2.9. TSCA § 8(e) Reporting

In the 1994 proposed rule and in its response to public comments, EPA reminded persons manufacturing, importing, processing, or distributing in commerce any TSCA-covered microorganisms of their responsibility under TSCA § 8(e) to immediately report to EPA any information the person obtains which reasonably supports the conclusion that the microorganisms present a substantial risk of injury to health or the environment. EPA, however, declined to develop guidance specifically for microorganisms, citing the broad nature of section 8(e) and the diverse types of studies and other information that can be required. EPA stated that it could not provide fully explicit reporting requirements that would cover every hypothetical circumstance involving the diversity of microorganisms and uses potentially subject to TSCA. Instead, EPA's interpretive guidance for section 8(e) reporting for traditional chemicals applies to microorganisms. *See* U.S. Environmental Protection Agency, *Microbial Products of Biotechnology, Final Regulations Under the Toxic Substances Control Act: A Summary of the Public's Comments and the Agency's Reponse*, March 26, 1997, at 109-110.

8.3. OVERLAP WITH OTHER STATUTES

Because several agencies regulate biotechnology, TSCA submitters should be aware of potential conflicts or overlap in statutory requirements and authority. Of particular interest are regulations issued by the FDA, EPA and the USDA under their respective regulatory programs. The latter two are discussed below. (FDA authority is discussed in Chapter 13.) Table VIII-1, at this end of this chapter, shows the agencies most significantly involved in regulating biotechnology.

8.3.1. Interplay between TSCA and FIFRA

Interaction between TSCA and FIFRA occurs primarily along jurisdictional lines. TSCA § 3(2)(B)(ii) specifically excludes from the definition of chemical substance "any pesticide (as defined in [FIFRA]) when manufactured, processed, or distributed in commerce for use as a pesticide." FIFRA section 2(u) defines a pesticide as any substance "intended for preventing, destroying, repelling or mitigating any pest."

On the same day EPA published the proposed TSCA biotechnology rule, EPA also published a final rule under FIFRA regarding the regulation of microbial pesticides. 59 Fed. Reg. 45,600 (Sept. 1, 1994). The FIFRA final rule altered the Experimental Use Permit (EUP) regulations. Previously, these regulations provided that a substance undergoing limited field trials (no more than ten acres of land or one surface acre of water) to determine its pesticidal properties "is not considered a pesticide within the meaning of FIFRA and no experimental use permit will be required." 40 C.F.R. § 172.3(a). EPA's prior regulation would have prevented EPA from regulating the release of new microorganisms in small-scale field tests under FIFRA because these microorganisms would not yet be pesticides. Instead, TSCA would control.

In the final FIFRA rule, section 172.3 was changed to read:

> An experimental use permit (EUP) is generally required for testing of any unregistered pesticide or any registered pesticide being tested for an unregistered use. However, as described in paragraph (b) of this section, certain of such tests [*i.e.*, limited field trials of products other than genetically modified microorganisms] are presumed not to involve unreasonable adverse effects and, therefore, do not require an EUP.

40 C.F.R. § 172.3(a). Now, EPA considers substances that are subject to limited field trials may be pesticides under FIFRA even if they will not be subject to an EUP. 59 Fed. Reg. at 45,608. In this way, EPA expanded the definition of pesticide to allow it to require EUPs for small-scale field testing of microbial pesticides.

Once a new microorganism becomes a pesticide under FIFRA it is no longer subject to TSCA jurisdiction. But, implicit in the EUP regulations is that not all *pesticides* are subject to EUP requirements. It is not clear, however, whether a genetically modified organism subject to an EUP and undergoing limited laboratory or field tests is being "use[d] as a pesticide" within the meaning of TSCA § 3(2)(B)(ii). The question also remains whether candidate pesticides not yet subject to EUPs are regulated under TSCA or FIFRA. (*See* discussion in Chapter 13.)

8.3.2. Interplay between EPA under TSCA, and the USDA

When it promulgated the 1997 Biotechnology Rule, EPA stated that products also subject to another statute need only be regulated by one agency. EPA has identified the Federal Plant Pest Act (FPCA) and Plant Quarantine Act (PQA), which are administered by the Animal and Plant Health Inspection Service (APHIS) within USDA, as presenting overlapping jurisdiction. Under the FPPA and the PQA, USDA regulates genetically altered microorganisms that are plant pests. 51 Fed. Reg. 23,352 (June 25, 1986). The term plant pest means:

> Any living stage (including active and dormant forms) of insects, mites, nematodes, slugs, snails, protozoa, or other

> invertebrate animals, bacteria, fungi, other parasitic plants or reproductive parts thereof; viruses; or any organisms similar to or allied with any of the foregoing; or any infectious agents or substances, which can directly or indirectly injure or cause disease or damage in or to any plants or parts thereof, or any processed, manufactured, or other products of plants.

7 C.F.R. § 340.1.

Thus, USDA and EPA have overlapping authority over genetically manipulated microorganisms that are or are believed to be plant pests or animal pathogens. But, to date, EPA and USDA are not aware of any specific products subject to overlapping jurisdiction. EPA has stated that if it learns of such a product EPA will work with APHIS to develop a proposed exemption from TSCA § 5; and, if other cases of duplicative oversight arise, EPA will work with the implicated agencies as appropriate. *See* 62 Fed. Reg. 17,909, 17,924.

8.3.3. Interplay with International Standards

The biotechnology policy of the United Nations Environment Programme (UNEP) has also generated substantial controversy. On 29 January 2000 in Montreal, Canada, the Parties to the UNEP "Convention on Biological Diversity" (CBD) adopted the "Cartagena Protocol on Biosafety to the Convention on Biological Diversity." The Cartagena Protocol regulates the transboundary movement of genetically engineered microorganisms (called "Living Modified Organisms" or "LMOs") among Parties. The United States is not a Party to either the CBD or the Cartagena Protocol, but exports from the United States to more than 100 Parties to the Protocol, which are subject to the Protocol in that they are bound by its import provisions.

The Protocol establishes rules and procedures for the transboundary movement, transit, handling and use of LMOs. *See* Article 4. The Protocol features a set of procedures for LMOs for contained use (*e.g.*, research materials) to be intentionally introduced into the environment, and for LMOs for use as food or feed or for further processing. These procedures and requirements are meant to provide importing Parties the necessary information to accept or reject LMO imports, and for handling them in a safe manner.

Procedurally, for a shipment of an LMO for intentional introduction into the environment, either the exporting Party or the exporter must follow the "Advance Informed Agreement" (AIA) procedure which was developed to ensure that importing Parties have both the opportunity and capacity to assess the risks associated with the LMO prior to its importation. This AIA requires the exporting country to notify the importing Party by providing a detailed written description of the LMO before the first shipment. The importing Party must acknowledge receipt within 90 days. Then, within 270 days of receipt, the importing Party must: (i) approve the import; (ii) prohibit the import; (iii) request additional relevant information; or (iv) extend the 270 days by a defined period of time. The Party of import must also state its reasons, unless it gives unconditional consent (*see* Article 7, Article 8, Article 9, and Article 10).

The Cartagena Protocol espouses the "precautionary principle," which is based on the "precautionary approach" as contained in Principle 15 of the Rio Declaration on Environment and Development, United Nations Conference on Environment and Development (June, 1992). Specifically, the Protocol affirms the precautionary approach contained in Principle 15 and states that "Lack of scientific certainty due to insufficient relevant scientific information and knowledge regarding the extent of the potential adverse effects of an LMO on biodiversity, taking into account risks to human health, shall not prevent a Party of import from taking a decision, as appropriate, with regard to the import of the LMO in question, in order to avoid or minimize such potential adverse effects." Article 10.6 and 11.8. Thus, in case of insufficient scientific information, the importing Party may use precaution to make import decisions. Parties may also take into account socio-economic considerations.

Non-Parties, such as the United States, are not bound by the provisions of the Protocol. Nevertheless, the Protocol addresses the obligations of Parties for the movements of LMOs to and from non-Parties. These movements must be carried out consistently with the Protocol's objectives. In transacting with non-Parties, Parties are encouraged to: notify the non-Party before export; make information required by the Protocol available on the Biosafety Clearing-House; ensure risk assessment; apply its domestic regulatory framework consistent with the Protocol; protect confidential information, and monitor and report transboundary movements with non-Parties, including difficulties and best-practices. In turn, non-Parties are encouraged to cooperate with Parties, voluntarily comply with the Protocol, and make information available to the Biosafety Clearing-House. The Protocol also includes a provision allowing Parties to enter into bilateral, regional and multilateral agreements and arrangements with non-Parties regarding transboundary movements of LMOs, so long as they are consistent with the objectives of the Protocol.

In light of the Protocol and other internal regulations, companies receiving U.S. regulatory approval for their biotechnology products should account for the regulatory requirements of their export markets. Thus, companies interested in exporting biotechnology products should seek specialized information. The Protocol established a "Biosafety Clearing-House" as one source of such information. The Biosafety Clearing-House allows both Parties and non-Parties alike to exchange scientific, technical, environmental and legal information, and is online at http://bch.biodiv.org/. Parties have numerous obligations to post information on the Biosafety Clearing-House. Since most Parties to date are developing countries or countries with economies in transition, however, there is a lack of capacity to ensure these obligations are met. Thus, the Biosafety Clearing-House does not yet serve as an up-to-date and complete source of information.

8.4. CONCLUSION - MCAN AND TERA SUBMISSION SUMMARY

On March 16, 1998, OPPT received the first two MCANs under the 1997 biotechnology regulations. Then, on May 6, 1998 OPPT approved the first three TERAs. To date, EPA has received six MCANs and approved 11 TERAs.

Copies of the nonconfidential versions of MCANs and TERAs can be obtained through the TSCA Non-Confidential Information Center (NCIC) by phone at 202-566-0280, by fax at 202-566-0282, and by e-mail at oppt.ncic@epa.gov.

TABLE VIII-1
AGENCY AUTHORITY OVER BIOTECHNOLOGY PRODUCTS

Subject	Responsible Agency(ies)
Foods/Food Additives	FDA* FSIS[1]
Human Drugs, Medical Devices and Biologics	FDA
Animal Drugs	FDA
Animal Biologics	APHIS[2]
Other Contained Uses	EPA
Plants and Animals	APHIS* FSIS[1] FDA[3]
Pesticide Microorganisms	EPA* APHIS[2]
Other Uses (Microorganisms) Released in the Environment:	EPA* APHIS[2]
Intergeneric Organisms:	EPA* APHIS
Intrageneric Combination:	
1. Agricultural Use	APHIS[2]
2. Non-Agricultural Use	EPA

Adapted from 51 Fed. Reg. 23,304 (1986).

* Lead agency.

1 The Food Safety and Inspection Service (FSIS), under the assistant secretary of agriculture for marketing and inspection services, is responsible for food use.

2 APHIS is involved when the microorganism is a plant pest, animal pathogen or regulated article requiring a permit.

3 FDA is involved when in relation to a food use.

CHAPTER 9
TESTING UNDER TSCA

One of Congress's stated objectives in 1976 when it enacted TSCA was to require chemical manufacturers and processors to develop data on the health and environmental effects of their products. TSCA § 2(b)(1). Thus, Congress authorized the Administrator to require manufacturers and processors of substances and mixtures regulated under TSCA to develop safety and environmental data when: (1) the chemical may present an unreasonable risk of injury; or (2) substantial quantities of the chemical are produced with the potential for substantial environmental or human exposure. TSCA § 4(a)(1). To require testing of mixtures, the Administrator must also find that the effects "may not be reasonably and more efficiently determined or predicted by testing the chemicals which comprise the mixture." TSCA § 4(a)(2).

To assist EPA in its testing function, Congress created the Interagency Testing Committee (ITC) "to make recommendations to the Administrator respecting the chemical substances and mixtures to which the Administrator should give priority consideration." TSCA § 4(e). Designees from eight federal government agencies serve on the ITC. The ITC must give priority consideration to substances suspected of causing or contributing to cancer, gene mutations, or birth defects. As of December, 2004, the ITC had submitted 55 reports to EPA transmitting the Priority Testing List and its revisions. Within twelve months after the ITC designates a chemical for testing, the Agency must initiate section 4 rule-making or publish its reasons for not doing so.

Since Congress enacted TSCA, EPA has issued or entered into approximately 221 test rules and consent agreements.[26] Before issuing a test rule, EPA must determine that the substance or mixture poses some degree of risk or that the potential for substantial exposure exists. In either case, the Agency also must find that insufficient data exists and that testing will provide the necessary data. This statutory standard is not especially difficult, but EPA's formal rule-making under TSCA § 4 has proved to be time consuming and problematic.

The Agency's initial delay in issuing its first two test rules prompted the Natural Resources Defense Council to sue EPA in 1979, resulting in a settlement that forced the Agency to develop a schedule for implementing section 4. To meet the schedule, EPA began to use negotiated testing agreements, which NRDC also challenged. *See Natural Resources Defense Council, Inc. v. EPA*, 595 F. Supp. 1255 (S.D.N.Y. 1984).

---

[26] EPA publishes a cumulative list of test rules and consent agreements and orders. This summary is available from the TSCA Assistance Office (tel: 202-554-1404) and from the EPA website at http://www.epa.gov/oppt/chemtest/sunsettable.htm.

Subsequent negotiations among industry, NRDC, and the Agency produced a procedure for negotiating test orders based upon a consensus of the involved parties. This procedure, though potentially more expeditious than formal rule-making, is not without its own difficulties and critics.

Although the process is time-consuming, EPA also uses its section 4 rulemaking authority to obtain data on substances of concern under TSCA and under other environmental statutes administered by EPA and by other federal agencies. For example, EPA has promulgated TSCA test rules to facilitate administering the Clean Air Act. *See* 61 Fed. Reg. 33,178 (June 26, 1996). EPA also has promulgated TSCA test rules to obtain dermal absorption data to facilitate administration of the Occupational Safety and Health Act. *See* 69 Fed. Reg. 22,402 (April 26, 2004).

Because the rulemaking process is time consuming, EPA has increasingly turned to voluntary initiatives to collect data on chemicals of concern. These initiatives include a program to collect and develop data for existing "high production volume" (HPV) chemicals. *See* 65 Fed. Reg. 81658 (Dec. 26, 2000). Under the HPV Initiative, which includes the voluntary HPV Challenge Program, international efforts, and potential rulemaking, EPA will collect or require development of screening level data concerning environmental fate and potential hazards of HPV chemicals. EPA will address data needs not met by the HPV Challenge Program through international efforts or section 4 rulemaking.

HPV chemicals are non-polymeric organic substances produced or imported in amounts equal to or greater than 1 million pounds per year. In 1998, EPA found that, based on 1990 reporting for EPA's Inventory Update Rule (IUR) (40 C.F.R. pt. 710) of over 2,800 HPV chemicals, only 7% had a full set of publicly available, internationally recognized, health and environmental fate/effects screening test data. EPA also found that 43% had no publicly available hazard data. For the remaining chemicals, only limited data were available. But, since EPA announced the HPV Challenge Program in late 1998, and as of January, 2005, approximately 382 companies, working either independently or through 98 consortia, have publicly committed to make health and environmental hazard data for approximately 2,242 chemicals publicly available by 2005.[27] Thus, the HPV Challenge Program represents a quantum leap for EPA fulfilling its TSCA testing obligations.

[27] This information is updated periodically and can be found on the EPA website at http://www.epa.gov/chemrtk/volchall.htm.

9.1. CANDIDATE CHEMICALS

9.1.1. Interagency Testing Committee

TSCA § 4(e) established an Interagency Testing Committee (ITC) to recommend chemicals and mixtures for test rule priority. Representatives from eight member federal agencies serve on the ITC:

- EPA
- Occupational Safety and Health Administration
- Council on Environmental Quality
- National Institute for Occupational Safety and Health
- National Institute of Environmental Health Sciences
- National Cancer Institute
- National Science Foundation
- Department of Commerce.

TSCA § 4(e)(2)(A). Additional federal agencies are represented as "Liaison Members":

- Agency for Toxic Substances and Disease Registry
- Consumer Product Safety Commission
- Department of Defense
- Department of the Interior
- Food and Drug Administration
- National Library of Medicine
- National Toxicology Program
- Department of Agriculture.

The ITC must give priority to substances or mixtures suspected of causing or contributing to cancer, gene mutation or birth defects. TSCA § 4(e)(1)(A). The ITC revises the section 4(e) Priority List at least every six months, and can designate at any time up to 50 chemicals or mixtures for priority consideration.

In recommending tests, the ITC must consider eight factors:

(i) the quantities in which the substance or mixture is or will be manufactured;

(ii) the quantities in which the substance or mixture enters or will enter the environment;

(iii) the number of individuals who are or will be exposed to the substance or mixture in their places of employment and the duration of such exposure;

(iv) the extent to which human beings are or will be exposed to the substance or mixture;

(v) the extent to which the substance or mixture is closely related to a chemical substance or mixture which is known to present an unreasonable risk of injury to health or the environment;

(vi) the existence of data concerning the effects of the substance or mixture on health or the environment;

(vii) the extent to which testing of the substance or mixture may result in the development of data upon which the effects of the substance or mixture on health or the environment can reasonably be determined or predicted; and

(viii) the reasonably foreseeable availability of facilities and personnel for performing testing on the substance or mixture.

TSCA § 4(e)(1)(A).

The ITC conducts a multi-step scoring exercise to identify substances for priority testing. The scoring-exercise algorithm combines information on production, release, use, structure-activity relationships and any known toxicity. Initially, the ITC lists substances suspected of presenting a risk to human health and the environment (Initial List). The ITC chooses these chemicals because: (1) they have been identified in previous reviews as presenting a toxicity concern for human health or the environment; (2) their structure-activity relationships suggest such a toxicity concern; or (3) they are produced in large volumes with a potential for substantial human or environmental exposure. The ITC then refines this Initial List into a smaller list called a "Master File," which the ITC compiles by eliminating chemicals not subject to TSCA, not judged likely to be commercially produced, or not otherwise considered to be a priority for testing.

From this Master File, the ITC then selects substances for further consideration, called the "Preliminary List." The ITC develops the Preliminary List by applying the eight factors listed in section 4(e)(1)(A) and assigning a score for each substance. From the Preliminary List, the ITC selects between 80 and 100 candidates for a detailed review based on potential exposure, biological activity, and the need for health, ecological, and chemical effects testing. Finally, the ITC determines the need for testing based on all available information on each candidate substance. The ITC then will make one of four decisions. Adding a chemical substance to any of the first *three* categories triggers automatic reporting under TSCA §§ 8(a) and 8(d):

A. *Designation for testing:* Substances in this category are placed on the Priority List submitted to the EPA Administrator, and require priority consideration and response within twelve months.

B. *Recommended with intent to designate:* Substances in this category warrant testing but not an expedited review, and do not require EPA to respond to the ITC by a certain deadline. This category takes advantage of automatic reporting requirements under § 8(a) and 8(d) that require submission to EPA of unpublished health and safety studies and any other relevant information. After receiving the § 8(a) and 8(d) data, the ITC decides whether to designate or not designate that chemical or chemical group for EPA to respond within twelve months.

C. *Recommended without being designated for response within twelve months:* Substances in this category are placed on the Priority List without a specified time for EPA response. EPA must respond in a "timely" manner.

D. *Deferral:* Substances are so categorized when the ITC believes that: (a) there is insufficient exposure to be of concern; (b) the chemical is not likely to be hazardous; or (c) sufficient information/test data are already available.

See 50 Fed. Reg. 47,603, 47,604 (Nov. 19, 1985).

Under the section 8(a) Preliminary Assessment Information Rule (PAIR), manufacturers must submit production and exposure data on ITC-listed chemicals within 90 days of EPA's publishing a *Federal Register* rule amendment adding the chemical to the manufacturers' PAIR reporting list at 40 C.F.R. part 712, subpart B. Similarly, under the section 8(d) Health and Safety Data Reporting Rule, manufacturers and processors must submit to EPA unpublished health and safety studies within 90 days of EPA's publishing a *Federal Register* notice adding the chemical to the reporting list at 40 C.F.R. part 716, subpart B. The list is not effective until 30 days after publication, and the reports are then required within 60 days of this effective date. The PAIR and health and safety data reporting applies to chemicals designated for testing, recommended with intent to designate, and recommended without designation.

After receiving the ITC's report, EPA must commence rule-making proceedings under TSCA § 4(a) for designated chemicals within twelve months or, "if such a proceeding is not initiated within such period, publish in the *Federal Register* the Administrator's reason for not initiating such a proceeding." TSCA § 4(e)(1)(B). No statutory time limit applies to an EPA response to chemicals that the ITC has recommended, but not designated, for testing. But, EPA is required to use its "best efforts." 40 C.F.R. § 790.20(b)(2). In determining whether to initiate rule-making in response to an ITC report, EPA uses the decision making process described in section 9.2.

9.1.2. Master Testing List

Since 1990, the Office of Pollution Prevention and Toxics (OPPT) has used the Master Testing List (MTL) to set its chemical testing program agenda. The MTL consolidates OPPT's Existing Chemical Testing Program priorities with chemicals brought to OPPT by the TSCA ITC, other EPA Program Offices, other federal agencies, and international organizations such as the Organization for Economic Cooperation and Development (OECD). According to the Agency:

> The purposes of the MTL are to (1) identify chemical testing needs of the Federal government (including EPA) and international programs of interest to the U.S., (2) focus limited EPA resources on the highest priority chemical testing needs, (3) identify and publicize EPA's testing priorities for industrial chemicals, (4) obtain broad public comment on EPA's Chemical Testing Program and its priorities, and (5) encourage voluntary initiatives by members of the U.S. chemical industry to provide EPA priority data identified via the MTL as being needed.

EPA, Office of Pollution Prevention and Toxics, *Master Testing List* (Dec. 1, 1996).[28]

The MTL provides companies an early warning of EPA's testing plans and thus affords them an opportunity to initiate voluntary activities to satisfy the Agency's test data needs for their affected chemicals. Where companies decline to take this opportunity, EPA considers promulgating TSCA § 4 test rules. *Id.*

9.1.3. EPA Program Offices

In addition to the ITC's testing nominations, EPA relies on other sources for candidate chemicals. For example, in 1987 EPA's Office of Solid Waste (OSW) identified a need for health effects or chemical fate data on 73 chemicals to support its effort under Resource Conservation and Recovery Act (RCRA) section 3001 to identify wastes which may pose a substantial hazard to human health and the environment. 52 Fed. Reg. 20,336 (May 29, 1987). RCRA does not authorize EPA to mandate testing on wastes. In 1988 the Agency published a final test rule under TSCA § 4(a)(1)(A) requiring or recommending that manufacturers and processors of 33 chemicals perform testing for human health effects or chemical fate to support EPA's hazardous waste regulatory program under RCRA. 53 Fed. Reg. 22,300 (June 15, 1988).

---

28 The MTL is available from: (1) TSCA Hotline: (202) 554-1404; (2) E-Mail: tsca-hotline@epa.gov; also tsca-hotline@epamail.epa.gov; and (3) URL: http://www.epa.gov/opptintr/chemtest/mtl.htm.

EPA justifies using its TSCA § 4 testing authority to support other EPA programs by stating that Congress intended EPA to do so where its other programs lack their own independent testing authority. 53 Fed. Reg. at 22,302. Other agencies are given an opportunity to review and comment on the testing program to avoid duplicative testing, which section 4(c)(2)(B) prohibits. See, *e.g.*, 60 Fed. Reg. 60,627, 60,629, (Nov. 28, 1995).

According to the MTL[29], EPA has targeted the following five chemical categories:

1. Persistent Bioaccumulators

According to EPA, many chemicals that possess persistent and bioaccumulative properties present significant environmental problems. Concerns in EPA's Office of Water focus on sediments contaminated with chemicals having these characteristics. OPPT plans to require environmental fate and ecotoxicity test data to support a more comprehensive risk assessment. OPPT is identifying the chemical set that will be addressed under this effort and the testing needed.

2. Clean Air Act Section 112 "Air Toxics" (Hazardous Air Pollutants)

EPA's Office of Air and Radiation (OAR) and Office of Research and Development (ORD) seek data to determine the "residual risk" posed by the 189 chemicals (Hazardous Air Pollutants (HAPs)) listed under section 112 of the Clean Air Act (CAA) Amendments of 1990. The MTL includes the 23 chemicals from this category for which TSCA § 4 testing has been proposed (*see* 61 FR 33,178; June 26, 1996). The final HAPS rule has not yet been issued, in part because EPA has pursued enforceable consent agreements (ECAs) on chemicals addressed in the proposed rule. OPPT, OAR and ORD are determining testing needs for other chemicals in this category. EPA primarily intends to use the test data to implement CAA section 112 by determining residual risks (*e.g.*, assessing risks remaining after imposing technology-based emission standards, estimating risks of accidental chemical releases, and determining whether subject chemicals should be removed ("delisted") from the CAA section 112(b) HAPs list. EPA also intends to use the data from this testing activity: 1) to inform communities and citizens about local chemical hazards; 2) to assist state and local permitting authorities to establish appropriate standards within their programs; and 3) to help other EPA Program Offices and other federal agencies to assess chemical risks and to take appropriate action.

3. SARA Section 104 "Priority Data Needs"

Section 104 of the Superfund Amendments and Reauthorization Act (SARA) requires EPA and the Agency for Toxic Substances and Disease Registry (ATSDR) to

---

[29] *See* http://www.epa.gov/opptintr/chemtest/mtladcat.htm.

list chemicals frequently identified in Superfund sites. ATSDR prepares "Toxicological Profiles" for these chemical substances, identifying data gaps and research needs, and developing a testing/research program. The list now includes 250 chemicals and categories, and ATSDR is preparing Toxicological Profiles on 215 of them. ATSDR has identified priority data needs for the first subset of 13 chemicals (3 metals and 10 organics). These chemicals are listed on the MTL with testing needs/testing action development underway, and with section 4 test rulemaking possible within the next two years.

4. Indoor Air Source Characterization - Interior Architectural Coatings

OPPT and OAR are coordinating efforts to characterize and determine specific needs for chemical emissions and total emissions testing for indoor air sources such as paints, varnishes and other interior architectural coatings.

5. Oxygenated Fuel Additives

Under Clean Air Act section 211, OAR has requested OPPT to use its TSCA § 4 testing authority to obtain health effects data on Oxygenated Fuel Additives (OFAs) such as ethyl t-butyl ether (ETBE) and t-amyl methyl ether (TAME). EPA is also exploring options to obtain toxicity data on diisopropyl ether (DIPE) and t-butyl alcohol (TBA) before these chemicals come into wide use as OFAs. EPA is also attempting to obtain test data needed by OAR on t-butyl formate (TBF), which is a possible breakdown product of methyl t-butyl ether (MTBE).

9.1.4. Other Federal Agencies

On May 26, 2004, EPA promulgated a section 4 test rule requiring manufacturers, including importers, of 34 chemicals to conduct *in vitro* dermal absorption rate testing. 69 Fed. Reg. 22,402. EPA requires that the 34 chemicals be tested to measure a permeability constant (Kp) and two *in vitro* dermal short-term absorption rates (10 minutes and 60 minutes) for the chemical substances in liquid form, using the test standard set forth in 40 C.F.R. section 799.5115(h). Manufacturers, including importers, had to submit a letter of intent to test, or apply for an exemption from testing, by June 25, 2004 and had to submit test results by June 27, 2005. In addition, TSCA § 12(b) export notice requirements apply to anyone who exports or intends to export any quantity of any chemical substance included in this final rule.

In the preamble to the test rule, EPA stated that the Agency has insufficient data to reasonably determine the dermal absorption rate on these chemicals, and that each substance in the final rule is produced domestically and/or imported in an amount equal to or greater than one million pounds per year, based on the 2002 TSCA Inventory Update Rule. Thus, these chemicals are produced in "substantial quantities" and it is reasonable to infer "substantial human exposure" warranting a test rule under TSCA § 4(a)(1)(B)(i)(II) (*see* section 9.2).

The test results will be used by the Occupational Safety and Health Administration (OSHA) to evaluate the need for "skin designations," which OSHA adds to OSHA's permissible exposure limits to alert industrial hygienists, employers and workers if OSHA determines that cutaneous exposure (through skin, eyes and mucous membranes) to a particular chemical may result in systemic toxicity.

9.2. TESTING TRIGGERS

The Administrator may require manufacturers and processors to test a chemical or mixture if EPA finds that it may pose a risk to human health or the environment, or that it will be produced in substantial quantities and may result in substantial or significant exposure to humans or substantial exposure to the environment. Whether the testing "trigger" is risk-based or exposure-based influences the type of testing required.

9.2.1. TSCA § 4(a)(1)(A): Risk Trigger

Section 4(a)(1)(A) authorizes EPA to require testing if the Agency finds that: (1) the chemical or mixture may present an unreasonable risk of injury to human health or the environment; (2) existing data on and experience with the chemical or mixture are insufficient to reasonably predict or determine the effects of the chemical substance; and (3) testing is necessary to obtain such data. EPA's first step, therefore, is to make a risk determination.

9.2.1.1. Risk Assessment

The Agency considers several factors in assessing the possible unreasonable risk of a chemical, including knowledge of the chemical's physical and chemical properties, structural relationships to other chemicals with demonstrated adverse effects, data from inconclusive tests, and case history data. As EPA uses the term, "risk" is a function of both hazard (toxicity) and exposure.

Although the Agency acknowledges that some exposure is required to support a section 4(a)(1)(A)(i) finding that a chemical "may present an unreasonable risk," EPA has advised manufacturers in some situations that risk may be significant, even when exposure is extremely low. Furthermore, to find exposure, EPA has stated that "it is sufficient for the Agency to show that there is a reasonable likelihood that exposure may arise because of activities associated with the manufacturing, processing, distribution, use or disposal of the chemical." 45 Fed. Reg. 48,524, 48,528 (July 18, 1980).

Two U.S. Circuit Courts of Appeal have considered the meaning of "may present an unreasonable risk," the statutory standard for supporting a TSCA § 4(a)(1)(A) test rule.[30] In *Ausimont U.S.A. Inc. v. EPA*, 838 F.2d 93 (3d Cir. 1988), the Third Circuit held that EPA may not base a testing requirement on mere "scientific curiosity." 838 F.2d at 97. EPA meets its burden, however, if its test rule is based on an "existing possibility of harm [raising] reasonable and legitimate cause for concern." *Id.*

In *Chemical Manufacturers Association v. EPA*, 859 F.2d 977 (D.C. Cir. 1988) (*CMA v. EPA*), the D.C. Circuit concluded that the Agency could require testing where an unreasonable risk of injury to health is "a substantial (*i.e.*, more than theoretical) probability." 859 F.2d at 988. "A test rule is warranted when there is a more-than-theoretical basis for suspecting that some amount of exposure occurs and that the substance is sufficiently toxic at that exposure level to present an 'unreasonable risk of injury to health.'" *Id.* at 988.

In the same decision, the D.C. Circuit also observed that the evidence supporting the Agency's finding of a probable risk need not be conclusive. For this reason, the Agency may note flaws in an existing toxicology study, but still conclude that the study suggests a possible risk. 859 F.2d at 995. The Third Circuit in *Ausimont* similarly concluded that "[i]f no doubt existed, testing would not be required." 838 F.2d at 97.

Even though a section 4(a)(1)(A) test rule is not exposure-based, the Agency still must demonstrate some potential exposure because exposure is a component of risk. In *CMA v. EPA*, however, the D.C. Circuit held that EPA could rely on inferences to establish exposure, "so long as all the evidence—including the industry evidence—indicates a more-than-theoretical probability of exposure." 859 F.2d at 989. Also, exposure can be based on non-recurrent, brief exposure if the record supports a finding that brief exposure could create an unreasonable risk. 859 F.2d at 995.

9.2.1.2. Insufficiency of Data

Not only must EPA determine that the chemical or mixture may present a risk, the Agency must also find that the existing data and experience are insufficient to determine or predict the effects of concern. TSCA § 4(a)(1)(A)(ii). To assess data sufficiency, EPA reviews and evaluates existing information on the substance. To be considered sufficient, these existing studies need not necessarily meet EPA test standards. See, *e.g.*, 45 Fed. Reg. 48,524 (July 18, 1980). The Agency in essence attempts to determine whether the available information, despite its inherent limitations, provides a sufficiently reliable basis for defining the hazard and/or exposure component of its risk equation.

---

[30] The Third Circuit reviewed a section 4(a)(1)(A) rule but did not assess the degree of risk that the Agency must demonstrate to support a section 4(a)(1)(A) test rule. *Shell Chemical Co. v. EPA*, 826 F.2d 295 (5th Cir. 1987). Instead, the court remanded the case to the Agency to consider additional exposure data. *Id.* at 298.

EPA places existing studies in one of four categories: (1) studies too flawed to be relied upon even as suggestive evidence; (2) studies that suggest an effect or suggest no effect; (3) studies adequate for qualitatively predicting a chemical's effects but inadequate for performing a quantitative risk assessment; and (4) studies adequate for performing a quantitative risk assessment. EPA has explained how it uses these categories in making its decision whether to require testing:

> If all of the existing studies for a given effect fall into the first category, we have no basis for finding that the chemical may present an unreasonable risk of that effect, although testing still may be required on other grounds. . . . If one or more studies fall into the second category, the studies are suggestive of an adverse effect, and there is exposure or the potential for exposure, we would quantitatively evaluate whether the weight of the evidence of all studies available for that effect suggests that the chemical may present an unreasonable risk. A study providing sound qualitative evidence of the effect, *i.e.*, falling into category three, would lead to testing to quantify the dose-response relationship for that effect unless we were to conclude that risk management decision for the chemicals ultimately would be made on the basis of other effects of far greater toxicological significance. If a study fell in category 4, data would be judged adequate and no testing would be required.

Gary R. Timm, *The Implementation of TSCA Section 4*, Remarks at The Toxicology Forum 1984 Annual Summer Meeting at 3-4 (July 16-20, 1984) (photocopy on file with author).

9.2.1.3. Necessity of Testing

Finally, the Agency must find that testing of the substance is necessary to develop the data. TSCA § 4(a)(1)(A)(iii). To do so, EPA will review any ongoing or completed studies. If the Agency decides that the ongoing or completed studies will enable EPA to determine whether a substance presents an unreasonable risk, no further testing will be required. But, EPA may determine that a serious defect in an ongoing study's design or execution exists, and require testing to replace the flawed study. 46 Fed. Reg. 30,301 (June 5, 1981).

EPA also must find that testing will produce the needed information. The Agency will not require chemical testing if "no testing methodology exists which would lead to the production of the necessary data." *Id.* Publishing a generic section 4 test standard for a particular effect constitutes the Agency's finding that tests conducted according to that standard will provide the needed data (*id.* at 30,302) or a standard may be created on a chemical-specific basis for a specific testing endpoint.

9.2.2. TSCA § 4(a)(1)(B): Exposure Trigger

Congress recognized the prudence of testing a substance produced in substantial quantities and that results in substantial environmental or human exposure, even in the absence of information that a chemical substance or mixture may present a risk. Section 4(a)(1)(B) provides the Administrator an alternative basis for requiring testing founded upon an exposure trigger. Under this section, EPA can require testing if it finds that: (1) a chemical substance or mixture is or will be produced in substantial quantities; (2) a substance or mixture enters or is reasonably expected to be released into the environment in substantial quantities, or there is or may be significant or substantial human exposure; (3) data or experience to reasonably predict the effects of human health or the environment are insufficient; and (4) testing is necessary to develop the data. Section 4(a)(1)(B) makes no reference to "risk," "injury," or "toxicity," as in section 4(a)(1)(A).

While the risk trigger for testing under section 4(a)(1)(A) also requires an exposure finding, that finding is "much lower" than required to satisfy the exposure trigger under section 4(a)(1)(B). 45 Fed. Reg. 48,524, 48,528 (July 18, 1980). EPA bases this difference on the fact that less exposure is necessary when the Agency has a scientific basis for suspecting potential toxicity under section 4(a)(1)(A). By its express terms, however, section 4(a)(1)(B) requires both substantial production and substantial or significant human exposure or substantial environmental exposure.

The phrase "substantial or significant" is not defined in TSCA or its legislative history. Historically, EPA had declined to quantify "substantial," contending it "neither feasible nor desirable to make strict numerical definitions of substantial exposure or release," and that production and exposure determinations should be made individually for each chemical. 50 Fed. Reg. 20,662, 20,664 (May 17, 1985).

Notwithstanding this pronouncement, however, EPA subsequently acquiesced in and published a final policy on TSCA § 4(a)(1)(B) findings in which it quantified "substantial" production, release and exposure. 58 Fed. Reg. 28,736 (May 14, 1993). EPA developed the policy in response to *Chemical Manufacturers Association v. EPA,* 899 F.2d 344 (5th Cir. 1990), in which the court instructed EPA to "articulate the standards or criteria on the basis of which it found the quantities of [the chemical] cumene entering the environment from the facilities in question to be 'substantial.' " 899 F.2d at 360. The policy established quantitative thresholds to serve as guidance for determining "substantial" production and release to the environment, and "substantial" and "significant" human exposure:

Category	*Threshold Value*
Substantial production	1 million pounds total/year
Substantial release	1 million pounds total/year
Substantial human exposure	
general population	100,000 people
consumers	10,000 people
workers	1,000 workers

Significant human exposure
- < 100,000 people population exposed more directly or on a routine or episodic basis
- < 10,000 people exposed more directly or on a routine or episodic basis
- < 1,000 workers exposed more directly or on a routine or episodic basis

58 Fed. Reg. at 28,746. In addition to finding substantial production volume, release and/or exposure under section 4(a)(1)(B), EPA also must determine that insufficient data exist and that testing is necessary to develop the needed information. These findings are identical to those under TSCA § 4(a)(1)(A), discussed above.

9.2.3. Elements of a TSCA § 4 Test Rule

After EPA determines that one or both of the triggers under TSCA § 4(a) has been met, the Agency publishes a proposed test rule. After a public comment period, EPA publishes the test rule in final form. A TSCA § 4 test rule must specifically identify the chemical substance or mixture to be tested, the standards for developing test data and, for existing chemicals, the time period during which the test data must be submitted. TSCA § 4(b)(1).

TSCA § 4(b)(1) requires EPA to consider "the relative costs of the various test protocols and methodologies which may be required under the rule." Section 4(b)(1) also requires EPA to consider "the reasonably foreseeable availability of the facilities and personnel needed to perform the testing required under the rule." In 1982 EPA conducted a study of laboratory availability, which it updated in 1990.[31] In response to an industry challenge to a final test rule on diethylenetriamine on the basis that laboratory space to conduct the mouse visible specific locus test (MVSL) was unavailable, EPA proposed to modify five final and proposed test rules to give the manufacturers the option to choose either the MVSL or the mouse biochemical specific locus test (MBSL). 53 Fed. Reg. 51,847 (Dec. 23, 1988).

---

[31] Booz, Allen, Hamilton, Inc., for Office of Policy Analysis, EPA, *EPA Census of the Toxicological Testing Industry* (1990).

9.3. STUDIES REQUIRED UNDER TSCA § 4

TSCA § 4 grants EPA wide latitude to decide the types and amount of testing to require. "The health and environmental effects for which standards . . . may be prescribed include carcinogenesis, mutagenesis, teratogenesis, behavioral disorders, cumulative or synergistic effects, and any other effect which may present an unreasonable risk of injury to health or the environment." TSCA § 4(b)(2)(A).

OPPT has published in the *Code of Federal Regulations* some TSCA test guidelines referenced in individual test rules. *See* 40 C.F.R. pts. 795-798. Since their publication, however, OPPTS has created a unified library of test guidelines harmonizing the requirements of the regulations, those of the Office of Pesticide Programs (OPP) that appeared in publications of the National Technical Information Service (NTIS), and the guidelines published by the Organization for Economic Cooperation and Development (OECD). *Id.* OPPTS harmonized these guidelines into a single set to minimize variations among the testing procedures that must be performed to meet data requirements under TSCA and the Federal Insecticide, Fungicide and Rodenticide Act (FIFRA) (7 U.S.C. 136 *et seq.*). As a result of the publication of the harmonized test guidelines, TSCA § 4 test rules now reference the Product Properties Test Guidelines (40 C.F.R. pt. 799, subpt. E; 65 *Federal Register* 78,751 (2000)) and the Health Effects Test Guidelines (40 C.F.R. pt. 799, subpt. H; 62 *Federal Register* 43,824 (1997)). If the manufacturer or processor subject to the rule is interested in seeking a modification of the applicable test guideline, EPA encourages it to consult the modification procedures outlined at 40 C.F.R. part 790.

The OPPTS harmonized guidelines are organized in the following 10 disciplinary series:[32]

Series 810 - Product Performance Test Guidelines
Series 830 - Product Properties Test Guidelines
Series 835 - Fate, Transport and Transformation Test Guidelines
Series 840 - Spray Drift Test Guidelines
Series 850 - Ecological Effects Test Guidelines
Series 860 - Residue Chemistry Test Guidelines
Series 870 - Health Effects Test Guidelines
Series 875 - Occupational and Residential Exposure Test Guidelines
Series 880 - Biochemicals Test Guidelines
Series 885 - Microbial Pesticide Test Guidelines

---

[32] These guidelines are available electronically in PDF on EPA's website under the heading "Information Sources," "Test Methods," "OPPTS Harmonized Test Guidelines" (http://www.epa.gov/OPPTS_Harmonized/) or in paper by contacting the OPPT Public Docket at (703) 305-5805 or by e-mail: opp-docket@epa.gov. Final guidelines are also available from the U.S. Government Printing Office Bookstore, 810 North Capitol St., NW., Washington, DC or by calling (202) 512-1800 and ordering ASCII disks or paper copies.

9.3.1. Health Effects

The health effects and studies usually required by EPA in section 4 test rules are summarized below.

9.3.1.1. Acute Toxicity

Acute toxicity tests determine a substance's mean lethal dose (LD_{50}) as a consequence of a single exposure by oral, dermal or inhalation routes of administration. Rats, rabbits or guinea pigs are used for acute dermal toxicity studies. Rats are used in acute oral and inhalation studies. Acute toxicity studies are conducted to assess the potential for skin and eye irritation or sensitization.

9.3.1.2. Subchronic

Subchronic studies determine the no-observed-effect level and toxic effects of repeated exposure to a test substance for periods of 28 to 90 days. Again, exposure may be oral, dermal or by inhalation. These studies are typically conducted in rats or dogs.

9.3.1.3. Chronic

Chronic studies determine the effects of a substance following prolonged and repeated exposure, typically one to two years. Chronic studies serve to define long term dose-response relationships. Testing is performed on two species, a rodent (typically the rat) and a non-rodent (typically the dog).

9.3.1.4. Oncogenicity

Oncogenicity studies observe test animals for a major portion of their life span for the development of neoplastic lesions during or after exposure to various doses of a test substance by an appropriate route of administration. Testing is performed in the rat and mouse.

9.3.1.5. Reproduction

Reproduction studies provide general information concerning the effects of a test substance on gonadal function, conception, parturition, and the growth and development of the offspring. The rat is the preferred species.

9.3.1.6. Developmental Toxicity

The developmental toxicity study is designed to determine the potential of the test substance to induce structural and/or other abnormalities in the offspring which may arise from exposure of the mother during pregnancy. Testing is typically performed in two species, rat and rabbit.

9.3.1.7. Mutagenicity Assays

Mutagenicity studies indicate the capacity of a substance to alter the genetic materials of a cell. EPA's test rule program extensively uses mutagenicity data in two ways: (1) as a screen to determine the oncogenic potential of a substance; and (2) as an endpoint to determine whether exposure to a substance may induce inheritable gene mutations or chromosome aberrations. Another use of mutagenicity data is to assist in determining the appropriate form of the risk assessment. For example, The March 2005 *Supplemental Guidance for Assessing Susceptibility from Early-Life Exposure to Carcinogens (EPA/630/R-03/003F)* prescribes a more conservative approach to the risk assessment of infants, children and adolescents for those carcinogens that are also mutagenic.

9.3.1.8. Neurotoxicity

Neurotoxicity studies develop data on changes in the nervous system after exposure to chemical substances, including a no-effect level, after acute or repeated exposures. Neurotoxicity studies may include neuropathology studies which develop data on morphologic changes, neurophysiologic studies which develop data on the peripheral nervous system, developmental neurotoxicity studies which assess effects in newborns and juveniles, and motor activity studies.

9.3.2. Environmental Effects

EPA's Environmental Effects Test Guidelines cover eight environmental studies to be used in test rules promulgated under TSCA § 4(a). 40 C.F.R. pts. 795, 797. These are:

- Daphnid Acute Toxicity Test;
- Daphnid Chronic Toxicity Test;
- Mysid Shrimp Acute Toxicity Test;
- Mysid Shrimp Chronic Toxicity Test;
- Algal Acute Toxicity Test;
- Fish Acute Toxicity Test;
- Fish Early Life Stage Toxicity Test; and
- Gammarid Acute Toxicity Test.

In the past, Environmental Effects Test Guidelines have incorporated numerous other studies, such as bioconcentration tests, seed germination/root elongation toxicity tests, avian dietary tests, and acute toxicity tests. These and others may be specified in the future as required.

9.3.3. Chemical Fate

The Agency's Chemical Fate Test Guidelines cover testing for physical and chemical properties, transport processes, and transformation processes, such as:

- Absorption in Aqueous Solution: Ultraviolet and Visible Spectra;
- Vapor Pressure;
- Sediment and Soil Absorption Isotherm;
- Biodegradation, Aerobic Aquatic;
- Hydrolysis as a Function of pH at 25° C;
- Indirect Photolysis Screening Test;
- Partition Coefficient; and
- Water Solubility.

40 C.F.R. pts. 795, 796, 799. Other chemical fate tests have been used in the past and may be used again in the future. These have included particle size distribution, fiber length and diameter distributions, disassociation constants in water, and pH. Transformation processes also have included anaerobic biodegradation, sewerage treatment biodegradation, and complex formation ability in water.

9.3.4. Multi-Chemical End-Point Testing

In 1991, EPA proposed its first multi-substance or multi-chemical test rule to require testing of ten substances for a single toxicological end point—neurotoxicity. 56 Fed. Reg. 9105 (Mar. 4, 1991). While most test rules require manufacturers to conduct a variety of tests on a single chemical, this test rule required testing of many chemicals for one specific end point or effect. EPA believes that end-point test rules will require fewer Agency resources to develop than individual test rules for each of the chemicals in question. EPA reasons that such a rule can be expanded easily by amending the rule to add more chemicals.

When EPA promulgated the final neurotoxicity test rule in 1993, subject chemical manufacturers immediately challenged it. *See* 60 Fed. Reg. 4516, 4516-17 (Jan. 23, 1995). EPA and the manufacturers settled the litigation, however, reaching a consent agreement that requires neurotoxicity testing for seven of the ten chemicals. *Id.* at 4517. Thereafter, EPA revoked the original test rule. 60 Fed. Reg. 4514 (Jan. 23, 1995). This litigation slowed EPA's progress in issuing other similar test rules and enforceable consent agreements (ECAs). Since the neurotoxicity consent agreement, EPA has issued one final multi-chemical, single end point test rule. *See* 69 Fed. Reg. 22,402 (Apr. 26, 2004) (in vitro dermal absorption rate testing for 34 chemicals).

9.4. GOOD LABORATORY PRACTICE STANDARDS

To satisfy a TSCA test rule, a study must meet EPA's Good Laboratory Practice (GLP) standards. EPA published TSCA's GLP standards on November 29, 1983 at 48 Fed. Reg. 53,922, codified at 40 C.F.R. pt. 792. Any person who submits to EPA a test required by a section 4 test rule also must submit a statement, signed by the submitter and the study director, that: (1) the study complies with GLP requirements; (2) the study describes the differences between the practices used in the study and TSCA's GLP requirements; or (3) the submitter did not sponsor the study, did not conduct the study and does not know whether the study complies with TSCA's GLP requirements.

TSCA's GLP standards prescribe the minimum requirements that the laboratory and sponsor must fulfill in the following areas:

1. Organization and personnel;
2. The physical requirements of the testing facility;
3. Equipment;
4. Testing facilities operation;
5. Test, control, and reference substances;
6. Protocol for and conduct of a study; and
7. Records and reports.

A section 4 test rule study sponsor should assure itself that the laboratory complies with TSCA GLP standards. EPA will deem the failure to comply with the GLPs a violation of TSCA § 15 if:

- the test is not conducted in accordance with GLP requirements;
- the submission contains false or misleading data or information, contains significant omissions, or otherwise does not fulfill a GLP requirement; or
- entry for auditing test data or inspecting facilities is denied.

40 C.F.R. § 792.17(a). In addition, a failure to comply with GLPs may lead EPA to conclude that a study does not reliably demonstrate a lack of risk from the test chemical or mixture. Further, if EPA required the test data by a TSCA § 4 test rule, EPA may determine that the sponsor has not fulfilled its section 4 obligations.

9.5. CONSENT AGREEMENTS

A 1980 federal court decision imposed on EPA a timetable for responding to ITC reports because to that point EPA had not responded to several ITC reports as required by TSCA § 4(e). *Natural Resources Defense Council v. Costle*, 14 Env't Rep. Cas.

(BNA) 1858 (S.D.N.Y. Feb. 4, 1980). In response to the *NRDC* decision, EPA developed a controversial "Negotiated Testing Program." Used by the Agency beginning in 1982, the Negotiated Testing Agreements (NTAs) offered EPA a degree of flexibility in developing test rules with affected manufacturers.

A second NRDC action, however, brought the NTA practice to a halt. *Natural Resources Defense Council v. EPA*, 595 F. Supp. 1255 (S.D.N.Y. 1984). This second *NRDC* case considered four features of the Agency's section 4 testing program: (1) the use of NTAs; (2) the use of advanced notices of proposed rule-making (ANPRs) instead of proposed test rules; (3) the two-phase test rule process (Phase I identifying testing end points and Phase II identifying testing protocols); and (4) the resultant delays in promulgating test rules.

The second *NRDC* court ruled that the Agency lacked the administrative discretion inherent in the NTA program because once the ITC has designated a chemical for testing, TSCA § 4(e) gives EPA only two choices: EPA can initiate rule-making or conclude that rule-making is not necessary. The court concluded that an Agency decision to opt for an NTA in lieu of initiating a rule-making constitutes a *de facto* finding that testing is required. Therefore, the NTA subverts the statutorily required rule-making. In addition, the court believed that EPA should evaluate the use of ANPRs or two-phased rule-making on a case-by-case basis to determine whether it has unreasonably delayed the final test rule.

Negotiations among EPA, NRDC, and the Chemical Manufacturers Association (now the American Chemistry Council) culminated in an interim final rule on consent agreements under TSCA § 4 (known as enforceable consent agreements, or ECAs). 51 Fed. Reg. 23,706 (June 30, 1986) (codified at 40 C.F.R. pt. 790, subpt. B). This rule reflects the Agency's policy that negotiations can play a constructive role in resolving testing issues, while introducing significant changes to expedite test rules and to make them legally binding.

Under this interim final rule, EPA evaluates testing candidates that were recommended with intent to designate by ITC, and conducts negotiations to develop ECAs where appropriate. EPA conducts rulemaking under section 4, however, whenever the Agency determines that testing should be required under section 4(a) and negotiations will not achieve a consensus about appropriate testing.

Once adopted, EPA considers the consent agreements to be "'orders issued under section 4 for purposes of section 15(1) of TSCA." 40 C.F.R. § 790.65(b). Therefore, signatories who violate any provision of a consent agreement are subject to civil and criminal liability under TSCA §§ 16 and 17.

Consent agreements include seventeen provisions, including:

- a specification of the technical or commercial grade of the test substance or mixture;

- standards for the development of test data;
- a requirement to conduct the testing according to GLPs;
- a requirement to submit a study plan to EPA before initiation of testing; and
- a provision acknowledging EPA's authority to conduct laboratory inspections and to audit studies.

40 C.F.R. § 790.60(a).

EPA has a schedule for developing ECAs and test rules. 40 C.F.R. pt. 790, subpt. E, app. A. A public comment period occurs one to four weeks after the ITC report is published in the *Federal Register*. The first public focus meeting is held during week four. After section 8(a) and 8(d) reporting, a second public meeting is held at week 20, and constitutes the deadline for requests to participate in the negotiations. At week 30, EPA decides whether to enter into an ECA or to publish a test rule. Finally, the schedule for promulgating the ECA or test rule is published in the *Federal Register*.

While the consent agreement process enables the Agency and industry to conserve resources that otherwise would be devoted to formal rule-making, the process is not without its limits and critics. Chief among these limits is that while enforceable against its signatories, a consent agreement is not enforceable against non-participants and does not trigger section 4 reimbursement procedures. Indeed, negotiations between industry and EPA fail on occasion because a single manufacturer grows dissatisfied with the direction of the negotiations and chooses not to bear the testing costs alone. On the other hand, the threat of onerous test rules, promulgated in formal rule-makings without the opportunity for informal input through the negotiation process, tends to promote negotiated consent agreements. The Agency continues to use voluntary, non-binding testing agreements for some non-ITC designated substances, where test sponsors are willing to cooperate. 58 Fed. Reg. 16,669 (Mar. 30, 1993).

9.6. IMPLEMENTING AND ENFORCING TEST RULES

In the absence of a consensus leading to a consent agreement, EPA will promulgate specific test rules either by a single-phase rule-making procedure or by a two-phase rule-making procedure. Today EPA uses the former almost exclusively.

EPA originally proposed to develop and codify in the C.F.R. standardized test methodologies for all major test types that might be required under section 4 test rules. In response to criticism that this approach would prove too rigid, EPA proposed to make test rule development a two-phase process. In the first phase, EPA would establish by rule the particular effects for which a given chemical must be tested. In addition, companies would be required to submit study plans. In the second phase, after considering public comment on the proposed rule, the Agency would by rule adopt the study plans as test standards. On October 10, 1984, EPA issued a procedural rule adopting this two-phase process for developing certain test rules. 49 Fed. Reg. 39,774 (Oct. 10, 1984) (codified at 40 C.F.R. §§ 790.1 to -.99).

In *NRDC v. EPA*, 595 F. Supp. 1255 (S.D.N.Y. 1984), the court upheld the two-phase process, but also held that the Agency must promulgate test rules within a reasonable time frame. In an attempt to shorten the rule-making process, EPA in 1985 issued guidelines and procedures for using single-phase rule-making, which has all but replaced the two-phase process. 50 Fed. Reg. 20,652 (May 17, 1985) (codified at 40 C.F.R. §§ 790.5, -.20 to -.39, -.80 to -.99). In the single-phase test rule, EPA proposes the pertinent OPPT test guideline as the required test standard in the initial notice of proposed rule-making. Industry and others may propose different methodologies during the public comment period. The final rule promulgates as the test standard either the OPPT test guideline or other suitable guidelines. The Agency uses single-phase rule-making for most TSCA § 4 rules, reserving the two-phase rule-making only for testing where no well-accepted test methodologies exist, such as with epidemiology studies.

9.6.1. Letters of Intent

Within 30 days after the effective date, each person subject to the test rule either must notify EPA by letter of his or her intent to conduct testing or must apply for an exemption. 40 C.F.R. § 790.45. Manufacturers or processors who continue their activities and who do not submit a letter of intent or apply for an exemption are in violation of the rule. *Id.*

If no person submits a letter of intent, EPA will follow one of three procedures, depending on who is subject to the rule. 40 C.F.R. § 790.48. If EPA is requiring testing solely to evaluate the risks associated with manufacturing, then the rule will state that only manufacturers are subject to the rule. If only manufacturers are subject to a test rule and no manufacturer notifies EPA within 30 days of its intent to test, EPA will so notify the manufacturers either by certified letter or *Federal Register* notice and provide an opportunity to take corrective action. 40 C.F.R. § 790.48(a)(2). If no manufacturer submits a letter of intent to test within 30 days after receipt of the certified letter or publication of the *Federal Register* notice, all subject manufacturers will be in violation of the rule.

If EPA is requiring testing to evaluate risks associated with manufacturing and processing or with distribution in commerce, use, or disposal of the chemical, then the rule will state that manufacturers and processors are subject to the test rule. If manufacturers and processors both are subject to the test rule and no manufacturer indicates an intent to test, EPA will first publish a notice in the *Federal Register* that no manufacturers have notified EPA of their intent to test. Within 30 days of this notice, processors and small quantity manufacturers must notify EPA of their intent to test or submit an exemption application. If no manufacturer or processor notifies EPA within 30 days of the *Federal Register* notice of its intent to test, then EPA will so notify the manufacturers and processors either by certified letter or *Federal Register* notice and provide an opportunity for corrective action. 40 C.F.R. § 790.48(b)(4). If no manufacturer or processor submits a letter of intent within 30 days of receipt of the certified letter of publication of the *Federal Register* notice, all subject manufacturers and processors will be in violation of the rule.

If EPA is requiring testing solely to evaluate risks associated with processing, then the rule will state that only processors are responsible for testing. If only processors are subject to the test rule and no processor subject to the rule has notified EPA within 30 days of its intent to test, EPA will so notify the processors by certified mail or publish a *Federal Register* notice. The letter or the notice will give the processors an opportunity to take corrective action. 40 C.F.R. § 790.48(c)(2). If no processor submits a letter of intent to conduct one or more of the required tests within 30 days after receipt of the certified letter or *Federal Register* publication, all subject processors will be in violation of the test rule.

9.6.2. Small Quantity Manufacturers

While legally subject to a test rule specifying manufacturers, persons who manufacture less than 500 kilograms (1,100 pounds) of a chemical annually, or small quantities solely for R&D, during the period from the effective date of the test rule to the end of the reimbursement period, are exempt from the procedural requirements of a test rule (*i.e.*, submission of letters of intent or exemption applications) unless the test rule directs them to comply, or unless EPA directs them to comply in a *Federal Register* notice announcing that no manufacturers have indicated their intent to test as described in 40 C.F.R. section 790.48. When so directed, these manufacturers are subject to reimbursement claims. 40 C.F.R. § 790.42(a)(4), (5); 40 C.F.R. § 791.2(a).

9.6.3. Study Plans

For testing under a single-phase test rule, those who notify EPA of their intent to test must submit proposed study plans to EPA within 90 days after the effective date of the test rule. 40 C.F.R. § 790.50. Processors complying with the test rule because no manufacturer has indicated its intent to test must submit proposed study plans within 90 days of the *Federal Register* notice alerting them to respond.

9.6.4. Test Standards

Each test rule must include standards that prescribe the manner in which data are to be developed, any test methodology, and any other requirements necessary to assure that the manufacturer produces reliable and adequate data. TSCA § 4(b)(1)(B). Any test sponsor who wishes to modify a test standard or schedule for any required testing must submit an application to EPA. 40 C.F.R. § 790.55(a). If EPA concludes that the modification "would not alter the scope of the test or significantly change the schedule for completing the test, EPA will not ask for public comment before approving the modification." 40 C.F.R. § 790.55(b)(2). Otherwise, EPA will publish a notice in the *Federal Register* requesting comment on the proposal, unless EPA believes that an immediate modification is necessary to preserve the validity of an ongoing test.

"Significant changes" include a change in the test species, route of administration, exposure period, or a delay of over twelve months in receiving the final report.

9.6.5. Enforcement

EPA considers failure to comply with a TSCA § 4 test rule or ECA to violate TSCA § 15(3). 58 Fed. Reg. 59,667, 59,678 (Nov. 10, 1993). Violators are subject to criminal and civil liability under sections 16 and 17, and EPA may proceed at its discretion against individuals as well as corporations. *Id.* Enforcement includes EPA authority to inspect the testing facility—defined as the place where the chemical is held or stored, including laboratories. *Id.* Such authority is derived from TSCA §§ 15(4) and 4(b)(1). The latter directs EPA to promulgate standards for developing test data, including reliability, which necessitates laboratory inspections.

9.7. EXEMPTIONS FROM TESTING

TSCA § 4(c)(2) authorizes the Administrator to exempt a manufacturer or processor from a test rule if EPA determines that the applicant's substance "is equivalent to a chemical substance or mixture for which data has been submitted" or for which data are being developed in response to a test rule.

> [O]ne properly designed and executed study will normally provide a sufficient basis for making a regulatory decision on a given characteristic or effect of a chemical and . . . all tests meeting [the testing] standards [will be considered] . . . duplicative of each other as long as the substances being tested [are] equivalent. Therefore, if an exemption applicant established that its chemical was equivalent to a substance which was to be tested according to the standards described in the test rule, the Agency would accept the contention that testing of that applicant's chemical would yield duplicative data.

49 Fed. Reg. 39,775 (Oct. 10, 1984).

The Agency has published a procedure for implementing the section 4(c) exemption. 40 C.F.R. pt. 790, subpt. E. Under the exemption rule, any manufacturer or processor subject to a test rule who wishes to file for an exemption must apply within 30 days either after the effective date of that rule, or after a *Federal Register* notice stating that no one has submitted a letter of intent to test. 40 C.F.R. § 790.80(b)(1). EPA will not grant a request for exemption if no one submits a letter of intent to test.

A person subject to a test rule may submit a request for exemption from any or all required tests. The exemption application must contain:

(a) the identity of the test rule, the chemical at issue, and its CAS number;

(b) the specific testing requirement(s) from which an exemption is sought and the basis for the exemption request;

(c) name, address, and telephone number of applicant;

(d) name, address, and telephone number of appropriate individual to contact for further information; and

(e) equivalence data as specified in the test rule.

40 C.F.R. § 790.82. The applicant also must submit a sworn statement agreeing to reimburse persons who actually generated the data. *Id.* § 790.99.

EPA will conditionally grant an exemption for single-phase rules if it has received a letter of intent to conduct the testing for which the exemption is sought. For two-phase test rules, EPA will grant an exemption if it has received and adopted a complete proposed study plan, has determined that the subject substance is equivalent to the test substance for which the required data have been or will be submitted, and has concluded that submitting the required test data would duplicate data which have been or will be submitted under the test rule. 40 C.F.R. § 790.87.

Generally, EPA only contacts the applicant when its application information is missing or unclear. Where two or more chemicals are to be tested, the applicant is notified that the equivalence claim has been accepted or rejected. If EPA questions the adequacy of the equivalence data, the applicant has 15 days to provide explanatory information to EPA. EPA may deny an exemption application if: (1) the applicant fails to demonstrate data equivalency; (2) the applicant fails to submit the required information; (3) EPA has not received a letter of intent or an adequate study plan; or (4) the study sponsors fail to submit the required data. 40 C.F.R. § 790.88.

An applicant can appeal EPA's denial of its exemption application. *Id.* § 790.90. An appeal, however, does not stay the applicant's section 4 obligations. The appeal must be filed within 30 days of receipt of EPA's denial, must state the basis for reconsideration, and may include a request for hearing. EPA will hold a hearing if it determines that issues of material fact exist. A denial of a hearing request will be based on the applicant's submission. EPA will render a decision on an appeal within 60 days of receipt or within 60 days after the close of a hearing.

Any exemption is only conditional. EPA will terminate an exemption if the Agency determines that: (1) the test upon which the approval was granted has not been initiated by the deadline in the test rule; (2) the data have not been generated in accordance with the test standards in the test rule; or (3) the testing has not been conducted in accordance with GLPs. 40 C.F.R. § 790.93. EPA will notify the exemption holder of its preliminary decision to terminate the exemption. The exemption holder then has 30 days after receipt or publication of a *Federal Register* notice to submit information to rebut the Agency's determination and/or request a hearing. Any hearing request must be in writing and must include the exemption holder's reasons for objecting to EPA's preliminary decision to terminate. 40 C.F.R. § 790.97. EPA will notify the exemption holder of its decision within 60 days after the hearing.

Persons who manufacture less than 500 kilograms (1,100 pounds) of a chemical annually are legally subject to a test rule, but are exempt from the procedural requirements of a test rule (*i.e.*, submission of letters of intent or exemption applications) unless EPA directs them to comply in a *Federal Register* notice announcing that no manufacturers have indicated their intent to test as described in 40 C.F.R. section 790.48, or if the test rule directs them to comply. As with processors, because these manufacturers are legally subject to the test rule despite this exemption from its procedural requirements, they are not exempt from reimbursement claims.[33]

9.8. REIMBURSEMENT PROCEDURES

TSCA § 4(c) provides that persons receiving an exemption before the reimbursement period ends must reimburse those who perform the required testing for a portion of the costs. The reimbursement period "refers to a period that begins when the data from the last non-duplicative test to be completed under a test rule is submitted to EPA and ends after an amount of time equal to that which had been required to develop that data or after 5 years, whichever is later." 40 C.F.R. § 791.3(h). EPA encourages the parties to reach a voluntary agreement on reimbursement.

Where the parties cannot agree, the Administrator must issue a reimbursement order directing those who received an exemption "to provide fair and equitable reimbursement" to those who incurred the costs. Before issuing the order, the Administrator must consult with the Department of Justice and the Federal Trade Commission. The Administrator must take into account all relevant factors, including competitive position and market share of the persons providing and receiving reimbursement. TSCA § 4(c)(4)(A).

To implement the section 4 reimbursement provisions, EPA issued a reimbursement rule. 48 Fed. Reg. 31,786 (July 11, 1983) (codified at 40 C.F.R. pt. 791). The reimbursement rule takes effect only when the parties cannot agree. Private agreements need not conform to EPA's reimbursement rule.

If the parties cannot agree, any party may request a hearing with the American Arbitration Association (AAA). A party requesting an AAA hearing must mail a copy to EPA and to each person from whom the party seeks reimbursement. The hearing request must contain: (1) the names and addresses of the filing party and its counsel; (2) identification of the test rule under which the dispute arose; and (3) a list of parties seeking reimbursement and from whom reimbursement is sought, a description of the

---

[33] 54 *Federal Register* 21,237 (1989); 40 C.F.R. § 790.42(a)(4).

efforts to reach an agreement, a concise explanation of the disputed issues, and a filing fee.

EPA will publish a *Federal Register* notice announcing a hearing request. Anyone wishing to participate must notify the Agency within 45 days. Any party may file a written answer to a request for a hearing with AAA. A party may request, or the AAA in its discretion may hold, a prehearing conference to expedite the proceeding by exchanging information and stipulating to uncontested facts. After receiving a complete list of the parties, AAA will provide a roster of potential hearing officers to all parties. Each party has 30 days to object to any of the names on the roster and to indicate its preferences. AAA will select a hearing officer from the parties' lists of preferences according to the designated order of mutual preference. Once the officer is selected, no additional or different claims can be asserted without his or her consent.

The hearing is conducted using a modified version of the AAA's Rules for Commercial Arbitration (Commercial Rules). The reimbursement rule differs from the AAA's Commercial Rules in several important respects. Most significantly, the hearing officer does not render a final and binding decision, but only a proposed order that may be appealed to EPA and to a federal court. The proposed order automatically becomes a final Agency order 30 days after issuance, unless one of the parties or the Administrator seeks review. EPA has provided a complete list of the differences between commercial and TSCA § 4 arbitrations in the preamble to the reimbursement rule. 48 Fed. Reg. at 31,787.

The proposed order will be based on the formula set forth at 40 C.F.R. section 791.40(b), which provides that:

> In general, each person's share of the test cost shall be in proportion to its share of the total production volume of the test chemical:
>
> $$R_X = C \frac{Vx}{Vt}$$
>
> Where:
>
> R_X = the reimbursement share owed by company X.
>
> C = the total cost of the testing required by the test rule.
>
> V_x = the volume of the test chemical produced or imported by company X over the period defined by § 791.48.
>
> V_t = the total volume of the test chemical produced or imported over the period defined by § 791.48.

Production volume includes the amount of the test chemical imported in bulk form and in mixtures, as well as the total domestic volume produced, including by-products. Impurities are excluded unless specifically included in the test rule. 40 C.F.R. § 791.48(b). Amounts of chemicals exported are not included in the production volume unless subject to TSCA § 12(a)(2). In addition, chemicals excluded from TSCA under section 3(2)(B) are not included in computing production volume.

EPA recognizes that allocating test costs based on market share may not always be equitable. For example, "[t]he relative amount of exposure attributable to each party may be a legitimate factor when different processes or end uses are used by different firms." 48 Fed. Reg. at 31,788. Thus, the Agency permits any party to propose factors besides market share. The party proposing a different factor, however, has the burden of demonstrating that its method will produce a fair and equitable result.

9.8.1. Reimbursement by Processors

TSCA § 4(b)(3)(B) requires processors to test when the exposure or risk results from processing, distributing, using, or disposing of a substance subject to a test rule. Under the reimbursement rule, however, processors have fulfilled their testing and reimbursement obligation indirectly "through higher prices passed on by those directly responsible, the manufacturers." 40 C.F.R. § 791.45(a).

Processors are responsible for directly reimbursing those incurring testing costs when: (1) a test rule or subsequent *Federal Register* notice pertaining to a test rule specifically obligates processors and manufacturers to assume direct testing and data reimbursement responsibilities; (2) a manufacturer demonstrates to a hearing officer that it is necessary to obligate processors directly to provide a fair and equitable reimbursement; or (3) a processor voluntarily agrees to reimburse a manufacturer for a portion of the test costs (only those processors who volunteer will incur the obligation). *Id.*

9.8.2. Section 8(a) Reporting Requirements and Reimbursement

Because the hearing officer or EPA may need additional information on production volume to calculate the reimbursement amount, each *Federal Register* notice announcing a request for hearing will include a proposed section 8(a) reporting rule. A section 8(a) reporting rule will be proposed only in those instances where a party has requested a hearing or the Agency has insufficient information. In general, only manufacturers will be subject to section 8(a) reporting rules. Processors may be required to report reimbursement information in those instances where such information is necessary to calculate the reimbursement amount.

9.8.3. Multiple Testing

When two or more firms submit or plan to submit the same type of data on equivalent chemicals, the test costs will be added together, and each exemption holder's market share will be applied to the total. 40 C.F.R. § 791.52.

9.8.4. Enforcement of Reimbursement Orders

TSCA does not restrict the rights that any person may have under state, federal law, or common law to seek enforcement of the Act or to seek any other relief. If no other remedy is available, the party seeking reimbursement may sue the party from whom it seeks payment directly under TSCA § 20. Section 20 allows "any person" to "commence a civil action against any person . . . who is alleged to be in violation of the Act."

Persons in violation of a final reimbursement order are in violation of an order issued under TSCA § 4. 48 Fed. Reg. at 31,790. EPA will use its own enforcement powers under TSCA § 16 or 17 where a TSCA § 20 remedy is unavailable and the person seeking reimbursement has no other available legal remedy. TSCA § 16 allows the Agency to impose a maximum penalty of $32,500 per day until compliance. TSCA § 17 authorizes EPA to bring an action in federal court to compel payment.

9.9. JOINT DATA DEVELOPMENT

Once manufacturers and processors learn that EPA may require section 4 testing, they should waste little time getting organized to effectively shape testing requirements. Although, as noted, the practical effect of the *NRDC* decisions was to force EPA to expedite the test rule development process and to require EPA to rely more heavily on single-phase test rules, EPA's procedures governing ECAs and test rules still afford manufacturers and processors ample opportunity to negotiate with EPA over the scope, requirements, and timing of test rules. Chemical companies, processors, and their trade associations often join to shape test rules and develop test data. Cooperative testing reduces costs and risks, and avoids duplicative testing. The most frequent questions that companies face once they decide to cooperatively test are: (1) what type of organization to use, (2) how to structure and manage the organization, (3) how to share testing costs, and (4) what to test.

9.9.1. The Organization

Most frequently, a joint venture is used to conduct cooperative testing. A joint venture is an unincorporated entity that operates like a partnership except that, unlike the partnership, the joint venture's life is limited to accomplishing the venture's objectives.

9.9.2. Organizing and Administering

Typically, the company with a substantial interest in the chemical and in developing the data will invite other manufacturers and processors to an organizational meeting. At the meeting, prospective members discuss data development agreement terms, including tests to be conducted, member rights and responsibilities, and cost allocation. Based on these discussions, a draft memorandum of understanding is circulated and executed by each participating company.

Most joint ventures have a business group headed by a business chairperson, and a technical group headed by a technical chairperson. The latter develops protocols, monitors the studies, and reviews the results. The former typically decides when assessments will be made for expenses and decides if and when the testing program should be expanded beyond the original tests. During joint venture development, special attention should be devoted to the cost sharing formula and to selecting the test substance.

9.9.3. Cost Sharing

Joint testing venture participants should carefully prepare and review its terms. The most important terms will be on sharing costs and testing. Generally, costs can be apportioned based on each participant's market share, equally (per capita), or a variation of these two. Each has its advantages and disadvantages. While the market share basis may appear more equitable, defining the relevant market and assessing and reassessing each member's market share can be complex, and can unnecessarily distract the venture from developing data. Moreover, sharing costs equally gives each company an equal voice.

9.9.4. The Test Substance

The joint venture can test only one substance. This one substance should "represent" all members' products, but must meet the test rule's requirements. A representative substance may mean only that its purity is similar to the purity of all the members' products, or it may mean that it includes the same contaminants as in the members' products. Each prospective member should understand how the test substance will be selected before joining the venture.

9.10. JUDICIAL REVIEW

9.10.1. Jurisdiction, Standing and Venue

TSCA § 19(a)(1)(A) authorizes judicial review of section 4(a) test rules:

> Not later than 60 days after the date of the promulgation of a rule under section [4(a)] . . . any person may file a petition for judicial review of such rule with the United States Court of Appeals for the District of Columbia Circuit or for the circuit in which such person resides or in which such person's principal place of business is located.

TSCA § 19 provides for appellate-type review—that is, the court reviews only the rule-making record, and the EPA's findings are conclusive if supported by substantial evidence.

Timing for judicial review is clear. The petition must be filed within 60 days of the final rule. But, two procedural provisions of section 19 deserve consideration: (1) who may petition for judicial review (*i.e.*, standing); and (2) where judicial review may be obtained (*i.e.*, choice of forum). Section 19's standing provision is unrestricted—"any person" may file a petition seeking review of a final rule. "Any person" would include a producer of a substance, or any other interested organization, such as a trade association or environmental group. No injury need be shown. Regarding forum, a petition for judicial review may be filed in: (1) the District of Columbia; (2) the federal circuit in which the petitioner resides; or (3) the federal circuit in which the petitioner has its principal place of business. TSCA § 19(a)(1)(A).

9.10.2. The Rule-Making Record

A TSCA test rule must be based on the rule-making record, and must be supported by substantial evidence. With one exception, section 19(b), the reviewing court will consider only the evidence contained in the rule-making record. The court will not hold a new (*de novo*) hearing on whether and how a chemical substance or mixture should be tested.

The rule-making record will consist of: (1) the final test rule; (2) the necessary findings; (3) transcripts of oral presentations; and (4) written public comment. The record also includes any other information which EPA considers relevant to the test rule and "which the Administrator identified, on or before the date of the promulgation of such rule, in a notice published in the Federal Register." TSCA § 19(a)(3)(E). Because the Administrator must identify all relevant information on or before the date of the final rule, EPA may not issue a test rule on the basis of one set of information and base the review in court on different information. Similarly, the petitioner seeking review of the rule or the Administrator can make additional oral or written submissions to the court only upon leave of the court and only on reasonable grounds (*i.e.*, newly discovered evidence) for the failure to make the submission during the rule-making proceeding. TSCA § 19(b).

9.10.3. Standard of Review

TSCA § 19(c)(1)(B) prescribes the standard of judicial review of section 4 test rules: "[T]he court shall hold unlawful and set aside such rule if the court finds that the rule is not supported by substantial evidence in the rule-making record . . . taken as a whole." "Evidence" is defined to be "any matter in the rule-making record." *Id.*

While Congress recognized that it imposed an arguably stricter standard of review for TSCA rules by prescribing the substantial evidence test, it cautioned that the Administrator need only demonstrate that the rule is "reasonably" supported:

> While the "substantial evidence" review extends to rules under section 4(a), it is not anticipated that this review standard will unduly hinder the Administrator. As testing requirements under section 4(a) will frequently be based on an insufficiency of data, it would ordinarily not be apporpriate

> [sic] for the Administrator to develop "substantial evidence" of that insufficiency.
>
> Nonetheless, if a reasonable effort to find data which indicates that the health or environmental effects of a chemical substance may be determined does not find such information, the Administrator should be deemed to have fulfilled the substantial evidence requirement.

122 Cong. Rec. S16,804 (daily ed. Sept. 28, 1976) (statement of Sen. Magnuson), *reprinted in* House Comm. on Interstate and Foreign Commerce, 94th Cong., *Legislative History of the Toxic Substances Control Act* 726 (1976).

The TSCA § 19(c) standard requires close judicial scrutiny of the rule-making record to assure that substantial evidence supports any factual findings and that the record fully and adequately explains why the Agency made its decisions. Courts agree that judicial review of section 4 test rules should be "demanding" and "fairly rigorous." *Chemical Manufacturers Ass'n v. EPA*, 859 F.2d 977, 992 (D.C. Cir. 1988); *Ausimont U.S.A. Inc. v. EPA*, 838 F.2d 93, 96 (3d Cir. 1988); *Shell Chemical Co. v. EPA*, 826 F.2d 295, 297 (5th Cir. 1987). Practically, however, the reviewing court will accord substantial deference to EPA on policy and scientific issues. If EPA finds data unavailable on a particular chemical substance or mixture, the rule-making record need only demonstrate that the Administrator made a reasonable effort to find the data.

9.11. TSCA § 4(f) FINDINGS OF SIGNIFICANT RISK

TSCA § 4(d) requires the Administrator to publish a notice of the receipt of test data submitted in response to a test rule, and TSCA § 4(f) governs the Agency's actions after test data receipt. If the Administrator receives test data or other information "which indicates to the Administrator that there *may* be a reasonable basis to conclude that a chemical substance or mixture presents or will present a significant risk of serious or widespread harm to human beings from cancer, gene mutations, or birth defects," the Administrator must within 180 days initiate the appropriate rule-making under section 4, 5, 6, or 7 or publish in the *Federal Register* the reasons for not taking action. TSCA § 4(f)(2) (emphasis added).

The purpose of section 4(f) is to focus the Agency's attention on those substances which pose significant risks, such as carcinogenicity, teratogenicity, and mutagenicity. The 180-day deadline forces the Agency to decide whether to initiate regulatory action. In evaluating whether a substance may present an unreasonable risk, the Agency uses the "weight of evidence" to examine toxicity and human and environmental exposure, and the technological, social, and economic feasibility of controlling those risks.

Estimating a substance's toxicity is only one component of the risk equation. Environmental and human exposure, including duration, also must be determined. EPA examines data on the rate of a chemical's absorption, its metabolic fate, the number of people exposed, the type of exposure (*e.g.*, dermal, inhalation), and the potential rates of exposure. EPA has explained the importance of exposure information:

> A § 4(f) finding will be based on data about one or more exposed populations. If a single population is subject to a risk that meets § 4(f) criteria the finding will be made even though risks to other populations have yet to be characterized and evaluated.

EPA, Office of Toxic Substances, *Guidance Document on Requirements of Section 4(f) of the Toxic Substances Control Act* 7 (June 1985) [Section 4(f) Guidance Document].

9.11.1. Criteria for Risk

Under TSCA § 4(f), EPA must take regulatory action when the chemical poses "a significant risk of serious or widespread harm to human beings." EPA considers this TSCA § 4(f) regulatory trigger to present a higher risk threshold than the TSCA § 6 trigger which requires a finding of "unreasonable risk." According to the Agency, the language of TSCA § 4(f) closely parallels the language of TSCA § 7 (imminent hazard provision):

> The language in § 7(f) is "risk of serious or widespread injury"; and the legislative history indicates that "risk of serious injury" means a high individual risk for a population, while "risk of widespread injury" means a somewhat lower risk, but for large numbers of people. We have taken this history into account in interpreting § 4(f).

Section 4(f) Guidance Document at 7.

9.11.2. Significant Risk of Serious Harm

Under this criterion, EPA examines whether a population whose members are at high individual risk from the substance can be identified. If the Agency estimates that humans will be exposed to doses that produced an effect observed in animals or humans, the Agency will make a section 4(f) finding. This same criterion also is met by situations where "human exposures are below the lowest level at which the effect has actually been observed in animals or humans under study, but nevertheless are at exposure levels at which high individual risk can be predicted." *Id.* at 8. This would suggest that the Agency will find a "significant risk of serious harm" where an exposed population does not enjoy an adequate margin of safety.

9.11.3. Significant Risk of Widespread Harm

Here, EPA examines whether a large number of persons are exposed to the substance at a level on which a significant aggregate population risk is predicated. *Id.*

Although the individual risk may not be as high as that needed under the previous criterion, the harm must be widespread and affect a large number of people.

9.11.4. Review Period

Once EPA determines that the section 4(f) criteria have been met, the Agency has 180 days to decide whether to initiate regulatory action. This 180-day period can be extended for an additional 90 days for "good cause." TSCA § 4(f)(2). The Agency will begin the 180-day review period when it receives sufficient information to make a section 4(f) finding. In general, EPA will not solicit public comments before making a section 4(f) finding. Instead, the Administrator will make the final section 4(f) finding and, if supported by the finding, will initiate an appropriate proceeding under TSCA § 4, 5, 6 or 7.

9.12. VOLUNTARY TESTING INITIATIVES

Due to the time required to promulgate a test rule, EPA and the chemical industry have recently pioneered several voluntary programs to increase EPA's data collection and testing capabilities.

9.12.1. High Production Volume (HPV) Chemicals

HPV chemicals are industrial non-polymeric chemicals manufactured in or imported into the United States in volumes of 1 million pounds or more per year. The U.S. HPV chemicals were identified through information collected under the TSCA Inventory Update Rule (IUR). The initial HPV Challenge Program Chemical List consisted of all the HPV chemicals reported during the 1990 IUR reporting year. In April 1998, EPA completed a study, entitled *Chemical Hazard Data Availability Study: What Do We Really Know About the Safety of High Production Volume Chemicals?,* evaluating whether health hazard data and environmental hazard/fate data for HPV chemicals was publicly available. The study analyzed public test data availability for 2,863 HPV chemicals. EPA's study found what it described as "major gaps" in basic HPV test data. EPA learned that most had never been tested for acute toxicity, repeat dose toxicity, developmental and reproductive toxicity, mutagenicity, ecotoxicity or environmental fate. Then, in June 1998, the American Chemistry Council (ACC, formerly the Chemical Manufacturers Association) issued a report on public data availability for HPV chemicals based on a study that included data sources in addition to those used by EPA. The ACC report, entitled *Public Availability of SIDS-Related Testing Data for U.S. High Production Volume Chemicals*, confirmed EPA's conclusions that the public domain contained only limited toxicity and environmental fate test data for many HPV substances.

When Vice President Gore unveiled EPA's "Chemical Right to Know" initiative in 1998, he included a challenge to industry to increase HPV chemical testing. EPA then announced that U.S. industry must test all HPV chemicals by 2001 or face mandatory TSCA test rules. The ACC proposed an alternative approach: a voluntary testing initiative that allowed flexibility, where scientifically appropriate, and called for increased international efforts, backed by potential section 4 test rulemaking. On October 9, 1998, EPA, joined by the ACC, the American Petroleum Institute (API), and the Environmental Defense Fund, announced the voluntary HPV Challenge Program, which adopted the ACC's approach.

The essential elements of the HPV Challenge Program are (1) a fixed timetable and fixed list of chemicals; (2) continuous public access to program status and results, over the Internet; and (3) internationally shared testing responsibility. 65 Fed. Reg. 81,686, 81,692 (Dec. 26, 2000). Under the Program, EPA invited U.S. HPV chemical manufacturers and importers to voluntarily "sponsor" chemicals. Sponsorship entails identifying and assessing the adequacy of existing information, conducting new testing if adequate information does not exist, and making the new and existing test results available to the public. Necessary testing should be completed by 2004, and all data available to the public by 2005. The Agency intends to consider specific chemicals that are not voluntarily sponsored in the HPV Challenge Program as candidates for test rules under section 4. *See* 65 Fed. Reg. 81,658 (Dec. 26, 2000).

To develop the testing requirements for HPV chemicals, EPA used information and sources in EPA's study and the ACC's report. HPV testing standards were derived from a test battery agreed upon by the international community as appropriate for screening international HPV chemical substances for toxicity. The Organization for Economic Cooperation and Development (OECD) adopted six basic testing endpoints as the required minimum. The testing endpoints, known as the OECD's "Screening Information Data Set" (SIDS)[34] include: acute toxicity, repeat dose toxicity, developmental and reproductive toxicity, mutagenicity (gene mutation and chromosomal aberration/damage assays), ecotoxicity (studies in fish, invertebrates, and algae), and environmental fate (including physical/chemical properties [melting point, boiling point, vapor pressure, n-octanol/water partition coefficient, and water solubility], photolysis, hydrolysis, transport/distribution, and biodegradation). The "SIDS battery" of tests can be used to conduct an initial hazard and risk assessment and to identify HPV chemicals needing more in-depth testing and assessment.

The HPV Challenge Program commenced with two initial time periods during which sponsors made commitments to sponsor HPV chemicals for testing. EPA assured companies that committed to the program before March 15, 1999 that sponsored HPV chemicals would not be listed in a proposed test rule. Thereafter,

---

[34] The SIDS program, operated under the auspices of the OECD, is a voluntary cooperative international testing program that began in 1989. The SIDs program is focused on developing base level test information on 600 international HPV chemicals. The SIDS data are used to screen the chemicals and set priorities for further testing or risk assessment and management. The OECD/SIDS test data set includes physical properties, chemical properties, and environmental fate, environmental effects, and health effects testing results. Because virtually all 600 chemicals on the SIDS list are produced by manufacturers in or imported into the United States, EPA considers the OECD/SIDS testing program to be an integral part of the TSCA chemical testing program.

companies still had a further opportunity to commit to the HPV Challenge Program until December 1, 1999, when the sign-up period for volunteering to sponsor chemicals ended. EPA is not currently planning to include in a TSCA § 4 HPV SIDS rulemaking any chemicals sponsored during these first two sign-up periods. But, EPA intends to issue a TSCA § 4 HPV SIDS rule to address unmet data needs for chemicals not sponsored during these phases.

Although the commitment phase of the voluntary HPV Challenge Program has ended, EPA will accept commitments to sponsor additional chemicals, which must be consistent with EPA's "viable commitment" guidance. EPA does not intend to include a chemical covered by a viable commitment in a final TSCA § 4 HPV SIDS rulemaking, if, during the regulatory phase of the Program, the sponsor agrees to the voluntary phase commitments and provides the following additional information:

- Evidence that work is underway and proceeding in a timely manner.
- Data required to complete the SIDS battery are developed within the time frame set by EPA in the proposed rule.
- Robust summaries and full copies of all study reports from new studies and existing data are submitted to EPA in a timely manner.

Since announcement of the HPV Challenge Program in late 1998, and as of January, 2005 over 382 companies, working either independently or through 98 consortia, have publicly committed to make screening level health and environmental hazard data available on approximately 2,242 chemicals by 2005. *See* footnote 2, herein. *See also* 65 *Federal Register* 248 (Dec. 26, 2000).

In 2005, EPA plans to finalize a TSCA § 4 test rule that the Agency proposed for certain unsponsored chemicals on December 26, 2000 (65 Fed. Reg. 81,685). EPA is considering additional TSCA § 4 test rules to fill data needs that are unmet in the voluntary HPV Challenge Program, the OECD HPV SIDS Program, and the ICCA HPV Initiative. The Agency will continue to evaluate unsponsored HPV chemicals for potential rulemaking under TSCA § 4.

9.12.2. The Voluntary Information Submission Innovative Online Network (VISION)

In its 41st Report (63 Fed. Reg, 17,658, April 9, 1998) and 42nd Report (63 Fed. Reg, 42,554, August 7, 1998), the ITC described its Voluntary Information Submission Innovative Online Network (VISION) and the Health and Safety Data Reporting Form. The ITC created VISION and the Health and Safety Data Reporting Form in response to chemical industry requests to offer more opportunities to provide voluntary information submissions. ITC intended to:

1. Encourage more voluntary information reporting and testing;

2. Facilitate retrieval of information to meet U.S. Government data needs;

3. Promote more efficient use of TSCA §§ 4, 8 and related resources; and

4. Foster participation in ITC dialogue groups and partnerships.

VISION and the Health and Safety Data Reporting Form did not meet the ITC's expectations in stimulating voluntary submissions. In its 50th Report (67 Fed. Reg. 45,929, July 30, 2002), the ITC asked for comments to make these tools more effective. In response, the ACC expressed concerns about the need to protect confidential business information, the problems of soliciting voluntary submissions on non-HPV chemicals, the potential that specific data may not exist in all cases, and the resources required to submit studies as PDF files.

The ITC reviewed its voluntary information submission procedures and considered these comments. As a result, the ITC is revising the VISION as outlined below.

1. The ITC will continue to acknowledge trade organizations and companies that voluntarily submit information in response to an ITC solicitation.

2. The ITC requested that EPA include ITC's solicitations for voluntary information submissions in the summary and body of the preambles of the ITC's *Federal Register* Reports, to allow companies to readily determine if the ITC is soliciting voluntary information.

3. The ITC will notify major chemical trade associations by e-mail that new ITC Reports have been posted to the ITC's website (http://www/epa.gov/optintr/itc/). The e-mails will include a summary of the Report and announcements of new information solicitations.

4. The voluntary information submissions should be submitted within 90 days of the date the ITC Report is published in the *Federal Register*. Failure to voluntarily submit information in a timely manner may lead ITC to request that EPA promulgate the appropriate TSCA § 8(a) and 8(d) reporting rules in a subsequent Report to the EPA Administrator.

5. Information submitted voluntarily need not be re-submitted under a TSCA § 8(d) rule.

6. The ITC is working with EPA to revise the Electronic Health and Safety Data Reporting Form, and to improve electronic reporting. To supplement the efforts to obtain studies in electronic format through the VISION, the ITC staff contacts the producers and importers of ITC-recommended chemicals to obtain voluntary information submissions.

7. Voluntary information may be submitted by mail, in person, by courier or electronically.[35]

9.12.3. The Voluntary Children's Chemical Evaluation Program (VCCEP)

In 2000, EPA announced the Voluntary Children's Chemical Evaluation Program (VCCEP) to develop data on potential health risks to children. *See* 65 Fed. Reg. 81699 (Dec. 26, 2000). EPA asked companies that manufacture or import 23 chemicals found in human tissues and the environment to volunteer to sponsor the evaluation of those chemicals. Thirty-five companies and ten consortia responded and volunteered to sponsor 20 of the 23 chemicals.

The VCCEP consists of three tiers, to which a sponsor could commit separately. EPA invited companies to volunteer to sponsor chemical(s) that they manufacture or import in Tier 1 of the VCCEP pilot. As part of their sponsorship, companies collect or develop health effects and exposure information on their chemical(s) and integrate that information in a risk assessment. The sponsor also develops a "data needs assessment." The data needs assessment discusses the need for additional data, which could be provided by the next tier, to fully characterize the risks the chemical may pose to children.

A group of scientific experts in toxicity testing and exposure evaluates the Tier 1 results in Peer Consultation. Toxicology Excellence for Risk Assessment (TERA) will organize and facilitate the Peer Consultations and forward the results to EPA and the sponsor(s). EPA will consider the Peer Consultation and announce whether additional higher tier information is needed. If so, sponsors will be asked to volunteer to provide it. If no more information is needed, EPA and the sponsors will conduct appropriate risk communication and, if necessary, risk management.

EPA designated a chemical to the VCCEP pilot if monitoring data indicated that humans had been exposed to the chemical, and that the chemical is present in the environment. To determine human exposure, EPA used biomonitoring data sets from samples from human blood, breast milk, and exhaled breath. To determine presence in

---

35 *See* http://www.epa.gov/opptintr/itc/vision.htm.

the environment, EPA used monitoring data indicating presence in indoor air or presence in drinking water as an unregulated contaminant.

The 23 chemicals in the VCCEP pilot are:

CAS No.	Chemical Name	CAS No.	Chemical Name
67-64-1	Acetone	108-88-3	Toluene
71-43-2	Benzene	108-90-7	Chlorobenzene
75-35-4	Vinylidenechloride	112-40-3	*n*-Dodecane
78-93-3	Methyl ethyl ketone	123-91-1	*p*-Dioxane
79-01-6	Trichloroethylene	124-18-5	Decane
80-56-8	*a*-Pinene	127-18-4	Tetrachloroethylene
95-47-6	*o*-Xylene	541-73-1	*m*-Dichlorobenzene
100-41-4	Ethylbenzene	1120-21-4	Undecane
106-46-7	*p*-Dichlorobenzene	1163-19-5	Decabromodiphenylether
106-93-4	Ethylene dibromide	32534-81-9	Pentabromodiphenyl ether
107-06-2	Ethylene dichloride	32536-52-0	Octabromodiphenyl ether
108-38-3	*m*-Xylene		

The health effects tests in the VCCEP listed by tier are:

Tier 1	Tier 2	Tier 3
Acute toxicity	Subchronic toxicity	Neurotoxicity screening battery
Repeated dose toxicity with reproductive and developmental toxicity screens	Prenatal developmental toxicity	Carcinogenicity
	Reproductive and fertility effects	Developmental neurotoxicity
Bacterial reverse mutation assay	Immunotoxicity	
In vitro <u>or</u> *in vivo* chromosomal aberrations <u>or</u> *in vivo* micronucleus test	*In vivo* chromosomal aberrations <u>or</u> *in vivo* micronucleus test	
	Metabolism and pharmacokinetics	

As of July, 2005, Tier 1 Peer Consultation Reports have been written for 9 of the 23 chemicals.

CHAPTER 10
REPORTING AND RETENTION OF INFORMATION

TSCA § 8 establishes reporting and record-keeping requirements to provide EPA with information on which to base regulatory and enforcement actions and to track patterns of adverse reactions to chemicals. Section 8 grants the Agency broad information-gathering authority because Congress thought that one of the most significant gaps in pre-TSCA environmental laws was EPA's lack of authority "for collection of data to determine the totality of human and environmental exposure to chemicals." H.R. Rep. No. 1341, 94th Cong., at 6, *reprinted in* House Comm. on Interstate and Foreign Commerce, *Legislative History of the Toxic Substances Control Act* (*TSCA Legislative History)* 409, 414 (1976). Section 8 was designed to provide:

> [A]n ongoing mechanism that would ensure that the EPA Administrator would continually have access to new information developed regarding adverse health or environmental effects associated with chemical substances.

122 Cong. Rec. S16,807 (daily ed. Sept. 28, 1976) (statement of Sen. Pearson), *reprinted in TSCA Legislative History* at 735.

Section 8(a) provides EPA with authority to promulgate rules requiring manufacturers to maintain records on their chemicals and to make reports concerning the chemical identities, categories of use, by-products, environmental and health effects, and numbers of workers exposed. As previously discussed in Chapter 4, TSCA § 8(b) requires EPA to publish and keep current a list or "inventory" of chemical substances that are manufactured in the U.S. or imported for any commercial purpose that could be subject to regulation under TSCA. Section 8(c) requires manufacturers and certain processors to maintain records of alleged adverse reactions to health or the environment. Section 8(d) requires manufacturers and processors to submit to EPA lists of health and safety studies in their possession and to provide copies of such studies upon request. Finally, TSCA § 8(e) requires manufacturers, processors, and distributors to inform EPA when they receive information that a chemical substance may present a substantial risk of injury to health or the environment.

EPA uses the information obtained under section 8: (1) to provide other EPA programs, industry, and citizens with reliable information on chemicals; (2) to evaluate existing data to determine its adequacy for risk assessment purposes, (3) to identify data gaps; and (4) to monitor ongoing activities with respect to specific chemicals. In order to accomplish these objectives, the Agency uses a number of approaches. First, EPA applies its section 8 authority as needed to specific chemicals and withdraws the reporting requirements when the information need ceases. Second, the Office of Pollution Prevention and Toxics (OPPT) coordinates its information-gathering activities with those of other EPA programs and other federal and state agencies. Finally, by using "model" rules and standardized forms, the Agency helps to reduce the cost of compliance to the regulated community, while minimizing possible reporting errors.

Beginning in 1986, the Agency began to use section 8 with increasing frequency to support not only regulatory activities by OPPT, but the regulatory activities of other EPA offices and other federal agencies as well. Also in 1986, EPA began to aggressively enforce all of the provisions of TSCA § 8, not just section 8(e). Enforcement actions have included the issuance of civil complaints against companies that allegedly violated one or more of the section 8 requirements.

In addition to its obvious relevance for EPA enforcement, a company's compliance record also could have a bearing on its "toxic tort" liability. A growing number of suits have been filed by plaintiffs seeking redress from risk or injury caused by "toxic" substances. Failure to comply with TSCA's section 8 reporting and record-keeping requirements may be cited by a plaintiff as evidence of negligence.

10.1. TSCA § 8(a): REPORTS

Under TSCA § 8(a), EPA may require companies to maintain records and to submit reports on their chemical manufacturing, importing and processing activities. EPA uses section 8(a) rules to determine what information exists on a particular chemical substance or mixture, and to set priorities for test rules under TSCA § 4 and/or regulatory action under TSCA § 6.

The Agency has used its section 8(a) authority to impose record-keeping and reporting requirements on specific chemicals, but its most significant use of section 8(a) has been the issuance of "model" rules that apply to multiple chemicals. The first of these model rules, the Preliminary Assessment Information Rule (PAIR), was issued in June 1982. 47 Fed. Reg. 26,992 (June 22, 1982) (codified at 40 C.F.R. pt. 712, subpt. B). The second, the Comprehensive Assessment Information Rule (CAIR), was issued on December 22, 1988 and, as explained below, initially was designed to replace the PAIR. Due to the controversy surrounding EPA's implementation of the CAIR, the rule never functioned as intended and finally on June 19, 1995, EPA removed the CAIR regulations from the C.F.R. 60 Fed. Reg. 31,917 (June 19, 1995).

TSCA § 8(a) authorizes the Administrator to require those who currently manufacture or process chemical substances, or who propose to do so in the future, to maintain records and submit reports as the Administrator "may reasonably require." TSCA § 8(a) also authorizes the Administrator to require those who currently manufacture or process, or propose to manufacture or process, mixtures or small quantities of research and development (R&D) chemicals to maintain records and to submit reports to the Agency only to the extent "necessary for the effective enforcement" of the Act. This same standard also applies to records and reports on changes in the proportions of the components of a mixture. The difference in these standards reflects Congress's belief that the Agency's need for information concerning mixtures and R&D chemicals is not as great as the need for information on basic chemical substances already in commerce. H.R. Rep. No. 1341, at 41, *reprinted in TSCA Legislative History* at 448.

"Small" manufacturers and processors generally are exempt from section 8(a).[36] The Administrator, however, can require section 8(a) reports from small manufacturers and processors of chemicals that are subject to test rules under section 4, that appear on the "risk list" under section 5(b)(4), or that are subject to limitations under section 5(e) or 6.

Section 8(a)(2) lists the kinds of information for which the Agency may require record-keeping and reporting. Such information can include chemical identity, categories of use, amounts manufactured or processed, by-products, data on environmental and health effects, and exposure information. Manufacturers and processors must provide this information to the extent they know of or can reasonably ascertain it.

10.1.1. The Preliminary Assessment Information Rule (PAIR)

When proposing the PAIR in 1980, the Agency viewed it as the first of a set of three progressively more detailed section 8(a) reporting rules intended to obtain information appropriate to the needs of initial, middle, and later stages of a comprehensive assessment of chemical substances. 45 Fed. Reg. 13,646 (Feb. 29, 1980). The two-page PAIR reporting form (EPA Form No. 7710-35) was intended to gather very preliminary exposure data to help the Agency set testing priorities.

10.1.1.1. Who Must Report

Manufacturers and importers must report on each listed chemical substance manufactured or imported (in bulk form) during the complete corporate fiscal year preceding listing. Processors are not subject to the PAIR. Manufacturers of chemical substances extracted from natural sources, such as oil and ore, need only report the manufacturing steps and uses of the extracted chemical. They do not have to describe the extraction of the natural source material or other crude precursors derived from the natural source. 40 C.F.R. § 712.5. For example, extraction of shale oil from a mine need not be reported, but the steps involved in retorting the ore and refining the shale oil into usable products must be reported.

---

[36] TSCA does not define "small manufacturers" or "small processors"; rather each reporting rule defines these terms separately.

EPA also exempts the following from reporting under the PAIR:

- persons who manufacture or import a listed substance solely for R&D, including commercial R&D;
- persons who, during the reporting period, manufactured or imported fewer than 500 kilograms of a chemical at a single plant site;
- small manufacturers or importers, which the PAIR defines as companies whose total annual sales from all sites owned by the foreign or domestic parent company were below $30 million for the reporting period *and* who produced less than 45,400 kg of the listed substance at the plant site;[37]
- persons who manufactured the chemical as a non-isolated intermediate, an impurity, or, under certain conditions, as a byproduct.

40 C.F.R. § 712.25.

10.1.1.2. Filling Out the Form

Manufacturers and importers subject to the PAIR must submit a two-page "Manufacturer's Report—Preliminary Assessment Information" form for each plant site manufacturing or importing (in bulk form) a chemical listed in 40 C.F.R. section 712.30. Completed reports can be submitted by either the individual plants or the company headquarters. The information must be provided to the extent it is "known to or reasonably ascertainable by" the respondent. EPA has interpreted this phrase to require "persons to report data that are readily obtainable by management and supervisory employees responsible for manufacturing, processing, distribution, technical services, marketing, and other related activities." 47 Fed. Reg. 26,994 (June 22, 1982). For each category of information, EPA has specified the accuracy level or range within which the information must be reported (*e.g.*, ± 50 percent, "best estimates from readily obtainable data," etc.).

10.1.1.3. Certification by Respondent

The respondent must certify the technical accuracy and confidentiality of the data reported. The physical location of the plant site and its mailing address must be identified along with any Dun & Bradstreet number. A technical contact familiar with the

---

[37] This exemption does not apply to manufacturers or importers of listed chemical substances that are designated as being of special concern. Such substances are marked with an asterisk in the table at 40 C.F.R. § 712.30.

information submitted also must be identified. EPA will send its acknowledgment of receipt of the form to this person.

10.1.1.4. *Chemical Identity*

If the chemical has a Chemical Abstract Service Registry Number (CASRN) and is listed in 40 C.F.R. section 712.30 by its specific chemical name, then the chemical substance must be identified on the form by its CASRN and the first 15 characters of its name. If the chemical identity is considered confidential, it must be reported by the category name listed in 40 C.F.R. section 712.30 and the number of the Inventory Reporting Form C on which the chemical was originally reported for the TSCA Inventory.

10.1.1.5. *Preliminary Assessment Information—Plant Site Activities*

Information on plant site activities must be based on "best estimates from readily obtainable data." (Here, no specific accuracy range is required.) EPA has adopted this accuracy standard because the Agency was:

> persuaded that manufacturers must routinely know their own production efficiencies and quantities in order to control their costs and price their products. Thus, when manufacturers report about their own activities, the best estimate from readily obtainable data would be sufficiently accurate. There is no need for the company to expend further effort to report more exactly.

47 Fed. Reg. 26,994 (June 22, 1982).

Reportable information on plant activities includes: (1) data pertaining to the amount of the chemical manufactured or imported; (2) the amount routinely lost during manufacturing operations; (3) a description of the amount processed in enclosed, controlled release, or open process operations; and (4) the number of workers involved in each process. The reporting company must specify the level of accuracy for losses of the chemical during manufacturing. EPA decided that companies should specify the level of accuracy in response to comments that the lack of measured data on such losses prevented respondents from meeting the "best estimates from readily obtainable data" standard.

In determining the number of workers involved, all persons employed directly in manufacturing, processing, and handling the chemical during the reporting period are to be counted. A worker is to be considered as working with only one process category. If someone works in several process categories, the category in which the worker spends the most time is the one for which that worker should be counted.

10.1.1.6. Quantity in Commercial Distribution

The quantity of the substance prepared for distribution in industrial and consumer products is to be reported. "Industrial" use means the manufacturing and service industries included in the Standard Industrial Classification (SIC) codes, while consumer products are those used primarily by the general population. Industrial and consumer products are divided into three types: (1) chemical substances or mixtures; (2) articles or products with no release; and (3) articles or products with some release. In addition, the quantity of chemical manufactured for export, consumed as a reactant, and sold for an unknown use also must be reported. This information must be accurate to within $\pm$ 50 percent. If the respondent cannot meet this accuracy level, the respondent should indicate on the form that the accuracy level is "unknown."

10.1.2. The Comprehensive Assessment Information Rule (CAIR)

In 1988, EPA published a second, more detailed reporting rule, the CAIR. EPA envisioned the CAIR as a single form that could be used by the Agency under a variety of situations to elicit information on chemical substances under TSCA § 8(a). 53 Fed. Reg. 51,698 (Dec. 22, 1988). In the initial rule, EPA listed nineteen substances that were to be subject to CAIR reporting. Companies that manufactured or processed these 19 chemicals during the reporting period (February 8, 1987 through February 5, 1989) would have been required to submit CAIR reports, but industry challenged the rule in court, resulting in a stay of the rule's effectiveness until EPA promulgated amendments. In 1993, EPA proposed amendments to the CAIR, but these proposed amendments were never finalized. In 1995, EPA removed the CAIR regulations from the C.F.R. because they are "not in effect and their presence in the C.F.R. is confusing to the public and the regulated community." 60 Fed. Reg. 31,918 (June 19, 1995).

10.1.3. Inventory Update Rule

In June 1986, EPA issued an Inventory Update Rule requiring manufacturers and importers of certain chemicals listed on the Inventory to report quadrenially current data on the production volume, plant site and site-limited status of the substances. In 2003 EPA promulgated extensive revisions to the IUR that dramatically expand the amount of information that must be reported. 68 Fed. Reg. 848, Jan. 7, 2003. *See* chapter 4 for a more detailed discussion of the Inventory Update Rule.

10.2. TSCA § 8(c): RECORDS OF SIGNIFICANT ADVERSE REACTIONS

TSCA § 8(c) requires manufacturers, processors, and distributors to keep records of significant adverse reactions to health and the environment alleged to have been caused by a chemical substance or mixture. Such allegations may be made by "any source," including employees, customers, surrounding neighbors, or other companies on behalf of their employees, or other organizations on behalf of their members. Occupationally derived allegations must be kept on file for 30 years, non-occupational allegations for five years. These allegations do not have to be reported to EPA unless the Agency specifically requests them.

EPA's rule implementing TSCA § 8(c) establishes a record-keeping and reporting system that will "[c]reate a historical record of significant adverse reactions alleged to have been caused by [a particular] substance or mixture" and to "[p]rovide a means to identify previously unknown chemical hazards and to reveal patterns of adverse effects" which previously might have gone undetected. 48 Fed. Reg. 38,178 (Aug. 22, 1983) (supplementary information to final rule) (codified at 40 C.F.R. pt. 717). The TSCA § 8(c) rule became effective November 21, 1983.

10.2.1. Persons Subject to the Rule

Manufacturers of chemical substances and mixtures covered by TSCA (with the exception of manufacturers involved solely in mining or other extractive functions—mineral, oil, petroleum, natural gas, coal, etc.) are subject to the provisions of 40 C.F.R. part 717. The manufacture of a chemical substance for commercial purposes at any site owned or controlled by a firm is sufficient to subject that corporate entity to the section 8(c) rule. If the United States manufacturing facility is the subsidiary of a foreign parent, the subsidiary is the "person" subject to section 8(c). United States parents with foreign subsidiaries, however, are responsible for recording allegations originating with the foreign subsidiary. The degree of a United States parent's involvement with the foreign subsidiary is irrelevant. Although federal agencies, such as the Department of Defense, generally do not engage in commercial activities and, therefore, are not themselves manufacturers for a commercial purpose, EPA has taken the position that government-owned, company-operated (GOCO) facilities are engaged in manufacturing for commercial purposes, making the GOCO contractor liable for section 8(c) compliance. EPA, Office of Toxic Substances, *TSCA Section 8(c) Questions and Answers* (question 6) (Nov. 1983).

The original rule made processors in SIC code 28 (chemicals and allied products) and SIC code 2911 (petroleum refining) subject to section 8(c). EPA later abandoned the use of SIC codes to identify processors who are subject to section 8(c). 50 Fed. Reg. 46,769 (Nov. 13, 1985). As amended, the rule exempts all processors except those who "process" chemical substances by using them to produce mixtures, or who repackage chemical substances or mixtures. 40 C.F.R. § 717.5(b). In other words, formulators and re-packagers are subject to section 8(c). EPA also has exempted from the rule's provisions persons who are solely distributors, defined as a person "solely engaged in the distribution of chemical substances," and retailers. There are no exemptions for small manufacturers or processors or for R&D substances.

10.2.2. What Constitutes a Significant Adverse Reaction

EPA has defined a significant adverse reaction to mean:

> reactions that may indicate a substantial impairment of normal activities, or long-lasting or irreversible damage to health or the environment.

40 C.F.R. § 717.3(i).

10.2.2.1. Human Health Reactions

This definition is intended to encompass not only damage that manifests itself physiologically, such as cancer or birth defects, but also includes "subjectively experienced adverse reactions" which, although not physically verifiable, may be indicative of a more serious effect. EPA intends that regulated entities file those reactions which initially appear less serious in nature, but could indicate a pattern of adverse effects. The Agency concedes that regulated entities must exercise a considerable amount of judgment in determining which adverse reactions are significant ones.

EPA has listed four groups of reactions at 40 C.F.R. section 717.12 which are intended to provide examples of the range of reactions that should be considered "significant." These types of reactions include:

> (1) Long-lasting or irreversible damage, such as cancer or birth defects.
>
> (2) Partial or complete impairment of bodily functions, such as reproductive disorders, neurological disorders or blood disorders.
>
> (3) An impairment of normal activities experienced by all or most of the persons exposed at one time.
>
> (4) An impairment of normal activities which is experienced each time an individual is exposed.

40 C.F.R. §§ 717.12(a)(1)-(4).

Groups three and four involve two criteria. First, they involve the impairment of a normal activity (which can be either job related or non-job-related). Second, they are "repeated," either in the sense that they are experienced by a group of persons, or in the sense that they are experienced by a single individual several times.

In order to place some limitation on what initially appears to be an open-ended recording obligation, EPA provided a narrow exemption for "known human health effects." *Id.* § 717.12(b). Known human health effects are defined as "commonly recognized human health effect[s] of a particular substance or mixture" as described in scientific articles and publications, or the firm's material safety data sheets. *Id.* § 717.3(c)(1). An effect is not considered to be a known human health effect, however, if the effect:

- Was a significantly more severe toxic effect than previously described.
- Was a manifestation of a toxic effect after a significantly shorter exposure period or lower exposure level than described.
- Was a manifestation of a toxic effect by an exposure route different from that described.

Id. §§ 717.3(c)(2)(i)-(iii).

EPA has stated that an effect is not a known human health effect if it has been observed only in *in vitro* or animal testing on the substance. Thus, an allegation that a chemical produced a chronic or subchronic effect in a human must be recorded if, at the time of the allegation, animal studies are the only evidence that the chemical can produce that effect. The Agency, however, has qualified this exclusion. In a "question and answer" document issued on the section 8(c) rule, the Agency stated that acute effects (*e.g.*, primary irritant effects) observed only in animal test species "may be considered known human effects because of the inevitability that such substance will have similar adverse acute effects on human tissue." EPA, Office of Toxic Substances, *Questions and Answers Concerning the TSCA Section 8(c) Rule* 45 (July 1984).

10.2.2.2. Environmental Reactions

Environmental reactions which must be recorded include:

(1) Gradual or sudden changes in the composition of animal life or plant life, including fungal or microbial organisms, in an area.

(2) Abnormal number of deaths of organisms (*e.g.*, fish kills).

(3) Reduction of the reproductive success or the vigor of a species.

(4) Reduction in agricultural productivity, whether crops or livestock.

(5) Alterations in the behavior or distribution of a species.

(6) Long lasting or irreversible contamination of components of the physical environment, especially in the case of ground water, and surface water and soil resources that have limited self-cleansing capability.

40 C.F.R. § 717.12(c)(1)-(6). These reactions are to be recorded even if the incident is restricted to a single plant or disposal site.

EPA has provided a limited exemption from the requirement to record environmental reactions. If the alleged cause of the significant adverse reaction is "directly attributable" to an accidental spill or discharge, an emission exceeding permitted levels, or other incidents which have been reported to the federal government under any applicable authority, then firms are not required to record the incident under section 8(c). 40 C.F.R. § 717.12(d). Environmental contamination incidents reported to local or state authorities, however, are not exempt unless the state or local government has been delegated responsibility for administering the federal law in question. EPA developed this exemption primarily to avoid the problem of duplicative record-keeping and reporting of environmental incidents. The Agency declined to exempt "known environmental effects" because environmental reactions are more widely variable than human reactions.

10.2.3. "Allegations" Trigger Recording Obligations

An "allegation" is defined as:

> a statement, *made without formal proof or regard for evidence*, that a chemical substance or mixture has caused a significant adverse reaction to health or the environment.

40 C.F.R. § 717.3(a) (emphasis added).

In order to constitute an allegation which triggers recording obligations under section 8(c), the statement must clearly state the alleged cause of the adverse reaction by identifying one or more of the following:

- A specific substance.
- A mixture or article that contains a specific substance.
- A company process or operation in which substances are involved.
- An effluent, emission, or other discharge from a site of manufacturing, processing or distribution of a substance.

See id. § 717.10(b)(2)(i)-(v). Under this definition, no proof or evidence, such as a doctor's report, is required for an allegation to be recordable. It is sufficient simply that the allegation has been made.

Allegations can be derived from a variety of sources. For example, a complaint in a lawsuit or other legal action may contain allegations that trigger recording requirements. Allegations made during discovery in a lawsuit also can trigger recording obligations. Allegations made to "off-duty employees at social functions," however, require action under section 8(c) only if the off-duty employee is an official who has knowledge of the company's section 8(c) responsibilities. Under such circumstances, EPA asserts that the official should request that the alleger submit the allegation in writing or contact the official during normal business hours.

Each allegation must be recorded separately, even if several identical or very similar allegations are received over a short period of time. It is important to remember also that a series of identical or very similar allegations about a particular substance may indicate a significant risk, which can trigger reporting requirements under section 8(e) (see below for a discussion of section 8(e)).

An oral allegation can be handled in one of two ways. A company may transcribe the allegation for record-keeping purposes. There is no requirement that company transcriptions be signed by the alleger. Alternatively, the company can request that the alleger submit the allegation in writing and sign it. 40 C.F.R. § 717.10(b)(1). The company request does not have to be in writing; an oral request is sufficient. If the alleger fails to respond to the company's request for a written allegation, the company is not required to record the allegation. EPA has provided a number of additional hypothetical examples to illustrate the rule's provisions in two question and answer documents. These documents are part of the official public rule-making record and are available from the EPA TSCA Assistance Office. *TSCA Section 8(c) Questions and Answers* (Nov. 1983) and (July 1984).

10.2.4. Record-Keeping Requirements

Only those allegations meeting the criteria of 40 C.F.R. § 717.10(b)(2) are required to be recorded. EPA does not require allegations to be recorded on a specific form. In general, firms are permitted to keep the information in a format of their own choosing as long as the original allegation is retained and an abstract of the allegation containing the following information is prepared and recorded:

(i) The name and address of the plant site which received the allegation.

(ii) The date the allegation was received at that site.

(iii) The implicated substance, mixture, article, company process or operation, or site discharge.

(iv) A description of the alleger (*e.g.*, "company employee," "individual consumer," "plant neighbor"). If the allegation involves a health effect, the sex and year of birth of the individual should be recorded, if ascertainable.

(v) A description of the alleged health effect(s). The description must relate how the effect(s) became known and the route of exposure, if explained in the allegation.

(vi) A description of the nature of the alleged environmental effect(s), identifying the affected plant and/or animal species, or contaminated portion of the physical environment.

40 C.F.R. §§ 717.15(b)(2)(i)-(vi).

The company must keep its 8(c) records at a location central to its chemical operations or at company headquarters. 40 C.F.R. § 717.15(a). Although a company can use a computer data base to manage its section 8(c) records, EPA requires that the original allegation or a microfiche copy be retained; a computer data base is not viewed as a suitable replacement for a hard copy. *8(c) Questions and Answers* 16 (July 1984). Firms are not required to investigate the allegations, but must record the results of any investigation that is conducted. Finally, copies of any required records or reports relating to the allegations must be kept. For example, if the allegation must be reported to OSHA, a copy of that OSHA report must be maintained in the section 8(c) file. An allegation must be recorded based upon its original contents, even if some aspect is incorrect. Once recorded and filed, such an allegation may not be removed even if a subsequent investigation reveals inaccuracies in the allegation. Rather, the results of any such further investigation may be placed in the allegation file.

Records of allegations made by employees must be maintained for 30 years from the date the reactions were first reported or known to the person maintaining the records. 40 C.F.R. § 717.15. All other records of significant adverse reactions must be maintained for a period of five years. The unintentional loss or destruction of a firm's section 8(c) files will be handled by the Office of Enforcement and Compliance Assurance on a case-by-case basis. If a firm ceases to do business, the successor firm must receive and maintain the section 8(c) records. If there is no successor firm, the records must be forwarded to EPA.

Section 8(c) records are subject to EPA inspection. In conducting an inspection, EPA will examine whether the company possesses a basic awareness of its obligations under section 8(c). Such a basic awareness is demonstrated by the presence of a system designed to forward allegations to a central record-keeping location. EPA also will inspect the actual records to determine if all the information requirements previously described are met, and whether allegations, when taken together, may reasonably support a conclusion of substantial risk under section 8(e).

EPA can require submission of copies of section 8(c) records to the Agency upon request, and employees can petition the Agency to collect and release section 8(c) information. In 1986, for example, EPA required two manufacturers to submit section 8(c) records on allegations relating to perfluoroalkyl resins. EPA's request was sent by letter to the two companies, not announced in a *Federal Register* notice. In 1988, EPA issued a *Federal Register* notice that called in section 8(c) records from manufacturers, importers, processors and even certain distributors of tri(alkyl/alkoxy)phosphates and diisocyanates. 53 Fed. Reg. 1408 (Jan. 19, 1988).

10.3. TSCA § 8(d): HEALTH AND SAFETY STUDIES

Section 8(d) authorizes EPA to promulgate rules under which the Agency can require any person who manufactures, processes, or distributes in commerce any chemical substance or mixture -- or even someone who proposes to manufacture, process, or distribute in commerce such a substance or mixture -- to submit to the Administrator lists and copies of health and safety studies on the substance or mixture conducted by, known to, or reasonably ascertainable by that person.

EPA may use information from submitted health and safety studies to support regulatory decisions under TSCA §§ 4, 5, and 6. For example, EPA may obtain exposure information on a chemical under section 8(a) and obtain existing health and safety studies under section 8(d) to determine whether the Agency should promulgate a section 4 test rule to require manufacturers to conduct additional testing.

10.3.1. Model Reporting Rule

In 1982, EPA issued a final Model Health and Safety Data Reporting Rule ("Model Reporting Rule" or "the Rule") to implement section 8(d). 47 Fed. Reg. 38,780 (Sept. 2, 1982) (codified as amended at 40 C.F.R. pt. 716). On September 15, 1986, EPA published a final rule amending the Model Reporting Rule. 51 Fed. Reg. 32,720 (Sept. 15, 1986). These initial versions of the Model Reporting Rule applied broadly to all manufacturers and processors of listed substances or mixtures and required submission of virtually any unpublished health and safety study on such substances and mixtures.

Between 1982 and 1998, EPA added hundreds of chemicals to the Model Reporting Rule, including any chemical that was designated or listed by the Interagency Testing Committee as being a priority for additional testing (*see* Chapter 9). In 1998, however, EPA promulgated substantial amendments to the Model Reporting Rule that: (1) ended reporting requirements for chemical substances and mixtures listed prior to 1998; (2) narrowed the scope of persons subject to the reporting requirements; and (3) generally limited the required reporting to studies conducted on a particular grade or purity of the chemical or mixture and which are health and safety studies of particular specified types. 63 Fed. Reg. 15765 (April 1, 1998).

10.3.1.1. Who Must Report

The 1982 and 1986 versions of the Model Reporting Rule set forth required reporting procedures and deadlines and a list of chemicals that were subject to reporting. The Rule required any person who manufactured or processed a listed substance or mixture, or who proposed to manufacture or process a listed substance or mixture at any time in the ten years preceding listing through ten years following listing to submit: (1) copies of any unpublished health and safety studies in their possession; (2) lists of all ongoing and previously initiated studies; (3) lists of studies previously sent to other federal agencies; and (4) lists of studies known to but not possessed by the submitter. In 1998, however, EPA narrowed the scope of the reporting obligation so that it now applies only to companies that fall into North American Industry Classification System (NAICS) Subsector 325 (chemical manufacturing and allied products) or Industry Group 32411 (petroleum refineries)[38] and who: (1) manufacture in the U.S. or import the chemical substance or mixture being added to the Model Reporting Rule as of the effective date that the substance or mixture is added to the Rule; (2) manufactured in the U.S. or imported the chemical being added within the ten years preceding the effective date of the listing of the chemical, or proposed to manufacture or import the chemical;[39] or (3) after the effective date on which the substance or mixture is added to the Model Reporting Rule, but still during the reporting period (generally the 60 days after listing) that EPA specifies for the substance or mixture, propose to manufacture (including import) the substance or mixture. 40 C.F.R. § 716.5(a). Note that for the vast majority of the hundreds of substances still listed in the C.F.R. under the Model Reporting Rule, the reporting period has ended. Thus, companies that are just now beginning to manufacture or import such substances are not subject to section 8(d) reporting. Processors and persons who propose to process a listed chemical substance or mixture are not required to submit studies on newly listed chemicals or mixtures unless EPA specifically states otherwise in a particular notice or rule promulgated under section 8(d). 40 C.F.R. § 716.5(c).

10.3.1.2. What Must be Reported

There are two phases to section 8(d) reporting. First, persons who have manufactured or imported the newly listed substance or mixture or who proposed to manufacture or import in the last 10 years, are required to submit copies of all non-exempt studies in their possession within 60 days after EPA adds the chemical substance or mixture to the subject chemical list. 40 C.F.R. § 716.30(a) and 716.60(a).

---

[38] *See* 1997 North American Industry Classification System – 1987 Standard Industrial Classification Replacement, 62 Fed. Reg. 17288 (April 9, 1997).

[39] EPA defines "propose to manufacture, import or process" as "a person has made a management decision to commit financial resources toward the manufacture, importation, or processing of a substance or mixture." 40 C.F.R. § 761.3.

Such persons also are required to submit within this 60-day period lists of: (1) ongoing studies that have not yet been completed; (2) studies that are initiated within the 60-day reporting period; (3) studies that are known to the submitter but for which the submitter does not possess copies; and (4) studies that the submitter has previously sent to federal agencies without claims of confidentiality. 40 C.F.R. §§ 716.35 and 716.60(a). Persons who submit lists of ongoing and/or initiated studies must submit copies of the studies within 30 days after they are completed. 40 C.F.R. § 716.60(b)(2). Second, EPA must be informed within 30 days of any study on a subject chemical *initiated* by or for such manufacturer or processor during the initial 60-day reporting period. The reporting period will last only 60 days after the listing unless otherwise specified, and EPA will not specify a reporting period longer than two years. 40 C.F.R. § 716.65.

As noted above, under the 1998 amendments to the Model Reporting Rule, each time EPA adds chemicals or mixtures to the Rule, the Agency will specify the particular types of health and safety studies that will be subject to reporting. All other types of health and safety studies will be considered "exempt" from reporting. In the first new listings published after the 1998 amendments, EPA added 15 chemicals to the Model Reporting Rule, identified for each chemical the particular types of studies that persons subject were require to submit, and stated "All other studies are exempt at this time from reporting. 69 Fed. Reg. 24517, 24520 (May 4, 2004).

10.3.1.3. Health and Safety Study

Section 8(d) provides EPA with authority to require reporting of any "health and safety study." TSCA § 3(6) defines the term "health and safety study" to mean:

> any study of any effect of a chemical substance or mixture on health or the environment or on both, including underlying data and epidemiological studies, studies of occupational exposure to a chemical substance or mixture, toxicological, clinical, and ecological studies of a chemical substance or mixture, and any test performed pursuant to [TSCA].

15 U.S.C. § 2602(6). EPA's Model Reporting Rule closely follows this definition. 40 C.F.R. § 716.3. EPA interprets the phrase broadly and has provided an extensive list of examples of the types of tests that the Agency asserts constitute "health and safety studies" within the meaning of the Model Reporting Rule. 40 C.F.R. § 716.3. These examples include toxicity tests, tests for ecological and other environmental effects, assessments of human and environmental exposure, and monitoring data.

Monitoring Reports. Monitoring efforts that attempt to define exposure levels of manufacturing or processing workers potentially are reportable if the data are "aggregated and analyzed" and their meaning discussed in the study report. For example, if a company monitors the exposure of workers involved in the manufacture of a subject chemical and discusses the monitoring data in a report that analyzes the data to draw conclusions about occupational or environmental exposure, EPA asserts that this constitutes a "health and safety study." In contrast, daily or routine monitoring data, even if tabulated, do not have to be submitted if the report "merely confirms that permissible levels of a chemical have or have not been exceeded." EPA, *Questions and Answers About Reporting under the TSCA § 8(d) Health and Safety Study Reporting Rule* 1 (Nov. 10, 1982).

In 1986, EPA brought its first and most important civil action under TSCA § 8(d) against Lonza, Inc., seeking a $1.5 million penalty. *Lonza, Inc.*, No. TSCA 87-H-03 (EPA July 20, 1987). The key question raised by the case was whether "routine" monitoring of employee health for insurance purposes constituted a section 8(d) health and safety study. EPA eventually dropped the complaint against Lonza, Inc. after finding that the Agency had earlier taken the position (in writing) that very similar reports were not subject to TSCA § 8(d) reporting. In the wake of *Lonza*, EPA recognized that there was considerable uncertainty regarding the reportability of monitoring studies. As a result, on February 16, 1989, EPA issued a question and answer guidance document to clarify when monitoring studies must be submitted under TSCA § 8(d).

Modeling Studies. EPA considers modeling studies that estimate actual or reasonably likely environmental or human exposure to be reportable as "assessments of human and environmental exposure." Accordingly, modeling studies based on very conservative or worst case exposures are not reportable, while those that use a company's best estimates of emission quantities and conditions could be. For example, a modeling study conducted in planning plant or equipment construction does not have to be reported because it does not estimate actual or reasonably likely levels of existing environmental releases. As elsewhere under TSCA § 8(d), only studies and not data, computer printouts or hand-written calculations need be submitted unless specifically requested by the Agency under 40 C.F.R. §§ 716.10(a)(4) and 716.40. EPA, Office of Pesticides and Toxic Substances, *Questions and Answers: Applicability of TSCA Section 8(d) Model Health and Safety Data Reporting Rule (40 C.F.R. pt. 176) to Modeling Studies* 3 (Dec. 29, 1988).

Company Operations Reports. Many companies routinely conduct surveys of their operations and report their findings in operations reports. These operations reports may contain portions discussing section 8(d) chemicals or mixtures. Only those portions which discuss section 8(d) chemicals or mixtures and which constitute a "study" are potentially reportable — not the entire report.

Clinical Tests on an Employee. An individual employee's clinical test results which appear in that employee's medical record need not be submitted. *8(d) Questions and Answers Feb. 1989* at 6. Reports that characterize and discuss the implications of a chemical in the blood levels of workers, however, potentially are reportable since such reports may constitute a study of exposure in the work force, and the results may have implications beyond a single individual.

Reporting Physical/Chemical Properties. EPA's Model Reporting Rule requires the reporting of studies on any of ten physical/chemical properties if the studies are for the purposes of determining the environmental or biological fate of the substance or mixture, but only if they are studies of the following physical or chemical properties:

- Water solubility.
- Adsorption/desorption on particulate surfaces, *e.g.*, soil.
- Vapor pressure.
- Octanol/water partition coefficient.
- Density/relative density (specific gravity).
- Particle size distribution for insoluble solids.
- Dissociation constant.
- Degradation by photochemical mechanisms—aquatic and atmospheric.
- Degradation by chemical mechanisms—hydrolytic, reductive, and oxidative.
- Degradation by biological mechanisms—aerobic and anaerobic.

See 40 C.F.R. § 716.50(a)-(j).

10.3.1.4. Exemptions From Reporting

EPA has provided a number of general exemptions from the reporting requirements of the Model Reporting Rule. 40 C.F.R. § 716.20.

1. *Studies Which Have Been Published in the Scientific Literature*. Any study which has been published in the scientific literature is exempt from reporting. According to EPA, the term "scientific literature" is defined as:

> any periodical, book or monograph which presents data obtained through a systematic pursuit of knowledge involving the recognition and formulation of a problem, the collection of data through observation and experiment, and the formulation and testing of hypotheses.

EPA, Office of Pesticides and Toxic Substances, *General Comments on the Proposed Section 8(d) Rule; Support Document for the Final Section 8(d) Rule* 4 (Sept. 1, 1982).

2. *Studies Previously Submitted to OPPT.* In 1986 EPA amended the exemption for studies previously submitted. 51 Fed. Reg. 32,720 (Sept. 15, 1986). As originally issued, the Module Reporting Rule exempted from reporting all studies previously submitted to any EPA office. Now, only studies previously submitted to OPPT under TSCA § 4 proceedings, as section 8(e) submissions, with premanufacture notices or significant new use notices, or submitted on a "For Your Information" (FYI) basis in support of the Existing Chemicals Program are exempt from reporting. Studies initiated pursuant to a section 4(a) test rule and for which the person has submitted a letter of intent to conduct testing are exempt from the list submission requirements of the Model Reporting Rule.

3. *Studies Previously Submitted to a Federal Agency.* Studies submitted to EPA offices other than OPPT or to other federal agencies with no claims of confidentiality are exempt only from the copy submission requirements. Lists of such studies still must be provided.

4. *Studies Conducted or Initiated by or for Another Person Subject to § 8(d).* Studies conducted on a chemical subject to the Model Reporting Rule, but conducted by or for another person who is subject to the Rule and will report the studies, need not be submitted. For example, in many instances studies are conducted by a parent for its subsidiary or vice versa. These studies must be submitted by the entity that manufactures or processes the section 8(d) chemical, but if both parent and subsidiary are subject to the Model Reporting Rule, only one of the two entities needs to submit the studies. Companies are not required to acquire copies of studies from their foreign subsidiaries. Companies are required, however, to list the studies known to them, but not in their possession, if they know copies of the studies will not be submitted by the person who initiated or conducted the studies. In addition, EPA does not require companies to search their files for studies on listed chemicals that have been manufactured only by their foreign subsidiaries.

5. *Studies of Chemical Substances Which Are Not on the TSCA Inventory.* EPA has exempted chemical substances that are not on the TSCA Inventory from the reporting requirements of the Model Reporting Rule. This exemption applies only to substances that otherwise would trigger reporting obligations because they fall within the reportable chemical categories listed as subject to section 8(d)). Thus, all new chemicals used solely for R&D are exempt from reporting. (*See* Chapter 5 for a discussion of what constitutes R&D.)

6. *Certain Acute Toxicity Studies.* EPA has exempted from reporting six types of acute and primary toxicity studies commonly performed using mammalian species. This exemption applies only when the substance tested was a mixture which either contained a listed chemical substance or a listed mixture. Acute oral, dermal, or inhalation toxicity studies, primary eye or primary dermal irritation studies, and dermal sensitization studies on such mixtures do not have to be submitted. Acute toxicity studies involving aquatic species such as fish, however, must be reported. Similarly, mutagenicity tests on mixtures also must be submitted.

7. *Physical and Chemical Properties.* Only studies involving one of ten particular physical/chemical characteristics listed at 40 C.F.R. section 716.50 need to be reported. Studies involving any other physical/chemical property are not subject to reporting.

8. *Analyzed Aggregations of Monitoring Data Acquired More Than Five Years Ago.* Monitoring data collected more than five years before the substance or mixture was added to the section 8(d) list need not be reported, even if the data have been aggregated and analyzed.

9. *Impurities.* Studies of listed chemicals or mixtures, where the listed chemical was manufactured or processed only as an impurity, are not subject to reporting requirements.

10. *Studies Previously Submitted by Trade Associations.* In the 1986 amendments to its Model Reporting Rule, EPA added an exemption for studies previously submitted by trade associations on behalf of their members. 51 Fed. Reg. 32,728 (Sept. 15, 1986). Thus, member companies whose trade association has submitted the required studies in accordance with the provisions of the Model Reporting Rule are exempt from both the copy and list submission requirements.

10.3.1.5. File Searches

Once a company determines that a new listing has resulted in the company becoming subject to the Model Reporting Rule, the company must search its files for the specified health and safety studies which EPA wants submitted on that substance or mixture. The Model Reporting Rule states, however, that the scope of a person's responsibility to search its files is limited to searching records in the locations where the required information is typically kept, and to the records kept by the company's employees who are responsible for keeping such records and advising the company on health and environmental effects of chemicals. In a question and answer document, EPA has stated that only sites in the United States must be searched. EPA, *Questions and Answers About Reporting under the TSCA § 8(d) Health and Safety Study Reporting Rule* 6 (Nov. 10, 1982). It remains unclear whether a foreign site must be searched if that is where a domestic company ordinarily keeps the required information. Companies are not required to search for reportable information dated before January 1, 1977 unless specifically required to do so in a rule. 40 C.F.R. § 716.25.

10.3.1.6. Submission of Copies of Studies

Persons who become subject to the reporting requirements must submit copies of reportable studies. Underlying data, however, do not have to be submitted initially. Underlying data include data such as medical or health records, individual files, lab notebooks, and daily monitoring records. 40 C.F.R. § 716.10(a)(4).

Copies of required studies must be submitted with a cover letter that identifies the name, job title, address and telephone number of the submitting office and the name and address of the manufacturing or processing establishment on whose behalf the submission was made. EPA has provided specific directions on how to report studies on listed substances and mixtures. 40 C.F.R. § 716.45. If the substance is listed individually in the Model Reporting Rule, studies of the substance of the grade/purity specified in the amendment adding the substance to the Rule and studies of mixtures known to contain the substance must be reported as studies of that substance, not as studies of a mixture containing the substance. Similarly if the study was conducted on the listed substance in an aqueous solution or if it contains a small amount of an additive added for purposes of maintaining the integrity or physical form of the test substance, the study must be reported as a study of the substance itself and not of a mixture. When two or more substances are listed as a mixture in the Model Reporting Rule, studies of the listed mixture (or of any mixture known to contain the listed mixture) must be reported. 40 C.F.R. § 716.45.

10.3.1.7. Submission of Lists of Studies

Persons who become subject to the Model Reporting Rule must submit lists of: (1) non-exempt ongoing health and safety studies being conducted by or for them; (2) non-exempt studies that they initiate during the reporting period; (3) non-exempt unpublished studies known to them, but for which they do not have copies; and (4) non-exempt studies previously submitted to EPA or other federal agencies without any claim of confidentiality. In the case of studies known to, but not in their possession, the submitter must provide the name and address of the person known to be in possession of each study.

Submission of lists of ongoing studies must be indexed by chemical name and CASRN (if any) and accompanied by a cover letter which identifies the name, address, and job title of the submitting official and the name and address of the manufacturing or processing establishment on whose behalf the list is submitted. 40 C.F.R. § 716.35.

10.3.1.8. Confidentiality Claims

If no claim of confidentiality is asserted at that time of submission, EPA will place the document in a public file without further notice to the submitter. Submitters may claim certain information as confidential under TSCA § 14. In addition, persons making submissions under the Model Reporting Rule may claim as confidential the company name, address, financial statistics, and product codes. 40 C.F.R. § 716.55(a)(3). Companies also may claim as confidential information that would be an unwarranted invasion of personal privacy, such as individual medical records. *Id.*

10.3.1.9. EPA Requests for Further Information

Following the initial reporting of copies and lists of studies, EPA may request submission of the underlying data on completed studies or preliminary reports on ongoing studies. In addition, for studies about which EPA was informed but not copied (because the person reporting did not possess a copy), EPA may request that the person who actually possesses the study to submit a copy even though that person may not be subject to section 8(d). 40 C.F.R. § 716.40.

10.4. SECTION 8(e): SUBSTANTIAL RISK INFORMATION

Section 8(e) provides:

> Any person who manufactures, processes, or distributes in commerce a chemical substance or mixture and who obtains information which reasonably supports the conclusion that such substance or mixture presents a substantial risk of injury to health or the environment shall immediately inform the Administrator of such information unless such person has actual knowledge that the Administrator has been adequately informed of such information.

There is little on section 8(e) in the legislative history of TSCA. Section 8(e)'s language, however, suggests that section 8(e) was designed to ensure that information which indicates a currently existing substantial risk is immediately reported to EPA so that the Agency can take prompt action to address the risk. It is the only section in TSCA that requires a person to "immediately" inform EPA.

Section 8(e) is "self-actuating" in the sense that the reporting obligation became effective immediately upon enactment of TSCA. The Agency was not required to promulgate any implementing regulations. In fact, TSCA does not contain any express grant of authority for EPA to issue regulations to implement this section. The Agency, however, has published in the *Federal Register* two statements of the Agency's interpretation of section 8(e): Statement of Interpretation and Enforcement Policy, 43 Fed. Reg. 11,110 (Mar. 16, 1978) ("1978 Policy Statement") and Notification of Substantial Risk; Policy Clarification and Reporting Guidance, 68 Fed. Reg. 33,129 (June 3, 2003) ("2003 Policy Statement"). EPA also has provided some limited policy guidance through section 8(e) Status Reports, and from time to time through its publication, "Chemicals in Progress Bulletin." The Status Reports are a summary of EPA's initial review of submitted section 8(e) and FYI reports and are available for public viewing in the OPPT Public Reading Room at EPA Headquarters in Washington, D.C.[40] Finally, the Agency published a 1991 Reporting Guide as part of the Compliance Audit Program under TSCA § 8(e).

---

[40] Copies of individual EPA section 8(e) Status Reports are available from the EPA TSCA Assistance Office. Biennial "Blue Book" volumes of Status Reports are available from the TSCA Assistance Office in Washington, D.C., or from the National Technical Information Service in Springfield, VA (tel: 703-487-4650). EPA also makes limited TSCA § 8(e) information available through the section 8(e) Triage Data Base, such as summary test information and EPA's preliminary classification of the chemical as high, medium or low toxicological risk. The Triage Data Base can be downloaded from EPA's web site at http://www.epa.gov or diskettes can be ordered from the TSCA Assistance Office.

10.4.1. 1991 Compliance Audit Program

In 1991, working in conjunction with the American Chemistry Council (then known as the Chemical Manufacturers Association), EPA developed a one-time voluntary Compliance Audit Program (CAP) designed to obtain any outstanding TSCA § 8(e) data. 56 Fed. Reg. 4128 (Feb. 1, 1991). Under the CAP, EPA and any interested company would enter into a CAP consent agreement by no later than July 1, 1991. 56 Fed. Reg. 28,458 (June 20, 1991). The agreement obligated the company to audit its files for information that should have been reported under section 8(e) but had not been, and to pay stipulated penalties for the late reports. Under pressure from industry to provide more specific detailed guidance regarding what studies do <u>not</u> trigger reporting obligations, and faced with the possible receipt under the CAP of thousands of not-very-useful studies showing little risk, in June 1991 EPA published the TSCA § 8(e) *Reporting Guide* (1991 Reporting Guide). The *1991 Reporting Guide* provides reference to both general and specific examples of information the Agency believes are reportable under section 8(e).

According to EPA, 123 companies participated in the CAP and the Agency received over 11,000 studies. These 11,000 studies received under the CAP represented approximately 90 percent of the studies that EPA received under section 8(e) between 1977, when TSCA was enacted, through 1996, when the CAP was completed.

10.4.2. Who Must Report

Any person who manufactures, processes, or distributes in commerce a chemical substance or mixture potentially is subject to the section 8(e) reporting requirements. According to the *1991 Reporting Guide*, “the term ‘person’ includes the following: any natural person, corporation, firm, company, sole-proprietorship, joint-venture, partnership, association, or any other business entity, any State or political subdivision of a State, any municipality, any interstate body, and any department or agency of the Federal Government.” *1991 Reporting Guide* at 3. Unlike many other TSCA reporting requirements, there is no small business exemption under section 8(e). On the other hand, persons who do not manufacture, process, or distribute chemicals are not obligated to report even if they obtain information about a particular chemical which appears to constitute substantial risk information. *Id.* Thus, trade associations and testing laboratories generally are not subject to section 8(e). These groups, however, often report such information to the Agency on an FYI basis. *Id.*

EPA asserts that both the company and individual employees are responsible for ensuring that any substantial risk information is reported to the Agency and may be subject to enforcement actions for failure to report. EPA considers a business entity to have obtained section 8(e) information if any officer or employee “capable of appreciating the significance of that information” obtains it. A company can relieve its officers or employees of their obligation as individuals to report the information directly to the Agency by “establishing, internally publicizing, and affirmatively implementing procedures for employee submission and corporate processing of pertinent information." 2003 Policy Statement at 33,137; *1991 Reporting Guide* at 4, 6.

10.4.3. What Constitutes Substantial Risk Information

TSCA § 8(e) requires the reporting of information which "reasonably supports" the conclusion that the chemical substance or mixture presents a "substantial risk." Neither TSCA nor its legislative history, however, defines the term "substantial risk," and EPA's *1991 Reporting Guide*, 1978 and 2003 Policy Statements, and Status Reports provide only limited guidance. According to EPA,

> [i]n deciding whether information is "substantial risk" information, one must consider 1) the seriousness of the adverse effect, and 2) the fact or probability of the effect's occurrence. In determining TSCA § 8(e) - applicability/reportability, these two criteria should be weighted differently depending upon the seriousness of the effect or the extent of the exposure, *i.e.*, the more serious the effect, the less heavily one should weigh actual or potential exposure, and vice versa.

1991 Reporting Guide at 2; *see also* 1978 Policy Statement at 11,111. The 1978 and 2003 Policy Statements list three broad categories of effects that are potentially serious enough to trigger reporting obligations: human health effects; environmental effects; and emergency incidents of environmental contamination.

10.4.3.1. Human Health Effects

EPA states that information should be reported under section 8(e) on the following human health effects:

> (1) Any instance of cancer, birth defects, mutagenicity, death, or serious or prolonged incapacitation, including the loss of or inability to use a normal bodily function with a consequent relatively serious impairment of normal activities, if one (or a few) chemical(s) is strongly implicated.
>
> (2) Any pattern of effects or evidence which reasonably supports the conclusion that the chemical substance or mixture can produce cancer, mutation, birth defects or toxic effects resulting in death, or serious or prolonged incapacitation.

2003 Policy Statement at 33,138. EPA asserts that any such effects must be reported if they occur in humans and a particular substance or mixture is strongly implicated. In addition, lesser effects on humans may be reportable if they are preliminary manifestations of more serious effects. In addition, EPA considers information indicating that a chemical causes serious toxicological effects in laboratory animals to constitute "evidence" which reasonably supports the conclusion that the chemical will produce such serious effects in humans.

10.4.3.2. Exposure Factors

It is generally recognized that risk is a function of both toxicity and exposure. As EPA has stated:

> Both hazard and exposure must occur for there to be any risk. If there is virtually no exposure, EPA will be unable to conclude that the chemical may present an unreasonable risk.

Gary R. Timm, "The Implementation of TSCA § 4," Remarks at The Toxicology Forum 1984 Annual Summer Meeting at 3 (July 16-20, 1984) (photocopy on file with author). EPA generally disregards exposure, however, when determining whether certain toxicity information reasonably supports a conclusion that a chemical may present a substantial risk. According to the Agency, the serious human health effects listed in the 1978 and 2003 Policy Statements "are so serious that relatively little weight is given to exposure; the mere fact the implicated chemical is in commerce constitutes sufficient evidence of exposure." 2003 Policy Statement at 33,138; *see also 1991 Reporting Guide* at 2. In practice, with respect to potential human health effects, EPA staff may interpret the phrase "relatively little weight" to mean "no weight."

The reportability of effects noted during tests on R&D chemicals has been a subject of particular confusion. Companies often perform or commission toxicity tests on chemicals before beginning commercial production.[41] If the results of these tests indicate that the chemical can cause a serious health effect, the language of section 8(e) suggests that the company would have to determine whether there is sufficient potential for exposure to reasonably support the conclusion that the chemical presents a substantial risk. In an oral question and answer session on section 8(e) that EPA sponsored on March 16, 1978, EPA officials reportedly stated that the Agency did not want to receive information on R&D chemicals that never left the laboratory. EPA recanted this statement several years later and since then has insisted that any test results showing that a chemical can produce a serious health effect will trigger section 8(e) reporting obligations even if the R&D chemical never leaves the laboratory.

---

[41] EPA has long asserted that section 8 applies to chemicals in the R&D phase. Although section 8(f) limits the application of section 8 to chemicals that are manufactured, processed or distributed "for a commercial purpose," EPA has argued that manufacture, processing or distribution for R&D is done for a commercial purpose, and this view has been affirmed by the United States Court of Appeals for the Third Circuit in Dow Chemical Co. v. EPA, 605 F.2d 673 (1979).

EPA first took this position in a January 1986 Status Report which arose from an FYI submission of preliminary results of a two-year oncogenicity study on a candidate pesticide that indicated that the chemical could cause liver tumors in mice. EPA, Status Report 8EHQ-0685-0583 S/8EHQ-1085-0583 S FLWP (Jan. 7, 1986). The FYI data submitter asserted that the test results did not trigger section 8(e) reporting obligations for several reasons, including the fact that the chemical was only produced in small quantities for laboratory research. EPA disagreed, and stated that the information should have been submitted as a formal section 8(e) report. EPA's Status Report does not explain, however, how substantial risk can be inferred solely from toxicity data. EPA did not take any enforcement action against the company for failure to submit the information as a formal section 8(e) report.

10.4.3.3. Acute Toxicity Data

EPA's 1978 and 2003 Policy Statements state that cancer, birth defects, mutagenicity, death and serious or prolonged incapacitation constitute reportable effects under section 8(e). The Policy Statements also say that evidence of such effects may be derived from designed, controlled studies. Death or serious or prolonged incapacitation, of course, can result from a chemical's acute toxicity. Thus, a frequent issue under section 8(e) is whether receipt of routine acute toxicity studies, which are designed to determine the dose of a chemical necessary to cause death, triggers section 8(e) reporting obligations or, conversely, whether there also must be evidence of substantial exposure to the chemical before any reporting obligation can arise.

Acute studies are routinely run on chemicals to determine appropriate safety measures for those exposed to the chemical. Commonly performed acute toxicity tests include the LD_{50} (defined as the dose of the compound which causes 50 percent mortality in a given population) and the LC_{50} (defined as the concentration which causes 50 percent mortality during a given exposure period). In responding to public comments concerning the reportability of routine tests such as the LD_{50}, EPA has stated that unknown effects occurring during a standard range-finding acute toxicity test may have to be reported if they meet the definition of substantial risk, but the Agency implies that the results of routine tests may not be reportable if they do not show any unexpected effect. 1978 Policy Statement at 11,114 (response to Comment 14).

EPA has avoided giving detailed guidance regarding the degree of exposure that must be shown before an acute toxicity test's results trigger a reporting obligation. EPA has indicated, however, the degree of toxic response that does and does not warrant consideration of the degree of exposure before making a report. In the *1991 Reporting Guide*, EPA provided the following guidelines for reporting acute toxicity data.

LD_{50} Oral Dose	LD_{50} Dermal Dose	4-Hour LC_{50} Inhalation Dose	Consider Exposure or other Factors?
≤5 mg/kg	≤20 mg/kg	≤50 ppm (≤0.5 mg/l)	No (Extremely Toxic)
>5 mg/kg to ≤50 mg/kg	>20 mg/kg to ≤200 mg/kg	>50 ppm (>0.5 mg/l) to ≤200 ppm (≤2 mg/l)	Only to Some Reasonable Degree (Highly Toxic)
>50 mg/kg	>200 mg/kg	>200 ppm (>2 mg/l)	Yes (Moderately Toxic)

1991 Reporting Guide at 31.

EPA also has stated that minor acute effects on humans need not be reported. For example, a company submitted information concerning an employee's reaction to fumes generated during the heating and molding of a certain compound. The Agency concluded that this reaction need not have been reported under section 8(e). In Status Report EHQ-1283-0502, EPA stated that such information, together with "another triggering piece of information," could constitute reportable information under section 8(e), but

> [c]onsidering that the acute human health effects reported in this submission do not appear to have been serious or to have resulted in prolonged incapacitation or serious impairment of normal bodily functions/activities, EPA does not believe that the information warranted submission under Section 8(e) of TSCA.

Status Report EHQ-1283-0502, at 4.

It should be noted that, although EPA does not consider minor symptoms of acute human toxicity to be reportable under section 8(e), such information, if reported by an employee, consumer, or other person, could constitute an "allegation of a significant adverse reaction" under section 8(c) of TSCA.

10.4.3.4. Subchronic Toxicity Data

EPA also has stated that serious toxic effects observed during the conduct of subchronic studies should be reported. This includes both readily observable serious effects and serious effects that are discussed only as the result of gross and/or histopathological examination. Although an organ weight change alone may not reflect serious or prolonged incapacitation, the reportability of such a finding could depend upon an evaluation of one or more factors, such as, but not limited to, the overall magnitude of the organ weight change, the biological significance of the change, blood chemistry, dose, route of administration, actual or expected exposure, etc. The more significant the magnitude of the organ weight change (*e.g.*, severe atrophy of the testes, thymus, kidneys), however, the less consideration one should give to other factors in determining reportability of the findings. Likewise, a statistically or biologically significant histopathologic finding indicating serious or prolonged incapacitation should be reported with little, if any, consideration given to factors such as exposure. When the histopathologic findings are of a less serious or less significant nature, however, other relevant factors (*e.g.*, actual/expected exposure, dose, etc.) should be considered in determining the reportability of the study results. *1991 Reporting Guide* at 37.

10.4.3.5. Neurotoxic Effects

Prior to the CAP another area of confusion was the reportability of neurotoxic effects, which EPA addressed in the *1991 Reporting Guide*. EPA acknowledges that it may not be possible to distinguish neurobehavioral effects or neurological signs in moribund animals from a direct neurotoxic action of the tested chemical substance. The Agency, however, asserts that statistically or biologically significant neurotoxic effects observed in non-moribund animals (including animals in groups receiving doses equal to or greater than lethal doses) in any type of study cannot be dismissed simply as reflecting a "system overload" and should be considered for immediate reporting to the Agency. Further, EPA believes that evidence of possible neurotoxic effects during an acute or other general toxicity test would indicate that additional studies designed to more specifically assess neurotoxic effects should be considered for that chemical. *1991 Reporting Guide* at 33.

To provide a sense of scale for the reportability of neurotoxic/neurobehavioral findings derived from acute and other types of animal toxicity studies (*e.g.*, 28-day studies, teratology studies), the Agency is most interested in receiving reports that involve "serious or prolonged effects." In general, the acute toxicity LD_{50} values listed in the table in section 10.4.3.3 should be consulted first and an appropriate level of consideration should be given to exposure and/or other factors in determining reportability based solely on lethality in acute or other types of animal toxicity studies. In those cases involving biological or statistically significant evidence of serious neurotoxicological effects (*e.g.*, paralysis, convulsions, ataxia), EPA asserts that exposure or other factors should be given virtually no consideration in determining the reportability. As neurotoxicologic observations become more limited or as confidence in the accuracy of such observations becomes more uncertain, the reportability of such findings diminishes. For example, in the absence of other more serious effects, observations of lethargy and/or salivation, in and of themselves, would not be viewed typically as providing reasonable support for a conclusion of substantial risk. Similarly, the reportability of effects such as convulsions or ataxia would be diminished if such effects (1) were seen only in moribund animals, or (2) were found simply to be transient rather than either intermittent or continuous in nature. *Id.*

10.4.3.6. Skin/Eye Irritation and Skin Sensitization Tests

EPA also has commented on the reportability of skin and eye irritation and skin sensitization tests. First, irritation and/or corrosivity findings from acute animal eye or skin irritation studies is generally not reportable. This should not be interpreted to mean, however, that EPA is not concerned about the irritation/corrosion findings from such studies. Previously unknown or unexpected effects that occur and are observed during such routine tests may have to be reported under section 8(e) if the effects are serious and meet the reporting criteria outlined in part V of the 1978 and 2003 Policy Statements (*e.g.*, lethality, neurotoxicity). Therefore, when evaluating the results of skin and eye irritation studies, EPA expects a company to consider such factors as lethal dose, pH of the test material, the route(s) of administration, occurrence of unexpected serious effects (which can be determined via "cage-side" observation or during necropsy), and the extent and pattern of the actual or potential exposure to the tested chemical or mixture. When evaluating such information for possible TSCA § 8(e) reporting, the greater the acute toxicity, the less heavily one should weigh the actual or potential exposure to the test materials, and vice versa. *1991 Reporting Guide* at 35.

With regard to sensitization studies, it must be noted that sensitization is a systemic reaction that is manifested in many cases locally (*i.e.*, directly at the site of re-exposure) but also may be manifested away from the site of exposure. Further, the nature of the reaction can vary from slight to severe and, in some cases, can result in death. In reviewing results of sensitization studies for submission under section 8(e), EPA expects companies to evaluate a variety of factors including, but not limited to, the severity of the response, the site(s) of the response, the number of animals affected, and/or the actual or potential exposure to the tested chemical substances. In general, the more severe the observed sensitization response(s) and the greater the number of animals affected, the less heavily one should weigh the actual or potential exposure to the tested chemicals, and vice versa. *Id.*

10.4.3.7. Non-Emergency Contamination and Environmental Effects

EPA's enforcement policy regarding possible reportability of non-emergency environmental contamination has undergone significant revision since the 1978 Policy Statement. Part V(b)(1) of the 1978 Policy Statement declared that EPA would consider reportable:

> widespread and previously unsuspected distribution in environmental media, as indicated by studies (excluding materials contained within appropriate disposal facilities).

1978 Policy Statement at 11,112. EPA later indicated that the Agency would consider groundwater to be included in the term "environmental media" (EPA, TSCA Chemicals in Progress Bulletin (Mar. 1985) (available from the TSCA Assistance Office), but EPA did not define "widespread" or "previously unsuspected."

The section 8(e) Compliance Audit Program (CAP) (*see* 10.4.1) brought to light the need for clarification of EPA's position. In early 1992, EPA announced that there would be a second phase of the CAP, during which companies could report information on releases of chemicals to the environment and detection of chemicals in environmental media, as well as the results of toxicity tasks on facility effluents. EPA twice issued draft revised guidance on such reporting, but after reviewing the extensive comments of CAP participants, in May 1996 EPA cancelled the second phase of the CAP. At the time, EPA stated in consent agreements signed with the CAP participants, and in a letter to the CAP participants, that the Agency intended to publish final guidance in the *Federal Register* and that any such information received prior to the effective date of that guidance would not be the subject of any section 8(e) enforcement action. EPA Letter to CAP Participants with Revised Addendum to TSCA § 8(e) CAP Agreement (May 15, 1997).

The 2003 Policy Statement contains the revised EPA guidance. Part V(b)(1) of the 2003 Policy Statement adds two important caveats to the statement that "widespread and previously unsuspected distribution in environmental media" is reportable. First, EPA notes that such information must be:

> coupled with information that widespread or significant exposure to humans or non-human organisms has occurred or that there is a substantial likelihood that such exposure will occur. . . .

68 Fed. Reg. 33, 129, 33, 138 (June 3, 2003). Second, the 2003 Policy Statement notes that the Agency often establishes a concentration of a particular chemical in a particular environmental medium that triggers a regulatory response or a concentration that is presumed to pose no risk, such as Maximum Contaminant Levels, Ambient Water Quality Criteria, and Reference Doses. EPA states that information regarding contamination found at or below those benchmarks does not trigger section 8(e) reporting obligations.

Part V(b) of the 2003 Policy Statement also contains the following examples of information environmental effects or data that the Agency will consider reportable:

> (b) *Environmental effects*
>
> (2) Measurements and indicators of pronounced bioaccumulation heretofore unknown to the Administrator (including bioaccumulation in fish beyond 5,000 times water concentration in a 30-day exposure or having an n-octanol/water partition coefficient greater than 25,000) should be reported when coupled with potential for widespread exposure and any non-trivial adverse effect.
>
> (3) Any non-trivial adverse effect, heretofore unknown to the Administrator, associated with a chemical known to have

bioaccumulated to a pronounced degree or to be widespread in environmental media.

(4) Ecologically significant changes in species' interrelationships; that is, changes in population behavior, growth, survival, etc. that in turn affect other species' behavior, growth, or survival.

Examples include: (i) Excessive stimulation of primary producers (algae, macrophytes) in aquatic ecosystems, *e.g.*, resulting in nutrient enrichment, or eutrophication, of aquatic ecosystems.

(ii) Interference with critical biogeochemical cycles, such as the nitrogen cycle.

(5) Facile transformation or degradation to a chemical having an unacceptable risk as defined above.

2003 Policy Statement at 33,138.

The *1991 Reporting Guide* notes that only actual exposure will trigger reporting, as evidenced by the following comment in

> modeling studies, including those based solely on theoretical exposure data (*e.g.*, 'worst case' scenarios), are *not* . . . sufficient in and of themselves to meet the Section 8(e) reporting requirements. Further, environmental or health risk assessments (including those using computer modeling) based on either 1) theoretical exposure data, or 2) actual exposure data submitted on a mandatory basis under an EPA-administered statute typically need *not* be reported under Section 8(e).

1991 Reporting Guide at 7 (emphasis in original).

EPA does not address in any of its policy statements, Reporting Guide, or questions and answers on 8(e) reporting, the reportability of biomonitoring data. Nevertheless, in 2004, the Agency brought an enforcement action in which it alleged that a company's failure to report certain blood monitoring data was a violation of section 8(e). EPA claimed that a sample taken from the umbilical cord of an employee's baby was substantial risk information because it confirmed the transplacental movement of a chemical. It also claimed that other blood samples taken from individuals that lived near the company's plant was substantial risk information because the data were "useful" to EPA in associating the presence of the chemical in the general population with a specific source of exposure.

EPA's position in the enforcement action suggests that the Agency may consider reportable any biomonitoring information that may be useful to the Agency in understanding exposure to a chemical. Without knowing what the Agency may consider useful, one approach would be to report all biomonitoring data, regardless of its significance. This approach, however, is at odds with the statutory language of section 8(e) and with EPA interpretive statements regarding section 8(e) reporting. Information indicating that a person has been potentially exposed to a chemical substance does not, standing alone, establish that the chemical presents a substantial risk to human health. The biomonitoring data must be considered in the context of what is known about the hazards associated with the chemical substance and the reported levels of exposure. Moreover, EPA has stated clearly that it does not want companies to simply "dump" information on the Agency. Instead, EPA directs industry to use judgment in determining whether information reasonably supports the conclusion that a chemical presents a substantial risk of injury to health or the environment.

In the absence of specific Agency statements on the reportability of biomonitoring data, EPA's criteria for reporting of non-emergency contamination set forth in the 2003 Policy Statement may provide some guidance. Factors to consider include:

- The hazards associated with the chemical substance. (Is it a carcinogen, mutagen, teratogen, or reproductive toxin?; known to cause other serious or irreversible health effects?; persistent or bioaccumulative?)

- Federal, state, or local risk values established for the chemical substance. (EPA Reference Dose (RfD)?; EPA Estimated Lifetime Cancer Risk?; EPA Maximum Contaminant Level (MCL)?; FDA Virtually Safe Dose?; state or local risk values?; company derived risk benchmarks?; company risk management actions related to the chemical?)

- Whether the biomonitoring data provide evidence of exposure to the chemical substance in potentially sensitive subgroups, *e.g.*, children, women of child-bearing age, developing adolescents, and prospective fathers.

- If biomonitoring data for a chemical substance is above an established benchmark or provide evidence of exposure in potentially sensitive subgroups, whether EPA is aware that the chemical substance has been measured in blood of workers or the general population or in potentially sensitive subgroups at or above the levels measured by the company.

- Whether biomonitoring data on the chemical substance has previously been reported to EPA under TSCA § 8(e).

- Whether EPA has published any reports that include biomonitoring data on the chemical substance.
- Published studies in the scientific literature reporting biomonitoring data on the chemical substance.

10.4.3.8. Emergency Incidents of Environmental Contamination

Emergency incidents of environmental contamination (EIEC) also may be reportable under section 8(e) if they meet the criteria set forth in part V(c) of EPA's 2003 Policy Statement:

> (c) *Emergency incidents of environmental contamination*— Any environmental contamination by a chemical substance or mixture to which any of the above adverse effects has been ascribed and which because of the pattern, extent, and amount of contamination (1) seriously threatens humans with cancer, birth defects, mutation, death, or serious or prolonged incapacitation, or (2) seriously threatens non-human organisms with large-scale or ecologically significant population destruction.

2003 Policy Statement at 33,138.

For example, incidents such as the accidental rupture of railroad tank cars containing hazardous chemicals, or the discovery of transformers leaking PCBs, are considered EIECs. In most cases, section 103(a) of the Comprehensive Environmental Response, Compensation and Liability Act (CERCLA) requires responsible parties to report such incidents immediately to the National Response Center for Oil and Hazardous Material Spills, and under the CERCLA implementing regulations, a written follow-up report may be required. 42 U.S.C.A. § 9603 (West 1995); 40 C.F.R. pt. 302. These reports may eliminate the obligation to make a submission under section 8(e), since under section 8(e) no report is required if the responsible party "has actual knowledge that the Administrator has been adequately informed of such information."

10.4.4. Information Not Reportable Under Section 8(e)

EPA has identified several kinds of information which it deems not reportable under section 8(e). In brief, information is not reportable if it was obtained in its entirety from: (1) an EPA study or report; (2) an official publication or official report (draft or final) published by another federal agency, or developed by another agency under a program in which EPA is collaborating; (3) scientific publications available electronically or in hard copy; (4) scientific databases; (5) a new publication with circulation in the United States; (6) a radio or television report broadcast in the United States; (7) a public scientific conference or meeting in the United States, if the information is captured accurately by records of the meeting and is cited in a bibliographic/abstract database within 90 days of the person's obtaining it; (8) a public scientific conference sponsored or co-sponsored by EPA, or is presented at such a conference by an EPA employee or contractor; or (9) a study that is corroborative (in terms of, for example, route of exposure, dose, species, time to onset, severity, species, strain, etc.) of a well established adverse effect. Information also is not reportable if it is reported to the Agency or to a State under certain specified mandatory reporting requirements of other federal statutes. 2003 Policy at 33,139.

10.4.5. Nature and Sources of Section 8(e) Information

EPA considers that information from designed, controlled studies as well as reports concerning, and studies of, undesigned, uncontrolled circumstances can "reasonably support" a finding of substantial risk. In fact, EPA has indicated that even informal communications between companies can trigger section 8(e) reporting obligations, if a company thereby "obtains" substantial risk information on a chemical it manufactures, processes or distributes in commerce. In section 8(e) Status Report 8EHQ-0585-0572/8EHQ-0985-0572 Follow-up (Status Report Follow-up), EPA stated that a company incurred reporting obligations when its official heard by telephone that another company had found teratogenic effects while doing a study of the first company's chemical. Accordingly, in the *1991 Reporting Guide*, EPA established that "reportable information can come from a variety of sources including, but not limited to draft, interim or final written reports (including study reports, letters, telegrams, telex reports) or verbal reports (received at meetings or by phone) that involve observations (including preliminary observations)," for example, from controlled or uncontrolled human or animal studies/events and environmental studies/events. *1991 Reporting Guide* at 7.

10.4.5.1. Designed, Controlled Studies

Studies which reasonably support a substantial risk finding include: (1) *in vivo* experiments and tests, (2) *in vitro* experiments and tests, (3) epidemiological studies, and (4) environmental monitoring studies. Status Report Follow-up. According to EPA, conclusions concerning effects on humans can be obtained directly or inferred from these designed studies. In certain instances, even preliminary results from incomplete studies would trigger section 8(e) reporting obligations, and the responsible parties should not await final results.

EPA has stated that serious *in vivo* genotoxic effects (*e.g.*, gene or chromosomal mutations) are reportable in and of themselves under section 8(e). On the other hand, a positive *in vitro* genotoxicity test, when considered alone, is usually insufficient to trigger reporting. EPA believes, however, that such information is of value in assessing the possible risk(s) posed by exposure to the tested chemical or mixture. Further, the Agency believes that a positive *in vitro* genotoxicity test result, in combination with other information (*e.g.*, knowledge of actual/potential exposure to and/or high production volumes of the tested chemical), would suggest the need, in many cases, to conduct further studies designed to determine the toxicity of or exposure to that chemical. EPA expects the results of such additional studies to be considered also for section 8(e) submission. *1991 Reporting Guide* at 23.

10.4.5.2. Undesigned, Uncontrolled Circumstances

Reports concerning and studies of undesigned or uncontrolled circumstances also may give rise to section 8(e) reporting obligations. Such reports and studies can include: (1) medical and health surveys, (2) clinical studies, and (3) reports concerning and evidence of effects in consumers, workers, or the environment. Status Report Follow-up. For example, a company medical survey may reveal a pattern of health effects among employees that would give rise to a section 8(e) reporting obligation even where none of the individual reports alone would be reportable.

EPA anticipates that most reports of undesigned, uncontrolled circumstances will be triggered because they reveal patterns of health effects correlated with exposure to a chemical. In some circumstances, however, a single report may reveal a more serious effect caused by a chemical, thereby triggering reporting obligations even in the absence of any pattern of effects. EPA has stated that "a single instance of cancer, birth defects, mutation, death, or serious incapacitation in a human would be reportable if one (or a few) chemical(s) was strongly implicated." *Id.*

10.4.6. Submission of Section 8(e) Information by Trade Associations

Many trade associations sponsor and report studies on chemicals, although they have no obligation to report under section 8(e) because they are not manufacturers, processors, or distributors. The information is generally communicated to their member companies who are subject to section 8(e). EPA has addressed the submission of section 8(e) information by trade associations in a section 8(e) Status Report:

> [T]he obligation to immediately report substantial risk information would apply to an organization/association such as SPI, CMA, API, CIIT, etc. only if such organization/association engages in the manufacture, import, processing, or distribution of the chemical substance or mixture about which substantial risk information has been obtained. However, it is more likely that a Section 8(e) reporting obligation would be incurred by a member (or non-member) company that obtains the results (including preliminary results) from studies conducted or sponsored by an organization/association, if the obtained results meet the reporting criteria outlined in the TSCA § 8(e) policy statement and pertain to a chemical substance or mixture that the company manufactures, imports, processes, or distributes in commerce.

EPA, Status Report 8EHQ-0185-0543, at 3 (Mar. 6, 1985).

10.4.7. FYI Submissions versus Section 8(e) Submissions

Many companies or persons have sent toxicological and other information to EPA on an FYI basis. These FYI submitters have determined that their information, while indicating some degree of risk, does not indicate a "substantial" risk. For example, acute toxicity and mutagenicity test results often are submitted on an FYI basis. These FYI submissions are available for review in the OPPT Public Reading Room at EPA Headquarters.

The FYI submissions are processed by EPA in a manner which is almost identical to a section 8(e) notice, except that a status report is not prepared on an FYI submission. Upon receipt of an FYI notice, the OPPT section 8(e) staff reviews it to determine whether the submission should have been submitted under section 8(e). If the staff determines that the information should have been submitted pursuant to section 8(e), the submitter is notified by EPA and given 20 working days in which to respond to EPA's findings and to explain why the information was not submitted pursuant to section 8(e). EPA then evaluates the response and, if the Agency still determines that the information constitutes section 8(e) information, the FYI is "converted" into a section 8(e) notice and enters the section 8(e) notice processing system. The history of the submission, however, also is forwarded to the Office of Enforcement and Compliance Assurance for evaluation of the situation and possible enforcement action. To date, EPA has not prosecuted anyone for submitting information as an FYI that EPA later determined should have been submitted under section 8(e), if the submission was made within the section 8(e) reporting deadline, *i.e.*, within 15 working days after the person received the information.

10.4.8. When to Submit Section 8(e) Reports

TSCA § 8(e) requires that substantial risk information be submitted "immediately" to the Agency. Neither TSCA nor its legislative history define the term. EPA initially stated in the 1978 Policy Statement that information had to be submitted within 15 working days from its receipt by the submitter. 1978 Policy Statement at 11,111. That 15 working day period was retained in the *1991 Reporting Guide*. *1991 Reporting Guide* at 11. In its 2003 Policy Statement, EPA states that most section 8(e) information must be submitted "not later than the 30th calendar day after the date the subject person obtained such information."

Reporting is not to be delayed while "conclusive" information is developed. EPA has recognized that the evidence generally will not be conclusive:

> Such evidence will generally not be conclusive as to the substantiality of the risk; it should, however, *reliably ascribe the effect to the chemical.*

1978 Policy Statement at 11,112 (emphasis added); *see also 1991 Reporting Guide* at 7.

Emergency incidents, however, are to be reported initially by telephone to the National Response Center (800-424-8802) or the appropriate EPA region within 24 hours. The 2003 Policy Statement lists telephone numbers for regional offices.

10.4.9. How to Make a TSCA § 8(e) Report

Section 8(e) submissions must be transmitted to EPA in a manner that permits the Agency to verify receipt of the submission (*e.g.*, certified or registered mail). In addition, the submission must state clearly that it is being provided under section 8(e) of TSCA. Further, the submission must contain the name, title and telephone number of the person sending the information, the name and address of the establishment with which the reporting person is affiliated, the name and CASRN of the subject chemical, and a summary describing the nature of adverse effects or exposure being reported together with the source of any supporting technical data. EPA has no specific section 8(e) reporting form. For emergency incidents, the initial telephone report must provide the time and location of the incident and as much of the above information as is known at the time.

10.4.10. Confidentiality Claims and Section 8(e) Reports

Persons submitting a section 8(e) notice may claim some or all of the information as confidential. Any information claimed as confidential will be disclosed only to the extent authorized in 40 C.F.R. part 2. If no information is claimed confidential, the entire notice will be placed in the public file.

In order to claim information confidential, the submitter must specifically indicate which information is claimed confidential by labeling each page "proprietary," "trade secret" or "confidential." If a submitter claims any information in the notice confidential, a second ("sanitized") copy of the notice must be submitted from which the confidential information has been deleted. This sanitized copy is then placed in the public file.

As a general rule, EPA discourages claims of confidentiality and attempts to make public as much information as possible from the reports submitted to EPA. While TSCA § 14(a) provides that trade secret information, which is privileged or confidential, shall not be disclosed, TSCA § 14(b) creates a limited exemption, allowing EPA to disclose "any health and safety study" of chemical "offered for commercial distribution." EPA's regulations construe this exemption broadly to include chemical substances distributed "for test marketing or for use in research and development."

EPA generally considers all information contained in a "health and safety study" submitted to the Agency under TSCA § 8(e), including the specific chemical identity, to be available for public disclosure. In the EPA policy on the enforcement of TSCA § 8(e) the Agency states as follows:

> EPA considers chemical identity to be part of, the underlying data to, a health and safety study. . . . Consequently, the confidential identity of a chemical substance will not be

> protected by EPA unless otherwise provided for under § 14 of TSCA and the interpreting regulations in 40 C.F.R. part 2.

68 Fed. Reg. 33,136 (June 3, 2003). Notwithstanding this statement and EPA's preference for restricting confidentiality claims, however, the Agency generally respects submitters' requests to keep confidential the identity of a chemical substance, including even the class of chemical to which the substance belongs, presumably in recognition of companies' legitimate concerns regarding the confidentiality of their chemicals' identities.

10.5. DEVELOPING A REPORTING AND RETENTION PROGRAM

In order to comply with the reporting and record-keeping provisions of section 8, companies must develop an internal section 8 compliance program. While each compliance plan should be tailored to a company's individual structure and needs, there are five key elements which must exist in any sound section 8 program.

First, a section 8 compliance program must be an ongoing activity that is well integrated into regular management and operations activities. Second, it is extremely important for the program to have very visible support from the company's top management. This emphasizes the importance of section 8 compliance to overall corporate success. Many companies achieve this top level support by having the company's chief executive officer sign major communications regarding section 8 compliance. Third, the compliance system must allow a two-way flow of information between personnel who track EPA developments and people who follow company activities. Fourth, people who are responsible for knowing about EPA requirements and those who actually will implement the compliance program in plants, laboratories, or other sites should be involved in developing or revising the program. Finally, the company should periodically remind people about their TSCA § 8 responsibilities through memos, training, or meetings.

10.5.1. Specific Compliance Suggestions

10.5.1.1. Section 8(a)

Under TSCA § 8(a), EPA may request several kinds of information regarding a chemical, including the amount a company produces, the number of people exposed, or the chemical's health effects. Someone in the company must be responsible for checking the *Federal Register* for new EPA reporting requirements. Some companies delegate this responsibility to their legal department, others to their regulatory affairs department.

Once aware of a new EPA requirement, the responsible person must identify and inform those persons in the company who likely have information about that chemical. The way this is done will depend on the company's structure. In a smaller company, it may be enough to identify and inform the plant manager who deals with the chemical. Larger companies sometimes have a steward assigned to each of their products, in which case that person should be informed. If a company maintains a computerized inventory of chemicals that includes information regarding where chemicals are being produced, the affected chemicals can be flagged. In other companies, it may be more convenient to identify people who have information about the chemical from the company's organizational chart. Regardless of how they are identified, those people who are likely to have the information needed in a section 8(a) report should be informed and required to gather the data. Someone also must be designated to review the information gathered and prepare it for submission to EPA.

Remember that section 8(a) reports can be one-time reports such as PAIR reports, or periodic reports such as inventory update rule (IUR) reports. In its IUR report, EPA will require information on plant production for past period (*e.g.*, the last year). Because of this, it is worthwhile to incorporate plant-level record-keeping into a company's section 8(a) compliance program.

10.5.1.2. Sections 8(c) and 8(e)

Since companies can use similar systems for complying with both section 8(c) and section 8(e), the two TSCA provisions are discussed together here. First, the company must have a system in place for gathering section 8(c) and section 8(e) information. This may be accomplished by having a system of product stewardship or responsibility built into the company's structure. Part of the product steward's responsibility would be to gather section 8(c) allegations and information regarding the product's health or environmental risks. Another way section 8(c) and section 8(e) information can be gathered is to have at each location in the company a TSCA coordinator who is trained in TSCA compliance and in turn is responsible for training people at his or her location in how to identify either section 8(c) allegations or section 8(e) substantial risk information. This TSCA coordinator also would have the responsibility of reporting to the corporate committee or committees responsible for section 8(c) and section 8(e).

Second, one or two committees should be formed at the corporate level to evaluate section 8(c) and section 8(e) information. At a minimum, the company's regulatory affairs, medical, industrial hygiene, toxicology, operations, and legal departments should be represented on such committees. These committees should have two major responsibilities: 1) educating plant level product stewards or TSCA coordinators regarding the requirements of section 8(c) and section 8(e) and the company's compliance policy, and 2) reviewing submitted information to determine whether it is a record that should be retained under section 8(c) or reported under section 8(e). The committee should see that several educational activities are incorporated into company practice.

Training in section 8 compliance should be included in the initial training of product stewards or TSCA coordinators. The committee could provide continuing training at yearly meetings. The section 8(c) and section 8(e) committees should send out memos, signed by the company's CEO annually, reminding people who may get section 8(c) or section 8(e) information of their reporting responsibilities and explaining both the company's compliance program and the EPA's reporting requirements. The committee responsible for section 8(c) should meet periodically (monthly, quarterly, or semi-annually) to review potential section 8(c) submissions and to determine which constitute section 8(c) allegations that should be retained in the company's files. Because section 8(e) information must be reported within 15 working days, the section 8(e) committee must meet on an *ad hoc* basis as potentially reportable information is discovered. The section 8(e) committee also should periodically review section 8(c) allegations to determine whether they show any pattern of effects indicating that a chemical may pose substantial risk of harm to health or the environment reportable under section 8(e).

Section 8(e) also requires prompt reporting of emergency incidents. Because a committee generally could not review and respond to such an incident quickly enough, the company should designate an individual as responsible for deciding whether an incident should be reported as an emergency. This person may be a committee member or someone at the plant level. This person also should know the company's emergency reporting responsibilities under other environmental laws. These laws may require reporting to the National Response Center or to state and local emergency response committees.

10.5.1.3. Section 8(d)

In order to ensure compliance with section 8(d), someone in the company must monitor the *Federal Register* for new health and safety study reporting requirements. This could be the same person who reviews the *Federal Register* for TSCA § 8(a) requirements. People who are responsible for the chemical must then be informed of the need to report. Again, these people could be identified via a computerized chemical inventory that identifies where the chemical is manufactured, or through a diagram of corporate responsibilities. A company also might consider maintaining a data base of all toxicological studies and a data base of all industrial hygiene studies. The databases could be labeled so they can retrieve studies by the chemical substances or mixtures examined. If this system is followed, the databases should be searched and the responsible people should be informed of the new reporting obligation.

Once the studies are gathered, they should be reviewed by legal or regulatory affairs personnel to see if they are reportable under TSCA and by operations personnel to see if they contain confidential business information. Someone, of course, must be responsible for submitting the reports to EPA.

EPA also requires ongoing reporting under TSCA § 8(d). The company person responsible for following the *Federal Register* should remind company personnel each year about their ongoing reporting obligations.

CHAPTER 11
EXISTING CHEMICAL REGULATION

Although much of EPA's regulatory activity under TSCA has been focused on premanufacture notification (PMN) review of new chemicals and on development of test data on existing chemicals, TSCA § 6(a) grants EPA broad authority to regulate existing chemicals that present unreasonable risks to health or the environment. During TSCA's near 30 years, however, EPA has promulgated only a handful of regulations under section 6(a).

Some attribute the Agency's limited use of section 6(a) to EPA's slow development of the section 4 testing program. EPA did not issue its first TSCA test rule until October 1984. EPA's slow implementation of the section 4 testing program has meant that the Agency has had little test data on those chemicals most likely to pose risks to human health or the environment. Thus, EPA has had no basis for making a finding that they present an unreasonable risk.

In a few instances, EPA has obviated the need for a section 6(a) rule by referring the situation to another agency for resolution. TSCA § 9(a) provides that if a risk can be adequately controlled by federal laws administered by other agencies, EPA may not act on its own under TSCA until it submits a report to the other agency, describing the risk and requesting an analysis of whether the risk may be prevented or reduced to a sufficient extent via action by the other agency. EPA may not take action if the other agency either finds that there is no unreasonable risk or initiates corrective action within 90 days. As of July 2005, EPA has used the section 9(a) referral mechanism only four times—twice in 1985, once in 1986, and once in 1990. The first three referrals were to OSHA, because in each case potential adverse health effects arose from workplace exposures to the chemical. The industrial chemicals involved were 4,4'-methylenedianiline (MDA) (50 Fed. Reg. 27,674 (July 5, 1985)), 1,3-butadiene (50 Fed. Reg. 41,393 (Oct. 10, 1985)) and glycol ethers (51 Fed. Reg. 18,488 (May 20, 1986)). In 1990, the Administrator referred dioxin in bleached wood pulp and paper products to the Food and Drug Administration because of concern about dioxin exposure from paper material used to package food (55 Fed. Reg. 53,047 (Dec. 26, 1990). (For further discussion of section 9, see chapter 13.)

Another often overlooked reason for the limited number of section 6(a) rules is the chemical industry's voluntary removal of potentially harmful chemicals from the market. Products often are withdrawn because of possible product liability concerns or simply as a matter of good product stewardship, eliminating any need for a section 6(a) rule.

11.1. EPA's AUTHORITY UNDER SECTION 6(a)

If the EPA Administrator "finds that there is a reasonable basis to conclude that the manufacture . . . use, or disposal of a chemical . . . presents or will present an unreasonable risk of injury to health or the environment," and the risks cannot be addressed by another agency under another statute, EPA must initiate section 6(a) rule-making to regulate the substance. TSCA § 6(a). Before the Agency can make such a finding, it must conduct a risk assessment on the chemical by examining the potential hazard associated with the chemical, the potential exposure to humans and the environment, the benefits of the chemical, the potential economic impacts of any proposed regulatory activity, and the availability of substitutes. TSCA § 6(c).

Once having found an unreasonable risk, EPA has a number of regulatory options under section 6(a), including:

- prohibition or limitation on the manufacture, processing, distribution, commercial use or disposal of the chemical;
- prohibition or limitation on the use of the chemical in a concentration above a specified level;
- requirement for adequate warnings and instructions with respect to the chemical's use, distribution in commerce or disposal;
- requirements for record-keeping;
- prohibition or other regulation of the disposal of the chemical; and
- requirement to notify the purchasers or the general public about the risks involved and to replace or repurchase a chemical substance or mixture if requested.

EPA must choose the least burdensome of these restrictions that is adequate to protect against the identified risk. TSCA § 6(a).

In addition to the foregoing regulatory options provided by section 6(a), EPA also may regulate the quality control procedures used in the manufacture or processing of a chemical substance or mixture under section 6(b). If EPA determines that chemical manufacture or processing occurs in a manner "which unintentionally causes the chemical substance or mixture to present or which will cause it to present an unreasonable risk of injury to health or the environment," EPA can order the manufacturer or processor to submit its quality control procedures for review.[42] If the

---

[42] This determination must be made on the record after opportunity for hearing in accordance with the Administrative Procedure Act, 5 U.S.C. § 554. TSCA § 6(b).

quality control procedures are inadequate to control the risk, the Agency can order the manufacturer or processor to give public notice of the risk and to replace or repurchase the substance. TSCA § 6(b).

11.2. PROCEDURES AND STANDARDS

Before regulating an existing substance under section 6(a), the Agency must demonstrate that the chemical presents or will present an unreasonable risk of harm to human health or the environment. TSCA § 6(c). Section 6(c) requires a risk/benefit comparison in which EPA must consider and publish a statement regarding:

- effects on health and the magnitude of human exposure;
- effects on the environment and magnitude of exposure of the environment;
- benefits of the substance for various uses and the availability of substitutes for these uses; and
- reasonably ascertainable economic consequences of the rule after consideration of the effect on the national economy, small business, technological innovation, the environment, and public health.

TSCA §§ 6(c)(1)(A)-(D). The rule must specify a date on which the rule will take effect, and TSCA requires any section 6(a) rule to be effective as soon as feasible. TSCA § 6(d). With respect to chemical substances that are undergoing PMN review, if EPA determines that the activities it is proposing to regulate will present an unreasonable risk before a section 6(a) rule can be promulgated, the Agency can propose its section 6(a) rule and invoke its section 5(f) authority to make the "proposed" rule final and effective as of the day it is published in the *Federal Register*. EPA's authority under section 5(f) is discussed in more detail in chapter 7.

When prescribing a rule under section 6(a), the Administrator must comply with the informal rule-making procedures of section 4 of the Administrative Procedure Act (APA), 5 U.S.C. § 553. These procedures include publishing a proposed rule, allowing an opportunity for written comment, providing an opportunity for an informal hearing, and promulgating a final rule with supporting findings of unreasonable risk. TSCA § 6(c)(2). If the Administrator determines that there are disputed issues of material fact, the Administrator may allow interested parties to cross-examine witnesses and to call rebuttal witnesses.

Congress enacted TSCA to "fill the gaps" in existing environmental laws rather than to supplant the then-existing programs for the control of toxic substances. Consequently, section 6(c) provides that EPA may not regulate an existing chemical under section 6(a) if the Administrator determines that the chemical's risks could be eliminated or reduced under another federal law administered in whole or in part by

EPA. For example, a health risk caused by the discharge of a toxic material into a stream most likely could be reduced or eliminated under section 307 of the Federal Water Pollution Control Act (commonly referred to as the Clean Water Act). Nevertheless, EPA may still find that it is in the public interest to regulate the discharge or otherwise control the risk by using the Agency's authority under TSCA. In making such a finding, however, EPA must consider all relevant aspects of the risk, compare the relative costs of complying with an action under TSCA as distinct from an action under another law or laws, and the relative efficiency of TSCA action versus action under another law to protect against such risk or injury.

TSCA § 21 allows any person to petition EPA to "initiate a proceeding for the issuance, amendment, or repeal of a rule under section [4, 6, or 8] or an order under section [5(e) or 6(b)(2)]." EPA has received many such petitions and their use appears to be increasing. Within 90 days after a petition is filed, EPA must either grant or deny the petition. A denial can be challenged in district court. If EPA grants the petition, however, section 21(b)(3) requires EPA to "promptly commence an appropriate proceeding in accordance with section [4, 5, 6, or 8]." Various petitioners have argued that a rule-making can only be "commenced" by a notice of proposed rule-making (NPRM) (*i.e.*, a proposed rule). In other words, if EPA grants the petition, it must immediately publish a proposed rule. *See Service Employees International Union (SEIU) v. Thomas*, No. 84-2790, 1987 WL 14598 (D.D.C. July 17, 1987) (mem.). In *SEIU*, the court remanded the case to EPA to initiate an "appropriate proceeding," and explained in a subsequent memorandum that the appropriate proceeding was the issuance of an NPRM. In that memorandum, the court interpreted EPA's procedural requirements for rule-making under section 6 (40 C.F.R. § 750.2(a)) to require a TSCA § 6 proceeding to *begin* with an NPRM.

In response to that ruling, EPA has amended section 750.2 to indicate that a proceeding under section 6 may begin with an NPRM, an advance notice of proposed rule-making (ANPR), or notice of other action, such as a formal regulatory investigation designed to lead to issuance of rules within a reasonable time. As support of this position, EPA cites *Natural Resources Defense Council v. EPA*, 595 F. Supp. 1255 (S.D.N.Y. 1984), where the court found that EPA may use an ANPR to initiate a rule-making proceeding under TSCA § 4.

11.3. SECTION 6(a) REGULATIONS

11.3.1. Chlorofluorocarbons

Chlorofluorocarbons (CFCs) were a concern to EPA because of their potential to deplete the protective ozone layer of the upper atmosphere. In 1978, EPA promulgated final regulations prohibiting almost all propellant uses of CFCs. 43 Fed. Reg. 55,241 (Nov. 27, 1978) (codified at 40 C.F.R. pt. 762). Under the regulations, the manufacture, processing, and distribution in commerce of fully halogenated chlorofluoroalkanes for aerosol propellant uses was prohibited, except for certain enumerated "essential" uses.

In late 1988, the Montreal Protocol on Substances That Deplete the Ozone Layer (Protocol) was ratified by a group of countries, including the United States, that account for more than two-thirds of the world's CFC production. Protocol, Sept. 16, 1987 (published at 52 Fed. Reg. 47,515 (Dec. 14, 1987)). The Protocol requires signatory countries immediately to freeze their production and consumption of CFCs at 1986 levels and gradually to reduce those figures by up to 50 percent by 1999. On August 12, 1988, EPA issued a final rule to implement the Protocol, but the rule was issued under EPA's Clean Air Act authority, not under TSCA. 53 Fed. Reg. 30,566 (Aug. 12, 1988). The rule regulates production and consumption of CFCs through an allotment system. On June 19, 1995, EPA revoked the TSCA § 6(a) regulations governing CFCs, noting that the Clean Air Act regulations have rendered the TSCA regulations obsolete. 60 Fed. Reg. 31,917.

11.3.2. Tetrachlorodibenzo-P Dioxin (TCDD)

At one time, EPA regulated the treatment and disposal of wastes containing tetrachlorodioxins (TCDD) (commonly referred to as "dioxin") under TSCA. *See* 40 C.F.R. pt. 775. EPA later acknowledged that the regulation of hazardous waste disposal more logically belonged under RCRA. In 1985, EPA promulgated RCRA regulations that prescribe land disposal and treatment standards (*i.e.*, incineration) for dioxin-contaminated wastes. As part of that rule, EPA revoked the TSCA regulation of dioxin-contaminated wastes. 50 Fed. Reg. 2006 (Jan. 14, 1985).

11.3.3. Metalworking Fluids

On three occasions EPA has used its section 6(a) authority to address potential hazards that could arise from mixing nitrosating agents with certain amides and salts. 49 Fed. Reg. 2772 (Jan. 23, 1984), 24,669 (June 14, 1984), and 36,855 (Sept. 20, 1984) (codified at 40 C.F.R. pt. 747). In each case, EPA used its section 5(f) authority and declared the "proposed" rule to be final and effective as of the day it was proposed in the *Federal Register*.

The three rules involved four PMN substances that were intended for use in metalworking fluids. The substances' specific chemical identities were claimed confidential by the PMN submitters. In each case, EPA determined that the common metalworking industry practice of adding anti-corrosive nitrosating agents to the fluids would result in the formation of N-nitrosodiethanolamine (NDELA), a potent animal carcinogen. Employees in metalworking facilities would be exposed to NDELA by inhalation and dermal contact when the fluids were used.

The rules prohibit mixing nitrosating agents with metalworking fluids that contain the PMN substances, and require distributors of the PMN substances to send advance warning letters and copies of the regulations to proposed recipients. In addition, distributors must affix warning labels to containers of the substances.

11.3.4. Asbestos

11.3.4.1. Asbestos in Schools

In 1982, EPA promulgated regulations under TSCA § 6(a) to protect users of school buildings from unwitting exposure to concentrations of airborne asbestos which occur when friable (capable of crumbling) asbestos-containing materials are damaged or disturbed. 47 Fed. Reg. 23,360 (May 27, 1982). These regulations have been replaced by regulations implementing the Asbestos Hazard Emergency Response Act of 1986. 52 Fed. Reg. 41,826 (Oct. 30, 1987) (codified as amended at 40 C.F.R. pt. 763, subpt. E)).

11.3.4.2. Asbestos Abatement Projects

In 1986 and 1987, EPA promulgated regulations that established requirements which must be followed by state and local government employers conducting asbestos abatement projects not covered by the Asbestos Standard of the Occupational Safety and Health Administration (OSHA), an asbestos standard adopted by a state as part of a state plan approved by OSHA, or a state asbestos regulation which EPA has determined is comparable to or more stringent than EPA's regulations. 51 Fed. Reg. 15,722 (Apr. 25, 1986); 52 Fed. Reg. 5623 (Feb. 25, 1987) (codified at 40 C.F.R. pt. 763, subpt. G (2004)). The 1987 rule replaced the 1986 rule; both cover employees who take part in asbestos abatement work. The 1986 rule extended to such employees provisions of the OSHA Asbestos Standard. The 1987 rule attempts to ensure that all public and private sector employees who participate in asbestos abatement projects enjoy similar levels of protection.

11.3.4.3. Asbestos Product Ban

In July 1989, EPA issued a final rule to ban the manufacture, import, processing, and distribution of approximately 94 percent of all asbestos-containing products manufactured in the United States. 54 Fed. Reg. 29,460 (July 12, 1989). Although most of the rule was set aside by the U.S. Court of Appeals for the Fifth Circuit (see discussion below), the asbestos ban rule illustrates a number of points about EPA's authority and procedures under TSCA § 6(a). First, the breadth of the rule illustrates EPA's view that section 6(a) gives the Agency authority to virtually shut down an industry when there is evidence of serious human health effects. EPA sought to impose the sweeping ban because exposure to asbestos fibers has been associated with pulmonary fibrosis (asbestosis), lung cancer, mesothelioma, gastrointestinal cancer, and other lung disorders and diseases, and because millions of people were exposed to airborne asbestos fibers through occupational exposure, the use of asbestos products, or release of asbestos to ambient air during milling and product manufacturing. The rule did not attempt to ban the remaining six percent of asbestos-containing products, including acetylene cylinders, arc chutes, asbestos diaphragms, battery separators, high-grade electrical paper, missile liners, packing, reinforced plastic, sealant tape, specialty industrial gaskets, and asbestos textiles. EPA found that these products did not create high risk of exposure, and that, unlike the other products, reasonably priced substitutes were not available.

Second, the asbestos ban rule demonstrates that TSCA § 21 petitions can be used to cause or at least affect section 6(a) rule-making. Glenn Scott, a private citizen, had petitioned EPA to ban further manufacture and distribution of asbestos cement water pipes, and the Natural Resources Defense Council (NRDC) had petitioned the Agency to ban the future use of asbestos in motor vehicle brakes. EPA granted both petitions, in 1979 and 1984, respectively, and incorporated the requests into the proposed rule in 1986 and then into the final rule. 44 Fed. Reg. 60,156 (Oct. 18, 1979); 49 Fed. Reg. 49,311 (Dec. 19, 1984); 51 Fed. Reg. 3738 (Jan. 29, 1986); 54 Fed. Reg. 29,461 (July 12, 1989).

Third, the rule is an example of an EPA decision not to refer a hazard to another agency. In this case, EPA determined that existing laws and regulations, including those based on the concept of "permissible exposure limits," were insufficient to control the risks from asbestos. Therefore, the Agency did not refer the matter to OSHA pursuant to TSCA § 9(a).

Under the asbestos rule, asbestos production and importation would have been phased out over a seven-year period, using a three-stage process. At each stage, the manufacture, importation, and processing of certain categories of asbestos products would be banned. When the ban took effect, a manufacturer, importer, or processor of those products would have to cease those operations, inventory all "stock-in-hand" of those products, and mark each product unit with a warning label. They also would have been required to retain copies of the labels for three years after the effective date of the ban. The rule also would have prohibited manufacture of asbestos solely for export. EPA determined that even such manufacture posed an unreasonable risk to human health.

Most of EPA's asbestos rule never took effect; it was set aside by the U.S. Court of Appeals for the Fifth Circuit. *Corrosion Proof Fittings v. EPA*, 947 F.2d 1201 (1991). The court noted first that EPA's rule-making procedures were defective, because EPA had not announced until after the close of the rule-making record that the Agency would use "analogous exposure" data—data on exposure to other chemicals—to estimate certain exposures to asbestos. The court stated that this deprived the public of the opportunity to analyze, comment on and influence a critical aspect of the proceedings. Second, the court found that EPA had not met the Agency's obligations under TSCA § 6(a) to promulgate a regulation consisting of the least burdensome regulatory options that would adequately protect human health. The court noted that EPA had not demonstrated that an intermediate level of regulation, such as workplace exposure controls, would be inadequate.

Third, the court criticized EPA's methodology for calculating benefits of the rule, and found unacceptable EPA's use of un-quantified "future benefits" of a ban to justify banning certain products where the quantified benefits of a ban were small. Fourth, the court found that EPA had not demonstrated a reasonable basis for the rule, given both the flaws in benefit calculation methods and EPA's refusal to consider (1) the lack of substitutes for some asbestos products and (2) the credible evidence presented that some of the existing substitutes actually posed more risk than asbestos. Finally, the court stated that in promulgating a rule that required spending $30-40 million per life saved, EPA had "basically ignored the cost side of the TSCA equation" and thus had not discharged the Agency's duty under TSCA to consider the economic impacts of its regulations.

The court allowed to stand portions of the rule that banned manufacture or importation of asbestos for new uses. The court noted that the rule contained provisions allowing companies to petition EPA for a waiver of the ban under appropriate circumstances.

11.3.5. Hexavalent Chromium

EPA has promulgated a rule that prohibits use of hexavalent chromium chemicals in comfort cooling towers (CCTs). 40 C.F.R. § 749.68. CCTs use ambient air to cool circulating water as part of heating, ventilation, air conditioning and refrigeration systems, and hexavalent chromium can be added to the water to prevent corrosion. EPA determined that hexavalent chromium compounds are human carcinogens, and that continued use in CCTs would create an unreasonable risk to human health. The rule does not ban the use of hexavalent chromium chemicals in industrial cooling towers or closed cooling water systems.

The rule also prohibits distribution of hexavalent chromium chemicals for use in CCTs. Distributors of hexavalent-chromium based water treatment chemicals are required to place on containers warning labels stating that use in CCTs is prohibited by federal law, and they also must report their existence to EPA and retain records of all shipments of hexavalent chromium-based chemicals for use in cooling systems.

While TSCA § 12(b) export notification requirements must be followed for hexavalent chromium chemicals that can be used for water treatment, either alone or in combination with other chemicals and where the mixture can be used to treat water cooling systems, other hexavalent chromium chemicals are not subject to section 12(b) export notification requirements. 59 Fed. Reg. 42,773 (August 19, 1994).

11.3.6. Lead- and Zinc-Containing Fishing Sinkers

Pursuant to citizen petition, EPA promulgated a proposed rule prohibiting the manufacture, import, and processing of fishing sinkers containing any lead or zinc and which are one-inch or less in any dimension for use in the United States. 59 Fed. Reg. 11,122 (Mar. 9, 1994). The proposed rule does not prohibit the manufacture and processing of lead- or zinc-containing fishing sinkers one-inch or less in any dimension solely for export.

EPA proposed prohibiting the manufacture, processing, and distribution of lead- or zinc-containing fishing sinkers because EPA believes they pose an unreasonable risk of injury to avian species such as waterbirds. Despite proposing the rule in 1994, EPA has not yet promulgated a final regulation. EPA's Spring 2005 Regulatory Agenda says, "EPA intends to publish a notice withdrawing the proposal." 70 Fed. Reg. 27,509, 27,625 (May 16, 2005). Meanwhile, however, the proposed rule continues to trigger section 12(b) export notification requirements.

11.4. TSCA § 6(e): POLYCHLORINATED BIPHENYLS (PCBs)

Polychlorinated biphenyls (PCBs) are a group of aromatic chemical compounds. As a class, PCBs possess a number of desirable characteristics such as low electrical conductivity, low water solubility, low flammability, and high chemical stability. Because of these properties, at one time PCBs were widely used in electrical transformer cooling liquids, capacitor fluids, heat transfer fluids, and hydraulic system fluids.

Unfortunately, the stability of PCBs makes them extremely persistent when released into the environment, and their low water solubility allows them to accumulate in the fatty tissues of exposed animals or humans. This persistence and bioaccumulation concerned EPA and Congress because the more heavily chlorinated forms of PCBs are known to cause toxic effects in laboratory animals, including cancer and birth defects.

11.4.1. TSCA § 6(e) Authority

Monsanto, the primary domestic PCB manufacturer, ceased production in 1971. Nevertheless, by that time, there were hundreds of millions of pounds of PCBs in existence. Because of the large amount of PCBs in existence and the perception that PCBs posed a significant health threat, Congress chose to single out PCBs for special treatment under TSCA.

TSCA § 6(e) directs EPA to regulate the manufacture, importation, processing, distribution in commerce, use, disposal, and labeling of PCBs and items containing PCBs. TSCA § 6(e), however, functions in a manner that is virtually the opposite of section 6(a). Unlike section 6(a), section 6(e) does not require EPA to find that an unreasonable risk exists before the Agency can act; rather, under section 6(e), Congress created a legal presumption that PCBs pose an unreasonable risk and banned most activities involving PCBs, while allowing EPA to permit activities only if the Agency finds they do not pose an unreasonable risk.

Section 6(e) generally prohibits manufacture, processing, or distribution in commerce of PCBs. TSCA § 6(e)(3)(A). Section 6(e) also prohibits use of PCBs other than in a "totally enclosed manner."[43] TSCA § 6(e)(2)(A). EPA can authorize a specific type of manufacture, processing, etc.—even a non-enclosed one—if the Agency finds by rule that the specific activity will *not* pose an unreasonable risk. TSCA § 6(e)(2)(B). In addition, any person may petition EPA to exempt a specific activity involving PCBs from the general ban. EPA can grant such an exemption for up to one year if the Agency determines that the specific activity will not present an unreasonable risk *and* that good faith efforts have been made to develop safe chemical substitutes for such PCBs. TSCA § 6(e)(3)(B).

11.4.2. EPA Regulation of PCBs

The Operations Branch/Chemical Management Division of OPPT is responsible for developing and implementing EPA's PCB control program. In general, EPA's PCB regulations, set forth at 40 C.F.R. part 761, cover the following areas: (1) prohibited and authorized commercial activities; (2) marking requirements; (3) storage, disposal and decontamination requirements; (4) exemptions from the general prohibitions; (5) spill cleanup policy; and (6) record-keeping requirements.

In 1998, EPA extensively amended the PCB regulatory framework. 63 Fed. Reg. 35,384 (June 29, 1998). These amendments were challenged by industry and environmental groups in *Central and South West Services v. United States EPA,* 220 F.3d 683 (5th Cir. 2000). Applying the arbitrary and capricious standard of review, the Fifth Circuit for the most part upheld the regulatory amendments. The court rejected petitioners' challenge to EPA's classification of PCB-containing transformers, which was critical to the application of regulatory use controls specific to such transformers. Based on EPA's stated commitment to reexamine PCB toxicity the court remanded sections 761.61(a) and 761.79(b) to give EPA the opportunity to complete its assessment of the non-cancer toxic effects of PCBs. The court also required EPA to provide further response to industry comments requesting a blanket exemption from EPA's "storage for reuse" restrictions. In 2004, EPA published its *Storage of PCB Articles for Reuse: Availability of Supplemental Response to Comments Document*, advising the regulated community of EPA's further response to industry's comments. 69 Fed. Reg. 54,025 (Sept. 7, 2004).

EPA has established controls, restrictions and prohibitions for PCB-related materials based on the known or assumed concentration of PCBs in such materials. *See, e.g.*, 40 C.F.R. § 761.30. Accordingly, a significant component of the regulatory amendments was the promulgation of criteria for the determination of PCB concentration. 40 C.F.R. § 761.1(b)(4). EPA also established specific assumptions for

---

[43] TSCA defines "totally enclosed manner" as any manner which will ensure that any exposure of human beings or the environment as a result of the activity will be insignificant, as determined by EPA by rule. TSCA § 6(e)(2)(C). EPA has defined "totally enclosed manner" as "any manner that will ensure no exposure of human beings or the environment to any concentration of PCBs." 40 C.F.R. § 761.3.

PCB concentrations in PCB materials, where the PCB concentrations have not been determined. 40 C.F.R.§ 761.2. For example, any person must assume that mineral oil-filled electrical equipment manufactured before July 2, 1979 contains more than 50 ppm, but less than 500 ppm PCBs (thereby designating such equipment as "PCB-Contaminated Electrical Equipment" subject to specific requirements and restrictions). 40 C.F.R § 761.2(a)(2). A transformer manufactured prior to July 2, 1979 and containing 3 or more pounds of fluid other than mineral oil must be assumed to contain PCBs in a concentration of 500 ppm or more (thereby designating it as a "PCB Transformer" subject to specific requirements and restrictions). 40 C.F.R. § 761.2(a)(3). Similarly, any person must assume that a capacitor manufactured prior to July 2, 1979 contains 500 ppm or more PCBs. 40 C.F.R. § 761.2(a)(4).

11.4.2.1. 50 ppm PCB Standard

In 1979, EPA promulgated a rule implementing section 6(e) that prohibited the manufacturing, processing, distribution in commerce, or use of any substance containing intentionally generated PCBs in concentrations above 50 parts per million (ppm) except in a "totally enclosed manner" or unless specifically exempted by EPA. 44 Fed. Reg. 31,514 (May 31, 1979) (codified at 40 C.F.R. pt. 761). In *Environmental Defense Fund, Inc. v. EPA*, 636 F.2d 1267, 1284 (D.C. Cir. 1980), the Environmental Defense Fund (EDF) successfully challenged EPA's 50 ppm regulatory cutoff as well as other provisions of the PCB rule. The court set aside EPA's 50 ppm cutoff and remanded the PCB regulations for further Agency rule-making proceedings. EPA, however, obtained an indefinite stay of the court's mandate pending the completion of additional rule-making to govern PCBs. 46 Fed. Reg. 16,090 (May 10, 1981); 46 Fed. Reg. 27,615 (May 20, 1981). As part of the 1998 regulatory amendments, EPA reaffirmed the 50 ppm cutoff for intentionally generated PCBs. With a few exceptions, substances containing PCBs in concentrations below 50 ppm are exempted from regulation. *Id.* Conversely, substances containing concentrations above 50 ppm cannot be manufactured, processed, used, or distributed in commerce unless expressly exempted by Agency rule. *See* 40 C.F.R. § 761.1(b). Persons may not avoid PCB regulations, however, by diluting PCBs to concentrations below 50 ppm. *Id.*

11.4.2.2. Prohibited and Authorized Commercial Activities

Subpart B of 40 C.F.R. part 761 establishes EPA's complex system for regulation of the manufacture, processing, distribution and use of PCBs. Subpart B prohibits manufacture, processing and distribution in commerce of PCBs for use in the United States or for export, and prohibits use of PCBs in any manner not authorized by EPA. 40 C.F.R. §§ 761.20(a)-(d). EPA recognizes, however, that some manufacturing processes inadvertently generate PCBs and allows such generation, subject to certain limits. EPA also permits importation of inadvertently generated PCBs. These generators and importers still are subject to certain record-keeping and reporting obligations, and can lose their "excluded manufacturing process" status if they fail to file required reports. 40 C.F.R. §§ 761.185, 761.187.

Subpart B also authorizes 16 specific uses of PCBs that EPA has determined do not pose an unreasonable risk to human health or the environment. 40 C.F.R. § 761.30. Virtually all of these authorizations are narrowly defined and some specifically require the user to comply with other portions of part 761, such as the marking or storage regulations, to maintain their "authorized use" status. *Id.*

In 1998, EPA amended subpart E of 40 C.F.R. part 761 to establish class exemptions for certain types of research and development activities involving PCBs. Generally, and in contrast to the R&D exemption from the PMN requirement, these exemptions impose specific quantity limits on the amount of PCBs that may be manufactured, imported, processed, distributed and/or exported for the designated research and development purposes. Other specific requirements, such as packaging, recordkeeping and disposal requirements, also are imposed, depending on the specific class exemption being invoked. Additionally, a person seeking a class exemption must file a petition requesting the exemption 60 days before engaging in the covered R&D activities. For example, section 761.80(e) establishes a class exemption allowing R&D facilities to manufacture and import PCBs solely for the manufacturer's own research to develop PCB disposal technologies. The quantity of PCB manufactured for this purpose cannot exceed 500 grams by total weight of pure PCBs. A person seeking to invoke this exemption must file a petition with EPA, such that EPA receives the petition 60 days prior to the person's engaging in this activity. Further, a person engaging in such exempted R&D activities also must maintain records of the PCB activities for three years after ceasing operations, among other requirements.

11.4.2.3. Marking of PCBs and PCB Items

Subpart C of 40 C.F.R. part 761 gives the standardized format for marking labels (40 C.F.R. § 761.45) and lists the types of items that must be marked with such labels (40 C.F.R. § 761.40). The list includes electrical, hydraulic and heat transfer equipment, containers, vehicles, and storage areas (including means of access to any area that contains such equipment). In addition to the items listed in 40 C.F.R. section 761.40, PCB marking regulations apply to the compressors and pipes of natural gas pipelines when the liquids in them contain any measurable concentration of PCBs. 40 C.F.R. § 761.30(i).

The standard formats for large and small PCB labels (known as M_L and M_S, respectively and set forth at 40 C.F.R. section 761.45) must be used whenever PCB warning marks are required, with one exception. Access to a PCB transformer can be marked with a non-conforming label if such labels were in place prior to August 15, 1985, the primary fire department that serves that area accepts the alternate label, and the EPA Regional Administrator approves its use. 53 Fed. Reg. 27,322, 27,329 (July 19, 1988) (codified at 40 C.F.R. § 761.40(j)).

In 1998, EPA amended its PCB marking regulations. Among other things, the regulatory amendments expanded the types of PCB-related items requiring marks, including PCB Large Low Voltage Capacitors in use (40 C.F.R. § 761.40(k)(1)), and all equipment containing PCB Transformers or PCB Large Capacitors (High or Low

Voltage), including equipment in use (40 C.F.R § 761.40(k)(2)). These marking provisions, however, do not apply to equipment containing PCB-Contaminated Electrical Equipment. *See* 63 Fed. Reg. at 35,400. Furthermore, 40 C.F.R. section 761.40(h), which requires the marking of various PCB items to be conspicuous, was amended to specifically include PCB storage units.

EPA further clarified marking requirements for transport vehicles. After having proposed to require markings on transport vehicles carrying PCBs in any phase, EPA rejected that proposal in the 1998 amendments, requiring transport vehicles instead to bear markings only if they carry PCB-containing liquid, in the amount of 45 kilograms or more. *See* 40 C.F.R. § 761.40(b). In that regard, EPA clarified that the 45 kilogram threshold is to be calculated by the total weight of liquid containing 50 ppm or more PCBs, not by the total weight of PCB molecules in the liqu*id.* 63 Fed. Reg. at 35,400. EPA also clarified that, transport vehicles do not include fork lifts used onsite (*e.g.*, not used on public roads). *Id.*

11.4.2.4. Disposal Requirements

The PCB regulation scheme that Congress and EPA have established is designed to eliminate potential harm from PCBs by ensuring that few, if any, new PCBs are created, and that those in existence are gradually disposed of by methods that virtually eliminate exposure. The disposal scheme is complicated, however, by the diversity of PCB contaminated wastes, which include: liquids; various types of equipment such as transformers, capacitors, or hydraulic machinery; other contaminated articles; containers that once held PCBs; dredged materials and sewage treatment sludges; and contaminated soil and/or concrete scrap from cleanup sites.

Promulgated as part of the 1998 PCB regulatory amendments, 40 C.F.R. section 761.50 sets forth the general scope of permitted and prohibited disposal activities. The regulation further clarifies that section 761.60 applies to PCB liquids and PCB Items, and not to other PCB wastes, which are regulated under 40 C.F.R. sections 761.61 and 761.62. In that regard, the regulation nevertheless does set forth certain general standards for disposal of PCB remediation waste. For example, open burning of PCBs is prohibited. The regulation also specifies the storage and disposal options for PCB/radioactive waste.

When assigning disposal methods to each type of waste, EPA attempts to achieve sufficient destruction or containment to be safe without being overly stringent. Subpart D of 40 C.F.R. part 761 sets forth categories of PCB wastes and the methods of disposal for each category; use of any other method is prohibited. Furthermore, the regulations define "disposal" so that virtually any release of PCBs to the environment in concentrations at or above 50 ppm will be considered a prohibited act of disposal.

> "Disposal" means intentionally or accidentally to discard, throw away, or otherwise complete or terminate the useful life of PCBs and PCB Items. Disposal includes spills, leaks, and other uncontrolled discharges of PCBs as well as

actions related to containing, transporting, destroying, degrading, decontaminating, or confining PCBs and PCB Items.

40 C.F.R. § 761.3. Unauthorized PCB disposal subjects the violator to civil and criminal penalties under TSCA § 16. *See Yaffe Iron & Metal Co. v. EPA*, 774 F.2d 1008 (10th Cir. 1985) (affirmed a $10,000 civil penalty against a scrap and warehousing business for improper storage and disposal of PCBs by using an incinerator which failed to meet the requirements of Annex I of the PCB regulations); *see also United States v. Ward*, 676 F.2d 94 (4th Cir. 1982), *cert. denied*, 459 U.S. 835 (1982) (affirmed criminal conviction for unlawful disposal of oil contaminated with PCBs); *see also Newell Recycling Co., Inc. v. United States EPA*, 231 F.3d 204 (5th Cir. 2000) (upholding penalty of $1.345 million for violations of disposal requirements).

The PCB disposal regulations list three permissible methods, with associated specific criteria, for disposal of PCB waste in the form of PCB liquids, PCB Articles and PCB Containers: incineration; placement in a chemical waste landfill; and burning in a high efficiency boiler, scrap metal recovery oven or smelter. 40 C.F.R. § 761.60. However, not all methods of disposal are appropriate for all types of PCB items and waste. For example, PCB Small Capacitors may be disposed of at municipal landfills (subject to certain exceptions), but PCB Large Capacitors may not. Additionally, packaging requirements may apply for waste. *See* subpart D of 40 C.F.R. part 761 for further information. Persons may not lawfully avoid a disposal requirement (or any other concentration-based PCB regulation) by diluting liquid PCBs to a lower concentration (40 C.F.R. § 761.1(b)(5)), or by processing them into a non-liquid form (40 C.F.R. § 761.50(a)(2)). In addition, EPA Regional Administrators have authority to approve alternative methods of disposal, provided those methods meet certain performance standards. 40 C.F.R. § 761.60(e). As an alternative to incineration, all 10 Regional Administrators have approved chemical dechlorination of liquids containing up to 10,000 ppm PCBs.

As part of the 1998 PCB regulatory amendments, EPA prohibited disposal of PCB-Contaminated mineral oil dielectric fluid, which has been stabilized on-site prior to disposal in accordance with section 761.75(b)(8), at a chemical waste landfill (63 Fed. Reg. at 35,402). Land disposal of PCB-contaminated liquids from incidental sources associated with non-liquid PCB waste is allowed, under certain conditions (§ 761.60(a)(3)). EPA also: (1) prohibited open burning of PCBs (§ 761.50(a)(1)); (2) required disposal of drained PCB-Contaminated Electrical Equipment and other drained PCB Articles, except capacitors, in scrap metal recovery ovens and smelters, municipal solid waste landfills or disposal facilities approved under part 761 (§ 761.60(b)(4)); (3) required fluorescent light ballasts containing PCBs in their potting material to be disposed of in a TSCA-approved disposal facility, as bulk product waste under section 761.62, as household waste under section 761.63 (where applicable), or in accordance with the decontamination provisions of section 761.79 (§ 761.60(b)(6)(iii)); and (4) regulated the disposal of PCB-containing pipes from natural gas pipelines (*see* § 761.60(b)(5) for further information).

Also in 1998, EPA promulgated section 761.61 to provide three cleanup and disposal options for PCB remediation waste: (1) self-implementing disposal similar to the PCB Spill Cleanup Policy, which is an enforcement policy codified at 40 C.F.R. part 761, subpart G; (2) existing, performance-based disposal technologies; and (3) risk-based disposal. Similarly, EPA established disposal standards for PCB bulk product waste (non-remediation waste): (1) performance-based disposal; (2) disposal in solid landfills; (3) risk-based disposal; and (4) disposal as daily landfill cover or roadbed. 40 C.F.R. § 761.62. Standards for disposal of household PCB waste and certain R&D-generated waste are set forth in sections 761.63 and 761.64, respectively.

Figure XI-1 at the end of this chapter shows the permitted disposal methods for various PCB wastes.

11.4.2.5. Import for Disposal

In 1997, the Ninth Circuit Court of Appeals overturned the Import for Disposal Rule, previously codified at 40 C.F.R. § 761.93, on the ground that EPA could not rely, as it did, on section 6(e)(1) of TSCA to authorize imports of PCBs for disposal. *Sierra Club v. EPA*, 118 F.3d 1324 (9th Cir. 1997). Consequently, in 1998 EPA amended section 761.93 such that EPA can now allow imports of PCBs only by issuing exemptions to importers via the petition process under TSCA § 6(e)(3)(B).

11.4.2.6. Storage for Disposal

When PCBs and PCB items (articles or containers) are removed from use, they must be disposed of (incinerated, placed in landfill, etc.) within one year. Persons storing PCBs or PCB Items subject to this limitation may obtain an extension of the one-year period under certain conditions. 40 C.F.R. § 761.65(b). PCB/radioactive waste removed from service for disposal is excluded from the 1-year storage for disposal requirement provided that continuing attempts to dispose of the waste are documented and the waste is managed in accordance with all applicable federal, state, and local laws and regulations. 40 C.F.R. § 761.65(a).

Certain restrictions apply to storage of PCBs that are awaiting disposal. 40 C.F.R. § 761.65. All PCBs and PCB items must be marked to indicate the date the PCBs were removed from service. The storage facility must be properly constructed to contain spills, and the operators must inspect stored PCBs every 30 days, keep records of those inspections, and prepare and maintain on file annual reports. 40 C.F.R. §§ 761.65(b), (c)(5), (c)(9), 761.180.

Non-leaking PCB items, leaking PCB items placed in non-leaking PCB containers and non-liquid PCB waste such as rags and soil in PCB containers can be stored for 30 days in areas that do not comply with the storage facility requirements. Liquid PCBs with concentrations at 50 ppm or greater may be stored in PCB containers in areas that do not comply with the storage facility requirements if a Spill Prevention, Control and Countermeasure Plan has been prepared in accordance with 40 C.F.R. part 112. 40 C.F.R. § 761.65(c)(1). Undamaged Large High Voltage Capacitors and non-leaking PCB-Contaminated Electrical Equipment (containing PCBs at concentrations between 50 and 500 ppm) can be stored on pallets next to proper storage facilities, if certain conditions are met. 40 C.F.R. § 761.65(c)(2).

11.4.2.7. PCB Activity Notification and Manifesting Rule

In the 1970s and early 1980s, many companies disposed of PCBs and PCB Items by giving them to PCB "brokers," who would arrange for disposal of the PCBs and possibly decontamination and recycling of the contaminated equipment or materials. Unfortunately, several of these brokers abandoned large quantities of PCBs on site; their facilities became Superfund sites; and the companies that generated the PCB waste incurred liability under the Comprehensive Environmental Response Compensation and Liability Act (CERCLA). *See* General Accounting Office, *GAO/RCED-87-127, Abandonment of PCBs Demonstrates Need for Program Improvements* (May 1987). As a result, many sources called for a cradle-to-grave manifesting system to allow EPA to track PCBs from the time they are taken out of service to the time of ultimate disposal.

Some states created tracking systems by listing PCBs as a RCRA hazardous waste, thereby subjecting them to the state's RCRA manifesting requirements. In 1989, EPA promulgated a rule to create a nationwide PCB manifesting system under TSCA. Polychlorinated Biphenyls; Notification and Manifesting for PCB Waste Activities, 54 Fed. Reg. 52,752 (Dec. 21, 1989).

Under the rule, all PCB disposal companies, transporters and commercial storers of PCB waste must notify EPA, identifying their facilities and activities, within sixty days after the effective date of the rule. Generators of PCB wastes who store their own wastes in a facility subject to the long-term storage requirements of section 761.65, or who operate a PCB storage tank subject to section 761.65(c)(7), also must notify EPA. All companies that notify EPA receive an EPA registration number. A company with more than one long-term storage facility must submit a separate notification for each such facility, and each facility will be assigned a different registration number.

If a company previously has notified EPA of its PCB waste handling activities and those activities change, the company must renotify EPA to reflect those changes no later than 30 days from when a change is made. For example, a company must renotify EPA when the company changes the location where it conducts PCB waste handling activities or when it wishes to change the kind of PCB waste handling activities that it does. 40 C.F.R. § 761.205(f).

The TSCA rule defines "generators" differently than under RCRA. Under the RCRA regulations, each individual site that is a source of hazardous waste is a separate "generator" with its own EPA identification number. Under the TSCA rule, however, a company is treated as a single generator with one EPA registration number, even if it disposes of PCBs from a number of different facilities. EPA took this approach because generator sites regulated under RCRA usually produce a regular stream of wastes for some time, but a PCB "site" may consist of a single transformer that is taken out of service only once. Registering each of the estimated 12 million such "sites" would create an unmanageable administrative burden on the Agency, as well as on industry. Under the PCB Manifesting Rule, a company is a "generator" if it: (1) produces PCB waste that is subject to the PCB disposal regulations; (2) first causes a PCB or PCB item to become subject to the disposal regulations; or (3) has physical control over PCBs when a decision is made that the use of the PCBs has been terminated. 40 C.F.R. § 761.3.

Under the rule, generators must prepare a manifest for any batch of PCB waste they create. However, a manifest is not required for PCB waste currently below 50 ppm which derives from pre-April 18, 1978 spills of any concentration; pre-July 2, 1979 spills of less than 500 ppm PCBs; or materials decontaminated in accordance with section 761.79. 40 C.F.R. § 761.207(j).

When the generator sends the PCB waste out for disposal, the generator keeps one copy of the manifest and sends an advance copy to the designated disposal facility. When the designated disposal facility receives the waste, the responsible official signs the manifest and returns it to the generator, who retains it on file for three years, or for five years if the generator is subject to the record-keeping provisions of 40 C.F.R. section 761.180(a) or (b).

Under the rule, generators must notify EPA if the signed manifest is not returned by the disposal facility. If disposal and commercial storage facilities receive unmanifested PCB waste, or if there is any discrepancy between the amount they receive and the amount listed on the corresponding manifest, they must attempt to contact the generator to resolve the discrepancies and, if unable to do so, they must notify EPA. 40 C.F.R. §§ 761.211(a), (b); 761.210(b).

A facility that commercially stores PCB wastes must submit for EPA's approval a closure plan and financial assurance of the facility's ability to close. If EPA does not accept the facility's closure plan or financial assurance, the facility cannot continue to store PCB wastes. Enforcement of the financial assurance requirement is currently a top national enforcement priority for the Agency, which also has developed a cost-estimating model for closure and post-closure costs. *See* http://www.epa.gov/compliance/resources/policies/data/planning/npmguidance2006.pdf for information about EPA's current enforcement of financial assurance requirements under TSCA § 6(e).

EPA has attempted to coordinate PCB regulation under this rule with state regulation under RCRA. PCB generators that are subject to state-administered RCRA programs are permitted to use the same Dun & Bradstreet Data Universal Numbering (DUN) system numbers for the manifesting and record-keeping requirements of both programs. The rule also allows PCB generators to utilize the RCRA Uniform Manifest, which has designated space for additional information requirements that states may impose under their RCRA program.

11.4.2.8. Records and Reports

By July 1st of each year the operators of a facility, including an operator that disposes of its own waste and does not receive or generate manifests, must prepare and keep at hand an annual report for the previous calendar year if their facility contains 45 kilograms or more of PCBs in PCB containers, one or more PCB transformers, 50 or more large PCB capacitors, or is used for PCB storage and/or disposal. 40 C.F.R. § 761.180, subpt. J. The annual report for the previous calendar year must be submitted to the appropriate EPA Regional Administrator by July 15 of each year. Subpart J also describes specific records that must be maintained by disposal and storage facilities, incineration facilities, chemical waste landfills, high efficiency boiler facilities, importers and persons who inadvertently generate PCBs. Scattered throughout part 761 are other record-keeping requirements that are imposed on persons who engage in specified activities involving PCBs.

11.4.2.9. PCB Spill Cleanup Policy

On April 2, 1987, EPA issued a final policy governing the reporting and cleanup of all spills occurring after May 4, 1987 and involving materials containing PCBs greater than 50 ppm. 52 Fed. Reg. 10,688 (Apr. 2, 1987) (codified at 40 C.F.R. §§ 761.120-761.135, subpt. G). This policy was issued in order to set a uniform cleanup standard among EPA regions, each of which previously had established its own respective cleanup standards, and in recognition that the risks posed by PCBs vary with the amount of PCBs and the location. 52 Fed. Reg. at 10,689.

The policy is not a legislative regulation whose violation would trigger liability. Rather, EPA asserts that any spill of material containing 50 ppm or more PCBs is an unlawful "disposal." Thus, in EPA's view, whenever a spill occurs, a violation of TSCA already has taken place. The PCB cleanup policy offers the responsible party an opportunity to avoid liability for the disposal violation because EPA states that compliance with both the procedural and substantive provisions of the PCB cleanup policy will "create a presumption against both enforcement action for penalties and the need for further cleanup under TSCA." 40 C.F.R. § 761.135(a). EPA specifically has preserved its rights to compel cleanup, however, when it determines that the cleanup levels specified in the policy have not been met, and to seek penalties if the Agency believes that the responsible party has not made a good-faith effort to comply with the cleanup policy. *Id.* The Agency also has stated that in some cases the PCB cleanup policy standards may be superseded by stricter standards established under other statutes. According to EPA:

> This policy does not affect cleanup standards or requirements for the reporting of spills imposed, or to be imposed, under other Federal statutory authorities, including but not limited to, the Clean Water Act (CWA), the Resource Conservation and Recovery Act (RCRA), and the Comprehensive Environmental Response Compensation and Liability Act of 1980 (CERCLA) as amended by the

> Superfund Amendments and Reauthorization Act (SARA). *Where more than one requirement applies, the stricter standard must be met.*

40 C.F.R. § 761.120(e)(1) (emphasis added). EPA has acknowledged that cleanups required by other statutes, such as RCRA and CERCLA, may have to meet different standards than those imposed by the TSCA PCB Spill Cleanup Policy. *Id.*

Among the "procedural" requirements that a company must meet to comply with the Spill Cleanup Policy are reporting provisions. Spills of any magnitude that directly contaminate surface waters, sewers, or drinking water supplies, or which directly contaminate grazing lands or vegetable gardens must be reported immediately to the appropriate EPA regional office. In addition, any spill that involves a release of more than ten pounds of PCBs *by weight* must be reported immediately. 40 C.F.R. § 761.125(a)(1). Note, also, that to comply with EPA's CERCLA and the National Contingency Plan spill reporting requirements, spills of over one pound PCBs by weight must be reported to the National Response Center. *Id.*

For purposes of cleanup, the Policy separates PCB spills into two categories:

- Low concentration spills (less than 500 ppm PCBs) which involve less than 1 lb. of PCBs by weight (less than 270 gallons of untested mineral oil).

- High concentration spills (greater than 500 ppm PCBs) or low concentration spills involving 1 lb. or more PCBs by weight (270 gallons or more of untested mineral oil).

40 C.F.R. §§ 761.125(b) and (c).

Under the PCB cleanup policy, required levels of cleanup depend upon which of the two categories (low or high) applies, the spill location, potential for exposure to residual PCBs remaining after the cleanup, concentration of PCBs initially spilled, and the nature and size of the population potentially at risk from exposure. The policy sets cleanup standards for surfaces, concrete, soil, and objects that have been exposed to PCBs. In general, the greater the potential human exposure, the more stringent the cleanup standard.

Several categories of spills are exempt from the cleanup standards of this policy, including spills that took place before the policy was published, and spills directly into surface water, drinking water, sewers, grazing lands, and vegetable gardens. For these latter types of spills, the Agency will set cleanup standards on a case-by-case basis, based upon site specific considerations. 40 C.F.R. § 761.120(d).

11.4.2.10. Decontamination of PCB Waste

In 1998, EPA promulgated new regulations regarding decontamination standards and procedures for removing PCBs from water, organic liquids, non-porous surfaces, concrete, and non-porous surfaces covered with a porous surface, such as paint or coating on metal. 40 C.F.R. § 761.79. Section 761.79 does not apply to intact electrical equipment, wood, soil, debris or sediments.

Decontamination standards and procedures can be substituted for PCB disposal and decontaminated materials can be distributed in commerce, used or reused. In addition, materials meeting the applicable decontamination standards are unregulated for disposal under subpart D of part 761. Nevertheless, when contaminated PCB materials are sent off-site for decontamination, they must be manifested to a commercial PCB storer or disposer.

FIGURE XI-1
PERMITTED DISPOSAL METHODS

PCB WASTE	PERMITTED DISPOSAL METHOD
Liquids containing 500 ppm or more of PCBs	Incineration Alternative methods approved by Regional Administrator
Liquids containing 50-499 ppm PCBs	Incineration Chemical waste landfill (for liquids from incidental sources, such as precipitation, condensation, leachate or load separation and are associated with PCB Articles or non-liquid PCB wastes) High efficiency boiler Alternative methods approved by Regional Administrator
PCB Transformers	Incineration Chemical waste landfill (if drained and flushed)
PCB Large Capacitors	Incineration (A reuse process has been approved by Region VII)
PCB Small Capacitors	Incineration Chemical waste landfill Municipal waste landfill
PCB Hydraulic Machines	Decontamination (in accordance with 40 C.F.R. § 761.79) Municipal waste landfill Scrap metal recovery oven or smelter (operating in compliance with 40 C.F.R. § 761.72) Disposal facility approved under 40 C.F.R. pt. 761
Natural Gas Pipeline Systems containing PCBs	Abandonment Removal with subsequent action
Fluorescent Light Ballasts containing PCBs in their Potting Material	TSCA-approved disposal facility (as bulk product waste under 40 C.F.R. § 761.62, as household waste under 40 C.F.R. § 761.63 (where applicable), or in accordance with the decontamination provisions of 40 C.F.R. § 761.79)

FIGURE XI-1 (continued)

PCB WASTE	PERMITTED DISPOSAL METHOD
Other PCB Articles (machinery, rags, soil, debris)	Incineration Chemical waste landfill
PCB Containers	Incineration Chemical waste landfill (if liquids are drained) Municipal solid waste landfill (if liquids in container had less than 500 ppm PCBs and liquids are drained)
Dredge spoils, sewage treatment sludges	Incineration Chemical waste landfill Alternative methods approved by Regional Administrator

Source: 40 C.F.R. § 761.60.

CHAPTER 12
IMPORTATION AND EXPORTATION

Importers of any chemical substance must comply with the same obligations imposed by TSCA on domestic manufacturers (TSCA defines manufacturer to include an importer) and in addition are subject to a certification requirement established pursuant to TSCA § 13. Similarly, exporters of chemicals intended solely for use abroad may be subject to the export notification obligations of TSCA § 12.

12.1. IMPORT REGULATION: TSCA § 13

TSCA § 13 requires the Secretary of the Treasury to refuse entry of any chemical substance into the U.S. customs territory if: (1) it fails to comply with any rule in effect under the Act; or (2) it is offered for entry in violation of (a) section 5 or 6, (b) a rule or order under section 5 or 6, or (c) an order issued in a civil action brought under section 5 or 7. TSCA § 13(a)(1). The U.S. customs territory includes the fifty States, the District of Columbia, Puerto Rico, the U.S. Virgin Islands, Guam, the Canal Zone, American Samoa, the Northern Mariana Islands or any other territory or possession of the U.S.[44]

12.1.1. Importer's Certification Requirement

Under the authority granted to the Secretary of the Treasury, the U.S. Customs Service issued regulations to implement the provisions of TSCA § 13. 48 Fed. Reg. 34,734 (Aug. 1,1983) (codified at 19 C.F.R. §§ 12.118 - 12.127 and 127.38). These regulations require an importer to certify at the port of entry that either (1) the shipment is subject to TSCA and complies with all applicable rules and orders thereunder or (2) it is not subject to TSCA. 19 C.F.R. § 12.121(a). Customs and EPA refer to the former as a "positive certification" and the latter as a "negative certification." Failure to certify as required under TSCA § 13 may subject an importer to an administrative civil penalty under section 16(a). *See* chapter 12. Between 1986 and 1996, EPA brought over sixty enforcement actions to impose civil penalties for failure to certify under section 13 ranging from $3,600 to $685,000 (including concurrent violations of TSCA § 5).

In most cases, the Customs entry documentation and TSCA certification will be filed with Customs at the same port at which the shipment is unloaded from an international carrier. It is not uncommon, however, for a shipment to be unloaded at one Customs port and to be transported inland under bond (in-transit bond) to another

---

[44] U.S. EPA Communication to T. B. Johnston, 2000.

Customs port where it is entered with Customs. The port of unloading from the international carrier is referred to as the port of arrival. The port where the certification and other entry documentation are filed is referred to as the port of entry. Customs has established approximately 90 ports where entry documents may be filed. They are listed in section 101.3(b) of the Customs Regulations. 19 C.F.R. § 101.3(b).

In some situations, chemicals are merely moved through the U.S. for export to another destination, such as from Mexico to Canada. Under these circumstances, no certification is required. Also, import certification is not required for entry into foreign trade zones. Customs does require certification, however, for withdrawal of the chemical substance from the foreign trade zone if the chemical is intended for United States consumption. *Toxic Substances Control Act—A Guide for Chemical Importers/ Exporters* 33 (Apr. 1991) [*Guide*].

EPA has issued a policy statement clarifying how the Agency will interpret and implement chemical substance import requirements. 48 Fed. Reg. 55,462, 55,464 (Dec. 13, 1983) (codified at 40 C.F.R. § 707.20). For guidance to assist importers and exporters, see: *Guide*; also, see *Introduction to the Chemical Import Requirements of the Toxic Substances Control Act, June 1999,* available at http://www.epa.gov/opptintr/chemtest/importguide.pdf. These documents are also available from the TSCA Assistance Office.

12.1.1.1. Importer Defined

Under Customs Regulations, an "importer" is defined as:

> [T]he person primarily liable for the payment of any duties on the merchandise, or an authorized agent acting on his behalf. The importer may be:
>
> > (1) The consignee, or
> >
> > (2) The importer of record, or
> >
> > (3) The actual owner of the merchandise, if an actual owner's declaration and superseding bond has been filed in accordance with § 141.20 of this chapter, or
> >
> > (4) The transferee of the merchandise, if the right to withdraw merchandise in a bonded warehouse has been transferred in accordance with Subpart C of Part 144 of [Chapter I of 19 CFR].

19 C.F.R. § 101.1. Generally, the consignee will make the certification.

12.1.1.2. Product Coverage

The importer is responsible for determining whether a chemical substance is on the TSCA Inventory. The importer can file a *bona fide* intent to import request with the Agency in order to have EPA search the Master Inventory (this includes the confidential Inventory). 40 C.F.R. § 720.25(b). The importer should file the *bona fide* intent to import request well in advance of the actual date of importation because *bona fide* requests take a minimum of 30 days to process. (*See* chapter 4.)

If the chemical substance is on the TSCA Inventory, the importer must then determine whether it has been the subject of any regulatory action under TSCA § 5, 6, or 7. After evaluation of the foregoing, the importer would then make a positive certification that the chemical is being imported in compliance with TSCA. *Guide* at 12. (Note that, as "manufacturers," importers also must comply with all reporting and recordkeeping requirements under TSCA §§ 4 and 8.)

If the chemical product is not on the Inventory but is being imported solely for research and development (R&D) purposes as defined by TSCA, the importer must make a positive certification that the chemical substance is imported in compliance with TSCA. *Guide* at 30. (For a detailed discussion of TSCA's R&D provisions see chapter 5.) If the chemical is not on the Inventory and is being imported for a non-exempt commercial purpose, the importer must comply with the TSCA § 5 premanufacture notification (PMN) requirements before importation.

12.1.1.3. Importation of Wastes

Wastes, both hazardous and non-hazardous, are covered by TSCA because they are "chemical substances" within the meaning of the Act. As such, they require a positive certification, even if accompanied by a hazardous waste manifest pursuant to the Resource Conservation and Recovery Act of 1976 as amended, 42 U.S.C. §§ 6901-6992k. For example, if the wastes are imported in order to be burned as a fuel, to be disposed of, or for extraction of component chemical substances under 40 C.F.R. section 720.30(g) (by-products), and the wastes consist of by-products as defined at 40 C.F.R. section 720.3(d), they are not subject to the section 5 PMN requirements. Therefore, an importer can file a positive certification even if the by-products are not on the Inventory. According to EPA:

> "[B]y-products" include by-products of use as well as of manufacture and processing. Therefore, spent solvents, spent cleaning agents, and used motor oil are classified as by-products in addition to manufacturing waste.

Guide at 34.

12.1.1.4. Unsolicited Samples

EPA recognizes that companies occasionally receive both solicited and unsolicited samples of chemical substances through the mail. Although such shipments appear to be subject to the TSCA § 13 import certification requirement, in practice U.S. Customs may not examine these packages (for example, shipments valued at less than $200 may be imported pursuant to informal customs entry procedures and escape U.S. Customs scrutiny). Whether unsolicited or solicited, such packages present a difficult problem of certification at the time of entry. Consequently, EPA has developed a procedure for "post importation" certification. *Guide* at 32. Import certifications for shipments received through the mail may be filed directly with EPA after receipt of the shipment. Such certifications should be sent to U.S. EPA, 1200 Pennsylvania Avenue, N.W., Washington, D.C. 20460, Att'n: TSCA § 13 Coordinator, Chemical Control Division (7405).

12.1.1.5. Exclusions

If a substance is excluded from the TSCA § 3(2)(B) definition of "chemical substance," and therefore not subject to TSCA, it is subject to a negative certification or to no certification at all, depending on which exclusion applies. EPA takes the position that in order for a food, drug, cosmetic, or device to be excluded from all certification requirements, they must be imported *solely* for such use under the Federal Food, Drug, and Cosmetic Act (FFDCA), 21 U.S.C.A. §§ 301-395. Customs has determined that foods, food additives, drugs, drug intermediates, cosmetics, cosmetic intermediates and devices are exempt from TSCA certification because they require certification under FFDCA. Furthermore, customs excludes chemicals from the certification requirement if they will be used solely in the manufacture of a food, food additive, etc. *Guide* at 28-29. Similarly, pesticides require no certification if they are accompanied by a Notice of Arrival of Pesticide (which is required for all pesticide imports). Nuclear source materials, special nuclear materials, nuclear by-product material, firearms, and ammunition require a negative certification, which states that the substance is not subject to TSCA. *Guide* at 25. Substances imported under a negative certification subsequently may be used by the importer for a TSCA purpose as long as such use was not contemplated at the time of importation and it otherwise complies with TSCA (*i.e.*, the chemical is listed on the TSCA Inventory or a PMN has been filed and cleared, and it is not otherwise regulated under TSCA § 5, 6 or 7). *Guide* at 29.

If a shipment is being imported for both a non-TSCA and a TSCA purpose, the importer must identify that portion of the shipment which is subject to TSCA and that portion which is not. For the former, the importer must certify that it complies with TSCA and for the latter (if required) must certify that it is not subject to TSCA.

12.1.1.6. Certification Content

The importer or its agent, a Customs broker, can fulfill the importer's obligation to certify compliance with TSCA by filing one of the two following statements, properly signed, with Customs at the port of entry:

[POSITIVE CERTIFICATION]

I certify that all chemical substances in this shipment comply with all applicable rules or orders under TSCA and that I am not offering a chemical substance for entry in violation of TSCA or any applicable rule or order under TSCA.

[NEGATIVE CERTIFICATION]

I certify that all chemicals in this shipment are not subject to TSCA.

19 C.F.R. § 12.121(a); *Guide* at 20.

The importer must use one of the statements as worded; no other language may be substituted. The certification may appear either on the appropriate entry document or commercial invoice, or on an attachment to the entry or invoice. *Guide* at 20. The certification may be signed by means of an authorized facsimile signature. 19 C.F.R. § 12.121(c). The Customs Regulations require the importer (or its agent, the Customs broker) to keep a copy of this certification along with other Customs entry documentation for five years. 19 C.F.R. §§ 163.3, 163.4.

12.1.1.7. Blanket Certification Procedures

An importer may use a "blanket" certification to cover several shipments of the same chemical made over a one-year period subject to the approval of the appropriate district director of the Customs Service. A blanket certification must be on the letterhead of the importer and signed by an authorized official (or imprinted with authorized facsimile signature). *Guide* at 21. Blanket certifications need only be filed with each Customs district where importation is anticipated, not at every port of entry within the district. *Id.* The commercial invoice for each shipment, however, must contain a reference to the blanket certification as described further below. The district director may revoke a blanket certification "for cause." A copy of each approved blanket certification is sent by the district director to the Cargo Control Program, Office of Inspection and Control, Customs Service Headquarters, Washington, D.C. *Id.*

EPA also has a blanket certification procedure for routine shipments of chemicals imported through the mail. Because such shipments are not inspected by U.S. Customs, EPA requires importers to submit the TSCA § 13 import certification directly to EPA. *See* section 12.1.1.4 above. Prior to April 1992, importers were required to submit a certification for each shipment. In order to reduce the administrative burden on both EPA and the importer, EPA established this blanket certification procedure in April 1992. EPA, *Chemicals in Progress Bulletin* No. 1, at 7 (Apr. 1992). Pursuant to the blanket certification procedure, importers must file a TSCA § 13 import certification with EPA the first time the chemical is imported and note in the certification the importer's intent to use this blanket certification procedure. Thereafter, the importer must submit an annual report to EPA, postmarked by January 31, identifying each shipment of the chemical imported during the preceding year. The initial certification and subsequent annual report(s) should be sent to: U.S. EPA, 1200 Pennsylvania Avenue, N.W., Washington, D.C. 20460, Att'n: TSCA § 13 Coordinator, Chemical Control Division (7405).

12.1.1.8. Blanket Certification Content

The following is EPA's suggested format for blanket positive certifications to Customs and for related invoice statements:

[MODEL POSITIVE BLANKET CERTIFICATION]

TO: District Director
U.S. Customs Service

____________________ ____________________
(city) (state)

CERTIFICATE

The undersigned, as an authorized officer or agent of (Importer), hereby certifies that all chemical substances in all shipments of product(s) listed herein and imported from suppliers listed below, namely:

PRODUCTS

(list name and HTS [Harmonized Tariff Schedule of the United States] item number)

SUPPLIERS

(list names and addresses)

comply with all applicable rules or orders under TSCA, and (Importer), is not offering a chemical substance for entry in violation of TSCA or any applicable rule or order thereunder.

Dated this __ day of _____, 20__.

____
(Authorized Signature)

____
(Title)

Guide at 22.

[COMMERCIAL INVOICE STATEMENT]
(COMPLYING PRODUCTS)

Importation of the products described above are subject to certificate on file with the District Director in respect of compliance with TSCA executed by (Importer), on ______, 20__, the terms of which, including the fact of its execution are incorporated herein by this reference.

Id. at 24.

The following is EPA's suggested format for blanket negative certifications and for related invoice statements:

[MODEL NEGATIVE BLANKET CERTIFICATION]

TO: District Director
U.S. Customs Service

______________________ ______________________
(city) (state)

CERTIFICATE

The undersigned, as an authorized officer or agent of (Importer), hereby certifies that all chemical substances in all shipments of product(s) listed herein and imported from suppliers listed below, namely:

PRODUCTS

(list name and HTS [Harmonized Tariff Schedule of the United States] item number)

SUPPLIERS

(list name and address)

are not subject to TSCA.

Dated this __ day of ________, 20__.

____
(Authorized Signature)

____
(Title)

Guide at 23.

[COMMERCIAL INVOICE STATEMENT]
(PRODUCTS NOT SUBJECT TO TSCA)

> Importation of the products described above are subject to certificate on file with the District Director indicating that they are not subject to TSCA executed by (Importer), on _____ , 20__, the terms of which, including the fact of execution are incorporated herein by this reference.

Guide at 24.

12.1.2. Chemicals Imported as Part of an Article

As more fully discussed in chapter 5, a manufacturer of any new chemical substance imported into the United States for commercial purposes must file a PMN "unless the substance is imported as part of an article." 40 C.F.R. § 720.22(b)(1). Thus, EPA has taken the position that importers of articles that contain chemical substances, which are not intended to be removed from the article, and which have no separate commercial purpose are excluded from the PMN requirements. Such chemical imports also are exempt from the TSCA § 13 import certification requirement. *Guide* at 5; 19 C.F.R. § 12.121(b). According to EPA, however, articles, which contain chemical substances designed to be used or released, such as ink in pens or toner in printers or photocopiers, are not encompassed by this exemption. *Guide* at 17. Accordingly, an importer of an article, which contains a chemical substance, must determine whether the substance is part of the article and as such exempt from the PMN and import certification requirements or is not part of the article and therefore is subject to those requirements.

12.1.3. Customs Detention of Shipments

The Customs Regulations specify when shipments can be detained:

Detention at Port of Arrival (Port of Entry if the Same)—The district director must detain shipments of chemical substances, mixtures, or articles:

> (1) Which have been banned from customs territory of the United States by a rule or order issued under section 5 or 6 of TSCA (15 U.S.C. 2604 or 2605); or
>
> (2) Which have been ordered seized because of imminent hazards as specified under section 7 of TSCA (15 U.S.C. 2606).

Detention at Port of Entry

> (1) Whenever the [EPA] Administrator has reasonable grounds to believe that the shipment is not in compliance with TSCA and notifies the port director to detain the shipment;

(2) Whenever the port director has reasonable grounds to believe that the shipment is not in compliance with TSCA; or

(3) Whenever the importer fails to certify compliance with TSCA as required by § 12.121.

19 C.F.R. § 12.122(a), (b); *Guide* at 2.

The district director must give prompt notice of the detention and the reasons therefore to both EPA and the importer. 19 C.F.R. § 12.122(c). The district director cannot hold a detained shipment for more than 48 hours after the date of detention. Thereafter, unless the shipment has been released to the importer on bond, the shipment must be turned over to EPA. 19 C.F.R. § 12.122(d).

The district director can release the shipment under bond when he has reasonable grounds to believe that the shipment may be brought into compliance with TSCA or when he deems it appropriate under 19 C.F.R. section 146.66 (transfer of merchandise from one zone to another). If released under bond, the shipment must not be used or disposed of until the Administrator makes a final determination on entry. 19 C.F.R. § 12.123(b).

12.1.4. Procedures After Detention

An importer whose shipment has been detained can submit a written explanation to EPA (with a copy to the district director) as to why the shipment should be permitted entry. This explanation must be submitted within 20 days after the importer receives a notice of detention. EPA then will make a decision within ten days on whether to allow entry, but "in any case shall allow or deny entry of the shipment within 30 days of the date of notice of detention." 19 C.F.R. § 12.123(a).

If EPA determines that the shipment is in compliance with TSCA, the district director will release it to the importer. If EPA determines that the shipment is not in compliance, however, the district director must take one of two actions:

(1) Refuse delivery to the importer, giving reasons for such refusal, or

(2) If the shipment has been released on bond, demand its redelivery under the terms of the bond, giving reasons for such demand. If the merchandise is not redelivered within 30 days from the date of the redelivery notice, the port director shall assess liquidated damages in the full amount of the bond.

19 C.F.R. § 12.123(c).

The importer must bring the shipment into compliance or export the shipment within 90 days after notice of detention or 30 days of demand for redelivery, whichever comes first. 19 C.F.R. § 12.124(a). The district director may grant an extension of not more than 30 days upon notification by EPA that: (1) for good cause, the importer is unable to bring the shipment into compliance within the required time period, or (2) the importer is unable to export the shipment within the time period. 19 C.F.R. § 12.124(b)(1), (2).

If the importer decides to export the non-complying shipment within the 30 days after notice of refusal of entry or within 90 days of the demand for redelivery, the importer must provide both EPA and the district director with written notice of the exportation. 19 C.F.R. § 12.125. This written notice must contain (a) the name and address of the exporter or his agent; (b) a description of the chemical substances, mixtures, or articles exported; (c) the country of destination; (d) the port of arrival at the destination; (e) the carrier; (f) the date of exportation; and (g) the bill of lading or airway bill number. *Id.*

Similarly, if the importer chooses to abandon the shipment, the importer must provide written notice of the abandonment to both the district director and EPA. Notification of abandonment operates as a waiver of any right to export the merchandise. The importer, moreover, remains liable for any expense incurred in conjunction with the storage and/or disposal of the abandoned merchandise. 19 C.F.R. § 12.126.

12.2. EXPORT REGULATION: TSCA § 12

TSCA § 12(a) generally exempts from most provisions of the Act any chemical substance, mixture or article manufactured, processed or distributed solely for export from the United States. The recordkeeping and reporting requirements of TSCA § 8, however, continue to apply to such chemical exports. TSCA § 12(a)(1). In order to qualify for the export exemption under section 12(a), the substance, mixture or article must bear a stamp or label stating that it is intended for export. TSCA § 12(a)(1)(B). The export exemption does not apply if the Administrator finds that the chemical substance, mixture or article "will present an unreasonable risk of injury to health within the United States or to the environment of the United States." TSCA § 12(a)(2). In making this determination, moreover, the Administrator may require testing under section 4. *Id.*

Additionally, section 12(b) requires exporters to notify EPA in writing before shipment abroad of any substance for which test data are required under section 4 or 5(b), a rule has been proposed or promulgated under section 5 or 6, an order has been issued under section 5, or an action is pending or relief has been granted under section 5 or 7. Thus, as an increasing number of chemicals are subject to section 4 test rules (*see* chapter 9), section 5(e) orders and SNURs (*see* chapter 7), more chemicals will require notification if exported. Upon notification of export of a regulated substance, EPA must notify the government of the importing country that there are data available (in the case of an applicable test rule under section 4 or 5(b)), or that a rule, order, action or relief exists under section 5, 6, or 7. EPA identifies those chemicals subject to export notification in its section 12(b) list. The section 12(b) list is available from the TSCA Assistance Information Service (also known as the TSCA Hotline) (tel: 202-554-1404) or on-line at http://www.epa.gov/opptintr/chemtest/main12b.htm.

12.2.1. Exporter's Notification Requirement

Pursuant to TSCA § 12(b), EPA promulgated its Export Notification Rule, 45 Fed. Reg. 82,844 (Dec. 16, 1980) (codified as amended at 40 C.F.R. pt. 707, subpt. D). The rule defines an "exporter" as:

> [T]he person who, as the principal party in interest in the export transaction, has the power and responsibility for determining and controlling the sending of the chemical substance or mixture to a destination out of the customs territory of the United States.

40 C.F.R. § 707.63(b). In addition to the export notices required under TSCA § 12(b), the rule requires exporters of PCBs or PCB articles to notify the Agency if the PCBs are being exported for purposes other than disposal. 40 C.F.R. § 707.60(c).

Export notification is required regardless of the intended foreign use of the regulated chemical. In other words, in determining whether export notification is required, EPA does not consider it relevant whether the chemical is being exported for use or in a manner that is not regulated domestically under a TSCA § 5, 6 or 7 action, rule, or order. 45 Fed. Reg. at 82,845.

As a matter of policy, EPA has exempted from the export notification requirements regulated chemical substances and mixtures that are exported in articles (except for PCB articles). Thus, export notification need not accompany export of an article, unless the Agency specifically requires export notification for such articles in the context of individual section 5, 6 or 7 rulemakings. 40 C.F.R. § 707.60(b).

The rule currently requires exporters to submit written notice of the first export or intended export to a particular country in a calendar year for substances for which data are required under TSCA § 5(b), an order has been issued under TSCA § 5, a rule has been proposed or promulgated under TSCA § 5 or 6, or an action is pending or relief has been granted under TSCA § 5 or 7. 40 C.F.R. § 707.65(a)(2)(i). For those substances subject to a test rule under TSCA § 4, the notice is required only for the first export or intended export to a particular country. *Id.* § 707.65(a)(2)(ii). In 1993 EPA changed the prior annual notification requirement for chemical substances and mixtures subject to section 4 test rules to a one-time notification for each country of destination. By this amendment, EPA sought to reduce the number of notifications and thereby enhance its ability to respond when foreign governments request additional information about the exported chemical. 58 Fed. Reg. 40,238 (July 27, 1993). Section 4 chemicals have a finite reporting period, after which these chemicals are "sunset" and no longer have a reporting requirement. EPA maintains a list of section 4 "sunset" chemicals at http://www.epa.gov/opptintr/chemtest/sunset.htm.

The notice must be postmarked by the date of export or within seven days of "forming the intent to export" any regulated chemical substance or mixture, whichever is earlier. Intent to export such regulated substances "must be based on a definite contractual obligation, or an equivalent intra-company agreement, to export the regulated chemical." 40 C.F.R. § 707.65(a)(3).

The export notice must contain: (a) the name and address of the exporter; (b) the name of the substance; (c) date(s) of export or intended export; (d) country or countries of import; and (e) specific section of TSCA (4, 5, 6, or 7) under which EPA has taken regulatory action. 40 C.F.R. § 707.67(a) - (e). It is significant that exporters are not required to divulge the name of the shipment consignee. In a letter to Congress, EPA acknowledged that TSCA § 12(b) does not authorize the Agency to require information on either the foreign customer or the intended use of the exported product. Notices must be marked "Section 12(b) Notice" and filed with the Document Control Office (7407), Office of Pollution Prevention and Toxics, U.S. EPA, Room G-099, 1200 Pennsylvania Avenue, N.W., Washington, D.C. 20460. 40 C.F.R. § 707.65(c).

Within five days of receiving a TSCA § 12(b) export notice, EPA will transmit the following information to the importing country: (1) the name of the regulated chemical; (2) a summary of the regulatory action the Agency has taken; (3) the name of an EPA official to contact for further information; and (4) a copy of the relevant *Federal Register* notice. 40 C.F.R. § 707.70(a), (b). EPA will send this notice to the country's ambassador in Washington, D.C. (or other official designated by the foreign government) and to the State Department. 40 C.F.R. § 707.70(c).

12.2.1.1. New Chemicals

A regulated substance within the meaning of TSCA § 12(b) does not include every new chemical substance subject to a PMN under section 5. Only if a new chemical substance is subject to a section 4 test rule, included on the section 5(b)(4) "risk" list, subject to an order under section 5(e) because of insufficient information or under section 5(f) because of an unreasonable risk finding, or subject to a proposed or final significant new use rule under section 5(a)(2), must it undergo export notification. 45 Fed. Reg. at 82,849. In the absence of such specific regulatory action, the export notification provisions do not apply to new chemical substances undergoing PMN review.

12.2.1.2. Mixtures and Testing

Despite industry requests for relief from the export notification requirement for any mixture that contains less than one percent of a regulated substance, EPA decided not to grant such a *de minimis* exemption. 58 Fed. Reg. at 40,240. Thus, if an exporter knows that a regulated substance is present in even trace amounts in the mixture intended for export, it must provide the required export notification. EPA has stated, however, that "exporters need not test their export products for impurities in order to comply with these regulations." 45 Fed. Reg. at 82,845.

12.2.1.3. Confidentiality

In response to industry's concerns over the lack of a confidentiality provision, EPA allows exporters to assert a confidentiality claim for any information contained in their export notices at the time the notice is submitted. 40 C.F.R. § 707.75(a). No proof of the confidentiality claim is required at the time of submission, but each page must be marked with a label which states that it is "confidential business information," "proprietary," or a "trade secret." *Id.* § 707.75(b). EPA will treat as confidential any information claimed as such in the notice and will disclose it to the public only according to the procedures set forth in 40 C.F.R. part 2. *Id.* § 707.75(c). Thus, an exporter's failure to mark the notice as confidential may result in it being placed in the public files, without further notice to the submitter. *Id.* § 707.75(d). If EPA receives a request under the Freedom of Information Act (FOIA) for confidential information contained in an export notice, the Agency will require the submitter to substantiate its confidentiality claims in accordance with its FOIA procedures under 40 C.F.R. part 2. 45 Fed. Reg. at 82,848-49.

Notwithstanding a confidentiality claim, however, EPA will disclose to the government of the receiving country the limited information contained in the export notice. 40 C.F.R. § 707.75(c). Should the foreign government request further information concerning the chemical being exported, EPA will provide only such information as can be disclosed within the limits of confidentiality prescribed in TSCA § 14 and 40 C.F.R. part 2. 45 Fed. Reg. at 82,847.

CHAPTER 13
RELATIONSHIP BETWEEN TSCA AND OTHER LAWS

Congress enacted TSCA to fill regulatory gaps among the various federal laws that regulate the manufacture, distribution, use and disposal of hazardous chemicals, but Congress did not want TSCA to overlap or duplicate these laws. (*See* chapter 1.) TSCA avoids overlap and duplication by: (1) excluding from the definition of "chemical substance" any chemical that is regulated under certain federal statutes; (2) requiring EPA to refer chemical regulation to that federal agency having primary authority to regulate the risk posed by the chemical in various applications; and (3) limiting the circumstances under which TSCA preempts state and local chemical regulation.

Even though TSCA's purpose is to fill regulatory voids, EPA only reluctantly foregoes its broad authority conferred by TSCA. For example, TSCA § 6 regulations require fewer resources than those of other laws, become effective immediately, and apply even before the chemicals enter the market or workplace. Over time, the original gap-filling function of TSCA has given way to a more pragmatic view favoring TSCA for its value in single agency coordination, under a single statute. Thus, TSCA's role and relationship to other environmental laws are unsettled issues. This chapter discusses the relationship between TSCA and other laws that regulate chemicals.

13.1. TSCA's EXCLUSION FOR SUBSTANCES REGULATED UNDER FIFRA AND FFDCA

TSCA § 3(2)(B) excludes from the definition of "chemical substance":

> (ii) any pesticide (as defined in the Federal Insecticide, Fungicide, and Rodenticide Act) when manufactured, processed, or distributed in commerce for use as a pesticide [;and]
>
> . . . .
>
> (vi) any food, food additive, drug, cosmetic, or device (as such terms are defined in [the Federal Food, Drug, and Cosmetic Act, 21 U.S.C.A. 321]) when manufactured, processed, or distributed in commerce for use as a food, food additive, drug, cosmetic, or device.

As a result, pesticides and FFDCA-regulated substances generally are exempt from regulation under TSCA, although determining whether the TSCA exclusion applies can require a complex case-by-case analysis.

13.1.1. Federal Insecticide, Fungicide, and Rodenticide Act (FIFRA)

EPA considers pesticide raw materials, precursors, and inert ingredients to be subject to TSCA until they are incorporated into a pesticide product, after which they become subject to FIFRA. In this regard, the TSCA exclusion for pesticides is consistent with the idea that TSCA should regulate only those chemicals not already regulated under other laws. Although the concept appears simple, several gray areas cloud the TSCA pesticide exclusion.

To qualify for the TSCA pesticide exclusion, a chemical must satisfy a two-pronged test. First, the chemical must fall within the FIFRA definition of a "pesticide." Second, the chemical must be "manufactured, processed, or distributed in commerce for use as a pesticide." TSCA § 3(2)(B)(ii). Semantically, the first prong of this test appears to subsume the second, because FIFRA defines a pesticide as a substance intended for use as a pesticide. FIFRA § 2(u). Unless and until the requisite pesticidal intent is established, however, a chemical is not considered a pesticide. Once intent to use a chemical as a pesticide is established, the chemical is subject to regulation as a pesticide under FIFRA and no longer regulated under TSCA. Significantly, non-pesticidal uses of the same chemical are subject to TSCA.

Determining when a chemical is intended for use as a pesticide is a complex issue that arises in a number of contexts. Consequently, EPA prefers to resolve the relationship between TSCA and FIFRA on a case-by-case basis. *See* 42 Fed. Reg. 64,585 (Dec. 23, 1977). To assist the regulated community, EPA has adopted positions on the status of certain categories of chemicals under the TSCA pesticide exclusion. These positions are discussed in the comments accompanying the 1977 TSCA Inventory Reporting Rules (42 Fed. Reg. at 64,585-86) (raw materials and inert ingredients); the 1986 Revisions of Premanufacture Notification Regulations (51 Fed. Reg. 15,098 (Apr. 22, 1986)) (R&D candidate pesticides); and the preamble to the 1988 Solid Waste Chemicals Test Rule (53 Fed. Reg. 22,300 (June 15, 1988)) (disposed chemicals).

13.1.1.1. End-Use Products and Technical or Manufacturing-Use Products

End-use pesticide products registered under FIFRA are pesticides by operation of law and not subject to TSCA. In addition, technical or manufacturing-use chemicals also are excluded from TSCA if they are intended for use as a pesticide active ingredient. 40 C.F.R. § 152.15. In general, "intention" must be supported by the circumstances of the putative pesticide's use. Use as an intermediate in manufacturing another pesticidal chemical would not qualify as a pesticidal use.

13.1.1.2. Raw Materials, Inert Ingredients, and Intermediates

The status of a chemical as "intended" or "not intended" for use as a pesticide may change as the chemical moves through the manufacturing process. EPA considers raw materials and inert ingredients to be subject to TSCA until they are incorporated into a pesticide product, at which time the Agency considers them to be subject to FIFRA. 42 Fed. Reg. at 64,586. Intermediates intended for production of a pesticide by chemical reaction with other substances, however, are not considered pesticides by EPA, and therefore are subject to TSCA. 43 Fed. Reg. 9256 (Mar. 1, 1978); 42 Fed. Reg. at 64,586. Even pesticides that are manufactured for use as an intermediate in the production of other pesticides are subject to TSCA. As a result, if a pesticide intermediate is not on the TSCA Inventory, the manufacturer must file a premanufacture notice (PMN) pursuant to TSCA § 5. *See* chapter 6.

13.1.1.3. R&D Candidate Pesticides

Candidate pesticides undergoing research and development (R&D) are subject to TSCA until an intent to use the chemical as a pesticide is established. EPA considers submission of an application for a FIFRA Experimental Use Permit (EUP) or an application for registration under FIFRA section 3 to be conclusive evidence that a chemical is intended for use as a pesticide, and thus excluded from TSCA. 42 Fed. Reg. 64,585 (Dec. 23, 1977). Prior to the submission of an application for an EUP or a FIFRA section 3 registration, EPA contends that TSCA's provisions, most importantly TSCA § 8(e) which requires notification of substantial risk, apply to R&D candidate pesticides. 51 Fed. Reg. 15,098 (Apr. 22, 1986); EPA, Office of Toxic Substances, *TSCA § 8(e) Reporting Guide* (June 1991).

Whether this interpretation remains consistent with EPA's view of the scope of its FIFRA jurisdiction is less certain. Prior to September 1, 1994, EPA's interpretation was entirely consistent with its position that pre-EUP chemicals undergoing laboratory or greenhouse tests or limited field trials to determine their value for pesticidal purposes *are not pesticides*, if no one receives any benefit in pest control. 40 C.F.R. § 172.3(a) (emphasis added). In 1994, however, EPA revised this regulation, which now states that EUPs are not required because such tests (*i.e.*, laboratory or greenhouse tests or limited field trials to determine the chemical's value for pesticidal purposes) "*are presumed not to involve unreasonable adverse effects.*" 40 C.F.R. § 172.3(a) (emphasis added). Under the new regulations, a pre-EUP chemical apparently is a pesticide and thereby excluded from TSCA jurisdiction even before an EUP application (or pesticide registration) is filed. Until EPA formally revises its policy under TSCA, however, pesticide producers should assume that their pre-EUP chemicals remain subject to TSCA jurisdiction.

R&D chemicals, including pesticides, are exempt from section 5 PMN requirements. Under TSCA § 5(h)(3), "small quantities" of new chemical substances that are manufactured or processed solely for scientific experimentation or analysis are exempt from PMN requirements. In April 1986, EPA adopted final regulations implementing this "R&D exemption." 51 Fed. Reg. 15,096 (Apr. 26, 1986) (codified at

40 C.F.R. § 720.36). *See* chapter 5. Although these regulations exempt R&D chemicals from most TSCA § 5 requirements, they do impose certain risk evaluation, notification, and record-keeping requirements. If the purpose of a company's R&D, however, is solely to determine whether the chemical can be used as a pesticide, then even the limited R&D requirements (risk evaluation, notification, and record-keeping) do not apply. 40 C.F.R. § 720.36(g).

The R&D pesticide exemption applies even if the potential pesticidal properties of the chemical are unknown at the time it is first produced. 51 Fed. Reg. at 15,098. EPA's rationale is that companies conducting only pesticide-oriented R&D need not comply with the TSCA R&D requirements applicable to non-pesticide chemicals, because such requirements place an unnecessary burden on development of pesticides, which are regulated comprehensively under FIFRA.[45] *Id.*

13.1.1.4. Pesticides Which Are "Disposed"

On June 15, 1988, EPA promulgated its TSCA § 4 Solid Waste Chemicals Test Rule, which requires manufacturers and processors of certain chemicals to test for human health effects and/or chemical fate in support of EPA's hazardous waste regulatory program under the Resource Conservation and Recovery Act. 53 Fed. Reg. 22,300 (June 15, 1988).[46] In the preamble to that rule, EPA determined that a pesticide does not fall within the TSCA § 3(2)(B)(ii) pesticide exclusion during the disposal process because the chemical is not being "manufactured, processed, or distributed in commerce for use as a pesticide." Thus, EPA concluded the disposed pesticide reverts to TSCA jurisdiction even though originally it was manufactured, processed, and distributed for use as a pesticide.

In keeping with this approach, EPA covered two pesticides, endrin and maleic hydrazide, under its Solid Waste Chemicals Test Rule. Recognizing that neither endrin nor maleic hydrazide was listed in the TSCA Inventory, EPA stated that "disposal of [these substances] does not constitute 'use as a pesticide,' and so is subject to regulation under TSCA." 53 Fed. Reg. at 22,306. Based on its section 4(a)(1)(A) finding that disposal of these two pesticides poses a potentially unreasonable risk of injury to health or the environment, the Agency subjected manufacturers and processors of endrin and maleic hydrazide to the test rule. *Id.*

---

45 EPA has indicated that the TSCA R&D exemption requirements apply to chemicals manufactured by companies whose R&D and marketing efforts include chemicals other than pesticides, unless the company has positive evidence showing that a particular substance is intended exclusively for pesticidal use. One way to demonstrate such intent would be to produce a patent for use exclusively as a pesticide.

46 As discussed in Chapter 9, TSCA § 4(a) directs the Administrator to require testing on any chemical substance or mixture if he finds that the manufacture, distribution in commerce, processing, use, or disposal of such substance or mixture may present an unreasonable risk of injury to health or the environment.

Never before nor since has EPA applied TSCA to chemicals like endrin and maleic hydrazide, which were manufactured, processed and distributed solely for use as a pesticide. Both chemicals appeared to fall within previous EPA and Interagency Testing Committee interpretations of the pesticide exclusion. As initially proposed, the rule stated that both chemicals had been identified as pesticides and therefore excluded by the final rule. 52 Fed. Reg. 20,336, 20,351 (May 29, 1987). In the final rule, however, EPA reversed its position.

As a practical matter, no one was required to test endrin, because its pesticide registration has been canceled, and its manufacture discontinued. Moreover, the costs of testing maleic hydrazide were relatively small. Consequently, no one challenged the rule, thereby leaving for another day judicial resolution of whether EPA's exercise of TSCA § 4 authority to test pesticides in order to evaluate their disposal risks is appropriate.

13.1.1.5. Biocides Are Treated Similar to Pesticides

In 1994, EPA implicitly extended this FIFRA rule to certain use of biocides, such that biocides would also fall within the TSCA § 3 pesticide exclusion from the definition of "chemical substances," and therefore from regulation under TSCA. The pesticide exclusion specifically includes chemicals "manufactured, processed, or distributed in commerce, for use as pesticides." In 1994, while responding to a petition from the International Union, United Automobile, Aerospace and Agricultural Implement Workers of America-UAW (UAW) for EPA to issue test rules under section 4 of TSCA to develop data to aid in the determination of whether machining fluids pose an unreasonable risk to public health or the environment, EPA explained that when biocides are added to machining fluids to act as pesticides, they would not normally be subject to a TSCA § 4 rule. Rather, they would be regulated by EPA under FIFRA, and EPA has authority to require health and environmental data under FIFRA. *See* 59 Fed. Reg. 18,535 (Apr. 19, 1994).

13.1.2. Federal Food, Drug, and Cosmetic Act (FFDCA)

TSCA § 3 also excludes foods, food additives, drugs, devices, and cosmetics subject to the FFDCA from the TSCA definition of "chemical substance." TSCA § 3(2)(B)(vi). EPA considers such substances to be exempt from TSCA regulation at the point where the Food and Drug Administration (FDA) assumes jurisdiction. 42 Fed. Reg. 64,586 (Dec. 23, 1977). EPA's position concerning intermediates and catalysts used in food and drug manufacture is different than when those same chemicals are used in pesticide manufacture, because FDA considers them to be integral components of the substances they are used to produce. *Id.* Consequently, EPA considers intermediates and catalysts intended solely for use in foods, food additives, or drugs to be excluded from TSCA. *Id.*

13.2. TSCA's RELATIONSHIP TO OTHER FEDERAL LAWS

TSCA § 9 addresses EPA's authority under TSCA to regulate chemicals that fall within the purview of both TSCA and other federal statutes. Congress adopted section 9 to ensure that TSCA would fill gaps in existing regulatory authority without overlapping the jurisdiction exercised under these other laws.

13.2.1. Laws Not Administered by EPA

Commonly called TSCA's "referral provision," section 9(a) establishes procedures by which EPA can refer regulation of chemical risks to other agencies that have adequate statutory authority to regulate the risks. The Administrator is required to refer a chemical risk when two determinations are made: (1) "[T]he Administrator has reasonable basis to conclude that . . . a chemical substance or mixture . . . presents or will present an unreasonable risk of injury to health or the environment," and (2) "[S]uch risk may be prevented or reduced to a sufficient extent by action taken under a Federal law not administered by the Administrator." TSCA § 9(a)(1). Referral is accomplished by sending a detailed report to the referral agency describing EPA's findings. To inform the public of its action, EPA publishes the report in the *Federal Register* at the time it is sent to the referral agency.

The referral agency must respond within 90 days. If the referral agency either issues an order declaring that the chemical's use described in the Administrator's report does not present a significant risk, or initiates an "action . . . to protect against such risk," EPA may not regulate the risk under TSCA § 6 or 7. TSCA § 9(a)(2). Section 9(a) precludes EPA from taking action under TSCA even if EPA believes that the referral agency's risk assessment is faulty or its regulatory action inadequate. If the referral agency determines that it lacks adequate authority to regulate the risk "to a sufficient extent," explicitly defers to EPA, or fails to respond within the 90-day deadline, then EPA may regulate under TSCA. The referral agency's response is published in the *Federal Register*.

To implement section 9(a), EPA has entered into memoranda of understanding (MOUs) with two federal agencies—the Occupational Safety and Health Administration (OSHA) and the Consumer Product Safety Commission (CPSC). The MOUs provide for pre-report and post-report consultations between EPA and the referral agencies.

EPA has used the section 9(a) referral mechanism only four times—twice in 1985, once in 1986, and once in 1990. The first three referrals were to OSHA, because in each case, potential adverse health effects arose from workplace exposures to the chemical. In each instance, OSHA initiated action under the Occupational Safety and Health Act to regulate the risk. The industrial chemicals involved were 4,4'-methylenedianiline (MDA) (50 Fed. Reg. 27,674 (July 5, 1985)), 1,3-butadiene (50 Fed. Reg. 41,393 (Oct. 10, 1985)), and glycol ethers (51 Fed. Reg. 18,488 (May 20, 1986)). In 1990, the Administrator referred dioxin in bleached wood pulp and paper products to the Food and Drug Administration, because of concern about dioxin exposure from paper material used to package food (55 Fed. Reg. 53,047 (Dec. 26, 1990)).

The most publicized section 9(a) referral actually never occurred. In 1985, EPA became embroiled in a controversy whether to regulate asbestos under TSCA, or to refer it to OSHA and CPSC. Because EPA never referred asbestos, a three-way debate ensued among EPA, the Office of Management and Budget (OMB), and Congress. At first, EPA appeared to adopt OMB's view that section 9 mandates referral to another agency if the other agency has statutory authority to regulate the risk. Ultimately, however, EPA yielded to congressional criticism and internal pressure from its own staff and concluded that the Administrator has broad latitude under section 9(a) to decide whether to refer regulation of a chemical risk to another agency.

The asbestos controversy produced at least two documents that provide guidance on the TSCA § 9(a) referral procedure and the circumstances under which EPA may defer to other agencies. The first, a June 1985 EPA Office of General Counsel (OGC) memorandum, replaced an earlier, more controversial version, and concludes that Congress intended EPA to err on the side of making referrals to other agencies, especially where occupational exposure is concerned. According to the memorandum, before making a referral, the Administrator can make a "rough cut" evaluation of the "sufficiency" of the other agency's statutory authority. The OGC memorandum acknowledges that after referral, EPA cannot second-guess the other agency's risk determination or actions.

The second document is an October 1985 House of Representatives report criticizing OMB's role in the asbestos controversy (the "Dingell Report"). Staff of House Subcomm. on Oversight and Investigations, Comm. on Energy and Commerce, 99th Cong., *Report on a Case Study on OMB Interference in Agency Rulemaking* (Comm. Print 1985). The Dingell Report explains that TSCA was intended to consolidate authority in EPA to address all human exposure to a chemical's use—in the home, the workplace, and the environment. Dingell Report at 54-55. Further, EPA is required to refer risk if the referral agency has sufficient statutory authority to regulate the risk over the entire life cycle of the chemical, including its manufacturing, processing, distribution, use, and disposal. This post-enactment legislative history suggests that Congress now believes broad-based chemical risks should be regulated under TSCA, rather than referred to another agency.

According to Agency officials in a 1994 GAO report on TSCA, the process of formally referring chemicals to other agencies has not been effective for three reasons: first, EPA rarely finds that an "unreasonable risk" exists, and consequently, the event triggering referral is infrequent; second, the "unreasonable risk" standard under TSCA § 9 may not be relevant under the referral agency's enabling legislation; and third, the Agency cannot significantly influence the agendas of other agencies, which have their own priorities. General Accounting Office, *GAO/RCED-94-103, Toxic Substance Control Act: Legislative Changes Could Make the Act More Effective* 23 (Sept. 1994).

13.2.2. Coordination With Other Agencies

Section 9(d) directs the Administrator to "consult and coordinate" with other federal agencies "for the purpose of achieving the maximum enforcement of [TSCA] while imposing the least burdens of duplicative requirements on those subject to [TSCA]." Such coordination is not a substitute for section 9(a) referrals to other agencies, but is more accurately characterized as information sharing. Section 9(d) referral differs from section 9(a) referral because informal referrals are based solely on policy grounds and considerations. Informal referrals occur prior to any EPA determination as to whether a chemical poses an unreasonable risk under TSCA § 4(f).

Under section 9(d), EPA announced termination of its investigations of occupational exposures to formaldehyde (51 Fed. Reg. 9469 (Mar. 19, 1986)), 4,4'-Methylene bis (2-chloroaniline) (MBOCA) (51 Fed. Reg. 22,836 (June 23, 1986)) and Toluenediamines (TDAs) (51 Fed. Reg. 25,070 (1986)), and sent investigatory records for those chemicals to OSHA.[47] On June 23, 1989, EPA's Assistant Administrator for Prevention, Pesticides and Toxic Substances sent a letter to OSHA recommending that OSHA consider a lower permissible exposure limit for para-dichlorobenzene.

13.2.3. Other Laws Administered by EPA

TSCA § 9(b), the intra-agency counterpart of section 9(a), requires the Administrator to "coordinate" actions taken under TSCA with actions taken under other statutes administered "in whole or in part" by EPA. If the Administrator determines that a chemical risk "could be eliminated or reduced to a sufficient extent by actions taken under the authorities contained in such other Federal laws, the Administrator shall use such authorities to protect against such risk." TSCA § 9(b). If the Administrator determines that "it is in the public interest to protect against such risk" by actions taken under TSCA, EPA is not required to regulate the risk under the other statute. *Id.* Further, TSCA § 6(c)(1) amplifies this public interest determination by requiring the Administrator to consider "all relevant aspects of the risk," a comparison of the costs of compliance under TSCA versus other statutes, and the "relative efficiency" of actions under TSCA § 6(a) versus other statutes.

To date, section 9(b) has had the greatest impact in the hazardous waste area. RCRA and other environmental laws provide EPA with broad authority to regulate a range of risks posed by a chemical. In such circumstances, using TSCA authority to regulate may be less efficient.

---

[47] TSCA § 9(c) provides that in taking action under TSCA, the Administrator shall not "be deemed to be exercising statutory authority to prescribe or enforce standards or regulations affecting occupational safety and health." This provision makes it clear that EPA actions under TSCA do not preempt OSHA from regulating the same chemical under the OSH Act. Section 4(b)(1) of the OSH Act otherwise would preempt OSHA from taking such action. 29 U.S.C. § 653(b)(1).

13.3. TSCA PREEMPTION OF STATE AND LOCAL LAWS

TSCA § 18 governs the relationship between TSCA and state and local laws that regulate chemical risks. Section 18(a)(1) provides that TSCA does not "affect [*i.e.*, preempt] the authority" of states or their political subdivisions to regulate the same chemicals covered by TSCA, subject to two exceptions. First, if EPA adopts a testing rule under TSCA § 4, state and local requirements for testing the same chemical are prohibited. TSCA § 18(a)(2)(A). Second, if EPA adopts a rule or order under TSCA § 5 or 6, state and local regulations of a chemical (other than disposal requirements) are prohibited, unless such regulations are identical to TSCA's; carry out a federal law (such as the Clean Air Act); or ban the use of the chemical (other than its use in manufacturing or processing other chemicals). TSCA § 18(a)(2)(B).

TSCA § 18(b) gives the Administrator authority to allow otherwise preempted state or local laws to be adopted or to continue in effect, if they are consistent with EPA's actions under TSCA, afford a higher degree of protection than TSCA, and do not unduly burden interstate commerce.

In two cases, the courts ruled that the local laws were preempted by TSCA § 18. Both involved local attempts to ban PCB disposal facilities. *Rollins Environmental Services (FS), Inc. v. St. James Parish*, 775 F.2d 627 (5th Cir. 1985); *Warren County v. North Carolina*, 528 F. Supp. 276 (E.D.N.C. 1981). In a third case, the constitutionality of TSCA's preemption provision was upheld, even though the local law survived because it was adopted to implement the federal Clean Water Act. *SED, Inc. v. Dayton*, 519 F. Supp. 979 (S.D. Ohio 1981). In a fourth case, the district court ruled that TSCA did not preempt the local law. *Potomac Electric Power Co. v. Sachs*, 639 F. Supp. 856 (D. Md. 1986). On appeal, the court of appeals reversed, holding that the federal district court should have declined to hear the preemption claim because it could be raised in subsequent state judicial proceedings. *Potomac Electric Power Co. v. Sachs*, 802 F.2d 1527 (4th Cir. 1986). The U.S. Supreme Court granted certiorari, but never reached the substantive issue. Instead the Court vacated and remanded the case for the court of appeals to consider whether the case had become moot, because the criminal investigation of PEPCO had been suspended while the petition for certiorari was pending. *Potomac Electric Power Co. v. Curran*, 484 U.S. 1022 (1988). On remand, the court of appeals dismissed the case as moot. *Potomac Electric Power Co. v. Sachs*, 841 F.2d 90 (4th Cir. 1988).

CHAPTER 14
TSCA INSPECTIONS AND ENFORCEMENT

14.1. THE ROLE OF EPA HEADQUARTERS AND REGIONAL OFFICES

Both EPA headquarters and the regional offices play a role in the enforcement process. At EPA headquarters, the Office of Enforcement and Compliance Assurance (OECA) has responsibility for enforcement and compliance matters. Within OECA are the Office of Compliance and the Office of Civil Enforcement, among other divisions.

The Office of Compliance is responsible for setting enforcement policy, providing policy and technical guidance to the regional offices, directing and overseeing the regional enforcement programs on national program priorities, establishing inspection priorities, and targeting compliance initiatives. EPA regional offices generally have the responsibility for performing inspections and gathering evidence, and have considerable autonomy in the selection of inspection targets.

The Office of Civil Enforcement is responsible for developing, bringing, managing, and resolving civil administrative enforcement cases. This office also acts as a liaison with the regional offices and the Department of Justice on enforcement matters. Cases can be initiated by either the Office of Civil Enforcement or by the regional offices. Most regional cases are handled by the regions with little direct involvement from headquarters.

Within the Office of Civil Enforcement, the Toxics and Pesticides Enforcement Division (TPED) is responsible for TSCA enforcement and the Division's Core TSCA Center (CTEC), which was established in 2001. On its website, TPED summarizes its role as follows:

> The Division provides national direction and leadership in the development of TSCA, EPCRA and FIFRA enforcement actions, as well as in case resolution, and appeals; provides technical and legal support to the Regions; has the lead in developing certain nationally significant cases; and manages the inspection and enforcement program for TSCA §§ 4, 5, 8, 12, and 13, at the Core TSCA Center, a Division office located in Lakewood, Colorado.
>
> The Lakewood Center was established in 2001 to serve as the focal point for the Core TSCA inspection program. Center personnel are responsible for 1) supporting participating EPA Regional TSCA inspection programs, 2) investigating industry-wide compliance status,

3) inspecting manufacturing facilities and importers in thirty states, 4) providing leadership for national compliance assistance and audit programs, 5) assuring continuity of compliance monitoring and enforcement on a national level, 6) tracking and investigating tips/referrals, and 7) providing TSCA inspector training and guidance.

EPA typically initiates hundreds of TSCA enforcement cases each year. For example, in 2001, the Agency issued 170 TSCA administrative orders or complaints; in 2002, 185 were issued; in 2003, 254 were issued; in 2004, 268 were issued; and from January through July 2005, 114 were issued. Further statistics regarding enforcement cases can be determined from reviewing the EPA website at: http://www.epa.gov/echo/compliance_report_icis.html.

14.2. TSCA INSPECTIONS

14.2.1. EPA's Authority to Inspect

TSCA § 11 gives EPA authority to inspect: (1) any establishment, facility, or other premises in which chemical substances or mixtures are manufactured, processed, stored or held before or after distribution in commerce; and (2) any conveyance being used to transport such materials in connection with distribution in commerce. Section 11(a) requires the EPA inspector to present his or her credentials and a written notice of inspection to the owner, operator, or agent in charge of the premises prior to conducting the inspection.

EPA has broad authority under section 11 to designate state employees or private contractors as EPA representatives for the purpose of conducting an inspection. *See Litton Industrial Automation Systems, Inc.*, TSCA Appeal No. 93-4, 1995 WL 38026 (EPA Jan. 27, 1995).

14.2.2. Permissible Scope of an Inspection

Under TSCA § 11(b), an inspection may extend to all things relevant to TSCA compliance within the premises or conveyances under inspection, including records, files, papers, processes, controls, and facilities. An EPA inspector cannot look at: (1) financial data; (2) sales data (other than shipment data); (3) pricing data; (4) personnel data; or (5) research data (other than data required by TSCA) *unless* the written notice of inspection describes with reasonable specificity the nature and extent of such data.

14.2.3. Consent

TSCA § 15 makes it unlawful for any person to fail or refuse to permit entry as required by section 11. An EPA administrative law judge (ALJ) also held that a facility operator cannot refuse to allow a lawful TSCA inspection, or the taking of samples during the inspection, by a duly authorized EPA inspector without risk of penalty. *Lefton*

Iron & Metal Co., No. TSCA-V-C-55-1991 (Feb. 23, 1996) (orders upon cross motion for summary judgment).

14.2.4. Administrative Search Warrants

The Fourth Amendment's protection against unreasonable searches and seizures may bar an EPA inspector from obtaining entry under TSCA § 11 for the purposes of inspecting a facility without a search warrant if the owner/operator of the facility refuses to voluntarily allow the inspector to enter. *See Marshall v. Barlow's, Inc.*, 436 U.S. 307 (1978).[48] One federal court has explicitly addressed the issue of administrative warrants under TSCA, and found that TSCA § 11 implicitly authorizes EPA to obtain search warrants where necessary to carry out its inspection duties under the Act. *Boliden Metech, Inc. v. EPA*, 695 F. Supp. 77 (D.R.I. 1988).

The Supreme Court in *Barlow's* noted that an industry which has a history of pervasive regulation, *e.g.*, the liquor or firearms industries, may be subject to warrantless searches, but declined to allow OSHA to conduct a warrantless search pursuant to this exception. Nevertheless, a New Jersey court held that the New Jersey Department of Environmental Protection was entitled to enter and search the business premises of a pesticide application business licensed by the state without a search warrant. *New Jersey v. Santiago*, 527 A.2d 963 (1986). The New Jersey court reasoned that this warrantless inspection was an appropriate exercise of state authority because of the pervasive and long-standing regulation of pesticides in the state. *See also In Re Environmental Protection Dep't.*, 426 A. 2d 534 (1981) (industrial wastewater treatment). A Pennsylvania court rendered a similar decision regarding the Commonwealth's Solid Waste Management Act. *Dept. of Environmental Resources v. Bilonski Disposal Service*, 566 A. 2d 845 (1989).

No federal court has addressed the issue of whether the chemical industry meets the *Barlow's* test of a pervasively regulated industry which is exempt from the normal warrant requirements in the TSCA context. In *Dow Chemical Co. v. United States*, 536 F. Supp. 1355 (D.C. Mich., 1982), however, the Court held that the chemical industry is not pervasively regulated under the Clean Air Act or the Federal Water Pollution Control Act. In New Jersey, moreover, the chemical industry is a business *not* pervasively regulated in the state. *See In Re Environmental Protection Dep't., supra.*

The EPA Environmental Appeals Board (EAB) has suggested that "it is not a certainty" that the Fourth Amendment would require the suppression of evidence

---

[48] If a company official consents to a warrantless inspection, the company cannot later contest the admissibility of the evidence if the inspectors are later discovered not to be properly authorized or not to have provided a proper notice of inspection, unless the consent was the product of duress or trickery. *See Litton Industrial Automation Systems, Inc.*, 1995 WL 38026.

obtained in an invalid warrantless search because the exclusionary rule has not been extended to all administrative proceedings. *Litton Industrial Automation Systems, Inc.*, 1995 WL 38026, at *7 n.9. Thus, there is still uncertainty as to whether TSCA-regulated industries are subject to the normal warrant requirements of the Fourth Amendment.

14.2.5. EPA Warrant Practices

EPA typically will obtain a warrant without first seeking voluntary entry where: (1) a suspected violation could be covered up between the time voluntary entry is sought and a warrant obtained; (2) prior experience or correspondence with the facility leads the Agency to believe that voluntary entry will be denied; or (3) the facility is unusually remote from a magistrate or district court and obtaining a warrant (after being denied entry) would require considerable travel time. *See* EPA, *Toxic Substances Control Act Inspection Manual: Part I*, at 3-11 to 3-12 (Gov't. Institutes 1982) (*TSCA Inspection Manual Part I*). A warrant may be issued either where there is specific evidence of an existing violation, or where a facility has been neutrally selected for inspection as part of a general enforcement plan. *Marshall*, 436 U.S. at 321. An inspector is not authorized to conduct a search beyond the scope of the specifications in the warrant. *Id.* at 323.[49] Material not described in a search warrant, however, quite possibly may be lawfully seized when it is in the same book or file folder as the information covered by the warrant. *United States v. Christine*, 687 F. 2d. 749 (3d Cir. 1982); *United States v. Beusch*, 596 F.2d 871 (9th Cir. 1979).

14.2.6. Types of Inspections

EPA can conduct inspections of a facility for compliance with TSCA § 5 (new chemical activities), § 6 (bans or limitations on manufacturing, processing or distribution in commerce), § 8 (reporting and record-keeping), § 12 (exports), and/or § 13 (imports). Often, the Agency will inspect a facility simultaneously for compliance with TSCA §§ 5, 8, and 13. A § 12 inspection also could be conducted at the same time. Typically, EPA will conduct a separate inspection for compliance with the section 6(e) PCB requirements.

A section 5 inspection can be either "specific," *i.e.*, targeting a specific premanufacture notice (PMN), or "general," *i.e.*, assessing overall PMN compliance for the facility. In a specific section 5 inspection, the inspector will trace the history of the PMN chemical substance from its synthesis, through research and development (R&D), and finally, its production and distribution in commerce. Inspectors will seek to determine, for example, (1) whether the PMN and NOC were filed in a timely manner; (2) whether any commercial production, distribution, or use took place during the R&D period; and (3) whether commercial production began prior to the expiration of the PMN

---

49 *See also, e.g.*, *United States v. Tamura*, 694 F.2d 591, 595 (9th Cir. 1982).

review period. A general section 5 inspection is conducted in much the same manner, except that an inspector will check on the TSCA status of all chemicals being produced.

Inspections under section 6 usually are intended to detect PCB marking, storage, disposal, and use violations. Inspectors typically will conduct a physical inspection of a PCB facility looking for obvious marking, storage, disposal, and use violations, as well as an examination of its records to determine compliance with the disposal, record-keeping, and other requirements.

The purpose of a section 8 inspection is to verify compliance with the reporting and record-keeping requirements. Among other things, EPA will check to see if the targeted company has set up a centralized system for tracking allegations of significant adverse effects about its chemicals under section 8(c), and has a well-publicized procedure for its employees to report significant risk information under section 8(e). The absence of such a system and procedure will engender suspicions about a company's compliance with section 8.

EPA may also conduct "multi-media" environmental compliance investigations of facilities that discharge, emit, prepare, manage, store, or dispose of pollutants. These inspections integrate the enforcement programs for air, water, solid waste, pesticides, and toxic substances, including toxic substances under TSCA. EPA, Office of Enforcement, *Multi-Media Investigation Manual* (March, 1992). The principles of inspection preparation and conduct discussed herein apply to both TSCA-specific inspections, and TSCA inspections conducted as part of a broader multi-media inspection.

14.2.7. Preparing for TSCA Inspections and Protecting CBI

A facility may receive notice of a routine inspection from three to four days to several weeks prior to the inspection.[50] The notification usually specifies the authority for the inspection, provides an outline of the areas covered by the inspection, and specifies any financial, sales, pricing, personnel, or research data that the Agency wishes to inspect (as stated above, section 11(b)(2) provides that these data may not be inspected unless specified in the notice of inspection). Typically, the Agency will not request information that is already available in regulatory files.

Along with the notice of inspection, the Agency provides a declaration of confidential business information (CBI) form. The company must use this form to

[50] Prior notification of the facility is not required when illegal activity, such as improper recordkeeping or violations of the PMN requirements, is suspected. This allows an inspection to be conducted before the violation can be concealed or records destroyed. In such a situation, the EPA inspector will likely arrive with a search warrant.

declare those types of information requested during an inspection that it deems to be CBI.

A company that receives a notice of inspection should designate one or more company officials to take responsibility to prepare for the inspection. The company should become knowledgeable about the inspection process by consulting with legal counsel and other individuals with appropriate expertise. Company employees should be informed about the inspection, and educated about the process. The responsible officials should interview company employees who perform(ed) duties relevant to the subject matter of the inspection in advance, and determine if there are any problem areas or concerns. The company may wish to provide counsel to employees regarding their rights in providing statements to the EPA inspectors during the inspection and the dangers of giving incomplete or incorrect information.

Prior to the inspection, the company should gather and review all pertinent records and designate an area free from clutter and irrelevant documents where the inspector can review the records which are the subject of the inspection. Any misplaced documents should be located and documents should be organized in a coherent manner. All relevant permits, regulatory approvals and extensions thereof should be collected to make sure that the inspector has access to all the necessary regulatory information. Ideally, the company should number-stamp each page of the documents produced for the EPA inspector, and make an identical copy of the documents for the company to maintain.

Documents that contain confidential business information should be clearly marked CBI *in advance of the inspection* to avoid any potential confusion or inadvertent release of CBI. A good method for protecting confidential business information is to mark each page containing CBI with a prominent "CBI" label and to attach a cover page to the documents stating that they contain CBI.

14.2.8. The Inspection

14.2.8.1. Entry and Documentation

TSCA § 11(a) requires that "[e]ach inspection shall be commenced and completed with reasonable promptness and shall be conducted at reasonable times, within reasonable limits, and in a reasonable manner."

Inspections generally are conducted during normal working hours, unless the focus of the inspection is on activities that occur at night. The EPA inspector is required to present his or her official agency credentials to the owner, operator, or agent in charge of the facility, along with a notice of inspection. TSCA § 11(a). The notice of inspection should be dated and must indicate the scope of the inspection. If the inspector is not using a warrant to gain entry, the inspector must obtain the consent of the facility officials to enter. Permission to enter can be revoked at any time during the inspection, but all information collected before permission is revoked remains in the possession of the inspector. *See generally TSCA Inspection Manual Part I*, at 3-7 to 3-10.

A qualified company representative should greet the EPA inspector(s) and assure that the inspector's credentials are in order. Once admitted, the inspector must present to facility personnel copies of three TSCA inspection forms: (1) the Notice of Inspection, which explains the scope of the TSCA inspection; (2) a TSCA Inspection Confidentiality Notice, which outlines the manufacturer's rights for making CBI claims;[51] and (3) the Declaration of CBI form used by the company to list documents containing CBI.

14.2.8.2. Opening Conference

The inspector will conduct an "opening conference" with facility officials during which he or she outlines the purpose and scope of the inspection, the areas of the facility, processes and records to be inspected, individuals to be interviewed, any sampling the inspector wishes to conduct, the order of activities in the inspection, the length of time the inspection should take, and any procedural issues specific to the inspection. The inspector also may request general background information about the facility and its operations, and discuss any new regulations which might affect the facility. *See generally TSCA Inspection Manual Part I*, at 3-15 to 3-19.

Company officials should discuss with the EPA inspector at the opening conference any confidentiality problems and procedural concerns, and raise any objections to the procedures that the inspector wishes to follow. For example, the facility may need to make a claim of confidentiality for any photographs taken by the inspector. Agreement should be reached on the procedures for sampling to assure that the company obtains a split sample of any physical samples collected during the inspection. If the EPA inspector takes samples or documents from the facility, he or she is required to provide company officials with a form entitled "Receipt for Samples and Documents," which identifies and describes each sample or document that the inspector takes from the facility.

14.2.8.3. Tour of Facility, Sampling, and Document Review

At least one, and preferably more than one, qualified company representative should accompany the inspector throughout the course of the inspection. The company official(s) accompanying the inspector should pay careful attention to the observations and statements of the inspector, and ensure that the inspector follows the agreed upon procedures for any sampling or other evidence taking activities, and proper procedures in taking statements from facility employees.

---

[51] EPA's procedures for handling CBI claims are found in 40 C.F.R. part 2, subpart B. Special rules governing CBI obtained under TSCA are at 40 C.F.R. § 2.306.

14.2.8.4. *Closing Conference*

At the conclusion of the inspection, the EPA inspector will discuss his or her specific factual observations, and present the facility with a receipt itemizing all samples and documents taken during the inspection. An inspector usually will not make statements as to his or her conclusions regarding compliance with TSCA or discuss the legal consequences of potential non-compliance. Inspectors, however, will inform facility personnel of problems that require immediate attention, and may discuss any observed deviations from recommended procedures and offer suggestions based on their preliminary findings.

Inspectors also may request additional data and ask follow-up questions regarding their observations and review of records during the inspection. Inspectors generally will not turn over their work papers to facility officials, but a copy of the final inspection report may be obtained through the EPA office that initiated the audit. The company should make a request for this report at the conclusion of the inspection.

14.2.8.5. *Company Memorandum of Inspection*

As soon as possible after the completion of the inspection, the company officials who accompanied the inspector should prepare a written report summarizing the inspection, including the areas and operations observed by the inspector, any statements made by the inspector, the length of time of the inspection, the questions asked by the inspector, statements made by company employees, sampling procedures, etc. Such a memorandum could prove very useful if EPA ultimately brings an enforcement action against the facility.

14.2.8.6. *EPA Follow-up to an Inspection*

The EPA inspection report records the procedures used in gathering the compliance data, and the factual observations and evaluations of the inspector(s). The EPA office that initiated the inspection will use the inspection report to determine whether to institute an enforcement action.

For a very minor first-time violation which can be easily corrected within 30 days, the Agency may issue a Notice of Noncompliance advising a company that a violation of TSCA has been found and request written verification that the violation has been corrected. *See* EPA, *TSCA Compliance/Enforcement Guidance Manual, Policy Compendium* (1984). The most frequently used remedy is the issuance of an administrative civil complaint under TSCA § 16(a). *Id.* If EPA believes there has been a knowing and willful violation that resulted or had the potential to result in serious harm to health or the environment, the Agency is likely to consider pursuing criminal charges under TSCA § 16(b). *Id.* at 91.

EPA has authority under TSCA § 17(a) to initiate an injunctive action in federal district court to restrain any violation of TSCA, to compel any action required by or under Title I of the Act, or to prevent a person from taking any action prohibited by

TSCA §§ 5 and 6. The Agency also has authority under TSCA §§ 7 and 17(b) to bring a seizure action under certain circumstances. *Id.* at 91-92.

14.3. EPA'S AUTHORITY TO ISSUE SUBPOENAS

14.3.1. *Alyeska* Decision

TSCA § 11(c) authorizes EPA to issue administrative subpoenas to require the attendance and testimony of witnesses, and the production of reports, papers, documents, answers to questions and such other information "that the Administrator deems necessary" to carry out TSCA's requirements. The U.S. Court of Appeals for the Ninth Circuit addressed the scope of EPA's subpoena authority under this provision in *EPA v. Alyeska Pipeline Service Co.*, 836 F.2d 443 (9th Cir. 1988), and held that EPA had the authority to require the president of a water treatment plant to testify and produce documents pertaining to the discharge of chemicals handled at the facility. The court rejected Alyeska's arguments that EPA had acted beyond its authority in using its TSCA subpoena authority to conduct an investigation under the Clean Water Act (which does not give EPA subpoena power), and held that the investigation of hazardous chemicals at the plant was within the Agency's TSCA authority. *Id.* at 446. The court did narrow the scope of the subpoena, however, to exclude documents that clearly would not have led to information relevant to a TSCA purpose.

The *Alyeska* court also held that EPA need not first allege any suspicion of a violation or knowledge of any facts suggesting a violation before using its subpoena authority to conduct an investigation. *Id.* at 447. Under the holding of the *Alyeska* court, a TSCA subpoena will be enforced by a federal court where the information sought is relevant and material to a TSCA investigation, unless the party receiving the subpoena can demonstrate that the inquiry is unreasonably overbroad or unduly burdensome. *Id.* at 446. *See also Reich v. Montana Sulphur & Chemical Co.*, 32 F.3d 440 (9th Cir. 1994). The "unduly burdensome" standard can be met by showing that responding to the subpoena would threaten the normal operation of the respondent's business. *EEOC v. Quad/Graphics, Inc.*, 63 F.3d 642, 645 (7th Cir. 1995).

14.3.2. Judicial Review of EPA Subpoena

An EPA subpoena is not self-enforcing. Rather, the Agency must petition a federal district court to order compliance. TSCA § 11(c). A recipient of an EPA subpoena may refrain from complying with it, without penalty, until directed otherwise by a federal court order. *Alyeska, supra*, 836 F. 2d. at 446.

14.3.3. New River Subpoenas

In 1994, EPA startled the regulated community by issuing expansive subpoenas to 95 U.S. companies believed to own or operate industrial facilities in Mexicali, Mexico. The subpoenas sought information regarding the manufacture, use, disposal and release of chemical substances to the environment for the purpose of determining whether chemicals exported by the U.S. companies to their Mexican facilities were contaminating the New River, which flows from Mexico into the United States.

Although the subpoenas were issued to U.S. companies, the inquiry clearly pertained to the activities of the facilities in Mexico. In many cases, moreover, the subpoena recipient had no direct ownership interest in, and no operational control over, the Mexicali facility. EPA's action was widely criticized as beyond the scope of its authority because U.S. legislation generally cannot be applied by executive agencies to activities outside the U.S. Rather than litigate this issue, however, subpoena recipients reached an agreement with EPA providing for the withdrawal of the subpoenas in exchange for a voluntary submission of information responsive to the Agency's concerns. The subpoena recipients thus provided information to EPA, and the Agency made no referrals to the Department of Justice for enforcement of any of the subpoenas. Nevertheless, the Agency's action raised an issue about the scope of EPA's authority under TSCA § 11 to demand information regarding activities outside the U.S., which is yet unresolved.

14.4. UNLAWFUL ACTS

TSCA § 15 makes it unlawful for any person to:

1. fail or refuse to comply with a section 4 test rule or order; or any rule, order, or requirement issued under section 5, section 6 or subchapter II (Asbestos Hazard Emergency Response);

2. use for commercial purposes a chemical substance or mixture which such person knew or had reason to know was manufactured, processed, or distributed in commerce in violation of section 5 or 6, a rule or order under section 5 or 6, or an order issued in an action brought under section 5 or 7;

3. fail or refuse to establish or maintain records; submit reports, notices, or other information; or permit access to or copying of records; or

4. fail or refuse to permit entry or inspection as required by section 11.

14.5. CIVIL PENALTIES

14.5.1. Statutory Authority

Section 16 authorizes the imposition of civil (and criminal) penalties for violations of section 15 of TSCA. Under section 16(a)(1), EPA can assess a civil penalty of up to

$32,500[52] for each violation of section 15, with each day that the violation continues constituting a separate violation. Section 16(a)(2)(B) requires the Agency to take into account the following factors in determining the amount of a civil penalty: the nature, circumstances, extent, and gravity of the violation(s); the violator's ability to pay; the effect of the penalty on the violator's ability to continue to do business; any history of "prior such violations," the degree of culpability; and "such other matters as justice may require."

EPA must give written notice of a proposed penalty and provide the affected "person" 15 days from the date of notice receipt to request a hearing. TSCA § 16(a)(2)(A). The hearing must be conducted in accordance with the requirements of section 554 of the Administrative Procedure Act. *Id.* The person who requested a hearing may challenge the Agency's final order following the hearing by filing for judicial review within 30 days of issuance of the order with the U.S. Court of Appeals for the District of Columbia Circuit, or any other circuit in which such person resides or transacts business. TSCA § 16(a)(3).

14.5.2. TSCA Civil Penalty Policy

EPA promulgated a general TSCA Civil Penalty Policy to provide guidance to enforcement officials in evaluating the statutory factors for determining the amount of a TSCA penalty. *See Guidelines for the Assessment of Civil Penalties Under Section 16 of the Toxic Substances Control Act*, 45 Fed. Reg. 59,770 (Sept. 10, 1980) (TSCA Civil Penalty Policy). In addition, the Agency has issued specific penalty policies each referred to as an Enforcement Response Policy, or ERP, for sections 4, 5, 8, 12, and 13, and for the PCB regulations.[53] These penalty policies establish a system for assessing civil penalties below the maximum statutory amount.

Under the TSCA Civil Penalty Policy, the Agency determines the amount of a proposed civil penalty in a two-step process. First, EPA calculates a gravity-based

---

52 Beginning March 15, 2004, EPA increased the maximum penalty that can be imposed under TSCA from the statutory maximum of $25,000 to $32,500 under the Debt Collection Improvement Act of 1996, Pub. L. No. 104-134, sec. 31001, 110 Stat. 1321-358 (1996) (31 U.S.C. §§ 3720B - D). 69 Fed. Reg. 7121 (Feb. 13, 2004). This increase applies to violations that occur after March 15, 2004. For violations occurring between January 30, 1997 and March 14, 2004, the maximum penalty is $27,500. *See* 61 Fed. Reg. 69, 360 (Dec. 31, 1996). OECA has implemented these penalty increases in its penalty and enforcement response policies.

53 *See Enforcement Response Policy For Test Rules Under Section 4 of The Toxic Substances Control Act* (May 28, 1986); *TSCA Section 5 Enforcement Response Policy* (Aug. 5, 1988 as amended June 8, 1989 and July 1, 1993); *TSCA Sections 8, 12, and 13, Enforcement Response Policy* (March 31, 1999); and *PCB Penalty Policy* (April 9, 1990, amending the 1980 *PCB Penalty Policy* at 45 Fed. Reg. 59,776). These policies may be accessed online at the EPA website at http://cfpub.epa.gov/compliance/resources/policies/civil/tsca.

penalty (GBP) using a matrix that takes into account the nature, extent, and circumstances of the violation. This matrix applies to all violations of TSCA and appears in each TSCA penalty policy. Second, the Agency adjusts the GBP to take into account culpability, history of prior such violations, cost to the government, benefits from non-compliance, the violator's ability to pay/ability to continue in business, and such other factors as justice may require.

The "nature" of a violation refers to its essential character, grouped into the following types: chemical control, control-associated data gathering, or hazard assessment. Chemical control violations include violations of EPA regulations promulgated under sections 6, 7, 12, 13, 5(e), and 5(f) to minimize the risk presented by chemical substances (by imposing measures ranging from labeling to total manufacturing bans). Record-keeping and/or reporting requirements associated with a chemical control regulation fall within the control-associated data gathering category. The hazard assessment category includes requirements pertaining to the development and gathering of data, such as section 5 premanufacture notification, section 4 testing requirements, and section 8 reporting and record-keeping requirements. The "nature" of a violation determines the "extent" and "circumstances" categories into which the violation is placed under the matrix.

The "extent" category reflects the potential for the violation to cause damage to human health or the environment. There are three extent categories: Major (indicating a potential for serious damage to human health or major damage to the environment); Significant (indicating a potential for a significant damage to human health or the environment); and Minor (indicating a potential for a lesser amount of damage to human health or the environment). For a chemical control violation, *e.g.* a violation of PCB storage or disposal requirements, the quantity of the regulated substance is the principal basis for determining the "extent."

The "circumstances" category represents the probability that damage to health or the environment actually will occur. Categorization is based on the risk inherent in the violation at the time of its occurrence, irrespective of whether the harm actually did occur. There are six circumstance levels: Levels 1 and 2 (High) for violations which are likely to cause damage, such as improper manufacturing, processing, use and disposal; Levels 3 and 4 (Medium) for violations from which there is a significant chance that damage will result, such as major shortage or recordkeeping violations; and Levels 5 and 6 (Low) for violations for which the likelihood of damage is small, such as minor recordkeeping violations.

14.5.2.1. Culpability

The two principal criteria used by EPA for assessing culpability are the alleged violator's knowledge of the TSCA requirement and his degree of control over the violation. 45 Fed. Reg. at 59,773. Under the TSCA Civil Penalty Policy, lack of knowledge warranting a reduction in the penalty would occur only where a reasonably prudent and responsible person in the violator's position would not have known that the conduct was hazardous or violated TSCA.

The Penalty Policy calls for an upward adjustment of 25 percent for willful violations. A downward reduction of 25 percent could be appropriate where the violator lacked sufficient knowledge of the potential hazard *and* lacked control over the situation. *Id.*

In a situation where the violator had sufficient knowledge to recognize the hazard or had significant control over the activities giving rise to the violation, there is no adjustment based on culpability or degree of control. Nevertheless, the violator's "attitude" can result in an upward or downward adjustment of the GBP by 15 percent. Factors considered in this "attitude" determination include: whether the violator is making good faith efforts to comply, whether the violator took prompt corrective actions, and whether the violator assisted EPA in minimizing any harm to the environment caused by the violation. *Id.*

14.5.2.2. History of Prior TSCA Violations

EPA takes the position that a penalty should be adjusted upward if a company has a prior history of TSCA violations. The TSCA Civil Penalty Policy calls for an upward adjustment of 50 percent for the first repetition of a similar provision or regulation, and a 100 percent upward adjustment for the second such repetition. A prior violation of a different TSCA provision or regulation results in an upward adjustment of 25 percent for a first repetition and 50 percent for the second repetition. 45 Fed. Reg. at 59,774. EPA cannot use a company's prior history of violations to raise a penalty above the maximum of $32,500 per violation.

To be considered a "prior such violation," the prior violation must have resulted in a final order against the violator and must have occurred within five years of the present violation. This five-year period begins when a final order is issued. 45 Fed. Reg. at 59, 773-59, 774.

EPA generally considers a company with multiple establishments as one company for the purpose of counting prior violations. Thus, violations committed by one facility owned by a company count as past violations for any other facility owned by the same company. For wholly or partly owned subsidiaries, the violation history of the parent corporation will apply to its subsidiaries, and that of the subsidiaries to the parent. Two companies held by the same parent corporation, however, do not necessarily share their violation histories if they are in substantially different lines of business, and if their management and boards of directors are substantially independent of one another. 45 Fed. Reg. at 59, 774.

14.5.2.3. Government Clean-up Costs

The TSCA Civil Penalty Policy calls for an upward adjustment to the GBP for reimbursement of government funds to investigate, clean up, or otherwise mitigate the effects of a violation, subject to the limitation that a civil penalty may not exceed $32,500 per day. EPA will seek this adjustment in situations where the Agency does not intend otherwise to sue the violator to recover costs under section 7 or section 17. 45 Fed. Reg. at 59,774.

14.5.2.4. Gains from Noncompliance

Another factor that may result in an upward adjustment is the economic gain that may result from noncompliance. Such a gain could include, for example, savings achieved by not following more costly operating procedures or investing in new equipment, or profits earned from the sale of illegally manufactured products. 45 Fed. Reg. at 59,774.

14.5.2.5. Ability to Pay and Ability to Continue in Business

EPA treats the ability to pay and the ability to continue in business as essentially the same factor. In issuing a complaint, the Agency assumes that a firm has the ability to pay. Thus, the burden falls on the respondent to raise the issue of inability to pay in its answer if it wishes this factor to be considered.

The Agency operates under the assumption that a firm can pay a penalty equal to 4 percent of its average gross sales, based on an average of the sales for the current year and three prior years. 45 Fed. Reg. at 59,775. EPA acknowledges that in some cases a company may not be able to pay a 4 percent fine, and that further adjustments may need to be made. *Id.* A company seeking to demonstrate that it does not have the resources to pay a penalty of 4 percent will have to present extensive documentation to the Agency, including balance statements, bank statements, tax returns, and other information.

14.5.2.6. "Other Matters as Justice May Require"

The "other matters as justice may require" category covers any other case-specific factors that should be taken into account. Among these factors are: (1) money spent by the violator in mitigating the harm or clean-up costs; (2) the unfairness of burdening a new owner with the past violation history of the old owner; (3) considerations of national defense or foreign policy; (4) conflict or ambiguity with other federal statutes and regulations; (5) environmentally beneficial expenditures that a violator offers to make in lieu of paying part of a civil penalty; and (6) disproportionality between a penalty under the GBP and an essentially minor offense. 45 Fed. Reg. at 59,775-59,776.

14.5.3. TSCA Section 4 Enforcement Response Policy

On May 28, 1986, EPA issued the TSCA Section 4 Enforcement Response Policy (ERP), which covers administrative penalties for failure to comply with section 4 test rules. The Section 4 ERP tracks the Agency's TSCA Penalty Policy.

Under the Section 4 ERP, EPA will issue notices of noncompliance for minor violations of the relevant section 4 test rule that are not considered substantive. An example would be the submission of a timely letter of intent to conduct testing or a timely request for exemption from testing for each required test, but failure to provide all information required for those documents. Should the submitter provide the missing additional information to the Office of Toxic Substances (OTS) by a date acceptable to and specified by OTS, that would be considered non-substantive. TSCA Section 4 ERP at 1.

The Section 4 ERP employs a matrix for purposes of making GBP determinations for violations of section 4 test rules. The "nature" of all violations are considered as "hazard assessment." The "extent" of a violation is based generally upon the disruption to an EPA review due to the increased time to generate acceptable data. Failure to submit studies requiring at least 90 days to perform is of "Major" extent. Examples include two-year bioassays and avian reproduction tests. Failure to submit studies requiring at least 14 but less than 90 days to perform is of "Significant" extent. Examples include a 21-day Daphnid chronic toxicity test and a 21 to 42 day hen acute delayed neurotoxicity test. Failure to submit studies requiring less than 14 days to perform is of "Minor" extent. Examples include a 48-hour EC50 Daphnid acute toxicity test and a rat oral LD50 test periods are the time spent in the laboratory exclusive. *Id.* at 2-3.

The matrix retains the "five" (sic) (*id.* at 3) levels of the "Circumstances" from the TSCA Penalty Policy:

High Range (Level 1) violations are those which seriously impair the Agency's ability to evaluate the hazards of chemicals. Level 1 violations include falsification of data; failure to test; failure to complete required testing after making a commitment to conduct testing; failure to adhere to test standards or failure to obtain written EPA approval on modifications to test standards; and failure to submit a letter of intent to test or a valid request for exemption from testing more than 60 days after the letter of intent to test is required. *Id.* at 3-4.

Middle Range (Levels 3 and 4) violations are those that impair the Agency's ability to evaluate chemicals in an important but less than critical way. Level 3 and 4 violations include completing a study but submitting it to EPA more than 30 days after the required date without written approval; failure to adhere to test standards or failure to obtain written EPA approval on modifications; failure to submit study plans or submitting study plans more than 30 days after the required date; submitting letters of intent to test or submitting a valid request for exemption from testing more than 30 but within 60 days after the letter of intent to test is required; and failure to submit or submitting interim progress reports more than 30 days after the documents are required. *Id.* at 4.

Low Range (Levels 5 and 6) violations are those which minimally impair the Agency's ability to evaluate the hazards of a chemical. Level 5 and 6 violations include completing a study and submitting it to EPA more than 15 but within 30 days after the required date but without EPA's written approval of a modification to the schedule; submitting a letter or intent to test or valid request for exemption from testing more than

15 but within 30 days after the letter of intent to test is required; submitting study plans, interim progress reports or submitting final reports more than 15 but within 30 days after the required date without an EPA written approval of a modification to the schedule; initiating a study after the date indicated in the approved study plan without an EPA written approval of a modification to the schedule if the final report is submitted by the required date and accepted by EPA; and other such documents submitted not more than 15 days after the required date. *Id.* at 5.

Under the Section 4 ERP, EPA may assess per-day penalties for continuing violations for falsification of data, failure to test, failure to complete tests after making a commitment to conduct testing, failure to adhere to test standards, failure to submit or late submissions of letters of intent to test, and failure to submit valid requests or submission of invalid requests for exemption from testing after the letter of intent to test is required. *Id.* at 5-6.

Once the gravity based penalty has been determined, upward and downward adjustments to the penalty amount may be made based on culpability, history of violations, ability to pay, and such other matters as justice may require, as described in the TSCA Civil Penalty Policy. In settling cases, the Agency will assure that the final penalty is greater than the economic gain for noncompliance. *Id.* at 7.

14.5.4. TSCA Section 5 Enforcement Response Policy

In August 1988, EPA issued the TSCA Section 5 Enforcement Response Policy (ERP) which covers administrative penalties for failure to submit premanufacture notifications (PMNs), noncompliance with TSCA § 5(e) or 5(f) orders, rules, or injunctions and significant new use rules, commercial use of a substance produced without a PMN or valid exemption, and noncompliance with various exemption restrictions.

The Section 5 ERP first assigns each type of violation to one of three categories for the nature of the offense, as follows:

<u>Chemical Control Violations</u>

> Noncompliance with: (1) TSCA § 5(e) or 5(f) orders, rules or injunctions; (2) the aspects of significant new use rules that deal with actual control; (3) R&D exemption warning and supervision requirements; and (4) chemical control provisions of test marketing or other exemptions.

<u>Control-Associated Data-Gathering Violations</u>

> Noncompliance with the record-keeping provisions of: (1) TSCA § 5 orders, rules, or injunctions; and (2) exemption restrictions.

Hazard Assessment Violations

> (1) All failures to notify EPA when such notice is required by law; (2) withholding material information from or submitting false or misleading information in a TSCA § 5 notice or exemption request; (3) commercial use of a substance produced without a PMN or valid exemption; and (4) noncompliance with reporting provisions of § 5(e) or § 5(f) orders, rules, or injunctions.

TSCA Section 5 ERP at 7-8.

Second, the policy assigns each type of potential violation to a circumstance level. *Id.* at 8-13. There are six different circumstance levels. Levels one and two are used where there is a high probability of harm. Levels five and six cover potential violations with a low probability of harm. Potential violations which fall between these high and low probabilities are put in levels three and four.

Third, the Agency assigns a potential violation to a major, significant, or minor extent level, based on an Extent Matrix. TSCA Section 5 ERP at 13. The extent categories depend on the "nature" of the violation and the amount of chemical involved.

Once the nature, circumstance and extent levels are determined, the GBP can be derived from the Gravity Based Penalty Matrix. TSCA Section 5 ERP at 16. The GBP is then adjusted in accordance with the adjustment factors discussed in the TSCA Civil Penalty Policy plus several factors specific to TSCA § 5 violations, as discussed below.

EPA will reduce a civil penalty by 25 percent if the violator voluntarily disclosed the section 5 violation, provided that disclosure to EPA is made before the violator received notice of a pending inspection. The disclosure cannot be one that is required under section 8(e) or one that is made after EPA has already received information about the violation. TSCA Section 5 ERP at 17. EPA may reduce a civil penalty by an additional 25 percent if a company reports the violation to EPA within 30 days from the time it has reason to believe a violation may have occurred. *Id.* EPA also treats any self-disclosed violation as a first time offense, regardless of any prior history of TSCA violations. *Id.* at 19.

The Agency may reduce a proposed penalty for a voluntarily disclosed violation by an additional 15 percent if the violator has taken all steps reasonably expected or requested by EPA to mitigate the violation, including a timely submission of information necessary for EPA to assess a violation. *Id.* at 18. Thus, if a company discloses a violation in a timely manner and takes all reasonable steps to mitigate the violation, the Section 5 ERP permits EPA to reduce the GBP by a total of 65 percent. However, EPA will not reduce the penalty below the amount of the economic benefit gained from noncompliance. *Id.*

The TSCA Civil Penalty Policy under section 5 also may allow the violator a reduction of an additional 15 percent for demonstrating "good attitude." (The TSCA Civil Penalty Policy also permits EPA to *increase* a penalty by up to 15 percent if the violator shows a "bad attitude," as long as the increased penalty does not exceed the statutory limit of $32,500 per day.) This brings the total potential reductions under both the TSCA Civil Penalty Policy and the Section 5 ERP to 80 percent. While 80 percent is the maximum downward adjustment available under the Section 5 ERP, the ALJ and EAB are free to reduce the penalty even further "as justice may require."

Even assuming a reduction of up to 80 percent, a penalty for a violation that has continued over a period of time can be quite substantial. For example, each day of production or importation of a new chemical substance in violation of the PMN requirement counts as a separate violation, with the GBP calculated based on the assigned circumstance level and the amount produced or imported on that day. The total GBP under these circumstances would be the sum of the GBPs for each day of production or importation.

14.5.5. TSCA Sections 8, 12, and 13 Enforcement Response Policy

On March 31, 1999, EPA issued a revised penalty policy for sections 8, 12, and 13. This policy follows the same approach as the TSCA Civil Penalty Policy in assigning a GBP and making appropriate adjustments. *See* TSCA Sections 8, 12, and 13 ERP at 8-11 for determination of circumstance and extent categories. In the circumstances chart, the Agency indicates whether a particular violation will be treated as a one-day violation, or whether penalties will be assessed on a per-day basis for the entire period of violation. *Id.* at 9-10. A key feature of the TSCA Sections 8, 12, and 13 ERP is a cap on the number of days a "per day" TSCA penalty can be levied for reporting and record-keeping violations. There are no caps, however, for violations of the substantial risk reporting provisions of section 8(e), but the rate of penalty assessment reduces over time.

The caps for per day violations are as follows:

Section or Subsection TSCA	Violation **on or before** January 30, 1997	Violation **after** January 30, 1997
§ 8(e)	**no caps**	**no caps**
§ 8(d) non or false reporting Major, level 1 (5 year cap)	**$278,333**	**$306,166**
§ 8(d) non or false reporting Significant, level 1 (3 year cap)	**$120,322**	**$132,354**
§ 8(d) non or false reporting Minor, level 1 (1 year cap)	**$15,111**	**$16,622**
§ 8(d) late reporting Major, level 4 (5 year cap)	**$111,333**	**$122,466**
§ 8(d) late reporting Significant, level 4 (3 year cap)	**$42,467**	**$46,714**

Section or Subsection TSCA	Violation **on or before** January 30, 1997	Violation **after** January 30, 1997
§ 8(d) late reporting Minor, level 4 (1 year cap)	**$3,022**	**$3,324**
§ 8(c) non or false reporting Significant, level 1 (1 year cap)	**$51,378**	**$56,516**
§ 8(c) Late reporting Significant, level 4 (1 year cap)	**$18,133**	**$19,946**
§ 8(a) Chemical Specific Rules non or false reporting Significant, level 1 (1 year cap)	**$34,189**	**$37,608**
§ 8(a) Chemical Specific Rules Late Reporting Significant, level 4 (1 year cap)	**$12,067**	**$13,273**
§ 13 Imports	flexible penalty not to exceed Circumstance level 3, Significant Extent (**$10,000**)	flexible penalty not to exceed Circumstance level 3, Significant Extent (**$11,000**)

TSCA Sections 8, 12 and 13 ERP, App. 1.

14.5.6. Audits and Compliance Management under EPA'S Self-Policing Policy

EPA's Final Policy Statement, "Incentives for Self-Policing: Discovery, Disclosure, Correction, and Prevention of Violations," 65 Fed. Reg. 19,618 (April 11, 2000) (Self-Policing Policy), is also often referred to as EPA's "Audit Policy." In addition to encouraging companies to develop compliance programs that reflect their due diligence, the Policy is designed to encourage companies to periodically audit their compliance with environmental laws. The Self-Policing Policy replaced EPA's 1995 Audit Policy (60 Fed. Reg. 66,706 (Dec. 22, 1995)).

14.5.6.1. Incentives to Audit Offered under the Policy

The primary incentives offered to encourage auditing are: (1) reductions in the amount of gravity-based civil penalties (even elimination of the penalty entirely if all of the policy's nine criteria are met) and (2) a pledge by EPA to not generally recommend criminal prosecution by the Department of Justice of the disclosing entity. The Self-Policing Policy continues what the Policy describes as "EPA's long-standing practice of not requesting voluntary audit reports to trigger Federal enforcement investigations." *Id.* Where appropriate, the Self-Policing Policy can be used to eliminate or reduce GBPs calculated under the Agency's TSCA ERPs.

14.5.6.2. Criteria for Eligibility

To receive a 100 percent reduction in the gravity-based civil penalty a company must satisfy each of the nine conditions outlined below. Companies that satisfy the last eight conditions but do not discover the violations through exercise of due diligence or an audit are eligible for a 75 percent penalty reduction, and may still receive the benefit of EPA's determination not to recommend criminal prosecution of the company. *Id.*

The nine conditions are:

1. **Systematic Discovery Through an Environmental Audit or Compliance Management System.** As noted above, the regulated entity may qualify for complete penalty elimination if the violation was discovered through an "environmental audit," defined as "a systematic, documented, periodic and objective review by regulated entities of facility operations and practices related to meeting environmental requirements." *Id.* at 19,625.

EPA previously identified the following non-binding, useful "yardsticks" as likely elements of an effective auditing system:

(1) An explicit written policy evidencing top management support for the environmental auditing program and a commitment to follow up on audit findings to correct identified problems and prevent their recurrence;

(2) An environmental auditing function sufficiently independent of audited activities to ensure objective and unobstructed auditing;

(3) Adequate team staffing and auditor education and training;

(4) An explicit written procedure setting forth scope, objectives, check-lists, protocols, resources, and frequency of the audit;

(5) A process which collects, documents, analyzes, and interprets information sufficient to achieve audit objectives;

(6) A process which includes detailed procedures to promptly prepare candid, clear, and appropriate written reports on audit findings, corrective actions, and schedules for implementation, and procedures for communication of these reports to management; and

(7) A process which includes quality assurance procedures to assure, through periodic review, the objectivity, accuracy, thoroughness, and effectiveness of the audit program.

51 Fed. Reg. at 25,004 (July 9, 1986). In addition, EPA has published a model protocol for auditing a facility's compliance with TSCA requirements for PCBs, asbestos, and lead-based paint, but the audit protocol does not address the requirements for non-PCB commercial chemical substances in Title I of TSCA and, therefore, will be of limited use to many facilities. EPA, Office of Enforcement and Compliance Assurance, *Protocol for Conducting Environmental Compliance Audits of Facilities with PCBs, Asbestos, and Lead-based Paint Regulated under TSCA* (March 2000).

Companies discovering violations through an institutional "compliance management system" also meet the requirement of this first condition. EPA defines "compliance management system" as "the regulated entity's documented systematic efforts, appropriate to the size and nature of its business, to prevent, detect and correct violations through all of the following":

> (a) Compliance policies, standards and procedures that identify how employees and agents are to meet the requirements of laws, regulations, permits, enforceable agreements and other sources of authority for environmental requirements;
>
> (b) Assignment of overall responsibility for overseeing compliance with policies, standards, and procedures, and assignment of specific responsibility for assuring compliance at each facility or operation;
>
> (c) Mechanisms for systematically assuring that compliance policies, standards and procedures are being carried out, including monitoring and auditing systems reasonably designed to detect and correct violations, periodic evaluation of the system, and a means for employees or agents to report violations of environmental requirements without fear of retaliation;
>
> (d) Efforts to communicate effectively the regulated entity's standards and procedures to all employees and other agents;
>
> (e) Appropriate incentives to managers and employees to perform in accordance with the compliance policies, standards and procedures, including consistent enforcement through appropriate disciplinary mechanisms; and
>
> (f) Procedures for the prompt and appropriate correction of violations, and necessary modifications to prevent future violations.

65 Fed. Reg. at 19,625.

2. **Voluntary Discovery.** The violation must be identified voluntarily and not through a legally mandated monitoring or sampling requirement. 65 Fed. Reg. at 19,625.

3. **Prompt Disclosure.** The regulated entity must fully disclose to EPA in writing a specific violation within 21 days (or a shorter period if provided by law) after the entity has discovered that the violation has occurred or may have occurred. This period may be extended with EPA's concurrence. *Id.* at 19,626.

4. **Discovery and Disclosure Independent of Government or Third Party Plaintiff.** The violation must be disclosed prior to commencement of a government inspection, investigation, or information request to the regulated entity. *Id.*

5. **Correction and Remediation.** The regulated entity must correct the violation within 60 days, certify in writing that the violations have been corrected, and take appropriate measures as determined by EPA to remedy any environmental or human harm due to the violations. *Id.*

6. **Prevent Recurrence.** The regulated entity must agree in writing to take steps to prevent a recurrence of the violation, which may include improvements to its auditing or due diligence efforts. *Id.*

7. **Repeat Violations Ineligible.** There must have been no such violation nor closely related violation at the same facility within the last three years, nor can the violation be part of a pattern of federal, state or local violations by the facility's parent organization (if any) within the last five years. *Id.*

8. **Violation Not Otherwise Excluded.** The violation must not be one that results in serious actual harm, presents an imminent and substantial endangerment to human health or the environment, or violates the terms of any judicial or administrative order or consent agreement. *Id.*

9. **Cooperation.** The regulated entity must cooperate with EPA and provide such information as is necessary and requested by EPA to determine the applicability of the Self-Policing Policy. For potential criminal violations, cooperation, at minimum, will include providing all requested documents, access to employees and assistance in investigating the violation. *Id.*

14.5.6.3. Voluntary Auditing Issues

Confessing a violation of environmental law to EPA in the hope of paying no civil penalty requires a certain amount of faith that the Agency will apply consistently and fairly the somewhat subjective criteria of the Self-Policing Policy. Similarly, EPA officials have acknowledged in public statements that the success of the Policy in encouraging auditing will depend in large part on the consistency of its decisions, because consistency provides regulated entities with greater assurance that they can accurately predict the enforcement consequences in advance of a decision to audit or confess. Still, certain areas of ambiguity remain. In deciding to audit, a company will need to be aware at a minimum of the following issues:

1. *EPA Discretion to Recover Economic Benefit*

EPA has stated that the Agency "reserves the right to collect any economic benefit that may have been realized as a result of noncompliance, even where the entity meets all other policy conditions." 65 Fed. Reg. at 19,620, 19,626. For PMN violations, EPA has sought to recover economic benefit based upon the savings associated with delayed preparation or avoidance of the PMN. EPA uses the BEN computer model to calculate the economic benefit that regulated entities obtain as a result of violating environmental requirements. In cases involving violations of the Inventory Update Rule, EPA has not attempted to collect any penalty based upon economic benefit, but the issue appears open with respect to other types of TSCA violations.

2. *Criminal Liability Issues*

EPA states that its policy "in general" is not to recommend criminal prosecution of a self-disclosing company. *Id.* at 19,621. Nevertheless, this assurance does not extend, for example, to cases where corporate officials were consciously involved in or willfully blind to violations, or concealed or condoned them. EPA also has declined to extend its "no criminal referral" policy to individual company employees, where the company has reported violations under the Policy. *Id.* at 19625. Thus, individual officers or employees could face criminal charges for egregious conduct uncovered by an audit. Finally, ultimate prosecutorial discretion resides with the U.S. Department of Justice. *Id.* at 19,620.

3. *Public Access to Audit Information*

The Self-Policing Policy, as a condition of penalty mitigation, requires that a regulated entity cooperate "as requested by EPA and provides such information as is necessary and requested by EPA to determine applicability of [the] policy." *Id.* at 19,626. Once documents are provided to EPA, there always is some potential that the Agency will not be able to protect them from disclosure under the Freedom of Information Act (FOIA). Confidential business information is exempt from release under FOIA, but non-confidential information in audit documents still might be subject to release. *Id.* at 19,624. In one case, EPA has even required a company to waive the attorney-client privilege with respect to its attorney's notes so that EPA could fully evaluate the company's entitlement to the benefits of the Self-Policing Policy.

14.6. INJUNCTIVE AUTHORITY AND SEIZURE ACTIONS

TSCA § 17(a), among other things, gives the federal district courts jurisdiction to restrain any violation of section 15, to restrain any person from violating a provision of TSCA § 5 or 6 or a rule or order issued under the authority of sections 5 or 6, or to compel the taking of any action required by Title I of the Act. *See United States v. Commonwealth Edison Co.*, 620 F. Supp. 1404 (N.D. Ill. 1985).

Section 7 gives EPA the authority to institute an action in a U.S. district court for seizure of "an imminently hazardous chemical substance or mixture or any article containing such a substance or mixture." The Agency also has authority under section 17(b) to seize any chemical substance, mixture or product subject to Title I which was manufactured, processed or distributed in commerce in violation of TSCA or a rule or order issued pursuant to TSCA.

14.7. ADMINISTRATIVE HEARING PROCEDURES

The rules at 40 C.F.R. part 22 govern administrative proceedings, including those initiated for TSCA violations.

14.7.1. The Complaint

The Agency initiates a TSCA § 16(a) administrative civil penalty action by issuing a formal complaint. The complaint may be issued by the EPA headquarters office or a regional office. It must include: the section of TSCA that authorizes the complaint; the provisions of TSCA, implementing regulations, permit or order alleged to be violated; a concise statement of the factual basis for each alleged violation; the requested relief; the proposed civil penalty; a statement explaining the basis for the proposed penalty; and notice to the respondent of its right to request a hearing. 40 C.F.R. § 22.14. The Agency follows the practice of including a statement in the complaint informing the respondent that it may seek a settlement conference.

14.7.2. The Answer

Under 40 C.F.R. section 22.15, the respondent must respond to the allegations in the complaint within 30 days after service.[54] The response is called an answer, which must address each of the factual allegations in the complaint by admitting, denying, or explaining each allegation. A statement by the respondent that it lacks knowledge regarding a particular allegation is treated as a denial. Failure to admit, deny, or explain a material fact will constitute an admission of that fact.

The answer also must contain the respondent's grounds for defense, the facts that the respondent wants to put in issue, the basis for opposing the proposed relief, and any request for a hearing. The respondent must file the answer with the hearing clerk (headquarters or regional, as appropriate) within the 30-day period, and serve the Agency attorney named in the complaint with a copy of the answer, in accordance with the requirements of 40 C.F.R. section 22.5. If the respondent fails to comply with the requirements specified in section 22.5, the hearing clerk can reject the answer.

---

[54] The EPA regulation extends the time to answer a complaint from 15 days, under TSCA § 16(a)(2)(A), to 30 days. 40 C.F.R. § 22.15(a).

An "ALJ is usually appointed to preside over the case shortly after the answer is filed. The rules refer to the ALJ as the 'Presiding Officer.' " *See* 40 C.F.R. § 22.21(a).

14.7.3. Settlement Conference

Typically, along with filing an answer, a respondent will request a settlement conference with the Agency attorney in charge of the case. The Agency usually is represented at the settlement conference by one or more enforcement attorneys as well as the case officer. At the settlement conference, the respondent will bring to the Agency's attention any information which demonstrates that the Agency's allegations are erroneous; try to clarify the basis for the action to the extent the complaint is unclear; and begin negotiations to settle the case. Often, a number of settlement conferences (either in person or by telephone) take place before the case proceeds further.

14.7.4. Motion for Accelerated Decision

Either party may move for an accelerated decision in favor of a party as to any or all parts of the proceedings. A respondent may file a motion for accelerated decision seeking dismissal, as a matter of law, of all or some of the allegations in the case. *See* 40 C.F.R. § 22.20. Respondent's motion may take the form of a motion for summary judgment, supported by affidavits, where there are no genuine issues of material fact in dispute, or may seek dismissal because of the complainant's (Office of Enforcement's) failure to establish a prima facie case or on other grounds. The Agency has 15 days after service to respond. 40 C.F.R. § 22.16(b). The respondent's reply to any written response must be filed within ten days and is limited to issues raised in the response. *Id.*

After briefing on any motions for accelerated decision is complete, the ALJ may conduct a conference call with the parties to determine the possibility of settlement. Rather than decide the motion, the ALJ may encourage settlement discussions to try to resolve the case. If the respondent and the Agency inform the ALJ that settlement cannot be reached, the ALJ will decide the motion.

If the ALJ issues a decision granting accelerated decision or dismissing the case in its entirety, the Agency can appeal the decision to the EAB as a matter of right. If the ALJ's decision only resolves some of the issues in a case, a party can request the ALJ to certify the decision to the EAB for interlocutory appeal. *See* 40 C.F.R. § 22.29(a). An ALJ may certify a ruling for interlocutory appeal when "(1) the order or ruling involves an important question of law or policy concerning which there is [sic] substantial grounds for difference of opinion; and (2) either an immediate appeal from the order or ruling will materially advance the ultimate termination of the proceeding, or review after the final order is issued will be inadequate or ineffective." 40 C.F.R. § 22.29(b). If the EAB agrees to hear the interlocutory appeal, the case typically will not proceed at the ALJ level until the EAB resolves the issues which are the subject of the interlocutory appeal.

14.7.5. Pre-Hearing Exchange

After the resolution of any preliminary motions, the ALJ will conduct a pre-hearing conference with the parties (often by telephone) to determine the likelihood of settling the case. *See* 40 C.F.R. § 22.19. If the parties inform the ALJ that they wish to proceed to trial, the ALJ will set a schedule for the submission of the pre-hearing exchange and a hearing date.

In the pre-hearing exchange, the parties provide the names of the witnesses, including experts, they intend to call, along with a brief narrative summary of their expected testimony, and copies of all documents and exhibits which they intend to introduce into evidence. 40 C.F.R. § 22.9(a)(2). Additional discovery is rare, and is permitted only upon motion and where the ALJ finds that such discovery will not unreasonably delay the proceeding, and the information is not otherwise obtainable and has significant probative value. 40 C.F.R. § 22.19(e). Each party has the duty to supplement or correct the exchange when it learns that the information is incomplete, inaccurate, or outdated. 40 C.F.R. § 22.19(f).

14.7.6. The Hearing

Before the hearing, the ALJ will hold another prehearing conference (sometimes by telephone) to determine whether there remains any possibility for settlement, to resolve any outstanding procedural issues, to set a hearing date, to determine whether the parties can simplify the proceedings by stipulating to facts not in dispute, and to issue any other rules necessary for the conduct of the hearing. 40 C.F.R. § 22.19(b).

A TSCA administrative hearing is a full evidentiary hearing with direct oral testimony and cross-examination under oath. The ALJ must admit all evidence "which is not irrelevant, immaterial, unduly repetitious, unreliable or of little probative value." 40 C.F.R. § 22.22(a). An ALJ is guided, but not bound, by the Federal Rules of Evidence. Hearsay evidence is admissible. The ALJ may issue a subpoena to compel the attendance of witnesses or the production of documentary evidence. 40 C.F.R. § 22.4(b).

At the conclusion of the evidentiary hearing, the ALJ will set a briefing schedule for the submission of initial and reply briefs. The rules direct the ALJ to issue his initial decision after the filing of the reply briefs. 40 C.F.R. § 22.27(a). If the ALJ determines that a violation has occurred, he must consider any penalty guidelines in determining the proper penalty. 40 C.F.R. § 22.27(b). If the ALJ decides to set a different penalty than that proposed by the complainant, the ALJ must state in the decision the specific reasons for altering the penalty amount. *Id.*

In *Employers Insurance Co. of Wausau*, TSCA Appeal No. 95-6 (EPA Feb. 11, 1997) (order affirming initial decision in part and vacating and remanding in part), the EAB emphasized that the ALJ is not constrained by the complainant's penalty proposal, even if the proposal has been shown to take into account each of the prescribed statutory factors. The ALJ can set a penalty different than that proposed by the complainant, as long as the ALJ provides specific reasons for rejecting the proposed penalty and sets a penalty which reasonably applies the statutory penalty criteria to the facts of the offense.[55] Hence, an ALJ is free to reject a proposed penalty because application of the TSCA § 16 criteria in the framework of the penalty policy does not yield an appropriate penalty, or reject an appropriate penalty calculated using the penalty policy in favor of another appropriate penalty better suited to the circumstances of the particular case.

14.7.7. Administrative Appeals

Within 30 days after service of the ALJ's initial decision, a party may appeal an adverse ruling by filing a notice of appeal and an accompanying appellate brief with the EAB. 40 C.F.R. § 22.30(a). The other party has 20 days to file a response brief, limited to the scope of the issues appealed. Further briefs may be filed only with EAB permission. *Id.* An issue which is not appealed to the EAB is not preserved for appeal even though other issues are appealed. The EAB may *sua sponte* (of its own accord), or upon request by a party, hear oral argument in an appeal. 40 C.F.R. § 22.30(d).

The EAB also has the right to review an ALJ decision *sua sponte*. In such a case, the EAB must notify the parties within 45 days after the issuance of the ALJ's initial decision and set a briefing schedule. 40 C.F.R. § 22.30(b).

If the final order requires payment of a penalty, the respondent must make payment within 30 days after the effective date of the final order, unless otherwise ordered. 40 C.F.R. § 22.31(b).

14.7.8. Judicial Review

A person who filed an answer contesting a complaint filed under TSCA § 16(a)(2)(A) and is "aggrieved by an order assessing a civil penalty" may file a petition for judicial review with the United States Court of Appeals for the District of Columbia Circuit, or any other circuit in which such person resides or conducts business. TSCA § 16(a)(3). The standard of review is set forth in section 706(2) of the Administrative

---

[55] The EAB decision overruled the ALJ's decision in *Wausau* that the Agency must support its penalty in each case with evidence showing that the proposed penalty is justified under the statutory penalty factors, rather than merely relying on the framework of the penalty policy as presumptively valid. *See Employers Insurance Co. of Wausau*, No. TSCA-V-C-62-90, 1995 WL 605784, at *15, *19 (EPA Sept. 29, 1995). In the *Wausau* case, the respondents had not challenged the penalty policy and the ALJ had not put the Agency on notice that it would have to present arguments or evidence justifying the underlying assumptions in the penalty policy. In its decision, the EAB noted that the ALJ can demand that the complainant provide additional evidence or argument, beyond reliance on the penalty policy, in situations where the ALJ concludes that he or she cannot otherwise evaluate the appropriateness of the proposed penalty or where the respondent challenges the appropriateness of the penalty policy to the facts of the situation.

Procedure Act. *See, e.g., ALM Corp. v. EPA*, 974 F.2d 380, 383 (3d Cir. 1992); *All Regions Chemical Labs, Inc. v. EPA*, 932 F. 2d 73 (1st Cir. 1991); *Yaffe Iron & Metal Co. v. EPA*, 774 F.2d 1008 (10th Cir. 1985).

14.8. FAIR NOTICE/WARNING

A respondent in a civil penalty proceeding cannot be said to have violated an agency rule or order except insofar as the rule or order has been published in the *Federal Register. See In Re: CWM Chemical Services, Inc., et al.*, Docket No. TSCA Appeal No. 93-1 (US EPA, Environmental Appeals Board, May 15, 1993), *citing* Administrative Procedure Act, 5 U.S.C. § 552(a)(1). The fair notice doctrine prohibits the enforcement of a government regulation or order against a private party for criminal or civil penalties where the regulation or order is vague or amenable to a reasonable interpretation that would render the conduct to be lawful. *See Diamond Roofing Co., Inc. v. Occupational Safety & Health Review Commission*, 528 F.2d 645, 649 (5th Cir. 1976) ("If a violation of a regulation subjects private parties to criminal or civil sanctions, a regulation cannot be construed to mean what an agency intended but did not adequately express."). *See also Gates & Fox Co., Inc. v. Occupational Safety & Health Review Commission,* 790 F.2d 154, 156 (D.C. Cir. 1986) ("Where the imposition of penal sanctions is at issue . . . the due process clause prevents . . . validating the application of a regulation that fails to give fair warning of the conduct it prohibits or requires.") "The test is not what [the agency] might possibly have intended, but what [it] sa*id.* If the language is faulty, the [agency] has the means and the obligation to amend." *Bethlehem Steel Corp. v. Occupational Safety & Health Review Commission,* 573 F.2d 869, 872 (10th Cir. 1974).

In a challenge to the imposition of liability under the fair notice doctrine, a contention that the respondent had notice of the Agency's intent, whether actual or constructive, is irrelevant. *See Gates & Fox Co., Inc. v. Occupational Safety & Health Review Commission,* 790 F.2d at 156 (rejecting government's argument that liability could be imposed because respondent had received actual notice of agency intent by virtue of warning prior to inspection and previous citation from agency for same alleged offense at another respondent facility.) *See also CWM Chemical Services, supra* at 9 (rejecting Agency contentions that CWM had actual and constructive notice of EPA intent, on grounds that such arguments are "without legal foundation and contrary to basic principles under the Administrative Procedure Act"). "To satisfy due process, the notice of the required conduct must come from the regulation itself or, if applicable, the [other regulatory] document." *Id.* at 11. "In other words, it is not enough that the interpretation of the regulation be reasonable, [rather] the regulation itself must provide the community with adequate notice of conduct required by the agency." *Id.* at 10, quoting *Southwestern Bell Telephone Co. v. Federal Communications Commission,* 10 F.3d 892, 896 (D.C. Cir. 1993). "Thus, although courts typically give deference to an agency's interpretation of its own regulation, "[w]here the imposition of penal sanctions is at issue, however, the due process clause prevents that deference from validating the application of a regulation that fails to give fair warning of the conduct it prohibits or requires." *Gates & Fox Co., supra* at 156.

The U.S. Court of Appeals for the District of Columbia Circuit has vacated TSCA penalty orders issued in the absence of fair warning of the regulatory requirements. In *General Electric Co. v. United States*, 53 F.3d 1324 (D.C. Cir. 1995), the court vacated the Agency's finding of liability and set aside a $25,000 fine for allegedly violating a PCB disposal regulation by operating a solvent distillation system without an alternate disposal permit. Although the court gave deference to the Agency's interpretation of the regulation, it concluded that the Agency's interpretation was "so far from a reasonable person's understanding of the regulations," *id.* at 1330, that the Agency had not provided "fair warning." The court held that a regulated party is not on "notice" of an agency's interpretation of a regulation where the regulation and interpretive policy statements are not clear, the regulated party's interpretation is reasonable, and the agency itself has struggled with its own interpretation of the regulatory requirements.

Likewise, in *Rollins Environmental Services v. EPA*, 937 F.2d 649 (D.C. Cir. 1991), the court, while giving deference to the Agency's interpretation of a PCB disposal regulation, set aside the penalty because of uncertainty in the meaning of the regulation. The *Rollins* court found this uncertainty in the ambiguous language of the regulation, coupled with documentation showing that: (i) there was disagreement within the Agency about the meaning of the regulation; (ii) Agency personnel had given conflicting advice about compliance with the regulation; and (iii) the Agency's Office of General Counsel had found that the regulatory language supported two different constructions.

In another PCB case, *CWM Chemical Services, Inc.*, No. TSCA-PCB-91-0213, 1995 WL 302356 (EPA May 15, 1995) (order on interlocutory appeal), the EAB itself dismissed a complaint because of the absence of fair warning of the analytical methodology requirements. Because the regulation at issue was silent as to whether PCB measurements must be made on a "wet weight" or "dry weight" basis, the EAB found that the regulated party could not be penalized based on "dry weight" measurements in the absence of any violation based on the "wet weight " levels.

14.9. STATUTE OF LIMITATIONS FOR CIVIL PENALTIES

Although TSCA does not contain a statute of limitations provision, the court of appeals in *3M Co. v. EPA*, 17 F.3d 1453 (D.C. Cir. 1994) held that 28 U.S.C. section 2462, which imposes a five-year statute of limitations for all civil actions initiated by the United States, applies to TSCA administrative civil penalty actions. Before the *3M* case, EPA asserted that no statute of limitations applied to TSCA. The Agency thus took the position in numerous administrative proceedings that there was no restriction on the time with which it must initiate an enforcement action and assess civil penalties for a violation of TSCA. The court also rejected EPA's contention that the period of limitations does not begin to run for TSCA violations until EPA discovers the violation; rather, the five-year period begins to run when the violation first accrues. Under this ruling, EPA must commence an action, suit, or proceeding within five years of the date of the violation giving rise to the penalty. The court did indicate that, in appropriate circumstances, the fraudulent concealment doctrine could toll the five-year statute of limitations.

EPA construes the *3M* decision narrowly. In particular, EPA contends that the statute of limitations does not apply to "continuing" violations. *See* "EPA Internal Guidance On Application Of Statute Of Limitations To Administrative And Judicial Civil Penalty Proceedings," BNA, August 31, 1994. To illustrate, EPA takes the position that a failure to submit "substantial risk" information under TSCA § 8(e) is continuing violation, and that the violation "continues" until the information is submitted to the Agency. Accordingly, in EPA's view, the statute of limitations does not expire after five years but continued to run for such a violation until the report is submitted. *See In re Union Carbide Corp.*, No. TSCA-III-322 (EPA Dec. 23, 1991) (order granting motion to dismiss). The Agency also has taken the position that, under a fraudulent concealment theory, the statute of limitations is tolled if an importer files a "false" certification of TSCA compliance when importing a noncomplying shipment of chemicals, even if the "falsity" of the certification is simply due to an inadvertent error. *In re Mobay Corp.*, No. TSCA-III-605 (EPA Mar. 1, 1995) (order denying motion for accelerated decision).

In *Newell Recycling Co., Inc. v. U.S. E.P.A.*, 231 F.3d 204, 206 (5th Cir. 2000), Newell argued that the EPA's improper PCB disposal claim "accrued" when the PCBs at issue were "taken out of service." Because Newell disposed of the PCBs before 1990, and thus they were "taken out of service" sometime before 1990, Newell asserted that the EPA's claim accrued more than five years before the filing of its TSCA complaint in 1995 and was time-barred. EPA argued that Newell's TSCA violation, excavating and stockpiling the soil and then leaving it on the site for ten years before disposing of it in accordance with 40 C.F.R. section 761.60(a), was a continuing violation. The Fifth Circuit held that the EAB did not abuse its discretion when it agreed with EPA's position, holding that the EPA's TSCA cause of action against Newell did not accrue until the violative course of conduct complained of no longer continued. Thus, EPA's PCB disposal claim did not accrue for limitations purposes until 1995, when the PCB's were disposed of properly.

Thus, litigants who defend against TSCA complaints should expect EPA to resist the application of the statute of limitations, especially in administrative proceedings. Several judicial and administrative cases, however, run counter to EPA's narrow interpretations.[56] Note also that there is a distinction between the ability to file a lawsuit

---

[56] *See, e.g., United States v. Trident Seafoods Corp.*, 60 F.3d 556 (9th Cir. 1995), where the Ninth Circuit found that a defendant's failure to notify EPA of its of intent to remove asbestos was a one-time violation of the Clean Air Act, rather than a continuous violation. The court concluded that the Agency could not charge Trident with a continuous violation in the absence of an express provision in the statute or the Agency's regulations stating that the penalty would be calculated based on the length of time between the breach and notification. *See also United States v. Telluride Co.*, 884 F. Supp. 404 (D. Colo. 1995), where the U.S. district court held that the statute of limitations begins to run at the time of unlawful discharge of pollutants under the Clean Water Act; *In the Matter of The Landmark Properties*, No. TSCA-

(Footnote continued on next page)

to remedy and collect penalties for a continuing violation and collecting penalties for violations more than five years before the action commenced. *See American Cause Ass'n, Inc. v. Dist. of Columbia Water and Sewer Authority*, 306 F. Supp. 3d 30 (D.D.C. 2004) (allowing Clean Water Act citizen suit as timely where continuing violation alleged, but barring recovery of civil penalties for violations committed more than five years before the suit commenced).

EPA does not always assert that violations are "continuing." In its enforcement of the Inventory Update Rule (IUR), the Agency appears to concede that the statute of limitations applies because the Agency has declined in many cases to seek penalties for a failure to file an IUR report more than five years prior to EPA's discovery of the violation. Presumably, this is because EPA treats IUR violations as "one-day" violations in the TSCA Sections 8, 12, and 13 Enforcement Response Policy. By this logic, however, EPA also should apply the statute of limitations broadly in the case of export notification or import certification violations because these also are characterized as "one-day" violations.

14.10. NEGOTIATED SETTLEMENTS

14.10.1. Settlement Discussions

EPA encourages settlements of civil penalty proceedings, where consistent with the objectives of TSCA and applicable regulations. 40 C.F.R. § 22.18(a). Typically, a respondent will request a settlement conference at the same time as the answer is filed, and a settlement conference will be held shortly thereafter. A settlement conference can be requested, however, at any time during the course of the administrative proceeding. On occasion, EPA is willing to hold a settlement conference before an answer is filed, and may agree to an extension for the filing of an answer pending the outcome of the settlement discussions. *See* 40 C.F.R. § 22.7(b).

At some point after the answer is filed, the ALJ assigned to the case will request the parties to report on the status of settlement discussions. The ALJ usually will not move the case forward until he or she is informed by the parties that there is no possibility of settlement. *See* 40 C.F.R. § 22.19; section 14.7.5, *supra*.

(Footnote continued from previous page)
07-2002-0220, 2002 WL 31745008 (E.P.A. Nov. 19, 2002) (administrative penalty actions under the Lead-Based Paint Disclosure requirements are subject to the five-year statute of limitations); *In Re: Lazarus, Inc.*, No. TSCA-V-C-32-93, Appeal No. 95-2 (E.A.B. Sep. 30, 1997) (violations of PCB registration requirements are continuing violations and thus an action for penalties is not barred where these violations continued into the five-year limitations period, but violations of the annual PCB documentation requirements are not continuing in nature, and the statute of limitations provides a complete defense).

14.10.2. The Consent Agreement and Consent Order

If a settlement is reached, the parties will sign a written consent agreement, which is filed at the conclusion of the case along with a consent order. A consent agreement typically includes: (1) a stipulation that EPA has jurisdiction over the subject matter alleged in the complaint; (2) a statement that the respondent admits, or neither admits nor denies, the factual allegations in the complaint; (3) a consent to any stated civil penalty, to any specified compliance or corrective action order, and to any stated permit action; (4) any other terms and conditions that are a part of the settlement; and (5) a statement that the respondent will not contest the Agency's reliance on the consent agreement and consent order as demonstrating a prior violation in a future enforcement action. *See* 40 C.F.R. § 22.18(b).

14.10.3. Supplemental Environmental Projects

As part of a consent agreement, EPA frequently permits a company to reduce the amount of the civil penalty by agreeing to perform a Supplemental Environmental Project (SEP), 63 Fed. Reg. 24,796 (May 5, 1998). A SEP is defined as an "environmentally beneficial project" which a defendant/respondent agrees to undertake in settlement of an enforcement action, but which the defendant/respondent is not otherwise legally required to perform. *Id.* at 24,797-24,798. The eight categories of SEPs are: public health, pollution prevention, pollution reduction, environmental restoration and protection, assessments and audits, environmental compliance promotion, emergency planning and preparedness, and a general category for projects that do not fit in the others but will benefit the environment nonetheless. An acceptable SEP must fulfill the requirements of one of these categories. *Id.*

To qualify as part of a consent agreement, the SEP must meet the following criteria. First, it must have an "adequate nexus" to the subject of the enforcement action. That is, the SEP generally must mitigate the impact of the violation or reduce the likelihood of similar future violations. Second, the SEP must further at least one objective of the law underlying the enforcement action and cannot be inconsistent with the law. Third, EPA must not play a role in managing the SEP or controlling its funds (although EPA will monitor or oversee respondent's performance), and federal funds cannot be used for the SEP. Fourth, the "what, where and when" of the project must be specifically outlined in the settlement agreement. Finally, a SEP can neither fulfill one of EPA's legal duties nor "appear to be an expansion of an existing EPA program." *Id.* While the SEP may provide the violator with some benefits, the SEP must primarily benefit public health or the environment.

If a SEP meets these criteria, the Agency may subtract up to 80 percent of the cost of the SEP from the gravity component of a proposed civil penalty, depending on how the SEP addresses the following six factors: benefit to the public or the environment; innovativeness; environmental justice; community input; multimedia impacts; and pollution prevention. EPA may reduce the proposed penalty by up to 100 percent of the cost of the SEP if the respondent is a small business, a government entity, or a non-profit organization, or if one of the results of the SEP is pollution prevention of outstanding quality. *Id.* at 24,802.

The terms and conditions of a SEP, including any monitoring and reporting requirements, will be detailed in the consent agreement. If the respondent fails to comply with these terms and conditions, it will be subject to penalties under the terms of the consent agreement (*e.g.*, the consent agreement could reinstate the original penalty if the SEP is not performed). *Id.* at 24,803.

14.10.4. Approval of Settlement

Before a consent agreement can become final and effective, it must be approved by the Administrator or a delegatee. In a case initiated by a regional office, the Regional Administrator must approve the settlement. In a case initiated at EPA headquarters, a consent agreement must be approved both by the Administrator or Deputy Administrator of OECA and the EAB (the delegatee for the Administrator for headquarters cases).

For headquarters cases, once the consent agreement is signed by the parties, OECA forwards the consent agreement and a proposed consent order (often referred to together as a CACO) to the EAB. *See* EPA, *Environmental Appeals Board Practice Manual* Appendix 4 (June 2004). OECA also must provide the EAB with an action memorandum explaining how the proposed agreement is consistent with the applicable penalty guidelines, or if not, why not; how each of the violations in the complaint is addressed; a summary of any human health or environmental concerns or lack thereof; the disposition of any substances or wastes; a brief description of any past or pending actions against the respondent; and a statement of how the agreement serves the public interest. *Id.* The settlement is not final until approved by the EAB. The EAB occasionally questions the appropriateness of settlements negotiated by the parties.

14.11. CRIMINAL LIABILITY

14.11.1. TSCA § 16(b)

Under TSCA § 16(b), EPA can seek criminal penalties against any person who "knowingly or willfully" violates any provision of section 15. The maximum penalty that can be imposed is a fine of $25,000 for each day of violation and/or imprisonment for not more than one year. The Agency can seek criminal penalties instead of, or in addition to, civil penalties.

To obtain a conviction against a company or an individual under section 16(b), the government must prove beyond a reasonable doubt that the defendant violated a requirement of TSCA and did so "knowingly or willfully." Criminal prosecutions under the Act may be expected to raise the following issues.

14.11.1.1. The Knowledge Requirement

The element that distinguishes a criminal offense from a civil one is referred to as *mens rea*, or knowledge of the violation. As a general principle, a person cannot be found guilty of a crime unless the government can prove that the act was committed willfully, or with knowledge.

Although *mens rea* is sometimes referred to as a "guilty mind," in the case of public welfare statutes, courts have consistently found that there is a diminished requirement to prove *mens rea.* Generally, it is necessary only to prove that the defendant had knowledge of the acts or omissions which constitute the violation, rather than knowledge that such conduct is in violation of a particular law or regulation. Where the public welfare is at issue, that is, where dangerous materials are regulated, the Supreme Court has determined that constitutionally adequate notice of criminal liability is derived from the hazardous nature of a substance, even if there is no proof that the defendant knowingly violated the statutory or regulatory requirement itself. The leading case is *United States v. International Minerals & Chemical Corp.*, 402 U.S. 558 (1971), where a shipper of sulfuric acid failed to list the chemical on the manifest, as required by the Interstate Commerce Commission (ICC) regulations. The shipper defended on the ground that he was not aware of the manifesting requirement for sulfuric acid. Nevertheless, the shipper was found criminally liable of a "knowing" violation, because he knew that he was shipping sulfuric acid, a dangerous substance. *See also United States v. Weitzenhoff*, 35 F.3d 1275, 1283-86 (9th Cir. 1993); *United States v. Dotterweich*, 320 U.S. 277, 280-81 (1943); *United States v. Holland*, 810 F.2d 1215, 1223 (D.C. Cir. 1987).[57]

The principle expressed by the Supreme Court in *International Minerals* has been applied to a number of environmental statutes designed to protect the public from hazardous substances. For example, in *United States v. Hopkins*, 53 F.3d 533 (2nd Cir. 1995), the court held that the Clean Water Act's felony prohibition of "knowingly" falsifying, tampering with, or rendering inaccurate any required monitoring device or method did not require that the defendant know that the Clean Water Act required accurate maintenance of the monitoring device or method. In *United States v. Ho*, 311 F.3d 589 (5th Cir. 2002) and *United States v. Weintraub*, 273 F.3d 139 (2nd Cir. 2001), the courts held that criminal liability for the Clean Air Act's asbestos abatement and work-practice provisions required only knowledge that the material contained asbestos, not knowledge of the provisions themselves. In *United States v. Dean*, 969 F.2d 187, 190-92 (6th Cir. 1992), the court stated that persons who handle hazardous waste have reason to know their activities are regulated by law and cannot rely on ignorance of the law as an excuse for unlawful conduct. In *United States v. Buckley*, 934 F.2d 84, 88

---

[57] The term "willfully" generally "refers to consciousness of the act, but not to consciousness that the act is unlawful." *Cheek v. United States*, 498 U.S. 192, 209 (1991); *see also Ratzlaf v. United States*, 510 U.S. 135 (1994).

(6th Cir. 1991), the court held that a conviction under the criminal provisions of the Clean Air Act requires knowledge of the emissions in question, rather than knowledge of the emissions standards.

Likewise, in *United States v. Weitzenhoff*, 35 F.3d at 1286 (9th Cir. 1993), knowledge of a permit requirement was found not to be a required element of proof for a criminal violation of the Clean Water Act ("The criminal provisions of the CWA are clearly designed to protect the public at large from the potentially dire consequences of water pollution and as such fall within the category of public welfare legislation" [citation omitted]). *See also United States v. Hoflin*, 880 F.2d 1033, 1037-39 (9th Cir. 1989) ("knowing" unlawful disposal of hazardous waste only requires knowledge of the act of disposing of the waste, not that a permit is required.)[58]

Knowledge of the facts may be inferred from circumstantial evidence, such as the position and responsibility of a corporate official, or information conveyed to the official on prior occasions. *United States v. MacDonald & Watson Waste Oil Co.*, 933 F.2d 35, 55 (1st Cir. 1991). The mere fact that an individual had official responsibility, however, is insufficient to establish knowledge of the facts constituting the offense, unless that individual exhibited willful blindness to the relevant facts. 933 F.2d at 51-55.

Notwithstanding these cases under other environmental statutes, the level of proof necessary to satisfy the *mens rea* requirement in a criminal prosecution under TSCA remains unclear. Among the major environmental statutes, TSCA is uniquely oriented toward reporting and record-keeping. Moreover, many of the TSCA requirements, the PMN requirement, for example, apply to all chemical substances without regard to whether they are hazardous. There is nothing inherent in the act of manufacturing a chemical substance that necessarily would put a person on notice of the specific TSCA requirements.

Indeed, there are few contested TSCA criminal cases from which to determine how the *mens rea* requirement is applied under TSCA. In *United States v. Catucci*, 55 F.3d 15 (1st Cir. 1995), a case arising from the unlawful disposal of PCBs, the knowledge requirement was met where the defendant, after being told that the cost of incineration of PCB transformers was $8,000-$10,000, disposed of the transformers by giving them to individuals who agreed to remove the transformers for free in return for the salvage value of the copper coils. The court concluded that, under these facts, the defendant knew the PCB transformers would not be incinerated in accordance with the requirements of the PCB disposal regulations. There are no reported decisions, however, of contested criminal prosecutions of other TSCA violations addressing the *mens rea* requirement.

---

[58] *See also United States v. Kelley Technical Coatings, Inc.*, 157 F.3d 432 (6th Cir. 1998); *United States v. Wagner*, 29 F.3d 264, 266 (7th Cir. 1994); *United States v. Baytank, Inc.*, 934 F.2d 599, 612 (5th Cir. 1991).

Further, in *United States v. Ahmad*, 101 F.3d 386 (5th Cir. 1996), the Fifth Circuit held that an alleged violator of an environmental statute cannot be held criminally liable, absent knowledge of facts establishing *all* statutory elements of the alleged violation. This case involved an alleged criminal violation of the Clean Water Act by a gas station owner who participated in the emptying of about 4,690 gallons of gasoline from an underground leaking storage tank into the public sewers. The court overturned his conviction based on improper instructions to the jury. Noting that the public welfare exception under which some regulatory crimes have been found not to require a showing of *mens rea* is narrow, the court held that the government had to prove that the defendant had knowledge of each and every fact that constituted a necessary element of the crime. *Id.* at 391. In its analysis, the court also noted that it was inappropriate to dispense with *mens rea* for crimes punishable by substantial penalties. *Id.* at 391-92. Thus, the law is still uncertain on the application of the *mens rea* requirement in TSCA.

14.11.1.2. Liability of Corporation for Acts of its Employees and Employee Liability

A corporation may be found liable for violations of its employees, acting within the scope of their employment, even if the corporate officers did not have knowledge of the violation. *See, Apex Oil Co. v. United States*, 530 F.2d 1291, 1295 (8th Cir. 1976). The knowledge of the employee is the knowledge of the corporation. *Id.* Furthermore, a corporation generally cannot escape criminal liability by claiming that no one corporate employee had sufficient knowledge of a corporation's specific activities or operations to comprehend its full import. Rather, a corporation is considered to possess the collective knowledge of its employees and is held responsible for the acts of corporate employees acting within the scope of their employment. *See, e.g., United States v. Josleyn*, 206 F.3d 144, 159 (1st Cir. 2000); *United States v. Bank of New England*, 821 F.2d 844, 856 (1st Cir. 1987). Corporations have been held criminally liable for acts of even menial employees. *See Standard Oil Co. of Texas v. United States*, 307 F.2d 120, 127 (5th Cir. 1962).

An employee's conduct generally falls within the scope of his employment if it is: (1) of the type that he or she is employed to perform; (2) conducted within authorized limits; and (3) has at least, in part, the purpose of providing a benefit to the employer. *United States v. Gold,* 743 F.2d 800, 823 (11th Cir. 1984). Corporations and their employees cannot avoid responsibility by failing to exercise responsibility to prevent or promptly correct a violation of a regulatory requirement with an important health and safety purpose. *United States v. Park*, 421 U.S. 658, 673-74 (1975). A corporation even may be held criminally liable for actions of an employee taken contrary to instructions or company policy. *See, e.g., United States v. Hilton Hotels Corp.*, 467 F.2d 1000, 1004 (9th Cir. 1972).[59]

Responsible corporate officers can also be held criminally liable for a corporation's violation of a criminal law. *United States v. Park*, 421 U.S. 658 (1975); *United States v. Dotterweich*, 370 U.S. 277 (1943). Both the corporation and the individual(s) responsible for the violation can be found criminally liable for the same violation. *Apex Oil*, 530 F.2d at 1294.

14.11.2. The False Statements Act

Individuals and corporations may be prosecuted under the False Statements Act, 18 U.S.C.A. section 1001, for making a false statement in connection with any of the filings required under TSCA, such as PMNs, various PMN exemption applications, notices of commencement of manufacture, or any of the section 8 reporting requirements. Under the False Statements Act, a person who "knowingly or willfully" makes "any false, fictitious or fraudulent statements or representations" is subject to a fine of not more than $10,000, and not more than five years' imprisonment. Thus, unlike TSCA, which is a misdemenor statute, the False Statements Act is a felony statute.

To obtain a conviction under section 1001, the government must prove: (1) that the defendant made a false statement; (2) that the statement was material; (3) that the defendant acted with specific intent to mislead; and (4) that the matter was within the purview of a specific government agency. *United States v. McCarrick*, 294 F.3d 1286 (11th Cir. 2002). To do so, the government must prove that a defendant "had the specific intent to make a false or fraudulent statement 'deliberately or at least with reckless disregard of the truth and with the purpose to avoid learning the truth.' " *United States v. Puente*, 982 F.2d 156, 159 (5th Cir. 1993). The false statement must be material as well as false to sustain a conviction. *See, e.g., United States v. Whitaker*, 848 F.2d 914, 916 (8th Cir. 1988); *United States v. Lopez*, 728 F.2d 1359, 1362 (11th Cir. 1984). A statement is "material" if it is capable of influencing an agency's function or decision. *United States v. Whitaker*, 848 F.2d at 916. Actual reliance on the statement is not required — a false statement is material even if the agency ignores or never reads the statement or an agency official knows the statement is false. *See, e.g., United States v. Diaz*, 690 F.2d 1352, 1358 (11th Cir. 1982). Further, there is no need for the government to show any loss or damage as a result of a false statement. *Morgan v. United States*, 301 F.2d 272, 275 (9th Cir. 1962).

---

[59] In some situations, a corporation may escape liability for acts of its employees which were not done to benefit the corporation. *See, e.g., United States v. Beusch*, 596 F.2d 871, 878 (9th Cir. 1979); *Standard Oil Co. of Texas v. United States*, 307 F.2d at 129.

14.11.3. EPA Criminal Enforcement Policy

14.11.3.1. Criminal Enforcement Priorities

EPA ordinarily brings criminal actions only in cases where there is evidence of "guilty knowledge or intent" (often referred to as "scienter") on the part of the defendant. *TSCA Compliance/Enforcement Guidance Manual* (1984) at 9-2. Of primary importance to the Agency in assessing whether to bring criminal charges is the extent of environmental contamination or human health hazard that resulted from, or was threatened by, the unlawful conduct. *Id.* at 9-3. Criminal sanctions become more appropriate where there is a past history of noncompliance. *Id.* at 9-4.

In its 1984 Guidance Manual, the Agency stated that it would place a "high investigative priority" on: violations that have a significant impact on the Agency's ability to act under section 4(f)(1); situations of falsified test data; violations of section 8(e) reporting requirements; violations of the premanufacture notification program; and knowing or willful violation of the PCB regulations resulting in, or threatening, significant environmental contamination or human health hazard. *Id.* at 9-5.

On January 12, 1994, EPA issued an internal guidance memorandum regarding the exercise of investigative discretion in criminal enforcement matters. Director, Office of Criminal Enforcement, *The Exercise of Investigative Discretion* (Jan. 12, 1994). This document states that the criminal case selection process will be guided generally by the extent of significant environmental harm and culpable conduct. *Id.* at 3. Significant environmental harm can be found where there is an illegal discharge, release or emission that has an identifiable and significant harm to human health or the environment, or where such significant harm is threatened. *Id.* An additional factor favoring criminal investigation is the failure to report an actual discharge, release or emission. EPA also may undertake criminal investigation where the single violation, although not itself rising to the level of significant harm, is indicative of general industry practices which, considered as a whole, would result in significant harm. *Id.* at 4.

The following may indicate culpable conduct: a history of repeated violations; deliberate misconduct resulting in violation; concealment of misconduct or falsification of required records; tampering with monitoring or control equipment; or operation of pollution-related activities by a business without a permit, license, manifest or other required documentation. *Id.* at 5.

In a criminal environmental inquiry, EPA may investigate both individual employees and their corporate employers. *Id.* at 6.

A company can reduce the risk of criminal prosecution by a policy of self-auditing, self-disclosure, and self-correction. In its 1994 guidance document, EPA stated that a violation discovered through a company audit, promptly remediated and fully and completely disclosed to EPA, generally will not be the subject of a criminal investigation. As discussed in section 14.5.6 above, under EPA's Self-Policing Policy, the Agency generally will not recommend criminal prosecution for a company that discovers violations through audits or due diligence assessments and discloses the violations to the Agency in accordance with the Policy.

14.11.3.2. EPA Procedures for a Criminal Investigation

EPA's Office of Criminal Enforcement, Forensics and Training (OCEFT), operating within the Office of Enforcement and Compliance Assurance, has responsibility for managing and directing EPA's criminal investigation program. Allegations of potential criminal activity are investigated by EPA criminal investigators at headquarters or a field office. Guidance Manual at 9-6. A criminal investigator is responsible for determining the basic investigative approach, which will include such activities as conducting interviews, assembling and reviewing records, planning and executing surveillance and searches, and coordinating with other law enforcement agencies. *Id.* at 9-7. An EPA enforcement attorney will work with the criminal investigator during the case development process. *Id.* at 9-6. OCEFT provides technical expertise and support for complex criminal investigations having a national impact.

If a case is referred to the Department of Justice for criminal prosecution, the EPA enforcement attorney will have responsibility for preparing a "referral package" for the Department of Justice (and/or local U.S. Attorneys' office). *Id.* at 9-7. OCEFT has the responsibility for coordinating with the Department of Justice to provide prosecutorial support.

14.12. SECTION 20 CITIZENS' SUITS

Subject to certain notice requirements, any person may commence a civil action in a U.S. district court under TSCA § 20 (unless the Agency or the Attorney General has commenced and is diligently prosecuting an administrative or a civil action, respectively) against: (1) any person, including the United States, alleged to be in violation of TSCA or any rule promulgated under section 4, 5, or 6 or a section 5 order; or (2) the Administrator to compel the performance of any non-discretionary act or duty under TSCA.[60] Reasonable attorneys fees and other court costs may be awarded if a court determines that such an award is appropriate. TSCA § 20(c)(2).

A TSCA § 20 citizens' suit can only be brought to remedy an ongoing violation. *Moreco Energy, Inc. v. Penberthy-Houdaille*, 682 F. Supp. 931 (N.D. Ill. 1987). There is no private right of action for money damages under TSCA. *Sanford Street Local Development Corp. v. Textron, Inc.*, 768 F. Supp. 1218, 1223 (W.D. Mich. 1991), *vacated on other grounds*, 805 F. Supp. 29 (W.D. Mich. 1991); *Welch v. Schneider National Bulk Carriers*, 676 F. Supp. 571, 577-78 (D.N.J. 1987). TSCA's citizen suit

---

[60] One court has found that a county is not a "person" for the purpose of filing a citizens' suit under TSCA § 20. *Warren County v. North Carolina*, 528 F. Supp. 276, 282-83 (E.D.N.C. 1981).

provision also does not authorize private citizens to file an action to compel the seizure or condemnation of chemical substances. *United States v. Holloway Oil Co.*, 28 Env't Rep. Cas. (BNA) 1190 (M.D. Fla. 1988).

14.13. CITIZENS' PETITIONS UNDER TSCA § 21

14.13.1. Statutory Authority

TSCA § 21 permits any person to petition the Administrator to initiate a proceeding for the issuance, amendment, or repeal of a rule under sections 4, 6, or 8 or an order under section 5(e) or section 6(b)(2).

The Administrator must either grant or deny the petition within 90 days of its filing. TSCA § 21(b)(3). If the petition is granted, the Administrator must promptly commence an appropriate proceeding under sections 4, 5, 6, or 8. *Id.* If the petition is denied, the Administrator must publish the reasons for such denial in the *Federal Register*. *Id.*

14.13.2. Legal Standard for Review

If the Administrator denies a section 21 citizens' petition, or fails to act upon such a petition within 90 days, the petitioner may seek judicial review in order to compel the Administrator to initiate the requested proceeding. To obtain such review, the aggrieved petitioner must file an action in a United States district court within 60 days of the Administrator's denial of the petition or within 60 days of the expiration of the 90-day period for action, if the Administrator has failed to act upon the petition. TSCA § 21(b)(4)(A).[61]

The type of Agency action sought in the petition will determine the legal standard under which the Administrator's denial or failure to act is reviewed.

The denial of a petition to initiate a proceeding to issue a rule under section 4, 6, or 8 or an order under section 5(e) or 6(b)(2) will receive *de novo* review. TSCA § 21(b)(4)(B). Under the *de novo* standard, the agency denial has no presumptive validity but the party appealing the denial of a petition must meet certain evidentiary standards.

To institute a section 4 test rule or a section 5(e) order (prohibiting or limiting the manufacturing, processing, distribution in commerce, use, or disposal of a chemical substance) the petitioner has an affirmative burden to prove by a preponderance of the

[61] The time frames set out in the statute for seeking judicial review are subject to Rule 6(a) of the Federal Rules of Civil Procedure. *Environmental Defense Fund v. Thomas*, 657 F. Supp. 302, 305-07 (D.D.C. 1987), *aff'd on other grounds sub nom. Environmental Defense Fund v. Reilly*, 909 F.2d 1497 (D.C. Cir. 1990).

evidence that (1) the information available to the Agency is insufficient to permit a reasoned evaluation of the health and environmental effects of the chemical substance; and (2) in the absence of such information, the substance may present an unreasonable risk to health or the environment or substantial quantities of the substance will enter the environment or there may be significant or substantial human exposure to the chemical. TSCA § 21(b)(4)(ii); *see Citizens for a Better Environment v. Thomas*, 704 F. Supp. 149 (N.D. Ill. 1989).

A party appealing the denial of a petition seeking a section 6 or section 8 rule must demonstrate by a preponderance of the evidence that "there is a reasonable basis to conclude that the issuance of such a rule or order is necessary to protect health or the environment against an unreasonable risk of injury to health or the environment." TSCA § 21(b)(4)(B)(ii).

The reviewing court's authority is to direct EPA to initiate rulemaking proceedings, not to direct EPA to adopt a rule. *Id.*[62] To meet the preponderance of the evidence test, a petitioner must establish that the requested rule actually will develop data useful in addressing the alleged health risk. *Citizens for a Better Environment v. Reilly*, 33 Env't Rep. Cas. (BNA) 1460 (N.D. Ill. 1991).

Review of the Agency's denial or failure to act upon a section 21 petition requesting the initiation of proceedings to amend or repeal an *existing* rule under section 4, 6, or 8 or order under section 5(e) or 6(b)(2) is governed by the "arbitrary and capricious" standard of the Administrative Procedure Act. *See Walker v. EPA*, 802 F. Supp. 1568, 1574-75 (S.D. Tex. 1992).

The court is authorized to award reasonable attorneys fees and other costs in an action brought under section 21. TSCA § 21(b)(4)(C).

14.13.3. Guidance for Preparing Citizens' Petitions

EPA has issued guidance for preparing citizens' petitions under TSCA § 21. *See* 50 Fed. Reg. 46,825 (Nov. 13, 1985). The Agency has requested that a section 21 petition contain the following information to facilitate the Agency's review:

(1) Name, address, and phone number of the petitioner, contact person for further information, and, if the petitioner is an organization, the nature of its purpose and membership;

[62] A petitioner who pursues a *de novo* review in district court cannot also seek review of the Agency's denial under the "arbitrary and capricious" standard of the Administrative Procedure Act. *Environmental Defense Fund v. Reilly*, 909 F.2d 1497 (D.C. Cir. 1990).

(2) A description of the relief requested, identifying the TSCA § under which relief is being sought and explaining how the action requested would solve the problem;

(3) A description of the problem to assist the Agency in making a finding regarding the potential for or presence of an unreasonable risk, including as much information as possible with regard to—

(a) The nature and severity of harm (toxicity) to humans or the environment from the subject chemical(s);

(b) Exposure data reflecting the actual or potential release of the chemical substance to the environment or its actual or potential contact with humans;

(c) The extent of harm that the subject chemical(s) present or may present, in terms of type, severity, and immediacy; and

(d) Risk reduction information indicating possible methods by which risk could be reduced, the degree of risk reduction that could be achieved, the costs of risk reduction methods, and the impacts of any regulation on the economy, small businesses, and other affected entities.

Id. at 46,826. The guidance also addresses the findings the Agency must make, depending on whether the petition seeks the initiation of proceedings for rules under section 4, 6(a), or 8 or orders under section 5(e) or 6(b)(2), and thus informs the petitioner of special considerations for each petition. *Id.* at 46,827.

CHAPTER 15
INDUSTRY COMPLIANCE PROGRAMS AND INTERNAL AUDITS

15.1. COMPLIANCE PROGRAMS

EPA has placed great emphasis on TSCA enforcement, and the Agency no doubt will continue to be aggressive in its efforts to ensure compliance with TSCA. As a result, industry compliance programs have become commonplace in companies potentially subject to TSCA requirements.

15.1.1. Why Institute a Compliance Program?

The are several reasons for instituting and implementing a TSCA compliance program. First, TSCA imposes a regulatory scheme that is extremely broad in scope, applying to virtually any type of company involved in today's diversified business economy. Companies engaged in the manufacture, processing, distribution, use, importation, or export of chemical substances—as those terms are expansively defined under TSCA—all are potentially subject to the varied requirements of TSCA. The inadvertent manufacture or importation of a chemical substance not listed in the TSCA Inventory, for example, can create a very serious enforcement problem for the unwary company. Consequently, chemical companies, as well as many business entities well outside the traditional notion of a "chemical manufacturer," are discovering the importance of TSCA compliance programs.

Second, the penalties assessed for noncompliance with TSCA can be staggering—up to $32,500 per day of violation.[63] The Agency's enforcement/response policy for TSCA violations is inflexible and mechanistic with little regard for actual environmental impact. Furthermore, TSCA is a "strict liability" statute, *i.e.*, knowledge of the Act's requirements or the existence of a violation is not necessary for the imposition of a civil penalty. *See Hodag Chemical Corp.*, No. TSCA-V-C-025-88, 1988 WL 236332 (EPA Nov. 16, 1988). Knowing or willful violations of TSCA, however, can subject the violator to potential criminal sanctions under section 16(b). Reductions in the civil penalties—in some cases complete elimination—are available to companies that voluntarily confess TSCA violations, resulting in a significantly lower penalty than would have been assessed if the subject violations had been discovered by EPA. (*See* chapter 14, TSCA Inspections and Enforcement.)

---

[63] *See* Chapter 13, footnote 5, p. 270.

Third, in addition to the threat of criminal and civil penalties, TSCA violations also may result in economic and operational effects which prove to be far more devastating than any EPA-imposed TSCA penalties. For example, a process for which a particular product is critical may be entirely shut down for months if it is discovered that the product contains a chemical substance not listed in the Inventory. Thereafter begins the time-consuming process of obtaining a new Inventory listing, which is required before the supplier can legally resume manufacturing the needed substance.

A well-designed TSCA compliance program and a general sensitization of employees to the importance of TSCA and the potential consequences of non-compliance can help to ensure a company's compliance with the Act and to avoid the enforcement problems discussed above.

15.1.2. Elements of a TSCA Compliance Program

The elements of a good TSCA compliance program generally have included commitment to compliance by upper management, devotion of adequate resources, written policies and standard operating procedures, clear assignment of responsibilities, and the education of employees regarding the existence and importance of TSCA compliance policies and procedures. EPA, however, has recently provided more detailed guidance on the general elements of a satisfactory environmental compliance program. On April 11, 2000, EPA published a final policy statement entitled: "Incentives for Self-Policing: Discovery, Disclosure, Correction and Prevention of Violations." 65 Fed. Reg. 19, 618 (April 11, 2000). This "Self-Policing Policy" (often referred to less accurately as EPA's "Audit Policy") provides companies with incentives to develop both "compliance management systems" and self-auditing plans, either of which may result in discovery and disclosure of violations of environmental laws.
Under the Self-Policing Policy, EPA will not seek gravity-based penalties for disclosing entities that meet all nine Policy conditions, including "systematic discovery," meaning "the detection of a potential violation through an environmental audit or a compliance management system that reflects the entity's due diligence in preventing, detecting and correcting violations." 65 Fed. Reg. at 19,620. (*See* section 15.2.2, Criteria for Eligibility, below). The Self-Policing Policy defines "compliance management system" as encompassing the following:

> [T]he regulated entity's documented systematic efforts, appropriate to the size and nature of its business, to prevent, detect and correct violations through all of the following:
>
> (a) Compliance policies, standards and procedures that identify how employees and agents are to meet the requirements of laws, regulations, permits, enforceable agreements and other sources of authority for environmental requirements;

(b) Assignment of overall responsibility for overseeing compliance with policies, standards, and procedures, and assignment of specific responsibility for assuring compliance at each facility or operation;

(c) Mechanisms for systematically assuring that compliance policies, standards and procedures are being carried out, including monitoring and auditing systems reasonably designed to detect and correct violations, periodic evaluation of the overall performance of the compliance management system, and a means for employees or agents to report violations of environmental requirements without fear of retaliation;

(d) Efforts to communicate effectively the regulated entity's standards and procedures to all employees and other agents;

(e) Appropriate incentives to managers and employees to perform in accordance with the compliance policies, standards and procedures, including consistent enforcement through appropriate disciplinary mechanisms; and

(f) Procedures for the prompt and appropriate correction of any violations, and any necessary modifications to the regulated entity's compliance management system to prevent future violations.

65 Fed. Reg. at 19,625. The ideal TSCA compliance program incorporates all elements mentioned in EPA's Self-Policing Policy, thereby enabling the regulated entity to claim entitlement to full penalty elimination for confessing TSCA violations.

15.2. AUDITS UNDER EPA's SELF-POLICING POLICY

The Self-Policing Policy is often referred to as EPA's "Audit Policy" because, in addition to encouraging companies to develop compliance management systems, the Policy is designed to encourage companies to periodically audit their compliance with environmental laws. The current Policy replaces a version originally issued on December 22, 1995 that took effect on January 22, 1996. The 1995 Policy explicitly superseded "any inconsistent provisions in . . . EPA's 1986 Environmental Auditing Policy Statement." 60 Fed. Reg. 66,706, 66,712 (1995). The current Policy revised the 1995 Policy to lengthen the prompt disclosure period to 21 days, clarify that the independent discovery condition does not automatically preclude penalty mitigation for multi-facility entities, and clarify how the prompt disclosure and repeat violation conditions apply to newly acquired companies.

15.2.1. Incentives to Audit Offered under the Policy

The primary incentives offered to encourage auditing are: (1) reductions in the amount of gravity-based civil penalties (even elimination of the penalty entirely if all of the policy's nine criteria are met) and (2) a pledge by EPA not to recommend criminal prosecution by the Department of Justice of any regulated entities that discover and disclose violations through due diligence or environmental audits. The Self-Policing Policy restates EPA's long-standing practice of not requesting copies of regulated entities' voluntary audit reports to trigger federal enforcement investigations. 65 Fed. Reg. at 19,618.

15.2.2. Criteria for Eligibility

To receive a 100 percent reduction in the gravity-based civil penalty and to be assured that EPA will not recommend criminal prosecution of the corporation, a company must satisfy each of the nine conditions outlined below. Companies that satisfy the last eight conditions but do not discover the violations through exercise of due diligence or an audit are eligible for a 75 percent penalty reduction. The nine criteria are set forth in section 14.5.6.2:

EPA has declined to spell out in detail how a voluntary auditing program ought to be organized, but has identified the following non-binding, useful "yardsticks" as likely elements of an effective auditing system:

(1) An explicit written policy evidencing top management support for the environmental auditing program and a commitment to follow up on audit findings to correct identified problems and prevent their recurrence;

(2) An environmental auditing function sufficiently independent of audited activities to ensure objective and unobstructed auditing;

(3) Adequate team staffing and auditor education and training;

(4) An explicit written procedure setting forth scope, objectives, check-lists, protocols, resources, and frequency of the audit;

(5) A process which collects, documents, analyzes, and interprets information sufficient to achieve audit objectives;

(6) A process which includes detailed procedures to promptly prepare candid, clear, and appropriate written reports on audit findings, corrective actions, and schedules for implementation, and procedures for communication of these reports to management; and

(7) A process which includes quality assurance procedures to assure, through periodic review, the objectivity, accuracy, thoroughness, and effectiveness of the audit program.

51 Fed. Reg. 25,004 (July 9, 1986).

15.3. AUDITS UNDER A VOLUNTARY AGREEMENT

Since 1998, EPA has entered into five voluntary TSCA audit agreements with companies. Compliance audit agreements allow companies to audit themselves and receive reduced civil penalties, which can be completely eliminated for violations that are properly corrected. Such agreements also demonstrate a company's commitment to environmental compliance.

Compliance audit agreements benefit EPA by conserving scarce resources while ensuring that the public and environment are protected. In addition, EPA obtains useful compliance information from a company's periodic status reports and from consultation with a company's representatives regarding violations and receives assurances that the company will remedy and prevent future violations.

A typical voluntary audit agreement with EPA includes provisions that are similar to those of the Agency's Audit Policy. Similar to the Audit Policy, the agreements establish deadlines for disclosing and correcting violations discovered during audits, but a company that negotiates a voluntary auditing agreement with EPA has an opportunity to propose non-standard reporting, remediation, or auditing deadlines to address the company's particular auditing needs.

15.4. AUDITS UNDER A CONSENT AGREEMENT

Prior to promulgation of the Self-Policing Policy, it had become common practice for companies served with an administrative complaint, alleging violations and seeking civil penalties, to negotiate with EPA a settlement via a consent agreement that included a binding commitment by the company to audit some element of its TSCA compliance. EPA's 1986 Audit Policy stated that the Agency may include environmental auditing provisions in consent agreements where auditing could resolve identified compliance problems and reduce the likelihood of their recurrence. 51 Fed. Reg. at 25,007.

EPA has developed an internal policy for Agency negotiators regarding the incorporation of environmental auditing provisions in consent agreements and other enforcement settlements. *See* Memorandum from Thomas L. Adams, Jr., Assistant Administrator for Enforcement and Compliance Monitoring, EPA, Final EPA Policy on the Inclusion of Environmental Auditing Provisions in Enforcement Settlements (Nov. 14, 1986) (Enforcement Audit Policy). The Agency considers that auditing requirements are appropriately included in consent agreements "where heightened management attention could lower the potential for noncompliance to recur." *Id.* at 2.

Specifically, EPA will most likely propose the inclusion of such auditing provisions in settlement negotiations where:

- A pattern of violations can be attributed, at least in part, to the absence or poor functioning of an environmental management system; or

- The type or nature of violations indicates a likelihood that similar noncompliance problems may exist or occur elsewhere in the facility or at other facilities operated by the regulated entity.

Id. (quoting 51 Fed. Reg. at 25,007). EPA asserts that it has the authority to request an administrative law judge or a court to order an audit as part of an enforcement proceeding if the company involved is unwilling to agree to conduct an audit voluntarily. *See* Enforcement Audit Policy at 2.

A typical auditing agreement includes commitments that the audit will be completed by an independent third party by a specified date, that the company will notify EPA whenever it discovers certain types of violations or "reportable events" such as potential violations, and/or make an interim report, and that the company will pay a stipulated penalty for each TSCA violation uncovered by the audit. As an incentive to audit, the stipulated penalties generally are set at an amount below the statutory maximum, and the parties agree that a single penalty will suffice for all violations involving the chemical in question and that total liability will be capped at a particular amount appropriate to the size of the company or division being audited.

If a regulated entity negotiating a settlement can adopt a policy of periodically auditing for TSCA compliance, and expect to eliminate civil penalties, the entity may have less incentive to agree to a mandatory audit under dictated terms with stipulated penalties for discovered violations.

15.5. AUDIT PROCEDURES

15.5.1. TSCA § 5 Audit Procedures

In conducting an audit of section 5 PMN requirements, the company should consider taking the following steps, modeled after the procedures incorporated into the Diamond Shamrock Consent Agreement.[64] Although the Diamond Shamrock Consent

---

[64] The Diamond Shamrock audit also included the following TSCA provisions:

§ 5 — Premanufacture Notification (PMNs)
§ 5(a)(2) — Significant New Use Rules (SNURs)
§ 6(e) — Polychlorinated Biphenyls (PCBs)

(Footnote continued on next page)

Agreement sets forth the procedures for an EPA-ordered TSCA audit, its provisions serve as useful guidance for the procedures to be used in conducting a voluntary internal audit.

Step 1: Review records and files to obtain information that will be used in the audit

Initially, the company should compile a list of all of the chemicals which it has manufactured or imported into the United States during the period the audit will cover, along with copies of all PMNs and Notices of Commencement of Manufacture (NOCs) submitted to EPA. In so doing, the company should examine records and files at all production sites and other locations where it is reasonably anticipated such materials would be retained. This step often will involve separate interviews with key corporate personnel connected with developing, marketing, and producing the chemical substance and complying with PMN requirements.

In settlement of its enforcement proceeding, American Hoechst agreed to use the preceding information: (1) to create a computerized data base which would assist the company in tracking all chemicals manufactured and imported; (2) to confirm (as a result of this computerized system) that "all orders submitted to foreign suppliers for product samples will include requests for specific information relating to TSCA compliance product safety, chemical properties, etc."; and (3) to create a model chemical substance order system in order to track samples of products being distributed or obtained for market evaluation. *American Hoechst Corp.*, No. TSCA-84-H-05, slip op. at 6 (EPA Sept. 19, 1985) (consent agreement and order). To assure that such a computerized system will work properly, it is important to tie the chemical tracking system to the company's purchasing system in order to maintain the information on an input/ output basis.

Step 2: Identify any chemicals that the company has manufactured (including importations into the U.S.) which are not included on the Inventory

The company then should compare the information gathered under Step 1 against the TSCA Inventory in order to determine whether the company has manufactured or imported any chemicals that are not listed on the Inventory. The company should begin this step by defining the chemical substances it has

(Footnote continued from previous page)

§ 8(a)	—	Reports
§ 8(b)	—	Inventory of Existing Chemical Substances
§ 8(c)	—	Records of Allegations of Significant Adverse Reactions
§ 8(d)	—	Health and Safety Studies
§ 12(a)	—	Exports — Exemptions
§ 12(b)	—	Exports — Notice
§ 13	—	Entry into the Customs Territory of the United States.

manufactured and imported. This exercise can be resource intensive, especially for imports which may include "hidden" chemical substances, such as inks in typewriter ribbons. For each chemical so identified, the company should take the steps described below.

Step 3: Review the records and files to obtain information that will be used in the audit

For each chemical identified in Step 2, the company must collect information on the purpose for manufacturing or importing, the sites of manufacture or import, and the amount manufactured or imported.

Step 4: Determine whether the company was excluded or exempted from submitting a PMN to EPA

The information obtained in Step 3 must be reviewed in order to determine whether the company was excluded or exempted from filing a PMN. For example, some chemicals manufactured or imported may be specifically excluded from TSCA (*e.g.*, chemicals used in food, drugs, or cosmetics), while other chemical substances, such as those used for R&D, are exempted from the section 5 PMN requirements but otherwise subject to TSCA.

Step 5: Determine whether the company submitted to EPA a timely PMN

If the chemical was not excluded or exempted from PMN filing, the company should determine whether a PMN was filed with EPA and whether the PMN was submitted at least 90 days prior to the commencement of commercial manufacture.

Step 6: Determine whether the company submitted a timely NOC to EPA

If a PMN was submitted to EPA (regardless of when submitted), the company should then determine if an NOC was submitted to EPA and whether the notice was timely (*i.e.*, whether the notice was submitted after the conclusion of EPA's review of the PMN and within the first 30 days of commercial manufacture). An NOC constitutes formal notice that *actual* commercial manufacture or importation has begun and therefore cannot be submitted before then. In addition, of course, the NOC cannot be submitted prior to the end of the PMN review period.[65]

---

[65] Failure to submit a timely NOC actually is not a violation of TSCA § 5, but of an EPA regulation promulgated under TSCA §§ 8(a) and (b), 44 Fed. Reg. 2242, 2249 (Jan. 10, 1979). Because NOC submission is so closely related to PMN submission, however, EPA often requires review of both under a "§ 5" audit.

Step 7: Determine whether the company has complied with all applicable requirements under sections 5(e) and 5(f)

The company must next determine whether any PMN submitted to EPA is subject to a requirement under section 5(e) or 5(f), and if so, whether the company has complied with such requirements. To date, EPA has issued many consent and unilateral orders under section 5(e) but only three rules under section 5(f).

In the now standard EPA audit agreements under TSCA § 5, the company must take additional steps where violations of TSCA § 5 are discovered. First, if the company determines that a reportable event exists, the company must notify EPA within 21 days, unless otherwise negotiated. Second, if there is a reportable event, the company immediately must cease manufacturing, importing, processing, distributing or using the chemical substance, except use in compliance with TSCA. Third, the company must undertake remedial measures for each reportable event. For example, if the company failed to file a PMN, the company must submit one and must cease commercial manufacture, importation, processing, distribution in commerce, or use until the chemical has cleared PMN review.

TSCA imposes no obligation to confess a violation. Nevertheless, to proceed with manufacture or importation upon discovery that the chemical is not listed on the Inventory places one at risk of "knowingly or willfully" violating section 15(1), which is punishable as a criminal offense under section 16(b).

15.5.2. TSCA § 8(c) Audit Procedures

In general, conducting an audit of compliance with section 8 would entail steps similar to those used in a section 5 audit, but the procedures to be followed must be tailored to the particular requirements and purposes of the various section 8 provisions. For example, the procedures for auditing compliance with section 8(c), which requires a company to maintain records of allegations of significant adverse reactions, should entail the following steps.

Step 1: Determine whether the company is in compliance with the general record-keeping requirements

In determining compliance with the general record-keeping requirements of section 8(c) and its implementing regulation at 40 C.F.R. section 717.15, the company should ascertain whether it retains records at a central location; whether the records are complete and accurate; whether the company has established an appropriate file structure; and whether the records are kept for the required length of time.

Step 2: Review records and files to obtain information that will be used to determine whether the company has properly recorded specific written allegations

The company then should review the information obtained under Step 1 in order to determine whether it has received any written allegations, as defined in 40 C.F.R. section 717.3(a), and if there are any materials which document or otherwise relate to the disposition of the allegation. The files reviewed should include the company's major relevant files, such as legal files (especially workers' compensation) and medical files.

Step 3: Determine whether specific written allegations were required to be recorded

The company should determine whether each written allegation was required to be recorded, based upon the information available to the company at the time the allegation was received. *See* 40 C.F.R. §§ 717.10, 717.12.

Step 4: Determine whether the company recorded specific written allegations

If the company was required to record the existence of the written allegation, the next step is to ascertain whether the company made a record of the allegation and whether the record is complete and accurate.

In the standard EPA provisions for section 8(c) audits, EPA requires the following two steps. First, upon determining that a recordable event exists, *i.e.*, that the written allegation should have been recorded but the company failed to do so, the company must notify EPA of this failure. Second, the company must develop and implement remedial measures appropriate for any reportable event. For example, if the company has failed to comply with the general record-keeping requirements of 40 C.F.R. section 717.15, then the company would have to establish and maintain records in compliance with these provisions and to notify EPA when this task has been accomplished.

15.6. MAINTAINING CONFIDENTIALITY

Facts discovered during an audit might be used to establish both corporate and individual liability for TSCA violations. TSCA imposes no duty to disclose a violation uncovered by a voluntary internal company audit, although the company must immediately discontinue the unlawful conduct or risk criminal liability under section 16(b) for "knowingly or willfully" violating the Act.[66] Nevertheless, a company may have a duty to report such facts under a myriad of authorities: federal and state laws and

66 As stated above, the disclosure of audit findings to EPA is ordinarily required under EPA-approved audits performed pursuant to a consent agreement.

regulations, tort law, professional codes of conduct[67] or, if the firm is publicly held, requirements under the federal securities acts. As explained earlier in the chapter, a company must disclose violations to EPA in order to obtain the benefit's of the Self-Policing Policy, and may have to provide EPA with copies of audit documents.

In order to minimize the risk or the obligation of having to disclose violations, the audit should be conducted under the direct supervision of an attorney to establish the basis for a claim that the information is protected under the attorney-client and attorney work-product privileges. If a motion to compel production of documents is attempted, the attorney-client privilege and the attorney work-product doctrine can be invoked to limit disclosure of sensitive information that has been generated by persons working directly under the attorney during the audit.

15.6.1. The Attorney-Client Privilege

To qualify for the attorney-client privilege, the documents in question must reflect a communication made in confidence to an attorney by a member of the client company for the purpose of seeking legal advice. *See Upjohn Co. v. United States*, 449 U.S. 383, 389 (1981). The attorney-client privilege is narrowly applied because it is an absolute privilege which, if applied too broadly, could suppress the search for truth. *See United States v. Nixon*, 418 U.S. 683, 709-10 (1974). When a communication is privileged, both the substance of the communication and the documentation reflecting the communication are considered privileged. The original facts underlying the communication, of course, do not become privileged by virtue of their confidential disclosure to an attorney. Thus, while the contents of a special audit report may be considered privileged communications, the original statements or records underlying the reports would not.

In order to fall under the attorney-client privilege, the primary purpose of TSCA audit reports must be legal rather than managerial. In *In re Grand Jury Subpoena*, 599 F.2d 504 (2d Cir. 1979), for example, a company claimed attorney-client privilege to protect memoranda concerning two internal investigations of an alleged bribery incident. The first memorandum was written by non-lawyer employees who had been "deputized" by the general counsel for the purpose of reporting the extent of the problem to the board of directors. The second memorandum was prepared by outside counsel hired by the company to conduct a follow-up investigation and to provide legal advice. The court held that the second memorandum was privileged but the first memorandum was not because it was prepared for a business purpose, not a legal

---

[67] The ABA has drafted Model Rules of Professional Conduct, including two disciplinary rules that are particularly relevant to the issue of whether a lawyer may or should disclose a client's environmental law violation: Rule 1.6 regarding future criminal acts and Rule 3.3 regarding candor towards a tribunal. The Accounting and Engineering codes may impose additional duties on these professionals to disclose unsafe or illegal activities in certain circumstances.

one. Accordingly, for TSCA audit reports to be privileged, they must be conducted under the direction of attorneys for the purpose of obtaining legal advice. To provide evidence of the legal nature of the audit, the company should send a formal written request to the in-house and/or outside attorneys asking them to conduct and direct an audit of the company's TSCA performance, policies, and procedures.

Furthermore, because the communication must be confidential, information arising from TSCA audits should not be distributed widely through normal business channels. Auditors and other non-lawyers assigned to assist the attorneys should limit distribution of information gathered to only those superiors who are involved in the investigation and have a need to know. If unnecessary distribution of the information is made, a court may find that the information was not confidential, or that the attorney-client privilege had been waived.

15.6.2. The Attorney Work-Product Doctrine

The attorney work-product doctrine applies only where documents are prepared in anticipation of litigation or for trial by an attorney or a non-lawyer working under the attorney's direct supervision. *See* Fed. R. Civ. P. 26(b)(3). In contrast to the attorney-client privilege, the attorney work-product doctrine creates a qualified, not an absolute, privilege. Edna Selan Epstein, *The Attorney-Client Privilege and the Work-Product Doctrine* 297-98 (3d ed. 1997). This privilege can be overcome if the party seeking discovery shows substantial need for the materials and an inability to obtain the substantial equivalent of the materials by other means. Although the attorney work-product privilege first arose in a civil setting, it may play an important role in criminal cases as well. *See* Fed. R. Crim. P. 16(b)(2) ("Except as to scientific or medical reports, this subdivision does not authorize the discovery or inspection of reports, memoranda, or other internal defense documents . . . .").

Compared to the attorney-client privilege, there are fewer pitfalls in applying the attorney work-product privilege to reports prepared by non-lawyer auditors or investigators under the direction of an attorney. For example, materials privileged according to the attorney work-product doctrine may be more widely disseminated within the company without effecting a waiver than would be the case with materials subject to the attorney-client privilege. The essential requirement of the work-product privilege is that the documents were prepared in anticipation of litigation. In the case of TSCA audit reports, the risk of litigation often may be real enough to satisfy the litigation requirement. *See In re Grand Jury Investigation*, 599 F.2d 1224, 1229 (3d Cir. 1979). The litigation requirement, however, necessarily excludes reports that have been prepared in the ordinary course of business, as well as special investigations conducted by non-lawyers for business purposes. *See In re Grand Jury Subpoena*, 599 F.2d at 510.

In light of EPA's emphasis on TSCA compliance monitoring, a company should take great care to protect the confidentiality legitimately afforded by these privileges. Counsel must become involved in the audit process immediately upon discovery of a potential problem. To lay a foundation for the privileges, paperwork should be prepared documenting that the TSCA audit is being conducted under the direction of an attorney for the purpose of obtaining legal advice, and, where appropriate, in anticipation of legal proceedings. The resulting report should clearly indicate that it is confidential and should not be widely distributed through normal business channels.

15.6.3. SEC's Disclosure Requirements

Under the SEC's disclosure requirements, publicly held companies may have a duty to disclose certain TSCA violations discovered during an internal audit. In their registration statements (filed under the authority of the Securities Act of 1933) and in annual and quarterly reports (filed pursuant to the Security Exchange Act of 1934), SEC registrants must disclose the material economic effects caused by company compliance with federal, state, and local environmental laws. Certain SEC regulations and Securities Act releases establish that publicly held companies have a legal obligation to disclose any and all environmental information that is material to investors and shareholders. All reports submitted to the SEC are then made available to the public.

In particular, public corporations must report information on (1) the material effects on the company of the costs of complying with environmental laws, (2) certain administrative environmental legal proceedings, and (3) company environmental compliance policies, if those policies are likely to result in substantial fines or penalties or have other significant effects on the corporation. *See* generally SEC Release Nos. 33-6130, 34-16224, 44 Fed. Reg. 56,924 (Oct. 3, 1979). To the extent that a TSCA audit uncovers information falling into these categories, which the SEC interprets broadly, a duty to report may arise.

The complications associated with environmental disclosures have increased substantially over the past few years with the changes precipitated by The Sarbanes-Oxley Act of 2002. One of the most important changes arises from the requirements of SOX section 404, which requires each annual report of a company to contain (1) a statement of management's responsibility for establishing and maintaining an adequate internal control structure and procedures for financial reporting; and (2) management's assessment, as of the end of the company's most recent fiscal year, of the effectiveness of the company's internal control structure and procedures for financial reporting. In the environmental context, this obligation to establish and maintain an adequate control structure is generally regarded to create three separate set of requirements: (1) additional rigor in estimating the nature and extent of contingent environmental liabilities; (2) creation of appropriate internal mechanisms to perform QA/QC checks on environmental cost estimates, including the assumptions built into those costs; and (3) greater detail in disclosures describing environmental liabilities, the costs to address those liabilities, and the assumptions on which the liabilities are based.

Although companies have made considerable progress in incorporating the section 404 requirements into most areas of SOX compliance, environmental disclosures are proving to be particularly difficult. There seem to be two reasons why the environmental component has proven troublesome. First, estimating environmental costs is a very technical and arcane process. Indeed, ASTM has published separate guidance on the topic (ASTM E-2137). Most engineering cost estimators are not well versed in the nuances of securities review and disclosure requirements. Second, most internal control processes are not well suited to dealing with the abstract and highly contingent nature of environmental liabilities and, unless the disclosure is based on a simple formula (such as, for example, the penalty assessment found under some environmental laws like TSCA, for which EPA provides substantial information on the likely penalty in its various TSCA ERPs), most accountants and auditors will not be well versed in the engineering technicalities that drive both the choice of a cost model and the assumptions on which it is based. On top of this, many companies have adopted the SEC's proposal to disclose their "critical accounting estimates," which only exacerbates the disconnect between the available information and ordinary corporate disclosure forms. The combination of these factors means that companies are often faced with cost estimating processes that cannot be easily reconciled with existing corporate controls and disclosure requirements that do not easily match the available cost data. Early attention to these sorts of difficulties can lead to great efficiencies down the road.

TOXIC SUBSTANCES CONTROL ACT

CONTROL OF TOXIC SUBSTANCES

Toxic Substances Control Act, 15 U.S.C. §§ 2601-2692

[from http://www.epa.gov/region5/defs/html/tsca.htm]

Subchapter I—Control of Toxic Substances

[TSCA § 2, 15 U.S.C. § 2601—] Findings, policy, and intent

(a) Findings

The Congress finds that—

(1) human beings and the environment are being exposed each year to a large number of chemical substances and mixtures;

(2) among the many chemical substances and mixtures which are constantly being developed and produced, there are some whose manufacture, processing, distribution in commerce, use, or disposal may present an unreasonable risk of injury to health or the environment; and

(3) the effective regulation of interstate commerce in such chemical substances and mixtures also necessitates the regulation of intrastate commerce in such chemical substances and mixtures.

(b) Policy

It is the policy of the United States that—

(1) adequate data should be developed with respect to the effect of chemical substances and mixtures on health and the environment and that the development of such data should be the responsibility of those who manufacture and those who process such chemical substances and mixtures;

(2) adequate authority should exist to regulate chemical substances and mixtures which present an unreasonable risk of injury to health or the environment, and to take action with respect to chemical substances and mixtures which are imminent hazards; and

(3) authority over chemical substances and mixtures should be exercised in such a manner as not to impede unduly or create unnecessary economic barriers to technological innovation while fulfilling the primary purpose of this chapter to assure that such innovation and commerce in such chemical substances and mixtures do not present an unreasonable risk of injury to health or the environment.

(c) Intent of Congress

It is the intent of Congress that the Administrator shall carry out this chapter in a reasonable and prudent manner, and that the Administrator shall consider the environmental, economic, and social impact of any action the Administrator takes or proposes to take under this chapter.

[TSCA § 3, 15 U.S.C. § 2602—]
Definitions

As used in this chapter:

(1) the term "*Administrator*" means the Administrator of the Environmental Protection Agency.

(2) (A) Except as provided in subparagraph (B), the term "*chemical substance*" means any organic or inorganic substance of a particular molecular identity, including—

(i) any combination of such substances occurring in whole or in part as a result of a chemical reaction or occurring in nature and

(ii) any element or uncombined radical.

(B) Such term does not include—

(i) any mixture,

(ii) any pesticide (as defined in the Federal Insecticide, Fungicide, and Rodenticide Act [7 U.S.C. 136 et seq.]) when manufactured, processed, or distributed in commerce for use as a pesticide,

(iii) tobacco or any tobacco product,

(iv) any source material, special nuclear material, or byproduct material (as such terms are defined in the Atomic Energy Act of 1954 [42 U.S.C. 2011 et seq.] and regulations issued under such Act),

(v) any article the sale of which is subject to the tax imposed by section 4181 of the Internal Revenue Code of 1986 [26 U.S.C. 4181] (determined without regard to any exemptions from such tax provided by section 4182 or 4221 or any other provision of such Code), and

(vi) any food, food additive, drug, cosmetic, or device (as such terms are defined in section 201 of the Federal Food, Drug, and Cosmetic Act [21 U.S.C. 321]) when manufactured, processed, or distributed in commerce for use as a food, food additive, drug, cosmetic, or device.

The term "*food*" as used in clause (vi) of this subparagraph includes poultry and poultry products (as defined in sections 4(e) and 4(f) of the Poultry Products Inspection Act [21 U.S.C. 453(e) and (f)]), meat and meat food products (as defined in section 1(j) of the Federal Meat Inspection Act [21 U.S.C. 601(j)]), and eggs and egg products (as defined in section 4 of the Egg Products Inspection Act [21 U.S.C. 1033]).

(3) The term "*commerce*" means trade, traffic, transportation, or other commerce (A) between a place in a State and any place outside of such State, or (B) which affects trade, traffic, transportation, or commerce described in clause (A).

(4) The terms "*distribute in commerce*" and "*distribution in commerce*" when used to describe an action taken with respect to a chemical substance or mixture or article containing a substance or

mixture mean to sell, or the sale of, the substance, mixture, or article in commerce; to introduce or deliver for introduction into commerce, or the introduction or delivery for introduction into commerce of, the substance, mixture, or article; or to hold, or the holding of, the substance, mixture, or article after its introduction into commerce.

(5) The term "*environment*" includes water, air, and land and the interrelationship which exists among and between water, air, and land and all living things.

(6) The term "*health and safety study*" means any study of any effect of a chemical substance or mixture on health or the environment or on both, including underlying data and epidemiological studies, studies of occupational exposure to a chemical substance or mixture, toxicological, clinical, and ecological studies of a chemical substance or mixture, and any test performed pursuant to this chapter.

(7) The term "*manufacture*" means to import into the customs territory of the United States (as defined in general note 2 of the Harmonized Tariff Schedule of the United States), produce, or manufacture.

(8) The term "*mixture*" means any combination of two or more chemical substances if the combination does not occur in nature and is not, in whole or in part, the result of a chemical reaction; except that such term does include any combination which occurs, in whole or in part, as a result of a chemical reaction if none of the chemical substances comprising the combination is a new chemical substance and if the combination could have been manufactured for commercial purposes without a chemical reaction at the time the chemical substances comprising the combination were combined.

(9) The term "*new chemical substance*" means any chemical substance which is not included in the chemical substance list compiled and published under section 2607(b) of this title.

(10) The term "*process*" means the preparation of a chemical substance or mixture, after its manufacture, for distribution in commerce—

(A) in the same form or physical state as, or in a different form or physical state from, that in which it was received by the person so preparing such substance or mixture, or

(B) as part of an article containing the chemical substance or mixture.

(11) The term "*processor*" means any person who processes a chemical substance or mixture.

(12) The term "*standards for the development of test data*" means a prescription of—

(A) the—

(i) health and environmental effects, and

(ii) information relating to toxicity, persistence, and other characteristics which affect health and the environment,

for which test data for a chemical substance or mixture are to be developed and any analysis that is to be performed on such data, and

(B) to the extent necessary to assure that data respecting such effects and characteristics are reliable and adequate—

(i) the manner in which such data are to be developed,

(ii) the specification of any test protocol or methodology to be employed in the development of such data, and

(iii) such other requirements as are necessary to provide such assurance.

(13) The term "*State*" means any State of the United States, the District of Columbia, the Commonwealth of Puerto Rico, the Virgin Islands, Guam, the Canal Zone, American Samoa, the Northern Mariana Islands, or any other territory or possession of the United States.

(14) The term "*United States*", when used in the geographic sense, means all of the States.

[TSCA § 4, 7 U.S.C. § 2603—] Testing of chemical substances and mixtures

(a) Testing requirements

If the Administrator finds that—

(1)(A)(i) the manufacture, distribution in commerce, processing, use, or disposal of a chemical substance or mixture, or that any combination of such activities, may present an unreasonable risk of injury to health or the environment,

(ii) there are insufficient data and experience upon which the effects of such manufacture, distribution in commerce, processing, use, or disposal of such substance or mixture or of any combination of such activities on health or the environment can reasonably be determined or predicted, and

(iii) testing of such substance or mixture with respect to such effects is necessary to develop such data; or

(B)(i) a chemical substance or mixture is or will be produced in substantial quantities, and (I) it enters or may reasonably be anticipated to enter the environment in substantial quantities or (II) there is or may be significant or substantial human exposure to such substance or mixture,

(ii) there are insufficient data and experience upon which the effects of the manufacture, distribution in commerce, processing, use, or disposal of such substance or mixture or of any combination of such activities on health or the environment can reasonably be determined or predicted, and

(iii) testing of such substance or mixture with

respect to such effects is necessary to develop such data; and

(2) in the case of a mixture, the effects which the mixture's manufacture, distribution in commerce, processing, use, or disposal or any combination of such activities may have on health or the environment may not be reasonably and more efficiently determined or predicted by testing the chemical substances which comprise the mixture;

the Administrator shall by rule require that testing be conducted on such substance or mixture to develop data with respect to the health and environmental effects for which there is an insufficiency of data and experience and which are relevant to a determination that the manufacture, distribution in commerce, processing, use, or disposal of such substance or mixture, or that any combination of such activities, does or does not present an unreasonable risk of injury to health or the environment.

(b) Testing requirement rule

(1) A rule under subsection (a) of this section shall include—

(A) identification of the chemical substance or mixture for which testing is required under the rule,

(B) standards for the development of test data for such substance or mixture, and

(C) with respect to chemical substances which are not new chemical substances and to mixtures, a specification of the period (which period may not be of unreasonable duration) within which the persons required to conduct the testing shall submit to the Administrator data developed in accordance with the standards referred to in subparagraph (B).

In determining the standards and period to be included, pursuant to subparagraphs (B) and (C), in a rule under subsection (a) of this section, the Administrator's considerations shall include the relative costs of the various test protocols and methodologies which may be required under the rule and the reasonably foreseeable availability of the facilities and personnel needed to perform the testing required under the rule. Any such rule may require the submission to the Administrator of preliminary data during the period prescribed under subparagraph (C).

(2)(A) The health and environmental effects for which standards for the development of test data may be prescribed include carcinogenesis, mutagenesis, teratogenesis, behavioral disorders, cumulative or synergistic effects, and any other effect which may present an unreasonable risk of injury to health or the environment. The characteristics of chemical substances and mixtures for which such standards may be prescribed include persistence, acute toxicity, subacute toxicity, chronic toxicity, and any other characteristic which may present such a risk. The methodologies that may be prescribed in such standards include epidemiologic studies, serial or hierarchical tests, in vitro tests, and whole animal tests, except that before prescribing epidemiologic studies of employees, the Administrator shall consult with the Director of the National Institute for Occupational Safety and Health.

(B) From time to time, but not less than once each 12 months, the Administrator shall review the adequacy of the standards for development of data prescribed in rules under subsection (a) of this section and shall, if necessary, institute proceedings to make appropriate revisions of such standards.

(3)(A) A rule under subsection (a) of this section respecting a chemical substance or mixture shall require the persons described in subparagraph (B) to conduct tests and submit data to the Administrator on such substance or mixture, except that the Administrator may permit two or more of such persons to designate one such person or a qualified third party to conduct such tests and submit such data on behalf of the persons making the designation.

(B) The following persons shall be required to conduct tests and submit data on a chemical substance or mixture subject to a rule under subsection (a) of this section:

(i) Each person who manufactures or intends to manufacture such substance or mixture if the Administrator makes a finding described in subsection (a)(1)(A)(ii) or (a)(1)(B)(ii) of this section with respect to the manufacture of such substance or mixture.

(ii) Each person who processes or intends to process such substance or mixture if the Administrator makes a finding described in subsection (a)(1)(A)(ii) or (a)(1)(B)(ii) of this section with respect to the processing of such substance or mixture.

(iii) Each person who manufactures or processes or intends to manufacture or process such substance or mixture if the Administrator makes a finding described in subsection (a)(1)(A)(ii) or (a)(1)(B)(ii) of this section with respect to the distribution in commerce, use, or disposal of such substance or mixture.

(4) Any rule under subsection (a) of this section requiring the testing of and submission of data for a particular chemical substance or mixture shall expire at the end of the reimbursement period (as defined in subsection (c)(3)(B) of this section) which is applicable to test data for such substance or mixture unless the Administrator repeals the rule before such date; and a rule under subsection (a) of this section requiring the testing of and submission of data for a category of chemical substances or mixtures shall expire with respect to a

chemical substance or mixture included in the category at the end of the reimbursement period (as so defined) which is applicable to test data for such substance or mixture unless the Administrator before such date repeals the application of the rule to such substance or mixture or repeals the rule.

(5) Rules issued under subsection (a) of this section (and any substantive amendment thereto or repeal thereof) shall be promulgated pursuant to section 553 of title 5 except that (A) the Administrator shall give interested persons an opportunity for the oral presentation of data, views, or arguments, in addition to an opportunity to make written submissions; (B) a transcript shall be made of any oral presentation; and (C) the Administrator shall make and publish with the rule the findings described in paragraph (1)(A) or (1)(B) of subsection (a) of this section and, in the case of a rule respecting a mixture, the finding described in paragraph (2) of such subsection.

(c) Exemption

(1) Any person required by a rule under subsection (a) of this section to conduct tests and submit data on a chemical substance or mixture may apply to the Administrator (in such form and manner as the Administrator shall prescribe) for an exemption from such requirement.

(2) If, upon receipt of an application under paragraph (1), the Administrator determines that—

(A) the chemical substance or mixture with respect to which such application was submitted is equivalent to a chemical substance or mixture for which data has been submitted to the Administrator in accordance with a rule under subsection (a) of this section or for which data is being developed pursuant to such a rule, and

(B) submission of data by the applicant on such substance or mixture would be duplicative of data which has been submitted to the Administrator in accordance with such rule or which is being developed pursuant to such rule,

the Administrator shall exempt, in accordance with paragraph (3) or (4), the applicant from conducting tests and submitting data on such substance or mixture under the rule with respect to which such application was submitted.

(3)(A) If the exemption under paragraph (2) of any person from the requirement to conduct tests and submit test data on a chemical substance or mixture is granted on the basis of the existence of previously submitted test data and if such exemption is granted during the reimbursement period for such test data (as prescribed by subparagraph (B)), then (unless such person and the persons referred to in clauses (i) and (ii) agree on the amount and method of reimbursement) the Administrator shall order the person granted the exemption to provide fair and equitable reimbursement (in an amount determined under rules of the Administrator)—

(i) to the person who previously submitted such test data, for a portion of the costs incurred by such person in complying with the requirement to submit such data, and

(ii) to any other person who has been required under this subparagraph to contribute with respect to such costs, for a portion of the amount such person was required to contribute.

In promulgating rules for the determination of fair and equitable reimbursement to the persons described in clauses (i) and (ii) for costs incurred with respect to a chemical substance or mixture, the Administrator shall, after consultation with the Attorney General and the Federal Trade Commission, consider all relevant factors, including the effect on the competitive position of the person required to provide reimbursement in relation to the person to be reimbursed and the share of the market for such substance or mixture of the person required to provide reimbursement in relation to the share of such market of the persons to be reimbursed. An order under this subparagraph shall, for purposes of judicial review, be considered final agency action.

(B) For purposes of subparagraph (A), the reimbursement period for any test data for a chemical substance or mixture is a period—

(i) beginning on the date such data is submitted in accordance with a rule promulgated under subsection (a) of this section, and

(ii) ending—

(I) five years after the date referred to in clause (i), or

(II) at the expiration of a period which begins on the date referred to in clause (i) and which is equal to the period which the Administrator determines was necessary to develop such data,

whichever is later.

(4)(A) If the exemption under paragraph (2) of any person from the requirement to conduct tests and submit test data on a chemical substance or mixture is granted on the basis of the fact that test data is being developed by one or more persons pursuant to a rule promulgated under subsection (a) of this section, then (unless such person and the persons referred to in clauses (i) and (ii) agree on the amount and method of reimbursement) the Administrator shall order the person granted the exemption to provide fair and equitable reimbursement (in an amount determined under rules of the Administrator)—

(i) to each such person who is developing such test data, for a portion of the costs incurred by each such person in complying with such rule, and

(ii) to any other person who has been required under this subparagraph to contribute with respect to the costs of complying with such rule, for a portion of the amount such person was required to contribute.

In promulgating rules for the determination of fair and equitable reimbursement to the persons described in clauses (i) and (ii) for costs incurred with respect to a chemical substance or mixture, the Administrator shall, after consultation with the Attorney General and the Federal Trade Commission, consider the factors described in the second sentence of paragraph (3)(A). An order under this subparagraph shall, for purposes of judicial review, be considered final agency action.

(B) If any exemption is granted under paragraph (2) on the basis of the fact that one or more persons are developing test data pursuant to a rule promulgated under subsection (a) of this section and if after such exemption is granted the Administrator determines that no such person has complied with such rule, the Administrator shall (i) after providing written notice to the person who holds such exemption and an opportunity for a hearing, by order terminate such exemption, and (ii) notify in writing such person of the requirements of the rule with respect to which such exemption was granted.

(d) Notice

Upon the receipt of any test data pursuant to a rule under subsection (a) of this section, the Administrator shall publish a notice of the receipt of such data in the Federal Register within 15 days of its receipt. Subject to section 2613 of this title, each such notice shall (1) identify the chemical substance or mixture for which data have been received; (2) list the uses or intended uses of such substance or mixture and the information required by the applicable standards for the development of test data; and (3) describe the nature of the test data developed. Except as otherwise provided in section 2613 of this title, such data shall be made available by the Administrator for examination by any person.

(e) Priority list

(1)(A) There is established a committee to make recommendations to the Administrator respecting the chemical substances and mixtures to which the Administrator should give priority consideration for the promulgation of a rule under subsection (a) of this section. In making such a recommendation with respect to any chemical substance or mixture, the committee shall consider all relevant factors, including—

(i) the quantities in which the substance or mixture is or will be manufactured,

(ii) the quantities in which the substance or mixture enters or will enter the environment,

(iii) the number of individuals who are or will be exposed to the substance or mixture in their places of employment and the duration of such exposure,

(iv) the extent to which human beings are or will be exposed to the substance or mixture,

(v) the extent to which the substance or mixture is closely related to a chemical substance or mixture which is known to present an unreasonable risk of injury to health or the environment,

(vi) the existence of data concerning the effects of the substance or mixture on health or the environment,

(vii) the extent to which testing of the substance or mixture may result in the development of data upon which the effects of the substance or mixture on health or the environment can reasonably be determined or predicted, and

(viii) the reasonably foreseeable availability of facilities and personnel for performing testing on the substance or mixture.

The recommendations of the committee shall be in the form of a list of chemical substances and mixtures which shall be set forth, either by individual substance or mixture or by groups of substances or mixtures, in the order in which the committee determines the Administrator should take action under subsection (a) of this section with respect to the substances and mixtures. In establishing such list, the committee shall give priority attention to those chemical substances and mixtures which are known to cause or contribute to or which are suspected of causing or contributing to cancer, gene mutations, or birth defects. The committee shall designate chemical substances and mixtures on the list with respect to which the committee determines the Administrator should, within 12 months of the date on which such substances and mixtures are first designated, initiate a proceeding under subsection (a) of this section. The total number of chemical substances and mixtures on the list which are designated under the preceding sentence may not, at any time, exceed 50.

(B) As soon as practicable but not later than nine months after January 1, 1977, the committee shall publish in the Federal Register and transmit to the Administrator the list and designations required by subparagraph (A) together with the reasons for the committee's inclusion of each chemical substance or mixture on the list. At least every six months after the date of the transmission to the Administrator of the list pursuant to the preceeding[1] sentence, the committee shall make such previsions in the list as it determines to be necessary and shall transmit them to the Administrator together with the committee's reasons for the revisions. Upon receipt of any such revision, the Administrator shall publish in the Federal Register the list with such revision, the reasons for such revision, and the designations made under subparagraph (A). The Administrator shall provide reasonable opportunity to any interested person to file with the Administrator written comments on the committee's list, any revision of such list by the committee, and designations made by the committee, and shall make such comments available to the public. Within the 12-month period beginning on the date of the first inclusion on the list of a chemical substance or mixture designated by the committee under subparagraph (A) the Administrator shall with respect to such chemical substance or mixture either initiate a rulemaking proceeding under subsection (a) of this section or if such a proceeding is not initiated within such period, publish in the Federal Register the Administrator's reason for not initiating such a proceeding.

(2)(A) The committee established by paragraph (1)(A) shall consist of eight members as follows:

(i) One member appointed by the Administrator from the Environmental Protection Agency.

(ii) One member appointed by the Secretary of Labor from officers or employees of the Department of Labor engaged in the Secretary's activities under the Occupational Safety and Health Act of 1970 [29 U.S.C. 651 et seq.].

(iii) One member appointed by the Chairman of the Council on Environmental Quality from the Council or its officers or employees.

(iv) One member appointed by the Director of the National Institute for Occupational Safety and Health from officers or employees of the Institute.

(v) One member appointed by the Director of the National Institute of Environmental Health Sciences from officers or employees of the Institute.

(vi) One member appointed by the Director of the National Cancer Institute

[1] So in original. Probably should be "preceding".

from officers or employees of the Institute.

(vii) One member appointed by the Director of the National Science Foundation from officers or employees of the Foundation.

(viii) One member appointed by the Secretary of Commerce from officers or employees of the Department of Commerce.

(B)(i) An appointed member may designate an individual to serve on the committee on the member's behalf. Such a designation may be made only with the approval of the applicable appointing authority and only if the individual is from the entity from which the member was appointed.

(ii) No individual may serve as a member of the committee for more than four years in the aggregate. If any member of the committee leaves the entity from which the member was appointed, such member may not continue as a member of the committee, and the member's position shall be considered to be vacant. A vacancy in the committee shall be filled in the same manner in which the original appointment was made.

(iii) Initial appointments to the committee shall be made not later than the 60th day after January 1, 1977. Not later than the 90th day after such date the members of the committee shall hold a meeting for the selection of a chairperson from among their number.

(C)(i) No member of the committee, or designee of such member, shall accept employment or compensation from any person subject to any requirement of this chapter or of any rule promulgated or order issued thereunder, for a period of at least 12 months after termination of service on the committee.

(ii) No person, while serving as a member of the committee, or designee of such member, may own any stocks or bonds, or have any pecuniary interest, of substantial value in any person engaged in the manufacture, processing, or distribution in commerce of any chemical substance or mixture subject to any requirement of this chapter or of any rule promulgated or order issued thereunder.

(iii) The Administrator, acting through attorneys of the Environmental Protection Agency, or the Attorney General may bring an action in the appropriate district court of the United States to restrain any violation of this subparagraph.

(D) The Administrator shall provide the committee such

administrative support services as may be necessary to enable the committee to carry out its function under this subsection.

(f) Required actions

Upon the receipt of—

(1) any test data required to be submitted under this chapter, or

(2) any other information available to the Administrator,

which indicates to the Administrator that there may be a reasonable basis to conclude that a chemical substance or mixture presents or will present a significant risk of serious or widespread harm to human beings from cancer, gene mutations, or birth defects, the Administrator shall, within the 180-day period beginning on the date of the receipt of such data or information, initiate appropriate action under section 2604, 2605, or 2606 of this title to prevent or reduce to a sufficient extent such risk or publish in the Federal Register a finding that such risk is not unreasonable. For good cause shown the Administrator may extend such period for an additional period of not more than 90 days. The Administrator shall publish in the Federal Register notice of any such extension and the reasons therefor. A finding by the Administrator that a risk is not unreasonable shall be considered agency action for purposes of judicial review under chapter 7 of title 5. This subsection shall not take effect until two years after January 1, 1977.

(g) Petition for standards for the development of test data

A person intending to manufacture or process a chemical substance for which notice is required under section 2604(a) of this title and who is not required under a rule under subsection (a) of this section to conduct tests and submit data on such substance may petition the Administrator to prescribe standards for the development of test data for such substance. The Administrator shall by order either grant or deny any such petition within 60 days of its receipt. If the petition is granted, the Administrator shall prescribe such standards for such substance within 75 days of the date the petition is granted. If the petition is denied, the Administrator shall publish, subject to section 2613 of this title, in the Federal Register the reasons for such denial.

[TSCA § 5, 15 U.S.C. § 2604—] Manufacturing and processing notices

(a) In general

(1) Except as provided in subsection (h) of this section, no person may—

(A) manufacture a new chemical substance on or after the 30th day after the date on which the Administrator first publishes the list required by section 2607(b) of this title, or

(B) manufacture or process any chemical substance for a use which the Administrator has determined, in accordance with paragraph (2), is a significant new use,

unless such person submits to the Administrator, at least 90 days before such manufacture or processing, a notice, in accordance with subsection (d) of this section, of such person's intention to manufacture or process such substance and such person complies with any applicable requirement of subsection (b) of this section.

(2) A determination by the Administrator that a use of a chemical substance is a significant new use with respect to which notification is required under paragraph (1) shall be made by a rule promulgated after a consideration of all relevant factors, including—

(A) the projected volume of manufacturing and processing of a chemical substance,

(B) the extent to which a use changes the type or form of exposure of human beings or the environment to a chemical substance,

(C) the extent to which a use increases the magnitude and duration of exposure of human beings or the environment to a chemical substance, and

(D) the reasonably anticipated manner and methods of manufacturing, processing, distribution in commerce, and disposal of a chemical substance.

(b) Submission of test data

(1)(A) If (i) a person is required by subsection (a)(1) of this section to submit a notice to the Administrator before beginning the manufacture or processing of a chemical substance, and (ii) such person is required to submit test data for such substance pursuant to a rule promulgated under section 2603 of this title before the submission of such notice, such person shall submit to the Administrator such data in accordance with such rule at the time notice is submitted in accordance with subsection (a)(1) of this section.

(B) If—

(i) a person is required by subsection (a)(1) of this section to submit a notice to the Administrator, and

(ii) such person has been granted an exemption under section 2603(c) of this title from the requirements of a rule promulgated under section 2603 of this title before the submission of such notice,

such person may not, before the expiration of the 90 day period which begins on the date of the submission in accordance with such rule of the test data the submission or development of which was the basis for the exemption, manufacture such substance if such person is subject to subsection (a)(1)(A) of this section or manufacture or process such substance for a significant new use if the person is subject to subsection (a)(1)(B) of this section.

(2)(A) If a person—

(i) is required by subsection (a)(1) of this section to submit a notice to the Administrator before beginning the manufacture or processing of a chemical substance listed under paragraph (4), and

(ii) is not required by a rule promulgated under section 2603 of this title before the submission of such notice to submit test data for such substance,

such person shall submit to the Administrator data prescribed by subparagraph (B) at the time notice is submitted in accordance with subsection (a) (1) of this section.

(B) Data submitted pursuant to subparagraph (A) shall be data which the person submitting the data believes show that—

(i) in the case of a substance with respect to which notice is required under subsection (a)(1)(A) of this section, the manufacture, processing, distribution in commerce, use, and disposal of the chemical substance or any combination of such activities will not present an unreasonable risk of injury to health or the environment, or

(ii) in the case of a chemical substance with respect to which notice is required under subsection (a)(1)(B) of this section, the intended significant new use of the chemical substance will not present an unreasonable risk of injury to health or the environment.

(3) Data submitted under paragraph (1) or (2) shall be made available, subject to section 2613 of this title, for examination by interested persons.

(4)(A)(i) The Administrator may, by rule, compile and keep current a list of chemical substances with respect to which the Administrator finds that the manufacture, processing, distribution in commerce, use, or disposal, or any combination of such activities, presents or may present an unreasonable risk of injury to health or the environment.

(ii) In making a finding under clause (i) that the manufacture, processing, distribution in commerce, use, or disposal of a chemical substance or any combination of such activities presents or may present an unreasonable risk of injury to health or the environment, the Administrator shall consider all relevant factors, including—

(I) the effects of the chemical substance on health and the magnitude of human exposure to such substance; and

(II) the effects of the chemical substance on the environment and the magnitude of environmental exposure to such substance.

(B) The Administrator shall, in prescribing a rule under subparagraph (A) which lists any chemical substance, identify those uses, if any, which the Administrator determines, by rule under subsection (a)(2) of this section, would constitute a significant new use of such substance.

(C) Any rule under subparagraph (A), and any substantive amendment or repeal of such a rule, shall be promulgated pursuant to the procedures specified in section 553 of title 5, except that (i) the Administrator shall give interested persons an opportunity for the oral presentation of data, views, or arguments, in addition to an opportunity to make written submissions, (ii) a transcript shall be kept of any oral presentation, and (iii) the Administrator shall make and publish with the rule the finding described in subparagraph (A).

(c) Extension of notice period

The Administrator may for good cause extend for additional periods (not to exceed in the aggregate 90 days) the period, prescribed by subsection (a) or (b) of this section before which the manufacturing or processing of a chemical substance subject to such subsection may begin. Subject to section 2613 of this title, such an extension and the reasons therefor shall be published in the Federal Register and shall constitute a final agency action subject to judicial review.

(d) Content of notice; publications in the Federal Register

(1) The notice required by subsection (a) of this section shall include—

(A) insofar as known to the person submitting the notice or insofar as reasonably ascertainable, the information described in subparagraphs (A), (B), (C), (D), (F), and (G) of section 2607(a)(2) of this title, and

(B) in such form and manner as the Administrator may prescribe, any test data in the possession or control of the person giving such notice which are related to the effect of any manufacture, processing, distribution in commerce, use, or disposal of such substance or any article containing such substance, or of any combination of such activities, on health or the environment, and

(C) a description of any other data concerning the environmental and health effects of such substance, insofar as known to the person making the notice or insofar as reasonably ascertainable.

Such a notice shall be made available, subject to section 2613 of this title, for examination by interested persons.

(2) Subject to section 2613 of this title, not later than five days (excluding Saturdays, Sundays and legal holidays) after the date of the receipt of a notice under subsection (a) of this section or of data under subsection (b) of this section, the Administrator shall publish in the Federal Register a notice which—

(A) identifies the chemical substance for which notice or data has been received;

(B) lists the uses or intended uses of such substance; and

(C) in the case of the receipt of data under subsection (b) of this section, describes the nature of the tests performed on such substance and any data which was developed pursuant to subsection (b) of this section or a rule under section 2603 of this title.

A notice under this paragraph respecting a chemical substance shall identify the chemical substance by generic class unless the Administrator determines that more specific identification is required in the public interest.

(3) At the beginning of each month the Administrator shall publish a list in the Federal Register of (A) each chemical substance for which notice has been received under subsection (a) of this section and for which the notification period prescribed by subsection (a), (b), or (c) of this section has not expired, and (B) each chemical substance for which such notification period has expired since the last publication in the Federal Register of such list.

(e) Regulation pending development of information

(1)(A) If the Administrator determines that—

(i) the information available to the Administrator is insufficient to permit a reasoned evaluation of the health and environmental effects of a chemical substance with respect to which notice is required by subsection (a) of this section; and

(ii)(I) in the absence of sufficient information to permit the Administrator to make such an evaluation, the manufacture, processing, distribution in commerce, use, or disposal of such substance, or any combination of such activities, may present an unreasonable risk of injury to health or the environment, or

(II) such substance is or will be produced in substantial quantities, and such substance either enters or may reasonably be anticipated to enter the environment in substantial quantities or there is or may be significant or substantial human exposure to the substance,

the Administrator may issue a proposed order, to take effect on the expiration of the notification period applicable to the manufacturing or processing of such substance under subsection (a), (b), or (c) of this section, to prohibit or limit the manufacture, processing, distribution in commerce, use, or disposal of such substance or to prohibit or limit any combination of such activities.

(B) A proposed order may not be issued under subparagraph

(A) respecting a chemical substance (i) later than 45 days before the expiration of the notification period applicable to the manufacture or processing of such substance under subsection (a), (b), or (c) of this section, and (ii) unless the Administrator has, on or before the issuance of the proposed order, notified, in writing, each manufacturer or processor, as the case may be, of such substance of the determination which underlies such order.

(C) If a manufacturer or processor of a chemical substance to be subject to a proposed order issued under subparagraph (A) files with the Administrator (within the 30-day period beginning on the date such manufacturer or processor received the notice required by subparagraph (B)(ii)) objections specifying with particularity the provisions of the order deemed objectionable and stating the grounds therefor, the proposed order shall not take effect.

(2)(A)(i) Except as provided in clause (ii), if with respect to a chemical substance with respect to which notice is required by subsection (a) of this section, the Administrator makes the determination described in paragraph (1)(A) and if—

(I) the Administrator does not issue a proposed order under paragraph (1) respecting such substance, or

(II) the Administrator issues such an order respecting such substance but such order does not take effect because objections were filed under paragraph (1)(C) with respect to it,

the Administrator, through attorneys of the Environmental Protection Agency, shall apply to the United States District Court for the District of Columbia or the United States district court for the judicial district in which the manufacturer or processor, as the case may be, of such substance is found, resides, or transacts business for an injunction to prohibit or limit the manufacture, processing, distribution in commerce, use, or disposal of such substance (or to prohibit or limit any combination of such activities).

(ii) If the Administrator issues a proposed order under paragraph (1)(A) respecting a chemical substance but such order does not take effect because objections have been filed under paragraph (1)(C) with respect to it, the Administrator is not required to apply for an injunction under clause (i) respecting such substance if the Administrator determines, on the basis of such objections, that the determinations under paragraph (1)(A) may not be made.

(B) A district court of the United States which receives an application under subparagraph (A)(i) for an injunction respecting a chemical substance shall issue such injunction if the court finds that—

(i) the information available to the Administrator is insufficient to permit a reasoned evaluation of the health and environmental effects of a chemical substance with respect to which notice is required by subsection (a) of this section; and

(ii)(I) in the absence of sufficient information to permit the Administrator to make such an evaluation, the manufacture, processing, distribution in commerce, use, or disposal of such substance, or any combination of such activities, may present an unreasonable risk of injury to health or the environment, or

(II) such substance is or will be produced in substantial quantities, and such substance either enters or may reasonably be anticipated to enter the environment in substantial quantities or there is or may be significant or substantial human exposure to the substance.

(C) Pending the completion of a proceeding for the issuance of an injunction under subparagraph (B) respecting a chemical substance, the court may, upon application of the Administrator made through attorneys of the Environmental Protection Agency, issue a temporary restraining order or a preliminary injunction to prohibit the manufacture, processing, distribution in commerce, use, or disposal of such a substance (or any combination of such activities) if the court finds that the notification period applicable under subsection (a), (b), or (c) of this section to the manufacturing or processing of such substance may expire before such proceeding can be completed.

(D) After the submission to the Administrator of test data sufficient to evaluate the health and environmental effects of a chemical substance subject to an injunction issued under subparagraph (B) and the evaluation of such data by the Administrator, the district court of the United States which issued such injunction shall, upon petition, dissolve the injunction unless the Administrator has initiated a proceeding for the issuance of a rule under section 2605(a) of this title respecting the substance. If such a proceeding has been initiated, such court shall continue the injunction in effect until the effective date of the rule promulgated in such proceeding or, if such proceeding is terminated without the promulgation of a rule, upon the termination of the proceeding, whichever occurs first.

(f) Protection against unreasonable risks

(1) If the Administrator finds that there is a reasonable basis to conclude that the manufacture, processing, distribution in commerce, use, or disposal of a chemical substance with respect to which notice is required by subsection (a) of this section, or that any combination of such activities, presents or will present an unreasonable risk of injury to health or environment before a rule promulgated under section 2605 of this title can protect against such risk, the Administrator shall, before the expiration of the notification period applicable under subsection (a), (b), or (c) of this section to the manufacturing or processing of such substance, take the action authorized by paragraph (2) or (3) to the extent necessary to protect against such risk.

(2) The Administrator may issue a proposed rule under section 2605(a) of this title to apply to a chemical substance with respect to which a finding was made under paragraph (1)—

(A) a requirement limiting the amount of such substance which may be manufactured, processed, or distributed in commerce,

(B) a requirement described in paragraph (2), (3), (4), (5), (6), or (7) of section 2605(a) of this title, or

(C) any combination of the requirements referred to in subparagraph (B).

Such a proposed rule shall be effective upon its publication in the Federal Register. Section 2605(d)(2)(B) of this title shall apply with respect to such rule.

(3)(A) The Administrator may—

(i) issue a proposed order to prohibit the manufacture, processing, or distribution in commerce of a substance with respect to which a finding was made under paragraph (1), or

(ii) apply, through attorneys of the Environmental Protection Agency, to the United States District Court for the District of Columbia or the United States district court for the judicial district in which the manufacturer, or processor, as the case may be, of such substance, is found, resides, or transacts business for an injunction to prohibit the manufacture, processing, or distribution in commerce of such substance.

A proposed order issued under clause (i) respecting a chemical substance shall take effect on the expiration of the notification period applicable under subsection (a), (b), or (c) of this section to the manufacture or processing of such substance.

(B) If the district court of the United States to which an application has been made under subparagraph (A)(ii) finds that there is a reasonable basis to conclude that the manufacture, processing, distribution in commerce, use, or disposal of the chemical substance with respect to which such application was made, or that any combination of such activities, presents or will present an unreasonable risk of injury to health or the environment before a rule promulgated under section 2605 of this title can protect against such risk, the court shall issue an injunction to prohibit the manufacture, processing, or distribution in commerce of such substance or to prohibit any combination of such activities.

(C) The provisions of subparagraphs (B) and (C) of subsection (e)(1) of this section shall apply with respect to an order issued under clause (i) of subparagraph (A); and the provisions of subparagraph (C) of subsection (e)(2) of this section shall apply with respect to an injunction issued under subparagraph (B).

(D) If the Administrator issues an order pursuant to subparagraph (A)(i) respecting a chemical substance and objections are filed in accordance with subsection (e)(1)(C) of this section, the Administrator shall seek an injunction under subparagraph (A)(ii) respecting such substance unless the Administrator determines, on the basis of such objections, that such substance does not or will not present an unreasonable risk of injury to health or the environment.

(g) Statement of reasons for not taking action

If the Administrator has not initiated any action under this section or section 2605 or 2606 of this title to prohibit or limit the manufacture, processing, distribution in commerce, use, or disposal of a chemical substance, with respect to which notification or data is required by subsection (a)(1)(B) or (b) of this section, before the expiration of the notification period applicable to the manufacturing or processing of such substance, the Administrator shall publish a statement of the Administrator's reasons for not initiating such action. Such a statement shall be published in the Federal Register before the expiration of such period. Publication of such statement in accordance with the preceding sentence is not a prerequisite to the manufacturing or processing of the substance with respect to which the statement is to be published.

(h) Exemptions

(1) The Administrator may, upon application, exempt any person from any requirement of subsection (a) or (b) of this section to permit such person to manufacture or process a chemical substance for test marketing purposes—

(A) upon a showing by such person satisfactory to the Administrator that the manufacture, processing, distribution in commerce, use, and disposal of such substance, and that any combination of such activities, for such purposes will not present any unreasonable risk of injury to health or the environment, and

(B) under such restrictions as the Administrator considers appropriate.

(2)(A) The Administrator may, upon application, exempt any person from the requirement of subsection (b)(2) of this section to submit data for a chemical substance. If, upon receipt of an application under the preceding sentence, the Administrator determines that—

(i) the chemical substance with respect to which such application was submitted is equivalent to a chemical substance for which data has been submitted to the Administrator as required by subsection (b)(2) of this section, and

(ii) submission of data by the applicant on such substance would be duplicative of data which has been submitted to the Administrator in accordance with such subsection,

the Administrator shall exempt the applicant from the requirement to submit such data on such substance. No exemption which is granted under this subparagraph with respect to the submission of data for a chemical substance may take effect before the beginning of the reimbursement period applicable to such data.

(B) If the Administrator exempts any person, under subparagraph (A), from submitting data required under subsection (b)(2) of this section for a chemical substance because of the existence of previously submitted data and if such exemption is granted during the reimbursement period for such data, then (unless such person and the persons referred to in clauses (i) and (ii) agree on the amount and method of reimbursement) the Administrator shall order the person granted the exemption to provide fair and equitable reimbursement (in an amount determined under rules of the Administrator)—

(i) to the person who previously submitted the data on which the exemption was based, for a portion of the costs incurred by such person in complying with the requirement under subsection (b)(2) of this section to submit such data, and

(ii) to any other person who has been required under this subparagraph to contribute with respect to such costs, for a portion of the amount such person was required to contribute.

In promulgating rules for the determination of fair and equitable reimbursement to the persons described in clauses (i) and (ii) for costs incurred with respect to a chemical substance, the Administrator shall, after consultation with the Attorney General and the Federal Trade Commission, consider all relevant factors, including the effect on the competitive position of the person required to provide reimbursement in relation to the persons to be reimbursed and the share of the market for such substance of the person required to provide reimbursement in relation to the share of such market of the persons to be reimbursed. For purposes of judicial review, an order under this subparagraph shall be considered final agency action.

(C) For purposes of this paragraph, the reimbursement period for any previously submitted data for a chemical substance is a period—

(i) beginning on the date of the termination of the prohibition, imposed under this section, on the manufacture or processing of such substance by the person who submitted such data to the Administrator, and

(ii) ending—

(I) five years after the date referred to in clause (i), or

(II) at the expiration of a period which begins on the date referred to in clause (i) and is equal to the period which the Administrator determines was necessary to develop such data,

whichever is later.

(3) The requirements of subsections (a) and (b) of this section do not apply with respect to the manufacturing or processing of any chemical substance which is manufactured or processed, or proposed to be manufactured or processed, only in small quantities (as defined by the Administrator by rule) solely for purposes of—

(A) scientific experimentation or analysis, or

(B) chemical research on, or analysis of such substance or another substance, including such research or analysis for the development of a product,

if all persons engaged in such experimentation, research, or analysis for a manufacturer or processor are notified (in such form and manner as the Administrator may prescribe) of any risk to health which the manufacturer, processor, or the Administrator has reason to believe may be associated with such chemical substance.

(4) The Administrator may, upon application and by rule, exempt the manufacturer of any new chemical substance from all or part of the requirements of this section if the Administrator determines that the manufacture, processing, distribution in commerce, use, or disposal of such chemical substance, or that any combination of such activities, will not present an unreasonable risk of injury to health

or the environment. A rule promulgated under this paragraph (and any substantive amendment to, or repeal of, such a rule) shall be promulgated in accordance with paragraphs (2) and (3) of section 2605(c) of this title.

(5) The Administrator may, upon application, make the requirements of subsections (a) and (b) of this section inapplicable with respect to the manufacturing or processing of any chemical substance (A) which exists temporarily as a result of a chemical reaction in the manufacturing or processing of a mixture or another chemical substance, and (B) to which there is no, and will not be, human or environmental exposure.

(6) Immediately upon receipt of an application under paragraph (1) or (5) the Administrator shall publish in the Federal Register notice of the receipt of such application. The Administrator shall give interested persons an opportunity to comment upon any such application and shall, within 45 days of its receipt, either approve or deny the application. The Administrator shall publish in the Federal Register notice of the approval or denial of such an application.

(i) "Manufacture" and "process" defined

For purposes of this section, the terms "manufacture" and "process" mean manufacturing or processing for commercial purposes.

[TSCA § 6, 15 U.S.C. § 2605—] Regulation of hazardous chemical substances and mixtures

(a) Scope of regulation

If the Administrator finds that there is a reasonable basis to conclude that the manufacture, processing, distribution in commerce, use, or disposal of a chemical substance or mixture, or that any combination of such activities, presents or will present an unreasonable risk of injury to health or the environment, the Administrator shall by rule apply one or more of the following requirements to such substance or mixture to the extent necessary to protect adequately against such risk using the least burdensome requirements:

(1) A requirement (A) prohibiting the manufacturing, processing, or distribution in commerce of such substance or mixture, or (B) limiting the amount of such substance or mixture which may be manufactured, processed, or distributed in commerce.

(2) A requirement—

(A) prohibiting the manufacture, processing, or distribution in commerce of such substance or mixture for (i) a particular use or (ii) a particular use in a concentration in excess of a level specified by the Administrator in the rule imposing the requirement, or

(B) limiting the amount of such substance or mixture which may be manufactured, processed, or distributed in commerce for (i) a particular use or (ii) a particular use in a concentration in excess of a level specified by the Administrator in the rule imposing the requirement.

(3) A requirement that such substance or mixture or any article containing such substance or mixture be marked with or accompanied by clear and adequate warnings and instructions with respect to its use, distribution in commerce, or disposal or with respect to any combination of such activities. The form and content of such warnings and instructions shall be prescribed by the Administrator.

(4) A requirement that manufacturers and processors of such substance or mixture make and retain records of the processes used to manufacture or process such substance or mixture and monitor or conduct tests which are reasonable and necessary to assure compliance with the requirements of any rule applicable under this subsection.

(5) A requirement prohibiting or otherwise regulating any manner or method of commercial use of such substance or mixture.

(6)(A) A requirement prohibiting or otherwise regulating any manner or method of disposal of such substance or mixture, or of any article containing such substance or mixture, by its manufacturer or processor or by any other person who uses, or disposes of, it for commercial purposes.

(B) A requirement under subparagraph (A) may not require any person to take any action which would be in violation of any law or requirement of, or in effect for, a State or political subdivision, and shall require each person subject to it to notify each State and political subdivision in which a required disposal may occur of such disposal.

(7) A requirement directing manufacturers or processors of such substance or mixture (A) to give notice of such unreasonable risk of injury to distributors in commerce of such substance or mixture and, to the extent reasonably ascertainable, to other persons in possession of such substance or mixture or exposed to such substance or mixture, (B) to give public notice of such risk of injury, and (C) to replace or repurchase such substance or mixture as elected by the person to which the requirement is directed.

Any requirement (or combination of requirements) imposed under this subsection may be limited in application to specified geographic areas.

(b) Quality control

If the Administrator has a reasonable basis to conclude that a particular manufacturer or processor is manufacturing or processing a chemical substance or mixture in a manner which unintentionally causes the chemical substance or mixture to present or which will cause it to present an unreasonable risk of injury to health or the environment—

(1) the Administrator may by order require such manufacturer or processor to submit a description of the relevant quality control procedures followed in the

manufacturing or processing of such chemical substance or mixture; and

(2) if the Administrator determines—

(A) that such quality control procedures are inadequate to prevent the chemical substance or mixture from presenting such risk of injury, the Administrator may order the manufacturer or processor to revise such quality control procedures to the extent necessary to remedy such inadequacy; or

(B) that the use of such quality control procedures has resulted in the distribution in commerce of chemical substances or mixtures which present an unreasonable risk of injury to health or the environment, the Administrator may order the manufacturer or processor to (i) give notice of such risk to processors or distributors in commerce of any such substance or mixture, or to both, and, to the extent reasonably ascertainable, to any other person in possession of or exposed to any such substance, (ii) to give public notice of such risk, and (iii) to provide such replacement or repurchase of any such substance or mixture as is necessary to adequately protect health or the environment.

A determination under subparagraph (A) or (B) of paragraph (2) shall be made on the record after opportunity for hearing in accordance with section 554 of title 5. Any manufacturer or processor subject to a requirement to replace or repurchase a chemical substance or mixture may elect either to replace or repurchase the substance or mixture and shall take either such action in the manner prescribed by the Administrator.

(c) Promulgation of subsection (a) rules

(1) In promulgating any rule under subsection (a) of this section with respect to a chemical substance or mixture, the Administrator shall consider and publish a statement with respect to—

(A) the effects of such substance or mixture on health and the magnitude of the exposure of human beings to such substance or mixture,

(B) the effects of such substance or mixture on the environment and the magnitude of the exposure of the environment to such substance or mixture,

(C) the benefits of such substance or mixture for various uses and the availability of substitutes for such uses, and

(D) the reasonably ascertainable economic consequences of the rule, after consideration of the effect on the national economy, small business, technological innovation, the environment, and public health.

If the Administrator determines that a risk of injury to health or the environment could be eliminated or reduced to a sufficient extent by actions taken under another Federal law (or laws) administered in whole or in part by the Administrator, the Administrator may not promulgate a rule under subsection (a) of this section to protect against such risk of injury unless the Administrator finds, in the Administrator's discretion, that it is in the public interest to protect against such risk under this chapter. In making such a finding the Administrator shall consider (i) all relevant aspects of the risk, as determined by the Administrator in the Administrator's discretion, (ii) a comparison of the estimated costs of complying with actions taken under this chapter and under such law (or laws), and (iii) the relative efficiency of actions under this chapter and under such law (or laws) to protect against such risk of injury.

(2) When prescribing a rule under subsection (a) the Administrator shall proceed in accordance with section 553 of title 5 (without regard to any reference in such section to sections 556 and 557 of such title), and shall also (A) publish a notice of proposed rulemaking stating with particularity the reason for the proposed rule; (B) allow interested persons to submit written data, views, and arguments, and make all such submissions publicly available; (C) provide an opportunity for an informal hearing in accordance with paragraph (3); (D) promulgate, if appropriate, a final rule based on the matter in the rulemaking record (as defined in section 2618(a) of this title), and (E) make and publish with the rule the finding described in subsection (a) of this section.

(3) Informal hearings required by paragraph (2)(C) shall be conducted by the Administrator in accordance with the following requirements:

(A) Subject to subparagraph (B), an interested person is entitled—

(i) to present such person's position orally or by documentary submissions (or both), and

(ii) if the Administrator determines that there are disputed issues of material fact it is necessary to resolve, to present such rebuttal submissions and to conduct (or have conducted under subparagraph (B)(ii)) such cross-examination of persons as the Administrator determines (I) to be appropriate, and (II) to be required for a full and true disclosure with respect to such issues.

(B) The Administrator may prescribe such rules and make such rulings concerning procedures in such hearings to avoid unnecessary costs or delay. Such rules or rulings may include (i) the imposition of reasonable time limits on each interested person's oral presentations, and (ii) requirements that any cross-examination to which a person may be entitled under subparagraph (A) be conducted by the Administrator on behalf of that person in such manner as the Administrator determines (I) to be appropriate, and (II) to be required for a full and true disclosure with respect to disputed issues of material fact.

(C)(i) Except as provided in clause (ii), if a group of persons each of whom under subparagraphs (A) and (B) would be entitled to conduct (or have conducted) cross-examination and who are determined by the Administrator to have the same or similar interests in the proceeding cannot agree upon a single representative of such interests for purposes of cross-examination, the Administrator may make rules and rulings (I) limiting the representation of such interest for such purposes, and (II) governing the manner in which such cross-examination shall be limited.

(ii) When any person who is a member of a group with respect to which the Administrator has made a determination under clause (i) is unable to agree upon group representation with the other members of the group, then such person shall not be denied under the authority of clause (i) the opportunity to conduct (or have conducted) cross-examination as to issues affecting the person's particular interests if (I) the person satisfies the Administrator that the person has made a reasonable and good faith effort to reach agreement upon group representation with the other members of the group and (II) the Administrator determines that there are substantial and relevant issues which are not adequately presented by the group representative.

(D) A verbatim transcript shall be taken of any oral presentation made, and cross-examination conducted in any informal hearing under this subsection. Such transcript shall be available to the public.

(4)(A) The Administrator may, pursuant to rules prescribed by the Administrator, provide compensation for reasonable attorneys' fees, expert witness fees, and other costs of participating in a rulemaking proceeding for the promulgation of a rule under subsection (a) of this section to any person—

(i) who represents an interest which would substantially contribute to a fair determination of the issues to be resolved in the proceeding, and

(ii) if—

(I) the economic interest of such person is small in comparison to the costs of effective participation in the proceeding by such person, or

(II) such person demonstrates to the satisfaction of the Administrator that such person does not have sufficient resources adequately to participate in the proceeding without compensation under this subparagraph.

In determining for purposes of clause (i) if an interest will substantially contribute to a fair determination of the issues to be resolved in a proceeding, the Administrator shall take into account the number and complexity of such issues and the extent to which representation of such interest will contribute to widespread public participation in the proceeding and representation of a fair balance of interests for the resolution of such issues.

(B) In determining whether compensation should be provided to a person under subparagraph (A) and the amount of such compensation, the Administrator shall take into account the financial burden which will be incurred by such person in participating in the rulemaking proceeding. The Administrator shall take such action as may be necessary to ensure that the aggregate amount of compensation paid under this paragraph in any fiscal year to all persons who, in rulemaking proceedings in which they receive compensation, are persons who either—

(i) would be regulated by the proposed rule, or

(ii) represent persons who would be so regulated,

may not exceed 25 per centum of the aggregate amount paid as compensation under this paragraph to all persons in such fiscal year.

(5) Paragraph (1), (2), (3), and (4) of this subsection apply to the promulgation of a rule repealing, or making a substantive amendment to, a rule promulgated under subsection (a) of this section.

(d) Effective date

(1) The Administrator shall specify in any rule under subsection (a) of this section the date on which it shall take effect, which date shall be as soon as feasible.

(2)(A) The Administrator may declare a proposed rule under subsection (a) of this section to be effective upon its publication in the Federal Register and until the effective date of final action taken, in accordance with subparagraph (B), respecting such rule if—

(i) the Administrator determines that—

(I) the manufacture, processing, distribution in commerce, use, or disposal of the chemical substance or mixture subject to such proposed rule or any combination of such activities is likely to result in an unreasonable risk of serious or widespread injury to health or the environment before such effective date; and

(II) making such proposed rule so effective is necessary to protect the public interest; and

(ii) in the case of a proposed rule to prohibit the manufacture, processing, or distribution of a chemical substance or mixture because of the risk determined under clause (i)(I), a court has in an action under section 2606 of this title granted relief with respect to such risk associated with such substance or mixture.

Such a proposed rule which is made so effective shall not, for purposes of judicial review, be considered final agency action.

(B) If the Administrator makes a proposed rule effective upon its publication in the Federal Register, the Administrator shall, as expeditiously as possible, give interested persons prompt notice of such action, provide reasonable opportunity, in accordance with paragraphs (2) and (3) of subsection (c) of this section, for a hearing on such rule, and either promulgate such rule (as proposed or with modifications) or revoke it; and if such a hearing is requested, the Administrator shall commence the hearing within five days from the date such request is made unless the Administrator and the person making the request agree upon a later date for the hearing to begin, and after the hearing is concluded the Administrator shall, within ten days of the conclusion of the hearing, either promulgate such rule (as proposed or with modifications) or revoke it.

(e) Polychlorinated biphenyls

(1) Within six months after January 1, 1977, the Administrator shall promulgate rules to—

(A) prescribe methods for the disposal of polychlorinated biphenyls, and

(B) require polychlorinated biphenyls to be marked with clear and adequate warnings, and instructions with respect to their processing, distribution in commerce, use, or disposal or with respect to any combination of such activities.

Requirements prescribed by rules under this paragraph shall be consistent with the requirements of paragraphs (2) and (3).

(2)(A) Except as provided under subparagraph (B), effective one year after January 1, 1977, no person may manufacture, process, or distribute in commerce or use any polychlorinated biphenyl in any manner other than in a totally enclosed manner.

(B) The Administrator may by rule authorize the manufacture, processing, distribution in commerce or use (or any combination of such activities) of any polychlorinated biphenyl in a manner other than in a totally enclosed manner if the

Administrator finds that such manufacture, processing, distribution in commerce, or use (or combination of such activities) will not present an unreasonable risk of injury to health or the environment.

(C) For the purposes of this paragraph, the term "totally enclosed manner" means any manner which will ensure that any exposure of human beings or the environment to a polychlorinated biphenyl will be insignificant as determined by the Administrator by rule.

(3)(A) Except as provided in subparagraphs (B) and (C)—

(i) no person may manufacture any polychlorinated biphenyl after two years after January 1, 1977, and

(ii) no person may process or distribute in commerce any polychlorinated biphenyl after two and one-half years after such date.

(B) Any person may petition the Administrator for an exemption from the requirements of subparagraph (A), and the Administrator may grant by rule such an exemption if the Administrator finds that—

(i) an unreasonable risk of injury to health or environment would not result, and

(ii) good faith efforts have been made to develop a chemical substance which does not present an unreasonable risk of injury to health or the environment and which may be substituted for such polychlorinated biphenyl.

An exemption granted under this subparagraph shall be subject to such terms and conditions as the Administrator may prescribe and shall be in effect for such period (but not more than one year from the date it is granted) as the Administrator may prescribe.

(C) Subparagraph (A) shall not apply to the distribution in commerce of any polychlorinated biphenyl if such polychlorinated biphenyl was sold for purposes other than resale before two and one half years after October 11, 1976.

(4) Any rule under paragraph (1), (2)(B), or (3)(B) shall be promulgated in accordance with paragraphs (2), (3), and (4) of subsection (c) of this section.

(5) This subsection does not limit the authority of the Administrator, under any other provision of this chapter or any other Federal law, to take action respecting any polychlorinated biphenyl.

[TSCA § 7, 15 U.S.C. § 2606—] Imminent hazards

(a) Actions authorized and required

(1) The Administrator may commence a civil action in an appropriate district court of the United States—

(A) for seizure of an imminently hazardous chemical substance or mixture or any article containing such a substance or mixture,

(B) for relief (as authorized by subsection (b) of this section) against any person who manufactures, processes, distributes in commerce, or uses, or disposes of, an imminently hazardous chemical substance or mixture or any article containing such a substance or mixture, or

(C) for both such seizure and relief.

A civil action may be commenced under this paragraph notwithstanding the existence of a rule under section 2603 of this title, 2604 of this title, 2605 of this title, or subchapter IV of this chapter or an order under section 2604 of this title or subchapter IV of this chapter, and notwithstanding the pendency of any administrative or judicial proceeding under any provision of this chapter.

(2) If the Administrator has not made a rule under section 2605(a) of this title immediately effective (as authorized by section 2605(d)(2)(A)(i) of this title) with respect to an imminently hazardous chemical substance or mixture, the Administrator shall commence in a district court of the United States with respect to such substance or mixture or article containing such substance or mixture a civil action described in subparagraph (A), (B), or (C) of paragraph (1).

(b) Relief authorized

(1) The district court of the United States in which an action under subsection (a) of this section is brought shall have jurisdiction to grant such temporary or permanent relief as may be necessary to protect health or the environment from the unreasonable risk associated with the chemical substance, mixture, or article involved in such action.

(2) In the case of an action under subsection (a) of this section brought against a person who manufactures, processes, or distributes in commerce a chemical substance or mixture or an article containing a chemical substance or mixture, the relief authorized by paragraph (1) may include the issuance of a mandatory order requiring (A) in the case of purchasers of such substance, mixture, or article known to the defendant, notification to such purchasers of the risk associated with it; (B) public notice of such risk; (C) recall; (D) the replacement or repurchase of such substance, mixture, or article; or (E) any combination of the actions described in the preceding clauses.

(3) In the case of an action under subsection (a) of this section against a chemical substance, mixture, or article, such substance, mixture, or article may be proceeded against by process of libel for its seizure and condemnation. Proceedings in such an action shall conform as nearly as possible to proceedings in rem in admiralty.

(c) Venue and consolidation

(1)(A) An action under subsection (a) of this section against a person who manufactures, processes, or distributes a chemical substance or mixture or an article containing a chemical substance or mixture may be brought in the United States District Court for the District of Columbia or for any judicial district in which any of the defendants is found, resides, or transacts business; and process in such an action may be served on a defendant in any other district in which such defendant resides or may be found. An action under subsection (a) of this section against a chemical substance, mixture, or article may be brought in any United States district court within the jurisdiction of which the substance, mixture, or article is found.

(B) In determining the judicial district in which an action may be brought under subsection (a) of this section in instances in which such action may be brought in more than one judicial district, the Administrator shall take into account the convenience of the parties.

(C) Subpoenas requiring attendance of witnesses in an action brought under subsection (a) of this section may be served in any judicial district.

(2) Whenever proceedings under subsection (a) of this section involving identical chemical substances, mixtures, or articles are pending in courts in two or more judicial districts, they shall be consolidated for trial by order of any such court upon application reasonably made by any party in interest, upon notice to all parties in interest.

(d) Action under section 2605

Where appropriate, concurrently with the filing of an action under subsection (a) of this section or as soon thereafter as may be practicable, the Administrator shall initiate a proceeding for the promulgation of a rule under section 2605(a) of this title.

(e) Representation

Notwithstanding any other provision of law, in any action under subsection (a) of this section, the Administrator may direct attorneys of the Environmental Protection Agency to appear and represent the Administrator in such an action.

(f) "Imminently hazardous chemical substance or mixture" defined

For the purposes of subsection (a) of this section, the term "imminently hazardous chemical substance or mixture" means a chemical substance or mixture which presents an imminent and unreasonable risk of serious or widespread injury to health or the environment. Such a risk to health or the environment shall be considered imminent if it is shown that the manufacture, processing, distribution in commerce, use, or disposal of the chemical substance or mixture, or that any combination of such activities, is likely to result in such injury to health or the environment before a final rule under section 2605 of this title can protect against such risk.

[TSCA § 8, 15 U.S.C. § 2607—] Reporting and retention of information

(a) Reports

(1) The Administrator shall promulgate rules under which—

(A) each person (other than a small manufacturer or processor) who manufactures or processes or proposes to manufacture or process a chemical substance (other than a chemical substance described in subparagraph (B)(ii)) shall maintain such records, and shall submit to the Administrator such reports, as the Administrator may reasonably require, and

(B) each person (other than a small manufacturer or processor) who manufactures or processes or proposes to manufacture or process—

(i) a mixture, or

(ii) a chemical substance in small quantities (as defined by the Administrator by rule) solely for purposes of scientific experimentation or analysis or chemical research on, or analysis of, such substance or another substance, including any such research or analysis for the development of a product,

shall maintain records and submit to the Administrator reports but only to the extent the Administrator determines the maintenance of records or submission of reports, or both, is necessary for the effective enforcement of this chapter.

The Administrator may not require in a rule promulgated under this paragraph the maintenance of records or the submission of reports with respect to changes in the proportions of the components of a mixture unless the Administrator finds that the maintenance of such records or the submission of such reports, or both, is necessary for the effective enforcement of this chapter. For purposes of the compilation of the list of chemical substances required under subsection (b) of this section, the Administrator shall promulgate rules pursuant to this subsection not later than 180 days after January 1, 1977.

(2) The Administrator may require under paragraph (1) maintenance of records and reporting with respect to the following insofar as known to the person making the report or insofar as reasonably ascertainable:

(A) The common or trade name, the chemical identity, and the molecular structure of each chemical substance or mixture for which such a report is required.

(B) The categories or proposed categories of use of each such substance or mixture.

(C) The total amount of each such substance and mixture manufactured or processed, reasonable estimates of the total amount to be manufactured or processed, the amount manufactured or processed for each of its categories of use, and reasonable estimates of the amount to be manufactured or processed for each of its categories of use or proposed categories of use.

(D) A description of the byproducts resulting from the manufacture, processing, use, or disposal of each such substance or mixture.

(E) All existing data concerning the environmental and health effects of such substance or mixture.

(F) The number of individuals exposed, and reasonable estimates of the number who will be exposed, to such substance or mixture in their places of employment and the duration of such exposure.

(G) In the initial report under paragraph (1) on such substance or mixture, the manner or method of its disposal, and in any subsequent report on such substance or mixture, any change in such manner or method.

To the extent feasible, the Administrator shall not require under paragraph (1), any reporting which is unnecessary or duplicative.

(3)(A)(i) The Administrator may by rule require a small manufacturer or processor of a chemical substance to submit to the Administrator such information respecting the chemical substance as the Administrator may require for publication of the first list of chemical substances required by subsection (b) of this section.

(ii) The Administrator may by rule require a small manufacturer or processor of a chemical substance or mixture—

(I) subject to a rule proposed or promulgated under section 2603, 2604(b)(4), or 2605 of this title, or an order in effect under section 2604(e) of this title, or

(II) with respect to which relief has been granted pursuant to a civil action brought under section 2604 or 2606 of this title,

to maintain such records on such substance or mixture, and to submit to the Administrator such reports on such substance or mixture, as the Administrator may reasonably require. A rule under this clause requiring reporting may require reporting with respect to the matters referred to in paragraph (2).

(B) The Administrator, after consultation with the Administrator of the Small Business Administration, shall by rule prescribe standards for determining the manufacturers and processors which qualify as small manufacturers and processors for purposes of this paragraph and paragraph (1).

(b) Inventory

(1) The Administrator shall compile, keep current, and publish a list of each chemical substance which is manufactured or processed in the United States. Such list shall at least include each chemical substance which any person reports, under section 2604 of this title or subsection (a) of this section, is manufactured or processed in the United States. Such list may not include any chemical substance which was not manufactured or processed in the United States within three years before the effective date of the rules promulgated pursuant to the last sentence of subsection (a)(1) of this section. In the case of a chemical substance for which a notice is submitted in accordance with section 2604 of this title, such chemical substance shall be included in such list as of the earliest date (as determined by the Administrator) on which such substance was manufactured or processed in the United States. The Administrator shall first publish such a list not later than 315 days after January 1, 1977. The Administrator shall not include in such list any chemical substance which is manufactured or processed only in small quantities (as defined by the Administrator by rule) solely for purposes of scientific experimentation or analysis or chemical research on, or analysis of, such substance or another substance, including such research or analysis for the development of a product.

(2) To the extent consistent with the purposes of this chapter, the Administrator may, in lieu of listing, pursuant to paragraph (1), a chemical substance individually, list a category of chemical substances in which such substance is included.

(c) Records

Any person who manufactures, processes, or distributes in commerce any chemical substance or mixture shall maintain records of significant adverse reactions to health or the environment, as determined by the Administrator by rule, alleged to have been caused by the substance or mixture. Records of such adverse reactions to the health of employees shall be retained for a period of 30 years from the date such reactions were first reported to or known by the person maintaining such records. Any other record of such adverse reactions shall be retained for a period of five years from the date the information contained in the record was first reported to or known by the person maintaining the record. Records required to be maintained under this subsection shall include records of consumer allegations of personal injury or harm to health, reports of occupational disease or injury, and reports or complaints of injury to the environment submitted to the manufacturer, processor, or distributor in commerce from any source. Upon request of any duly designated representative of the Administrator, each person who is required to maintain records under this subsection shall permit the inspection of such records and shall submit copies of such records.

(d) Health and safety studies

The Administrator shall promulgate rules under which the Administrator shall require any person who manufactures, processes, or distributes in commerce or who proposes to manufacture, process, or distribute in commerce any chemical substance or mixture (or with respect to paragraph (2), any person who has possession of a study) to submit to the Administrator—

(1) lists of health and safety studies (A) conducted or initiated by or for such person with respect to such substance or mixture at any time, (B) known to such person, or (C) reasonably ascertainable by such person, except that the Administrator may exclude certain types or categories of studies from the requirements of this subsection if the Administrator finds that submission of lists of such studies are unnecessary to carry out the purposes of this chapter; and

(2) copies of any study contained on a list submitted pursuant to paragraph (1) or otherwise known by such person.

(e) Notice to Administrator of substantial risks

Any person who manufactures, processes, or distributes in commerce as chemical substance or mixture and who obtains information which reasonably supports the conclusion that such substance or mixture presents a substantial risk of injury to health or the environment shall immediately inform the Administrator of such information unless such person has actual knowledge that the Administrator has been adequately informed of such information.

(f) "Manufacture" and "process" defined

For purposes of this section, the terms "manufacture" and "process" mean manufacture or process for commercial purposes.

[TSCA § 9, 15 U.S.C. § 2608—] Relationship to other Federal laws

(a) Laws not administered by the Administrator

(1) If the Administrator has reasonable basis to conclude that the manufacture, processing, distribution in commerce, use, or disposal of a chemical substance or mixture, or that any combination of such activities, presents or will present an unreasonable risk of injury to health or the environment and determines, in the Administrator's discretion, that such risk may be prevented or reduced to a sufficient extent by action taken under a Federal law not administered by the Administrator, the Administrator shall submit to the agency which administers such law a report which describes such risk and includes in such description a specification of the activity or combination of activities which the Administrator has reason to believe so presents such risk. Such report shall also request such agency—

(A)(i) to determine if the risk described in such report may be prevented or reduced to a sufficient extent by action taken under such law, and

(ii) if the agency determines that such risk may be so

prevented or reduced, to issue an order declaring whether or not the activity or combination of activities specified in the description of such risk presents such risk; and

(B) to respond to the Administrator with respect to the matters described in subparagraph (A).

Any report of the Administrator shall include a detailed statement of the information on which it is based and shall be published in the Federal Register. The agency receiving a request under such a report shall make the requested determination, issue the requested order, and make the requested response within such time as the Administrator specifies in the request, but such time specified may not be less than 90 days from the date the request was made. The response of an agency shall be accompanied by a detailed statement of the findings and conclusions of the agency and shall be published in the Federal Register.

(2) If the Administrator makes a report under paragraph (1) with respect to a chemical substance or mixture and the agency to which such report was made either—

(A) issues an order declaring that the activity or combination of activities specified in the description of the risk described in the report does not present the risk described in the report, or

(B) initiates, within 90 days of the publication in the Federal Register of the response of the agency under paragraph (1), action under the law (or laws) administered by such agency to protect against such risk associated with such activity or combination of activities,

the Administrator may not take any action under section 2605 or 2606 of this title with respect to such risk.

(3) If the Administrator has initiated action under section 2605 or 2606 of this title with respect to a risk associated with a chemical substance or mixture which was the subject of a report made to an agency under paragraph (1), such agency shall before taking action under the law (or laws) administered by it to protect against such risk consult with the Administrator for the purpose of avoiding duplication of Federal action against such risk.

(b) Laws administered by the Administrator

The Administrator shall coordinate actions taken under this chapter with actions taken under other Federal laws administered in whole or in part by the Administrator. If the Administrator determines that a risk to health or the environment associated with a chemical substance or mixture could be eliminated or reduced to a sufficient extent by actions taken under the authorities contained in such other Federal laws, the Administrator shall use such authorities to protect against such risk unless the Administrator determines, in the Administrator's discretion, that it is in the public interest to protect against such risk by actions taken under this chapter. This subsection shall not be construed to relieve the Administrator of any requirement imposed on the

Administrator by such other Federal laws.

(c) Occupational safety and health

In exercising any authority under this chapter, the Administrator shall not, for purposes of section 653(b)(1) of title 29, be deemed to be exercising statutory authority to prescribe or enforce standards or regulations affecting occupational safety and health.

(d) Coordination

In administering this chapter, the Administrator shall consult and coordinate with the Secretary of Health, and Human Services and the heads of any other appropriate Federal executive department or agency, any relevant independent regulatory agency, and any other appropriate instrumentality of the Federal Government for the purpose of achieving the maximum enforcement of this chapter while imposing the least burdens of duplicative requirements on those subject to the chapter and for other purposes. The Administrator shall, in the report required by section 2629 of this title, report annually to the Congress on actions taken to coordinate with such other Federal departments, agencies, or instrumentalities, and on actions taken to coordinate the authority under this chapter with the authority granted under other Acts referred to in subsection (b) of this section.

[TSCA § 10, 15 U.S.C. § 2609—] Research, development, collection, dissemination, and utilization of data

(a) Authority

The Administrator shall, in consultation and cooperation with the Secretary of Health and Human Services and with other heads of appropriate departments and agencies, conduct such research, development, and monitoring as is necessary to carry out the purposes of this chapter. The Administrator may enter into contracts and may make grants for research, development, and monitoring under this subsection. Contracts may be entered into under this subsection without regard to section 3324(a) and (b) of title 31 and section 5 of title 41.

(b) Data systems

(1) The Administrator shall establish, administer, and be responsible for the continuing activities of an interagency committee which shall design, establish, and coordinate an efficient and effective system, within the Environmental Protection Agency, for the collection, dissemination to other Federal departments and agencies, and use of data submitted to the Administrator under this chapter.

(2)(A) The Administrator shall, in consultation and cooperation with the Secretary of Health and Human Services and other heads of appropriate departments and agencies design, establish, and coordinate an efficient and effective system for the retrieval of toxicological and other scientific data which could be useful to the Administrator in carrying out the purposes of this chapter. Systematized retrieval shall be developed for use by all Federal and other departments and agencies with responsibilities in the area of regulation or study of chemical

(B) The Administrator, in consultation and cooperation with the Secretary of Health and Human Services, may make grants and enter into contracts for the development of a data retrieval system described in subparagraph (A). Contracts may be entered into under this subparagraph without regard to section 3324(a) and (b) of title 31 and section 5 of title 41.

(c) Screening techniques

The Administrator shall coordinate, with the Assistant Secretary for Health of the Department of Health and Human Services, research undertaken by the Administrator and directed toward the development of rapid, reliable, and economical screening techniques for carcinogenic, mutagenic, teratogenic, and ecological effects of chemical substances and mixtures.

(d) Monitoring

The Administrator shall, in consultation and cooperation with the Secretary of Health and Human Services, establish and be responsible for research aimed at the development, in cooperation with local, State, and Federal agencies, of monitoring techniques and instruments which may be used in the detection of toxic chemical substances and mixtures and which are reliable, economical, and capable of being implemented under a wide variety of conditions.

(e) Basic research

The Administrator shall in consultation and cooperation with the Secretary of Health and Human Services, establish research programs to develop the fundamental scientific basis of the screening and monitoring techniques described in subsections (c) and (d) of this section, the bounds of the reliability of such techniques, and the opportunities for their improvement.

(f) Training

The Administrator shall establish and promote programs and workshops to train or facilitate the training of Federal laboratory and technical personnel in existing or newly developed screening and monitoring techniques.

(g) Exchange of research and development results

The Administrator shall, in consultation with the Secretary of Health and Human Services and other heads of appropriate departments and agencies, establish and coordinate a system for exchange among Federal, State, and local authorities of research and development results respecting toxic chemical substances and mixtures, including a system to facilitate and promote the development of standard data format and analysis and consistent testing procedures.

[TSCA § 11, 15 U.S.C. § 2610—] Inspections and subpoenas

(a) In general

For purposes of administering this chapter, the Administrator, and any duly designated representative of the Administrator, may inspect any establishment, facility, or other premises in which chemical substances, mixtures, or products subject to subchapter IV of this chapter are manufactured, processed, stored, or held before or after their distribution in commerce and any conveyance being used to transport chemical substances, mixtures, such products or such articles in connection with distribution in commerce. Such an inspection may only be made upon the presentation of appropriate credentials and of a written notice to the owner, operator, or agent in charge of the premises or conveyance to be inspected. A separate notice shall be given for each such inspection, but a notice shall not be required for each entry made during the period covered by the inspection. Each such inspection shall be commenced and completed with reasonable promptness and shall be conducted at reasonable times, within reasonable limits, and in a reasonable manner.

(b) Scope

(1) Except as provided in paragraph (2), an inspection conducted under subsection (a) of this section shall extend to all things within the premises or conveyance inspected (including records, files, papers, processes, controls, and facilities) bearing on whether the requirements of this chapter applicable to the chemical substances, mixtures, or products subject to subchapter IV of this chapter within such premises or conveyance have been complied with.

(2) No inspection under subsection (a) of this section shall extend to—

(A) financial data,

(B) sales data (other than shipment data),

(C) pricing data,

(D) personnel data, or

(E) research data (other than data required by this chapter or under a rule promulgated thereunder),

unless the nature and extent of such data are described with reasonable specificity in the written notice required by subsection (a) of this section for such inspection.

(c) Subpoenas

In carrying out this chapter, the Administrator may by subpoena require the attendance and testimony of witnesses and the production of reports, papers, documents, answers to questions, and other information that the Administrator deems necessary. Witnesses shall be paid the same fees and mileage that are paid witnesses in the courts of the United States. In the event of contumacy, failure, or refusal of any person to obey any such subpoena, any district court of the United States in which venue is proper shall have jurisdiction to order any such person to comply with such subpoena. Any failure to obey such an order of the court is punishable by the court as a contempt thereof.

[TSCA § 12, 15 U.S.C. § 2611—] Exports

(a) In general

(1) Except as provided in paragraph (2) and subsection (b) of this section, this chapter (other than section 2607 of this title) shall not apply to any chemical substance, mixture, or to an article containing a chemical substance or mixture, if—

(A) it can be shown that such substance, mixture, or article is being manufactured, processed, or distributed in commerce for export from the United States, unless such substance, mixture, or article was, in fact, manufactured, processed, or distributed in commerce, for use in the United States, and

(B) such substance, mixture, or article (when distributed in commerce), or any container in which it is enclosed (when so distributed), bears a stamp or label stating that such substance, mixture, or article is intended for export.

(2) Paragraph (1) shall not apply to any chemical substance, mixture, or article if the Administrator finds that the substance, mixture, or article will present an unreasonable risk of injury to health within the United States or to the environment of the United States. The Administrator may require, under section 2603 of this title, testing of any chemical substance or mixture exempted from this chapter by paragraph (1) for the purpose of determining whether or not such substance or mixture presents an unreasonable risk of injury to health within the United States or to the environment of the United States.

(b) Notice

(1) If any person exports or intends to export to a foreign country a chemical substance or mixture for which the submission of data is required under section 2603 or 2604(b) of this title, such person shall notify the Administrator of such exportation or intent to export and the Administrator shall furnish to the government of such country notice of the availability of the data submitted to the Administrator under such section for such substance or mixture.

(2) If any person exports or intends to export to a foreign country a chemical substance or mixture for which an order has been issued under section 2604 of this title or a rule has been proposed or promulgated under section 2604 or 2605 of this title, or with respect to which an action is pending, or relief has been granted under section 2604 or 2606 of this title, such person shall notify the Administrator of such exportation or intent to export and the Administrator shall furnish to the government of such country notice of such rule, order, action, or relief.

[TSCA § 13, 15 U.S.C. § 2612—] Entry into customs territory of the United States

(a) In general

(1) The Secretary of the Treasury shall refuse entry into the customs territory of the United States (as defined in general note 2 of the Harmonized Tariff Schedule of the United States) of any chemical substance, mixture, or article containing a chemical substance or mixture offered for such entry if—

(A) it fails to comply with any rule in effect under this chapter, or

(B) it is offered for entry in violation of section 2604 of this title, 2605 of this title, or subchapter IV of this chapter, a rule or order under section 2604 of this title, 2605 of this title, or subchapter IV of this chapter, or an order issued in a civil action brought under section 2604 of this title, 2606 of this title, or subchapter IV of this chapter.

(2) If a chemical substance, mixture, or article is refused entry under paragraph (1), the Secretary of the Treasury shall notify the consignee of such entry refusal, shall not release it to the consignee, and shall cause its disposal or storage (under such rules as the Secretary of the Treasury may prescribe) if it has not been exported by the consignee within 90 days from the date of receipt of notice of such refusal, except that the Secretary of the Treasury may, pending a review by the Administrator of the entry refusal, release to the consignee such substance, mixture, or article on execution of bond for the amount of the full invoice of such substance, mixture, or article (as such value is set forth in the customs entry), together with the duty thereon. On failure to return such substance, mixture, or article for any cause to the custody of the Secretary of the Treasury when demanded, such consignee shall be liable to the United States for liquidated damages equal to the full amount of such bond. All charges for storage, cartage, and labor on and for disposal of substances, mixtures, or articles which are refused entry or release under this section shall be paid by the owner or consignee, and in default of such payment shall constitute a lien against any future entry made by such owner or consignee.

(b) Rules

The Secretary of the Treasury, after consultation with the Administrator, shall issue rules for the administration of subsection (a) of this section.

[TSCA § 14, 15 U.S.C. § 2613—] Disclosure of data

(a) In general

Except as provided by subsection (b) of this section, any information reported to, or otherwise obtained by, the Administrator (or any representative of the Administrator) under this chapter, which is exempt from disclosure pursuant to subsection (a) of section 552 of title 5 by reason of subsection (b)(4) of such section, shall, notwithstanding the provisions of any other section of this chapter, not be disclosed by the Administrator or by any officer or employee of the United States, except that such information—

(1) shall be disclosed to any officer or employee of the United States—

(A) in connection with the official duties of such officer or employee under any law for the protection of health or the environment, or

(B) for specific law enforcement purposes;

(2) shall be disclosed to contractors with the United States and employees of such contractors if in the opinion of the Administrator such disclosure is necessary for the satisfactory performance by the contractor of a contract with the United States entered into on or after October 11, 1976, for the performance of work in connection with this chapter and under such

conditions as the Administrator may specify;

(3) shall be disclosed if the Administrator determines it necessary to protect health or the environment against an unreasonable risk of injury to health or the environment; or

(4) may be disclosed when relevant in any proceeding under this chapter, except that disclosure in such a proceeding shall be made in such manner as to preserve confidentiality to the extent practicable without impairing the proceeding.

In any proceeding under section 552(a) of title 5 to obtain information the disclosure of which has been denied because of the provisions of this subsection, the Administrator may not rely on section 552(b)(3) of such title to sustain the Administrator's action.

(b) Data from health and safety studies

(1) Subsection (a) does not prohibit the disclosure of—

(A) any health and safety study which is submitted under this chapter with respect to—

(i) any chemical substance or mixture which, on the date on which such study is to be disclosed has been offered for commercial distribution, or

(ii) any chemical substance or mixture for which testing is required under section 2603 of this title or for which notification is required under section 2604 of this title, and

(B) any data reported to, or otherwise obtained by, the Administrator from a health and safety study which relates to a chemical substance or mixture described in clause (i) or (ii) of subparagraph (A). This paragraph does not authorize the release of any data which discloses processes used in the manufacturing or processing of a chemical substance or mixture or, in the case of a mixture, the release of data disclosing the portion of the mixture comprised by any of the chemical substances in the mixture.

(2) If a request is made to the Administrator under subsection (a) of section 552 of title 5 for information which is described in the first sentence of paragraph (1) and which is not information described in the second sentence of such paragraph, the Administrator may not deny such request on the basis of subsection (b)(4) of such section.

(c) Designation and release of confidential data

(1) In submitting data under this chapter, a manufacturer, processor, or distributor in commerce may (A) designate the data which such person believes is entitled to confidential treatment under subsection (a) of this section, and (B) submit such designated data separately from other data submitted under this chapter. A designation under this paragraph shall be made in writing and in such manner as the Administrator may prescribe.

(2)(A) Except as provided by subparagraph (B), if the

Administrator proposes to release for inspection data which has been designated under paragraph (1)(A), the Administrator shall notify, in writing and by certified mail, the manufacturer, processor, or distributor in commerce who submitted such data of the intent to release such data. If the release of such data is to be made pursuant to a request made under section 552(a) of Title 5 such notice shall be given immediately upon approval of such request by the Administrator. The Administrator may not release such data until the expiration of 30 days after the manufacturer, processor, or distributor in commerce submitting such data has received the notice required by this subparagraph.

(B)(i) Subparagraph (A) shall not apply to the release of information under paragraph (1), (2), (3), or (4) of subsection (a) of this section, except that the Administrator may not release data under paragraph (3) of subsection (a) of this section unless the Administrator has notified each manufacturer, processor, and distributor in commerce who submitted such data of such release. Such notice shall be made in writing by certified mail at least 15 days before the release of such data, except that if the Administrator determines that the release of such data is necessary to protect against an imminent, unreasonable risk of injury to health or the environment, such notice may be made by such means as the Administrator determines will provide notice at least 24 hours before such release is made.

(ii) Subparagraph (A) shall not apply to the release of information described in subsection (b)(1) of this section other than information described in the second sentence of such subsection.

(d) Criminal penalty for wrongful disclosure

(1) Any officer or employee of the United States or former officer or employee of the United States, who by virtue of such employment or official position has obtained possession of, or has access to, material the disclosure of which is prohibited by subsection (a) of this section, and who knowing that disclosure of such material is prohibited by such subsection, willfully discloses the material in any manner to any person not entitled to receive it, shall be guilty of a misdemeanor and fined not more than $5,000 or imprisoned for not more than one year, or both. Section 1905 of title 18 does not apply with respect to the publishing, divulging, disclosure, or making known of, or making available, information reported or otherwise obtained under this chapter.

(2) For the purposes of paragraph (1), any contractor with the United

States who is furnished information as authorized by subsection (a)(2) of this section, and any employee of any such contractor, shall be considered to be an employee of the United States.

(e) Access by Congress

Notwithstanding any limitation contained in this section or any other provision of law, all information reported to or otherwise obtained by the Administrator (or any representative of the Administrator) under this chapter shall be made available, upon written request of any duly authorized committee of the Congress, to such committee.

[TSCA § 15, 15 U.S.C. § 2614—] Prohibited acts

It shall be unlawful for any person to—

(1) fail or refuse to comply with (A) any rule promulgated or order issued under section 2603 of this title, (B) any requirement prescribed by section 2604 or 2605 of this title, (C) any rule promulgated or order issued under section 2604 or 2605 of this title, or (D) any requirement of subchapter II of this chapter or any rule promulgated or order issued under subchapter II of this chapter;

(2) use for commercial purposes a chemical substance or mixture which such person knew or had reason to know was manufactured, processed, or distributed in commerce in violation of section 2604 or 2605 of this title, a rule or order under section 2604 or 2605 of this title, or an order issued in action brought under section 2604 or 2606 of this title;

(3) fail or refuse to (A) establish or maintain records, (B) submit reports, notices, or other information, or (C) permit access to or copying of records, as required by this chapter or a rule thereunder; or

(4) fail or refuse to permit entry or inspection as required by section 2610 of this title.

[TSCA § 16, 15 U.S.C. § 2615—] Penalties

(a) Civil

(1) Any person who violates a provision of section 2614 or 2689 of this title shall be liable to the United States for a civil penalty in an amount not to exceed $25,000 for each such violation. Each day such a violation continues shall, for purposes of this subsection, constitute a separate violation of section 2614 or 2689 of this title.

(2)(A) A civil penalty for a violation of section 2614 or 2689 of this title shall be assessed by the Administrator by an order made on the record after opportunity (provided in accordance with this subparagraph) for a hearing in accordance with section 554 of title 5. Before issuing such an order, the Administrator shall give written notice to the person to be assessed a civil penalty under such order of the Administrator's proposal to issue such order and provide such person an opportunity to request, within 15 days of the date the notice is received by such person, such a hearing on the order.

(B) In determining the amount of a civil penalty, the Administrator shall take into account the nature, circumstances, extent, and gravity of the violation or violations and, with respect to the violator, ability to pay, effect on ability to continue to do business, any history of prior such violations, the degree of culpability, and such other matters as justice may require.

(C) The Administrator may compromise, modify, or remit, with or without conditions, any civil penalty which may be imposed under this subsection. The amount of such penalty, when finally determined, or the amount agreed upon in compromise, may be deducted from any sums owing by the United States to the person charged.

(3) Any person who requested in accordance with paragraph (2)(A) a hearing respecting the assessment of a civil penalty and who is aggrieved by an order assessing a civil penalty may file a petition for judicial review of such order with the United States Court of Appeals for the District of Columbia Circuit or for any other circuit in which such person resides or transacts business. Such a petition may only be filed within the 30-day period beginning on the date the order making such assessment was issued.

(4) If any person fails to pay an assessment of a civil penalty—

(A) after the order making the assessment has become a final order and if such person does not file a petition for judicial review of the order in accordance with paragraph (3), or

(B) after a court in an action brought under paragraph (3) has entered a final judgment in favor of the Administrator,

the Attorney General shall recover the amount assessed (plus interest at currently prevailing rates from the date of the expiration of the 30-day period referred to in paragraph (3) or the date of such final judgment, as the case may be) in an action brought in any appropriate district court of the United States. In such an action, the validity, amount, and appropriateness of such penalty shall not be subject to review.

(b) Criminal

Any person who knowingly or willfully violates any provision of section 2614 or 2689 of this title, shall, in addition to or in lieu of any civil penalty which may be imposed under subsection (a) of this section for such violation, be subject, upon conviction, to a fine of not more than $25,000 for each day of violation, or to imprisonment for not more than one year, or both.

[TSCA § 17, 15 U.S.C. § 2616—] Specific enforcement and seizure

(a) Specific enforcement

(1) The district courts of the United States shall have jurisdiction over civil actions to—

(A) restrain any violation of section 2614 or 2689 of this title,

(B) restrain any person from taking any action prohibited by section 2604 of this title, 2605 of this title, or subchapter IV of this chapter, or by a rule or order under section 2604 of this title, 2605 of this title, or subchapter IV of this chapter,

(C) compel the taking of any action required by or under this chapter, or

(D) direct any manufacturer or processor of a chemical substance, mixture, or product subject to subchapter IV of this chapter manufactured or processed in violation of section 2604 of this title, 2605 of this title, or subchapter IV of this chapter, or a rule or order under section 2604 of this title, 2605 of this title, or subchapter IV of this chapter, and distributed in commerce, (i) to give notice of such fact to distributors in commerce of such substance, mixture, or product and, to the extent reasonably ascertainable, to other persons in possession of such substance, mixture, or product or exposed to such substance, mixture, or product, (ii) to give public notice of such risk of injury, and (iii) to either replace or repurchase such substance, mixture, or product, whichever the person to which the requirement is directed elects.

(2) A civil action described in paragraph (1) may be brought—

(A) in the case of a civil action described in subparagraph (A) of such paragraph, in the United States district court for the judicial district wherein any act, omission, or transaction constituting a violation of section 2614 of this title occurred or wherein the defendant is found or transacts business, or

(B) in the case of any other civil action described in such paragraph, in the United States district court for the judicial district wherein the defendant is found or transacts business.

In any such civil action process may be served on a defendant in any judicial district in which a defendant resides or may be found. Subpoenas requiring attendance of witnesses in any such action may be served in any judicial district.

(b) Seizure

Any chemical substance, mixture, or product subject to subchapter IV of this chapter which was manufactured, processed, or distributed in commerce in violation of this chapter or any rule promulgated or order issued under this chapter or any article containing such a substance or mixture shall be liable to be proceeded against, by process of libel, for the seizure and condemnation of such substance, mixture, product, or article, in any district court of the United States within the jurisdiction of which such substance, mixture, product, or article is found. Such proceedings shall conform as nearly as possible to proceedings in rem in admiralty.

[TSCA § 18, 15 U.S.C. § 2617—] Preemption

(a) Effect on State law

(1) Except as provided in paragraph (2), nothing in this

chapter shall affect the authority of any State or political subdivision of a State to establish or continue in effect regulation of any chemical substance, mixture, or article containing a chemical substance or mixture.

(2) Except as provided in subsection (b) of this section—

(A) if the Administrator requires by a rule promulgated under section 2603 of this title the testing of a chemical substance or mixture, no State or political subdivision may, after the effective date of such rule, establish or continue in effect a requirement for the testing of such substance or mixture for purposes similar to those for which testing is required under such rule; and

(B) if the Administrator prescribes a rule or order under section 2604 or 2605 of this title (other than a rule imposing a requirement described in subsection (a)(6) of section 2605 of this title) which is applicable to a chemical substance or mixture, and which is designed to protect against a risk of injury to health or the environment associated with such substance or mixture, no State or political subdivision of a State may, after the effective date of such requirement, establish or continue in effect, any requirement which is applicable to such substance or mixture, or an article containing such substance or mixture, and which is designed to protect against such risk unless such requirement (i) is identical to the requirement prescribed by the Administrator, (ii) is adopted under the authority of the Clean Air Act [42 U.S.C. 7401 et seq.] or any other Federal law, or (iii) prohibits the use of such substance or mixture in such State or political subdivision (other than its use in the manufacture or processing of other substances or mixtures).

(b) Exemption

Upon application of a State or political subdivision of a State the Administrator may by rule exempt from subsection (a)(2) of this section, under such conditions as may be prescribed in such rule, a requirement of such State or political subdivision designed to protect against a risk of injury to health or the environment associated with a chemical substance, mixture, or article containing a chemical substance or mixture if—

(1) compliance with the requirement would not cause the manufacturing, processing, distribution in commerce, or use of the substance, mixture, or article to be in violation of the applicable requirement under this chapter described in subsection (a)(2) of this section, and

(2) the State or political subdivision requirement (A) provides a significantly higher degree of protection from such risk than the requirement under this chapter described in subsection (a)(2) of this section and (B) does not, through difficulties in marketing, distribution, or other factors, unduly burden interstate commerce.

[TSCA § 19, 15 U.S.C. § 2618—] Judicial review

(a) In general

(1)(A) Not later than 60 days after the date of the promulgation of a rule under section 2603(a), 2604(a)(2), 2604(b)(4), 2605(a), 2605(e), or 2607 or under subchapter II or IV of this chapter, any person may file a petition for judicial review of such rule with the United States Court of Appeals for the District of Columbia Circuit or for the circuit in which such person resides or in which such person's principal place of business is located. Courts of appeals of the United States shall have exclusive jurisdiction of any action to obtain judicial review (other than in an enforcement proceeding) of such a rule if any district court of the United States would have had jurisdiction of such action but for this subparagraph.

(B) Courts of appeals of the United States shall have exclusive jurisdiction of any action to obtain judicial review (other than in an enforcement proceeding) of an order issued under subparagraph (A) or (B) of section 2605(b)(1) of this title if any district court of the United States would have had jurisdiction of such action but for this subparagraph.

(2) Copies of any petition filed under paragraph (1)(A) shall be transmitted forthwith to the Administrator and to the Attorney General by the clerk of the court with which such petition was filed. The provisions of section 2112 of Title 28 shall apply to the filing of the rulemaking record of proceedings on which the Administrator based the rule being reviewed under this section and to the transfer of proceedings between United States courts of appeals.

(3) For purposes of this section, the term "rulemaking record" means—

(A) the rule being reviewed under this section;

(B) in the case of a rule under section 2603(a) of this title, the finding required by such section, in the case of a rule under section 2604(b)(4) of this title, the finding required by such section, in the case of a rule under section 2605(a) of this title the finding required by section 2604(f) or 2605(a) of this title, as the case may be, in the case of a rule under section 2605(a) of this title, the statement required by section 2605(c)(1) of this title, and in the case of a rule under section 2605(e) of this title, the findings required by paragraph (2)(B) or (3)(B) of such section, as the case may be and in the case of a rule under subchapter IV of this chapter, the finding required for the issuance of such a rule;

(C) any transcript required to be made of oral presentations made in proceedings for the promulgation of such rule;

(D) any written submission of interested parties respecting the promulgation of such rule; and

(E) any other information which the Administrator considers to be relevant to such rule and which the Administrator identified, on or before the date of the promulgation of such rule, in a notice published in the Federal Register.

(b) Additional submissions and presentations; modifications

If in an action under this section to review a rule the petitioner or the Administrator applies to the court for leave to make additional oral submissions or written presentations respecting such rule and shows to the satisfaction of the court that such submissions and presentations would be material and that there were reasonable grounds for the submissions and failure to make such submissions and presentations in the proceeding before the Administrator, the court may order the Administrator to provide additional opportunity to make such submissions and presentations. The Administrator may modify or set aside the rule being reviewed or make a new rule by reason of the additional submissions and presentations and shall file such modified or new rule with the return of such submissions and presentations. The court shall thereafter review such new or modified rule.

(c) Standard of review

(1)(A) Upon the filing of a petition under subsection (a)(1) of this section for judicial review of a rule, the court shall have jurisdiction (i) to grant appropriate relief, including interim relief, as provided in chapter 7 of title 5, and (ii) except as otherwise provided in subparagraph (B), to review such rule in accordance with chapter 7 of title 5.

(B) Section 706 of title 5 shall apply to review of a rule under this section, except that—

(i) in the case of review of a rule under section 2603(a), 2604(b)(4), 2605(a), or 2605(e) of this title, the standard for review prescribed by paragraph (2)(E) of such section 706 shall not apply and the court shall hold unlawful and set aside such rule if the court finds that the rule is not supported by substantial evidence in the rulemaking record (as defined in subsection (a)(3) of this section) taken as a whole;

(ii) in the case of review of a rule under section 2605(a) of this title, the court shall hold unlawful and set aside such rule if it finds that—

(I) a determination by the Administrator under section 2605(c)(3) of this title that the petitioner seeking review of such rule is not entitled to conduct (or have conducted) cross-examination or to present rebuttal submissions, or

(II) a rule of, or ruling by, the Administrator under section 2605(c)(3) of this title limiting such petitioner's cross-examination or oral presentations, has precluded disclosure of disputed material facts which was necessary to a fair determination by the Administrator of the rulemaking proceeding taken as a whole; and section 706(2)(D) shall not apply with respect to a determination, rule, or ruling referred to in subclause (I) or (II); and

(iii) the court may not review the contents and adequacy of—

(I) any statement required to be made pursuant to section 2605(c)(1) of this title, or

(II) any statement of basis and purpose required by section 553(c) of title 5 to be incorporated in the rule

except as part of a review of the rulemaking record taken as a whole.

The term "evidence" as used in clause (i) means any matter in the rulemaking record.

(C) A determination, rule, or ruling of the Administrator described in subparagraph (B)(ii) may be reviewed only in an action under this section and only in accordance with such subparagraph.

(2) The judgment of the court affirming or setting aside, in whole or in part, any rule reviewed in accordance with this section shall be final, subject to review by the Supreme Court of the United States upon certiorari or certification, as provided in section 1254 of title 28.

(d) Fees and costs

The decision of the court in an action commenced under subsection (a) of this section, or of the Supreme Court of the United States on review of such a decision, may include an award of costs of suit and reasonable fees for attorneys and expert witnesses if the court determines that such an award is appropriate.

(e) Other remedies

The remedies as provided in this section shall be in addition to and not in lieu of any other remedies provided by law.

[TSCA § 20, 15 U.S.C. § 2619—] Citizens' civil actions

(a) In general

Except as provided in subsection (b) of this section, any person may commence a civil action—

(1) against any person (including (A) the United States, and (B) any other governmental instrumentality or agency to the extent permitted by the eleventh amendment to the Constitution) who is alleged to be in violation of this chapter or any rule promulgated under section 2603, 2604, or 2605 of this title or subchapter II or IV of this chapter, or order issued under section 2604 of this title or subchapter II or IV of this chapter to restrain such violation, or

(2) against the Administrator to compel the Administrator to perform any act or duty under this chapter which is not discretionary.

Any civil action under paragraph (1) shall be brought in the United States district court for the district in which the alleged violation occurred or in which the defendant resides or in which the defendant's principal place of business is located. Any action brought under paragraph (2) shall be brought in the United States District Court for the District of Columbia, or the United States district court for the judicial district in which the plaintiff is domiciled. The district courts of the United States shall have jurisdiction over suits brought under this section, without regard to the amount in controversy or the citizenship of the parties. In any civil action under this subsection process may be served on a defendant in any judicial district in which the defendant resides or may be found and subpoenas for witnesses may be served in any judicial district.

(b) Limitation

No civil action may be commenced—

(1) under subsection (a)(1) of this section to restrain a violation of this chapter or rule or order under this chapter—

(A) before the expiration of 60 days after the plaintiff has given notice of such violation (i) to the Administrator, and (ii) to the person who is alleged to have committed such violation, or

(B) if the Administrator has commenced and is diligently prosecuting a proceeding for the issuance of an order under section 2615(a)(2) of this title to require compliance with this chapter or with such rule or order or if the Attorney General has commenced and is diligently prosecuting a civil action in a court of the United States to require compliance with this chapter or with such rule or order, but if such proceeding or civil action is commenced after the giving of notice, any person giving such notice may intervene as a matter of right in such proceeding or action; or

(2) under subsection (a)(2) of this section before the expiration of 60 days after the plaintiff has given notice to the Administrator of the alleged failure of the Administrator to perform an act or duty which is the basis for such action or, in the case of an action under such subsection for the failure of the Administrator to file an action under section 2606 of this title, before the expiration of ten days after such notification.

Notice under this subsection shall be given in such manner as the Administrator shall prescribe by rule.

(c) General

(1) In any action under this section, the Administrator, if not a party, may intervene as a matter of right.

(2) The court, in issuing any final order in any action brought pursuant to subsection (a) of this section, may award costs of suit and reasonable fees for attorneys and expert witnesses if the court determines that such an award is appropriate. Any court, in issuing its decision in an action brought to review such an order, may award costs of suit and reasonable fees for attorneys if the court determines that such an award is appropriate.

(3) Nothing in this section shall restrict any right which any person (or class of persons) may have

under any statute or common law to seek enforcement of this chapter or any rule or order under this chapter or to seek any other relief.

(d) Consolidation

When two or more civil actions brought under subsection (a) of this section involving the same defendant and the same issues or violations are pending in two or more judicial districts, such pending actions, upon application of such defendants to such actions which is made to a court in which any such action is brought, may, if such court in its discretion so decides, be consolidated for trial by order (issued after giving all parties reasonable notice and opportunity to be heard) of such court and tried in—

(1) any district which is selected by such defendant and in which one of such actions is pending,

(2) a district which is agreed upon by stipulation between all the parties to such actions and in which one of such actions is pending, or

(3) a district which is selected by the court and in which one of such actions is pending.

The court issuing such an order shall give prompt notification of the order to the other courts in which the civil actions consolidated under the order are pending.

[TSCA § 21, 15 U.S.C. § 2620—] Citizens' petitions

(a) In general

Any person may petition the Administrator to initiate a proceeding for the issuance, amendment, or repeal of a rule under section 2603, 2605, or 2607 of this title or an order under section 2604(e) or 2605(b)(2) of this title.

(b) Procedures

(1) Such petition shall be filed in the principal office of the Administrator and shall set forth the facts which it is claimed establish that it is necessary to issue, amend, or repeal a rule under section 2603, 2605, or 2607 of this title or an order under section 2604(e), 2605(b)(1)(A), or 2605(b)(1)(B) of this title.

(2) The Administrator may hold a public hearing or may conduct such investigation or proceeding as the Administrator deems appropriate in order to determine whether or not such petition should be granted.

(3) Within 90 days after filing of a petition described in paragraph (1), the Administrator shall either grant or deny the petition. If the Administrator grants such petition, the Administrator shall promptly commence an appropriate proceeding in accordance with section 2603, 2604, 2605, or 2607 of this title. If the Administrator denies such petition, the Administrator shall publish in the Federal Register the Administrator's reasons for such denial.

(4)(A) If the Administrator denies a petition filed under this section (or if the Administrator fails to grant or deny such petition within the 90-day period) the petitioner may commence a civil action in a district court of the United States to compel the Administrator to initiate a rulemaking proceeding as requested in the petition. Any such action shall be filed within 60 days after the Administrator's denial of the petition or, if the Administrator fails to grant or deny the petition within 90 days after filing the petition, within 60 days after the expiration of the 90-day period.

(B) In an action under subparagraph (A) respecting a petition to initiate a proceeding to issue a rule under section 2603, 2605, or 2607 of this title or an order under section 2604(e) or 2605(b)(2) of this title, the petitioner shall be provided an opportunity to have such petition considered by the court in a *de novo* proceeding. If the petitioner demonstrates to the satisfaction of the court by a preponderance of the evidence that—

(i) in the case of a petition to initiate a proceeding for the issuance of a rule under section 2603 of this title or an order under section 2604(e) of this title—

(I) information available to the Administrator is insufficient to permit a reasoned evaluation of the health and environmental effects of the chemical substance to be subject to such rule or order; and

(II) in the absence of such information, the substance may present an unreasonable risk to health or the environment, or the substance is or will be produced in substantial quantities and it enters or may reasonably be anticipated to enter the environment in substantial quantities or there is or may be significant or substantial human exposure to it; or

(ii) in the case of a petition to initiate a proceeding for the issuance of a rule under section 2605 or 2607 of this title or an order under section 2605(b)(2) of this title, there is a reasonable basis to conclude that the issuance of such a rule or order is necessary to protect health or the environment against an unreasonable risk of injury to health or the environment.[2]

the court shall order the Administrator to initiate the action requested by the petitioner. If the court finds that the extent of the risk to health or the environment alleged by the petitioner is less than the extent of risks to health or the environment with respect to which the Administrator is taking action under this chapter and there are insufficient resources available to the Administrator to take the action requested by the petitioner, the court may permit

[2] So in original. The period should probably be a semicolon.

the Administrator to defer initiating the action requested by the petitioner until such time as the court prescribes.

(C) The court in issuing any final order in any action brought pursuant to subparagraph (A) may award costs of suit and reasonable fees for attorneys and expert witnesses if the court determines that such an award is appropriate. Any court, in issuing its decision in an action brought to review such an order, may award costs of suit and reasonable fees for attorneys if the court determines that such an award is appropriate.

(5) The remedies under this section shall be in addition to, and not in lieu of, other remedies provided by law.

[TSCA § 22, 15 U.S.C. § 2621—] National defense waiver

The Administrator shall waive compliance with any provision of this chapter upon a request and determination by the President that the requested waiver is necessary in the interest of national defense. The Administrator shall maintain a written record of the basis upon which such waiver was granted and make such record available for in camera examination when relevant in a judicial proceeding under this chapter. Upon the issuance of such a waiver, the Administrator shall publish in the Federal Register a notice that the waiver was granted for national defense purposes, unless, upon the request of the President, the Administrator determines to omit such publication because the publication itself would be contrary to the interests of national defense, in which event the Administrator shall submit notice thereof to the Armed Services Committees of the Senate and the House of Representatives.

[TSCA § 23, 15 U.S.C. § 2622—] Employee protection

(a) In general

No employer may discharge any employee or otherwise discriminate against any employee with respect to the employee's compensation, terms, conditions, or privileges of employment because the employee (or any person acting pursuant to a request of the employee) has—

(1) commenced, caused to be commenced, or is about to commence or cause to be commenced a proceeding under this chapter;

(2) testified or is about to testify in any such proceeding; or

(3) assisted or participated or is about to assist or participate in any manner in such a proceeding or in any other action to carry out the purposes of this chapter.

(b) Remedy

(1) Any employee who believes that the employee has been discharged or otherwise discriminated against by any person in violation of subsection (a) of this section may, within 30 days after such alleged violation occurs, file (or have any person file on the employee's behalf) a complaint with the Secretary of Labor (hereinafter in this section referred to as the "Secretary") alleging such discharge

or discrimination. Upon receipt of such a complaint, the Secretary shall notify the person named in the complaint of the filing of the complaint.

(2)(A) Upon receipt of a complaint filed under paragraph (1), the Secretary shall conduct an investigation of the violation alleged in the complaint. Within 30 days of the receipt of such complaint, the Secretary shall complete such investigation and shall notify in writing the complainant (and any person acting on behalf of the complainant) and the person alleged to have committed such violation of the results of the investigation conducted pursuant to this paragraph. Within ninety days of the receipt of such complaint the Secretary shall, unless the proceeding on the complaint is terminated by the Secretary on the basis of a settlement entered into by the Secretary and the person alleged to have committed such violation, issue an order either providing the relief prescribed by subparagraph (B) or denying the complaint. An order of the Secretary shall be made on the record after notice and opportunity for agency hearing. The Secretary may not enter into a settlement terminating a proceeding on a complaint without the participation and consent of the complainant.

(B) If in response to a complaint filed under paragraph (1) the Secretary determines that a violation of subsection (a) of this section has occurred, the Secretary shall order (i) the person who committed such violation to take affirmative action to abate the violation, (ii) such person to reinstate the complainant to the complainant's former position together with the compensation (including back pay), terms, conditions, and privileges of the complainant's employment, (iii) compensatory damages, and (iv) where appropriate, exemplary damages. If such an order issued, the Secretary, at the request of the complainant, shall assess against the person against whom the order is issued a sum equal to the aggregate amount of all costs and expenses (including attorney's fees) reasonably incurred, as determined by the Secretary, by the complainant for, or in connection with, the bringing of the complaint upon which the order was issued.

(c) Review

(1) Any employee or employer adversely affected or aggrieved by an order issued under subsection (b) of this section may obtain review of the order in the United States Court of Appeals for the circuit in which the violation, with respect to which the order was issued, allegedly occurred. The petition for review must be filed within sixty days from the issuance of the Secretary's order. Review shall conform to chapter 7 of title 5.

(2) An order of the Secretary, with respect to which review could have been obtained under paragraph (1), shall not be subject to judicial

review in any criminal or other civil proceeding.

(d) Enforcement

Whenever a person has failed to comply with an order issued under subsection (b)(2) of this section, the Secretary shall file a civil action in the United States district court for the district in which the violation was found to occur to enforce such order. In actions brought under this subsection, the district courts shall have jurisdiction to grant all appropriate relief, including injunctive relief and compensatory and exemplary damages.

(e) Exclusion

Subsection (a) of this section shall not apply with respect to any employee who, acting without direction from the employee's employer (or any agent of the employer), deliberately causes a violation of any requirement of this chapter.

[TSCA § 24, 15 U.S.C. § 2623—] Employment effects

(a) In general

The Administrator shall evaluate on a continuing basis the potential effects on employment (including reductions in employment or loss of employment from threatened plant closures) of—

(1) the issuance of a rule or order under section 2603, 2604, or 2605 of this title, or

(2) a requirement of section 2604 or 2605 of this title.

(b) Investigations

(1) Any employee (or any representative of an employee) may request the Administrator to make an investigation of—

(A) a discharge or layoff or threatened discharge or layoff of the employee, or

(B) adverse or threatened adverse effects on the employee's employment,

allegedly resulting from a rule or order under section 2603, 2604, or 2605 of this title or a requirement of section 2604 or 2605 of this title. Any such request shall be made in writing, shall set forth with reasonable particularity the grounds for the request, and shall be signed by the employee, or representative of such employee, making the request.

(2)(A) Upon receipt of a request made in accordance with paragraph (1) the Administrator shall (i) conduct the investigation requested, and (ii) if requested by any interested person, hold public hearings on any matter involved in the investigation unless the Administrator, by order issued within 45 days of the date such hearings are requested, denies the request for the hearings because the Administrator determines there are no reasonable grounds for holding such hearings. If the Administrator makes such a determination, the Administrator shall notify in writing the person requesting the hearing of the determination and the reasons therefor and shall publish the determination and the reasons therefor in the Federal Register.

(B) If public hearings are to be held on any matter involved in an investigation conducted under this subsection—

(i) at least five days' notice shall be provided the person making the request for the investigation and any person identified in such request,

(ii) such hearings shall be held in accordance with section 2605(c)(3) of this title, and

(iii) each employee who made or for whom was made a request for such hearings and the employer of such employee shall be required to present information respecting the applicable matter referred to in paragraph (1)(A) or (1)(B) together with the basis for such information.

(3) Upon completion of an investigation under paragraph (2), the Administrator shall make findings of fact, shall make such recommendations as the Administrator deems appropriate, and shall make available to the public such findings and recommendations.

(4) This section shall not be construed to require the Administrator to amend or repeal any rule or order in effect under this chapter.

[TSCA § 25, 15 U.S.C. § 2624—] Studies

(a) Indemnification study

The Administrator shall conduct a study of all Federal laws administered by the Administrator for the purpose of determining whether and under what conditions, if any, indemnification should be accorded any person as a result of any action taken by the Administrator under any such law. The study shall—

(1) include an estimate of the probable cost of any indemnification programs which may be recommended;

(2) include an examination of all viable means of financing the cost of any recommended indemnification; and

(3) be completed and submitted to Congress within two years from the effective date of enactment of this chapter.

The General Accounting Office shall review the adequacy of the study submitted to Congress pursuant to paragraph (3) and shall report the results of its review to the Congress within six months of the date such study is submitted to Congress.

(b) Classification, storage, and retrieval study

The Council on Environmental Quality, in consultation with the Administrator, the Secretary of Health and Human Services, the Secretary of Commerce, and the heads of other appropriate Federal departments or agencies, shall coordinate a study of the feasibility of establishing (1) a standard classification system for chemical substances and related substances, and (2) a standard means for storing and for obtaining rapid access to information respecting such substances. A report on such study shall be completed and submitted to Congress not later than 18 months after the effective date of enactment of this chapter.

[TSCA § 26, 15 U.S.C. § 2625—] Administration

(a) Cooperation of Federal agencies

Upon request by the Administrator, each Federal department and agency is authorized—

(1) to make its services, personnel, and facilities available (with or without reimbursement) to the Administrator to assist the Administrator in the administration of this chapter; and

(2) to furnish to the Administrator such information, data, estimates, and statistics, and to allow the Administrator access to all information in its possession as the Administrator may reasonably determine to be necessary for the administration of this chapter.

(b) Fees

(1) The Administrator may, by rule, require the payment of a reasonable fee from any person required to submit data under section 2603 or 2604 of this title to defray the cost of administering this chapter. Such rules shall not provide for any fee in excess of $2,500 or, in the case of a small business concern, any fee in excess of $100. In setting a fee under this paragraph, the Administrator shall take into account the ability to pay of the person required to submit the data and the cost to the Administrator of reviewing such data. Such rules may provide for sharing such a fee in any case in which the expenses of testing are shared under section 2603 or 2604 of this title.

(2) The Administrator, after consultation with the Administrator of the Small Business Administration, shall by rule prescribe standards for determining the persons which qualify as small business concerns for purposes of paragraph (1).

(c) Action with respect to categories

(1) Any action authorized or required to be taken by the Administrator under any provision of this chapter with respect to a chemical substance or mixture may be taken by the Administrator in accordance with that provision with respect to a category of chemical substances or mixtures. Whenever the Administrator takes action under a provision of this chapter with respect to a category of chemical substances or mixtures, any reference in this chapter to a chemical substance or mixture (insofar as it relates to such action) shall be deemed to be a reference to each chemical substance or mixture in such category.

(2) For purposes of paragraph (1):

(A) The term "category of chemical substances" means a group of chemical substances the members of which are similar in molecular structure, in physical, chemical, or biological properties, in use, or in mode of entrance into the human body or into the environment, or the members of which are in some other way suitable for classification as such for purposes of this chapter, except that such term does not mean a group of chemical substances which are grouped together

(B) The term "category of mixtures" means a group of mixtures the members of which are similar in molecular structure, in physical, chemical, or biological properties, in use, or in the mode of entrance into the human body or into the environment, or the members of which are in some other way suitable for classification as such for purposes of this chapter.

(d) Assistance office

The Administrator shall establish in the Environmental Protection Agency an identifiable office to provide technical and other nonfinancial assistance to manufacturers and processors of chemical substances and mixtures respecting the requirements of this chapter applicable to such manufacturers and processors, the policy of the Agency respecting the application of such requirements to such manufacturers and processors, and the means and methods by which such manufacturers and processors may comply with such requirements.

(e) Financial disclosures

(1) Except as provided under paragraph (3), each officer or employee of the Environmental Protection Agency and the Department of Health and Human Services who—

(A) performs any function or duty under this chapter, and

(B) has any known financial interest (i) in any person subject to this chapter or any rule or order in effect under this chapter, or (ii) in any person who applies for or receives any grant or contract under this chapter,

shall, on February 1, 1978, and on February 1 of each year thereafter, file with the Administrator or the Secretary of Health and Human Services (hereinafter in this subsection referred to as the "Secretary"), as appropriate, a written statement concerning all such interests held by such officer or employee during the preceding calendar year. Such statement shall be made available to the public.

(2) The Administrator and the Secretary shall—

(A) act within 90 days of January 1, 1977—

(i) to define the term "known financial interests" for purposes of paragraph (1), and

(ii) to establish the methods by which the requirement to file written statements specified in paragraph (1) will be monitored and enforced, including appropriate provisions for review by the Administrator and the Secretary of such statements; and

(B) report to the Congress on June 1, 1978, and on June 1 of each year thereafter with respect to such statements and the actions taken in regard thereto during the preceding calendar year.

(3) The Administrator may by rule identify specific positions with the Environmental Protection Agency, and the Secretary may by rule identify specific positions with the Department of Health and Human Services, which are of a nonregulatory or nonpolicymaking nature, and the Administrator and the Secretary may by rule provide that officers or employees occupying such positions shall be exempt from the requirements of paragraph (1).

(4) This subsection does not supersede any requirement of chapter 11 of title 18.

(5) Any officer or employee who is subject to, and knowingly violates, this subsection or any rule issued thereunder, shall be fined not more than $2,500 or imprisoned not more than one year, or both.

(f) Statement of basis and purpose

Any final order issued under this chapter shall be accompanied by a statement of its basis and purpose. The contents and adequacy of any such statement shall not be subject to judicial review in any respect.

(g) Assistant Administrator

(1) The President, by and with the advice and consent of the Senate, shall appoint an Assistant Administrator for Toxic Substances of the Environmental Protection Agency. Such Assistant Administrator shall be a qualified individual who is, by reason of background and experience, especially qualified to direct a program concerning the effects of chemicals on human health and environment. Such Assistant Administrator shall be responsible for (A) the collection of data, (B) the preparation of studies, (C) the making of recommendations to the Administrator for regulatory and other actions to carry out the purposes and to facilitate the administration of this chapter, and (D) such other functions as the Administrator may assign or delegate.

(2) The Assistant Administrator to be appointed under paragraph (1) shall be in addition to the Assistant Administrators of the Environmental Protection Agency authorized by section 1(d) of Reorganization Plan No. 3 of 1970.

[TSCA § 27, 15 U.S.C. § 2626—] Development and evaluation of test methods

(a) In general

The Secretary of Health and Human Services, in consultation with the Administrator and acting through the Assistant Secretary for Health, may conduct, and make grants to public and nonprofit private entities and enter into contracts with public and private entities for, projects for the development and evaluation of inexpensive and efficient methods (1) for determining and evaluating the health and environmental effects of chemical substances and mixtures, and their toxicity, persistence, and other characteristics which affect health and the environment, and (2) which may be used for the development of test data to meet the requirements of rules promulgated under section 2603 of this title. The Administrator shall consider such methods in prescribing under section

2603 of this title standards for the development of test data.

(b) Approval by Secretary

No grant may be made or contract entered into under subsection (a) of this section unless an application therefor has been submitted to and approved by the Secretary. Such an application shall be submitted in such form and manner and contain such information as the Secretary may require. The Secretary may apply such conditions to grants and contracts under subsection (a) of this section as the Secretary determines are necessary to carry out the purposes of such subsection. Contracts may be entered into under such subsection without regard to section 3324(a) and (b) of title 31 and section 5 of title 41.

[TSCA § 28, 15 U.S.C. § 2627—] State programs

(a) In general

For the purpose of complementing (but not reducing) the authority of, or actions taken by, the Administrator under this chapter, the Administrator may make grants to States for the establishment and operation of programs to prevent or eliminate unreasonable risks within the States to health or the environment which are associated with a chemical substance or mixture and with respect to which the Administrator is unable or is not likely to take action under this chapter for their prevention or elimination. The amount of a grant under this subsection shall be determined by the Administrator, except that no grant for any State program may exceed 75 per centum of the establishment and operation costs (as determined by the Administrator) of such program during the period for which the grant is made.

(b) Approval by Administrator

(1) No grant may be made under subsection (a) of this section unless an application therefor is submitted to and approved by the Administrator. Such an application shall be submitted in such form and manner as the Administrator may require and shall—

(A) set forth the need of the applicant for a grant under subsection (a) of this section,

(B) identify the agency or agencies of the State which shall establish or operate, or both, the program for which the application is submitted,

(C) describe the actions proposed to be taken under such program,

(D) contain or be supported by assurances satisfactory to the Administrator that such program shall, to the extent feasible, be integrated with other programs of the applicant for environmental and public health protection,

(E) provide for the making of such reports and evaluations as the Administrator may require, and

(F) contain such other information as the Administrator may prescribe.

(2) The Administrator may approve an application submitted in accordance with paragraph (1) only if the applicant has established to the satisfaction of the Administrator a priority need, as determined under rules of the Administrator, for the

grant for which the application has been submitted. Such rules shall take into consideration the seriousness of the health effects in a State which are associated with chemical substances or mixtures, including cancer, birth defects, and gene mutations, the extent of the exposure in a State of human beings and the environment to chemical substances and mixtures, and the extent to which chemical substances and mixtures are manufactured, processed, used, and disposed of in a State.

(c) Annual reports

Not later than six months after the end of each of the fiscal years 1979, 1980, and 1981, the Administrator shall submit to the Congress a report respecting the programs assisted by grants under subsection (a) of this section in the preceding fiscal year and the extent to which the Administrator has disseminated information respecting such programs.

(d) Authorization

For the purpose of making grants under subsection (a) of this section there are authorized to be appropriated $1,500,000 for each of the fiscal years 1982 and 1983. Sums appropriated under this subsection shall remain available until expended.

[TSCA § 29, 15 U.S.C. § 2628—] Authorization of appropriations

There are authorized to be appropriated to the Administrator for purposes of carrying out this chapter (other than sections 2626 and 2627 of this title and subsections (a) and (c) through (g) of section 2609 of this title) $58,646,000 for the fiscal year 1982 and $62,000,000 for the fiscal year 1983. No part of the funds appropriated under this section may be used to construct any research laboratories.

[TSCA § 30, 15 U.S.C. § 2629—] Annual report

The Administrator shall prepare and submit to the President and the Congress on or before January 1, 1978, and on or before January 1 of each succeeding year a comprehensive report on the administration of this chapter during the preceding fiscal year. Such reports shall include—

(1) a list of the testing required under section 2603 of this title during the year for which the report is made and an estimate of the costs incurred during such year by the persons required to perform such tests;

(2) the number of notices received during such year under section 2604 of this title, the number of such notices received during such year under such section for chemical substances subject to a rule, and a summary of any action taken during such year under section 2604(g) of this title;

(3) a list of rules issued during such year under section 2605 of this title;

(4) a list, with a brief statement of the issues, of completed or pending judicial actions under this chapter and administrative actions under section 2615 of this title during such year;

(5) a summary of major problems encountered in the administration of this chapter; and

(6) such recommendations for additional legislation as the Administrator deems necessary to carry out the purposes of this chapter.

ACRONYMS

Acronym	Description
AAA	American Arbitration Association
ABA	American Bar Association
ACC	American Chemistry Council
AFL-CIO	American Federation of Labor and Congress of Industrial Organizations
AHERA	Asbestos Hazard Emergency Response Act of 1986
ALJ	Administrative Law Judge
ANPR	Advanced Notice of Proposed Rule-making
APA	Administrative Procedure Act
APHIS	Animal & Plant Health Inspection Service
CA	Chemical Abstracts
CAA	Clean Air Act
CACO	Consent Agreement Consent Order
CAIR	Comprehensive Assessment Information Rule
CAP	Compliance Audit Program
CAS	Chemical Abstracts Service
CASRN	Chemical Abstracts Service Registry Number
CBD	Convention on Biological Diversity
CBI	Confidential Business Information
CCD	Chemical Control Division
CCT	Comfort Cooling Tower
CEB	Chemical Engineering Branch
CEQ	Council on Environmental Quality
CERCLA	Comprehensive Environmental Response, Compensation, and Liability Act
CFC	Chlorofluorocarbons
CIS	Chemical Inventory Section
CMA	Chemical Manufacturers Association
CMD	Chemical Management Division
CORR	Chemicals on Reporting Rules
CPSA	Consumer Product Safety Act
CPSC	Consumer Product Safety Commission
CSPA	Consumer Specialty Products Association
CSRAD	Chemical Screening and Risk Assessment Division
CWA	Clean Water Act
DCO	Document Control Officer
EAB	Exposure Assessment Branch
EAD	Environmental Assistance Division
EBC	Environmental Biosafety Committee
ECA	Enforceable Consent Agreement
EETD	Economics, Exposure and Technology Division

EIEC	Emergency Incidents of Environmental Contamination
EPA	Environmental Protection Agency
EPCRA	Emergency Planning and Community Right-to-Know Act
ERP	Enforcement Response Policy
EU	European Union
EUP	Experimental Use Permit
FDA	Food & Drug Administration
FFDCA	Food, Drug, and Cosmetic Act
FIFRA	Federal Insecticide, Fungicide, and Rodenticide Act
FOIA	Freedom of Information Act
FPB	Field Programs Branch
FPPA	Federal Plant Pest Act
FSIS	Food Safety and Inspection Service
FWPCA	Federal Water Pollution Control Act
FYI	For Your Information
GAO	General Accounting Office
GBP	Gravity Based Penalty
GLP	Good Laboratory Practice Standards
GOCO	Government-Owned, Company-Operated
GPC	Gel Permeation Chromatography
HAP	Hazardous Air Pollutants
HCS	Hazard Communication Standard
HERD	Health and Environmental Review Division
ICB	Industrial Chemistry Branch
ICC	Interstate Commerce Commission
IMD	Information Management Division
ITC	Interagency Testing Committee
IUR	Inventory Update Rule
IURA	Inventory Update Rule Amendments
LC_{50}	Lethal Concentration
LD_{50}	Lethal Dose
LoREX	Low Release Low Exposure
LVE	Low Volume Exemption
MBSL	Mouse Biochemical Specific Locus test
MCAN	Microbial Commercial Activity Notice
M_L	PCB Marking Large
MOU	Memorandum of Understanding
M_S	PCB Marking Small
MSDS	Material Safety Data Sheet
MTL	Master Testing List
MVSL	Mouse Visible Specific Locus test
NCB	New Chemicals Branch
NCI	National Cancer Institute
NEIC	National Enforcement Investigations Center
NIEHS	National Institute of Environmental Health Sciences
NIH	National Institutes of Health

NIOSH	National Institute for Occupational Safety and Health
NOC	Notice of Commencement of Manufacture or Import
NON	Notice of Noncompliance
NPC	National Program Chemicals
NPRM	Notice of Proposed Rule-Making
NRC	National Response Center
NRDC	Natural Resources Defense Council
NSF	National Science Foundation
NTA	Negotiated Testing Agreements
NTIS	National Technical Information Service
OCE	Office of Criminal Enforcement
OCEFT	Office of Criminal Enforcement, Forensics and Training
OCM	Office of Compliance Monitoring
OECA	Office of Enforcement and Compliance Assurance
OECD	Organization for Economic Cooperation and Development
OECM	Office of Enforcement and Compliance Monitoring
OGC	Office of General Counsel
OMB	Office of Management and Budget
OPB	Operations Branch
OPP	Office of Pesticide Programs
OPPT	Office of Pollution Prevention and Toxics
OPPTS	Office of Prevention, Pesticides and Toxic Substances
ORE	Office of Regulatory Enforcement
OSH Act	Occupational Safety and Health Act
OSHA	Occupational Safety and Health Administration
OSW	Office of Solid Waste
PAB	Policy Analysis Branch
PAIR	Preliminary Assessment Information Rule
PCB	Polychlorinated Biphenyls
PDB	Program Development Branch
PFAS	Perfluoroalkyl sulfonates
PIB	Prevention Integration Branch
PM	Program Manager
PMN	Premanufacture Notification
PPA	Pollution Prevention Act
PPD	Pollution Prevention Division
PQA	Plant Quarantine Act
QSAR	Quantitative Structure-Activity Relationships
R&D	Research and Development
RCRA	Resource Conservation and Recovery Act
RIB	Regulatory Impacts Branch
RM	Risk Management
SAR	Structure-Activity Analysis
SARA	Superfund Amendments and Reauthorization Act of 1986
SAT	Structure-Activity Team
SEIU	Service Employees International Union

SEP	Supplemental Environmental Project
SIC	Standard Industrial Classification
SNUN	Significant New Use Notice
SNUR	Significant New Use Rule
SOCMA	Synthetic Organic Chemical Manufacturers Association
STNI	Scientific and Technical Network International
TERA	TSCA Experimental Release Application
TME	Test Marketing Exemption
TPB	Technical Programs Branch
TQI	Technically Qualified Individual
TRI	Toxic Release Inventory
TSCA	Toxic Substances Control Act
UNEP	United Nations Environment Programme
USDA	U.S. Department of Agriculture
UVCB	Unknown, Variable composition, Complex reaction product, and Biological materials
VPO	Vapor Pressure Osmometry

INDEX

D

E

J

K

L

M

N

O

Q

R

S

U

V

W

X

Y

Z

McKenna Long & Aldridge LLP Attorneys at Law   Technology Sciences Group Inc.

McKenna Long & Aldridge LLP is an international law firm with over 350 lawyers in Atlanta, Georgia; Washington, D.C.; Los Angeles, San Diego and San Francisco, California; Philadelphia, Pennsylvania; Denver, Colorado; and Brussels, Belgium. The firm is active in the fields of environmental regulation, environmental, civil and criminal litigation, government contracts, international trade and business, food and drug law, health care law, labor and employment law, antitrust, financial services, and general business and corporate law.

The firm's environmental practice group, with over 30 attorneys, embraces all of the federal and state environmental statutes, including TSCA, FIFRA, CSPA, FHSA, CERCLA, RCRA, EPCRA, and state laws in the states and regions in which we practice. McKenna has long been one of the preeminent firms in the TSCA field, having represented many of the largest chemical, specialty chemical, and equipment manufacturers in the world. In addition to providing TSCA compliance counseling, we have defended many of the most significant TSCA enforcement actions prosecuted by the U.S. Environmental Protection Agency. We routinely perform TSCA systems and compliance audits and assist companies in developing their own TSCA compliance programs. We also have extensive experience with TSCA counterparts in the European Union (REACH) and in countries around the world. Our international reach has allowed us to serve clients in this increasingly globalized marketplace.

Technology Sciences Group Inc. (TSG), a wholly owned subsidiary of McKenna Long & Aldridge LLP, is a multi-disciplinary consulting firm providing scientific and regulatory expertise to chemical, agrochemical, pharmaceutical, and consumer product companies, as well as industry groups and law firms.

TSG offers a wide-range of toxicology, chemistry, exposure assessment, risk assessment, and registration services to the regulated community. TSG combines innovative approaches, precise regulatory analysis, strategic planning, and state-of-the-art scientific knowledge to provide value-added services to its customers.

TSG provides advice on U.S. regulatory compliance issues relating to FIFRA, FFDCA, TSCA, EPCRA, and other federal, state, and local laws. Drawing upon an extensive global network of affiliates, TSG can also provide advice regarding regulatory matters in Canada, Europe, Asia, and Latin America. TSG's offices in Washington D.C., California and Canada keep TSG staff close to decision makers and the decision-making process.

TSG's consulting team features skilled professionals from industry, government, international organizations and consulting. This mix provides for synergy and creativity in crafting solutions to client problems. The consulting staff includes former senior state and federal officials, board-certified toxicologists, chemists, certified environmental specialists and regulatory affairs experts